CARL A. DAUTEN
Professor of Finance
Washington University

MERLE T. WELSHANS
Professor of Finance
Washington University

SOUTH-WESTERN PUBLISHING COMPANY

Cincinnati 27 Chicago 5 San Francisco 3 Dallas 2 New Rochelle, N. Y.

F10

PRINCIPLES of

FINANCE

Functions • Problems • Institutions

Library of Congress Catalog Card Number: 58-7186

H260

Printed in the United States of America

Preface

Principles of Finance is intended for the first course in finance. It is a survey of the whole field of finance, both private and public. Emphasis is placed on current problems in the field as well as on basic principles that have been developed from past experience. Financial institutions and the instruments and procedures used to make loans and investments are described and discussed, and loan and investment practices are analyzed. A book of this nature provides the necessary background for courses in monetary theory, banking problems, public finance, business finance, agricultural finance, security markets, and related courses.

Principles of Finance is organized by the major types of financing. The first four parts are concerned with business financing, both short-term and long-term; agricultural financing; foreign trade financing; and consumer financing. The next part covers governmental activities in the field of finance with special emphasis on the role of governmental agencies in the monetary field. The last part analyzes the effects of financial activities and governmental policies in this field on the level of prices, interest rates, and economic activity.

This plan of organization was adopted for several reasons. For one, it shows the alternatives that may be available to a businessman, a farmer, or a consumer having a demand for money. This arrangement has been used also because it helps to show how specialized institutions and procedures have been developed to meet new demands for financing. Furthermore it provides a meaningful basis for analyzing trends and current problems in the various fields of financing. The expanded loan activities of commercial banks, for example, and the problems currently confronting bankers can be understood only when their activities in short-term business lending, real estate financing, consumer lending, and in other areas of financing are studied, field by field, in relationship to the activities of competing agencies in each field.

At one time commercial banks handled most of the short-term business financing. Today other institutions have developed to such a degree that a study of banking alone no longer provides an adequate picture of short-term business financing, to say nothing of the other areas of finance. Nor can banking be understood clearly without a knowledge of the workings of other financial institutions. For example, fluctuations in the volume of bank credit can be understood only if the loan practices and procedures and the factors affecting the volume of financing of these other agencies are understood.

The approach in *Principles of Finance* is thus appropriate not only for a first course in finance for any student, but also for the student who will take only one course in the field. Moreover, it is uniquely suited for students in schools of business. It provides the same comprehensive approach to finance as is given in the first course in other business fields such as marketing, personnel, production, and accounting. *Principles of Finance* provides the background that all citizens and especially prospective businessmen need for understanding the financial structure of the economy in which they will live and work.

The authors have benefited greatly from discussions with their colleagues at Washington University and elsewhere. Especially significant have been the contributions of John W. Bowyer, Jr., Charles Gilliland, Jr., Elmer Lotshaw, Arthur W. Mason, Jr., Robert J. Oppitz, R. Miller Upton, and Arthur G. Vieth.

The authors are particularly indebted to Lloyd M. Valentine of the University of Cincinnati whose careful reading, penetrating analysis, and helpful comments enabled them to make many improvements not only in content, but also in clarity of presentation.

CARL A. DAUTEN
MERLE T. WELSHANS

Contents

CHAPTER 1, NATURE AND ROLE OF FINANCE IN OUR ECONOMY, 1

BASIC REQUIREMENTS OF AN EFFECTIVE FINANCIAL SYSTEM, 2; FUNCTIONS OF FINANCE, 3; Creation of Money, 3; Transferring Money, 4; Accumulation of Savings in Financial Institutions, 4; Lending and Investing Money, 4; Marketing of Claims to Wealth, 5; Facilitating the Lending and Investing Process, 5; THE DEVELOPMENT OF THE MONETARY SYSTEM, 5; Barter, 5; Early Development of Money, 6; The Use of Precious Metals as Money, 7; Paper Money, 8; Checks, 9; Recent Developments, 9; PRESENT-DAY PROCESSES OF EXCHANGE AND OF TRANSFERRING SAVINGS TO INVESTORS, 10; Individuals, 10; Businesses, Institutions, and Government Units, 12; THE PLAN OF STUDY, 12

CHAPTER 2, THE NATURE OF BUSINESS FINANCE, 17

THE BALANCE SHEET, 17; Current Assets, 18; Fixed Assets, 21; Current Liabilities, 21; Fixed Liabilities, 22; Owners' Interests, 23; RELATIONSHIP OF SOURCES OF FINANCING TO ASSETS, 23; Short-Term Financing, 24; Long-Term Financing, 24; NET WORKING CAPITAL AND SHORT-TERM FINANCING, 26; The Current Ratio, 26; Necessity for Adequate Net Working Capital, 28; Advantages of Adequate Net Working Capital, 30; Why Short-Term Financing? 30

CHAPTER 3, COMMERCIAL BANKS, 35

DEVELOPMENT OF BANKING IN THE UNITED STATES, 35; Banking in America Before the Civil War, 36; Banking in America from the Civil War to the Present, 38; FUNCTIONS OF COMMERCIAL BANKS, 39; ESTABLISHMENT AND ORGANIZATION OF THE COMMERCIAL BANK, 40; Application for Charter, 40; Minimum Capital Requirements, 41; Bank Deposits, 41; Relationship of Capital to Deposits, 42; Nonearning Bank Assets, 44; Concentration in Banking Control, 44; BANK FAILURES AND DEPOSIT INSURANCE, 48; Early State Plans for Insurance of Bank Notes and Deposits, 48; Failure of State Plans of Deposit Protection, 49; The Federal Deposit Insurance Corporation, 50

CHAPTER 15, INTERNATIONAL FINANCE, 289

CHAPTER 16, INTERNATIONAL FINANCE (CONCLUDED), 309

CHAPTER 17, CONSUMER CREDIT IN THE FINANCIAL STRUCTURE, 329

CHAPTER 18, INSTITUTIONS FINANCING THE CONSUMER, 351

CHAPTER 19, INSTITUTIONS FINANCING THE CONSUMER (CONCLUDED), 377

CHAPTER 24, TREASURY POWERS AFFECTING THE SUPPLY OF MONEY AND CREDIT, 499

CHAPTER 25, MONETARY POLICIES AND THE PRICE LEVEL, 519

CHAPTER 26, MONETARY POLICIES, INTEREST RATES, AND THE MONEY MARKET, 537

CHAPTER 27, MONETARY POLICIES AND BUSINESS FLUCTUATIONS, 553

CHAPTER 28, RECENT MONETARY AND CREDIT PROBLEMS AND POLICIES, 571

Chapter 1

Nature and

Role of Finance

in Our Economy

Finance is so important in a free enterprise economy that our system is frequently referred to as finance capitalism. Finance deals with the principles, institutions, instruments, and procedures involved in making payments of all types in our economy. These payments include those for goods and services which are bought for cash and those that are bought on credit and paid for later. It also includes payments when intangible claims to wealth such as stocks and bonds are purchased. Finance is also concerned with making available for investment in business and government money that has been saved.

A highly developed financial system is at the very heart of an economy such as ours. Large-scale production and a high degree of specialization of labor can function only if an effective system exists for paying for goods and services whether they are needed in production or are offered for sale. Business can obtain the money it needs to buy such capital goods as machinery and equipment only if the necessary institutions, instruments, and procedures have been established for making savings available for such investment. Similarly, the federal government and other governmental units can carry out their wide range of activities on the domestic and international scene only if efficient means exist for making payments and for borrowing money when such a policy has been decided upon.

A free-enterprise economy can function only if the price system is instrumental in determining which goods shall be produced and sold. The producer who can make and sell a product

1

at a price that yields him a volume of sales large enough to cover all costs and still make enough profit to attract capital for his business stays in business and grows; the producer who cannot do so stands still or is forced out of business. In short, our economy could not function as it does without an effective financial system.

BASIC REQUIREMENTS OF AN EFFECTIVE FINANCIAL SYSTEM

A financial system needs an efficient monetary system, facilities for creating capital by channeling savings into investment, and markets in which to buy and sell claims to wealth to facilitate the investment process.

The financial system must provide an efficient medium for exchanging goods and services. A basic feature of such a system is a unit in which to measure prices, that is, a unit of account, such as the dollar in our economy or the pound sterling in the British economy. This unit of account must be universally accepted in the economy if exchange is to function smoothly. It must also be a reasonably stable unit if it is to be used widely. There must be convenient means for making payments for goods and services purchased whether the purchase is a pack of chewing gum or a complete business worth millions of dollars. This means that the monetary system must operate with monetary institutions, instruments, and procedures geared to the needs of the economy.

Another essential feature in a highly developed economy is a financial system that makes possible the creation of capital on a scale large enough to meet the demands of the economy. Capital creation takes place whenever production facilities are used to produce buildings, machinery, or other equipment to be used in the production of goods for consumer or producer use. In a simple economy such as that on a largely self-sufficient one-man farm, this process, in part at least, takes place directly. The farmer creates capital when he takes time during the winter months to build a new barn or to fashion a new ax handle. In a highly developed economy this process takes place when some individuals, businesses, or governmental units do not spend all of their current income. They save some of it and make such savings available to others who use them to buy buildings, machinery, or equipment. This indirect process of capital creation can work only if the proper legal instruments and financial institutions exist so that savers are willing to transfer the ownership of their savings to businesses having a demand for them.

A third essential feature in the financial system of a highly developed economy is that it provide markets and procedures for the transfer of claims to wealth, such as promissory notes and shares of ownership in a business, and for the conversion of such claims into cash. Such markets and procedures facilitate the process of capital creation since savings will be made available for investment in sufficient sums by a large group of investors only when the saver can quickly and easily convert his claim into cash when he has a need or desire to do so. For example, over a million individuals are willing to invest billions of dollars in the American Telephone and Telegraph Company because the facilities of the New York Stock Exchange make it possible to sell their shares of ownership to other investors easily and quickly.

FUNCTIONS OF FINANCE

In our economy the government and private financial institutions of many kinds have developed instruments and procedures to perform the following functions:

1. Creation of money.
2. Transferring money.
3. Accumulation of savings in financial institutions.
4. Lending and investing money.
5. Marketing of claims to wealth arising out of the lending and investing process.
6. Other activities that facilitate the lending and investing process.

(1) Creation of Money

One of the most significant functions of the financial system is that of creating the money used as a medium of exchange and in the savings-investment process. This money creation function is carried on by agencies of the federal government and also by the banking system.

(2) Transferring Money

Another function performed by some financial institutions is that of transferring money. When money is put into a checking account at a commercial bank, it can easily be used to make payments by writing checks. Many types of financial institutions carry on the other functions of finance, but in the United States only commercial banks are allowed by law to handle checking accounts.

(3) Accumulation of Savings in Financial Institutions

A function performed by many different types of financial institutions is the accumulation or gathering together of individual savings. For example, a commercial bank handles the accounts of many businesses and individuals, many of them small. When all are accumulated in one place, however, they are available in amounts much larger than any individual depositor could supply. From time to time banks conduct advertising campaigns to secure savings deposits.

A part of this function of the gathering together or accumulation of savings is that of acting as a custodian of the savings and cash balances of the public. Most individuals, businesses, and organizations do not want to take the risks involved in having large amounts of cash on hand. They therefore put them into a bank or other financial institution for safekeeping.

(4) Lending and Investing Money

Another basic function of financial institutions is the lending and investing function. The money that has been put into these institutions may be loaned to businesses, farmers, consumers, institutions, and governmental units. It may be loaned for different purposes, such as to buy buildings or equipment, or to pay current bills. This money may also be loaned for varying time periods. Some financial institutions make loans of almost all types to all groups of borrowers; others specialize in only one or perhaps several types since procedures are different in different types of lending. Some financial institutions invest all or part of the savings that have been put into them in shares of ownership in a business.

(5) Marketing of Claims to Wealth

Savings may be placed with financial institutions that invest them, or they may be invested directly. For example, a business may want to sell shares of ownership to the general public. It could do so directly, but the process of finding individuals interested in investing funds in that business might be difficult and time-consuming. A type of financial institution (the investment bank) has been developed to sell these shares of ownership, or shares of stock as they are called. This function is essentially a merchandising function. This function is also involved at times in other fields of financing.

(6) Facilitating the Lending and Investing Process

In the process of lending and of selling securities, several types of institutions serve as facilitating agencies. For example, if shares of stock are to be sold to the general public, it is desirable to have a ready market in which such stocks can be resold later if the investor no longer wants to hold them. The several stock exchanges serve this purpose. If lending is to be done effectively, it is desirable to have information on the applicants for loans readily available on an up-to-date basis. Various types of credit-checking agencies have been developed to meet this need.

THE DEVELOPMENT OF THE MONETARY SYSTEM

Our monetary system developed to meet the changing needs of the economy. Adequate records to trace the early developments of the system do not exist, but these can be inferred from such evidence as is available and practices that are still in use in the more primitive economies in our world.

Barter

Primitive economies consisted largely of self-sufficient units or groups that lived by means of hunting, fishing, and simple agriculture. There was little need or occasion to exchange goods or services. Even in such economies, however, some trade took place.

As economies became more developed and some men specialized to a degree at least in herding sheep, others in raising grain, others as goldsmiths and silversmiths, and the like, the process of exchange became more important. To help facilitate such exchanges of goods for goods, or *barter* as is it known, tables of relative values were developed from past experience. For example, the table might show the number of furs, measures of grain, amount of cloth, and the like equal to one animal.

This arrangement helped facilitate exchanges, but the process still had many serious drawbacks. For example, if a man had a cow he wanted to trade for some nuts and some furs, he would need to find someone who had an excess of both of these items to trade.

Early Development of Money

Money is anything that is generally accepted as a means of paying for goods and services and of discharging debts. The record of the early development of money is very sketchy. In all probability traders found that some items, such as furs and grain, were traded more frequently than other items. Therefore they could afford to accept these items in exchange even when they did not have an immediate need for them since they could always trade them for goods they wanted. They probably also found it convenient to figure the value of goods less frequently traded in terms of these more frequently traded items because such a system gave them a familiar yardstick with which to value them.

This development took place in much this same way in some American prisoner of war camps in Germany during World War II. Cigarettes were used as a general medium of exchange of goods and services since they could always be traded for other goods. Values of all types of goods were also quoted in cigarettes even when there was no intention of exchanging them for the equivalent number of cigarettes.

Records in early economies show many items that were useful for food or clothing which were used as a general medium of exchange and, to some degree at least, probably also as a unit for measuring value. Included were grain, salt, skins, spices, tea, seeds, and cattle. Some early economies made use of such commodities as beads, ivory, the plumage of birds, gold, and silver for which there was a general demand for ornamentation. Some items that were useful as tools or in making tools, such as animal claws, fishhooks, shark teeth, and stone discs, were also used. All of these items were generally accepted in exchange because there was a demand for them since they could be usd for further exchange or as food, clothing, tools, or ornamentation.

These items were accepted by traders as long as they felt certain that they could use them again in future trading. This meant that the supply of the item had to be limited in relation to the desires of individauls in the economy to have the item. In early economies this was generally true of such items as grains, cattle, and tools. Items of ornamentation could likewise be used as a general medium of exchange only if there was an unfilled demand for them. For example, the American Indians valued wampum beads as a decoration and were not able to get enough of them to meet the desires of everyone. Therefore such beads could serve as a general medium of exchange.

The Use of Precious Metals as Money

When commodities were used as a medium of exchange, goods could be valued in terms of the item used as money and could be exchanged for it. This process, however, was still clumsy and time-consuming. For example, if furs were used, they were bulky and difficult to carry around. Furthermore arguments could arise over the quality of the furs. It was also necessary to make a trade of goods equal to one, two, three, or more furs since furs lost their value when cut into pieces.

The transition from the use of such commodities as money to the use of precious metals was probably a gradual one, but the advantages of precious metals eventually led to their general usage. Gold and silver were in great demand for ornamentation due to their durability, malleability, and beauty. The supply of these metals was limited enough so that they had great value, which made them easy to carry around as money. They could also be refined into the pure metal rather easily so that their quality was rather uniform. Various quantities could also be weighed out so that exchanges of varying values could be made. In time, coins with a certain weight of metal in them were developed.

Since an unscrupulous trader could cover baser metals with gold or silver or put in short weight, however, this process of coinage needed regulation if coins were to be generally acceptable. For that reason coining money and determining the value thereof has been a governmental function since the earliest days of recorded history.

Paper Money

Each of the commodities used as money served as a medium of exchange because of its intrinsic value. Its value as a commodity made it useful for money purposes. Even in early days, however, things were used at times that had value only as money. For example, large stones that were too big to be moved were used as money in some of the islands in the Pacific. They were useful, potentially at least, for making building blocks or grinding wheels, but they were not used in this way. Their value as money arose out of the general acceptance of these stones as representing wealth.

Since early modern times governments have issued money in the form of paper. Gold and silver coins are cumbersome to carry around when large transactions are to be made. To facilitate exchange, governments issued paper money to represent certain quantities of gold or silver that were kept on deposit by the government to back such paper. The paper was generally accepted as a medium of exchange because the persons accepting it knew they could get the precious metal when and if they wanted it. Banks also issued paper money backed by precious metals. This was done at first without specific authorization by governmental authorities; but as time went on, governments regulated the issuance of paper money by the banks. Such paper money backed by gold or silver, or *representative paper money* as it is called, circulated freely. As long as individuals felt certain they could exchange it for the precious metal behind it, there was no inclination to do so.

The general acceptance of paper money as a medium of exchange, with no intention of redeeming it for the precious metal behind it, made possible the issuance of paper money with no such backing. From time to time money was issued based only on the general credit of the government and on the legal provision that such money was acceptable to pay taxes and to fulfill contracts calling for payment in lawful money.

Banks also issued paper money without metallic backing. As such issues were brought under regulation, the banks were required to have some metallic backing for their paper money and to have some form of collateral, such as government bonds, for the remainder of the face value of the money they issued. The privilege of private banks to issue paper money of any type became more and more restricted in all countries and has been abolished in recent years. The only banks that issue any significant amounts of paper money today are central banks, which are owned or controlled by the national government of the country.

Checks

The process of making exchange more and more convenient did not cease with the widespread use of paper money. Today most transactions for any but small amounts are made by means of checks drawn on banks. Funds that an individual or a business has on deposit in a bank are transferred by means of an order to the bank to pay the amount of money stated on its face to a designated person. Most claims between banks as a result of the use of checks are settled by bookkeeping transactions rather than by actual transfer of funds.

Recent Developments

In recent years facilities have been developed for transferring funds in a matter of minutes by wire service. This may be done through Western Union by giving a check to the sending office. The receiving office in turn gives a check to the recipient of the funds. Some banks also have facilities for transferring funds to other banks by wire.

In the last few years procedures have been developed that simplify the process of exchange still further. The federal government found that most employees in the area of Washington, D. C., in which most government offices are located, deposited or cashed their pay checks in one or two banks in the area. This created peak work loads and poor service at the banks each payday. To eliminate this difficulty, some agencies now send an order to the bank to make funds available to the persons listed in the amounts shown and to withdraw the sum total of such funds from the government account. The employees upon proper identification can obtain the money due them at the bank. Those who have checking accounts at the bank may have their money credited directly to their accounts. This system eliminates the writing, distributing, cashing, and depositing of many checks, thus simplifying the process of exchange still further.

Plans have also been worked out, especially in smaller towns, whereby consumers can charge goods bought at a group of stores under a single charge plan and pay for them once a month at the local bank. A member store sends copies of its sales slips to the bank, and the bank credits the store's accounts with the amount of the sales less a service charge by the bank. The bank is repaid when the consumers pay the bank for their bills. Thus bookkeeping entries are replacing the use of checks in some transactions.

PRESENT-DAY PROCESSES OF EXCHANGE AND OF TRANSFERRING SAVINGS TO INVESTORS

The present-day processes of exchanging goods and services developed to meet the changing needs of the economy as it progressed from a simple nomadic culture to our modern way of economic life. Payments for most transactions are made by means of checks drawn on bank deposits; but currency is still used for many day-to-day transactions.

Individuals

An individual builds up a claim for funds against his employer as he performs services for him. On payday he presents his pay check to his bank and may ask for part of it in cash to pay for day-to-day purchases and deposit the balance in his checking account. His bank then has a claim against the employer's bank for funds equal to the face amount of the check. The employee writes checks to pay bills for merchandise bought on charge accounts, for utilities, and for professional services. The recipients of these checks then have a claim against the funds on deposit at the employee's bank. They use these claims in turn to make further payments for goods and services, and so on in a circular process. Thus, the cash withdrawn for minor day-to-day purchases and the checks drawn against the bank deposit account serve as the means of exchange.

The pocket money and the funds an individual keeps in his checking account not only serve as a means of exchange, but they also serve as a cushion between the receipt of funds and the making of payments. Income may be received weekly, biweekly, monthly, or at even longer intervals of time. Some payments must be made daily, others less frequently. Goods bought on charge accounts and bills for services are usually paid once a month. Some bills are paid only once or twice a year, as for example, property taxes. An individual should build up sufficient funds in his checking account to handle his regular monthly payments and also the payments to be made at longer intervals. He may also build up funds to act as a cushion against unforeseen payments, such as unexpected doctor bills, or to tide him over periods in which he may be unable to earn money.

The funds an individual has on hand and in his checking account, therefore, can be divided into two parts. The active balances are used to handle his regular transactions. Funds in excess of the active balances are used to cushion expected and unexpected imbalances between receipts and disbursements.

From time to time an individual may want to make a purchase that requires a payment larger than the funds he has on deposit in his checking account, as for example, when he decides to buy a new automobile. He now has the problem of obtaining a loan from someone who has excess money that he is willing to lend. He could get a loan from an individual directly, but in our economy the demand for such funds is so great that institutions have been developed to facilitate this process of borrowing money.

On the other hand, an individual may find that he has more funds in his checking account than he needs to handle his ordinary transactions and to provide what he feels is a reasonable cushion for emergencies. He then has the problem of using such funds in a profitable manner. He may invest them directly in a business, or he may loan them to a businessman or a consumer who has need for extra funds. In our economy, however, he will probably put them into one of the many financial institutions that have been developed to invest funds.

Businesses, Institutions, and Government Units

Businesses, institutions, and governmental units, like individuals, use checking accounts to handle transactions and to cushion any imbalance between receipts and disbursements. They also at times borrow funds and at other times invest excess funds. Like individuals, they usually perform these activities in our economy through financial institutions.

Since the funds that are saved and invested give rise to economic activity, the total volume of investment is an important economic variable. Since investment cannot take place unless funds are available, the supply of available savings is also of major significance. The relationship between the available supply of savings and the demand for them for investment funds is one of the most important factors in determining the status of economic activity.

THE PLAN OF STUDY

The subject matter of this book includes the functions of finance and the principles, institutions, instruments, and procedures developed to carry on these functions. The development of the monetary system and present-day methods for making payments have been considered briefly in this chapter.

The first four parts of the text are devoted to the functions of finance as they are carried on in the private sector of our economy. They have been organized around the various types of financing that are available in our economy to meet the needs of business, agriculture, and the consumer. This has been done to show how different institutions have been developed and have adapted their practices and procedures to the changing environment. It has also been done to show the alternatives available to the individual or institution having a need for funds.

The last two parts of the book deal with the monetary system in more detail than has been done in this chapter and with the financing of government. They also deal with monetary and financial policy and its effect on economic activity.

Part I deals with short-term business financing. The nature of such financing is first considered. Then the organization and the operation of commercial banks is presented in some detail because these banks are the major suppliers of short-term business funds. The practices and procedures of other institutions supplying such funds are also considered. A chapter is devoted to the organization of the Federal Reserve System and to its activities in facilitating the transfer of funds and the lending process. The last chapter in this part considers other facilitating agencies and also some whose major function is in the merchandising area.

Part II is concerned with long-term business financing. The nature of such financing and the instruments and procedures used are first developed. Then various sources of long-term funds are explored. Finally, attention is directed to the merchandising and facilitating agencies in this area of financing.

Part III covers the institutions and procedures developed to supply short-term and long-term funds in specialized areas. The first to be considered is the financing of agriculture, and the second, the financing of international trade and foreign investment.

Part IV deals with the financing of the consumer, both for short-term and long-term needs. The first chapter develops the role of consumer financing in the economy. The following chapters cover the development, practices, procedures, and problems of institutions that provide short-term and intermediate-term consumer credit, as well as long-term credit to finance the purchase of residential real estate.

Part V deals with the structure and the administration of the monetary system of the United States and with government financing. The first chapter explores the nature of the monetary system more fully than has been done in this chapter. The next chapter describes the process of the expansion and contraction of purchasing media, that is, the money- and credit-creation function of financial institutions and the government. The third chapter considers the role of the Federal Reserve System in this process. The last chapter deals with the financing of governmental units and the effect that such financing has on the monetary system.

Part VI analyzes the policies and problems in the broad area of monetary and financial policy. The relationships of monetary policies to the price level, to interest rates and the money market, and to business fluctuations are explored in turn. The last chapter considers recent monetary and credit policies in the light of their effects on the economy at large.

QUESTIONS

1. Discuss the role of finance in the American economy.
2. Describe the features that are basic in the financial structure of a highly developed economy.
3. Outline and discuss the functions of finance.
4. Discuss the use of barter as a method of exchange and show how experience with it probably led to the development of money.
5. Which characteristics did the items used as money in early times have in common? Why did these characteristics make them suitable for use as money?
6. Discuss the qualities needed in a good unit of account in a monetary system.
7. Discuss the probable development of precious metals as money. Account for this development.
8. Describe the development of paper money. Why was it accepted in exchange in place of coins?
9. Discuss the use of checks and bookkeeping transactions as a means of exchange.
10. Describe the role of currency and checking accounts as a cushion to meet imbalances between receipts and disbursements of funds.
11. Describe the adjustments that have to be made when cash receipts and disbursements do not balance for a period of time.

SUGGESTED READINGS

ANGELL, NORMAN. *The Story of Money*. New York: Frederick A. Stokes Company, 1929.

BURNS, A. R. *Money and Monetary Policy in Early Times*. New York: Alfred A. Knopf, Inc., 1927.

COPELAND, MORRIS. *A Study of Moneyflows in the United States*. New York: National Bureau of Economic Research, Inc., 1952. Chapters 2, 3, 11.

"U. S. A.—Permanent Revolution"—*Fortune* (February, 1951).

Short-Term

Business

Financing

Chapter 2

The Nature of

Business Finance

Business finance may be described as those activities which have to do with the provision and management of funds for the satisfactory conduct of business operations. As such, business finance is concerned with the alternative ways by which funds for business operations may be obtained, with the financial aspects of acquiring land, buildings, equipment, and materials, and with the payment of wages and salaries and other monetary obligations. The accumulation of funds for these purposes may come from the owners of the business, from accumulated profits, and from funds borrowed from other persons or institutions.

In this chapter we shall explore the principal sources of funds for business operations. In so doing, it will be necessary to explore the specific uses to which such funds are put. This is necessary because, as we shall see more clearly in the following pages, the uses to which funds are put are often related closely to the nature of the sources of funds. The role of short-term business finance will also be discussed in this chapter.

THE BALANCE SHEET

For purposes of exploring the interrelationship of uses and sources of funds for business enterprises, it will be helpful to refer to the balance sheet. The *balance sheet* is a summary or report that shows the assets, the liabilities, and the owners' interests of a business at a particular time. It reveals two broad categories of information: the properties owned by a business, referred to as *assets,* and the creditors' and the owners' rights or interests in the business assets. The creditors' rights or interests, which are the financial obligations of the business, are referred to as *liabilities.*

The balance sheet is in the nature of a snapshot, revealing the condition of a business as of a given date. Like a cutaway section of an automobile motor, however, much of the dynamic quality of the structure is revealed. The various classes of assets indicate at once the result of recent business operations and the capacity for future operations. The creditors' and the owners' interests in the assets reveal the sources from which the assets of the business were derived. The term "balance sheet" itself conveys a relationship of equality between the assets of the business and the sources of funds for their acquisition that may be expressed as follows:

$$\text{ASSETS} = \text{LIABILITIES} + \text{OWNERS' INTERESTS}$$

Business operations represent a continuous flow of funds from cash into noncash items, which are then reconverted into cash. Cash is paid out as wages and salaries, reducing the amount of cash in the enterprise. Sales of goods or services may provide an increase in cash. A large cash expenditure is made for the acquisition of additional buildings and equipment, providing greater productive capacity and reducing for the moment the funds of the business. To determine the dynamic nature of business finance we, in effect, stop the processes momentarily in order that we may study their movement and composition. The balance sheet is our medium through which this is accomplished.

The simplified balance sheet of a merchandising firm on page 19 reveals this equality of assets and the financial interests in the assets. The financial interests in the assets, as noted above, comprise the creditors' claims and owners' interests. We shall in the following pages discuss the composition of this balance sheet with the specific objective of relating the assets to the sources of funds for their acquisition.

Current Assets

The balance sheet of the ABC Merchandising Company reveals, among other things, that the business had assets as of December 31, 1958, of $375,000. The assets of the company have been classified into two major groups: current assets and fixed assets.

The *current assets* of a business enterprise include cash and other assets that may reasonably be expected to be converted into

Figure 2-1
ABC MERCHANDISING COMPANY
BALANCE SHEET
December 31, 1958

ASSETS

Current Assets:

Cash	$ 25,000.00	
Notes Receivable	25,000.00	
Accounts Receivable	75,000.00	
Merchandise Inventory	120,000.00	
Prepaid Expenses	5,000.00	
Total Current Assets		$250,000.00

Fixed Assets:

Equipment	$ 50,000.00	
Land and Buildings	75,000.00	
Total Fixed Assets		125,000.00
Total Assets		$375,000.00

LIABILITIES AND OWNERS' INTERESTS

Current Liabilities:

Notes Payable (to bank)	$ 25,000.00	
Accounts Payable	50,000.00	
Accrued Liabilities	25,000.00	
Total Current Liabilities		$100,000.00

Fixed Liabilities:

Mortgage Payable (due 1978)		60,000.00
Total Liabilities		$160,000.00
Owners' Interests [1]		215,000.00
Total Liabilities and Owners' Interests		$375,000.00

[1] The student with a knowledge of accounting will understand that in practice the owners' interests are shown in the balance sheet as the proprietorship, partnership, or capital and surplus accounts, depending upon the legal form of organization of the enterprise.

cash, sold, or used in the near future through the normal operations of the business. The principal current assets of a business are typically its cash, notes receivable, accounts receivable, inventories, and prepaid expenses.

Cash. In addition to cash on hand and on deposit with banks, such items as postal money orders, bank checks not yet deposited, and bank drafts are included under this heading.

Notes Receivable. A *note receivable* is a written promise by a debtor of the business to pay a specified sum of money on or before a stated date. Such notes are ordinarily made payable to the order of a specified firm or person or to "bearer." Notes receivable may come into existence from the settlement of accounts receivable, from the sale of goods and services when required by the seller, and from short-term loans made by the business to its employees or to other persons or businesses. These notes may be held until maturity or converted into cash immediately through their sale to a bank or other purchaser.

Because most credit sales of goods and services by businesses in the United States are made on the basis of accounts receivable financing, as described in the following paragraph, notes receivable are typically of minor importance. For the bank, loan company, or other such financial institution, however, notes receivables represent one of the principal assets since their customers are required to sign notes as evidence of the loans.

Accounts Receivable. *Accounts receivable* generally arise from the sale of merchandise or services on credit, that is, the oral promise of the customer to pay. An account receivable is not based on a note and is carried on the books of the seller as a claim against the buyer. The buyer generally pays his debts to the business according to the credit terms of the sale. Overdue accounts receivable may be converted to notes receivable at the insistence of the seller or upon special request by the buyer.

Merchandise Inventory. The goods that a merchandising enterprise has on hand for sale are generally shown as merchandise inventory on the balance sheet. A manufacturing firm has raw materials and goods in the process of manufacture as well as finished goods. The balance sheet of a manufacturing firm usually reveals the amount of inventory in each of these categories.

Prepaid Expenses. Supplies on hand and prepayment of operating expenses, such as rent, insurance, and taxes, are current assets of the business. Without them it would be necessary to make early expenditures in approximately equal amounts to support business operations. Although the trend is toward inclusion of such items in the current assets section of the balance sheet, they frequently are to be found under "deferred charges."

Fixed Assets

Fixed assets are the physical facilities used in the production, storage, display, and distribution of the products of a firm. These assets normally provide many years of service to the firm. The principal fixed assets are equipment, land, and buildings.

Equipment. In a manufacturing enterprise much investment exists in equipment. In merchandising operations also much equipment is required, such as display cases, cash registers, book-keeping machines, and delivery equipment.

Land and Buildings. The special characteristic of land and buildings is that they are relatively fixed or permanent. Although the buildings of a firm slowly outlive their usefulness, either from structural deterioration or lack of adaptability to new business methods, their life is generally far greater than that of the most permanent of the equipment and other assets of the firm.

Current Liabilities

The liabilities of a business come into existence through direct borrowing, the purchase of goods and services on a credit basis, and the accrual of obligations for such purposes as wages of employees and income taxes. Like the firm's assets, liabilities are classified as current and fixed.

The *current liabilities* of a business may be defined as those obligations that must be satisfied within a period of one year. They are the liabilities that are to be met out of current funds and operations of the business. Although the cash on hand for the ABC Merchandising Company is only $25,000 compared with current liabilities of $100,000, it is expected that normal business operations will convert receivables and inventory into cash in sufficient time to meet current liabilities as they become due. In addition to notes and accounts payable, a third general group of current liabilities, known as "accrued liabilities," are described below.

Notes Payable. A *note payable* is a written promise to pay a specified amount of money to the order of a creditor on or before a certain date. These notes may arise from the purchase of goods or services on a credit basis, from direct short-term borrowing, or in settlement of accounts payable that have not been satisfied according to the terms of the purchase agreement. The most common situation giving rise to a note payable is the borrowing of money from a bank on a short-term basis for the purchase of merchandise for resale or for other current operating requirements. The transaction that gives rise to the note payable on our balance sheet is reflected as a note receivable on the balance sheet of the firm to which the money is owed.

Accounts Payable. Accounts payable arise primarily from the purchase of goods by a business on credit terms. The account payable is not evidenced by a note. Although it lacks some of the certainty of the note, its convenience and simplicity have resulted in a considerable popularity in its use. Accounts payable, as well as notes payable, arising from the purchase of inventory on credit terms represent "trade credit" financing as opposed to direct short-term borrowing from banks and other lenders. An account payable shown in our balance sheet is reflected as an account receivable on the balance sheet of the firm from which we have acquired the goods.

Accrued Liabilities. Amounts owed but not yet due for such items as wages and salaries, taxes, and interest on notes are classified as *accrued liabilities* and as such are included in the current liabilities section of the balance sheet. Of special importance is the tax accrual, which often is the largest single current liability of the business.

Fixed Liabilities

The *fixed liabilities* of a business represent long-term debts, repayment of which is not required within a period of one year. The long-term debts of a business may extend from one to one hundred years or more, depending upon the confidence of lenders in the business and the nature of the security that the business may offer for such loans. As a long-term debt approaches the date it is to be paid, ordinarily within a year from its maturity date, the debt is transferred to the current liabilities section of the balance sheet to call attention to the fact that its settlement must be made within the year.

One of the most common methods of obtaining a long-term loan by a business establishment is to offer a mortgage to a lender. A *mortgage* may be described as a conveyance or transfer of title to property given by a debtor to a creditor as security for the payment of the debt, with a provision that such conveyance or transfer of title is to become void on the payment of the debt according to the terms of the mortgage. In the event that the borrowing business fails to meet the obligations of the loan contract, the mortgage may be foreclosed, that is, the property may be seized through appropriate legal channels and sold in order to satisfy the indebtedness.

Owners' Interests

All businesses have an ownership interest in one form or another. These ownership interests initially result from a cash outlay for the purchase of assets with which to operate the business. In other cases the owners of a business may simply place physical assets, such as machinery, real estate, or equipment, with the firm for its operation. Owners' interests are also increased by allowing profits of the business to remain with the business rather than by additional direct contributions of cash or property. On the balance sheet the amount of owners' interests is always represented by the difference between total assets and total debts of the business. It reflects the owners' claims on the assets of the business as opposed to the creditors' claims.

RELATIONSHIP OF SOURCES OF FINANCING TO ASSETS

Although we have classified the sources of funds for the ABC Merchandising Company into liabilities and owners' interests, the fixed liabilities of the business are in some respects more akin to the owners' interests than to the current liabilities. Short-term financing on the part of a business, reflected in the current liabilities section of the balance sheet, is generally utilized to obtain current assets for the business. Long-term financing, on the other hand, may be undertaken to obtain either or both current assets and fixed assets. The fixed liabilities and the owners' interests in a business both represent a form of long-term financing and in this respect they are similar. Legally, however, the fixed liabilities and the current liabilities are similar.

Short-Term Financing

The principal sources of short-term financing are banks, commercial finance companies, and sellers of goods on a credit basis. These sources of financing are discussed in detail in the following chapters. It is sufficient at this point to stress that financing from these sources is generally available to businesses for periods of less than one year and often for a maximum of two or three months. Business enterprises engage in short-term financing for such purposes as the acquisition of merchandise inventory for resale, the payment of salaries and wages, and the payment of other financial obligations that become due. This form of financing permits the business to meet the expenses of operations until the proceeds from the sale of merchandise are finally received. Hence, short-term financing facilitates the coordination of the flow of income and cash expenditures of the firm.

The firm that finds it possible to meet all cash expenditures out of the normal flow of income from operations requires no current financing. The firm that has a relatively long period of time involved in the manufacturing process and sells its goods on a basis that does not require the customer to meet his payment for several weeks may require considerable short-term financing to make possible the payment of current obligations while waiting for its receipt of income from customers. Short-term financing is ordinarily undertaken for current asset purposes rather than for the acquisition of fixed assets.

Long-Term Financing

The fixed liabilities and the owners' interests in a business constitute its long-term financing. Such financing may be undertaken to provide funds for all business purposes, such as the acquisition of current assets, equipment, buildings, and land. It may be observed, therefore, that while short-term financing is undertaken for the acquisition of current assets, long-term financing may be undertaken for the acquisition of either current or fixed assets. It should also be observed that while all short-term financing represents debt financing, long-term financing may be either debt financing (fixed liabilities) or equity financing (owners' interests).

The mortgage payable of the ABC Merchandising Company, the sole fixed liability item in our example, was probably issued in order to acquire a part of the land, buildings, or equipment, since the mortgage lien (or claim) itself is generally against the real estate, buildings, and certain equipment that is considered part of the real property.

In businesses other than banks and other financial institutions the owners' interests are typically greater than the combination of all current liabilities and fixed liabilities. The balance sheet of the ABC Merchandising Company reveals that current liabilities have contributed only $100,000 of the $250,000 invested in current assets, and that the mortgage payable of $60,000 is far short of the $125,000 invested in the fixed assets of the business. In both cases the difference is provided by the owners' investments.

The owners' interests in the business, sometimes referred to as *owners' equity* or *net worth,* is more than an incidental contribution to the business; the availability of both short-term financing and long-term borrowing is predicated upon the existence of substantial owners' interests in the business. The owners' interests in the ABC Merchandising Company represent $215,000 of the $375,000 invested in the business. This represents a percentage relationship of approximately 57 per cent for ownership financing and 43 per cent for debt financing. The business with a large proportion of its assets obtained through ownership financing is able to obtain additional financing more readily and on far better terms than if the business were financed with an unusually large proportion of borrowed capital.

In addition to the influence that the asset structure of a business exerts on the sources of financing of a business, many other factors come into play, such as the relative stability of the income of the business during periods of depression and prosperity, the importance of seasonal influences on production and sales during the year, and the reputation of the management. For example, the firm that experiences a relatively stable flow of income irrespective of general business conditions, that has a production and sales schedule that is closely related to the seasons of the year, and that has the reputation of meeting obligations promptly will find it possible to engage in short-term financing and long-term borrowing to a far greater extent than would otherwise be possible. Notwithstanding the fact that such a firm might engage heavily in debt financing, management attitudes have an important bearing on the extent of debt financing.

NET WORKING CAPITAL AND SHORT-TERM FINANCING

That part of total current assets provided through long-term financing is referred to as the *net working capital* of the firm. This amount is determined by subtracting the total of current liabilities shown on the balance sheet from the total of current assets. If short-term financing were relied upon entirely by a business for its current asset requirements, the total current assets of the firm would be equal to the total current liabilities. The balance sheet of a successful nonfinancial business enterprise, however, will reveal an excess of current assets over current liabilities. This excess reflects the extent to which long-term financing has contributed to the support of the current asset requirements of the business.

The net working capital is a measure of the financial soundness of a firm, since it provides additional resources from which the short-term liabilities may be paid. In general, the greater the net working capital of a firm the less burdensome are the problems of meeting short-term obligations. So important is the existence of an adequate net working capital to a firm that it has become one of the prime tests of strength, and creditors place great emphasis on it in determining whether or not to extend credit to their customers.

The appropriate amount of net working capital for a firm depends upon the individual firm in question as well as upon the industry within which it operates. For example, a firm that does a large proportion of its business on a cash sale basis and which has a stable volume of sales throughout the year may be able to conduct its affairs with only a very modest net working capital position. On the other hand, a firm that has a large volume of receivables outstanding and whose sales are subject to wide seasonal variations may find it necessary to maintain a large net working capital position in order to be assured of meeting its obligations promptly throughout the year.

The Current Ratio

The net working capital or short-term financial position of a firm is expressed not only in terms of a dollar quantity, that is, the difference between total current assets and total current liabilities, but also in relative terms. This relationship is determined by dividing total current assets by total current liabilities, the quotient being the *current ratio* of the firm. Although the net working capital position and the current ratio are simply alternative ways of expressing the short-term financial position of the firm, each has its particular usefulness.

The current ratio concept is particularly useful in comparing the financial positions of firms of varying sizes. For example, a firm may have total current assets of $200,000 and total current liabilities of $100,000, in which case the current ratio is 2 to 1 and the net working capital is $100,000. Another firm, engaged in similar business activities, may have total current assets of $400,000 and total current liabilities of $200,000, the current ratio being 2 to 1 and the net working capital $200,000. In this example, the net working capital of the latter firm is twice that of the former, yet it is clear that it is a matter of proportion, that the latter firm may simply be a larger enterprise doing a larger volume of business. The current ratio of each firm, however, is 2 to 1, revealing the similarity of short-term financial positions. It is the current ratio, therefore, that facilitates comparisons with other firms, while it is the net working capital position that is of primary interest to the management of the firm and in particular to those persons in the firm who are charged with the responsibility for budgeting and controlling the flow of funds into the business and the payment of short-term obligations.

Table 2-1 reveals the relationship between current assets and current liabilities for several industries. These ratios, compiled by Dun & Bradstreet, Inc., cover five-year averages for a representative sampling of firms within each industry for the years 1951 through 1955. Since the current ratios shown in this table represent averages for many firms in each industry, it is to be expected that in most industries there is a wide range of prevailing current ratios—from those of the financially weak enterprises to those of superior financial strength. For example, the median current ratio for manufacturers of automobile parts and accessories in 1954 was 3.0 to 1. This figure is based on a sample of 71 firms. Among the firms in this industry with current ratios far in excess of the median is the McCord Corporation with a current ratio of 8.1 to 1. At the other extreme, the Bendix Aviation Corporation in that year had a current ratio of 1.8 to 1.

Table 2-1

CURRENT RATIOS FOR 22 LINES OF BUSINESS
FIVE-YEAR AVERAGES FOR THE YEARS 1951-1955

LINE OF BUSINESS	RATIO OF CURRENT ASSETS TO CURRENT DEBT
Manufacturers:	
Cotton Cloth Mills	3.78
Paints, Varnishes and Lacquers	3.51
Confectionery	3.44
Drugs	3.36
Hardware and Tools	3.20
Furniture	3.20
Automobile Parts and Accessories	2.64
Paper	2.62
Meats and Provisions, Packers	2.16
Breweries	2.10
Bakers	1.95
Soft Drinks and Carbonated Water, Bottlers	1.89
Wholesalers:	
Hosiery and Underwear	3.70
Furnishing's, Men's	3.53
Hardware	3.23
Groceries	2.70
Wines and Liquors	1.95
Retailers:	
Clothing, Men's and Boys'	3.66
Furniture	3.57
Department Stores	3.55
Shoes	3.15
Women's Specialty Shops	2.72

SOURCE: Dun & Bradstreet, Inc.

Necessity for Adequate Net Working Capital

The importance of providing for part of the current asset requirements of a business through long-term financing may be illustrated by a theoretical and highly improbable situation in which long-term financing has not been provided for this purpose. The balance sheet of the firm might appear as in Figure 2-2. In this balance sheet the total of current liabilities equals the total of current assets; there is no net working capital.

By their nature, the current liabilities of such a firm would be falling due periodically and would have to be paid out of the cash funds of the business. Since the cash is $25,000, only that amount of current indebtedness could be retired on the date of the bal-

Figure 2-2

ABC MERCHANDISING COMPANY

BALANCE SHEET

December 31, 1958

ASSETS

Current Assets:

Cash	$ 25,000.00	
Notes Receivable	25,000.00	
Accounts Receivable	75,000.00	
Merchandise Inventory	120,000.00	
Prepaid Expenses	5,000.00	
Total Current Assets		$250,000.00

Fixed Assets:

Equipment	$ 50,000.00	
Land and Buildings	75,000.00	
Total Fixed Assets		125,000.00
Total Assets		$375,000.00

LIABILITIES AND OWNERS' INTERESTS

Current Liabilities:

Notes Payable (to bank)	$ 75,000.00	
Accounts Payable	150,000.00	
Accrued Liabilities	25,000.00	
Total Current Liabilities		$250,000.00

Fixed Liabilities:

Mortgage Payable (due 1978)		60,000.00
Total Liabilities		$310,000.00
Owners' Interests		65,000.00
Total Liabilities and Owners' Interests		$375,000.00

ance sheet. It is true, of course, that the accounts receivable and the inventory would in time be converted into cash. It is even possible to work out a schedule of conversion into cash of receivables and inventory at such a rate that obligations falling due could theoretically be met. The business would be in an extremely precarious position, however, and, in the event of failure of the conversion of receivables and inventory into cash on schedule, the firm would be unable to meet promptly its current obligations. Nor is it probable that this or any other firm, with such a relatively large volume of short-term obligations, could always schedule its inflow of funds in such a way as to match perfectly its outflow of payments.

The answer to this problem is to provide part of the current asset requirements through long-term financing. Under these circumstances the total of the current liabilities will be less than the total of the current assets. With current assets amounting to perhaps twice current liabilities, as in the balance sheet in Figure 2-1, the chance of the business having too little cash to meet its own obligations is reduced materially.

Advantages of Adequate Net Working Capital

An adequate net working capital makes it possible for the firm to meet its debts promptly and to take discounts that may be available if early payment is made for purchases of raw materials and other goods.[2] Also, the firm that is in a position to make cash payments may pay a lower price for its purchases, or it may have access to a better quality of merchandise at the same price because of the better bargaining position it enjoys. Suppliers of materials as well as banks regard more highly the firm with a strong net working capital position, insuring a continuing flow of funds and supplies during peak periods of seasonal activity and making it possible for the firm to take advantage of over-all expansion as long-term growth opportunities become available. Finally, insofar as an adequate net working capital position insures a continuous supply of raw materials and production, steady work is available for employees. The firm that offers steady employment will usually benefit from greater efficiency on the part of its employees.

Why Short-Term Financing?

In the light of the several advantages of a strong net working capital position the question may be asked, why engage at all in short-term financing? Despite the comfortable financial position that a firm would enjoy if it had no obligations arising from short-term financing, there are several reasons why there is scarcely a business in operation which does not engage in this form of financing from time to time. Among these reasons are:

[2] Cash discounts and other trade credit terms are discussed in detail in Chapter 6.

1. Lower cost of short-term financing.
2. Lack of sufficient long-term financing.
3. Advantage of establishing a credit record.
4. Greater flexibility.

(1) Lower Cost of Short-Term Financing. The lower costs of short-term financing may be explained by discussing the following three points: short-term financing vs. long-term borrowing; short-term financing vs. equity financing; and the influence of seasonal variations in business as they relate to financing costs.

From the beginning of the depression of the 1930's until late 1955, short-term interest rates on business loans were consistently lower than long-term interest rates. During this 25-year period, because of economies of cost, much incentive existed to use short-term financing, where such financing was suitable, as an alternative to long-term borrowing. By mid-year 1956 the cost of short-term borrowing was approximately the same as for that of long-term borrowing; however, in future periods when short-term interest rates may be less than long-term interest rates, the incentive for short-term financing will again exist.

It is usually less costly to engage in short-term financing than to sell additional equity (ownership) interests in the business. Persons who purchase additional ownership interests in the business, like the existing owners, will share in the profits of the business. During periods of normal business activity, these profits will generally represent a return on investment far greater than the costs of short-term financing. Hence, the existing owners of the business can increase their own earnings through short-term financing to the extent that the earnings on assets acquired through short-term financing exceed the costs of such financing. Even if the owners of a business are in a position to provide the business with needed funds from their personal accounts, that plan may represent a costly investment, since these funds might be employed far more profitably in other uses where equity capital is in great demand. Both forms of long-term financing, debt and equity, may therefore be more costly than are the usual forms of short-term financing.

Many business enterprises are subject to seasonal influences that result in a concentration of sales activity during certain months of the year. Department stores, for example, experience substantial increases in sales volume during October, November, and December, and again in the spring and early summer. Such periods of brisk activity must be preceded by an accumulation of inventory. Much of this inventory may be purchased with the aid of short-term financing. The advantages of short-term financing under these circumstances are readily apparent when it is recognized that such financing may extend over only a few months, at the end of which time the obligations may be repaid by a business out of the proceeds of sales.

The very nature of most business operations is such that the disbursements of the firm do not coincide with the receipts so far as timing is concerned. The cost of short-term financing is largely confined to the periods during the year when expenses are being incurred or inventories accumulated without a corresponding flow of receipts from sales. If long-term financing were undertaken for this purpose, these funds would be idle during several months of the year and of little use until the next period of increasing seasonal activity. The cost of long-term financing would continue throughout the year, while in short-term financing the costs exist only during the periods when such financing is actually needed and used.

(2) Lack of Sufficient Long-Term Financing. In many situations the availability of financing rather than the cost is the relevant factor. For example, the owners of a business may have exhausted their personal resources in the process of investing directly in their venture. They may have, in addition, mortgaged their real estate and otherwise obtained as much long-term borrowed capital as lenders are willing to provide.

(3) Advantage of Establishing a Credit Record. The firm that depends almost entirely upon long-term financing for its needs will not enjoy the close relationship with its bank that it otherwise would. A record of frequent borrowing from and prompt repayment to its bank by an enterprise is an extremely important factor in sound financial management. Under these circumstances, a bank will make every effort to accommodate its business customers with loans at all times. The enterprise that has not established such a working relationship with its bank will scarcely

be in a position to seek special loans during its periods of emergency needs. Also the credit experience of a business in connection with its short-term financing may be the only basis on which potential long-term lenders to a business can judge the enterprise. Hence, the business that intends to seek long-term loans may wish to establish a good credit reputation based on its short-term financing.

(4) Greater Flexibility. Periodic phases of business activity—expansion, prosperity, contraction, depression, and expansion again—generally extending over a time span of several years, have been a normal part of this nation's economy throughout most of its history. To the extent that an individual enterprise experiences similar fluctuations in its business activity, it will at times require substantial increases in its current assets. Just as short-term financing may serve an enterprise during periods of high seasonal demand during the year, it also may be utilized to advantage as a supplement to long-term financing during periods of general business expansion and prosperity.

The increased sales activity that accompanies a period of business expansion makes it necessary for the firm to maintain a larger volume of inventory, an increased volume of notes and accounts receivable (if the firm sells on credit terms), and larger sums of cash for day-to-day operations. At other times, because of declining sales activity resulting from depression influences, the total of current asset requirements may decline substantially.

If during periods of general business expansion an enterprise obtains its additional current asset requirements entirely through long-term financing, it might be burdened with excessive funds during a subsequent period of general business contraction or depression. In using short-term financing along with long-term financing, therefore, a flexibility of operations is possible that does not exist with long-term financing alone. As the need for assets decreases, the firm may simply retire its short-term obligations. Although the long-term obligations of the business may in some cases be retired when the funds provided through such financing are no longer required, such an action may be awkward and often a penalty must be paid for prepayment of the obligation.

QUESTIONS

1. Describe the function of finance as it applies to the operation of a business enterprise.
2. In what way are the sources of financing influenced by the firm's asset structure?
3. What are the principal sources of short-term financing?
4. Distinguish between short-term and long-term business financing?
5. What are the principal forms of long-term business financing?
6. Define the concept of net working capital. Describe the significance of net working capital.
7. Discuss the factors that influence the requirements for net working capital.
8. In what way is the current ratio related to the net working capital of a firm?
9. What benefit may be gained from a study of current ratios as well as net working capital levels?
10. Why is it important for a business enterprise to maintain an adequate net working capital?
11. Is it possible for a firm to have too much net working capital?
12. Compare the costs of short-term versus long-term business borrowing.
13. Why would a business engage in short-term financing if ample sources of funds were available through long-term financing?
14. How does the use of short-term financing introduce flexibility into the financial operations of a business?

SUGGESTED READINGS

DAUTEN, CARL A. *Business Finance;* Second Edition. Englewood Cliffs, New Jersey: Prentice-Hall, Inc., 1956. Chapters 1 and 13.

GERSTENBERG, CHARLES W. *Financial Organization and Management of Business;* Third Edition. Englewood Cliffs, New Jersey: Prentice-Hall, Inc., 1951. Chapter 18.

GUTHMANN, HARRY G., AND DOUGALL, HERBERT E. *Corporate Financial Policy;* Third Edition. Englewood Cliffs, New Jersey: Prentice-Hall, Inc., 1955. Chapter 1.

HOWARD, BION B., AND UPTON, MILLER. *Introduction to Business Finance.* New York: McGraw-Hill Book Company, Inc., 1953. Chapter 1.

HUSBAND, WILLIAM H., AND DOCKERAY, JAMES C. *Modern Corporation Finance;* Third Edition. Homewood, Illinois: Richard D. Irwin, Inc., 1952. Chapter 26.

NATIONAL INDUSTRIAL CONFERENCE BOARD. *The Duties of Financial Executives,* Studies in Business Policy, No. 56, New York, 1952.

WESTON, J. FRED. "The Finance Function," *The Journal of Finance,* IX, No. 3 (September, 1954), 265-82.

Commercial Banks

The importance of the nation's banking system to the processes of a modern industrial economy can hardly be exaggerated. The banking system is an integral part of the monetary system, accumulating and lending idle funds, facilitating the transfer of money, and providing for its safekeeping. As an indication of the importance of the banking system to business, more than $38 billion was outstanding in loans to business by the banks of the United States at midyear, 1957. The banking system also provides part of the long-term financing required by industry, by commerce, and by the farmer. It plays an important part, too, in financing the construction of the nation's millions of homes, and it is an important source of personal loans.

It is necessary to distinguish between commercial banks and the many other types of bank organizations, such as savings banks and investment banks. Briefly, *commercial banks* may be described as those banking institutions that provide "checking deposit" facilities. Although the modern commercial bank performs many functions and services that are provided by other banking and nonbanking establishments, the checking account gives to the commercial banking system its unique significance.

In this chapter the development, the functions, and the organization of commercial banks will be described, followed by a discussion of bank failures and insurance of bank deposits. In the following chapter, the operations of commercial banks will be explained.

DEVELOPMENT OF BANKING IN THE UNITED STATES

The structure of the modern commercial banking system is the result of historical forces as well as of modern-day banking requirements. Banking, like most forms of economic activity, is more subject to the forces of tradition than to those of innovation. Yet, despite the great influence of early banking practices and legislation on present-day banking, the evolution of commercial banks to meet the requirements of the modern industrial economy has been effective and successful. Nor may we assume that the present structure of commercial banking has achieved permanence. To meet the requirements of a dynamic economy, changes are constantly taking place with respect to banking practices, regulation, and legislation. An understanding of banking in the United States today, therefore, requires an understanding of the development of banking in the economic history of the country.

Banking in America Before the Civil War

Early banking in the United States developed under circumstances that explain much of the apparent confusion and difficulty that accompanied such development. The population lived for the most part on farms, families were self-sufficient, and transportation and communications were poor. The friction between proponents of a strong central government as opposed to state government existed in the early years of our history as it does today. Much controversy raged over the power to charter and regulate banks. The country had little experience in money and financial management.

Early Chartered Banks. During the colonial period banking took the form of small unincorporated banks that were established to ease the shortage of capital in businesses. Their operations consisted largely in the issue of their own notes. Outside of the larger towns deposit banking was of minor significance. It was not until 1782 that the first incorporated bank was created along modern lines. The Bank of North America was established in Philadelphia then by Robert Morris to assist in the financing of the Revolutionary War. This bank set a good example for successful banking. Its notes served as a circulating monetary medium, it loaned liberally to the United States Government, and it redeemed its own notes in specie upon demand. Two years later the Bank of Massachusetts and the Bank of New York were established. These three incorporated banks constituted the total of such banks until 1790.

The First Bank of the United States. Alexander Hamilton, the first Secretary of the Treasury of the United States, had for several years harbored the idea of a federally chartered bank that would adequately support the rapidly growing economy and would give financial assistance to the government during its crises. His recommendations were submitted to the House of Representatives of the United States in 1790, and in 1791 a 20-year charter was issued to the First Bank of the United States. Although this bank served the nation effectively in the issuance of notes, in the transfer of funds from region to region, in providing useful service to the government, and in curbing the excessive note issues of state banks by presenting such notes periodically for redemption, strong opposition existed to the renewal of its charter and it ceased operations in 1811. The antagonism of state banking interests was an important cause of the failure of the Bank to have its charter renewed.

Following the expiration of the charter of the First Bank of the United States, the number of state banks increased rapidly, as did the volume of their note issues. Most of the state banks ceased redeeming their notes in gold and silver, and the abuses of banking privileges were extensive.

The Second Bank of the United States. The Second Bank of the United States was chartered primarily to restore order to the chaotic banking situation that had developed after the First Bank of the United States ceased operations. Like the First Bank of the United States, it received a 20-year charter. It began operations in 1816 and, after a short period of mismanagement, set upon a course of reconstruction of sound banking practices. It ably served individuals, businesses, and the government by accepting deposits, making loans, issuing notes, and restraining the note-issuing practices of state banks by presenting periodically the notes of such banks for redemption. The Second Bank of the United States also played a most important and efficient role as fiscal agent for the government.

In 1833 President Andrew Jackson and many of his associates embarked upon such a vigorous campaign against the Second Bank of the United States that it became apparent that its charter would not be renewed upon expiration in 1836. Not until 1863 was another bank in the United States to receive a federal charter.

State Banks from 1836 to the Civil War. Following expiration of the Second Bank's charter, the excesses that had plagued the period 1811-16 again came into play. This period is characterized as one of "wildcat" banking. Although many state banks during this period from 1836 until the Civil War operated on a conservative and very sound basis, the majority of them engaged in risky banking practices through excessive note issues, lack of adequate bank capital, and insufficient reserves against their notes and deposits.

Because the notes of even the well-established banks were often of inferior quality, it was easy for skillful counterfeiters to increase the denomination of notes. Also, because of the poor communications that existed between various sections of the country, it was quite often difficult for a banker to be certain of the nature of the notes presented to him. Skillfully prepared counterfeit notes frequently circulated with greater freedom than did the legitimate notes of weak and little-known banks.

In spite of the many abuses of state banks during this period, New York, Massachusetts, and Louisiana originated banking legislation of a highly commendable nature, much of which provided the basis for the establishment of the National Banking System in 1863.

Banking in America from the Civil War to the Present

In 1863 the National Banking Act again made it possible for banks to receive federal charters. So many amendments were submitted for the improvement of the National Banking Act of 1863 that it was repealed in its entirety in 1864. The National Banking Act of June 3, 1864, represented a complete revision of the Act of 1863. This legislation provided the basis for our present national banking laws.

As for the First Bank and the Second Bank of the United States, the reasons for federal interest in the banking system were to provide for a sound banking system and to curb the excesses of the state banks. Probably an important additional purpose of this legislation was to provide for the financing of the Civil War. Secretary of the Treasury, Salmon P. Chase, and others believed that government bonds could be sold to these nationally chartered banks, which could in turn issue their own notes based in part on the government bonds so purchased.

Through the National Banking Act various steps were taken to promote safe banking practices. Among other things, minimum capital requirements were established for banks with federal charters, loans were regulated with respect to safety and liquidity, a system of supervision and examination was instituted, and minimum reserve requirements against notes and deposits were established. These reform measures, in general, were constructive; but, in some instances, they have been regarded as altogether too restrictive, as in the case of real estate against which all loans were forbidden. Much of the criticism of the national banking system, in fact, was derived from the inflexibility of its limitations, many of which were either modified or eliminated in 1913 with the establishment of the federal reserve system.

The National Banking Act did not establish a system of central banks; it only made possible the chartering of banks by the federal government. The Federal Reserve Act of 1913 brought to the American economy a system of central banks. The Federal Reserve System was designed to eliminate many of the weaknesses that had persisted under the National Banking Act and to increase the effectiveness of commercial banking in general. It brought with it not only strong central domination of banking practices but also many services to commercial banks. The influence of the federal reserve system is described in Chapter 5.

FUNCTIONS OF COMMERCIAL BANKS

The basic functions of the modern commercial bank are (1) the acceptance of deposits and (2) the granting of loans to business borrowers and to others. In accepting deposits, the commercial bank provides an alternative to the hoarding of funds for future use on the part of the public. Individuals and businesses seldom wish to spend their money as it becomes available, and without the depositary facilities of the bank such funds may lie idle. Having accumulated deposits, the commercial bank puts them to use through loans to persons and businesses having immediate use for them. The result of the pooling of funds by the commercial banks is a more effective utilization of funds.

Corollary to the acceptance of deposits by commercial banks are the functions of (3) safekeeping for depositors, (4) the efficient and economical transfer of claims to deposits through check-writing procedures, and (5) the record of transactions provided the depositor through the regular bookkeeping and reporting procedures of the bank.

In the granting of business loans the commercial bank accomplishes a desirable objective of (6) selection of risks. The banker's refusal to finance an ill-conceived venture is in the interest of the bank in protecting its assets, but it may also be in the interest of the prospective operators of the new venture, preventing them from engaging in an activity that will result in loss to them. Furthermore, the careful apportionment of loan funds to those businesses with the best apparent chances of success makes possible the development of the nation's resources to the greatest possible advantage.

ESTABLISHMENT AND ORGANIZATION OF THE COMMERCIAL BANK

In organizing a bank, the first decision to be made is whether the charter application will be made to a state or to the federal government. Many factors enter into this decision. In some states the requirements for bank operation may be considerably less restrictive than those of the federal government. If it is the intention of the bankers to affiliate their bank with the Federal Reserve System, however, or to carry bank deposit insurance provided by the Federal Deposit Insurance Corporation, some of the advantages that would otherwise accrue to a bank through a state charter may be eliminated since both the Federal Reserve System and the Federal Deposit Insurance Corporation insist upon the right to supervise and examine all participating banks. Many states, on the other hand, have banking laws that are quite as restrictive as are those of the federal government. The prestige of a charter from the federal government may also be an important factor in the determination of a choice of national bank versus state bank status.

Application for Charter

Assuming that a national bank is to be organized, a formal application must be submitted to the Comptroller of the Currency in the United States Treasury Department by the persons desiring to establish the new bank. A complete examination is made of the proposal. The examination includes not only the possibilities for success of the new venture and the need for such banking facilities in the community, but also an investigation into the background and qualifications of the persons who will operate the bank. If the report of the examiners is favorable, the venture is permitted to issue its stock to subscribers and cash may be paid into the organization. When the appropriate amount of cash has been paid in and the minimum paid-in surplus established, a certificate of authority to commence business is issued.

Minimum Capital Requirements

One of the requirements of banks with federal charters relates to the amount of capital. If the bank under consideration is to be established in a community having a population of less than 6,000, a minimum capital of $50,000 is required. In cities of more than 6,000 and less than 50,000 population, $100,000 is the minimum capital requirement. In cities of more than 50,000 population, at least $200,000 is required.

National banks are required to begin operations with paid-in surplus of at least 20 per cent of the capital stock, to be obtained, of course, through the sale of stock at a premium. (Further, national banks must add not less than one tenth of their net profits to surplus until the surplus is equal to the common stock.) The initial paid-in surplus is to provide for the costs of organization and early losses that may be realized. The organizers of the bank must then decide whether funds secured from the sale of capital stock are to be used to purchase land, buildings, or equipment, or whether such facilities will be leased and the capital funds invested directly in earning assets. The *earning assets* of a bank include all of its investments that provide an income, such as promissory notes, government bonds, and real estate mortgages.

Bank Deposits

Up to this point, the activities of the bank in question differ but little from those of an industrial enterprise. It is here, however, that we diverge from the pattern of industrial operations. Earnings on bank capital alone are hardly sufficient to provide a satisfactory profit to the stockholders; in fact, it would be impossible to operate on a satisfactory basis with no other funds to invest. To increase the earning assets of a bank, other persons and businesses are invited to become customers of the bank and to deposit their funds with the bank. As such deposits are presented to the bank, both the assets and the liabilities of the bank are increased. On *checking-account or demand deposits* no interest is paid, and the money earned on the reinvestment of these deposits serves to defray the expenses of bank operations and to provide a net return to the stockholders of the bank.

On time or savings deposits, which are not legally subject to immediate withdrawal, the depositors may receive a return on their deposits. In the case of either demand deposits or time deposits, however, the specific identity of the items deposited is lost. A claim exists only to a certain amount of money. The bank, therefore, is free to invest the depositor's money and to shift such investments from one form to another within the limits permitted by regulation. The more money a bank attracts from depositors, the larger the possible volume of earning assets the bank will have and, of course, the larger the earnings to the stockholders, other things remaining the same.

Relationship of Capital to Deposits

Although a large volume of deposits makes possible greater earnings for the stockholders of the bank, the larger the volume of deposits in relation to the capital contribution of the stockholders, the smaller the margin of safety for the depositors. The function of the stockholders' cash contribution in the purchase of stock is to provide a cushion for possible bank losses. The depositors of a bank, in fact, are creditors and hence have a claim prior to that of the stockholders in case of liquidation. The depositors of a bank lose nothing until the entire stockholder contribution and accumulation is exhausted, at which time the bank is rendered insolvent. Therefore, one of the important factors that bank examiners stress today is the maintenance of a minimum ratio between bank deposits and capital.

When the deposits of a bank are high in relation to capital funds, it may be said that the stockholders are assuming a small proportion of the risk of the bank and the depositors a large share of the risk. When the deposits of a bank are low relative to its capital funds, the bank will probably be in a poor position to pay satisfactory dividends to the stockholders unless the assets of the bank provide an unusually high yield.

For many years the Federal Deposit Insurance Corporation recommended a ratio of deposits to capital funds of no more than 10 to 1.[1] In recent years, however, few banks have been able to qualify with respect to this recommended ratio. The outstanding reason for the failure of banks to maintain such a ratio was the tremendous monetary expansion during and following World War II, which resulted in a corresponding expansion of deposits in the banking system. Many banks, in an effort to maintain a favorable relationship between deposits and capital funds, have sold additional stock. Other banks have established a policy of retaining a substantial part of their earnings in their surplus account in order to boost the ratio; however, this serves to reduce the amount of dividends paid to stockholders and hence makes it more difficult to sell additional stock to the general public.

That the two methods whereby capital may be increased have not provided an increase sufficiently great to maintain the recommended ratio is indicated by the fact that the average ratio of deposits to capital funds for the banks of the country at the end of 1956 was approximately $13\frac{1}{2}$ to 1. While this violates the 10 to 1 rule, the composition of a bank's earning assets is more important than the simple relationship between the volume of deposits and its capital funds. For example, if the bulk of a bank's deposits and capital is invested in government bonds, high-grade municipal securities, and government guaranteed real estate mortgages, the high ratio between total deposits and capital funds is not as serious as would be the case if the bank had the bulk of its funds invested in less well-secured assets. By the same token, if a bank has most of its earning assets invested in extremely safe securities, the yield from such investments will be rather modest and a high ratio between total deposits and capital funds will be necessary in order to avail the stockholders of a competitive rate of return on their investment. There is little doubt, however, that the insistence of a reasonable relationship between deposits and

[1] The deposits to capital ratio of 10 to 1, for which there appears to be little scientific basis, was in use long before the Federal Deposit Insurance Corporation came into existence. This organization is described later in the chapter.

capital funds is an extremely important one, assuming that some consideration is given to the composition of the earning assets of a bank.

Nonearning Bank Assets

Not all of a bank's funds are available for profitable investment. A bank will maintain a certain amount of vault cash to meet the day-to-day cash transactions, deposits with other banks, and legal reserves as established by regulatory authorities.[2] These funds provide no interest return for the bank.

Concentration in Banking Control

Concentration in banking control has taken a number of forms as banks, like other businesses, have increased their scope and volume of operations to accommodate the growing economy. Yet, commercial banks in the United States are typically single-unit organizations, each bank having its own board of directors and stockholders, exercising no control over branch offices, and in turn being responsible to no parent organization. At midyear 1956, of the 13,615 commercial banks in the United States, probably no more than 1,100 operated branch offices in any form. The laws of some states, in fact, prevent the operation of branch banking. Other states permit the operation of branch offices only within limited areas, and still others permit branch operation on a statewide scale. (See Table 3-1) A description of various forms that nonindependent banking takes will permit some general conclusions regarding their advantages or disadvantages relative to independently owned and operated banks.

In contrast, the branch banking system is predominant in Canada and Britian. Canada, for example, has only 10 chartered banks, which in turn operate over 3,000 branch offices; England has approximately 13 incorporated banks, of which 5 account for most of the deposits of that nation. These incorporated banks operate more than 8,000 branches throughout that country.

Branch Banking. Branch banks are those banking offices that are controlled by a single parent bank. One board of directors and one group of stockholders control the home office and the

---

[2] The individual classes of bank assets are described in greater detail in Chapter 4.

Table 3-1

SUMMARY OF STATE BRANCH BANKING LAWS

STATES PERMITTING STATE-WIDE BRANCH BANKING	STATES PERMITTING BRANCH BANKING WITHIN LIMITED AREAS	STATES PROHIBITING BRANCH BANKING	STATES WITH NO LEGISLATION REGARDING BRANCH BANKING
Arizona	Alabama	Colorado	Kentucky
California	Arkansas	Florida	New Hampshire
Connecticut	Georgia	Illinois	Oklahoma
Delaware	Indiana	Kansas	Wyoming
District of	Iowa	Minnesota	
Columbia	Louisiana	Missouri	
Idaho	Massachusetts	Nebraska	
Maine	Michigan	Texas	
Maryland	Mississippi	West Virginia	
Nevada	Montana	Wisconsin	
North Carolina	New Jersey		
Oregon	New Mexico		
Rhode Island	New York		
South Carolina	North Dakota		
South Dakota	Ohio		
Utah	Pennsylvania		
Vermont	Tennessee		
Virginia			
Washington			
Total, 18	Total, 17	Total, 10	Total, 4

SOURCE: Division of Research and Statistics, Board of Governors of the Federal Reserve System.

branches. Some of our branch banking systems are very small, involving perhaps only two, three, or four branches. Others are quite large, extending over an entire state and having many branches.

As to the merits of branch banking, one of the most important is that branch banking systems are less likely to fail than are independent unit banks. In a branch banking system more adequate diversification of investments can be made, and the temporary reverses of a single community are not so likely to cause complete failure of the entire banking chain. This would be true primarily of those branch systems that operate over wide geographical areas rather than in a single metropolitan area. The independent bank cannot rely on other banks to offset local economic reverses.

It is on this score that the branch banking operations appear to have their strongest argument, for the record of bank failures in the United States has been one of which the banking system as a whole cannot be proud; but there have been few failures in those systems of banks that have engaged in branch banking practices. Opponents of this form of banking have pointed out, however, that failure of a system of banks, although less frequent, is far more serious.

The record of bank failures in both Canada and England is far superior to the record in the United States in spite of the fact that those countries have also been subject to extreme economic pressures.

In addition to the matter of safety, a system of branch banks may provide more adequate banking service to the local community than the independently owned bank because it has the resources of its other branches on which it may draw. The independently owned unit bank, of course, may have access to larger banks for assistance when requests are made for loans beyond the capacity of the bank.

Other advantages that have been claimed for branch banking systems are the greater convenience to customers that results from the quick placement of branches in newly developed centers of population, the greater uniformity of interest rates throughout the area of branch banking activities due to the mobility of funds from branch to branch, and the operational advantages of bigness in business activity. For example, it may be possible to achieve economies through the large-scale purchase of bank supplies, through the establishment of elaborate operating systems, through the extensive training of personnel, and through the employment of more competent management.

Among the objections that are raised to branch banking are the fear of concentration in control of banking operations, the lack of sincere interest in community affairs of branch managers who may be transferred to other areas, the possibility of loan delays while obtaining approval from main offices, and the possible withdrawal of funds from small towns and rural areas for the benefit of larger cities.

These objections lack substance in the light of experience both in this country and in Canada. Although branch banking does result in some degree of concentration of control, competition remains intense in branch banking areas. With respect to delays in loan approvals, most branch bank managers have the authority to approve practically all loan applications coming to them and can facilitate approval of most of the remaining applications by telephone. Since branch managers establish a successful record of operations through cooperation with and service to the communities which they serve, it is doubtful that lack of interest in local affairs would exist. Finally, the flow of funds from rural areas to the cities is contrary to normal expectations; typically, the higher interest rates prevailing in rural areas result in a flow of funds from the cities to these areas.

Group Banking. *Group banking* involves the use of the holding-company device, whereby two or more individual banks are controlled through a company that holds the voting control of the individual banks. The policies of banks thus controlled by such a holding company are determined by the parent company and coordinated for the purposes of that organization. The holding company itself may or may not engage in direct banking activities, and the banks that are controlled by the holding company may operate branches. The liberalization of branch banking laws in many states during the last 25 years has resulted in a shift to branch banking, as opposed to group banking, for purposes of multiple-unit banking.

Chain Banking. The third general classification, that of *chain banking,* refers to an arrangement whereby two or more banks are brought under the direction and control of a group other than a holding company. This may be accomplished by several banks being owned by the same individual or group of individuals or through having the same members on the board of directors of each of the banks. Such organizations are generally built around one of the larger banks in an area or community. The principal bank is generally referred to as a "key bank," since it sets a pattern for general banking operations in the area or community.

BANK FAILURES AND DEPOSIT INSURANCE

Like all forms of business enterprise, the commercial bank may be subject to failure if improper management or unfortunate economic conditions prevail for a long enough period of time. Furthermore, the commercial bank must enjoy the complete confidence of the public. Commercial banks secure their profits largely through the investment of funds that have been deposited with them for safekeeping. These invested funds are necessarily unavailable for a period of time; and immediate withdrawal demand on the part of a large number of depositors, because of a lack of confidence or other reasons, inevitably would lead a commercial bank to insolvency unless help were forthcoming from other quarters. It is necessary, therefore, for the sound and continued operation of a bank that its customers retain confidence in the bank.

The failure of one bank in a community may precipitate the loss of confidence in other banks in the same area, giving rise to panic and demands for withdrawals. Bank failures not only present a hardship to individual depositors but also materially affect business within the community. The smooth flow of business intercourse is interrupted by bank failures through the loss of confidence on the part of the bankers themselves in their ability to meet withdrawals. Few new business loans may be made, and many existing business loans may be called or renewal refused.

Whatever the causes of bank failures, until recently the rate of failures in the United States was as high as, or higher than, that in any other highly industrialized country of the world. This has been an intolerable situation for the simple reason that a smoothly operating and highly efficient system of commercial banks is essential to the development of our industrial potential. To the extent that bank failures have retarded business development, the economy as a whole has suffered accordingly.

Early State Plans for Insurance of Bank Notes and Deposits

Although the federal system of deposit insurance is relatively new, state plans of insurance date back for more than a century. New York in 1829 adopted a plan by which it was to afford protection to both the notes issued by banks in that state and the deposits of the bank customers. The initiation of bank insurance by New York was followed by the establishment of insurance systems by Vermont, Indiana, Michigan, Ohio, and Iowa. The plans of insurance in these states varied from an assessment arrangement, in which participating banks were assessed to take care of the liabilities of a failed bank at the time such failures developed, to the establishment of an initial insurance or "safety" fund. In other states these two plans were combined, providing for both an initial insurance fund and assessments contingent upon the demand for additional funds to meet liabilities of participating banks that failed.

These early insurance plans were developed primarily to insure the notes issued by the banks of that period, and in a few of the states that attempted such insurance no provision whatsoever was made for the protection of deposits. Because bank notes played a dominant role as the circulating medium of that period, it is easy to understand the primary concern for insurance of these notes. These early state plans came to an end shortly after the passage of the National Banking Act. In 1865 a prohibitive tax was placed on state bank notes by the federal government, which ended their issuance. The notes of national banks were guaranteed by the federal government, and the need for further insurance was eliminated.

It was not until 1907 that another state insurance plan was to be provided. In that year Oklahoma, followed in later years by Kansas, Nebraska, Texas, Mississippi, South Dakota, North Dakota, and Washington, established bank insurance plans for the protection of depositors. These plans differed in detail but generally provided for the establishment of a guarantee fund to meet the liabilities of participating failed banks. In some of the states the participating banks were permitted to retain their proportionate contribution, while in other states such funds were collected and invested by an administrative agency of the state. The state deposit insurance plans of that period were stimulated by the financial losses encountered during the panic of 1907.

Failure of State Plans of Deposit Protection

All of these various state plans of deposit insurance failed. Among the reasons for their failure is the fact that supervision of the plans was generally faulty. Also, generally distressed conditions caused more bank failures than had been anticipated, which created an undue strain on the rather meager resources of the insurance plans. Finally, in most of the states that established deposit insurance plans, there was economic dependence primarily upon one agricultural crop with little diversification to offset the risk resulting from a poor year or two for that crop.

Following the stock market crash in 1929 and the accompanying large number of bank failures, there again developed an insistent demand for some form of deposit insurance. This demand followed each such period of major bank failures. A total of 150 bills for guaranty or insurance were introduced in Congress from 1886 to 1933. The proponents of a federal system of deposit insurance finally exercised considerable influence. They contended that in spite of the failure of the state plans of deposit insurance, a plan established on a national basis would prove successful as a result of the diversification which it would entail—diversification that would permit one or more sectors of the economy or geographical areas to experience difficulty, while the system of deposit insurance as a whole would remain sound.

The proponents also argued that, if established on a federal basis under very strict supervision and with liberal provision for the accumulation of a reserve from which losses could be met, the chances of success on the part of the deposit insurance fund would be considerably enhanced. Also, they alleged that many of the difficulties which the commercial banks of the country faced resulted from the intense competition between national banks and state banks. A federal system of deposit insurance that would permit participation by both state banks and national banks would tend to eliminate much of this competition and provide a sounder basis for banking operations.

The Federal Deposit Insurance Corporation

The forcefulness of the arguments by the proponents of a national plan of deposit insurance and the intense demand of the general public for such protection caused the Congress to adopt a temporary form of deposit insurance to become effective in 1934. The plan, which resulted from the Steagall Amendment to the Glass Bill of 1933, received the support of a large majority in both houses of Congress. This first plan of federal deposit insurance provided protection of deposits up to $2,500 for each depositor. It continued in effect until 1935, during which time the various interested parties in Congress managed to reach agreement on the form of operation of a permanent plan of deposit insurance. The permanent plan provided for the establishment of a corporation to be known as the Federal Deposit Insurance Corporation. The stock was to be held jointly by the United States Treasury and the federal reserve banks.

Sources of Capital. The Secretary of the Treasury subscribed to $150 million of stock of the Federal Deposit Insurance Corporation (hereafter referred to as the FDIC), and each federal reserve bank was required to subscribe for an amount equal to one half of its surplus on January 1, 1933. The total stock purchased by the Treasury and the federal reserve banks was approximately $290 million. This stock did not provide for voting privileges nor for the payment of dividends. For the purpose of meeting emergency financial claims against it, the FDIC was authorized to issue debentures in an amount aggregating not more than three times the sum of its paid-in capital stock plus the amount received as assessments from insured banks. All capital stock of the FDIC has now been retired. Although part of the original stock of the FDIC was purchased by the federal reserve banks, the Corporation is not a part of the Federal Reserve System. The FDIC has its own board of directors of three members. One of these is the Comptroller of the Currency of the United States Department of the Treasury, and the other two are appointed by the President with the advice and consent of the Senate. The term of office is six years.

Deposit Protection. Until 1950 the maximum amount of deposit insurance afforded a single depositor under the permanent plan of deposit insurance was $5,000. In 1950 the maximum was increased to $10,000 due largely to the generally increased size of the deposits during the war and postwar years. The costs of such deposit insurance are borne by the member banks of the insurance system.

Although membership in the FDIC is necessary for all banks holding national charters and for member banks of the Federal

Reserve System, membership is available for state banks that are not members of the Federal Reserve System. On December 31, 1956, 95 per cent of the nation's banks were insured by the FDIC.[3] To protect depositors in state banks from having insurance withdrawn arbitrarily without notice to the depositors, it is provided that although the insured status of a bank is terminated when it ceases to be a member bank of the insurance system, for two years thereafter the bank remains liable for assessments and retains the insurance on insured deposits held by it when it ceased to be a member bank. Deposits received by such a bank after its insured status has been terminated are, of course, not protected under this provision.

The FDIC not only serves to minimize and eliminate the hardships resulting from bank failures, but it also serves to establish sound banking practices and to minimize the chance of such losses developing in the first place. It is empowered among other things to pass on applications for deposit insurance, to examine and supervise the general operations of member banks, and to make loans to insured banks or facilitate mergers or consolidations of banks when such actions are in the interest of the depositors.

Evaluation of the Federal Deposit Insurance Corporation. The FDIC has served a very useful purpose. Having minimized the hardships of loss on the part of the depositors in the banks that have failed during the history of the FDIC, the Corporation has also contributed to the present high degree of public confidence in the banking system in general. Such confidence is, of course, an essential factor in the successful operation of any banking system.

Among the criticisms of the present system of deposit insurance may be included the claims that the premium paid by the banks is too high and that the FDIC could not withstand the financial pressure resulting from a major depression, and the fact that a large part of the average bank's assets today are either direct or indirect obligations of the federal government anyway. With respect to the first and third points, only future events will determine whether the FDIC is accumulating too

---

[3] *Annual Report of the Federal Deposit Insurance Corporation,* December 31, 1956, Washington, D. C., p. 3.

great a volume of reserves to meet periods of economic distress on the part of the banks. It is doubtful, however, whether the FDIC could withstand the financial pressure of an economic depression similar to that of the early Thirties. It has been suggested that the support given to the banking system by the FDIC during the course of a depression may actually prevent economic conditions in general from deteriorating as much as would otherwise be the case. There is little doubt that the depression of the early Thirties was made all the more burdensome by the accompanying failure of many banks.

Loss Experience of the Federal Deposit Insurance Corporation. From the beginning of deposit insurance on January 1, 1934, to December 31, 1956, the FDIC made disbursements to protect depositors in 431 insured banks. Disbursements for the protection of depositors totaled $340 million.[4] The FDIC in turn has recovered approximately 90 per cent of its disbursements through the liquidation of assets taken over from closed banks, leaving a net estimated loss of 10 per cent on its disbursements.

QUESTIONS

1. Discuss the relationship of commercial banking to the processes of a modern industrialized economy.

2. How vital a role did commercial banking play in the development of the United States economy? Has its importance decreased or increased with industrialization?

3. Describe the principal functions of commercial banks.

4. Why do regulatory authorities insist on certain minimum capital requirements on the part of banks before they may begin banking operations?

5. What are the sources of capital for a bank? Why would the bank wish to increase its capital after operations had begun and its initial capital requirements had been met?

6. Compare the relative merits of independent unit banking as opposed to branch banking.

7. Distinguish between branch, group, and chain banking.

4 *Ibid,* p. 10.

8. What are the principal causes of bank failures? Have bank failures been unusual in the history of United States commercial banking? Are bank failures frequent at the present time?

9. Discuss the development of deposit insurance in commercial banking in the United States.

10. Evaluate the significance of the Federal Deposit Insurance Corporation to commercial banking in the United States.

SUGGESTED READINGS

CAGLE, C. E. "Branch, Chain, and Group Banking," in *Banking Studies*. Washington: Board of Governors of the Federal Reserve System, 1941. Pages 113-140.

CHANDLER, LESTER V. *The Economics of Money and Banking;* Revised Edition. New York: Harper & Brothers, 1953. Chapters 10 and 11.

DEWEY, D. R. *Financial History of the United States;* Twelfth Edition. New York: Longmans, Green & Company, 1934.

HALM, GEORGE N. *Economics of Money and Banking.* Homewood, Illinois: Richard D. Irwin, Inc., 1956. Chapters 15, 18, 19, and 20.

HART, ALBERT GAILORD. *Money, Debt, and Economic Activity;* Second Edition. Englewood Cliffs, New Jersey: Prentice-Hall, Inc., 1953. Chapters 1 and 2.

JACOBY, NEIL H., AND SAULNIER, RAYMOND J. *Business Finance and Banking.* New York: National Bureau of Economic Research, 1947. Chapters 2 and 3.

KENT, RAYMOND P. *Money and Banking;* Third Edition. New York: Rinehart & Company, Inc., 1956. Chapters 9, 10, 11, and 19.

PROCHNOW, HERBERT V. *American Financial Institutions.* Englewood Cliffs, New Jersey: Prentice-Hall, Inc., 1951. Chapters 1, 2, and 4.

STEINER, W. H., AND SHAPIRO, ELI. *Money and Banking;* Third Edition. New York: Henry Holt & Company, Inc., 1953. Chapters 5 and 11.

THOMAS, ROLLIN G. *Our Modern Banking and Monetary System;* Second Edition. Englewood Cliffs, New Jersey: Prentice-Hall, Inc., 1950. Chapters 5, 6, and 16.

Chapter 4

Operations of

Commercial Banks

The tremendous resources of the commercial banking system of the nation make it the largest provider of short-term loan funds for business. In this chapter, we shall study the operations of a single bank through its financial statements to determine its manner of operation and its sources of income.

CHANGES IN LOAN POLICIES

According to an early and widely held theory, the only appropriate loans for a commercial bank to make were those for short-term productive purposes to businessmen and farmers exclusively. It was believed that the commercial bank should serve simply as a depositary or a pooling place for the surplus cash funds of the community and that these funds should be available to businessmen and farmers of the community in such form that they could be repaid out of current operations. For example, the use of bank loans by a business to purchase inventory makes possible their repayment from sales. Such loans, it was believed, would provide a high degree of liquidity for the bank in meeting depositor withdrawal demands. Nor was this attitude wholly theoretical, for much of our banking legislation specifically restricted the banks with respect to other forms of loans. The National Banking Act of 1863 prohibited completely the lending of money on the basis of real estate. Later legislation modified this extreme limitation.

Although commercial banks remain the primary source of short-term business funds, there has been a noticeable drift away

Chart 4-1

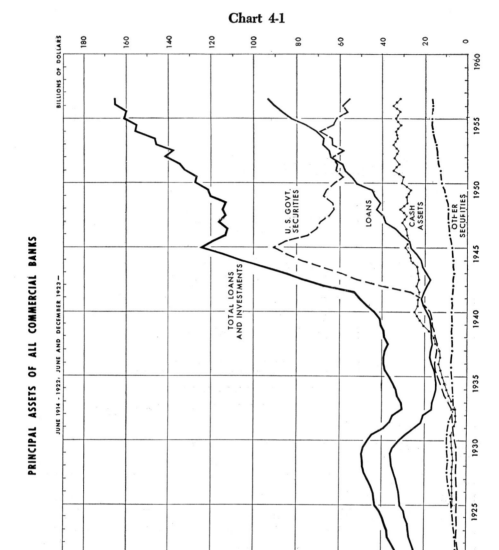

SOURCE: *Federal Reserve Chart Book on Financial and Business Statistics—Historical Supplement*, September, 1957, Board of Governors of the Federal Reserve System, p. 12.

from this traditional theory of banking practice. This change in attitude became noticeable during World War I when the banks were encouraged to lend to individuals for the purpose of purchasing government bonds. This type of lending, of course, represents a far cry from the traditional type of loan for production use. Following World War I there was much speculation in inventory accumulation by the business enterprises of the country, and many of the loans extended to businesses ostensibly for production purposes were, in fact, loans for speculative purposes. Later, during the stock-market boom of the late Twenties, the commercial banks played an important part in providing funds for the purchase of stocks and bonds, again representing a considerable shift from the traditional practices of banking. During the period from January, 1922, to September, 1929, when the Standard and Poor's Corporation index of common stock prices increased by 284 per cent, loans to brokers and others for purchasing securities finally became the largest class of bank loans.

During this period many of the nation's large companies were becoming more and more self-sufficient financially and required less assistance from the banking system for their short-term financial requirements. This, of course, meant that many commercial banks suffered from a lack of adequate demand for short-term business loans. During World War II the banks were encouraged to purchase large quantities of government bonds. Chart 4-1 shows that commercial banks continue to hold a large amount of government bonds. Although commercial banks at mid-year 1957 had only approximately 34 per cent of their total loans and investments in the form of government bonds, in the immediate postwar period the percentage was as high as 72 per cent.

THE BANK BALANCE SHEET

The balance sheet shown in Figure 4-1 is typical of the balance sheets of commercial banks in the United States. The resources and funds of a bank are obtained from stockholders' investments, profits from operation, and customers' deposits. The total of these three items plus "Other Liabilities and Deferred Credits" and "Reserve for Contingencies" equals the total assets of the bank. The assets (resources) for this particular bank are shown on the left-hand side of Figure 4-1, and for all commercial banks in the United States they are shown in Chart 4-1.

Figure 4-1

THE NATIONAL BANK

CONDENSED STATEMENT OF CONDITION—DECEMBER 31, 1958

RESOURCES

Cash: In our vaults	$ 5,240,538.21	
In Federal Reserve Bank	17,641,943.38	
In correspondent banks in New York and other cities	5,227,419.78	
		$ 28,109,901.37
Securities: U. S. Government Securities	$47,838,112.83	
Other Public Securities	3,436,606.24	
Other Bonds	789,687.50	
Capital Stock of the Federal Reserve Bank	150,000.00	
		52,214,406.57
Loans: Secured loans payable on demand	$ 5,851,310.96	
Secured loans with definite maturities	1,082,958.33	
Unsecured loans and discounts with definite maturities	17,341,182.51	
Real estate loans on first mortgages	7,769,897.27	
		32,045,349.07
Interest accrued on bonds and notes to date of this statement		396,787.13
Overdrafts		5,186.36
Bank premises owned (Main Office and five branches) and furniture and fixtures—less allowance for depreciation		1,248,358.06
Property acquired for branch building		179,110.82
Other resources, including prepaid expenses		44,579.46
Total Resources		$114,243,678.84

Bank Assets

The principal assets of a commercial bank are cash, securities, and loans, as shown in Figure 4-1.

Cash. The first category of assets on the "Resources" side of the balance sheet for a bank is Cash. *Cash* includes funds in the bank's vaults, in a federal reserve bank, and in correspondent banks.

A bank must keep a certain minimum of vault cash to meet the day-to-day currency requirements of the bank's customers.

Figure 4-1

THE NATIONAL BANK

CONDENSED STATEMENT OF CONDITION—DECEMBER 31, 1958

LIABILITIES

Deposits:

U. S. Government Deposits	$ 2,249,319.22	
Other demand deposits	81,269,505.04	
Savings and other time deposits	23,446,308.18	
		$106,965,132.44

Other Liabilities and Deferred Credits:

Dividend declared, but not yet payable	125,000.00
Interest on deposits, taxes and other expenses accrued to date of this statement	99,758.87
Discounts collected but not earned	237,997.20
Reserve for Federal Income Taxes	391,789.85
Other Liabilities	None
Total Liabilities	$107,819,678.36
Reserve for Contingencies	71,012.23

CAPITAL FUNDS

Capital—100,000 shares at $20.00 par value	2,000,000.00
Surplus	3,000,000.00
Undivided Profits	1,352,988.25
Total Capital Funds	$ 6,352,988.25
Total Liabilities and Capital Funds	$114,243,678.84

The amount of such cash requirements may be small relative to the total of a bank's resources, for the simple reason that the typical day's operations will result in approximately the same amount of cash deposits as cash withdrawals. A margin of safety, however, is required to take care of those periods when for one reason or another withdrawals exceed deposits by more than an average amount.

The appropriate amount of cash that a bank should carry depends largely upon the character of its banking operations and on the distance of the bank from its depositary for legal reserves.

For example, a bank that has a few very large accounts might be expected to have a larger volume of unanticipated withdrawals (and deposits) than a bank that has only small individual accounts. An erratic volume of day-to-day withdrawals requires, of course, a larger cash reserve. A bank that is located a great distance from its depositary for legal reserves also must maintain larger cash reserves than a bank that can in a matter of minutes or hours draw on such reserves.

The second cash item, designated "In Federal Reserve Bank," is considerably greater than vault cash. Members of the federal reserve system are required to keep minimum reserves, as a percentage of their deposits, with the federal reserve bank of their district.[1] As withdrawals are made and total deposit balances are decreased, the amount of the required reserves also decreases. These reserves that have been freed may be used by the bank to help meet withdrawal demands. State banks that are not members of the Federal Reserve System are required by state law to maintain minimum reserves. The laws of the states differ as to the form that such reserves may take. In general, however, state required reserves include vault cash, deposits with other banks, and in some cases bonds of the federal government.

Cash "In correspondent banks in New York and other cities" refers to the common practice of keeping substantial deposits with other banks, particularly those banks in large cities. Such correspondent relations with other banks facilitate the clearing of drafts and other credit instruments, and provide an immediate access to information regarding the money markets of the large cities.

The cash items of this bank total approximately $28 million as compared with total resources of approximately $114 million; hence, slightly less than 25 per cent of the total resources of this bank are held in such form as to produce no yield whatsoever.

Securities. Securities comprise the second major group of resources on the balance sheet. These securities held by the bank include those of the United States government, those of state governments, and of municipalities. Also included are other bonds and capital stock of the federal reserve bank. The bonds owned by this bank are held as investments. The capital stock of

[1] The system of fractional reserves is discussed in Chapter 5.

the federal reserve bank owned by the bank is a requirement for all member banks of the Federal Reserve System.

Loans. The third group of resource or asset items includes several classifications of loans: first, those loans that are payable on demand and which are secured; second, those secured loans that have definite maturities; third, and by far the most important, unsecured loans and discounts with definite maturities; and finally, real estate loans on first mortgages.

In a *secured loan* specific property is pledged as collateral for the loan. In the event of the failure of the borrower to repay his loan, the bank has recourse to the assets pledged as collateral for the loan. In all cases, the borrower is required to sign a note specifying the details of the indebtedness; but unless specific assets are pledged for the loan, it is classified as unsecured. An *unsecured loan* represents a general claim against the assets of the borrower. It is the typical arrangement between the business-men of the community and the bank whereby periodic amounts are borrowed for the purposes of meeting a payroll, accumulating an inventory, or for other short-term working capital purposes. This section reflects the most important single activity of the commercial bank and, except for the real estate component, it was often thought to be the sole type of activity in which the commercial banks should be permitted to engage. Through these loans the bank has gained its reputation as being the most important single source of short-term funds for businesses.

The Federal Deposit Insurance Corporation reports that, for all insured commercial banks at December 31, 1956, earnings from interest on loans accounted for approximately 59 per cent of total earnings, although such loans comprised only 44 per cent of total assets.[2] Total earnings include not only interest from loans and from other securities, but also service charges and fees on loans, service charges on deposit accounts, commissions, trust department earnings, and other current earnings.

The distinction between loans and discounts is an important one. A loan customarily includes a specified rate of interest that must be paid with the principal amount of the loan at the maturity of the loan contract. A discount, on the other hand, is

[2] *Annual Report of the Federal Deposit Insurance Corporation,* December 31, 1956, pp. 28, 38.

customarily made with no interest rate specified on the note, a deduction being made from the face amount of the note at the time the money is loaned. The borrower receives less than the face of the note, but he repays the full amount of the note when it matures.

A given discount rate means a higher real cost of borrowing than an interest loan made for the same rate. This is true because under the discount arrangement less actual money is received by the borrower, although the amount paid for its use is the same. For example, if $500 is borrowed on a loan basis at an interest rate of 4 per cent for one year, at the maturity of the loan $500 plus $20 interest is repaid. On the other hand, if the $500 is borrowed on a discount basis and the rate is 4 per cent, a deduction of $20 from the face of the note is made and the borrower receives only $480. At the end of the year, he returns to the lender the face amount of the note, $500. In the first case, the borrower has paid $20 for the use of $500; in the second case, he has paid $20 for the use of only $480. The effective rate of interest, therefore, on the discount basis is approximately 4.2 per cent in contrast with the even 4 per cent paid when the $500 was borrowed on a loan basis.

Other Bank Assets. The remaining items on the Resources side of the balance sheet are of less importance than the foregoing groups. A brief look, however, should be taken at these individual items. *Interest accrued on bonds and notes* refers to earnings that have not been received although they were earned during the period covered by the statement. *Overdrafts* are, in effect, short-term loans to customers who have overdrawn their bank balances. Banks in general disapprove of this practice and often will refuse to honor overdrafts. For a good customer, however, the bank may accept the check and carry the overdraft temporarily until the customer is able to make the necessary adjustments. During the period that overdrafts are accepted by the bank they are carried as assets.

The next item, *Bank premises owned, and furniture and fixtures,* is self-explanatory. These are the bank's physical properities. This particular bank has acquired other real estate that is to be used in the future for additional bank buildings. The final item, *Other resources, including prepaid expenses,* is a catchall account that includes such items as prepaid insurance and expenditures made for supplies which have not been completely used.

Bank Liabilities

The most important liability of a commercial bank consists of its deposits of various kinds, but a bank's other liabilities should be understood also.

Deposits. Three groups of deposits—U. S. Government, demand, and savings and time—make up the principal liabilities of all commercial banks. U. S. Government deposits are shown separately because by law banks must provide for a segregation of assets to protect such deposits. Demand deposits, representing the checking accounts of individuals, businesses, and other institutions, constitute the bulk of all deposits. Such deposits are withdrawable by check without the depositor having to go to the bank.

Savings and time deposits are segregated because they are payable on notice of thirty days or more, although most banks now permit customers to draw on their savings accounts as readily as on their checking accounts. *Savings deposits* differ from time deposits in that they are generally represented by a passbook, while *time deposits* are usually represented by printed receipts called *certificates of deposits.* Savings deposits are payable only after thirty days notice on the part of the depositor unless the bank chooses to reduce or eliminate the waiting period; time deposits are to be withdrawn only at specified times. A familiar time deposit plan is that of so-called "Christmas Clubs," which permits annual deposits to be withdrawn shortly before Christmas.

Other Liabilities and Deferred Credits. The second category of liabilities is represented by items having a far smaller dollar significance than that of deposits. For this bank, these items total nearly $1 million. In brief, this section represents liabilities not yet payable and the receipt of fees and other charges for which service has not yet been rendered. Funds borrowed from the federal reserve bank or other banks are also reflected in this section.

Reserve for Contingencies. Reserves set aside out of profits may be established by bank management to provide for unusually large risks. When a bank engages in lending practices that are not common to the bank, such reserves may be established to protect capital and surplus. Such reserves also are established to absorb possible losses from declining prices of bonds and other investments that the bank holds.

Bank Capital Funds

The capital funds section of the bank balance sheet includes capital, surplus, and undivided profits. This bank has 100,000 shares of common stock at $20 par value per share for a total of $2,000,000. Surplus of $3,000,000 was accumulated from the sale of capital stock at a price above its par value and from the earnings retained by the bank. The undivided profits section differs from surplus in that it is not considered to be a permanent part of capital. When dividends are paid, this account is reduced. These three capital accounts constitute the total capital funds of the bank.

LOAN OPERATIONS OF THE COMMERCIAL BANK

The typical loan made by a bank to a businessman is on an unsecured basis; that is, the prospects for the future of the business is such that the bank believes it to be unnecessary to require the pledge of specific assets of the business as security for the loan. Bankers for many years have held the opinion that if a loan does not qualify on an unsecured basis, it should not qualify on a secured basis. In recent years this attitude has been changing, and we find many banks lending on the basis of a pledge of specific assets. The unsecured loan, however, remains the primary type of bank loan arrangement.

The Bank Line of Credit

There is often an agreement between the business and the bank regarding the amount of credit that the business will have at its disposal. The loan limit that the bank establishes for each of its business customers is called a *line of credit*. These lines of credit cost the businessman only the normal interest for the

period for which money is actually borrowed. Under this arrangement, the businessman does not wait until he needs money to
negotiate for the loan, but rather he files the necessary financial
statements of his business and other evidences of financial condition with the bank in order that the credit may be available
when needed. The banker, of course, is interested not only in
how well the business has fared in the past, but also in the probable future of the business, since the line of credit itself is generally extended in advance for a year at a time. The banker may
require that other debts of the business be subordinated to the
claim of the bank.

Under a line-of-credit program, major changes in the operation of a business may be subject to the approval of the bank. A
major shift or change in management personnel or a major
change in the manufacture or sale of particular products can have
a material influence on the future success of a company; hence,
the bank, having contributed substantially to the resources of the
business, is necessarily interested in such business activities. The
bank may also seek information on the business through organized
credit bureaus, contact with other businesses having relations
with the enterprise in question, and other banks.

In the event that the businessman requires more money than
was anticipated at the time the line of credit was established, he
may request the bank to increase the limit on his line of credit.
He must be prepared, however, to offer very sound evidence not
only of the need for additional funds but also of the ability of the
business to repay the increased loan from business operations.
A request for an increased line of credit frequently occurs when
a business is growing and must have ever-increasingly large
amounts of capital to make such growth possible. Although banks
generally insist that expansion be financed with long-term capital,
they do frequently assist such growth by providing a part of increased capital needs. The businessman who is unable to secure
additional credit from his bank on an unsecured loan basis may
seek funds from other lenders or from his bank on a secured basis.
These other forms of borrowing are discussed later in this chapter.

A *compensating balance* (on deposit by the business) of from
10 to 20 per cent of unsecured loans outstanding under bank
lines of credit is required by nearly all banks. The most frequently cited justification for this requirement is that since banks

cannot lend without deposits, bank borrowers should be required
to be depositors also.

Banks require their business customers to "clean up" their
lines of credit for specified periods of time during the year,
generally a minimum time span of two weeks, that is, to eliminate
their indebtedness to the bank for this period of time.

The Revolving Credit Agreement

Although a businessman may feel rather certain that the line
of credit which has been agreed to will provide the necessary
capital requirements for the coming year, there is always the possibility that conditions will change to the extent that the bank
may have to reduce or withdraw its extension of credit. This
possibility is normally part of the original agreement, whereby
the bank is obligated to make good on its line of credit only so
long as conditions do not change materially.

The well-established business that has an excellent credit
rating may find it possible, however, to obtain a commitment in
the form of a stand-by agreement for a guaranteed line of credit.
This arrangement is referred to as a *revolving credit agreement.*
In addition to paying interest for the use of money for the period
of the loan, the business must pay a commission or fee to the
bank based on the amount of money it has on call during the
agreement period. This additional commission or fee is required
since the bank must provide for such loan demands regardless
of changes in business conditions and is, therefore, from time to
time denied flexibility in the use of its own funds for other
lending purposes.

Bank Credit Groups

The Postwar Small Business Credit Commission of the American Bankers Association (ABA) was largely responsible for the development of bank credit groups. Under this arrangement, if
a businessman applies to any bank that is a member of a bank
credit group and the bank is not in a position to make the loan
at that time, either because of other loan commitments or because the required loan is too large for the bank to handle, other
members of the bank credit group stand ready to participate in
the loan.

Accounts Receivable Financing

For the businessman whose credit does not warrant a loan on the part of the bank on an unsecured basis or for the businessman who has emergency needs for funds in excess of his line of credit, a pledge of his accounts receivable may be offered as security. Accounts receivables, as distinct from notes receivables, represent claims against customers to whom credit sales have been made without requiring the signing of a note or other credit instrument. This development in banking is rather recent and stems in part from the competition offered the banks by the specialized finance companies that have come into existence in recent decades.[3]

In extending loans on this basis, banks of course make the same sort of credit investigation that is made for businesses which are applying for unsecured loans. Particular attention is given to the collection practices of the company and to certain characteristics of the company's accounts receivables. The bank also spot-checks the receivables of the firm and may in some cases analyze each account to determine the promptness of the customers of the firm in making payments. In addition, the bank will study the type and the quality of goods that are sold, for if the merchandise is of inferior quality, there may be more objections from the customers and hence slower payment on the bills than would otherwise be the case. Accounts receivable are of little value as the basis of a loan if large quantities of merchandise are returned and the amount of accounts receivable reduced accordingly. It is also important for the bank to know something of the customers of the business since their ability to pay their debts will have an important influence or bearing on the actual collection success of the business applying for the loan.

Accounts Receivable Loan Limits. The Bank Management Commission of the ABA recommends that a loan based on the security of accounts receivables should generally be no more than 80 per cent of the gross receivables and that this amount should

---

[3] These specialized finance companies, commonly referred to as commercial credit companies, are discussed in detail in Chapter 6. In addition to competing against non-banking institutions by lending against the security of receivables, a very few banks undertake the practice of purchasing such receivables outright—a process referred to as "factoring." Factoring activities, also discussed in Chapter 6, are usually engaged in solely by highly specialized nonbanking finance organizations.

be reduced by any trade discounts allowed to customers and by the normal percentage of the merchandise returns. If there is reason to believe that many of the customers of the business which is applying for the loan are not suitable risks, or if adequate credit ratings are not available, the bank will be inclined to lend a correspondingly lower percentage of the face value of such receivables.

Technical Features of Accounts Receivable Financing. Under the accounts receivable loan arrangement, there is, in addition to the basic interest charge, a fee to cover the extra work that such a loan entails. The banks must periodically check the books of a business that has borrowed on the basis of its receivables in order to see that the business is, in fact, living up to the terms of the agreement. At the time the loan is made, it is generally provided that individual accounts on the ledger of the business will be clearly designated as having been pledged for the bank loan. Only those accounts that are suitable for collateral purposes for the bank are earmarked, and these accounts are replaced by other accounts as the accounts are paid in full or in the event one or more of the accounts become unsatisfactory.

In addition to "earmarking" pledged accounts in the ledger of the borrowing firm, the bank also requires a schedule of the accounts so pledged along with a copy of each of the invoices involved in the shipment of goods. The businessman must also execute an assignment of the accounts involved. A specimen copy of a note for such a loan is shown in Figure 4–2.

As remittances are received by the business on the individual accounts that have been assigned, they must be turned over to the bank separately from other business funds. The bank also reserves the right to make a direct audit of the books of the business from time to time and to have an outside accounting firm examine the books periodically. The accounting firm frequently verifies a certain percentage of the accounts by mail, much as it does in a regular audit. By verifying the accounts in a routine manner, customers of the business are not made aware of the fact that their accounts have been pledged as collateral for a loan.

In this connection, it is interesting to note that businesses utilizing their receivables as collateral for bank loans often prefer

Figure 4-2

```
$24,744.00                                   CLEVELAND, OHIO    October 15, 19 58

  Ninety days                                              AFTER DATE FOR VALUE RECEIVED THE UNDERSIGNED
PROMISES TO PAY TO THE ORDER OF
                        CENTRAL NATIONAL BANK of CLEVELAND
  Twenty-four thousand seven hundred forty-four and no/100 - - - - -     DOLLARS.
  AT ITS OFFICE IN THE CITY OF CLEVELAND, OHIO, WITH INTEREST AT THE RATE OF    6    % PER ANNUM, PAYABLE MONTHLY ON THE FIRST DAY
  OF EACH MONTH AFTER DATE HEREOF, UNTIL THE PRINCIPAL IS PAID.
        THIS NOTE IS SECURED BY THE PLEDGE OF ACCOUNTS RECEIVABLE PURSUANT TO AGREEMENT BY AND BETWEEN THE UNDERSIGNED AND CENTRAL
  NATIONAL BANK OF CLEVELAND, DATED  September 5  19 58
        THE UNDERSIGNED HEREBY AUTHORIZES ANY ATTORNEY-AT-LAW IN THE STATE OF OHIO OR ANY STATE OR TERRITORY OF THE UNITED STATES AT
  ANY TIME AFTER THE ABOVE SUM BECOMES DUE, TO APPEAR FOR THE UNDERSIGNED IN ANY COURT OF RECORD IN THE STATE OF OHIO, OR ANY STATE OR
  TERRITORY OF THE UNITED STATES, AND TO WAIVE THE ISSUING AND SERVICE OF PROCESS AND CONFESS JUDGMENT AGAINST THE UNDERSIGNED IN FAVOR
  OF THE PAYEE OR ANY HOLDER OF THIS NOTE FOR THE AMOUNT APPEARING DUE, TOGETHER WITH COSTS OF SUIT, AND THEREUPON TO RELEASE ALL
  ERRORS AND WAIVE ALL RIGHT OF APPEAL AND STAY OF EXECUTION.
                                                     THE NOBEL CORPORATION
TELEPHONE NO.                                        Authorized Signer
ADDRESS                              SIGNATURE
3-14                                 SIGNATURE                          TITLE
                                                                        TITLE
```

Promissory Note

to keep such knowledge from their own customers because this may be interpreted as an indication of weakness on the part of the business. Although businesses participating in this form of loan arrangement are frequently in a financially weak condition, this is not always the case. Some firms that are on a sound basis use accounts receivable financing as a permanent arrangement since they feel it has advantages for them which would not be available through other loan arrangements.

Manufacturing concerns appear to be the largest users of accounts receivable financing. In particular, this is true of manufacturers of food, textiles, leather products, furniture, paper, iron, steel, and machinery.[4]

Inventory Loans

A business enterprise may borrow on the basis of its inventory as collateral in much the same manner that it may borrow on its receivables. A study is made by the bank not only of the physical condition of the inventory but also of the general composition of the inventory that the firm owns. Staple items that have a ready marketability serve well as collateral for a loan; style and fashion items do not serve well as collateral except for brief periods of time. Firms that use inventory as collateral are generally not in a position to procure further funds on an unsecured basis.

[4] Raymond J. Saulnier and Neil H. Jacoby, *Accounts Receivable Financing* (New York: National Bureau of Economic Research, Inc., 1943), pp. 54-55.

The bank may protect itself when lending to a business on the basis of inventory as collateral either by having title to the goods assigned to the bank or by taking a chattel mortgage against the inventory. In other cases, a trust receipt instrument may be used. When an assignment of title of the inventory to the bank is made, no clear title can pass from the businessman to his customer until proper arrangements with the bank have been made, either by paying off the loan or by substituting other collateral for the merchandise sold. Under a trust receipt arrangement the bank retains ownership of the goods until they are actually sold in the regular course of business.

Warehousing of Inventory. In some cases the bank, when lending on the basis of inventory as collateral, may insist that the business deposit the inventory in a bonded and licensed warehouse. The receipt issued by the warehouse is then turned over to the bank, which in turn holds it until such time as the loan is repaid. A specimen copy of a warehouse receipt for stored merchandise is shown in Figure 4-3.

It is frequently inconvenient for a business to deliver large bulky items of inventory to a warehouse for storage. This problem is solved through the use of *field warehouses.* A field warehousing enterprise has the power to establish a bona fide warehouse on the premises of the borrowing business establishment. Field warehouses differ from the typical public warehouse in that they serve a single customer, that customer on whose property the field warehouse is established. The field warehouse could be a cattle ranch, a grain elevator, or a lake for the temporary storage of logs.

In establishing the field warehouse, it is generally necessary first for the warehousing establishment to obtain a lease on that portion of the property of the business which is to be used for warehousing purposes. It is then necessary to establish fences, barriers, walks, and other postings to indicate clear possession of the property by the warehouseman in order to avoid accidental or deliberate removal of items by employees of the business during the general course of the business operations. A guard may be posted in order to check on the safety of the goods warehoused, or a room may be sealed and the seal inspected periodically to determine whether or not the company is honoring its agreement.

Figure 4-3

Lawrence Warehouse Company

SPECIMEN **ORIGINAL** WAREHOUSE RECEIPT № **W** 76612

NOT INSURED

San Francisco, California DATE September 25, 1958

RECEIVED EX. Sun Belt Canning Company
FOR STORAGE IN Drumm Street, San Francisco   WAREHOUSE NO. 40
LOCATED AT 345 Drumm   STREET.

SUBJECT TO ALL THE TERMS AND CONDITIONS CONTAINED HEREIN AND ON THE REVERSE HEREOF, FOR THE ACCOUNT OF AND TO BE DELIVERED, WITHOUT SURRENDER OF THIS WAREHOUSE RECEIPT UPON WRITTEN ORDER OF

THE FIRST NATIONAL BANK -

CODE NO.	ITEM	NO. UNITS	SAID TO BE OR CONTAIN
		Cases	
77	1	983	24/2½ Peaches-Choice Halves Y. C.
77	2	2,160	24/2½ Peaches-Choice Halves Y. C.
77	3	390	24/2½ Peaches-Choice Halves Y. C.
77	4	928	24/2½ Peaches-Choice Halves Y. C.
77	5	1,804	24/2½ Peaches-Choice Halves Y. C.
78	6	581	24/2½ Peaches-Choice Sliced Y. C.
78	7	799	24/2½ Peaches-Choice Sliced Y. C.
78	8	1,262	24/2½ Peaches-Choice Sliced Y. C.
		8,907	Total Cases
			Goods cased and unlabeled.

NON-NEGOTIABLE

SUBJECT TO LIEN FOR STORAGE, HANDLING AND OTHER CHARGES, AS PER CONTRACT AND LEASE WITH THE INDUSTRY SERVED.

=(DO NOT ACCEPT THIS WAREHOUSE RECEIPT IF ANY CORRECTIONS OR ERASURES APPEAR HEREON)=

Lawrence Warehouse Company

TRANSFERS NOT COMPLETE UNLESS MADE UPON THE BOOKS OF THE WAREHOUSE COMPANY.

PER **SPECIMEN**   BONDED WAREHOUSE MANAGER

RECORD OF RELEASES AND BALANCE ON HAND

	ITEM 1				ITEM 2				ITEM 3				ITEM 4		
DATE	RELEASE	DELIVERY	BALANCE	DATE	RELEASE	DELIVERY	BALANCE	DATE	RELEASE	DELIVERY	BALANCE	DATE	RELEASE	DELIVERY	BALANCE

	ITEM 5				ITEM 6				ITEM 7				ITEM 8		
DATE	RELEASE	DELIVERY	BALANCE	DATE	RELEASE	DELIVERY	BALANCE	DATE	RELEASE	DELIVERY	BALANCE	DATE	RELEASE	DELIVERY	BALANCE

Warehouse Receipt

There must also be a complete statement of the commodities or items that are to be warehoused. Agreements must also be made as to the maintenance of the property, proper fire precautions, insurance, and other necessary physical requirements. Under certain circumstances the warehouseman is authorized to release a certain quantity of goods either by the day, by the week, or by the month to make possible a rotation of merchandise. Under this arrangement, periodic physical inventories must be taken.

Extent of Field Warehousing. Field warehouses are in operation throughout the United States with a concentration of such activities in the central and Pacific Coast regions. In 1957 it was estimated that from 10,000 to 12,000 field warehouses were in existence. Nearly all forms of merchandise that may be safely warehoused have at one time or another been used for this purpose. Canned goods, miscellaneous groceries, lumber, timber, and building supplies fill about two fifths of all field warehouses in this country. Those banks that make commodity loans will generally accept field warehouse receipts as collateral for loans.

Cost of Inventory Loans. Inventory loans are somewhat more expensive than are the unsecured loans. The increased cost is due in part to the cost of the warehousing operation itself and in part to the fact that the borrower's credit rating may be low. When warehousing facilities must be utilized anyway, there is little additional cost involved in the arrangement. Bank interest rates for warehouse receipt loans in 1957 were from 5.5 to 6.5 per cent. In addition, a warehouse fee of from $3/4$ to $2\frac{1}{2}$ per cent of the loan, depending upon size and other factors, must be paid.[5]

Inventory loans, like accounts receivable loans, have become popular due to the increasing demand for working captial additions. Also, business firms are understandably anxious to take advantage of cash discounts in their purchases when the money for cash payments can be secured at nominal rates. Unemployment insurance taxes under the federal social security laws have made it advantageous for many firms to stabilize both production and employment of labor throughout the year, rather than to bear part of the burden of seasonal employment layoffs. Stabi-

[5] Inventory loans, like receivable loans, are made also by commercial credit or sales finance companies. Interest rates charged by these companies are generally higher than are those charged by the banks.

lized production throughout the year rather than production just prior to anticipated sales of the products results in the firm's carrying a larger average inventory. In turn, a larger commitment of funds by the company for carrying inventories is required. Such funds for inventory accumulation may be obtained by placing the inventories in a field warehouse, thus using the inventory itself as the basis for a bank loan.

Loans Secured by Stocks and Bonds

Stocks and bonds constitute a very popular type of collateral for short-term loans. Such securities, when pledged as collateral for a loan, are of interest to the banker primarily because of their marketability and their value. If the securities are highly marketable, and if the value is satisfactory to cover the amount of the loan requested and to provide a substantial margin for shrinkage in value, the banker may have little hesitancy in extending such a loan. The banker, of course, gives preference to those securities that are listed on one of the national security exchanges since frequent quotations of the value of such securities are available. Banks will usually lend from 50 to 60 per cent of the market value of listed stocks, and from 60 to 70 per cent of the market value of high-grade bonds. Since 1934, however, the Board of Governors of the Federal Reserve System has established maximum loan limits when the purpose of the loan is to purchase or deal in listed stocks.[6]

Only assignable stocks and bonds are eligible for this type of collateral financing. This restriction excludes United States Savings Bonds that are not assignable. When assignable securities are placed with the bank, a *stock power* or *bond power* is executed that authorizes the bank to sell or otherwise dispose of the securities should it become necessary to do so to protect the loan. (See Figure 4-4).

Other Forms of Security for Short-Term Bank Loans

Security for bank loans may also include such things as the cash surrender value of life insurance policies, guarantee of a loan by a party other than the borrower, and notes and acceptances.

[6] The operations of the securities exchanges and the limitations on borrowing for purposes of dealing in securities are discussed in Chapter 13.

Figure 4-4

| IRREVOCABLE STOCK POWER | Law Reporter Blank No. 43-A |
| Adopted by Washington Stock Exchange | All Rights Reserved |

Know All Men by These Presents

That

For Value Received *have granted, bargained, sold, assigned, and fully and irrevocably transferred and do by these presents grant, bargain, sell, assign and fully and irrevocably transfer for all purposes unto* The Citizens National Bank of Washington, D. C.

- - - - - - - - - - one hundred- - - - - - - - - - - - *shares*

of the   common   *Stock of the* United States

     Copper and Brass Company of Baltimore   *standing in*   my   *name on the books of*   United States Copper and Brass Company of Baltimore

And   I   *do hereby constitute and appoint* The Citizens

National Bank of Washington, D. C.   *to be*   my   *true and lawful attorney, irrevocable, for*   me   *and in*   my   *name and stead to sell, hypothecate or dispose of in any manner and for any purpose, assign, transfer and set over to any person or persons the whole or any parts of said stock, at once or from time to time, and for that purpose to make all necessary acts of assignment or transfer, and with power to substitute one or more persons in*   their   *stead, as to the whole or parts of said stock, with all the powers herein mentioned,* and I do   *hereby ratify and confirm all acts that*   my   *said attorney or any substitute or substitutes under*   this power   *shall lawfully do by virtue hereof.*

has
In Witness Whereof   John Smith
~~have~~ *hereunto set*   his   *hand and seal this*   17th   *day of*
   June   *A. D. 19* 58
Signed, sealed and delivered in the presence of—

Roy Jones   *John Smith* [SEAL]
                                   (Seal affixed)

Made and Sold by Law Reporter Ptg. Co., 518 5th St., Wash., D. C.

Stock Power

Life Insurance Loans. Small business establishments frequently find it possible to obtain needed short-term bank loans by a pledge of the cash surrender value of life insurance policies. Such policies must be of the assignable type, and many insurance companies insist that assignment forms prepared by the company be used for such purposes. Because of the safety afforded the bank through the use of these cash surrender values, such loans usually carry a moderate interest rate. Another reason for the favorable rates is the fact that the borrower has the alternative of borrowing directly from the insurance company. Since the insurance companies have not encouraged borrowing on the part of their policyholders, the rates at which they are willing to extend such funds have remained somewhat higher than the rates available from most banks for similar types of loans.[7]

Comaker Loans. Many small businesses find it necessary to provide the bank with a guarantor in the form of a cosigner to their notes. It is to be expected that the cosigner would have to have at least as satisfactory a credit rating as, and usually a far better rating than, the firm requesting the loan.

Discounting Notes and Acceptances. Although the act of discounting a credit instrument with a bank technically may be considered as a sale rather than a pledge of collateral, the fact that such discounted instruments are endorsed by the seller renders the seller contingently liable. We may, therefore, consider the discount of credit instruments by a firm with its bank as a form of bank credit.

The promissory note signed by the customer may be used by a firm when it is not certain of the credit standing of its customer. The use of the promissory note to bind a credit sale, however, as noted earlier, is not common in most fields of business activity. Notes have the advantage to a business of not requiring further proof of the claim against a customer as may be the case for the open-book account. The further advantage of negotiability makes it possible for the business to sell these notes to its bank or other financing agency. Except for the few lines of business activity where the use of the note is customary, however, banks are cautious in their purchase of such instruments because they often arise out of weak credit situations.

Another type of receivable instrument that arises out of the sale of merchandise to a business customer and which may be sold to a bank is the acceptance. *Acceptances* come into the possession of a business through the sale of merchandise on the basis of a draft or bill of exchange drawn against the buyer or the buyer's bank. The accepted draft or bill of exchange is returned to the seller of the merchandise where it may be held until the date of its maturity. During this period the business may see fit to discount such acceptances with its bank. Again the seller is contingently liable for these discounted acceptances.[8]

[7] Chapter 11 is devoted entirely to the functions and financial operations of insurance companies.

[8] The use of the banker's acceptance is shown in detail in connection with an international shipment of goods in Chapter 15.

QUESTIONS

1. To what extent have commercial banks changed their lending policies? Do you believe that commercial banks have been wise in altering their original lending practices?
2. Describe the principal types of assets owned by commercial banks at the present time.
3. What bearing does the asset structure of a commercial bank have on the proportion of capital to deposits?
4. What is meant by an "unsecured loan"? Are such loans important as a form of bank lending?
5. Describe what is meant by a "bank line of credit." Describe the "revolving credit agreement" and compare it to the bank line of credit.
6. Describe the nature of accounts receivable lending on the part of commercial banks.
7. What safeguards may a bank establish to protect itself when it lends on the basis of customers' receivables pledged as collateral for the loans?
8. When a business establishment uses its inventory as collateral for a bank loan, how is the problem of storing and guarding the inventory accomplished for the bank?
9. Discuss other forms of collateral that a business may use in securing loans from a commercial bank.

SUGGESTED READINGS

CHANDLER, LESTER V. *The Economics of Money and Banking;* Revised Edition. New York: Harper & Brothers, 1953. Chapter 12.

HART, ALBERT GAILORD. *Money, Debt, and Economic Activity;* Second Edition. Englewood Cliffs, New Jersey: Prentice-Hall, Inc., 1953. Chapter 3.

KENT, RAYMOND P. *Money and Banking;* Third Edition. New York: Rinehart & Company, Inc., 1956. Chapters 12, 13, 14, 16, 17, and 18.

PROCHNOW, HERBERT V. *American Financial Institutions.* Englewood Cliffs, New Jersey: Prentice-Hall, Inc., 1951. Chapters 2 and 4.

ROBINSON, ROLAND I. *The Management of Bank Funds.* New York: McGraw-Hill Book Company, Inc., 1951.

STEINER, W. H., AND SHAPIRO, ELI. *Money and Banking;* Third Edition. New York: Henry Holt & Company, Inc., 1953. Chapters 7 through 9.

THOMAS, ROLLIN G. *Our Modern Banking and Monetary System;* Second Edition. Englewood Cliffs, New Jersey: Prentice-Hall, Inc., 1950. Chapters 7, 8, 9, 11, 12, 13, and 14.

WOODWORTH, GEORGE WALTER. *The Monetary and Banking System.* New York: McGraw-Hill Book Company, Inc., 1950. Chapter 7.

Chapter 5

The Federal

Reserve System

The Federal Reserve Act of 1913 was the culmination of a long series of bills, proposals, and public debates arising from dissatisfaction with the National Banking Act. Although the National Banking Act resulted in substantial improvement in banking practices, certain weaknesses persisted and new problems developed as the economy expanded.

WEAKNESSES OF THE BANKING SYSTEM

One of the principal weaknesses of the banking system late in the nineteenth century appeared to be the inappropriate arrangement for the holding of reserves. A large part of the reserve balances of banks were held in the form of deposits with the large city banks, in particular with the large New York City banks. During periods of economic stress the position of these large city banks was precarious because they had not only the problem of meeting deposit withdrawals by their own customers but also the deposit withdrawals of their correspondent banks. The frequent inability of the large banks to meet such deposit withdrawal demands meant extreme hardship for their correspondent banks whose reserves they held.

Another weakness of the banking system under the National Banking Act was the inflexibility of the note issue system. In an effort to provide the nation with a sound national currency, no provision had been made for the expansion or contraction of national bank notes with variations in business activity. The volume of national bank notes was governed not by the needs of business but rather by the availability and the price of government bonds.[1]

The National Banking Act provided that national banks could issue their own notes only against deposit with the Treasury of United States Government bonds. Note issues were limited to 90 per cent of the par value (as stated on the face of the bond) or the market value of the bonds, whichever was lower. When bonds sold at prices considerably above their par value, it meant that the advantage of purchasing bonds for the issue of notes was eliminated. For example, if a $1,000 par value bond were available for purchase at a price of $1,150, the banks would not be inclined to make such a purchase since a maximum of $900 in notes could be issued against the bond (90 per cent of par value in this case). The interest that the banker could earn from the use of the $900 in notes would not be great enough to offset the premium price of the bond. When government bonds sold at par or at a discount, on the other hand, the prospective earning power of the note issues would be quite attractive and encourage purchase of bonds for note issue purposes. The volume of national bank notes, therefore, depended on the government bond market rather than the seasonal or cyclical needs of the nation for currency.

In addition to the foregoing two weaknesses of banking under the National Banking Act, the collection of out-of-town checks continued to be a cumbersome process. The Federal Reserve System has contributed much to the check clearance and collection process.

CENTRAL BANKING

In the last analysis the financial system of the United States during this period appeared to suffer not so much from the shortcomings of the National Banking Act as it did from the lack of an effective banking structure. Yet throughout the welter of proposals and counterproposals that preceded the enactment of the Federal Reserve Act ran a single theme: that of opposition to a strong central banking system. Although the nation had experienced central banking under the First and Second Banks of the United States, the national banking system itself did not provide for any form of central banking. The opening of the vast western

[1] J. Marvin Peterson and D. R. Cawthorne, *Money and Banking* (2nd ed.; New York: The Macmillan Company, 1949), p. 117.

frontiers along with the local autonomy of the southern areas presented an atmosphere of distrust of centralized financial control. This distrust was made all the more pointed by the fact that during the years immediately preceding enactment of the Federal Reserve Act, an era of trust busting under President Theodore Roosevelt was experienced and many of the practices of the large corporate combinations were being made public through legislative commissions and investigations.

Although the United States was one of the last major industrial nations to adopt a system of central banking, many financial and political leaders had long recognized the advantages of such a system. These proponents of central banking were given immense assistance by the dissatisfactions arising out of the panic of 1907. It must be acknowledged, however, that the central banking system adopted by the United States was, in fact, a compromise between the system of independently owned unit banks in existence in this country and the central banking systems of such countries as Canada, Great Britain, Spain, and Germany. This compromise took the form of a series of central banks, each to represent a specific regional area of the United States and hence to be more responsive to the particular financial problems of the region concerned.

In many respects, a central bank resembles the commercial bank with regard to services performed. A central bank lends money to its members; it is required to hold reserves; it is given the responsibility of creating credit, generally through bank notes and deposits; and it has stockholders and a board of directors as well as other characteristics of the commercial bank. In contrast with the commercial bank, a central bank does not necessarily operate for a profit, but it has a primary responsibility for influencing the cost, the availability, and the supply of money. It facilitates the operations of the commercial banks in their relationships with the business community and with the government.

THE FEDERAL RESERVE SYSTEM

Under the authority of the Federal Reserve Act twelve federal reserve districts were established. Each federal reserve district is served by a federal reserve bank, and the activities of the twelve banks are in turn coordinated by a Board of Governors in Wash-

Chart 5-1

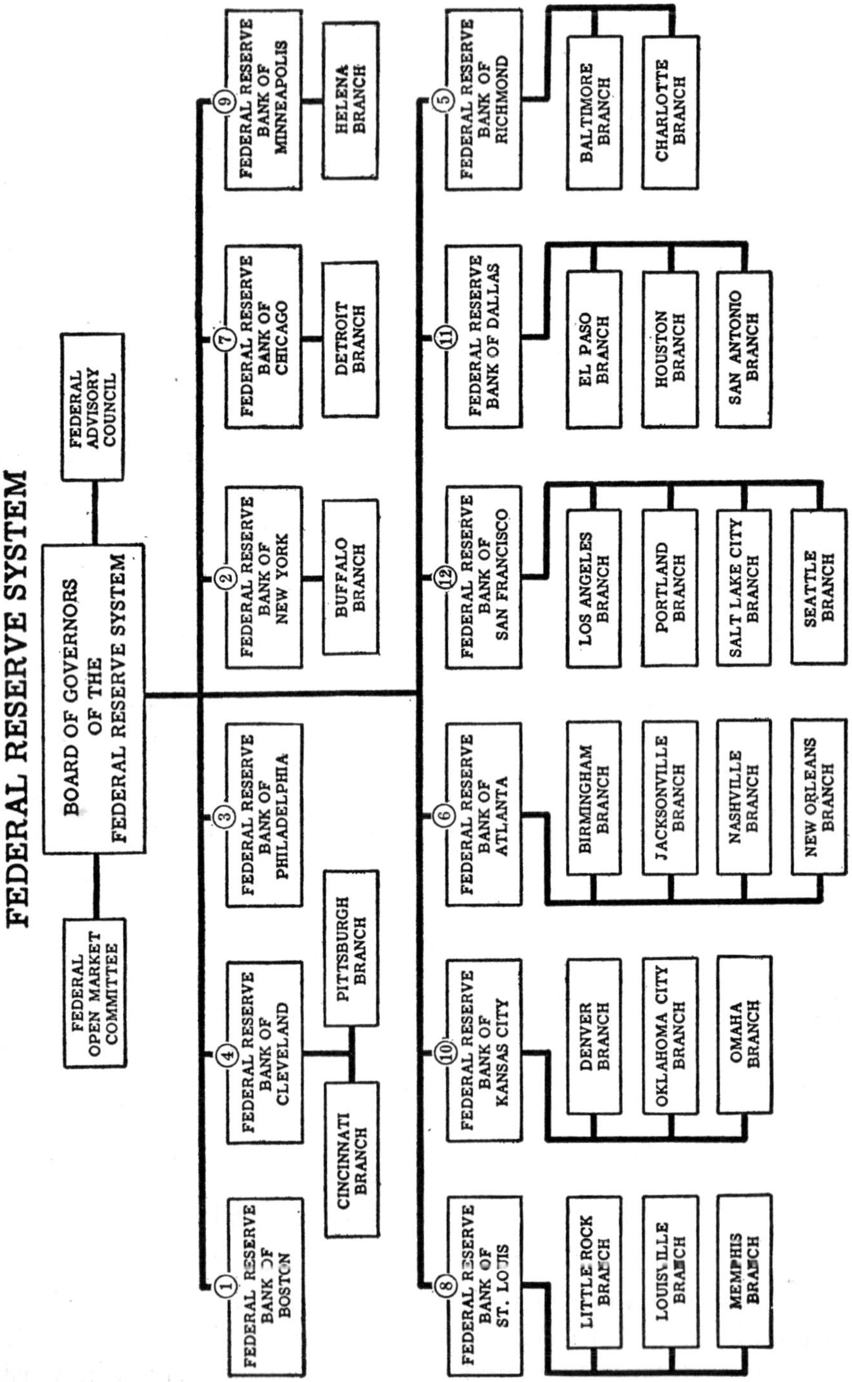

FEDERAL RESERVE SYSTEM

FEDERAL OPEN MARKET COMMITTEE

BOARD OF GOVERNORS OF THE FEDERAL RESERVE SYSTEM

FEDERAL ADVISORY COUNCIL

- ① FEDERAL RESERVE BANK OF BOSTON
- ② FEDERAL RESERVE BANK OF NEW YORK
  - BUFFALO BRANCH
- ③ FEDERAL RESERVE BANK OF PHILADELPHIA
- ④ FEDERAL RESERVE BANK OF CLEVELAND
  - PITTSBURGH BRANCH
  - CINCINNATI BRANCH
- ⑤ FEDERAL RESERVE BANK OF RICHMOND
  - BALTIMORE BRANCH
  - CHARLOTTE BRANCH
- ⑥ FEDERAL RESERVE BANK OF ATLANTA
  - BIRMINGHAM BRANCH
  - JACKSONVILLE BRANCH
  - NASHVILLE BRANCH
  - NEW ORLEANS BRANCH
- ⑦ FEDERAL RESERVE BANK OF CHICAGO
  - DETROIT BRANCH
- ⑧ FEDERAL RESERVE BANK OF ST. LOUIS
  - LITTLE ROCK BRANCH
  - LOUISVILLE BRANCH
  - MEMPHIS BRANCH
- ⑨ FEDERAL RESERVE BANK OF MINNEAPOLIS
  - HELENA BRANCH
- ⑩ FEDERAL RESERVE BANK OF KANSAS CITY
  - DENVER BRANCH
  - OKLAHOMA CITY BRANCH
  - OMAHA BRANCH
- ⑪ FEDERAL RESERVE BANK OF DALLAS
  - EL PASO BRANCH
  - HOUSTON BRANCH
  - SAN ANTONIO BRANCH
- ⑫ FEDERAL RESERVE BANK OF SAN FRANCISCO
  - LOS ANGELES BRANCH
  - PORTLAND BRANCH
  - SALT LAKE CITY BRANCH
  - SEATTLE BRANCH

SOURCE: Board of Governors of the Federal Reserve System.

80

ington, D. C. The members of the Board of Governors are also members of the Federal Open Market Committee. The Federal Advisory Council provides advice and general information to the Board of Governors. The organizational structure of the Federal Reserve System is shown in Chart 5-1.

The Federal Reserve System did not supplant the system that existed under the National Banking Act but rather was superimposed upon it. Certain provisions of the National Banking Act, however, were modified to permit greater flexibility of operations.

Federal Reserve Membership

The Federal Reserve Act provided that all national banks were to become members of the Federal Reserve System. In addition, state chartered banks, as well as trust companies, were permitted to join the system upon the presentation of evidence of a satisfactory financial condition. It was provided further that all member banks would be required to purchase capital stock of the federal reserve bank of their district up to a maximum of 6 per cent of their paid-in capital and surplus. It has been necessary, however, for the banks to pay in only 3 per cent, but the remainder is subject to call at the discretion of the Federal Reserve System. Member banks are limited to a maximum of 6 per cent dividends on the stock of the federal reserve banks that they hold. The federal reserve banks, therefore, are private institutions owned by the many member banks of the Federal Reserve System.

State chartered banks and trust companies are permitted to withdraw from membership with the Federal Reserve System six months after written notice has been submitted to the federal reserve bank of their district. In such cases, the stock originally purchased by the withdrawing member is canceled and a refund is made for all money paid in.

As of mid-year 1957, 6,438 of the nation's 13,615 commercial banks were members of the Federal Reserve System. Of this number, approximately 4,700 were national banks. Compared with the 95 per cent of all commercial banks that carried insurance under the provisions of the Federal Deposit Insurance Corporation as of mid-year 1957, the Federal Reserve System's coverage included only 48 per cent of all commercial banks. As an indication of their size and importance, however, member banks of the Federal Reserve System hold approximately 85 per cent of the deposits of all commercial banks.

Structure of the Federal Reserve Banks

Each federal reserve bank has corporate officers and a board of directors. The selection of officers and directors, however, is unlike that of other corporations.

Directors and Officers. As in the case of member banks, each federal reserve bank has its own board of directors. These nine directors must be residents of the district in which they serve. The directors serve terms of three years, the appointments being staggered in such a way that three directors are appointed each year. In order to assure that the various economic elements of the federal reserve districts are represented, the nine members of the board of directors are divided into three groups: Class A, Class B, and Class C.

Both Class A and Class B directors are elected by the member banks of the federal reserve district. The Class A directors represent member banks of the district while the Class B directors represent nonbanking interests. These nonbanking interests are commerce, agriculture, and industry. There is a further subdivision of Class A and Class B directors to represent the small banks, the medium-sized banks, and the large banks. Each of these groups is permitted to elect one Class A director and one Class B director. We have, therefore, a wide diversification of interests on the board of directors of each federal reserve bank. The Class C directors are appointed by the Board of Governors of the Federal Reserve System, and it is provided that these persons may not be stockholders, directors, or employees of existing banks.

Although the majority of the directors of the federal reserve banks are elected by the member banks of each district, the three members of each board appointed by the Board of Governors are in a strategic position relative to the other board members. One member appointed by the Board of Governors is designated chairman of the board of directors and a second member is appointed deputy chairman. Despite the precautions taken in establishing the method by which board members are chosen to represent diverse interests of the economy, there is seldom a conflict of interest among board members. Little interest is usually shown by member banks in the election of members for the board of directors.

Each federal reserve bank also has a president and first vice-president who are appointed by the board of directors with the approval of the Board of Governors. A federal reserve bank may have several additional vice-presidents. The president is responsible for the execution of the policies established by the board of directors and for general administration of the affairs of the federal reserve bank. All other officers and personnel of the federal reserve bank are subject to the authority of the president.

Federal Reserve Branch Banks. In addition to the twelve federal reserve banks, 24 branch banks have also been established. These branch banks are located, for the most part, in geographical areas not conveniently served by the federal reserve banks themselves; hence, the geographically large western federal reserve districts have a majority of the federal reserve branch banks. The San Francisco district has four, the Dallas district has three, and the Atlanta district has four branch banks. The New York federal reserve district, on the other hand, has only one branch bank, while the Boston district has no branches. The federal reserve districts and the cities in which federal reserve banks and their branches are located are shown in Chart 5-1.

The Board of Governors

The Board of Governors of the Federal Reserve System, previously known as the Federal Reserve Board, is composed of seven members. Each member is appointed for a term of fourteen years. The purpose of the fourteen-year term undoubtedly was to make possible as little partisan political pressure on the Board as possible. This Board need not be bipartisan in nature, nor is there any specific provision with respect to the qualifications a member must have. All members are appointed by the President of the United States with the advice and consent of the Senate, one member being designated as the chairman and another as vice-chairman.

The primary purpose of the Board of Governors is to give direction and coordination to the activities of the twelve federal reserve banks under its jurisdiction. The Board of Governors is also responsible for passing upon the applications of state-chartered banks applying for membership in the system and for recommending the removal of officers or directors of member banks because of infraction of rules established by the Federal Reserve System and other regulatory authorities. The Board of Governors must approve changes in the level of the rediscount rates of the federal reserve banks, and it implements many of the credit control devices that have come into existence in recent decades.

The Federal Open Market Committee

As early as 1922 efforts were made to coordinate the timing of purchases and sales of securities by the federal reserve banks in order to achieve desirable credit objectives. The Banking Act of 1933 formalized the early committees that had been established to coordinate these activities by the creation of the Federal Open Market Committee. This Committee, with the additional powers granted to it by the Banking Act of 1935, now has full control over all open market operations of the federal reserve banks.

The Federal Advisory Council

In an effort to keep the members of the Board of Governors in close contact with local business conditions, the Federal Advisory Council was created. This organization meets at least four times a year to consult with and to advise the members of the Board of Governors in matters relating to general business conditions, banking operations, and general questions of policy relative to the Federal Reserve System.

FUNCTIONS OF THE FEDERAL RESERVE SYSTEM

The primary responsibility of a central bank is to influence the cost, the availability, and the supply of money. By exercising such influence on the monetary system of the United States, the Federal Reserve System performs its most unique and important function—the promotion of economic stability. The functions of the Federal Reserve System that relate directly to the control of the cost, the availability, and the supply of money are the establishment of reserve requirements for member banks, loans and discounts to member banks, and open market operations. In addition, the Federal Reserve System exercises selective controls, such as the regulation of credit available for the purpose of purchasing listed stocks and the payment of interest on time deposits of member banks. The Federal Reserve System has also at times exercised control over consumer credit. These responsibilities involve policy decisions. Other functions of the Federal Reserve System, such as the collection of checks and issuance of currency, are regarded as services or chores.

In the remainder of this chapter we shall divide the functions of the Federal Reserve System into those that relate directly to member banks and those that relate to the economy in general. Two of the policy functions relate directly to member bank activities; the other two policy functions are implemented through other channels as well as through commercial banks. The policy functions are described in greater detail in Part V in connection with the discussion of monetary policies and problems.

The functions to be discussed are as follows:

> Bank Related Functions
> > Issuance of Currency
> > Bank Reserves
> > Loans and Discounts
> > Clearance and Collection of Checks
> > Supervision and Regulation
>
> General Functions
> > Open Market Operations
> > Selective Credit Controls
> > Direct Business Loans
> > Government Fiscal Agent
> > Reports, Publications, and Research

BANK RELATED FUNCTIONS OF THE FEDERAL RESERVE SYSTEM

Issuance of Currency

The federal reserve banks are the main source of currency in the United States. Individuals usually receive paper money and coin by making withdrawals from a bank or from the sale of merchandise or services. In either case the bank must provide such money, either directly or through the intermediary of the purchaser of goods or services. Although the flow of currency from the banks to the public is usually matched by a flow of currency deposits, at times the demand for currency by the public may exceed the banks available supply. At such times member banks depend upon the federal reserve banks for replenishment of their supply. As currency is ordered from a federal reserve bank, the reserves of the bank ordering the currency are charged. Non-member banks usually obtain their currency from member banks.

The federal reserve banks maintain large stores of paper money and coin on hand at all times to meet the demands of member banks. Approximately 85 per cent of all currency in circulation is represented by federal reserve notes, the remainder being made up of United States Treasury paper money and coin. Federal reserve notes are the obligations of both the United States government and of the issuing federal reserve banks, and they are backed by specified collateral, such as notes and government bonds. At least 25 per cent of the collateral for federal reserve notes must be in the form of gold certificates.

When the United States Treasury purchases silver from either domestic or foreign sources, it issues currency known as silver certificates. These silver certificates are delivered to the federal reserve banks, and they in turn credit the deposits of the United States Treasury. In like manner, as additional coin is required by the federal reserve banks for distribution to member banks it is received from the mints and the deposit balances of the Treasury with the federal reserve banks are credited. The cost of issuing federal reserve currency, as well as all transportation costs involved in the shipment of paper money and coin to or from the federal reserve banks, is borne by the federal reserve banks.

The issuance of currency by the federal reserve banks, therefore, eliminated one of the major weaknesses of banking under the National Banking Act prior to the establishment of the Federal Reserve System, that of an inflexible monetary system. As the demand for additional currency is now made by the public and by the banks of the nation, the federal reserve banks increase the flow of such currency from their reservoir of funds. Such increased demands for currency usually accompany an expansion in general business activity. As the economy contracts and the large additional supplies of currency are no longer required, the unnecessary currency is shipped back to the federal reserve banks.

Bank Reserves

One of the basic measures provided by the Federal Reserve Act was the institution of a more appropriate system of maintaining reserves by the banks of the nation. The shortcomings of the system of holding reserves as permitted under the National Banking Act had been recognized, and it was apparent that a remedy would have to be provided before substantial progress could be made toward stabilizing the banking system of the country. To accomplish this, member banks were to keep on reserve with the federal reserve bank of their district a specified percentage of the volume of deposits of the bank.

Although all member banks were subject to the same minimum reserve requirements on time and savings deposits, the member banks were divided into three groups for purposes of determining reserve ratios on demand or checking deposits. These three groups were based on the division established earlier by the National Banking Act: central reserve city banks, reserve city banks, and country banks. The importance of cities as national or regional money centers provided the basis for their classification. Although under the provisions of the Federal Reserve Act a part of the minimum reserves was permitted to be held as cash in the member bank's own vault, this provision was changed in 1917 by an act of Congress that required all legal reserves against time and demand deposits to be kept with the federal reserve banks.

Although the Board of Governors has the power to alter the legal reserve requirements, Congress establishes the range within which these changes can be made. At the present time, it is provided by law that the range of required reserves for central reserve city banks may be from 13 to 26 per cent of their demand deposits; for reserve city banks, from 10 to 20 per cent; for country banks, from 7 to 14 per cent; and for time deposits of all member banks, 3 to 6 per cent is the range.

Note from Table 5-1 that the legal reserves have been changed frequently. These changes have been effected for the purpose of countering either inflationary or deflationary influences.

Table 5-1

FEDERAL RESERVE MEMBER BANK RESERVE REQUIREMENTS

(PER CENT OF DEPOSITS)

EFFECTIVE DATE OF CHANGE	NET DEMAND DEPOSITS			TIME DEPOSITS	
	CENTRAL RESERVE CITY BANKS	RESERVE CITY BANKS	COUNTRY BANKS	CENTRAL RESERVE AND RESERVE CITY BANKS	COUNTRY BANKS
1917—June 21	13	10	7	3	3
1936—Aug. 16	19½	15	10½	4½	4½
1937—Mar. 1	22¾	17½	12¼	5¼	5¼
May 1	26	20	14	6	6
1938—Apr. 16	22¾	17½	12	5	5
1941—Nov. 1	26	20	14	6	6
1942—Aug. 20	24	....	....	....	....
Sept. 14	22	....	....	....	....
Oct. 3	20	....	....	....	....
1948—Feb. 27	22	....	....	....	....
June 11	24	....	....	....	....
Sept. 16	26	22	16	7½	7½
1949—May 1	24	21	15	7	7
June 30	....	20	14	6	6
Aug. 1	23½	19½	13	5	....
Aug. 16	23	19	12	....	5
Aug. 25	22½	18½	....	....	....
Sept. 1	22	18	....	....	....
1951—Jan. 11	23	19	13	6	6
Jan. 25	24	20	14	....	....
1953—July 1	22	19	13	....	....
1954—June 16	21	....	....	5	5
July 29	20	18	12	....	....
In effect Sept. 1, 1957 ..	20	18	12	5	5

SOURCE: *Federal Reserve Bulletin*, September, 1957, Board of Governors of the Federal Reserve System, Washington, D. C., p. 1044.

Loans and Discounts

It was believed that if the federal reserve banks were to serve effectively as banker's banks, they would have to provide facilities for lending to their member banks at times when additional funds were required by the banks. Such a lending arrangement was to meet one of the principal objections to the National Banking Act, that of an inflexible currency system. Loans to member banks by the federal reserve banks may take two forms: first, the bank may receive an "advance" secured by the promissory note of the bank together with eligible paper owned by the bank, or second, the bank may "discount" its eligible paper with the federal reserve bank. Eligible paper, which is defined in considerable detail by the Board of Governors, includes such items as the promissory notes, bills of exchange, and banker's acceptances of customers that member banks hold. Bonds and notes of the United States government and obligations of instrumentalities of the United States government that carry the guarantee of the government are also acceptable as collateral for advances. The federal reserve banks may make advances to banks that are not members of the Federal Reserve System and to certain nonbanking institutions when direct obligations of the United States government are offered as security.

The use of eligible paper as collateral for a loan from a federal reserve bank involves a contingent liability on the part of the member bank in the case of either a discount or an advance. In discounting eligible paper, the member bank is required to endorse each item. For an advance, the bank must sign a promissory note in addition to submitting eligible paper as collateral. The promissory note, of course, represents a general claim against the bank over and above the value of the eligible paper.

Member banks have generally found that in borrowing from a federal reserve bank the use of the advance arrangement, as opposed to the discount arrangement, is more convenient since the maturity of the various items of eligible paper may not coincide with the needs of the member bank. Under the advance arrangement, paper held by the federal reserve bank as collateral that matures before the due date of the advance is simply replaced by other eligible paper. Also, under the advance arrangement a single interest rate is calculated on the loan while discounted eligible paper may require varying discount rates, depending upon the quality, length of maturity, and general character of each item. Because of the large bank holdings of United States Government securities in recent years, however, and because of their convenience, member banks have generally used these securities instead of eligible paper as collateral for federal reserve bank advances.

The rate charged by all federal reserve banks on advances and discounts as of October 1, 1957, was 3.5 per cent. The rate may be lowered or raised from time to time to encourage or discourage, as may be desired, member banks' participation in the loan program. Also, at times the rate will vary from one federal reserve bank to another. Such variations in rates between banks generally result from a desire to equalize the general flow of credit throughout the nation.

Until late in 1952 the volume of lending operations of the federal reserve banks had reached significant proportions only during World War I and the period thereafter and during the stock market boom of 1928 and 1929. Late in 1952 member banks obtained over $1.5 billion in loans from the federal reserve banks in order to meet the unusually large demand for funds by their business customers.

Clearance and Collection of Checks

One of the important contributions of the Federal Reserve System to the smooth flow of financial interchange has been that of facilitating the clearance and collection of checks of the banks of the nation. Each federal reserve bank serves as a clearinghouse for all banks in its district, provided that they agree to remit at par on checks forwarded to them for payment. The importance of this service to the banking system of the United States can be readily understood by a brief review of clearance practices prior to the Federal Reserve System.

Although local clearinghouses made it possible for banks within the same city to effect an efficient exchange of customers checks, it was often difficult and time-consuming to provide for the settlement of claims when checks were drawn on out-of-town banks or when checks drawn on the local banks were presented to out-of-town banks for payment. In addition to the time consumed in routing checks from one bank to another for payment, many banks on which checks were drawn made payment only at a discount; that is, instead of remitting the face value of the check, they would deduct $\frac{1}{8}$ to $\frac{1}{2}$ of 1 per cent of the face value of the check as a clearance charge. This practice resulted in the establishment of correspondent banking relations between banks in the important commercial centers of the United States.

Correspondent arrangements generally provided that checks exchanged between the two banks would be accepted at par. In this way, a local bank that had received a check drawn on a bank in another community, in order to avoid having the other bank remit at less than par, would send the check instead to a correspondent bank in the same community as the bank on which the check was drawn. That bank, in turn, would either send the check directly to the bank on which it was written, if it were a correspondent of that bank, or pass it on to another bank that might have correspondent relations with it, thus avoiding the penalty. As such checks were forwarded to correspondent banks, the reserves of the forwarding bank were increased because deposits with correspondents were considered to be part of required reserves. The many days required to clear checks under this arrangement meant that the reserves of banks were greatly padded, increasing their potential for bank lending.

Although it may seem that the bank on which the check was originally presented would be able to pass on such charges to its customers, such practice was avoided if at all possible because of the intense competition for the accounts of businesses and other customers at that time. Hence, banks frequently attempted to absorb these costs, when they could not otherwise be avoided, rather than to pass them on to their customers.

Check Clearance Through the Federal Reserve Banks. Member banks of the Federal Reserve System and nonmembers alike may utilize the check-clearance facilities of the federal reserve banks. Nonmember participating banks, however, like member banks, must remit at par on checks presented to them for payment and must keep a small deposit with the federal reserve bank for check-clearance purposes. As of mid-year 1957 the number of banks that continued to charge exchange fees on checks presented for payment was 331. These banks are small and unimportant, and their number is continually decreasing. The Board of Governors of the Federal Reserve System has at times encouraged state legislatures to outlaw this practice. For the vast majority of commercial banks, the federal reserve banks provide an efficient and economical system of check clearance. For member banks the service is particularly appropriate since they must hold legal reserves with the federal reserve banks anyway. As checks are sent through federal reserve banks for collection, the reserve balances of participating banks are decreased or increased, depending upon the day's total of checks drawn against or in favor of a particular bank.

An example of the check-clearance process through the federal reserve banks will demonstrate the facility with which these clearances are made at the present time. Assume that a businessman in Sacramento, California, places an order for merchandise from a distributor in San Francisco. His order is accompanied by a check drawn on his bank in Sacramento. This check is deposited by the distributor with his bank in San Francisco, at which time he receives a corresponding credit to his account with the bank. The distributor's bank will then send the check to the federal reserve bank of its district, also located in San Francisco, which will in turn forward the check to the bank in Sacramento on which the check was originally drawn. The adjustment of accounts is accomplished at the federal reserve bank through an alternate debit and credit to the accounts of the banks concerned in the transaction. The San Francisco bank, which has honored the check of its customer, will receive an increase in its reserve with the federal reserve bank, while the bank in Sacramento will have its reserve decreased by a corresponding amount. The bank in Sacramento, of course, will reduce the account of the businessman who wrote the check. Hence, the exchange has been made with no transfer of currency.

In the event that the Sacramento bank found its legal reserve reduced below the point required by its total deposits, it would then be necessary, in one way or another, to supplement its reserves with the federal reserve bank. For the vast amount of check clearance that takes place, however, a negligible amount of cash shipment is required. Although the distributor in this case received an immediate increase in his account for the amount of the check deposited with his bank as is customary, the bank did not receive an immediate increase in its reserves with the federal reserve bank on which it could draw. Had the bank on which the check was drawn been located in San Francisco, there would have been an immediate credit to the account of the depositing bank. The length of time that a bank must wait before checks deposited with a federal reserve bank are added to their active accounts depends on the distance of the banks on which the checks are drawn from the federal reserve bank. A schedule of zones exists in which these waiting periods for various geographical areas are specified. In no case, however, is a bank required to wait more than two days before a check deposited with the federal reserve bank will be entered to its credit.

Check Clearance Between Federal Reserve Districts. If at the time the businessman placed his order with the San Francisco distributor, he also placed an order with a distributor of goods in Chicago, Illinois, his check would be subject to an additional step in being cleared through the Federal Reserve System. The Chicago distributor, like the San Francisco distributor, deposits the check with the bank of his choice and in turn receives an increase in his account. The Chicago bank deposits the check for collection with the Federal Reserve Bank of Chicago, which in turn forwards the check to the Federal Reserve Bank of San Francisco. The Federal Reserve Bank of San Francisco, of course, then presents the check for payment to the bank on which it was drawn. There are, therefore, two routes of check clearance: the intradistrict settlement where the transaction takes place entirely within a single federal reserve district, and the interdistrict settlement in which there are relationships between banks of two federal reserve districts.

The Interdistrict Settlement Fund. Just as the federal reserve banks are able to minimize the actual flow of funds by increasing or decreasing reserves of the participating banks, the federal reserve banks are able to avoid the flow of funds between the federal reserve banks to effect interdistrict settlements. This is accomplished through the Interdistrict Settlement Fund in Washington, D. C.

The Interdistrict Settlement Fund has a substantial deposit from each of the federal reserve banks. These deposit credits are alternately increased or decreased, depending upon the clearance balance of the day's activities on the part of each federal reserve bank. At a certain hour each day, each federal reserve bank informs the Interdistrict Settlement Fund by direct wire the amount of checks it has received the previous day that were drawn on banks in other federal reserve districts. The deposit of each federal reserve bank with the Interdistrict Settlement Fund is increased or decreased according to the balance of the day's check clearance activities. The Interdistrict Settlement Fund also makes it possible for large sums to be transferred for member banks to banks in other federal reserve districts through the deposit balances of the federal reserve banks with the Fund.

Check Clearance Through Federal Reserve Branch Banks. Branch banks of the federal reserve banks enter into the clearance process in a very important way. If the check is deposited with a bank located nearer to a federal reserve branch bank than to a federal reserve bank, the branch bank, in effect, takes the place of the federal reserve bank.

Check Routing Symbols. The magnitude of the task of assisting in the check-clearance process by the Federal Reserve System is attested to by the fact that over one quarter of the total personnel of the twelve federal reserve banks are engaged in this function. Great effort has been exercised to make this task easier, and much timesaving machinery has been introduced into the operation. A check routing symbol plan, jointly sponsored in 1945 by the American Bankers Association and the federal reserve system, is of great assistance in the more rapid and accurate sorting of out-of-town checks. These symbols, in the opinion of some banking authorities, represent one of our greatest advances in recent times in the check-clearance process.

The purpose of the symbol is to reveal to check sorters at a glance the identity, the location, and the proper check collection route to the bank on which the check is drawn. Preceding the hyphen, in the numerator of the symbol, are to be found numbers ranging from 1 through 99. Numbers 1 through 49 are assigned to major cities, while numbers 50 through 99 apply to states and United States territories. The number following the hyphen identifies a specific bank in the locality. The first digit of the denominator (or the first two digits in the case of the tenth, eleventh, and twelfth districts) identifies the federal reserve district. The next digit designates the federal reserve office serving the territory, that is, whether it is a federal reserve bank or one of its branches. The final figure in the denominator is a dual-purpose one. A zero means that credit will be given to the collecting of bank's reserve account as soon as the check is received by the appropriate federal reserve office. Any other final number signifies that reserve credit will be deferred because the paying bank is far enough away from

Figure 5-1

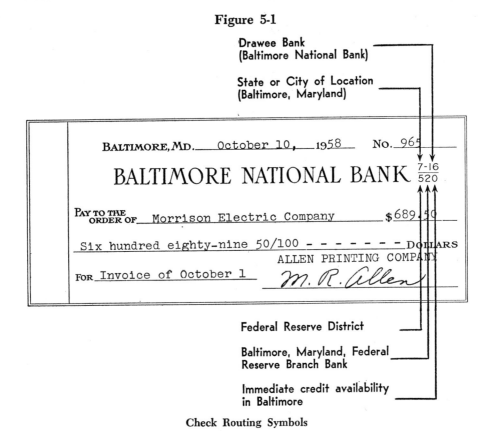

Drawee Bank
(Baltimore National Bank)

State or City of Location
(Baltimore, Maryland)

BALTIMORE, MD.____October 10,____19<u>58</u>____ No._96__

BALTIMORE NATIONAL BANK $\frac{7\text{-}16}{520}$

PAY TO THE
ORDER OF___Morrison Electric Company_____ $689.50

Six hundred eighty-nine 50/100 — — — — — — — DOLLARS

ALLEN PRINTING COMPANY

FOR_Invoice of October 1___   *M. R. Allen*

Federal Reserve District

Baltimore, Maryland, Federal
Reserve Branch Bank

Immediate credit availability
in Baltimore

Check Routing Symbols

the federal reserve office so that one or more days will elapse before the check can be physically presented to that bank for payment. In addition, if a "deferred availability" number (a final number other than zero) appears, it also indicates the district state within which the paying bank is located. In the Seventh District, a final number of 1 signifies Illinois; 2, Indiana; 3, Iowa; 4, Michigan; and 5, Wisconsin. In the Baltimore Branch Territory of the Fifth District, a final number of 1 signifies Maryland (outside of Baltimore); 2, West Virginia. An example of a check routing symbol is shown in Figure 5-1.

Federal Reserve Transfer of Credit. The Federal Reserve System provides for the transfer of hundreds of millions of dollars in bank credit about the country daily. In 1953 the Federal Reserve System put into operation a near-automatic system of teletype through which bank credit can be transferred. The communication system, referred to as the *federal reserve leased system,* spans approximately 11,000 miles and makes it possible for the 12 federal reserve banks and their 24 branches to maintain facilities for almost instantaneous transfer of bank credit. Headquarters for the communication system is in Richmond, Virginia.

Supervision and Regulation

Few fields of activity are so strongly regulated and supervised as that of the banking system. This regulation, of course, results in part from the strategic role played by the commercial banking system in the nation's economy and the sensitivity of business conditions in general to undue disturbances in the banking system. Regulation and supervision are exercised by several different agencies. For example, national banks are subject to examination by the Comptroller of the Currency, and because all national banks must be members of the Federal Reserve System, they are also subject to examination and regulation by the Federal Reserve System. Also, since members of the Federal Reserve System must be insured by the Federal Deposit Insurance Corporation, they are subject to possible examinations by that organization.

Regulation of State Chartered Banks. If a member bank is a state-chartered institution, although not subject to the supervision of the Comptroller of the Currency, it is subject to the laws of the state in which it is chartered as well as the regulation of the Federal Reserve System and the Federal Deposit Insurance Corporation. Insured state banks that are not members of the Federal Reserve System are subject to examination by the Federal Deposit Insurance Corporation, while nonmember uninsured state banks are subject only to state examination.

Delegation of Federal Reserve Examination Responsibilities. Examination of member banks by the Federal Reserve System is generally delegated to the regional federal reserve banks; however, the Board of Governors of the Federal Reserve System is authorized by law to examine member banks if it so chooses. In practice, national banks are seldom examined by the staff of the Federal Reserve System since they are normally subject to examination also by the Comptroller of the Currency. National bank examiners, responsible to the Comptroller of the Currency, gener-ally submit a copy of the examination report of each national bank to the examination department of the district reserve bank, and normally no further examination is made by the federal reserve bank. The federal reserve bank may, however, dispatch its own examiners to one of the national banks to secure information not covered by the examination of the national bank examiners. The principal activities of the examination department of the federal reserve banks is that of examining state-chartered member banks of the district.

As in the case of national banks and the national bank exami-ners, federal reserve authorities cooperate closely with the state banking authorities in an effort to minimize the burden of bank examination on banking operations and in order to simplify the procedure. In many states, state bank officials accept the report of the federal reserve examiners and concentrate their own examina-tion activities on nonmember state banks. State and federal reserve bank examiners may appear jointly for purposes of examination to minimize the inconvenience to bank operations. The Federal Deposit Insurance Corporation confines its examination activities largely to insured state banks that are not members of the Federal Reserve System.

GENERAL FUNCTIONS OF THE FEDERAL RESERVE SYSTEM

Open Market Operations

Open market operations are regarded as the most important single instrument available to the Federal Reserve System for pur-poses of credit control. By purchasing large quantities of securi-ties in the open market, the federal reserve banks increase the flow of funds in circulation. By selling securities, funds are with-drawn from circulation. Obligations of the United States govern-ment are the principal kind of securities that the federal reserve banks buy and sell. The Open Market Committee is responsible for such activities.

As an example of an Open Market Committee action, assume that the Committee decides to buy $50 million of United States government securities. These securities are purchased in the open market from whatever source they may be available. A check drawn on the federal reserve bank making the purchase is delivered to the seller of the securities. The seller deposits the check with a member bank, which in turn delivers the check to the federal reserve bank. The seller of the securities has had an increase in his deposit balance with the member bank, and the member bank in turn has increased its reserves with the federal reserve bank. On the basis of the expanded reserves of the member bank with the federal reserve bank, loans and investments may also be expanded. The net effect, therefore, of the purchase of securities is to expand the reserves of member banks and in turn their credit-creating potential.

If it is the desire of the Federal Reserve System to restrain credit expansion and growth in money supply, the federal reserve banks may sell securities in the open market. The purchasers of the securities pay for them by drawing checks on their balances with member banks. This, in turn, reduces the reserves of the member banks with the federal reserve banks, and they must adjust their loan and investment operations to the lower level of reserves on deposit with the federal reserve bank. In this way pressure is brought to bear on the loan and investment activities of commercial banks.

Selective Credit Controls

To supplement the general methods of regulating the flow of funds, the Federal Reserve System has special powers to regulate the credit terms on which transactions in stock market securities are financed. The terms of consumer credit and certain real estate credit has also been regulated by the Federal Reserve System from time to time. In contrast with the other methods of monetary control, selective credit controls act directly on credit rather than on the reserves of member banks. They are also directed to specific lines of business activity to the exclusion of all others. Much controversy has existed as to the merits of a system of monetary control that imposes special restriction on individual segments of the economy.

Margin Requirements on Stock Market Credit. Since 1934 the Board of Governors of the Federal Reserve System has had the responsibility of curbing the excessive use of credit for the purpose of purchasing or carrying securities. It discharges this responsibility by limiting the amount that brokers and dealers in securities, banks, and others may lend on securities for that purpose. Brokers are limited in their lending for the purpose of purchasing or carrying any type of security. The restriction on banks applies only to loans for purchasing or carrying securities registered on national security exchanges. Such limitations do not apply to loans secured by stocks if the purpose of the loans is for regular business activities. Current margin requirements for the purchase of listed securities are discussed in Chapter 13.

Consumer Credit. The Federal Reserve System has resorted to regulation of consumer credit only in times of emergency to supplement general credit measures. Its first use in 1941 was for the purpose of curbing the use of credit for the purchase of automobiles, household goods, and other such consumer durables. The problem faced by the nation at that time was one of an acute shortage of consumer goods and services accompanied by an increase in consumer purchasing power. Without restrictive measures, the result of such a situation could only be increasing prices. By 1952 all restrictions on the use of consumer credit were eliminated.

Real Estate Credit. Because of the tremendous inflationary pressure on prices in the post-World War II period, it was necessary to restrict the flow of credit for home purchase. Failure to do so would have meant a substantial diversion of manpower and materials from essential defense requirements. In 1950 the Board of Governors of the Federal Reserve System issued Regulation X for real estate credit. It specified the maximum amount that could be borrowed, the maximum length of time the loan could run, and the minimum periodic payments that had to be made to pay off the principal amount of the loan. Restrictions on real estate credit were removed in 1952, and they have not been utilized since that time.

Direct Business Loans

The Federal Reserve Act provides that the federal reserve banks may in certain instances make direct business loans for working capital purposes to industrial or commercial businesses in their district. Such loans may be made only when they appear to be warranted and when the business is unable to secure adequate financial assistance on a reasonable basis from other sources. As of October 1, 1957, interest rates charged by the federal reserve banks for such direct loans have been within the range of 3.5 to 6.0 per cent. As of that date the total of all industrial loans outstanding by the federal reserve banks was approximately $600 thousand. The relatively small volume of direct business loans made by the federal reserve banks is due in large part to the fact that such facilities have never been actively promoted. Also, until 1953 the well-publicized efforts of the Reconstruction Finance Corporation in lending directly to business enterprises and more recently the efforts of the Small Business Administration have tended to obscure the availability of direct loans from the federal reserve banks.

A federal reserve bank may also join with a member bank in making a working capital loan to a business, or a member bank may make a loan and secure from the federal reserve bank a commitment to the effect that it will take over the loan upon the request of the member bank. A federal reserve bank in taking over a loan from a member bank will not absorb losses in excess of 80 per cent of the loan. There is, of course, a fee charged by the federal reserve bank of the member bank for this deferred commitment.

The federal reserve banks are authorized to discount short-term agricultural paper for the Federal Intermediate Credit banks.[2] Also, the federal reserve banks are authorized to make advances to business and agricultural interests based on their notes for periods not to exceed 90 days. These notes must be secured by United States government securities.

Government Fiscal Agent

A substantial proportion of the employees of the Federal Reserve System hold duties that are directly related to the provision of fiscal services for the United States government. These services, provided without charge to the government, include the holding of the principal checking accounts for the Treasury of the United States, assisting in the collection of taxes, the transfer of money

[2] The Federal Intermediate Credit banks are discussed in Chapter 14.

from one region to another, the sale and redemption of federal securities, and the paying of interest coupons. These duties, undertaken in addition to the general functions of the Federal Reserve System, make it possible for the United States government, in spite of its increased complexity, to handle the mechanics of its fiscal affairs more efficiently and safely than before the establishment of the Federal Reserve System.

Reports, Publications, and Research

The federal reserve banks publish a weekly statement of condition for each reserve bank as well as a consolidated statement for all of the reserve banks. This information has become valuable for purposes of studying business conditions in general and for the formulation of forecasts of business activity. In addition to the weekly statement, all twelve of the federal reserve banks, as well as the Board of Governors, engage in intensive research in monetary matters. The Board of Governors makes available the *Federal Reserve Bulletin,* which not only carries articles of current interest to economists and businessmen in general, but also it offers a convenient source of the statistics compiled by the federal reserve system. The *Bulletin* is also a convenient secondary source for certain statistical series and data prepared by other organizations.

QUESTIONS

1. Describe the background of commercial banking activities that resulted in the passage of the Federal Reserve Act of 1913.
2. The Federal Reserve Act of 1913 provided for the establishment of a group of "central banks." How do the operations of a central bank differ from those of a commercial bank?
3. Describe the organizational structure of the Federal Reserve System.
4. Describe the circumstances and conditions under which a commercial bank may become a member of the Federal Reserve System.
5. The board of directors of each federal reserve bank is constituted in such a way that representation is given to banking and to business of large, intermediate, and small size. Explain how this is accomplished.
6. What is meant by a "federal reserve branch bank"? How many such branches exist, and where are most of them located geographically?
7. The Federal Reserve System is under the general direction and control of the Board of Governors of the Federal Reserve System in Washington,

D. C. How are members of the Board of Governors appointed? To what extent are the members of the Board of Governors subject to political pressures?

8. What is the number of the federal reserve district in which you reside? In what city is the federal reserve bank of your district located?

9. Discuss the structure, the functions, and the importance of the Federal Open Market Committee.

10. Why did Congress give to the Board of Governors the power to change within a limited range the legal reserve of member banks?

11. With respect to their lending power, federal reserve banks have at times been described as bankers' banks. What is meant by this statement?

12. Describe the process by which a check drawn on a commercial bank but deposited for collection in another bank in a distant city might be cleared through the facilities of the Federal Reserve System.

13. What is meant by "check routing symbols"?

14. Explain the usual procedures for examining national banks. How does this process differ from the examination of member banks of the Federal Reserve System holding state charters?

15. In what way do the federal reserve banks serve as fiscal agents for the United States government?

SUGGESTED READINGS

CHANDLER, LESTER V. *The Economics of Money and Banking*; Revised Edition. New York: Harper & Brothers, 1953. Chapter 13.

Federal Reserve System. *The Federal Reserve System—Purposes and Functions*. Washington, D. C.: Board of Governors of the Federal Reserve System, 1954.

HALM, GEORGE N. *Economics of Money and Banking*. Homewood, Illinois: Richard D. Irwin, Inc., 1956. Chapters 20 through 25.

KENT, RAYMOND P. *Money and Banking*; Third Edition. New York: Rinehart & Company, Inc., 1956. Chapters 20 through 22.

PROCHNOW, HERBERT V. *American Financial Institutions*. Englewood Cliffs, New Jersey: Prentice-Hall, Inc., 1951. Chapter 3.

ROOSA, ROBERT V. *Federal Reserve Operations in the Money and Government Securities Markets*. New York: The Federal Reserve Bank of New York, July, 1956.

THOMAS, ROLLIN G. *Our Modern Banking and Monetary System*; Second Edition. Englewood Cliffs, New Jersey: Prentice-Hall, Inc., 1950. Chapters 17 and 18.

WOODWORTH, GEORGE WALTER. *The Monetary and Banking System*. New York: McGraw-Hill Book Company, Inc., 1950. Chapters 10 and 11.

Chapter 6

Other Sources of

Short-Term Business

Financing

Although the commercial banking system is of great importance to the business community as a source of short-term funds, it is by no means the only source. Trade credit, commercial finance companies, factors, and the Small Business Administration also provide significant amounts of short-term financing for business. In this chapter each of these sources of short-term business credit will be discussed.

TRADE CREDIT

The most important single form of short-term business financing is that of credit extended by one business organization to another. The open accounts receivable, together with notes receivable, taken by manufacturers, wholesalers, jobbers, and other business units as sellers of goods and services to other businesses are known as *trade credit*. This discussion excludes credit established as a result of sale of goods to the ultimate consumer, which is considered in Part IV as consumer credit.

Characteristics of Trade Credit

The establishment of trade credit is the least formal of all forms of financing. It involves only an order for goods or services by one business and the delivery of goods or performance of service by the selling business. The purchasing business receives an invoice stating the terms of the transaction and the time period within which payment is to be made. The purchaser enters the liability as an

103

addition to accounts payable; the seller enters the claim as an addition to accounts receivable. In some situations, the seller of goods or services may insist upon written evidence of the liability on the part of the purchaser. Such written evidence generally takes the form of a note and is carried as a note payable by the purchaser and as a note receivable by the seller. In either situation, whether through open account or through the use of the note, trade credit as a form of short-term financing has been utilized.

Before a business organization delivers goods or performs a service for another business, it must determine, of course, the ability and willingness of the purchaser to pay for the order. The responsibility for such credit analysis in most businesses is that of the credit manager.

Terms for Trade Credit

Sales may be made on such terms as *cash*, *E.O.M.* (end of month), *M.O.M.* (middle of month), or *R.O.G.* (receipt of goods). In other situations, such terms as *2/10, net/30* may be provided, in which case the purchaser may deduct 2 per cent from the purchase price if payment is made within 10 days; but if not paid within 10 days, the net amount of the purchase is due within 30 days of shipment. Such discounts for early payment are common and are designed to provide incentive for prompt payment of bills by the purchaser. Occasionally net terms, such as net/30 or net/60, may be provided.

A cash sale, contrary to its implication, does involve the element of credit since the purchaser is generally permitted a certain number of days within which to make payment. For example, a sale of merchandise in which the purchaser is permitted up to ten days to remit may be considered a cash transaction, although credit is outstanding to the purchaser for that period of time. Even for the firm that purchases goods and services entirely on a cash basis of this nature, the volume of accounts payable outstanding on its books at any one time may be of a very sizable amount.

E.O.M. terms and M.O.M. terms are designed primarily for the convenience of frequent purchasers of goods from a given company. Rather than requiring payment for purchases after a specified number of days, such as 10 days, 20 days, or 30 days, all sales made to a customer during the month are payable during the following month. For example, under terms of 2/10, net/60 E.O.M., all sales made to a customer during the month of April become payable during the month of May, the discount period running from May 1 through May 10. This arrangement makes it possible for the customer to pay for his many purchases from a particular company with a single remittance. In order to shorten the time lag for payment of credit purchases, terms of M.O.M. may be used instead of E.O.M. Under this arrangement the discount period begins to run from the fifteenth day of the month for sales made from the first to the fifteenth of the month and from the first of the following month for sales made from the fifteenth to the end of the month.

R.O.G. terms signify that payment is to be made upon "receipt of goods." These terms are used when shipment of goods is made over long distances, during which period of shipment the seller of the merchandise finances the credit transaction.

Cost of Trade Credit

When trade credit terms provide for no discount for early payment of obligations, there is, of course, no cost for such financing. Even when discounts are available to the purchaser, it may appear that there is no charge for trade credit since failure to take the discount by early payment simply requires the purchaser to pay the net purchase price. An implicit cost is involved, however, when a discount is not taken. For example, with terms of 2/10, net/30 the cost is measured directly by the loss of the discount that might otherwise be taken if payment were made within the first 10-day period. During the first 10-day period, however, the buyer does have trade credit without direct cost.

In order to calculate the comparative cost of trade credit to a business firm as opposed to bank credit, the cost of the trade credit must be reduced to an annual interest rate basis. For example, if the terms of sale are 2/10, net/30, the cost of the trade credit is the sacrifice of the 2 per cent discount that the purchaser fails to take if he allows his credit to run for the full 30-day period. Since the buyer may take his discount if payment is made within the first 10 days after purchase, payment on the thirtieth day would result in a sacrifice of the discount for the privilege of extending the payment period by 20 days. The loss of the discount of 2 per cent may then be represented as the cost of trade credit for 20 days under terms of 2/10, net/30. Two per cent for 20 days is at the rate of 36 per cent for 360 days, the relevant figure for comparison with bank loan rates. Had the terms of the sale been 2/10, net/60, the cost of the trade credit would have been 2 per cent for the use of credit for 50 days. Two per cent for 50 days bears the same relationship as 14.4 per cent for 360 days. In like manner, terms of 2/10, net/20 presents a cost of trade credit on an annual basis of 72 per cent. The cost of such trade credit, therefore, is clearly far in excess of bank rates.

Volume of Trade Credit

As an indication of the importance and dominance of trade credit as a form of short-term financing, as of June 30, 1957, trade credit outstanding for a group of 9,200 manufacturing corporations was $16.8 billion compared with short-term bank loans of $8 billion.[1] Earlier studies have revealed similar comparisons. A study conducted in 1939 by the National Bureau of Economic Research revealed that trade debt was about $2\frac{1}{2}$ times as large as bank debt for manufacturing, trade, construction, and service industries. Further, at the beginning of World War II it was estimated that 80 per cent of the nonfinancial businesses of the nation had outstanding trade credit, while only about 35 per cent of the businesses had outstanding debt to financial institutions. Trade credit was particularly heavy in the construction industry and in wholesaling operations.[2]

Sources of Funds for Trade Credit

Trade credit, unlike other forms of short-term finance, does not involve the conveyance of money to the user. The net effect as far as the user of trade credit is concerned, however, is very much the same since it enables him to acquire goods or services without an immediate payment therefor. The firm that provides trade credit must be able to do so from its general resources. If the firm has such a strained financial position that it is unable

---

[1] FTC-SEC *Quarterly Financial Report*, United States Manufacturing Corporations, 2nd Quarter, 1957 (Washington, D. C., 1957), p. 30.

[2] Carl Kaysen, *Industrial and Commercial Debt—A Balance Sheet Analysis* (New York: National Bureau of Economic Research, unpublished manuscript, 1942), p. 30.

to extend credit terms in line with other firms of its industry, it operates at a severe if not impossible competitive handicap. Since the trade credit provided by a firm is reflected in its balance sheet as a current asset, in particular as notes receivable and accounts receivable, sources of funds for carrying such trade credit are very much the same as for carrying other current assets; namely, through the purchase of its own goods and services on the basis of trade credit, short-term borrowing, long-term financing, and retained profits from operations.

Reasons for Use of Trade Credit

Because the cost of trade credit in most lines of business activity is high, it may be difficult to understand why such a tremendous volume of trade credit would be taken by business. Trade credit is used by financially weak concerns because they have no adequate alternative sources of credit. In any event, it may not be assumed that, because of the high cost of trade credit, it is an undesirable source of short-term financing for the business. It may be, in fact, the most essential form of financing for small and growing business enterprises that are unable to qualify for short-term credit through customary financial channels.

Few of the business enterprises in operation today would have been able to reach their present size and scope of operations without the help of trade credit during the growth stages of their development. For the firm that does not have recourse to a line of credit with a bank or other financial institution, the question is not the cost of trade credit as compared with unavailable bank credit but rather the relationship between the profit that can be made from the sale of the goods so acquired through trade credit as compared with the cost of the trade credit itself. For the firm that does have access to low-cost bank credit and credit from other financial institutions, it appears reasonable to expect a wise management to take advantage of available discounts.

The firm in a weak financial condition will find trade credit more readily available than bank credit because the bank as a lender of money stands only to gain the stipulated interest on the loan if repayment is made in accordance with the terms of the agreement. It stands to lose up to the total of the sum loaned in the event of the failure of the borrower to meet his obligation.

The manufacturer or the merchant, on the other hand, who sells on the basis of trade credit has a profit margin on the goods sold. Failure of the purchaser to meet his obligation results, at most, in the loss of the cost of the goods so delivered to the purchaser. The seller of the merchandise also is encouraged to open up a new account, although it may be weaker than his average customer because he anticipates repeated orders from the customer. Hence, his profit from the first transaction is measured not simply by the markup but also by the future business that may be brought in by opening up the account.

COMMERCIAL FINANCE COMPANIES

Shortly after the turn of the century the first commercial finance company was chartered. Since that time the number of such institutions has increased to more than five hundred. Some of these organizations are small, offering limited financial services to their customers, while others have vast resources and engage in broadly diversified programs of business lending. The *commercial finance company* has been defined as an agency without a bank charter that performs one or more of the following functions: advances funds to business concerns by discounting accounts receivable, usually without notice to the trade debtor; makes loans secured by chattel mortgages on machinery or liens on inventory; and finances deferred-payment sales of commercial and industrial equipment.[3] These companies are also frequently referred to as commercial credit companies, commercial receivables companies, and discount companies.

Commercial finance companies, represented by such organizations familiar to the business world as Commercial Investors Trust Financial Corporation of New York City, the Commercial Credit Company of Baltimore, Maryland, and the Pacific Finance Corporation of Los Angeles, California, offer much the same sort of service to business concerns as do the commercial banks in connection with accounts receivable financing and inventory financing. Accounts receivable financing was, in fact, originated by the commercial finance companies and only later was it adopted by commercial banks.

---

[3] Neil H. Jacoby and Raymond J. Saulnier, *Business Finance and Banking* (New York: National Bureau of Economic Research, 1947), p. 113.

The commercial finance companies gained a foothold in the financial markets and grew to their present size as a result of many factors. Among these factors may be included the fact that they were completely free to experiment with new and highly specialized types of credit arrangements, that state laws were generally more favorable to these nonbanking organizations in lending on the basis of accounts receivable, and finally that these organizations were able to charge rates of such a level as to make possible a profitable return for high-risk loans. Frequently these rates were far above those bankers would want or were permitted to charge their own customers.

As noted in the definition of the commercial finance companies, these organizations also lend money on the basis of inventory as collateral and finance the sale of commercial and industrial equipment on a deferred-payment basis. These companies concentrate their attention, however, on receivables as a form of collateral for their loans. This type of financing is used primarily in fields where there are large numbers of small businesses, such as home appliances, hardware, plastics, drugs, paper, food products, paint, wall paper, and leather.

Operating Characteristics of Commercial Finance Companies

When a commercial finance company sets up a loan secured by receivables, it enters into a contract with the borrower that provides for the acceptance of the borrower's open accounts receivable as collateral for a loan. The company specifies those accounts that are acceptable to it as collateral and, as a rule, will lend to the borrower an amount less than the total of such receivables pledged for the loan. The excess of the total volume of receivables pledged over the actual amount of the loan provides a margin of safety in the event that the borrower fails to repay the loan, and it also facilitates adjustments in outstanding accounts resulting from the return of goods by customers of the borrowing company.

As in the case of receivables financing with the commercial banks, the commercial finance companies require their borrowers to mark clearly their ledgers to indicate those accounts that have been assigned as collateral for the loan, and all payments received on such accounts must be immediately turned over to the company.

As a further protection to the finance company, it is generally provided that the borrower may not assign any of his other accounts to other lenders without appropriate notice to the finance company. Also, representatives of the finance company may make periodic audits of the borrower's books.

Terms and Charges for Commercial Finance Company Financing

The cost of loans offered by the commercial finance companies on the basis of receivables as collateral varies widely with the size of the lending company. In recent years the effective rates per annum on loans by the largest companies have fallen within the range of 10 to 15 per cent. The volume of business of these large companies represents a major portion of all accounts receivable financing by finance companies. Higher rates of interest up to 18 per cent are not uncommon on that part of the business which is handled by small finance companies. The small firms generally deal with local firms whose receivables are small in amount and more expensive to handle proportionally than the receivables of the firms financed by the larger companies. Also, the small finance company cannot achieve the economies of large-scale operation.[4]

In comparing the costs of loans secured by receivables that are extended by commercial finance companies with the typical unsecured line of credit, another factor is commonly ignored. In the case of a bank loan the term is for a fixed period, such as 30, 60, or 90 days. During the period of the loan the borrower must accumulate a sufficient sum to repay the loan at its maturity, during which time the accumulating funds lie idle. The borrower pays interest on the total loan and may be required to maintain with the bank a compensating deposit balance. The bank's insistence that borrowers maintain in their deposit accounts some specified balance, usually 20 per cent of the amount borrowed from the bank, is a well-established banking practice. The net effect of such a required compensating balance is to increase the cost of borrowing from the bank. In accounts receivable financing, however, each item collected from the customer is immediately turned over to the finance company, and the amount of the loan is reduced

---

[4] Clyde William Phelps, *Accounts Receivable Financing as a Method of Business Finance* (Baltimore: Educational Division, Commercial Credit Company, Studies in Commercial Financing, No. 2, 1957), p. 41.

accordingly because financing charges are based entirely on the actual number of days the borrowed funds are outstanding.

Volume of Commercial Finance Company Lending

As of 1956, banks did about as much accounts receivable financing as did the commercial finance companies; however, there was some indication that the proportion of such financing handled by the commercial finance companies was increasing at that time relative to that of the commercial banks of the nation. It has been estimated that the volume of accounts receivable financing done by nonbank lenders was approximately $5.6 billion in 1956.[5]

Sources of Funds for Commercial Finance Companies

The equity position of the commercial finance companies is considerably greater than that of the commercial banks of the nation; however, these organizations do not operate on equity capital alone. Additional capital is acquired through the sale of debenture bonds. In addition, commercial banks lend a large volume of money at wholesale rates to the commercial finance companies, which in turn lend it to business borrowers at retail rates. In many cases banks have been known to refer customers to finance companies for their loans, when the bank itself does not prefer to engage in receivables or inventory financing.

As a source of funds for the commercial finance company, it is obvious why bank credit would be advantageous. It permits the commercial finance company to meet its peak loan demands during the year without encumbering the company with long-term debt, only part of which would be used during slack lending seasons.

Reasons for the Use of Commercial Finance Company Facilities

In view of the average cost of commercial finance company loans as noted above, the question may arise as to why a businessman would under any circumstances utilize the facilities of these companies. As a matter of fact, the businessman who has ample

[5] William J. Drake, "The Commercial Finance Industry's Trade Group," *Proceedings of the Twelfth Annual Convention of the Commercial Finance Industry* (New York: National Commercial Finance Conference, 1956), p. 5.

current assets and is in a highly liquid position may be well advised to restrict his borrowing activities to his local bank. The business that is without a short-term financial problem at one time or another, however, is the exception rather than the rule. During periods when business is most brisk and growth possibilities most favorable, the need for additional funds on a short-term basis becomes unusually pressing. The businessman's first action is to request an increase in his customary line of credit at his bank. Failing this, he may secure an additional loan from his bank by pledging either inventory or his receivables as collateral for such an increased loan.

As noted in Chapter 4, however, not all banks engage in this type of financial arrangement, and it may be necessary to deal with a commercial finance company if recourse to this form of financing is required. Also, under federal banking laws no bank may lend more than 10 per cent of its capital and surplus to any one borrower. Since two thirds of the nation's approximately 15,000 banks are capitalized for less than $150,000, it is entirely possible that the businessman's bank may be unable to provide additional short-term funds even though it considers the customer deserving of such increased credit. For the banks with capital and surplus of $150,000, the maximum loan would be no greater than $15,000 to each borrower. Because the commercial finance companies are able to operate through a system of branches on a regional, and in a few cases on a national, basis unhampered by restrictions on branch operations to which commercial banks are subject, they can acquire a volume of business necessary to cover overhead expenses and to provide the needed diversification of risks to undertake high-risk financing.

FACTORS

The *factor*, like the commercial finance company, engages in accounts receivable financing for business enterprises. In contrast with the commercial finance companies, however, the factor purchases the accounts outright and assumes all credit risks. Under this arrangement customers whose accounts are sold are notified that their bills are payable to the factor. The task of collection of accounts is thus shifted from the seller of the accounts to the factor.

Despite the long history of operations of these companies, their growth has taken place largely within the last twenty years. The origins of factoring are imbedded deeply in the textile industry, and since most of the selling agencies and credit-reporting agencies in the textile field are located in New York City, most of the nation's factors are also located there. In addition to serving the textile industry, factors have also proved useful in such fields as furniture, shoes, bottle producers, paper, men's clothing, and furs.

Operating Characteristics of Factors

Assume that a business organization in a field which is amenable to the factoring operation finds that, for the first time in several years because of increasing levels of inventory and receivables, the firm is experiencing financial difficulties. Although the firm is well managed and has for several years been able to secure adequate financing through an unsecured line of credit with its bank, in order to take advantage of expanded business opportunities it is now necessary to supplement its usual sources of current funds. The factor draws a contract establishing the duties and the obligations of each party. This contract includes the conditions under which accounts may be sold to the factor, the responsibility for the payment of all such accounts, the collection procedures to be followed, and the method of reporting balances due. The contract also provides that the daily invoices for sales of goods to customers, together with the original shipping documents, be delivered to the factor and that the accounts so established be assigned to the factor. The names of customers for all proposed sales must be approved before delivery by the factor, and they are subject to rejection in the event that the credit rating of the customer does not meet the necessary standards of the factor. Daily reports must be rendered to the factor of all credits, allowances, and returns of merchandise. The contract also indicates the charges to be made for the factoring service.

The credit analysis department of the factor is the heart of that organization since it must serve in such a way as to conserve the factor's assets and also to be in constant contact with the factor's clients. Members of the credit department of the factor not only must be extremely prompt and accurate in their credit analyses but also, because they work closely with the firm's clients, must retain the goodwill of the companies that use the services of the factor.[6]

Terms and Charges for Factoring

The charge for factoring is in two parts. First, interest is charged on the money advanced, generally 6 per cent per annum, based on the actual daily net debit balance. Second, a factoring commission or service charge is figured as a percentage of the face amount of the receivables. Such service charges typically range from ¾ of 1 per cent to 1½ per cent of the face amount of the accounts financed. The commission charge is determined after taking into consideration such things as the volume of sales of the client, the general credit status of the accounts being factored, and the average size of individual accounts.

In addition to the interest and commission charges, the factor will also reserve from 5 to 15 per cent of the total amount of receivables factored for purposes of making adjustments, such as merchandise that is returned to the seller. This amount is not a charge, however, and is returned to the seller after it has served its purpose as an adjustment account.

Volume of Factoring

About $4 billion of financing is being supplied to American business firms each year through the factoring of open accounts receivable. The dollar volume of such factoring operations is increasing and spreading into many lines of business where it was formerly unknown.[7] About eighteen firms in the United States engage exclusively in factoring, and each has capital funds of $1 million or more. Several additional firms with capital funds in excess of $1 million engage in both open accounts receivable financing and factoring operations.

Sources of Funds for Factors

Like the commercial finance companies, factors obtain their funds for operations through a combination of equity capital, long-

    [6] Raymond V. McNally, "The Factor at Work," *Credit and Financial Management* (March, 1951), p. 24.
    [7] Clyde William Phelps, *The Role of Factoring in Modern Business Finance* (Baltimore: Commercial Credit Company, 1956), p. 11.

term borrowing, short-term borrowing, and profits from operations. Although most factors obtain equity capital directly from the small group of persons actively engaged in the factoring operations, at least one factor has sold common stock to the general public.

Reasons for Use of Factoring Services

Although the services of the factor may be used by a firm that is unable to secure financing through customary channels, financially strong companies may also at times use their services to good advantage. In fact, these facilities are of greatest benefit to those companies that are enjoying unprecedented success with respect to sales and growth. It has been noted before that during such periods companies experience extreme shortages of working capital. The sale of receivables without recourse (no contingent liability for their collection) has the effect of substituting cash for accounts receivable, which may make possible even greater growth and profitability in the long run.

Some firms factor their receivables not because it is the only form of financing available to them but because of other considerations. First, the cost of doing business through credit sales is definite and determinable in advance, since the factor assumes all risks of collection. This is in effect a form of credit insurance. Second, it eliminates overhead expenses that would otherwise be required if the task of collection were retained by the firm. Such overhead expenses include bookkeeping costs, the maintenance of a credit department, and the expenses of collection of delinquent accounts. Unless a firm factors all of its receivables, however, the complete elimination of the expenses of credit department operation could not be accomplished. As a corollary of these two advantages, but of a somewhat less tangible nature, is the fact that the management of a business is freed from concern with financial matters and is permitted to concentrate on production and distribution.

Although factoring services are regarded highly by some business firms, others offer several objections to their use. The two reasons cited most frequently are the cost and the implication of financial weakness. The cost of factoring is admittedly higher than the cost of borrowing from a bank on the basis of an unsecured loan; however, it is difficult to conclude without reservation that the net cost is higher. The elimination of overhead costs that would otherwise be required of a business plus the fact that management need not concern itself with financial matters may completely offset the additional cost involved in the factoring process. With respect to the implication of financial weakness, many businessmen prefer to avoid the factoring plan in favor of the nonnotification plan available through the commercial finance companies. In this way they avoid having their customers make their payments to the factor.

In the textile field where factoring has long played an important part, there is less reluctance to engage in factoring. In most other fields, as a rule, the businessman makes every effort to avoid letting his customers know that he is using their accounts in order to secure financing because of the implication of financial weakness.

TRENDS IN ACCOUNTS RECEIVABLE FINANCING AND FACTORING

Following the great depression of the 1930's many financial institutions began to broaden their activities and functions. The factors began to engage in lines of activity other than that of the textile industry, which had been their special field for nearly a hundred years. During this period several commercial finance companies that were originally established to finance open accounts receivable on a nonnotification basis and without assumption of risk began to undertake factoring operations of much the same nature as those of the factors. In addition, a few commercial banks began to undertake regular factoring functions for the textile industry and for a few other fields on much the same basis as that provided by the factors.[8] One of the most important commercial banks engaged in direct factoring operations is the First National Bank of Boston, which because of its immediate interest in the textile industry of New England very early engaged in this type of operation to accommodate its customers.

In addition to the commercial finance companies that engage in both factoring operations and open accounts receivable financing, many of the companies which are solely engaged in factoring

[8] Jacoby and Saulnier, *op. cit.*, pp. 120-21.

operations are in fact wholly owned subsidiaries of larger commercial finance companies. At the present time, therefore, the commercial banks, the commercial finance companies, and the factors have much in common, and in many situations they offer identical services; but each retains a special emphasis and a primary interest that allows it to be identified with a basic type of financial operation.

SMALL BUSINESS ADMINISTRATION

The Small Business Administration was established by the federal government to provide financial assistance to small firms that are unable to obtain loans through private channels on reasonable terms. It limits its activities entirely to small firms in contrast with its predecessor, the Reconstruction Finance Corporation, which ceased its lending activities on September 30, 1953. The Small Business Administration, created June 30, 1953, was authorized to make loans of up to $150,000 to each borrower. In 1955 the maximum loan was increased by Congress to $250,000. The agency has 30 regional offices through which applications for loans are accepted. Preference is given to applicants engaged in producing for military, defense, or essential civilian requirements.

If a firm is able to obtain financing elsewhere, applications for loans to the Small Business Administration are rejected. An applicant for a loan must prove that such funds are not available from his own bank or a competing bank in an appropriate amount, that no other private lending sources are available, that the issuance of securities is not practicable, that financing cannot be arranged through the disposal of assets of the business, and that personal credit of the owners cannot be used. Such loans may not be used to pay off existing creditors or for speculative purposes.

Operating Characteristics of the Small Business Administration

The Small Business Administration assists in the financing of small enterprises in three ways: it may make direct loans to businesses; it may participate jointly with private banks in extending loans to businesses; or it may agree to a deferred participation contract with a bank. Under a deferred participation contract the Administration agrees to take over at the request of the lending bank a certain percentage of the total loan. In this way a bank may commit its funds; and if it should later need additional funds, it may turn over its qualifying Small Business Administration deferred participation loans to the Administration.

Terms and Charges for Small Business Administration Financing

In addition to short-term working capital loans to business by the Small Business Administration, loans of up to 10 years may be made. Interest rates on loans were initially set at 6 per cent and have remained at that figure. The Administration allows the cooperating bank or banks to set the interest rate on participation loans, but the rate may not exceed 6 per cent. It was assumed that by letting the bank or banks establish the rate of interest that prevailing rates in the area where the money was being loaned would be reflected.

Volume of Lending Activity by the Small Business Administration

During the first four months of operation of the Small Business Administration, emphasis was placed upon encouraging lending to small businesses by local credit pools throughout the country. A change in policy, however, resulted in more active direct lending by the Administration. From the start of the Administration's lending program in October, 1953, through December 31, 1956, 2,270 business loans were approved for a gross amount of over $114 million. Approximately two thirds of the loans were made on a participation basis with commercial banks, rather than independently by the Administration. Although the $114 million extended by the Small Business Administration during this period may seem small relative to the total flow of bank loans for business purposes, it was never intended that the volume of such loans would ever compare in volume to private lending. The 2,270 business loans made by the Administration, however, may have been of critical importance to those businesses receiving the loans.

Sources of Funds for the Small Business Administration

The Small Business Administration operates on a revolving fund of $105 million provided by Congress. The total of business loans, which have been approved for a gross amount of more than $114 million, exceeds the $105 million appropriated to the revolving fund because a portion of the amount approved is the banks' share of participations.

Reasons for Use of Small Business Administration Loans

The reason for the use of Small Business Administration loans by businesses is explained by the stated objectives of the Administration, that is, to enable small businesses to obtain financial assistance otherwise not available through private channels on reasonable terms. When the Small Business Administration was established, it was recognized that the economic development of the nation has depended in large part upon the freedom of entry of new business ventures into active operation. Yet the increased concentration of investable funds in the possession of the large institutional investors, such as life insurance companies, investment companies, and others, has made it increasingly difficult for new and small business ventures to attract investment capital. Through the Small Business Administration it is presumed that deserving small businesses may have access to borrowed capital on reasonable terms.

QUESTIONS

1. Describe the nature of trade credit as a form of short-term business financing.
2. Why do trade credit terms tend to be similar between firms within each industry?
3. Businesses that purchase all of their supplies on a cash basis frequently show sizable amounts as "accounts payable" in their balance sheets. Explain.
4. What is meant by the abbreviation E.O.M., as it applies to trade credit terms? Why would such terms be used?
5. Explain how the cost of financing through trade credit may be compared with financing through bank loans.
6. Compare the importance of trade credit as a form of short-term financing with other forms of short-term financing.
7. What are the principal reasons for the use of trade credit as a form of short-term financing?
8. Compare the operations of commercial finance companies with those of commercial banks.

9. Why is it difficult to compare the costs of short-term borrowing through a commercial finance company with short-term financing from commercial banks?

10. What are the sources of funds for commercial finance companies?

11. Under what circumstances would a business secure its financing through a commercial finance company?

12. Why are commercial finance companies able to provide their business customers with more liberal financing than are commecial banks?

13. Explain the operations of the factor.

14. Why is it difficult to make a direct comparison of short-term financing through a factor as compared with bank financing or commercial finance company financing?

15. Why would a business utilize the services of a factor?

16. Discuss the place of the Small Business Administration in the field of finance.

SUGGESTED READINGS

BECKMAN, THEODORE N., and BARTELS, ROBERT. *Credits and Collections in Theory and Practice*; Fifth Edition. New York: McGraw-Hill Book Company, Inc., 1949. Chapter 14.

DAUTEN, CARL A. *Business Finance*; Second Edition. Englewood Cliffs, New Jersey: Prentice-Hall, Inc., 1956. Chapters 6 and 20.

GREEF, ALBERT O. *The Commercial Paper House in the United States.* Cambridge: Harvard University Press, 1938.

GUTHMANN, HARRY G., and DOUGALL, HERBERT E. *Corporate Financial Policy*; Third Edition. Englewood Cliffs, New Jersey: Prentice-Hall, Inc., 1955. Pp. 442-445.

HOWARD, BION B., and UPTON, MILLER. *Introduction to Business Finance.* New York: McGraw-Hill Book Company, Inc., 1953. Pp. 337-345 and pp. 374-378.

PHELPS, CLYDE WILLIAM. *The Role of Factoring in Modern Business Finance.* Baltimore: Educational Division, Commercial Credit Company, Studies in Commercial Financing, No. 1, 1956.

PHELPS, CLYDE WILLIAM. *Accounts Receivable Financing as a Method of Business Finance.* Baltimore: Educational Division, Commercial Credit Company, Studies in Commercial Financing, No. 2, 1957.

PROCHNOW, HERBERT V. *American Financial Institutions.* Englewood Cliffs, New Jersey: Prentice-Hall, Inc., 1951. Chapter 22 and pp. 217-221.

SILBERT, THEODORE H. "Financing and Factoring Accounts Receivable," *Harvard Business Review* (January and February, 1952).

Chapter 7

Merchandising and Facilitating Agencies for Short-Term Financing

Short-term financing is provided directly by the nation's banks, commercial finance companies, factors, and other agencies and institutions discussed in the previous chapters. Other organizations contribute to the flow of short-term funds from lender to borrower by serving as media through which this flow takes place. For example, commercial paper houses serve merely to distribute or merchandise to lenders the obligations taken from borrowers, lending no money for their own account. Other organizations serve the business world through a system of insurance on the receivables held by business firms as a result of credit sales. These credit insurance companies serve as facilitating agencies, as do the many forms of special organizations established for the purpose of reporting on the credit standing of prospective customers. The federal reserve system, discussed in Chapter 5, although providing direct loans in some cases, is basically a facilitating agency in that it serves to make the commercial banking system more effective in its operation and service to the business community. Commercial paper houses, credit insurance companies, and credit reporting agencies are discussed in this chapter.

COMMERCIAL PAPER HOUSES

The *commercial paper house* purchases the promissory notes of reputable business organizations for the purpose of resale to banks and other lenders. A fee based on the amount of notes purchased, charged to the issuer of the notes, provides the basic income of the commercial paper house.

Operating Characteristics of Commercial Paper Houses

The businessman who wishes to use the services of the commercial paper house must have an unquestioned reputation for the sound operation of his firm. If after thorough investigation of the firm's financial position by the commercial paper house it appears that the notes of the firm can be sold with little difficulty, an agreement is made for the outright sale of a block of the firm's promissory notes to the commercial paper house. The commercial paper house will resell these notes as quickly as possible to banks and in some cases to managers of pension funds, and even to other business corporations that have surplus funds. The notes are usually prepared in denominations of $5,000, $10,000, or $25,000 in order that they may be resold in amounts convenient for the purchaser. In a few cases, denominations of $2,500 and $50,000 have also been used in preparing the notes.

Terms and Charges for Commercial Paper House Financing

The commercial paper house will pay to the borrower the face amount of the notes less the interest charge and a fee of from ¼ to ½ of 1 per cent of the face value of the notes. The interest charge is determined by the general level of prevailing rates in the money market and the strength of the borrowing company. When these notes are resold to banks and other lenders, only the prevailing interest rate is deducted from the face value of the notes; hence, the commercial paper house receives the ¼ to ½ of 1 per cent as compensation for the negotiation.

Although the paper is sold without recourse, that is, the commercial paper house has no liability in the event that the terms of the notes are not met by the borrowers, it is generally provided that a bank has ten days after purchase of the notes to investigate the credit standing of the company whose notes are purchased. If the bank determines the credit of the company to be unsatisfactory, it is permitted to return the notes to the commercial paper house. During this ten-day period the purchaser of the notes may contact other banks for information regarding the borrowing company and make direct inquiries of the company itself for additional information that may be desired. In addition, the purchaser of the notes may request information from the National

Credit Office, a specialized mercantile concern discussed in detail later in this chapter, regarding the strength of the company. One of the special activities of the National Credit Office is that of evaluating continuously the standing of companies using the facilities of the commercial paper houses.

Since a fee of $\frac{1}{4}$ of 1 per cent on a group of notes in the total amount of $100,000 is only $250, a commercial paper house has little interest in dealing regularly in transactions of this size, but it may occasionally do so in order to develop a new account.

Volume of Commercial Paper House Financing

Although the activities of the commercial paper houses date back nearly 150 years, in recent decades there has been a general decline in their volume of business. From a volume of well over $1 billion shortly after World War I, the amount of commercial paper decreased to less than $160 million in 1945. From this volume in 1945, however, there has been more than a threefold increase in its use by the end of 1956. Although this recent increase has been due in part to the tremendous over-all demand for business credit, there is reason to believe that commercial paper houses may regain permanently some of their former importance in the financial markets. In 1957, 11 commercial paper houses, located for the most part in New York City, served approximately 400 corporations.

The National Credit Office reports that about half of the companies that borrow on the basis of commercial paper are manufacturers, consisting of textile companies, millers, leather processors, fabricators, and food processors, in the order of their importance. The other half of the users consist primarily of various types of finance companies and wholesalers of hardware and food products. Most of these companies have net worth of from $1 million to $25 million. Among the larger firms that have used this form of short-term financing are General Mills, Inc., General Electric Supply Corporation, and the May Department Stores Company.

Reasons for Use of Commercial Paper House Financing

Businesses use funds secured through the commercial paper houses in much the same manner as those funds secured through regular banking channels: accumulation of inventory during peak seasons, carrying large volumes of receivables, and general working capital purposes. Funds secured through the commercial paper houses, however, are seldom regarded as an alternative to bank credit, but rather as a supplementary source of short-term financing. Any business that is in a strong enough position to make use of commercial paper facilities would be expected to have a firm line of bank credit. Funds secured through the commercial paper houses may be used to take advantage of special situations that require capital in excess of the regular line of bank credit. They may also be used periodically to retire all bank indebtedness, a measure that many banks require.

The most important reason for the use of facilities of the commercial paper houses, however, is the fact that the cost of such borrowing is generally less than regular bank rates, despite the fact that a commission on the face amount of the notes is charged. The companies borrowing through the commercial paper houses are generally able to obtain interest rates of from $\frac{1}{8}$ to $\frac{3}{8}$ of 1 per cent under regular bank rates because of their credit reputation.

Because the commercial paper houses distribute these notes over wide geographical areas, they are able to place them with banks that have less profitable alternative uses of their funds at that particular time. It is understandable that a bank would be willing under certain circumstances to purchase commercial paper through a commercial paper house at a lower rate of interest than they would charge their regular customers, even though their regular customers may be as strong as the company whose notes are being purchased. If the demand for business loans by the bank's regular customers is insufficient to absorb completely the loanable funds of the bank, the alternative may be to place these funds in low-yielding government securities. The purchased commercial paper in recent years has provided a yield slightly above that of short-term government securities but somewhat less than the yield obtainable from high-grade business loans. As evidence of the strength of the companies that have access to the facilities of the commercial paper houses, there were no recorded losses by lenders on commercial paper from 1936 through 1952, and there were only five cases of delayed payments.

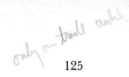

CREDIT INSURANCE COMPANIES

Like all forms of insurance, credit insurance serves to spread the risk of loss on the part of a few persons among many persons. A definite and ascertainable cost, the insurance premium, is substituted for an uncertain and perhaps unlimited loss. Just as fire and other forms of property insurance protect the businessman against loss due to damage to his physical properties, *credit insurance* offers similar protection against unusual losses resulting from the sale of merchandise on a credit basis. Credit insurance is written only on trade credit accounts, that is, the accounts receivable that are established from the sale of goods to another business. The history of credit insurance in one form or another has been traced back to 1837. Despite a rather intense demand for such facilities on the part of some companies, the use of credit insurance has never become widespread. It makes its contribution to the field of finance as a facilitating factor in the flow of credit between borrower and lender and is considered as such in this chapter.

Types of Credit Insurance

Although many types of credit insurance policies have been used in the past, at present credit insurance companies offer two broad types of policies. These are the *general coverage policy,* which insures the company against unusual losses on all of its insurable accounts, and the *extraordinary coverage policy,* which offers protection only against loss from a small proportion of the firm's accounts and often from a single account. The general coverage policy is used when the accounts of the firm are numerous with no single account being of such a size as to have a substantial effect in the event of the customer's failure to meet his obligation. The extraordinary policy, on the other hand, is used by firms having only a few very large accounts, any one of which could cause substantial difficulties to the firm extending the credit should a default in payments occur. In some instances, when a firm has many small accounts and only one or two large accounts, it may use the extraordinary coverage policy to good advantage to protect it against default of these large accounts. Policies are generally written for periods of one year and all losses to be covered must occur during the term of the credit insurance policy. Policies are renewable annually.

The Risk

The purpose of insurance companies offering credit policies is not to substitute the benefits of risk diversification for thorough and systematic credit investigation. In determining the insurability of accounts, the insurance companies depend heavily upon the regular merchantile credit reporting agencies, and on Dun and Bradstreet, Inc., in particular. In general, accounts are classified as either preferred or inferior, the preferred accounts alone qualifying for regular credit insurance. In some instances, both preferred and inferior accounts may be insured on a special combination-policy basis. Under a combination policy the amount of insurance extended on inferior accounts is severely limited and the cost considerably higher than on preferred risks.

In addition to dividing individual accounts into preferred and inferior categories, the credit insurance companies also classify types of businesses as to their desirability for credit insurance purposes based on past experience. These lines or types of businesses range from those dealing in agricultural implements, dairy products, and railroad supplies, which have the most desirable risk characteristics, to businesses dealing in diamonds and patent medicines, which are considered to have generally unsatisfactory risk characteristics and hence are not insurable.

Normal Loss and Coinsurance

Credit insurance attempts to insure only against losses that are in excess of the normal volume of such losses to be expected. Since losses on bad debts are a part of all credit sale operations, it would be expecting too much to depend upon credit insurance to eliminate all losses. To do so, it would be necessary for the insurance company to charge a premium equivalent to the normal loss to offset the expected costs of the insurance plus an additional premium to cover excess losses. Such an arrangement would be unacceptable, for the most part, to both the insured and the insurance company. In determining the normal loss of a firm above which losses are insurable, the insurance companies consider two factors: the line of trade of the applicant, and the past credit experience of the particular firm. An applicant with an excellent record of account collections is afforded a relatively low normal loss volume above which all accounts are insurable. The firm with a poor record, of course, can expect the establishment of a higher volume of normal losses, rendering a smaller percentage of total losses insurable.

In addition to the protection afforded the insurance company through the establishment of a normal loss ratio, additional protection is provided through the coinsurance clause. The *coinsurance clause* provides that, although all accounts above the normal loss volume are insurable, the insured must bear a portion of the losses that do occur. Such participation in losses on the part of the insured are generally limited to 10 per cent. Of the insurable accounts, therefore, the insurance company ordinarily will bear 90 per cent of the loss. The coinsurance clause makes possible a lower premium for the insurance and also avoids the complete shift of risk to the insurance company. It is assumed that a complete shift of risk to the insurance company would in some instances encourage laxity in extending credit sales.

Reasons for Use of Credit Insurance

Among the reasons for the use of credit insurance by business firms may be included the desire to establish a definite loss expense with the accompanying advantage of not having to establish large reserves to care for unusual losses, the ability to undertake a larger volume of business in selling to credit customers, and the success of the insurance companies in collecting overdue accounts.

Attitudes toward the use of credit insurance vary in great measure, however; the apparent advantages of its use by one firm may be regarded as disadvantages by other firms. In general, the credit managers of business firms display little liking for such insurance, possibly because it shifts much of their own function, that of credit analysis, to the insurance company. The major objection to the use of credit insurance lies in its cost. Over a period of years credit insurance adds to the cost of doing business by an amount equal to the premiums paid out over and above the amounts received by the business for losses under the policies.

CREDIT REPORTING AGENCIES

A highly refined system of banking and finance is essential to the processes of a modern industrial economy; it is no less true

that the field of finance could not possibly function effectively
without readily available sources of credit information. The history of the development of our credit reporting institutions is, in
fact, part and parcel of the development of our financial institutions themselves; and it is not surprising that there now exist many
large and efficient organizations devoted to the objective of determining the credit position of virtually every person and business
organization in the United States and to some extent throughout
the world. Nor are the services of these organizations used only
by lenders of money and firms selling goods and services on credit.
Insurance companies often require credit reports on individuals
when considering issuance of life or property insurance contracts
and when issuing fidelity bonds protecting against dishonest acts of
individuals in the performance of their jobs. Physicians, lawyers,
and other professional groups seek such information to determine
the ability of prospective clients to pay their bills. The Federal
Housing Administration and other government agencies, which
lend or insure loans to individuals and businesses, require that
all applications be accompanied by appropriate credit reports.
During World War II the United States government used the
services of many credit reporting firms to supplement the efforts
of the Federal Bureau of Investigation in determining the suitability and loyalty of individuals for positions of trust.

The sources of credit information are numerous and varied in
nature, ranging from informal personal contact with the person or
firm requesting credit to the detailed and thorough investigations
that are conducted by highly specialized credit reporting agencies.
In the remainder of this chapter we shall discuss the operations
of credit interchange bureaus, Dun & Bradstreet, Inc., the National
Credit Office, and the Retail Credit Company as representative of
the various types of credit reporting agencies.

Credit interchange bureaus are generally established as nonprofit institutions by the businesses they are intended to serve.
Such credit interchange bureaus exist to obtain information regarding both business firms and individuals. We shall in this
chapter refer to credit information on business firms as *mercantile
credit* and credit information on individuals as *retail credit*. Dun
& Bradstreet, Inc., is discussed because it is the only mercantile
credit reporting agency that provides information on businesses
in any line of activity; the National Credit Office is discussed

because it is representative of the type of mercantile agency that provides information on businesses in special lines of activity; the Retail Credit Company has been chosen as representative of the type of agency that provides information on individuals.

Credit Interchange Bureaus

Information obtained from other creditors of a prospective customer is often of substantial importance for both mercantile and consumer credit purposes. For local business operations it is common for the credit manager of one firm to phone his counterpart with another firm for advice and recommendations regarding applicants for credit. In addition to direct contact with other creditors, various attempts have been made to provide a more systematic and effective means of communicating credit information between firms.

Local Mercantile Credit Interchange Bureaus. The *local mercantile credit interchange bureau* provides a central record in the community for credit information on business firms. The typical local credit interchange bureau is a nonprofit organization whose expenses are paid by member businesses. One requirement of membership in the local credit bureau is that a complete list of the firm's customers must be given to the bureau. The bureau can determine from these lists the credit standing of a local business by contacting members who have extended credit to the business. In this way member firms need only to contact their credit bureau for information on prospective business customers rather than to write or phone many other firms in search of such information.

National Mercantile Credit Interchange System. As the scope of business operations expanded with better communication and transportation systems, it became increasingly important to have access to the credit experience of firms in other geographical areas, as well as within the area served by the local credit interchange bureau. This problem was solved through the establishment of centralized bureaus to which the records of local bureaus could be forwarded for broader distribution throughout the country. The exchange of mercantile credit information from bureau to bureau is accomplished through the National Credit Interchange

System. This system with a central bureau has 55 member credit interchange bureaus. These bureaus have a relationship with the central bureau much like that of the member firms with the local credit interchange bureaus.

Reports of credit exchange bureaus are factual rather than analytical, and it is the responsibility of each credit analyst to interpret these data.

Local Retail Credit Interchange Bureaus. Early retail merchants found that the rapid growth of cities and the increased mobility of consumers from community to community throughout the nation rendered it impracticable to rely on a direct exchange of credit information with other merchants. As for mercantile credit, the local merchants established retail credit bureaus for the purpose of consolidation and distribution of credit information regarding consumers in the community. These organizations are generally owned and operated by participating members on a nonprofit basis. The types of service rendered by the retail credit bureaus differ to a considerable extent, although basically they all provide credit information in one form or another. Some bureaus collect only derogatory information from their members, and this information in turn is distributed to other members. Other bureaus provide a complete reporting service on all customers. In addition, some bureaus publish rating books, cooperate with detective agencies, and operate collection services. A central organization known as the Associated Credit Bureaus of America serves as a medium through which the nearly 1,500 retail credit bureaus in the United States are able to transmit credit information from bureau to bureau.

Dun & Bradstreet, Inc.

This organization, with more than a 100-year history of operations, serves commerce and industry as a general credit agency covering all fields of business activity. The information that is assembled and evaluated by Dun & Bradstreet, Inc., is brought into the company through many channels. The company employs full-time and part-time employees for the purposes of direct investigation, communicates directly with business establishments by mail to supplement their informational files, and obtains the financial statements of companies upon which reports are to be made. In addition, careful analysis is made of all information filed with public authorities and all financial and trade papers in order to gather bits of information that would be pertinent to a credit analysis. The basic service supplied to the manufacturers, wholesalers, banks, and insurance companies who are subscribers to Dun & Bradstreet, Inc., is rendered in two ways—through written reports on individual businesses and through a Reference Book.

Written Credit Reports. Dun & Bradstreet, Inc., prepares three types of reports of interest to the businessman. The first type is the *regular* or *general report,* which is written on businesses where the owner's investment is below $75,000. The second type of report is the *analytical report.* This report is written on the larger businesses and those with a complex financial structure, such as firms with subsidiaries. The *key account report* is written for the express need of one subscriber to help him solve a credit problem.

A Dun & Bradstreet, Inc., report is typically divided into five sections as follows: (1) Rating and Summary, (2) History, (3) Operation and Location, (4) Financial Information, (5) Payments. An example of a typical report is shown in Figure 7-1. If a subscriber requests a report on a business about which the company does not have up-to-date information, it will send the latest available report with the notation, "Under further investigation, later will follow." The company then forwards a new up-to-date report as soon as it is becomes available. Then for the following twelve-month period any subsequent reports written on the case are sent automatically to the subscriber.

The upper right-hand corner of the report is colored so that the subscriber may know at a glance the nature of the report he is receiving. A green corner indicates that the rating is the same as a previous report, an amber corner indicates that the rating has changed, and a red corner on pink paper indicates that the report is a special notice of importance.

Reference Book. Dun & Bradstreet, Inc., publishes six times yearly a composite reference book of ratings on more than 2,900,000 manufacturers, wholesalers, retailers, and other businesses on which credit reports have been written. Figure 7-2 illustrates a sample section from one of the Dun & Bradstreet, Inc., reference books. The Standard Industrial Classification Code

Figure 7-1

Dun & Bradstreet, Inc. *Report* RATING CHANGE

5912
KENT DRUGS

CD 1 May 3 1958

BROOKLYN 19 NY
1246 KENT ROAD

Miles Gross, Partner   Hannah (Mrs. Miles) Gross, Partner

RATING: F 2½ to E 2

STARTED: 1947   PAYMENTS: Discount
NET WORTH $22,901   SALES: $89,232

SUMMARY
SALES ARE INCREASING AND OPERATIONS ARE PROFITABLE. THE CONDITION IS SOUND.

HISTORY
Style was registered by the partners on April 30, 1947.

This firm was formed April, 1947. Starting capital consisted of $10,500 savings, a $3,500 loan from Teachers Credit Union, and a $3,000 loan from partners' families, making a total of $17,000. Loans have since been repaid.

Miles Gross 41, native born and registered pharmacist. Graduated from Columbia College of Pharmacy in 1935. Employed as pharmacist by Liggett Drug Co. and by Ray Drug Co. until this business was started.

Hannah (Mrs. Miles) Gross is 36. She was a New York school teacher prior to formation of this firm.

OPERATION-LOCATION
Operates a pharmacy and soda fountain. Drugs and prescriptions account for 50% of sales, with balance equally divided among fountain, sundries, and confectionery. Fixtures and a twenty-foot soda fountain are new. Both partners active and two employed.

Rents first floor of a two-story building in good condition. Store measures about 20 x 50 feet. Located in recently developed residential section.

FINANCIAL INFORMATION
A financial statement at December 31, 1957--cents omitted:

ASSETS		LIABILITIES	
Cash on Hand	$ 304	Accts Pay	$ 3,724
Cash in Bank	1,872		
Merchandise	14,450		
Total Current	$16,626	Total Current	$ 3,724
Fixt & Equip	9,913		
Deposits	86	NET WORTH	22,901
Total Assets	$26,625	Total	$26,625

Net sales from January 1, 1957, to December 31, 1957, $89,232; gross profit $26,181; salaries and drawings of partners $6,732; net profit over and above salaries and drawings of partners $3,457. Monthly rent $150. Lease expires 1962.

Signed: April 20, 1958 KENT DRUGS By Miles Gross, Partner
Received by mail. No accountant indicated.

-----0-----

Residential construction has stepped up in this section with the result that both sales and profits of this business have mounted steadily. Part of earnings have been re-invested in the business to finance its steady growth.

PAYMENTS

HC	OWE	P DUE	TERMS	Mar 20 1958		
2431	2146		10th of mo	Disc		Sold 3 yrs to date
340	230		2-10-N30	Disc		Sold 1947 to 3-58
250			2-10	Disc		Sold 4 yrs
136	136		2-10 Prox	Disc		Sold yrs to date
75			2-10-EOM	Disc		
15			30	Ppt		Sold 1-49 to 12-57

5-3-58 (241 73) Five

Specimen Copy of a Typical Dun & Bradstreet Report

Figure 7-2

```
50 53 Mervine Poultry Co* ......    C+1          Name of town
59x69 Mills Supply Co FrmsupMch 7  E 2½          Name of county
22 94 New Process Fibre Co*......   E 3

TALISMAN (See Bingham)                           Standard Industrial Classification
TANNERVILLE (See Hargreaves)                     Code number gives business line

TAPPAN ▲ Lynch 81                                NR means near this town
50 ZJ B & O Co      ....... Petrpdt  G 3½         Estimated annual sales rating—See Key
59 EA Baber Henry H NR......Mus 7   F 3
52 51 Hamilton William T NR..  Hwr  D 2           The letter "C" in front of listing indicates
59 12 Hickman John ........Drg 8    3x            a change of rating
55 41 Hudson Harry Jr    Sstn 5   G 3½
53 93 Hurlock Frank A & Co RD   Gs  D 1½          The letter "A" in front of listing identifies
C 52 62 Johnson Bros Farm Supply Co   H 3½        name added to this edition
54 51 Joseph's Dairy .......  2   F 3½
59 BA Lawson Clifford W......Flor 1   4x
56 65 Mason Lawrence G    Sh 3   H 4
50 53 Paramount Poultry Co NR    5   .2           Current investigation incomplete when this
A 57 12 Patten Fred K ........ Frn 3  D+ 2        edition went to press
52 11 Paul Benjamin ........ Lbr   F 3
22 51 Paul Richard Inc ........ llsy  C+ 1
17 31 Phillips Raymond C ..... Elc 7   J 4
54 12 Veasey C Courtland ...  Gr   E 3
65 61 Warrington Edward & Co . Bldr  Inv          Town population

TAYLORSVILLE 2,113 Merrimac 42
1st NAT BK OF TAYLORSVILLE    $220M              Name of bank, its officers, and its capital
Y I Masten Pr T H Harrington Cas
GUARANTEE TR          ......  $163M              Abbreviation of the line of business
Solomon L Sapp Pr Randall W Knox Cas
34 63 Ace Mfg Co ........Metpdt  D 2             Rating of "Estimated Financial Strength" and
52 51 Andrews John E........  Hwr   2            "Composite Credit Appraisal"—See Key
54 52 Bailey Fred S Jr .....Milk  F 3
58 13 Blechman's Kopy Kat......Tav  D 2½
```

Page Section of Dun & Bradstreet Reference Book with Explanations

placed at the left of each concern's name indicates the type of business in which the firm is engaged. The symbols at the right of the firm name indicate the capital and the credit rating. The key to the Dun & Bradstreet, Inc., ratings is shown in Figure 7-3.

In addition to the activities of the Credit Reporting Division, Dun & Bradstreet, Inc., provides additional services to the business world through the operation of collection facilities for overdue accounts, the publication of a business magazine, and intensive research and statistical study on business trends.

The National Credit Office

The National Credit Office, which was organized in 1900, originally confined its activities to the textile industry. At present it is perhaps the largest and best known of the specialized credit agencies in the United States. This agency not only provides credit information in the textile field, but also it has extended its reporting on manufacturing to rubber goods, paints and varnishes, leather products, furniture, floor coverings, and a few other fields. It submits no reports on retail concerns with the exception of certain chain stores in the industries in which it is interested, depart-

Figure 7-3

KEY TO RATINGS

ESTIMATED FINANCIAL STRENGTH			COMPOSITE CREDIT APPRAISAL			
			HIGH	GOOD	FAIR	LIMITED
Aᴀ	Over	$1,000,000	A I	I	1½	2
A+	Over	750,000	A I	I .	1½	2
A	$500,000 to	750,000	A I	I	1½	2
B+	300,000 to	500,000	I	1½	2	2½
B	200,000 to	300,000	I	1½	2	2½
C+	125,000 to	200,000	I	1½	2	2½
C	75,000 to	125,000	1½	2	2½	3
D+	50,000 to	75,000	1½	2	2½	3
D	35,000 to	50,000	1½	2	2½	3
E	20,000 to	35,000	2	2½	3	3½
F	10,000 to	20,000	2½	3	3½	4
G	5,000 to	10,000	3	3½	4	4½
H	3,000 to	5,000	3	3½	4	4½
J	2,000 to	3,000	3	3½	4	4½
K	1,000 to	2,000	3	3½	4	4½
L	Up to	1,000	3½	4	4½	5

CLASSIFICATION AS TO BOTH
ESTIMATED FINANCIAL STRENGTH AND CREDIT APPRAISAL

FINANCIAL STRENGTH BRACKET			EXPLANATION
1	$125,000 to	$1,000,000 and Over	When only the numeral (1, 2, 3, or 4) appears, it is an indication that the estimated financial strength, while not definitely classified, is presumed
2	20,000 to	125,000	to be within the range of the ($) figures in the corresponding bracket and
3	2,000 to	20,000	that a condition is believed to exist which warrants credit in keeping
4	Up to	2,000	with that assumption.

NOT CLASSIFIED OR ABSENCE OF RATING

The absence of a rating, whether as to estimated financial strength or as to credit appraisal, and whether expressed by the **dash** (—), or by the (x) sales listing (see below), or by the omission of any symbol, is not to be construed as unfavorable but signifies circumstances difficult to classify within condensed rating symbols and should suggest to the subscriber the advisability of obtaining additional information.

ESTIMATED ANNUAL SALES BRACKET

1x	$500,000 and Over Annual Sales		3x	$10,000 to $75,000 Annual Sales	
2x	75,000 to $500,000 " "		4x	Up to 10,000 " "	

Key to Dun & Bradstreet Ratings

ment stores, and the larger furniture stores. The National Credit Office provides a special service to banks whereby it reports on the quality of commercial paper offered to the banks for their purchase. This company is, in fact, an affiliate of Dun & Bradstreet, Inc., having its main office in New York City, with branches in Boston, Philadelphia, Atlanta, Cleveland, Chicago, and Los Angeles.

The first section of National Credit Office reports gives certain factual information, such as background information on the key personnel of the company, a description of the company and its method of operation, and the name or names of the concern's banking connections. The second section of their report involves a summarization of the financial statements of the company for the past three years, ledger information provided by some of the company's suppliers, and a complete analysis based on available information by the Credit Office. In these reports a recommended maximum line of credit is included. In addition, the National Credit Office has promoted credit discussion groups in several key industries. These groups meet periodically, generally each month, and discuss the latest news that relates to the credit situation of the industry. Also the National Credit Office provides a market planning service as a separate division of the company. The information provided by this division is of great value as an aid in planning sales by subscribing companies.

The Retail Credit Company

This organization, which is more than 50 years old, gathers information not only within this country but throughout the world. Information provided by this organization is almost exclusively restricted to individuals rather than business firms. Although the services of the Retail Credit Company are used primarily by insurance companies, during World War II many corporations and government agencies depended upon the company to screen applicants for employment. The services of this company are also used by mortgage lenders and trade creditors in general. This organization has more than 125 offices and over 800 direct reporting stations. It has been reported that this company has on file the credit records of more than 20 million individuals. These files are maintained through personal investigation, clippings from newspapers, and information from numerous governmental offices. As reports are requested on individuals who are not currently in the files of the Retail Credit Company, special investigations are made by the representatives of the company.

QUESTIONS

1. Describe the operations of a commercial paper house.
2. In what manner may the commercial paper houses be considered as facilitating institutions in the field of business finance?
3. What is the commercial paper house's source of profits?
4. Describe a typical commercial paper house transaction.

5. Compare the cost of borrowing through the facilities of a commercial paper house with direct bank borowing.

6. How important are the operations of commercial paper houses as a part of the entire field of short-term business financing?

7. What are the advantages to a business of financing through a commercial paper house?

8. What is the special role of the credit insurance company in the field of short-term business finance?

9. Describe the principal types of credit insurance policies offered by the credit insurance companies.

10. To what extent does a credit insurance policy reduce the risk of loss on accounts receivable?

11. Of what significance are the terms "normal loss" and "coinsurance" in the credit insurance policy?

12. Explain the special circumstances that would induce a business to utilize the services of a credit insurance company.

13. In what way do credit reporting agencies serve the field of finance as facilitating media?

14. Describe the various types of credit reporting institutions that are available to a business in seeking credit information on its business customers.

15. How does Dun & Bradstreet, Inc., accumulate its information on which to base its credit reports?

16. Distinguish between mercantile credit information and retail credit information.

SUGGESTED READINGS

BECKMAN, THEODORE N., and BARTELS, ROBERT. *Credits and Collections in Theory and Practice*; Fifth Edition. New York: McGraw-Hill Book Company, Inc., 1949. Chapters 15, 16, 17, and 34.

DAUTEN, CARL A. *Business Finance*; Second Edition. Englewood Cliffs, New Jersey: Prentice-Hall, Inc., 1956. Chapter 6.

GUTHMANN, HARRY G., and DOUGALL, HERBERT E. *Corporate Financial Policy*; Third Edition. Englewood Cliffs, New Jersey: Prentice-Hall, Inc., 1955. Chapter 21.

HOWARD, BION B., and UPTON, MILLER. *Introduction to Business Finance*. New York: McGraw-Hill Book Company, Inc., 1953. Chapters 14 and 17.

PROCHNOW, HERBERT V., and FOULKE, ROY A. *Practical Bank Credit*; Second Edition. Englewood Cliffs, New Jersey: Prentice-Hall, Inc., 1950. Chapter 17.

Long-Term

Business

Financing

Tax situation —

Single proprietor or partnerships may elect not to be taxed as
corporation

Corporations with 10 or less stockholders may elect to be
taxed as unincorporated firm.

Chapter 8

Business Organization
and
Long-Term Financing

In Part I many sources of short-term financing were discussed in detail; yet for all of the importance of this form of credit, with its elaborate adaptations to special situations and conditions of business, it must be preceded by long-term financing in one form or another. A banker would scarcely be willing to advance short-term funds for the purchase of inventory or to meet a payroll if the businessman were not able to show that arrangements had been made for the accumulation of the fixed assets necessary for the operation of the business.

NATURE OF LONG-TERM FINANCING

We have defined all financial arrangements requiring settlement or repayment within one year as short-term financing; those financial arrangements requiring settlement over a period of time of more than one year, as long-term financing.

Long-term financing may be classed broadly into two categories: equity financing and long-term debt financing. *Equity financing* refers to the arrangements under which owners of a business enterprise contribute their resources to its establishment or operation. The proprietor of the corner grocery who invests part of his personal savings in a new cash register is engaging in long-term financing by increasing his equity in the business. The members of a partnership who contribute to the resources of their enterprise through additional investment are also engaged in equity financing. On the other hand, the purchase of the cash

139

register by the proprietor under arrangements whereby it is to be paid for over a period of eighteen months is a form of debt financing; in particular, a form of long-term debt financing, according to our definition, since the period of repayment extends for more than one year.

The nature of long-term financing for a business establishment depends upon several factors. For the small business, long-term debt financing will probably be effected through negotiation with a single lender, who often takes a mortgage on the real estate of the firm. A large firm, on the other hand, has at its disposal the facilities of the securities markets through which many thousands of investors may be brought into contact with the business. The alternative methods and sources of long-term financing are discussed in the chapters of this part.

PURPOSES OF LONG-TERM FINANCING

A business firm may undertake long-term financing for several reasons. A firm obtains its original productive or distributive facilities through long-term financing; hence, this is one of the first matters to be considered in connection with the establishment of a new enterprise. Thereafter, such financing may be undertaken to permit expansion of the business or the replacement of existing physical facilities. At a time when the business establishment is expanding, it is generally necessary to increase the current assets of the firm as well as the fixed assets. Although some of the increase in current assets may be taken care of through short-term financing, part of the increase should generally come through long-term financing. A complete dependence upon short-term financing for this purpose would result in a reduced current ratio and in due time make it difficult for the business to meet its current obligations as they mature. In order to maintain a reasonable balance between current assets and current liabilities, therefore, it is necessary to undertake long-term financing as well as short-term financing during periods of expansion.

Long-term financing in one form or another is also required for the renewing of existing debt when the debt is not to be retired at its contractual payment date. Another reason for long-term financing is to retire certain types of ownership shares that are no longer desirable in the capital structure of the enterprise or to provide the funds necessary to effect a merger or to acquire the assets of another business organization.

SOURCES OF LONG-TERM FUNDS

Insurance companies, trust companies, managers of pension funds, and investment companies are examples of organizations that have a primary interest in long-term investments. Each of these organizations may engage in some short-term investing, either as a temporary measure until a sum of money is accumulated to make a desired long-term investment or when short-term investments are more profitable. There is little doubt, however, that the primary use to which the investable funds of these institutions are put is long-term investments. Likewise, wealthy individuals, while having some funds invested in short-term securities, invest most of their resources in long-term securities.

The significance of long-term financing can be measured only in terms of the total productivity of the nation's economy. Such productivity has been achieved through the channeling of savings of many thousands of firms and millions of persons to those individuals and institutions that can use them effectively. This process of converting the savings of individuals and firms into productive assets, commonly referred to as the process of *capital formation*, is made possible through a smoothly functioning system of financial institutions that has developed over the years in the United States.

FORMS OF BUSINESS ORGANIZATION

The nature of long-term investments and the sources of long-term funds are influenced in large measure by the form of business organization of the enterprise. Of the many forms of business organization, each has its special characteristics that must be considered in determining its suitability for specific business objectives. Under certain circumstances, the sole proprietorship, with its emphasis on simplicity, may be entirely appropriate. At the other extreme, the corporate form of organization with its complex legal framework may be most appropriate. In any event, the choice of an organizational form for a business involves the consideration of many factors.

Chart 8–1

DISTRIBUTION OF FIRMS BY TYPE OF ORGANIZATION WITHIN EMPLOYEE-SIZE CLASSES
January 1, 1947

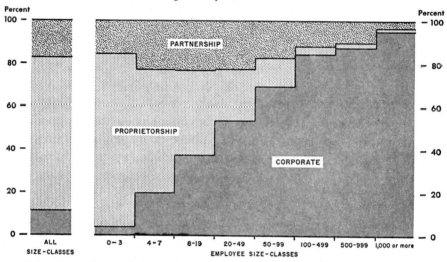

SOURCE: U. S. Department of Commerce, Office of Business Economics.

For the small business, the simplicity of operation and the importance of avoiding complicated legal details often cast the weight of advantage on the side of the noncorporate form. As the business increases in size and as additional capital is needed, the advantages of the corporate form of organization become more and more apparent. The business that needs much capital equipment will require a form of organization which makes convenient the acquisition of large sums of money. Although there are advantages of the corporate form other than those pertaining to finance, its convenience as a medium through which large sums of capital may be raised is perhaps its most important attribute.

The corporate form of organization is considerably less important in the retail and the service fields where the capital-equipment requirements are of less significant proportions. Chart 8-1, based on data from the 1947 *Census of Manufactures*, indicates the direct relationship between percentage of businesses incorporated and number of employees of such businesses. Partial and tentative information for the years since 1947 indicates that the distribution of firms by type of organization has changed very little. Although incorporated businesses comprise only about 9 per cent of firms of all size-classes, they account for approximately 72 per cent of all firms with more than 50 employees. This relationship appears to bear out the assumption that the corporate form of organization is particularly appropriate for those lines of activity that are most subject to beneficial application of large-scale production techniques. In some fields of activity, such as electric light and power, the corporate form of organization accounts for practically all business. [1]

In the following pages, the specific characteristics of the primary forms of business organization will be discussed, with particular emphasis on the financial aspects of business operations.

The financial aspects of the principal forms of business organization will be considered in the following order:

1. Ability to obtain capital
2. Liability of owners for debts of the business in the event of failure
3. Tax considerations
4. Expense of organizing the business

In addition, certain aspects having less direct financial implications will be discussed, as follows:

5. Delegation of duties
6. Permanence of the organization
7. Freedom from regulation
8. Transferability of ownership

Each of these factors will be considered as it relates to the more common forms of business organization in this country—the sole proprietorship, the partnership, and the corporation.

Sole Proprietorship

The *sole proprietorship* is a business venture that is owned by a single individual who receives all of the profits and assumes personal responsibility for the debts and the losses of the business. Although the number of business enterprises that take the pro-

[1] Albert Ralph Koch, *The Financing of Large Corporations* (New York: National Bureau of Economic Research, Inc., 1943) p. 9. Also see Betty C. Churchill, "The Business Population by Legal Form of Organization," *Survey of Current Business* (Washington, D. C.: United States Department of Commerce, Office of Business Economics, April, 1955), pp. 14-20.

prietorship form of organization far outnumbers all other forms of business organization, the economic power of these enterprises, as measured by number of employees and amount of payrolls, is far less than that of the corporations of the nation. Because of the simplicity of this form of business organization and because of its convenience for small business ventures in general, we shall discuss it first.

Ability to Obtain Capital. The savings of the businessman together with the funds that he may be able to borrow from friends, relatives, and his bank may be sufficient for the operations of the typical small business. As the volume of business increases, however, and as larger investments in capital equipment are required, the owner may reach the point where he cannot borrow additional funds without increasing his equity investment. As increased demands are made for borrowed capital, lenders will generally insist on an increase in the equity capital as well, since the equity of a firm provides a margin of safety for the lender. At this point the sole proprietorship form of organization displays its basic weakness. In many cases the owner's original investment exhausts his personal resources and often those of his friends and relatives; and unless profits from the operation of the venture have proved sufficient to meet increased equity needs, the business either is prevented from achieving its maximum growth or is required to adopt a more appropriate form of organization for capital-raising purposes.

Liability of the Proprietor. The sole proprietor's position as it relates to liability for debts of the business is an unfavorable one. Creditors have recourse not only to the assets of the business for the settlement of their claims but also to the personal assets of the proprietor. Thus, the sole proprietor may find his home and personal property under claim by his creditors in the event that the assets of the business are not sufficient to meet the demands of creditors. This unlimited liability of the proprietor is, therefore, one of the serious disadvantages of the sole proprietorship. In many cases it is possible to shift the risk of loss through various forms of insurance, but it is seldom possible to avoid risks in connection with contractual relations with large suppliers of inventories or with customers. Changing business conditions may render a contract impossible to fulfill, and creditors may take action to the extent of their claims against the owner of the business.

Tax Considerations. All profits of the sole proprietorship are subject to federal personal income taxes, whether they are withdrawn from the business by the proprietor or reinvested in assets of the business. Although the sole proprietorship is not subject to corporate income taxes, it is required to file a statement of income in order that the personal income taxes applicable to the owner of the business may be determined correctly.

Expense of Organizing the Sole Proprietorship. Undoubtedly one of the primary reasons for the prevalence of the proprietorship form of business organization among small establishments is the fact that there are virtually no expenses in connection with its formation. It may be necessary to pay a fee for a license to engage in business, as for example, a barber's permit or a plumber's certification, but such fees are usually quite small and would be required of any business irrespective of its legal form of organization. No formal charter for operations is required for the sole proprietorship.

Delegation of Duties. The sole proprietor has complete control with respect to the delegation and assignment of duties within his organization, just as he is the final authority with respect to all actions of the business. He may employ or discharge employees at will and otherwise enjoy an authority not present in any other form of business organization. Unless the proprietor conveys to the general public the impression that one or more of his employees has been granted the power to bind the business contractually, he has no liability for the unwarranted acts of employees.

Permanence of the Organization. The sole proprietorship is created at the will of the proprietor and ends with his death or at such time before his death as he may choose. Not only does the death of the proprietor terminate the legal status of the business organization, but it often means liquidation of the enterprise itself in order that death tax levies may be met. The prospect of liquidation of an enterprise for estate and inheritance taxes has encouraged the absorption of small firms by larger organizations. Once a small firm has been absorbed by a larger organization and the proprietor has received stock in the purchasing company, subsequent death taxes can be met by the former proprietor's heirs through a partial liquidation of the enterprise itself.

Freedom from Regulation. Except for complying with general requirements, such as the registration of fictitious titles (required in some states when a business title other than that of the owner's name is used), the renewal of licenses, and the reporting of business income to the appropriate tax authorities, the sole proprietorship is subject to no special regulation.

Transferability of Ownership. Although the sole proprietor is free to transfer his ownership interest at will, subject only to the claims of creditors, he may have difficulty in finding a prospective buyer who has both the desire and the necessary money to accomplish the transfer. The lack of permanence of this form of business organization, combined with the difficulty of transfer of ownership, may at times be an important reason for the inability of the proprietorship to obtain large sums of loan capital.

The Partnership

The *partnership* form of business organization exists when an association of two or more persons own a business operated for profit. Although the partnership differs from the sole proprietorship in a technical sense to only a small degree, joint ownership introduces many important differences.

Ability to Obtain Capital. Undoubtedly one of the important reasons for the popularity of the partnership arrangement is the fact that it enables businessmen to pool their resources without the complications that often accompany incorporation. In some instances the partnership form of organization exists from the beginning of business operation, the property, equipment, knowledge, and skills for business purposes being acquired through the joint contributions of two or more persons. In other cases, an enterprise that began as a sole proprietorship may reach the point where additional growth is impossible without an increase in equity capital, and conversion to the partnership arrangement is one method of increasing the equity capital of the enterprise.

Although the number of partners that may be taken into a business venture is theoretically unlimited, the managerial difficulties and conflicts arising as a result of a large number of partners limits effectively the number of such co-owners. The partnership, therefore, like the proprietorship, eventually suffers from a lack of command over large sums of capital because of the practical limit to the number of partners that a business venture may have. Although it is true that some types of businesses have dozens and even hundreds of partners, a modification of the general partnership arrangement is generally utilized. It is extremely rare to find more than a few partners involved in an industrial or commercial enterprise.

Liability of the Partners. Like the sole proprietor, the members of a partnership team risk their personal assets as well as their investment in the business venture. In addition, if one of the partners negotiates a contract that results in substantial loss, each partner suffers loss in proportion to the previously agreed upon terms of distribution of profits and losses. This is true whether the partner responsible for the loss was pursuing his specified responsibilities or whether he was violating his authorized functions as set out in the articles of copartnership. The other partners may, however, take action against the offending partner because of his violation of the articles of copartnership.

More serious, perhaps, is a partner's liability for the actions of the business. Under partnership law each partner has *joint and several liability* for the debts of the business, a situation that permits creditors to seek satisfaction from a single partner if the remaining partners are unable to bear their share of the loss. For example, assume that the three partners in a business venture have made equal investments in the business and have agreed to share profits and losses equally. After a period of unsuccessful business operations, the venture is dissolved and the cash obtained from liquidation of the assets is used to reduce the debt obligations of the enterprise; however, $30,000 remains due to creditors after liquidation of assets and payment of the proceeds to the creditors. Since profits and losses are to be divided equally, each partner owes $10,000 as his share of the liabilities of the business. If only one of the partners has personal property free of debt, however, this partner may have to sacrifice his personal property up to the limit of the liability established against the entire part-nership. The partner bearing the brunt of the loss then has a residual claim against his partners for their share of the loss, a claim that seldom has any immediate value.

Tax Considerations. The partnership, like the sole proprietor-ship, is subject to no special income tax, but profits of the part-nership are taxable as personal income in the proportion that they are claimed by the partners. For example, if the articles of copartnership specify a $\frac{1}{2}$-$\frac{1}{4}$-$\frac{1}{4}$ division of profits for partners *A, B,* and *C,* respectively, in a three-person partnership, then re-ported profits of $100,000 would accrue to partner *A* in the amount of $50,000; partner *B,* $25,000, and partner *C,* $25,000. As in the case of the sole proprietorship, it is immaterial whether the reported profits of the business venture are retained in the busi-ness and invested in additional assets or withdrawn for the per-sonal use of the partners because all profits are subject to federal personal income taxes. For the business enterprise that has no prospect of growth, this does not present a serious disadvantage, since it is to be expected that most of the profits from operations will be distributed irrespective of the form of organization.

Expense of Organizing the Partnership. Like the sole proprie-torship, the establishment of a general partnership requires little, if any, expense. Yet, in contrast with the sole proprietorship, there is excellent reason for some degree of formality in establishing the basic rules under which the partnership is to be operated. Despite the fact that the partners feel they have a complete and common understanding of their duties, privileges, and obligations, the careful formulation of articles of copartnership will serve to resolve many uncertainties that otherwise would arise. Although the partnership form requires no written agreement, the legal expense required for the proper preparation of the articles of copartnership is generally considered a wise investment.

Delegation of Duties. Agreements as to the division of duties and responsibilities of the partners are binding only between the partners and not on outsiders. The partnership form of organiza-tion, therefore, lacks the certainty of the sole proprietorship as well as the convenience and certainty offered by the corporation with respect to the delegation of duties.

Permanence of the Organization. The partnership arrangement ceases to exist with the death, withdrawal, or legal incapacity of one or more of the partners. Furthermore, should no agreement exist to the contrary, one partner may arbitrarily force the other partners either to purchase his share of the business or to be allowed to purchase their shares. The alternative is a forced liquidation of the business and a division of the proceeds. The articles of copartnership should include provisions for the dissolution of the partnership. In addition, the method of valuing assets for purposes of dissolution should be clearly established.

The claim of death taxes against the estate of the deceased partner may force the beneficiaries to claim the share of the deceased partner in the business. A common method of avoiding the necessity of a partial or complete liquidation as a result of the death of a partner is to maintain insurance on the life of each partner with the other partners named as beneficiaries. Upon the death of a partner, the proceeds of the policy may be used to pay to the beneficiaries the cash value of the share in the business of the deceased partner.

Freedom from Regulation. One of the important advantages of the partnership form of business organization is the lack of special regulation by government authorities. As in the case of the sole proprietorship, however, the partnership must report business income to tax authorities and otherwise meet the usual requirements for licenses and certifications.

Transferability of Ownership. One general partner may not sell his share to another person unless that person is acceptable to each of the other general partners. A disgruntled partner would otherwise be at liberty to dispose of his share of ownership to a competitor or to a person whose financial responsibility was in question. The partners could scarcely be expected to subject their investments to the possibilities that such action would make possible. In disposing of a partnership share, therefore, it is necessary to find a person who not only has the desire and necessary capital to buy into the business, but one who is also acceptable to the other general partners. Once a new partner is taken into the business, the old partnership ceases to exist and a new partnership comes into being.

The Corporation

In the Dartmouth College Case in 1819 Chief Justice John Marshall described the status of the corporation so explicitly and clearly that this description has since become the generally accepted definition of the corporation. It reads in part as follows:

> A corporation is an artificial being, invisible, intangible, and existing only in contemplation of law. Being the mere creature of law, it possesses only those properties which the charter of its creation confers upon it, either expressly, or as incidental to its very existence . . . [Dartmouth College vs. Woodward, 4 Wheaton (U. S.) 518 (1819)]

Being a creature of law, the corporation possesses many advantages for purposes of business operations. Along with the advantages enjoyed by the corporation, some distinct disadvantages also often exist.

Ability to Obtain Capital. The small corporation that has been in existence only a short time, like most new ventures, usually finds it extremely difficult to attract investment funds from outsiders. It is only after the corporation has become well established and offers attractive prospects for investors that the special features of the corporate form of organization become significant. One of the important reasons for the suitability of the corporate form of organization as a medium through which large sums of capital may be accumulated is that capital stock may be offered to its existing stockholders or to investors in amounts suited to their purposes. The corporate form of organization, however, does not by itself assure the flow of investment funds into the business. Rather, it removes several of the impediments to the flow of capital that exist for other forms of business organization. Among the characteristics enjoyed by the corporate form of organization that may facilitate the accumulation of capital are limited liability of the owners for business debts, continuity of corporate existence, and ease in transferring ownership.

Liability of Stockholders. One of the principal advantages to the stockholders is the limitation on liability. Ordinarily creditors and other claimants may look only to the assets of the corporation for satisfaction of their claims and do not have recourse to the personal assets of the owners. This advantage is particularly appealing to the owner of the business who has built up considerable wealth and has diverse business interests over which he cannot exercise complete personal control. The limitation on liability may also make it possible for the promoters of new ventures to attract the interest of wealthy investors who would otherwise be unwilling to risk possible claims against their personal property. Unlimited liability may be avoided under certain circumstances in some of the noncorporate forms of organization, but the certainty provided by the corporate form is not present.

The limitation on stockholder liability for debts of the corporation is seldom sufficient reason for incorporation of the small business in which there is an individual owner whose personal assets are largely invested in the business. In this situation there is little risk on the part of the owner beyond his investment in the corporation. Nor is the corporate form of organization necessarily effective in protecting stockholders from personal risk beyond their investment when the business is relatively new or in a weak financial condition. Creditors may simply require that one or more of the stockholders add their personal signatures to the obligation of the corporation, rendering them personally liable for the obligation. After a corporation has established a good credit reputation, creditors and suppliers seldom insist on personal guarantees on the part of the stockholders.

Tax Considerations. The corporation pays further for its government-conferred advantages through special taxes levied against its income. Income taxes are levied by some states against all corporations doing business within their borders and by other states on the entire income of corporations holding charters of those states, irrespective of the source of their profits. More important, however, are the taxes on corporate income levied by the federal government. The schedule of federal taxes for 1958 provided for a normal tax of 30 per cent on the first $25,000 of a corporation's net income and a combined normal tax and surtax of 52 per cent on all net income in excess of $25,000.

After payment of corporate income taxes, the remaining profits or a portion thereof may be distributed to the owners of stock in the form of dividends. The stockholders must then report these dividends as part of their own personal income, and as such the dividends are subject to federal personal income taxes. The distributed earnings of corporations, therefore, are subject to double taxation.[2] In general it may be concluded that the burdensome nature of this double taxation on corporation profits often renders a substantial advantage to the partnership or the proprietorship form of organization. Where other advantages of the corporate form are not considered to be essential, the owners of the business may be inclined to avoid incorporation. In recent years there have been several instances where corporations have sacrificed their charters and reverted to the partnership form of organization for tax reasons.

One aspect of the tax structure may offer an advantage for the corporation. If it is the intention of the controlling stockholders to allow corporate profits to remain in the business, these profits are not subject to federal personal income taxes as is the case for sole proprietorships and partnerships. These retained profits, however, are subject to the regular corporate income taxes. After the accumulation of such profits in a business, a subsequent sale of a share of stock by a stockholder at a higher price than that paid for the stock involves the payment of a capital gains tax on the appreciation in value of the stock.

As early as 1913 it was recognized that the opportunity to allow profits to remain with the corporation might lead to abuse in order to avoid the payment of personal income taxes. "Unreasonable" accumulations of earnings, as determined by the Federal Internal Revenue Service, are now discouraged through Section 102 of the Internal Revenue Code. Under this Section the first $100,000 of unreasonable earnings accumulation is taxed at the rate of $27\frac{1}{2}$ per cent, plus $38\frac{1}{2}$ per cent of all additional unreasonable accumulations. The objective of this legislation is to prevent through taxation the accumulation of profits within a corporation for which there is no appropriate use. Briefly then, the tax pattern applied to the corporate form of organization serves as the principal limiting factor to the general desirability of this form of organization.

Expense of Organizing the Corporation. The corporation requires greater expenditure of money and effort in its establishment than is required for noncorporate forms of organization.

---

[2] The Internal Revenue Code of 1954 provides some relief for this problem of double taxation by excluding the first fifty dollars of an individual's dividend income from taxable income; and if husband and wife each have dividends of fifty dollars or more, the exclusion is one hundred dollars. In addition, a tax credit of 4 per cent of the remaining dividend income is allowed against the taxpayer's final tax bill.

The governmental unit issuing the charter charges an initial incorporation fee as well as annual franchise taxes or fees for the privilege of retaining the corporate charter from year to year. Although these fees are seldom burdensome, they do represent an excess of cost over other forms of business organization.

Delegation of Duties. The delegation of duties, responsibilities, and authority within the corporate form of organization may be accomplished to suit the specific requirements of the owners of the business. The stockholders, who are the owners, elect a board of directors. The board of directors, as the elected representatives of the stockholders, is responsible for the establishment of general policy of the business and for the election of officers. The officers select the personnel of the business and specify the particular duties of such personnel. The officers and personnel of the company have only such authority as may be delegated to them, and the corporation may not be legally held liable for actions of their personnel that represent a violation of their granted authority. For example, only those persons within the firm that have been granted the authority to purchase supplies for the corporation may bind the corporation to such contracts. The flexibility and certainty with which duties, responsibilities, and authority may be established in the corporation is, therefore, one of the important attributes of this form of business organization.

Permanence of the Organization. The death of a stockholder does not affect the legal continuity of existence of the corporation; his stock is transferred to his heirs and they in turn become the stockholders of record after the corporation has been notified of the transfer. Where permanence of the organization is an important requirement, the corporation is undoubtedly the most desirable form of business organization.

Freedom from Regulation. Because the corporation depends upon its state-granted charter for its very existence, it is subject to many regulatory measures. It must submit reports of its activities to the state, pay annual taxes for the privilege of retaining its charter, and obtain permission from states other than the state from which the charter has been obtained before business may be conducted on a corporate basis in those states. In short, the corporation is subject to considerable regulation. The businessman who considers secrecy of operations and freedom from limitations and frequent reports on his business activities to be desirable will, other things being equal, prefer one of the noncorporate forms of organizations.

Transferability of Ownership. Corporate stock may be transferred freely from one person to another, and the purchaser of such stock receives all the rights and privileges held by the seller by virtue of his ownership of the stock. Transferability, therefore, is important in making it possible for the corporation to accumulate large sums of money since the investor knows that he may, as a rule, dispose of his investment when he wishes or finds it necessary to do so.

Other Forms of Business Organization

In addition to the sole proprietorship, the partnership, and the corporation, there are a variety of somewhat less well-known forms of business organization that combine to varying degrees some of the advantages and the disadvantages of the forms of organization which have been discussed. The *business trust*, for example, also known as the Massachusetts trust, the voluntary association, or common-law trust, combines the advantage of limited liability with convenience in raising capital. Yet, the utilization of the business-trust form of arrangement is limited, for the most part, to a few of the New England states. Under the business-trust arrangement, assets of the company are held by a trustee, the beneficiaries of the company holding trust certificates as evidence of their beneficial interest. Profits of the company are distributed to holders of trust certificates much as dividends are distributed to stockholders. In spite of the convenience of the business-trust arrangement, its general lack of familiarity to persons outside of the New England states renders it a less desirable form of business organization than the corporation for purposes of raising capital for business operations. Although the business-trust arrangement is noncorporate in form, it is subject to federal income taxes at the same rate as corporations.

The *limited partnership*, another minor form of business organization, is a statutory modification of the common-law partnership in which one or more general partners combine with one or more limited partners. The limited partner, much like the shareholders in a corporation, have liability for debts of the business only to the extent of their investment. The general partners are governed by the usual laws relating to partnerships while the limited partners are governed by state statutes. The limited partnership form of organization comes into existence only after proper application by the partners and acceptance and approval of the application by the state. Many states have adopted the Uniform Limited Partnership Act under which limited partnership operations may be conducted. Most of the remaining states have enacted their own statutory provisions relative to the limited partnership form of organization. One of the important limitations to the usefulness of this arrangement is the fact that the limited partners may not participate in the management of the business nor may the business capitalize upon the reputation or the credit standing of the limited partners for purposes of gaining more acceptable credit for the business. Aside from this limitation, there is a substantial advantage in that the limited partner, although perhaps the only member of the group with large personal financial resources, is afforded limited liability. He may also participate in the profits of the firm according to any prearranged terms that may be agreed upon among the partners.

In addition to the limited partnership and the business trust, there are many other forms of business organization that attempt to combine the advantages of the more common forms, each of which has its particular place and advantages. Some of these minor forms of business organization include the joint-stock company, the joint venture, the mining partnership, and the partnership association.

QUESTIONS

1. Discuss the possible reasons for long-term financing on the part of a business venture after it has already been in operation for several years.
2. Describe the procedures by which owners may invest in the sole proprietorship, the partnership, or the corporation.
3. For what type and size of business does the sole proprietorship, the partnership, and the corporation play the most important role?
4. Describe a business venture in which the circumstances would clearly indicate the sole proprietorship form of organization as being the most appropriate.
5. The ability of a business to obtain capital is in part a function of its legal form of organization. Explain.

6. Compare the practical significance of unlimited liability in the sole proprietorship with that of the partnership.

7. Compare the over-all tax situation of the sole proprietorship with that of the corporation.

8. Discuss the effectiveness with which duties, responsibilities, and authority may be delegated in the sole proprietorship, the partnership, and the corporation.

9. Why do not all business ventures incorporate in order to obtain the advantages of limited liability?

10. Explain how the members of a partnership may protect the business against possible forced liquidation in the event of the death of one of the partners.

11. Describe the practical difficulty of transferring an ownership share in a partnership.

12. In what manner are the profits of corporations doubly taxed by the federal government?

13. Since the business trust form of business organization provides many of the practical advantages of the corporate form of organization, account for its limited use.

14. Describe a business venture in which the limited partnership form of organization would be particularly appropriate.

SUGGESTED READINGS

Bradley, Joseph F. *Fundamentals of Corporation Finance.* New York: Rinehart & Company, Inc., 1953. Chapters 2 and 3.

Dauten, Carl A. *Business Finance;* Second Edition. Englewood Cliffs, New Jersey: Prentice-Hall, Inc., 1956. Chapters 2 and 3.

Gerstenberg, Charles W. *Financial Organization and Management of Business;* Third Edition. Englewood Cliffs, New Jersey: Prentice-Hall, Inc., 1951. Chapters 1-3.

Guthmann, Harry G., and Dougall, Herbert E. *Corporate Financial Policy;* Third Edition. Englewood Cliffs, New Jersey: Prentice-Hall, Inc., 1955. Chapters 2 and 3.

Howard, Bion B., and Upton, Miller. *Introduction to Business Finance.* New York: McGraw-Hill Book Company, Inc., 1953. Chapter 2.

Long-Term Financing for the Corporation

In the preceding chapter the corporation was described as a creature of the law, whose powers are derived entirely from a charter granted by the government. Early corporate charters in England were granted by the Crown. As the powers of the Crown were restricted, however, Parliament assumed this authority and later general incorporation acts were adopted. In the United States colonial governors originally granted charters, a responsibility that was later taken over by colonial legislatures, and still later by the states. The first state to enact general incorporation laws was North Carolina, which in 1795 enacted a law to provide for the establishment of canal companies. All of the states and the District of Columbia now have general incorporation laws; and for certain types of institutions, such as commercial banks and savings and loan associations, the federal government issues charters.

ESTABLISHMENT OF THE CORPORATION

The procedure by which the corporate form of business organization comes into existence involves the filing of articles of incorporation by the interested parties, the election of a board of directors, and the drafting of corporate bylaws. The financing of the corporation is then carried out within the authority and limitations established in the charter and bylaws. Careful selection of a state of incorporation is important since the regulation and taxation of corporations differ from state to state.

157

The Corporate Charter

When the articles of incorporation are accepted by the appropriate government official, a corporate charter is issued. The *charter*, which is the official statement of relationship between the government and the business, establishes the privileges as well as the responsibilities of the corporation.

Among the most important of the provisions of the corporate charter are the official title of the company, the purposes for which it is formed, the location of the principal office of the corporation, the length of life of the corporation, the names and the addresses of the incorporators or directors of the company, and certain matters relating to the financing of the company. It is with the financial matters of the company that we are primarily concerned in this chapter.

Directors and Officers

After the charter has been issued by the appropriate governmental authority, a meeting of the incorporators is held to select a *board of directors*, which is responsible for the broad managerial responsibilities of the corporation. In a small enterprise, and most new ventures are small, the incorporators elect themselves as members of the board of directors.

The details of business management, however, are delegated by the directors to the officers of the company. The officers generally include the president, the secretary, the treasurer, and frequently one or more vice-presidents. Again, in a small enterprise the incorporators may serve as officers of the company. Frequently a person may serve a dual official function in the company, for example, as both secretary and treasurer.

The Bylaws

Because the corporate charter itself does not concern itself with the day-to-day operations of the business, the board of directors generally adopts a set of bylaws at its first meeting. The *bylaws* provide the corporate officers with a statement of their duties and responsibilities. In addition, the bylaws generally specify the time and the place of the meetings of the owners of the corporation, the procedure for election of new directors, the appointment of committees, the names of banks that are to serve the business, and the names of persons authorized to sign checks and to take other actions for the corporation. In short, the bylaws provide for matters of internal management and control.

In both the corporate charter and the bylaws provisions are found that relate to the financing of the organization. For example, the number and the types of ownership shares that are to be authorized are described in the charter. The procedure by which these ownership shares may be transferred is usually described in the bylaws. Limits to the total debt that may be incurred by the corporation may also be established in the bylaws.

SOURCES OF LONG-TERM FINANCING

The long-term sources of capital funds for the corporation are of two broad groups: equity capital and debt capital. Equity capital is obtained through the sale of shares of stock in the corporation. These shares may be divided into several classes, each having specified benefits and privileges with respect to ownership status in the corporation.[1] As opposed to the equity capital of a corporation, debt capital represents funds obtained from creditors rather than from owners. Such capital may be obtained through direct negotiation with a lender or through the sale of notes or bonds to many lenders.

Equity Capital

Equity capital is the capital supplied by the owners of the enterprise. This ownership claim in a corporation is evidenced by the *stock certificate*. The stock certificate shows the type of stock held by the owner, the name of the company, the name of the owner of the stock, and the names of certain of the company officers. The stock certificate also carries space for its assignment in the event that it is transferred to another person. As a protection against forgery, all signatures on stock certificates must generally be certified by a representative of a commercial bank, a stockbroker, or other authorized person. In the event of the loss of a stock certificate, however, an individual may request a

---

[1] Profits of a business that are retained rather than paid out as dividends are also a form of equity capital since they represent ownership capital reinvested in the business. The importance of this source of financing is discussed later in this chapter.

Figure 9–1

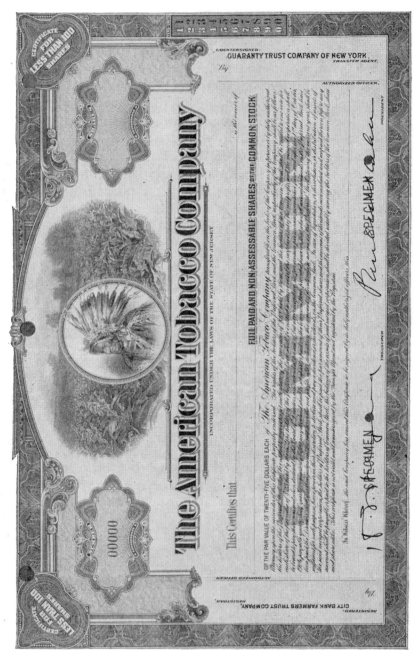

Common Stock Certificate

160

duplicate certificate of the corporation. In order to protect itself, the corporation, in turn, will generally require that a bond or surety be posted by the stockholder to protect the corporation in the event that the lost certificate should later be presented.

Stock certificates are generally made out in terms of one hundred shares or multiples thereof. Stock certificates representing less than one hundred shares are generally referred to as *fractional certificates*. The holder of an odd number of shares, as for example, 523, will probably hold one stock certificate representing the ownership of 500 shares and a fractional stock certificate representing an ownership of 23 shares. An example of a common stock certificate is shown in Figure 9-1.

When the holder of stock sells his shares, the assigned stock certificate is forwarded to the company by the purchaser, at which time the old certificate is destroyed by the secretary of the corporation and a new one issued to the new owner whose name will then be carried on the record. In the larger corporations, an official transfer agent, generally a trust company or a bank, is appointed to accomplish this task. The larger corporations may also have an independent stock registrar to supervise transfer of the securities.

The capital stock of a corporation may be assigned a *par value* (a fixed value) in the certificate of incorporation. If the corporation sells the stock for less than the par value, the owners of the stock may become liable to creditors for the difference between the selling price and the par value in the event of failure of the company. Thus the limited liability of the stockholders may be defeated under these circumstances. This technicality seldom creates any difficulty, however, since most stock is sold initially at or above its par value. In addition certain legal devices may be used to protect against such contingent liability even in those instances when the stock must be sold at less than its par value.

Aside from this significance, par value usually bears little relationship to the current price or book value of the stock. Most states permit corporations to issue no-par stock.

Types of Equity Instruments

Equity instruments of the corporation may be grouped broadly into two classes: common stock and preferred stock.

Common Stock. The outstanding characteristics of *common stock* is its complete claim to the profits of the business that remain after the holders of all other classes of debt and equity instruments have received their stipulated returns. Also, it is generally the voting privilege of the common stockholders that governs the selection of the board of directors of a corporation; the board of directors, in turn, exercises general control of the enterprise. For these reasons, the holders of common stock may be regarded as the basic owners of the corporation.

The favorable position of the common stockholders with respect to dividends and control of the corporation is offset by the fact that during periods when profits from operations are low, the claims of others may completely absorb available funds, leaving little or nothing for the common stockholders. The common stockholders, therefore, may expect less stability with respect to the amount of their dividends, often receiving considerably greater yield than the holders of other instruments during prosperous periods and generally less than other security holders during periods of distress.

Just as the common stockholder receives dividends only after all other classes of security holders have received their specified return, so too the common stockholders have low priority when a business venture is liquidated. All creditors must receive their claims in full and preferred stockholders must, as a rule, be paid in full before common stockholders may participate in the proceeds of liquidation. As in the case of dividends, all proceeds of liquidation remaining after the settlement of prior obligations accrue to the common stockholders. It is seldom, however, that an enterprise which has been forced to liquidate because of unfortunate business experience will provide enough proceeds to take care of the claims of creditors and preferred stockholders. Common stockholders generally receive little, if anything, from liquidation proceedings. The common stockholders, therefore, suffer the brunt of business failure just as they enjoy the primary benefits of business success.

Common stock may be divided into special groups, generally Class A and Class B, in order to permit the acquisition of additional capital without diluting the control of the business. When a corporation does issue two classes of common stock, it quite often will give voting rights only to one class, generally Class B. Owners of Class A stock, then, have most, if not all, of the other rights and privileges of the common stockholders with the exception that they have no vote in the affairs of the corporation. This tendency on the part of some corporations to issue nonvoting equity securities is opposed by some government agencies as well as some authorities in the field of corporate finance on the basis that it permits the concentration of ownership control. The New York Stock Exchange refuses to list the common stock of corporations that issue nonvoting classes of common stock.

Preferred Stock. *Preferred stock,* in contrast with common stock, generally carries a limited dividend specified as either a percentage of par value or as a fixed number of dollars per year. For example, a preferred stock may be referred to as a 5 per cent preferred, meaning that its annual dividend participation is limited to 5 per cent of its par or stated value. The dividend priority for no-par preferred stock is stated in terms of a dollar amount, for example, "preferred as to dividends in the amount of $5 annually." The holder of the preferred stock accepts the limitation on the amount of dividends as a fair exchange for the priority he has in the earnings of the company.

As has been noted, before the common stockholders receive any dividends, preferred stockholders must be paid the total of their prior claim. The preferred stock, therefore, offers the investor something of a compromise between the basic equity instruments of common stock and credit instruments such as bonds and long-term notes. Because preferred stocks are frequently of a nonvoting nature, the managements of many corporations favor their issuance as a means of obtaining equity capital without diluting the control of the present stockholders. An example of a preferred stock certificate is shown in Figure 9-2.

As in the case of common stock, preferred stock may be classified into Class A, Class B, or alternatively, First Preferred and Second Preferred. The Class A Preferred or First Preferred usually has priority over other classes of preferred stock of a company in the distribution of dividends and in the proceeds of assets that result from the liquidation of the company.

Preferred stock may have special features. For example, it may be cumulative or noncumulative. *Cumulative preferred stock*

Figure 9–2

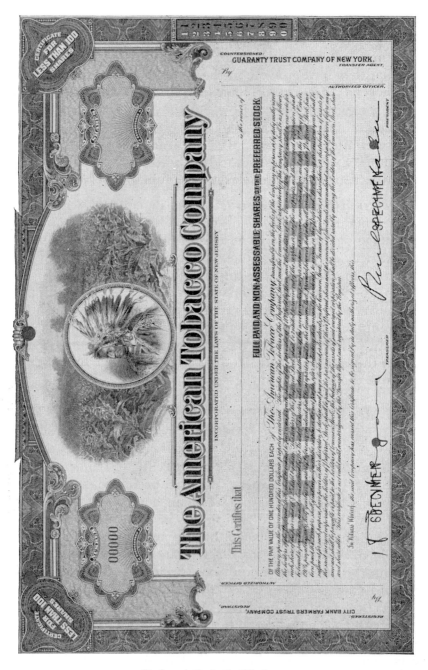

Preferred Stock Certificate

requires that before common stock dividends may be paid, preferred dividends must be paid not only for the dividend period in question but also for all previous periods in which no preferred dividends were paid. It is important to remember that, since the preferred stockholder technically is an owner of the business, he cannot force the payment of a dividend. The preferred stockholder may be made to wait until such time as earnings are adequate for that purpose, the cumulative preferred stock offering protection for those periods during which dividends were not declared. *Noncumulative preferred stock*, on the other hand, makes no provision for the accumulation of unpaid dividends with the result that management may at times be tempted to declare preferred dividends only when it appears that sufficient earnings are available to make possible common stock dividends also. Practically all modern preferred stock is cumulative.

A preferred stock may be participating or nonparticipating. A *participating preferred stock* is one that is entitled to some residual participation in the profits of a corporation after it has received the basic amount of dividends specified in the stock certificate. A common agreement of this sort involves first, the payment of a specified dividend to the preferred stockholders, after which the common stockholders receive a comparable amount per share of stock, followed by an equal share-for-share participation between preferred stockholders and common stockholders in any residual profits. Very few issues of modern preferred stock carry a participation clause.

Preferred stock also may be callable, in which case the corporation may retire the preferred stock at its option. Preferred stock may also carry a conversion clause that makes it possible to convert the preferred stock into common stock of the corporation at the stockholder's option.

Many special features that preferred stocks may carry exist primarily as an added attraction to investors to permit the sale of securities at times when distribution would otherwise be difficult.

Corporate Control

Although the control of a corporation is administered generally by its board of directors, ultimate control rests with those stockholders who hold classes of stock with voting rights. The stockholders are responsible for the election of the members of the board of directors, and the members of the board of directors are in turn responsible to the stockholders. Many stockholders in large corporations have little interest in their voting rights, owning such stocks purely for income. Under such circumstances it is possible and generally true that stockholders owning only a small proportion of the total stock are able to control the election of the members of the board of directors, and hence effect ultimate control over all activities of the corporation.

The device of classifying common stock as voting and non-voting shares facilitates the control of corporate affairs by the ownership of only a small part of all capital investment, and the same is true in some cases of the issue of nonvoting preferred stock. Some states require that all stock, regardless of its class, be voting stock, a provision apparently designed to permit participation on the part of all stockholders in corporate activity. This apparent protection to the stockholders in exercising their voting rights may easily be defeated by numerous devices, such as establishing the par value of the preferred stock or of one class of common stock at a much higher amount than that of the basic common stock. Since the stockholder is entitled to one vote for each share that he owns, an investment in the basic common stock will provide a considerably greater number of votes than would an equal investment in the preferred stock or other class of common stock. The ill-fated promotion and financing of the Tucker Motor Car Company in the post-World War II period serves as an example of the use of classified common stock. This company issued both Class A and Class B stock. The Class A stock, although carrying voting rights, was offered to the public at $5 a share; the Class B stock, also carrying voting rights, had a nominal value of 10 cents a share. Practically all of the Class B stock was held by the promoter of the enterprise. It is obvious, therefore, that a $5 investment in the Class A stock would bring one vote, while the same investment in Class B stock would bring fifty votes.

Although it is true that most corporations have done little to encourage stockholders to participate actively in the election of members of the boards of directors, in recent years some corporations have made very definite efforts to stimulate such activity. One company, The General Mills Corporation, has not only publicized its stockholders' meetings widely in an effort to encourage attendance, but it has also held regional meetings to permit greater attendance on the part of stockholders located in out-of-the-way areas. Wide interest on the part of the stockholders in the affairs of the corporation not only provides a greater feeling of ownership and a sympathy for the problems of the corporation, but also it provides a broadened market for the sale of new securities when such is desirable or necessary. The publicity value of favorable stockholder relationships is also to be considered since the larger corporations have many thousands of stockholders, each a potential medium of good public relations.

Debt Capital

In addition to the capital provided by the owners of the corporation, funds may be secured also from creditors on a long-term basis. Debt capital, however, must be preceded by an equity investment in the corporation on the part of the stockholders, inasmuch as creditors generally require a contribution on the part of owners before entrusting their own funds to the use of the corporation. Uses for borrowed funds may be the same as the uses for equity funds, for example, the acquisition of additional land, buildings, and equipment. Debt capital, however, has certain rights and privileges not possessed by the holders of equity capital in a corporation. The holder of a debt instrument issued by a corporation may force the business to abide by the terms of the contract even though it may mean reorganization or dissolution of the enterprise. The periodic interest payments due the holders of such debt instruments must be paid, therefore, if the corporation is to survive. The holders of debt instruments have priority over stockholders up to the limit of their claim against the corporation in the event of liquidation of the concern.

To offset the advantage of this preferred position on the part of the creditors of a corporation, it is generally true that the yield to which they are entitled is considerably less on the average over a period of years than that available to the owners of the various classes of equity securities. Also, as long as the corporation meets its contractual obligations the creditors have little voice in the matters of management and control of the corporation, except for those covenants and restrictions that are a part of the loan contract.

Types of Debt Instruments

Long-term corporate debt instruments may be classified into two categories—secured obligations and unsecured obligations, generally referred to as *mortgage bonds* and *debenture bonds.* In contrast with the stockholder whose ownership of shares of stock may be evidenced by a single stock certificate, the holder of bonds has a separate instrument for each bond owned. The bond itself will on the face of the instrument establish the pertinent facts relating to the rights and the obligations of the corporation and the bondholder. It will, among other things, specify the denomination of the bond (generally $1,000), the maturity, the interest rate, the periods of interest payment, and the specific nature of the claim of the particular debt instrument.

The bond contract is generally rather complicated and the ramifications of the contract itself are too extensive to be included on the face of the bond. This supplementary information is set out in a document referred to as the *trust indenture.* This document is generally quite voluminous and includes in the greatest detail the various provisions of the loan arrangement. Although the indenture is seldom seen or utilized by the average bondholder, it is available to the creditor who inquires for its use. The trust indenture, then, provides the basis for the settlement of disputes relative to the responsibilities and the rights of the parties to the contract and as such it is essential that it be carefully preserved. The trust indenture is generally in the possession of a trustee designated by the corporation for this purpose. The responsibility of the trustee is not only to protect the indenture but also to enforce its provisions on behalf of the bondholders, should it become necessary to do so.

The importance of the function of the trustee is such that in 1939 government legislation came into existence to establish specific duties and obligations of the trustee in this respect. This legislation, known as the Trust Indenture Act of 1939, provides, among other things, that the trustee act impartially in behalf of the creditors of the corporation in such a manner as required by the terms of the Act. Also, the trustee must have a combined capital and surplus of not less than $150,000, must be corporate in form, and must have interests not in conflict with those of the holders of the securities.

When there is a direct loan arrangement established between a borrowing corporation and a single lending institution, corporate notes may be used rather than bonds. Although long-term corporate notes are less formal in nature than bonds, they generally include many restrictive covenants not required in connection with the typical short-term promissory note. Long-term corporate notes may also be used when a group of institutions negotiate jointly with a borrowing corporation.

Mortgage Bonds. The property specifically pledged to secure the mortgage bonds may include all of the assets of a corporation or it may include only a part thereof. As a rule, however, the mortgage applies only to the real estate, buildings, and other assets that are classed as real property. For the corporation that is expanding its plant facilities, the mortgage so offered for expansion purposes usually includes only a lien on the additional property acquired. The opposite has been true of most railway expansions. Originally, railway construction was of a piecemeal nature, providing for extensions of road and facilities over a period of many years. Mortgage bonds issued to finance such extensions of track often included a lien on all of the roadbed previously constructed as well as the additional track.

When a parcel of real estate has more than one mortgage lien against it, the mortgage first filed for recording at the appropriate government office, generally the county recorder's office, has priority and the bonds outstanding against the mortgage are known as *senior liens*. The bonds outstanding against all mortgages subsequently recorded are known as *junior liens*. Inasmuch as senior liens have priority with respect to distribution of assets in the event of failure of the business, they generally provide a lower yield to investors than do the junior liens. The junior liens of a strong company, however, may be considered by investors to be safer than the senior liens of another less well-established company.

Mortgage bonds may differ to a considerable extent. For example, the mortgage may prevent the issuance of additional securities against the mortgage over and above those authorized to be issued in the initial flotation. The term *closed-end mortgage* applies to this arrangement. Alternatively, the mortgage may provide for continuing sale of bonds against the same mortgage. As a rule when such an *open-end mortgage* exists, there is also a stipulation to the effect that additional real property which the company acquires automatically becomes a part of the property secured under the mortgage.

Debenture Bonds. These bonds are dependent upon the general credit and strength of the corporation for their security. They represent no specific pledge of property, but rather their holders are classed as general creditors of the corporation on a par with the holders of promissory notes and trade creditors that have sold merchandise to the corporation. Debenture bonds are used by governmental bodies and by many industrial and utility corporations as well. Since mortgage bonds would otherwise have a prior claim against the fixed assets of a corporation, even though they are sold subsequent to the debenture bonds, the debenture bonds are sometimes afforded protection against such subsequent sale of senior securities through a covenant of equal coverage. Such a covenant provides that the debenture bonds will be accorded equal rank with any subsequent senior issues of securities.

Like preferred stock, corporate bonds may carry such special provisions as conversion rights and participation rights in order to enhance their original sale. Most modern industrial bond issues are callable at the option of the company. An example of a debenture bond is shown in Figure 9-3.

REASONS FOR LONG-TERM DEBT FINANCING

Unlike equity financing, which provides the ownership capital for all businesses, long-term debt financing may be avoided completely by business management. Since World War II, however, the corporations of the nation whose securities were registered with the Securities and Exchange Commission have acquired a substantially larger volume of long-term funds through bond financing than through stock financing. Among the principal reasons for this favorable attitude toward long-term debt financing may be included the desire to avoid sharing control with additional investors, the fact that at times equity financing may not be feasible, and that the cost of long-term debt financing may be less than equity financing.

Figure 9–3

Debenture Bond

To Avoid Sharing Corporate Control

A growing enterprise that has prospered under its existing management may lack the capital necessary to take advantage of the opportunities available. Yet the prospect of bringing additional stockholders into the enterprise may not be attractive to management because of the voting privileges that such new investors in the business would acquire. The volume of additional funds required might make necessary the sale of so much new stock that the existing stockholders would lose control of the affairs of the company because of the concentration of voting power in the hands of the new stockholders. Many firms have avoided expansion rather than risk loss of control through the sale of stock.

In other cases, the existence of a minority stockholder group would be objectionable to the existing owners even though the minority stockholder group would be ineffective, insofar as they might influence the affairs of the company. Although it may be suggested that a nonvoting form of stock can be issued, circumstances might make it impossible to sell such stock to outsiders.

Corporate bonds and notes, on the other hand, provide no voting privilege for their holders; hence, management frequently prefers this form of financing because it avoids a dilution of their own voting control. Although the holders of bonds and notes have no direct voting privilege, however, there are frequently contractural provisions that limit the managerial actions of the existing owners of the business. For example, before the loan is made, the borrower may be required to agree that dividends will not be distributed to stockholders if the net working capital of the firm falls below some stipulated minimum. Once the debt is retired, of course, the management is freed from such restrictions.

Equity Financing May Not Be Feasible

At times, although the prospect of reward from business expansion may be extremely attractive to the owners of the business, investors may have little interest in stock investments because of the prevailing state of the securities market. Such a market condition may result from a loss of confidence in stock investments because of heavy losses previously experienced. At such times investors may confine their attention entirely to high-grade corporate bonds or notes, since these securities provide greater stability of market value during periods of uncertainty than is true of stock investments. Also, for many small enterprises the prospects for permanent existence may be so uncertain that outside interests will avoid ownership investment. Long-term credit may be obtained, however, on the basis of the security of the assets of the business.

Lower Cost of Long-Term Debt Financing

Although management may be able to finance either through equity capital or debt capital, the decision may favor debt financing because of its lower cost. The cost of long-term borrowed capital, for example, may be only 4 per cent, as compared with a possible

8 or 10 per cent return that might otherwise be paid to new stock investors in the business. Borrowing the funds at a lower cost to the corporation than the return obtained on the use of the funds in the business permits the existing stockholders to retain the added income for their own account and to increase accordingly the return on their investment.

The lower cost to a corporation of financing through bonds and notes results from the lower risk involved in such investments from the viewpoint of the investor. Both the interest on and the redemption of the debt is fixed by contract; and if the corporation is to remain in operation, these obligations must be met. From the viewpoint of the corporation, equity claims are willingly subordinated to the claims of creditors in return for the use of creditors' money at a lower rate than that for which the corporation can in turn use the money. The investor, on the other hand, is willing to sacrifice the higher yields that are available on equity investments in return for the greater safety and certainty of income.

Trading on the Equity and Leverage. The process of borrowing long-term capital in order to increase the percentage return on the investment of existing stockholders in a business is termed *trading on the equity.* This term is apparently derived from the fact that equity investment must precede debt financing in a business enterprise; hence, the bonds or notes are being sold on the strength of the underlying equity. Frequently a company that is engaged heavily in trading on the equity is referred to as a *high-leverage company;* a company with little or no trading on the equity, as a *low-leverage company.* An example of the effects of this leverage on income is illustrated in Figure 9-4. In this illustration, two companies have similar asset structures and incomes. The Low Leverage Operating Company is financed entirely with equity capital. The $1,000,000 return on the $10,-000,000 investment of the stockholders of this company provides a percentage return of 10 per cent. The assets of the High Leverage Operating Company, on the other hand, were acquired by the sale of $4,000,000 of 4 per cent bonds and $6,000,000 of common stock. The income of this company before interest and dividends, like that of the Low Leverage Operating Company, is $1,000,000. Of this amount $160,000 must be paid to the bond-

Figure 9–4

LOW LEVERAGE OPERATING COMPANY

BALANCE SHEET
December 31, 1958

ASSETS		LIABILITIES AND CAPITAL	
Current Assets	$ 7,000,000	Liabilities	(none)
Fixed Assets	3,000,000	Common Stock	$10,000,000
Total Assets	$10,000,000	Total Liab. & Cap.	$10,000,000

* Earnings $1,000,000 (all earnings paid out)

Return to common stockholders expressed as a percentage
($1,000,000 ÷ $10,000,000) = 10%

HIGH LEVERAGE OPERATING COMPANY

BALANCE SHEET
December 31, 1958

ASSETS		LIABILITIES AND CAPITAL	
Current Assets	$ 7,000,000	Bonds @ 4%	$ 4,000,000
Fixed Assets	3,000,000	Common Stock	6,000,000
Total Assets	$10,000,000	Total Liab. & Cap.	$10,000,000

* Earnings $1,000,000 before interest and dividends (all earnings paid out)

Bondholders receive $160,000 (4% of $4,000,000)
Stockholders receive   840,000 ($1,000,000 earnings less bond interest)

Return to common stockholders expressed as a percentage
($840,000 ÷ $6,000,000) = 14%

---

* For purposes of simplification, tax matters have been ignored.

---

holders (4 per cent of $4,000,000), leaving $840,000 for the common stockholders. The $840,000 return on stockholders' investment of $6,000,000 provides a return of 14 per cent. The trading on the equity of the High Leverage Operating Company has increased the percentage return to the common stockholders by 4 per cent of their investment.

Trading on the Equity and Corporate Taxation. The cost advantage to a corporation of financing through long-term debt arrangements is even more striking when the influence of the federal corporate income tax is considered. This tax is levied against the net income figure of the corporation after deductions for interest expense but before dividends. Interest costs, therefore, reduce the amount of income against which the corporation must pay taxes, while dividends paid out by the corporation have no such effect. In our illustration, the federal corporate income tax would be levied against the entire $1,000,000 of the Low Leverage Operating Company, while the tax would be levied against the "after interest" figure of $840,000 for the High Leverage Operating Company. At the 1957 federal corporate income tax rate of 52 per cent, this would mean a tax saving of $83,200 (52 per cent of $160,000).

LIMITATIONS TO LONG-TERM DEBT FINANCING

The leverage effect of long-term corporate debt should be recognized as a two-edged weapon. Just as the percentage return to the stockholders is increased substantially during periods of profitable operations, so too the percentage return to stockholders is depressed during periods of low profits. During periods of low income, the fixed charges must be met irrespective of the effect on stockholders, even if it means ultimate liquidation of the business. The student may test the validity of this statement by determining the percentage return to the stockholders of the two companies in our illustration above if earnings before interest and dividends should fall to $200,000.

A study of the relationship of equity capital to borrowed capital for various types of businesses reveals a wide range of practice. Inasmuch as the obligations relating to borrowed capital are of a fixed nature, it is to be expected that if a corporation is wisely managed, fixed charges which would be difficult or impossible to meet during periods of unfavorable business experience will be avoided. Lenders, too, of course, try to avoid making loans that impose a dangerous financial burden on the borrower because of the possibility of loan default. In those industries that are subject to only minor economic fluctuations and reverses over the business cycle we generally find a greater use of borrowed capital than in those concerns that are subject to wide swings in cyclical experience. The utility companies that have relatively stable revenues can capitalize to a much larger extent through borrowed capital than do most industrial corporations.

INTERNAL CORPORATE FINANCING

No mention has been made of the benefit that a corporation derives from being able to retain earnings within the business rather than paying them out to the stockholders. Earnings so retained are not subject to personal income taxes as they are in the partnership and the proprietorship. Also, while corporations often make considerable effort to sustain their record of dividend payments, they also attempt to retain a portion of their earnings within the business to permit internal growth without being forced to secure funds from other sources. During periods when profits are high, as might be expected, corporations generally retain a larger percentage of their earnings than during periods when profits are low. In fact, one reason for so retaining earnings is to permit the establishment of reserves for the purpose of maintaining dividends during periods when earnings are not adequate. Only a very small part of the total earnings retained by corporations, however, are designated for this purpose; the bulk of the funds are used to build up permanently the asset structure of the company.

For the post-World War II years, 1946 through 1951, manufacturing corporations retained approximately three fifths of their after-tax profits. These retained earnings accounted for more than 43 per cent of the total sources of funds for manufacturing corporations in this period. By 1956, manufacturing corporations were in a position to pay out a larger proportion of their earnings, having accomplished their primary expansion of the postwar period. Retained earnings for 1956 provided approximately 25 per cent of the total sources of funds for manufacturing corporations.

Table 9-1 shows the sources and uses of new capital for all corporations except banks and insurance companies for 1956. Note that the combined amount of capital acquired by the corporations of the country through the public sale of stocks and bonds provided only 27.5 per cent of the total capital utilized for expansion purposes. Furthermore, the bulk of the funds utilized by the corporations came from two sources: retained earnings and depreciation reserve allowances. From the viewpoint of management, the retention of earnings by the corporation not only permits the stockholders to avoid paying a personal income tax on the dividends that would otherwise be distributed, but it also avoids the cost of public flotation of securities on the part of the corporation in accumulating additional capital.

Table 9–1

SOURCES AND USES OF CORPORATE FUNDS [1]
UNITED STATES, 1956

	BILLION DOLLARS	PER CENT OF TOTAL USES
Uses:		
Plant and equipment	$29.9	71.7%
Inventories	7.9	18.9%
Receivables	7.6	18.2%
Cash and U. S. Government securities	− 4.0	− 9.6%
Other current assets	.3	.8%
Total	$41.7	100.0%
Sources:		
Depreciation	$16.7	39.8%
Retained earnings (includes depletion)	8.1	19.3%
Net new issues:		
Bonds and other long-term debt	8.5	20.3%
Stocks	3.0	7.2%
Short-term debt	5.6	13.4%
Total	$41.9	100.0%
Discrepancy: [2]		
Uses less sources	$− .2	

SOURCE: U. S. Department of Commerce, Office of Business Economics, *Survey of Current Business*, September, 1957, p. 9.

[1] Excluding banks and insurance companies.
[2] The total funds used should equal the sources of financing; the small discrepancy is due to inadequacies in the estimating materials.

LONG-TERM FINANCING—AN EXAMPLE

In Figure 9-5 the long-term debt and equity capital section of the balance sheet of a large corporation is shown. The long-term debt capital consists of unsecured debenture bonds and notes; hence, the property of this firm is not under a special pledge or lien to any of its creditors. The reputation and general strength

Figure 9–5

LONG-TERM DEBT AND EQUITY CAPITAL

CELANESE CORPORATION OF AMERICA

(and domestic subsidiary companies)
December 31, 1956

Long-term debt (exclusive of amounts due
  within one year):

3% Debentures, due October 1, 1965 (semi-annual sinking fund requirements $1,000,000)	$ 24,000,000	
2.85% Debentures, due December 1, 1966 (semiannual sinking fund requirements $625,000)	16,188,000	
3½% Debentures, due October 1, 1976 (semi-annual sinking fund requirements $500,000, increasing to $1,000,000 on October 1, 1966)	48,428,000	
Notes payable to banks.....................	10,500,000	
Other notes, payable by a subsidiary—due 1958 to 1961............................	440,000	
Total long-term debt..................		$ 99,556,000

Preferred stocks

Preferred Stock, Series A (4½% cumulative, convertible), par value $100 per share—authorized and issued 1,000,000 shares)....	$100,000,000	
7% Second Preferred Stock (cumulative), par value $100 per share—authorized 148,179 shares; issued 35,708 shares, less 3,305 shares in treasury	3,240,300	
Total preferred stock..................		103,240,300

Equity of common stock

Common Stock—authorized 10,000,000 shares without par value; issued 5,844,954 shares.	$ 2,337,982	
Capital surplus	42,963,275	
Earned surplus	71,777,919	
Total common stock and surplus.......		117,079,176
TOTAL LONG-TERM DEBT AND EQUITY.....................		$319,875,476

SOURCE: Data taken from the Annual Report of the Celanese Corporation of America, 1956.

of this company is such that the investing public is willing to buy its debt instruments on an unsecured basis. Although there is no priority of claim between the various issues of debentures and notes, the rates of interest shown therefor differ to some extent. The prevailing level of interest rates in the investment market at the time each of these issues of securities were sold and the length of time each issue was to run account for the differing interest rates.

It should be observed that all three issues of the debentures require a regular and systematic retirement of the debt through sinking funds. The *sinking fund* provision requires the company to set aside regularly a certain sum for the purpose of retiring the outstanding bonds. Such sinking fund payments are generally paid to the trustee of the bond issue.

The preferred stock of the company consists of two issues. The Series A issue, which carries a dividend rate of 4½ per cent, is both cumulative and convertible. It is convertible into common stock at the conversion price of $55 per share of common stock and is callable at the option of the company at a price of $105 up to and including May 1, 1961, $102 thereafter to and including May 1, 1966, and $100 thereafter, plus accrued dividends. The 7 per cent Second Preferred Stock is not callable and the corporation has no choice but to maintain it or purchase the stock in the open market at current market prices. The 7 per cent Second Preferred Stock has a preference in liquidation of $100 per share plus unpaid cumulative dividends.

The equity of this company includes not only the common stock but also the capital surplus and earned surplus. Only a portion of the total authorized stock is now outstanding. The unissued common stock is being reserved for issuance at such time as the preferred stock may be converted and also for sale to officers and employees of the company. The capital surplus came into existence as a result of the sale of common stock at a price in excess of its stated value, and the earned surplus represents the accumulation of retained earnings.

QUESTIONS

1. Discuss the fundamental difference between equity capital and debt capital as it applies to corporate financing.
2. List the principal features of a stock certificate. How are such certificates transferred from person to person?
3. Discuss the characteristics of common stock as opposed to preferred stock.

4. (a) Why do corporations issue preferred stock? (b) Why would an investor invest in preferred stock? (c) Would you as an important stockholder in a corporation prefer to raise additional capital through the issue of preferred stock or common stock if either form of stock could be sold on favorable terms? (d) If the corporation should decide to issue and sell preferred stock for expansion purposes, what types of provisions would you as a common stockholder like to see included in the preferred stock issue? (e) As a prospective purchaser of the preferred stock, what provisions would you like to have included in the issue?

5. In such a state as Illinois, where all stock must have voting rights, why would a corporation ever classify its stock into Class A and Class B?

6. Distinguish between the types of corporate debt instruments.

7. What type of property is generally under lien in a mortgage bond issue?

8. Debenture bonds, although unsecured in a technical sense, are not necessarily insecure. Discuss.

9. List and explain the possible reasons for the use of long-term debt financing on the part of a corporation.

10. Explain and develop an illustration of the nature of trading on the equity in long-term corporate financing.

11. List as many industries as you can in which firms might well engage in trading on the equity to a substantial degree. In what types of industries would you expect to find little trading on the equity in long-term corporate financing?

12. Discuss the limitations to long-term corporate debt financing.

13. Discuss the relative importance of the various sources of long-term corporate financing.

SUGGESTED READINGS

BRADLEY, JOSEPH F. *Fundamentals of Corporation Finance.* New York: Rinehart & Company, Inc., 1953. Chapters 4 through 13.

DAUTEN, CARL A. *Business Finance*; Second Edition. Englewood Cliffs, New Jersey: Prentice-Hall, Inc., 1956. Chapters 4 and 9.

DEWING, ARTHUR STONE. *The Financial Policy of Corporations*; Fifth Edition. New York: The Ronald Press Company, 1953. Volume I, Chapters 3, 4, 6, 7, and 8.

GERSTENBERG, CHARLES W. *Financial Organization and Management of Business*; Third Revised Edition. Englewood Cliffs, New Jersey: Prentice-Hall, Inc., 1951. Chapters 4 through 8.

GUTHMANN, HARRY G., and DOUGALL, HERBERT E. *Corporate Financial Policy*; Third Edition. Englewood Cliffs, New Jersey: Prentice-Hall, Inc., 1955. Chapters 4 through 10.

HOWARD, BION B., and UPTON, MILLER. *Introduction to Business Finance.* New York: McGraw-Hill Book Company, Inc., 1953. Chapters 19 through 21.

Chapter 10

Investment Companies

and

Trust Institutions

Institutional investors, encouraged over the past twenty-five years by social and economic developments, have played an increasingly important role in financing the long-term capital needs of industry. Two of the institutions that have participated substantially in the growth of institutional long-term financing are the investment companies and the trust companies.

INVESTMENT COMPANIES

Investment companies engage principally in the purchase of stocks and bonds of other corporations. The investment company permits the pooling of funds of many investors on a share basis for the primary purpose of obtaining expert management and wide diversification of security investments. As of December 31, 1957, members of the National Association of Investment Companies held total assets, consisting primarily of stocks and bonds, of approximately $10.5 billion. Furthermore, the number and the size of the investment companies have been increasing rapidly in recent years.

Development of Investment Companies

Forerunners of the modern investment company existed in the United States during the early part of the 19th century when insurance companies, in addition to their insurance activities, accepted deposits from individuals for the purpose of professional administration of these funds. Following World War I the tremendous growth of the industrial component of the nation's economy and the interest in stock-market activity in general gave support for the first time to large-scale development of the investment companies. Such companies in the United States were both the victim and the cause of the speculative excesses in the securities market that existed during the 1920's, much like the situation which had developed at the close of the 19th century in Great Britain. Following the depression of the 1930's, the investment companies, strengthened by the introduction of a new form of operation, again attracted public attention and began to increase in numbers and to grow in strength.

A close resemblance may be observed between the modern-day savings and loan associations, the mutual savings banks, and the investment companies, in that they all pool the savings of the public, provide professional investment management for such savings, and diversify investments. In contrast with the savings and loan association and mutual savings banks, however, funds of investment companies may be invested in equity shares as well as debt instruments in order to provide an increased income for the investor. The depositor or the holder of shares in a mutual savings bank or savings and loan association has a return based entirely upon the yield of real-estate mortgages, governmental obligations, and other fixed income securities.

Many of our present-day investment companies represent an outgrowth of businesses originally established for other purposes. For example, in 1952 both the Electric Bond and Share Company and The United Corporation, having been ordered by the Securities and Exchange Commission to divest themselves of their utility holdings, stated their intention to become investment companies.[1] Until that time these companies had operated as public-utility holding companies. The Adams Express Company, organized in 1854, disposed of its express business to the American Railway Express Company in 1918, and has conducted business as an investment company since that time.

Classification of Investment Companies

Because of the lack of common understanding of the nature of various types of investment companies, the Securities and

---

[1] *Annual Report of the Securities and Exchange Commission*, 1952, pp. 87, 94, 103.

Exchange Commission was authorized to conduct an investigation of these organizations. As a result, the Commission presented a detailed classification of these companies. Of primary interest for our purposes is the distinction drawn between those investment companies that operate for the purpose of influencing or controlling the companies in which they invest, classified as *management investment holding companies* by the SEC, and the companies that invest for the primary purpose of securing diversification and yield, classified as *management investment companies*. We are primarily concerned with the latter classification in this chapter.

The legal form of organization taken by most investment companies today is either the corporation or the business trust. The company issues securities either for public distribution or for sale to selected individuals and in turn invests the proceeds in the securities of other companies. Although the trend is for investment companies to issue a single class of common stock for sale to the public, some companies have sold bonds and preferred stock as well.

Investment companies are classified also into the fixed trust type, the closed-end fund type, and the open-end fund type. Although all three types have the common objective of securing intelligent diversification for the pooled funds of individuals, the methods by which this objective is accomplished differ to a considerable degree.

The Fixed Trust Investment Company. *The fixed trust investment company* operates with a fixed trust fund, which involves an initial selection of a group of securities that are deposited in trust for a fixed number of years. Against this fund are issued shares that remain outstanding for the duration of the trust. Fixed trusts may consist entirely of common stocks of companies of a single type, such as oil stocks, motor stocks, or railroad stocks. Other fixed trusts may have a diversification of investment, including not only diversification with respect to industries but also with respect to type of security, that is, common stocks, preferred stocks, and bonds.

The fixed trust arrangement was particularly popular during the twenties when there was confidence in the future of common stocks in general. Well-chosen stocks of strong companies were expected to become more and more valuable, and it appeared to be unnecessary to provide for the continuous re-evaluation of such securities. Since the twenties, however, experience has revealed the importance of continuing attention to the position of each individual stock.

Investment companies of the management type dispose of the securities of companies whose prospects have become less favorable, replacing such investments with the securities of other companies whose positions are strong. The continuous purchase and sale of securities by an investment company, based on exhaustive analysis of the position of the securities market in general and of each individual security, is referred to as *portfolio management.* Because of the fixed trust's lack of portfolio management, it has become relatively unimportant as a form of investment company and only a very small number of such funds have been established in recent years. Although the volume of assets of fixed trusts is not available, the Securities and Exchange Commission reports that there were 79 such funds registered with the Commission as of June 30, 1956.[2]

The Closed-End Investment Company. In contrast with the fixed trust, the *closed-end fund investment company* places great emphasis on portfolio management. Ordinarily, the securities issued by a closed-end fund are sold at one time and additional securities seldom are issued. The total asset value of the closed-end fund increases only through the appreciation in the market value of the securities that it holds or through the retention of a small proportion of the earnings obtained by the company. The holder of the securities of a closed-end fund may liquidate his investment much as the holder of a security in any corporation may do so, that is, through the sale of the securities to other investors.

Bonds and preferred stocks, as well as common stocks, may be issued by the closed-end fund company. The holders of these senior securities have the same relative priority to earnings as the holder of senior securities in any organization. The bonds issued by the closed-end fund, however, seldom represent a claim against specific securities held by the fund, but rather take the debenture form. The holders of the debenture bonds of the closed-end funds, therefore, have only a general claim against the assets of the com-

[2] *Annual Report of the Securities and Exchange Commission,* 1956, p. 182.

pany. This arrangement makes possible the frequent sale and purchase of securities by the investment company without the necessity of securing a release of pledged collateral, as would be required if secured bonds were issued against the portfolio of securities. The closed-end investment funds that have outstanding senior securities as well as common stock, provide earnings leverage in the same way that leverage is provided by operating companies. An added leverage effect, however, may be obtained through investment companies that hold the common stock of operating companies that have financed their own long-term requirements in part through bonds and preferred stock. An example of this double-leverage effect is shown in Figure 10-1. It should be remembered that just as leverage works to the disadvantage of common stockholders when earnings are low, double leverage makes that disadvantage much more severe.

Like the fixed trust fund, the closed-end fund enjoyed its greatest popularity during the twenties and has since derived its importance from the continuation of its activities begun earlier. As of June 30, 1956, there were 106 closed-end funds registered with the Securities and Exchange Commission.[3] Closed-end investment companies that were members of the National Association of Investment Companies had total assets of $1.3 billion on December 31, 1957.

The Open-End Fund Investment Company. The *open-end fund investment companies*, commonly referred to as mutual funds, are of American origin. In contrast with closed-end funds they generally offer only a single class of shares to investors. These shares, held by the public, may be returned to the company for redemption at any time. The by-laws or trust agreement of the investment company provides for the redemption of such shares at the liquidation or net asset value of the investment company. Hence, the price at which shares tendered for redemption to an investment company will be redeemed depends upon the market value of the securities held by the investment company. New shares are offered to the public continuously. The price of these new shares is determined, as is true for shares that are being redeemed, by the current value of the securities held by the investment company.

[3] *Ibid.*

Figure 10-1

HIGH-LEVERAGE OPERATING COMPANY

BALANCE SHEET

ASSETS		LIABILITIES AND CAPITAL	
Current Assets	$ 7,000,000	Bonds @ 4%	$ 4,000,000
Fixed Assets	3,000,000	Common Stock	6,000,000
		Total Liab. &	
Total Assets	$10,000,000	Capital	$10,000,000

* Earnings $1,000,000 before interest and dividends (all earnings paid out)

Bondholders receive $160,000 (4% of $4,000,000)
Common Stockholders receive $840,000 ($1,000,000 less bond interest)

Return to Common Stockholders expressed as a per cent 14% ($840,000 ÷ $6,000,000)

Had this company been financed entirely through common stock, the rate of return would have been 10%. The leverage gain is 4% of total assets.

HIGH-LEVERAGE INVESTMENT COMPANY

BALANCE SHEET

INVESTMENTS		LIABILITIES AND CAPITAL	
Common stock of high-leverage operating company	$2,000,000	Bonds @ 4%	$1,000,000
		Common Stock	1,000,000
Total Assets	$2,000,000	Total Liab. & Cap.	$2,000,000

* Earnings on common stock of operating company $280,000 ($2,000,000 @ 14%)

Bondholders receive $ 40,000 (4% of $1,000,000)
Common Stockholders receive $240,000 ($280,000 earnings less interest)

Return to Common Stockholders expressed as a per cent 24% ($240,000 ÷ $1,000,000)

Had both of these companies been financed entirely with common stock, the return to common stockholders of both companies would have been 10%. The gain to investment company stockholders as a result of the double leverage is 14% of the investment company's assets.

* For purposes of simplification, tax matters have been ignored.

The shares of the open-end funds are generally sold at a price that includes a selling charge of from 7 to 9 per cent with a prevailing average for all companies of about 8 per cent. This means that the purchase of shares having a market value of $1,000 would require an additional fee or premium of approximately $80. As larger volumes of shares are purchased, the selling charge as a percentage of the purchase price is reduced accordingly.

Because the shares of the open-end funds are redeemable with the company, they are not listed on the exchanges. It is unnecessary to find other buyers for the shares when they can be promptly and easily redeemed by the investment company itself. In order to know the price at which shares should be redeemed or sold, the investment company must calculate at frequent intervals the total value of its portfolio of securities. Usually a formula that gives due weight to the amount of securities held in the different companies makes possible a quick and ready calculation of the total value of the portfolio. The legal form of organization taken by the open-end fund is generally that of the corporation or the business trust.

Open-end funds may differ radically with respect to objectives of management. In some cases, an extremely conservative portfolio is maintained, comprised largely of high-grade fixed-income senior securities of well-known companies. In other cases, the objective is to maximize the profits to be obtained through the purchase and sale of securities during changes in the market. Then, the bulk of the fund's investments is placed in common stocks. Between these extremes fall the objective of obtaining a somewhat above-average yield combined with reasonable stability of market value. This type of company objective is generally described as a "balanced-fund operation." Such portfolios generally include both bonds and stocks of leading companies.

For convenience and safety, a custodian is appointed to hold the assets of the fund. The duties of the custodian include safekeeping as well as the acquisition or disposition of specified securities upon instruction by the management of the fund. Custodians chosen by the open-end investment companies are generally banking institutions. The custodian may also be given the responsibility of serving as transfer agent or registrar. The *transfer agent* is generally responsible for the cancellation of old certificates tendered for redemption, the issuance of new shares, and the distribution of dividends at regular intervals.

The Riggs National Bank of Washington was appointed custodian of funds and assets for the Washington Mutual Investor's Fund, Inc. This Fund, which began operations in 1952, also appointed the American Security and Trust Company of Washington, D. C., as the transfer and dividend-disbursing agent. By delegating these responsibilities, the management of the fund has more time to devote to the management of the fund's portfolio and to the problems of distribution of the securities. Just as the details relative to the holding and transfer of the fund's assets may be delegated, however, so too may the investment-analysis and management tasks be assigned to others. For example, the fund just mentioned has contracted with the Capital Research and Management Company of Los Angeles, Detroit, and New York to render management service for the fund. The immediate management of the Washington Mutual Investor's Fund, Inc., is devoted primarily to the matter of promotion of the fund and to the distribution of the fund's securities.

The Washington Mutual Investor's Fund, Inc., like many open-end funds, is sponsored by an investment banking firm. This fund is therefore afforded the benefits of an established distributive system for the sale of its securities.

Other open-end investment funds have come into being through the efforts of research and management firms. Examples of this type of development are the Eaton and Howard Balanced Fund, which is sponsored by Eaton and Howard, Inc., investment managers; and the Scudder, Stevens & Clark Fund, Inc., sponsored by the investment management firm of Scudder, Stevens & Clark. Eaton and Howard Balanced Fund was established as a trust form of organization in which five trustees were appointed for the purpose of employing the managers, the custodian, and the transfer agent. Scudder, Stevens & Clark Fund, Inc., utilizes the typical corporate arrangement. The charge ordinarily made by the investment management firm for counsel given to the mutual funds ranges from $1/8$ of 1 per cent to $1/2$ of 1 per cent of the net asset value of the fund per year, depending upon the range of services provided.

As of June 30, 1956, there were 201 open-end funds registered with the Securities and Exchange Commission.[4] Open-end investment companies that were members of the National Association of Investment Companies had total assets of $9.2 billion as of December 31, 1957.

Tax Status of Investment Companies

Under the Revenue Act of 1936, corporations are subject to a tax on the dividends they receive. Strictly applied, this tax would make it almost impossible for investment companies to function in their present form, since it would mean triple taxation: taxation first of the operating corporation, again when the investment company receives its dividends or interest, and finally when these profits are distributed to the holders of the shares of the investment company. A special supplement (Supplement Q) to the Revenue Act of 1936, however, provides that under certain circumstances investment companies are considered as mere conduits through which earnings of a corporation flow to the ultimate shareholders of the investment companies. In order to be so regarded as a conduit for the flow of money, the investment company must register with the Securities and Exchange Commission and otherwise qualify as a *regulated investment company.* The regulated investment company is exempted from federal corporate income taxes on earnings distributed to shareholders.

Relative Popularity of Investment Funds

As indicated earlier, the fixed-trust fund and the closed-end fund enjoyed their primary popularity during the twenties. Since that time, the open-end funds have almost completely dominated the investment company field as far as the establishment of new companies is concerned. The growth of the open-end funds has in fact been so rapid as to make them a subject of popular discussion throughout the financial world. *The New York Journal of Commerce* and *Barron's* weekly have added special sections to their publications devoted entirely to the affairs of open-end funds. Some states now permit savings banks and fiduciaries to invest in the shares of some of the mutual funds.

[4] *Ibid.*

Economic Significance of the Investment Companies

In comparison with the $46 billion invested by savings and loan associations, the $34 billion invested by mutual savings banks, and the more than $98 billion of assets of life insurance companies at midyear, 1957, the assets of the investment companies appear to be rather small. However, the assets of the savings and loan associations are invested primarily in real-estate mortgages, the assets of the mutual savings banks also are alloted heavily to real-estate mortgages as well as high-grade corporate and government bonds, and the life insurance companies also have a primary interest in high-grade fixed-income investments. In contrast with the pattern of investment of these financial institutions, the investment companies provide a substantial amount of equity capital to the business establishments of the nation.

In 1949, the President's Council of Economic Advisors suggested that the development of the open-end funds offered a possible solution to what they considered to be the equity-capital problem prevailing at that time. It is also interesting to note that the open-end funds, through wide publicity and distributive effort, have extended the degree of securities market participation on the part of the general public. A study completed in 1949 revealed that the average value of shares held per individual was approximately $2,000. In the reports that have been submitted by some open-end funds and through one general survey of the field, there is some indication that women shareholders predominate in this type of company. A special study by Arthur Wiesenberger & Co. of shares of investment companies sold between 1946 and 1948 revealed that approximately 69 per cent of all the shares sold were in geographical areas which accounted for only 31 per cent of the volume of trading on the New York Stock Exchange. This indicates a broadening of the market for securities.

TRUST INSTITUTIONS

Trust institutions administer and control large amounts of wealth and account for a significant portion of all securities purchased. A *trust institution* serves in a fiduciary capacity for the administration or disposition of assets, or for the performance of specified acts for the beneficiaries of the trust arrangement. A *fiduciary*, in turn, is one who acts in a capacity of trust and undivided loyalty for another. It implies integrity and fidelity of the person or institution trusted, and it contemplates good faith rather than legal obligation as the dominant basis for transactions.

In this chapter we are concerned primarily with trust institutions rather than with individual trustees, but it was not until approximately one hundred years ago that the institutional form of trustee became important. In earlier times these duties were performed primarily by family friends or attorneys. With the growth of the country and the increased complexity of legal and financial matters, however, it is becoming increasingly difficult to find individuals who are capable of administering properly the matters required of trustees. The amount of trust business administered by individuals in the United States at the present time is of minor importance relative to that undertaken by such institutional trustees as trust companies and trust departments of banks.

Advantages of Institutional Trustees over Individual Trustees

Many small trusts or trusts of a very personal nature are well suited for administration by individuals as trustees. For most trusts, however, the institutional trustee offers important advantages. These advantages relate to the matters of convenience, permanence, experience, responsibility, and regulation.

Convenience. Persons served by a trust company or trust department know exactly when they may have access to the facilities of the company. Regular hours of business are specified, and the individual is never inconvenienced because of unexpected lack of availability of trust facilities.

Permanence. In contrast with the individual trustee, the trust company or trust department has a continuity of existence that is not interrupted by the death of a single member of the establishment. Sudden death of an individual trustee may bring about substantial inconvenience to the parties to a trust agreement.

Experience. Because of the specialization that institutional trustees may achieve, a high degree of competence is to be expected. The trust institution is able to employ persons with many divergent professional specialities, making it possible to serve completely the needs of the person whose assets are placed in trust.

Responsibility. The institutional trustee will generally provide greater financial responsibility and larger financial resources than will the individual trustee. Also, trust companies and trust departments must make every effort to uphold their standards of operation and reputation.

Regulation. Corporate trustees are subject to strict regulation. This regulation is exercised in many different ways, depending upon the form or type of organization in which the trust duties have been established. For the individual trustee, there is only an accountability at the end of the fiscal period or at the termination of the trust for the funds so entrusted. Individuals are not required to be licensed nor are they supervised except to the extent just mentioned.[5]

Forms of Trust Institutions

Most of the estimated 2,900 corporations actively engaged in the trust business of the United States are also engaged in the banking business. This is accounted for by the fact that the experiences and skills required for banking and trust work are very much the same. Nearly half of all the corporations engaged in the trust business are national banks that operate trust departments. State chartered banks having trust departments account for most of the remaining institutional trustees. In addition, a few independent trust companies are engaged solely in the trust business. Also, trust business is carried on by other organizations of a nonbanking nature, such as title companies, property insurance companies, and real estate firms. Finally, a few corporate trust institutions operate as affiliates of banks. The banks may own the trust company or the trust company may own the bank. In other circumstances, the stock of both the trust company and the bank may be owned by a holding company.

It is estimated that no more than 100 firms are represented by those corporate trustees not also engaged one way or another in

---

[5] James B. Trant, *Bank Administration* (New York: McGraw-Hill Book Company, 1931), p. 304.

banking activities.[6] Most banks that provide trust services include the words "and Trust Company" in the corporate title. In some cases, "and Trust Company" may be found to accompany the title even though the bank has ceased to offer trust services. Although the total volume of assets held by trust institutions is not available, an indication of the importance of these institutions is given by the Comptroller of the Currency of the United States Treasury Department in his 1956 annual report. As of December 31, 1956, the total trust assets of national banks was $39 billion. Since national banks account for slightly less than one half of all institutions engaged in trust services, it is apparent that the total assets of all trust institutions is much greater than the above figure.

Classification of Trusts

Trusts may be classified according to their functions. These functions may be broadly grouped between those of a personal trust nature and those of a corporate trust nature. Under both classifications, the functions are of tremendous importance to the financial structure of the economy in that they involve the transfer and the management of huge sums of wealth or the provision of services that make possible the administration of such wealth on the part of others. The personal trust is established for the direct benefit of one or more persons, while the corporate trust exists to handle certain affairs of corporations.

Personal Trust Business

Personal trust business is confined largely to the care of assets included in trust estates and to settling estates of deceased persons. The three principal types of personal trusts are living trusts, trusteeships under will, and insurance trusts.

Living Trusts. In recent years there has been a tremendous increase in the number of living trusts. The increasing popularity of the living trust arrangement is due to many factors. In the first place, it provides a convenient means of providing a reasonably assured income for a person's family without immediately conveying the property to the family. Under these circumstances, the

---

[6] Gilbert Thomas Stephenson, *Estates and Trusts* (New York: Appleton-Century-Crofts, Inc., 1949), p. 362.

beneficiary of the trust, who may be a widow or a minor child, will receive only the income from the trust principal during the term of the trust. The principal itself is conveyed to the beneficiary only upon the happening of some specified event set forth in the trust agreement. The trust agreement is often used by persons of advanced age who have reason to doubt their continuing ability to manage their financial affairs. In other cases, trusts may be established for the benefit of minor children or for persons who are incapable of managing their affairs for reasons of physical disability or mental incompetence. A businessman may establish a trust that will provide a reasonably comfortable income for a specified period of years to protect against undue hardship that might result from a particularly risky business venture.

Under the laws of most states, living trusts can be either revocable, irrevocable, or something in between that may be referred to as short-term trusts. As the term implies, a *revocable trust* is one in which the maker of the trust has the right to revoke the trust arrangement after its creation. Such an agreement makes it possible to plan the transfer of assets and reduces the time required in passing the property to the beneficiaries at the time of death of the maker of the trust. Also probate expenses may be reduced and the publicity of a will avoided.

An *irrevocable trust,* on the other hand, provides for the complete and final transfer of assets to the trustee. In addition to the advantages cited for the revocable trust, the irrevocable trust may involve substantial tax advantages. As a rule, the maker of the trust can free himself from taxation on the income from the assets transferred to the trust institution. In addition, the property in trust usually escapes estate taxes upon the death of the maker of the trust. The maker of such a trust must pay a gift tax when the trust is established, but the rate on gift taxes is approximately 25 per cent lower than that on estate taxes.

The irrevocable trust, because of its fixed and definite nature, presents some disadvantages also. First, the maker of the trust may be so tax-economy minded that he may dispossess himself of an unduly large proportion of his assets, making him dependent upon the beneficiaries of the trust for his care. In other cases, an increase in the general cost of living may leave the beneficiaries of the trust with too little income for their needs since trustees place primary emphasis on safety of principal in the administration of trust funds. Such a policy of trust administration generally provides a steady but rather low yield on trust investments.

A *short-term trust* represents a compromise between the revocable and irrevocable trust. In brief, it is an irrevocable trust established for a specified number of years. The reason for the establishment of the short-term trust is often for tax purposes. If the trust meets all of the requirements of the tax laws, the maker is free of tax on the income derived from the assets while the trust exists, assuming such income is paid to a person or institution other than the maker of the trust; and at the end of the trust term, the maker of the trust gets back his assets that have been placed in trust. Short-term trusts can be used for many purposes, such as the support of parents, contributions to charities, the accumulation of an estate for one's family, or carrying insurance on some other person's life.

Trusteeships Under Will. The trusteeship under will represents a second major classification of personal trust business. For the person who prefers that his estate be maintained and administered for the benefit of the heirs rather than be turned over to the heirs directly, a *testamentary trust* may be established. The person establishing such a trust is reasonably assured that his beneficiaries will be properly cared for and at the same time will be protected against acts of irresponsibility with respect to administration of the estate. A trust institution may be designated as the executor in a will. The duties of the executor are, of course, to handle the estate with respect to the accountability of all the assets, liquidating all of those assets of a perishable nature, paying all debts including tax claims that may exist against the estate, and distributing the assets of the estate in accordance with the provisions of the will. The trust institution may also act as administrator, guardian, or conservator under court appointment.

Insurance Trusts. The *insurance trust* represents a third classification of personal trust business. These trusts come into existence through the voluntary act of placing in trust one or more insurance policies with an agreement that the proceeds of the insurance will be paid to the trust institution upon the death of the maker of the trust. The trust institution is then, as a rule, bound by the terms of the agreement to administer the benefits of the insurance policies for the specified beneficiaries of the trust. Such an arrangement is generally provided when the maker of the trust has reason to doubt the ability of the beneficiary to handle properly the large sum of money that would otherwise accrue to him under the terms of the life insurance policy.

The maker of the trust may deposit along with the life insurance policies a group of securities, the income from which will maintain the premiums on the policies. Although most life insurance policies permit the policyholder to specify the manner in which benefits from the policy are to be distributed to beneficiaries, the individual may prefer to concentrate all of his policies under the supervision of a single trustee. Not all life insurance companies have the facilities for distributing benefits of a policy in the form of periodic payments, in which case it becomes necessary to establish a trust if such a distribution of policy benefits is desired.

Investment Policies of Trust Institutions

State laws that apply to the administration of trust funds are many and varied and are generally considered to be very restrictive. In addition to the law, the terms of the trust agreement itself may establish restrictive limitations on the trustee's management of the assets placed in trust. Traditionally, trust institutions have been required to limit the investment of assets placed in their trust to a mandatory legal list prepared by the state. Such a list includes only high-grade bonds and other designated forms of fixed-income investments. Only a few states continue to impose restrictions of this nature on trust institutions. Most states now follow what is referred to as the *prudent-man rule,* which requires that a trust institution be held responsible for the same degree of judgment that a prudent man would be expected to exercise in investing his own funds. This rule, therefore, represents a substantial liberalization from the legal-list concept.

Several states have taken an intermediate position between the legal-list and prudent-man-rule policies by permitting trust institutions to invest only a portion of their trust assets according to the prudent-man rule. This remainder of the assets must be invested in the securities included on the legal list published by the state.

Generally, the proportion of assets permitted in these states for investment under the prudent-man-rule concept is less than half. Investment in highly speculative securities would obviously be barred as a possibility under the prudent-man rule since the primary objective in any event, with respect to the administration of the trust assets, is the preservation of the estate and the earning of a reasonable yield. Many trust institutions operating in prudent-man-rule states have increased yields to beneficiaries by adding high-grade corporate stocks to their portfolios.

The Common Trust Fund

Of particular importance to the administration of trust assets was the modification of the law to permit national banks to comingle the trust funds of their customers. Since one of the long-established legal principles required that assets of separate trusts should not be mingled, this represented a major step or modification in trust administration activities. Amendments to the federal tax laws were also necessary in order that income from such invested assets would not be taxed first as income to the trust institution and again to the individuals named as beneficiaries.

Although the assets invested under the common-trust-fund plan are subject to the same regulatory limitations as the investment of individual trust assets, substantial advantages are offered both to the trust institution and to the beneficiaries. One primary advantage is that the common trust fund makes it possible for trust institutions to solicit smaller trusts. Principal amounts of only a few thousand dollars, placed under control of the trust institution under common trust agreement, receive the same competent supervision as much larger trusts. Costs are reduced and better diversification is obtained through the common-trust arrangement than is possible for the individual handling of assets for small trusts. Total assets of the comingled trusts are administered under the centralized supervision of the investment department of the trust department. The common trust fund was established, as a matter of fact, primarily for the benefit of the smaller trusts. This is evidenced by the fact that originally under the regulations of the Federal Reserve System the maximum amount of any single trust which could be placed in a common trust fund was $25,000. This was raised in 1945 to $50,000, and later to $100,000.

Several trust companies offer three separate common trust funds. One of the funds will ordinarily have all of its assets invested in bonds, the second fund will have all of its assets in common stocks, and the third fund will have its assets in both bonds and common stocks. The person establishing the trust, therefore, may choose between a fund with emphasis primarily on stability of principal as opposed to a fund with higher income and appreciation possibilities. Ordinarily a person may invest up to $100,000 in each of these funds without violating the limitations on amount established by federal regulations. Under this arrangement of multiple common trust funds the similarity to the operations of investment companies is readily apparent.

In addition to the common-trust-fund-operations of national banks, as of December 31, 1956, forty-seven states had authorized state-chartered corporations engaged in trust business to operate common trust funds. At that time there were 243 common trust funds in the United States operated by 195 trust institutions in 40 states, the District of Columbia, and the Territory of Hawaii. Total assets administered under the common-trust-fund arrangement totaled approximately $2 billion. Approximately 50 per cent of the assets of common trust funds were in the form of common stock, 11 per cent in preferred stock, and the remainder in United States obligations and corporate bonds.[7]

Trust Services for Corporations

One of the principal forms of trust service provided for corporations is that of *trusteeship under indenture*. This form of trusteeship was referred to in an earlier chapter under the description of the Trust Indenture Act of 1939. There it was explained that under the provisions of the Act, a trustee of a registered company, among other things, was required to be corporate in form, to have no less than the specified minimum of capital and surplus, and that there be no conflict of interest between the corporation issuing the securities and the investing public. Trust service for corporations is an important phase of the trust business since under the law all corporations subject to regulation by the Securities and Exchange Commission must seek the services of trust corporations.

---

[7] *Federal Reserve Bulletin*, June, 1957, Board of Governors of the Federal Reserve System, Washington, D. C., pp. 622 through 625.

The duties of the trust institution, when serving in a capacity of trusteeship under indenture, generally involves the holding of the mortgage against which bonds are issued by the corporation and the enforcement and accountability of all provisions relating to the mortgage. In addition, trustees under these circumstances may also handle the registration and transfer of ownership of registered securities, may enforce or supervise the insurance requirements that are established in the mortgage, may execute various releases, and may supervise the administration of sinking funds that may be provided in the mortgage.

As described in connection with the establishment of an investment company, trust institutions serve corporations as transfer agents to handle the details relating to the issuance and recording of stock and as dividend disbursing agents to avoid the details relating to the distribution of dividends. Trust institutions may also serve corporations as registrars. Many of the stock exchanges require that corporations having stock listed on their exchanges maintain separate registrars and transfer agents. The registrar's responsibility, among other things, involves supervision over issuance of new stock of the corporation in order that the corporation will not issue more stock than is authorized by the charter. The transfer agent and the registrar, therefore, provide an effective check on the operations of the other and assure the security holder that his interests are being responsibly administered.

In the event of corporate reorganization, it is customary for creditors, pending the final reorganization, to deposit bonds and other credit instruments with a corporate trustee. In return, the depositors of these securities are given transferable certificates of deposit. The property of a corporation in bankruptcy is generally conveyed to a trust institution, which provides, if necessary, for the liquidation and the disbursing of funds to the creditors of the corporation.

Trust institutions maintain safe-deposit facilities, administer security holdings, provide complete records of all security transactions, make monthly reports to customers, and provide investment counsel. The numerous additional services provided by trust institutions for corporations cannot be covered in this text. Further reference, however, is made to trust activities later in this part in connection with corporate financing through the use of equipment trust obligations and in connection with pension funds.

QUESTIONS

1. Describe the development of investment companies in the United States.

2. Identify the principal differences between investment companies and other savings institutions such as mutual savings banks and savings and loan associations.

3. Distinguish between the three principal types of investment companies. Compare their present relative popularity.

4. Although closed-end investment companies usually sell no additional securities after their initial authorization of securities has been distributed, many such companies have increased substantially in size as measured by the value of their assets. Explain.

5. Closed-end investment companies may trade on the equity in financing their operations in much the same manner as do operating companies. The earnings leverage obtained by such trading on the equity for the closed-end investment company, however, has a special significance. Explain.

6. Explain how the price of open-end investment company shares is determined in contrast with closed-end investment company shares.

7. The price at which a share of an open-end investment company may be purchased differs from the price at which the share may be redeemed with the company. Explain.

8. Describe the tax status of investment companies.

9. Explain the advantage of institutional trustees over individual trustees.

10. Identify the types of institutions that may engage in trust activities.

11. Describe three situations in which one of the forms of living trust would be appropriate.

12. Explain why the irrevocable trust arrangement is utilized since it removes control over trust assets by the maker of the trust.

13. Explain the operation of insurance trusts.

14. Discuss the significance of a trust institution's investment of funds under the legal-list limitation as opposed to the prudent-man rule.

15. Explain the development and significance of the common trust fund.

16. Describe the principal trust services provided for corporations.

SUGGESTED READINGS

PROCHNOW, HERBERT V. (ed.). *American Financial Institutions*. Englewood Cliffs, New Jersey: Prentice-Hall, Inc., 1951. Chapter 16 by Douglas H. Bellemore.

ROBBINS, SIDNEY M. *Managing Securities*. New York: Houghton Mifflin Company, 1954. Chapters 33 and 34.

STEPHENSON, GILBERT THOMAS. *Estates and Trusts*. New York: Appleton-Century-Crofts, Inc., 1949. Chapters 6 through 8.

WEISSMAN, RUDOLPH LEO. *The Investment Company and the Investor*. New York: Harper & Brothers, 1951.

Insurance Companies

The basic purpose of insurance is to establish a degree of certainty with respect to the plans and activities of individuals and institutions. This certainty is provided not through the elmination of the hazards that face the insured but by providing protection against financial loss that may result from such hazards. It is true, however, that insurance companies have done much to reduce the perils of both business and personal life through such activities as accident, health, fire prevention, and driver education. Aside from the financial aspects of insurance, many other benefits are observable. For example, the peace of mind and feeling of security that is derived from the knowledge that one's property and life are insured adequately may contribute in a significant way to the individual's effectiveness in his work as well as to the condition of his health. It is with the financial aspects of insurance, however, that we are primarily concerned in this chapter.

FINANCIAL ASPECTS OF INSURANCE

For purposes of this book, the contributions of insurance companies to the financial affairs of the nation may be broadly classified into two groups: first, a source of capital for business and government; and second, a provider of direct benefits to the insured. With respect to the provision of capital for business and government, the insurance companies serve in three ways: (1) they encourage saving by individuals; (2) they accumulate and invest vast sums of money through the normal course of their business operations; and (3) they provide a basis for the extension of credit on the part of other lenders.

(1) Encourage Saving

Most types of life insurance policies provide for a combination of insurance and savings programs. Periodic payments to the insurance company include both a fee for insurance protection and a contribution toward the savings element or cash value of the contract. The advantage for many people of an insurance contract that combines a savings program with insurance protection lies in the fact that the insured forms the habit of budgeting out of his income regular payments to the company. It is possible, of course, to contribute to a savings plan outside of the life insurance contract, but the individual may omit payments to his savings plan from time to time or he may simply abandon the plan altogether. The stability of an individual's savings program gained through an insurance contract stems from the attitude of individuals in meeting their payments of insurance premiums. Many people regard their insurance payments as a debt obligation. Under these circumstances policies are not allowed to lapse and the accompanying savings programs abandoned except under unusual circumstances. For many people the sole claim to cash savings involves accumulations of cash reserves in their life insurance policies.

(2) Accumulate and Invest Funds

The funds accumulated by the life insurance companies through their necessary reserves have reached tremendous proportions. These funds, which are paid to the companies by millions of individual policyholders, are reinvested by the insurance companies in many types of business organizations which, in turn, use the funds for constructing buildings and acquiring equipment, and for other business uses. Such financing results in increased productivity for the businesses in particular and for the over-all economy in general. Insurance companies also invest large sums of money in residential mortgages and government bonds.

(3) Basis for Credit

The lender of money is able to reduce some of the risk involved in the lending process through the use of various forms of insurance. To the extent that his risks are reduced, the lender is encouraged to increase his volume of lending activities. For example, it is important to the residential mortgage lender that properties on which loans are made be adequately insured against damage due to such things as fire and windstorm that might reduce the value of the property to less than the amount of the outstanding loan against the property. Institutions financing the sale of automobiles always require that the automobiles be insured until the indebtedness is completely retired. When a loan is to be made to an organization whose prosperity and continued operation are dependent upon the talents and efforts of one person, the lender may insist that the business maintain insurance on the life of that person with the lender designated as beneficiary. In these and many other instances, insurance contributes to the flow of credit between lender and borrower.

CLASSIFICATION OF INSURANCE

The field of insurance is a broad one, encompassing nearly every phase of our national economy. Most people think of insurance in terms of the type of policy that is purchased to protect income or property and which is purchased from private companies. However, our vast structure of old-age and survivor's insurance and employment security insurance, as well as many other forms of insurance administered by the federal government or by the state governments, is also part of the national pattern of insurance coverage. We may, therefore, divide the field of insurance broadly into that of public or government insurance and that of private insurance. In this chapter only the private insurance plans will be considered. These plans may be classified as personal insurance and property insurance.

Personal insurance includes all arrangements whereby the risk of loss of earning power as a result of death, accident, sickness, or retirement is avoided or reduced through insurance contracts. These contracts may be classified as life insurance and accident and sickness insurance.

LIFE INSURANCE

One of the most important functions of life insurance is that of providing an immediate estate for the dependents of the head of a household in the event that he dies before sufficient personal fortune has been accumulated to provide for his dependents. Where the amount of life insurance is quite small, the objective may be that of a "clean-up fund" which will defray the last medical expenses and the cost of the funeral and other costs incident to the death of the insured.

Life insurance may also play an important role in business affairs. For example, where the business organization is a partnership, it is frequently desirable to insure the lives of the partners and to specify the other members of the partnership as the beneficiaries. This arrangement permits the survivors in a partnership to buy the interests of the heirs of a deceased member without serious cash drain on the business. A businessman may carry life insurance for the purpose of settling business debts that may exist at the time of his death; and finally life insurance provides a means of minimizing the drain on an individual's estate as a result of death taxes imposed upon his business assets at his death.

Types of Life Insurance

The many applications of life insurance to special requirements and situations requires the availability of a wide variety of types of policies. The principal types of contracts sold by life insurance companies are term insurance, whole-life insurance, endowment insurance, and annuities.

Term Insurance. The basic feature of *term life insurance* is that the policy is issued for a specified period of time after which time no obligation exists on the part of the insurance company toward the insured. During the period of the insurance contract, however, the insured is entitled to protection to the extent of the face amount of the policy. Term life insurance policies are usually issued for one, five, ten, or twenty years.

The National Service Life Insurance policies issued during World War II by the United States Government to members of the armed services were of a term nature. Provision has since been made to permit the holders of these policies to convert their policies to other types of life insurance contracts. One of the popular applications of term insurance is that of *mortgage term insurance*. The mortgage term insurance policy is written in an amount and for a time period sufficient to cover the mortgage on a home. In the event of the death of the purchaser of the home, the benefits of the policy apply to the amount remaining due on the mortgage. The dependents of the insured, therefore, are freed from further mortgage obligations on the property.

Term life insurance is seldom recommended in its basic form as an appropriate contract for general family protection. Because no investment program is combined with this type of insurance contract, the annual premiums paid are less than for any other type of life insurance policy.

Many companies offer term policies that are renewable without the requirement of an additional physical examination. The renewal privilege, of course, adds to the insurance premium. At the time a term insurance policy is renewed, a higher premium based on the attained age of the insured is established. Since insurance premiums are based on the expected number of deaths per 1,000 persons in each age group, the older the person to be insured the higher the premium. The number of deaths per 1,000 persons and expectation of life-years at selected ages is shown in Table 11-1.

Table 11-1

COMMISSIONERS 1941 STANDARD ORDINARY MORTALITY TABLE—SELECTED AGES

Age	Deaths per 1000 Persons	Expectation of Life-Years
20	2.43	46.54
25	2.88	42.12
30	3.56	37.74
35	4.59	33.44
40	6.18	29.25
45	8.61	25.21
50	12.32	21.37

Another common modification of the term life insurance contract is that of the conversion privilege. For the typical five-year convertible term policy, conversion to other types of policies written by the company may be effected within the first three years of the policy. For the ten-year convertible term policy, the period during which the conversion may be effected is usually the first seven years. Some companies, however, permit conversion throughout the life of their term contracts.

Term life insurance with a renewable or convertible feature (or both) holds a substantial advantage over the straight term insurance in that physical disabilities which occur after the original contract has been issued do not prevent the insured from continuing with insurance protection. Hence, for the individual with large financial responsibilities and a low income, the modified forms of term life insurance may be appropriate.

Most term life insurance contracts, however, whether they are renewable or convertible, provide no accumulation of savings or cash value. Also, the renewal of term policies periodically at higher premium rates eventually reaches a point where it may be extremely burdensome to maintain the contract. It is true, of course, that the insured may need less insurance as his age becomes greater and his dependents fewer. As his insurance premiums increase, therefore, he may reduce the amount of protection.

One of the fastest growing forms of life insurance in the United States is that of *group insurance*. Although group insurance policies are not necessarily of term insurance type, more than 95 per cent of such policies fall in this category. Group insurance is generally purchased by individuals through the company for which they work. In view of the fact that such insurance eases the financial burden on the family of deceased workers and relieves the company of responsibility it might otherwise feel obligated to assume, employers generally pay part or all of the cost of group insurance in order to encourage its purchase.

Whole-Life Insurance. The *whole-life insurance* policy differs from term insurance in that the benefits under the provisions of the policy are payable to the beneficiaries irrespective of the time of death, while for the term policy such benefits are payable only if the insured dies during the specified term of the insurance. The whole-life insurance contract differs from term insurance in another important respect; it combines an investment program with the insurance contract. The premiums are generally for a fixed sum each payment period throughout the life of the insured or for a specified number of years. That portion of the premium which applies toward the protection part of the contract represents only a small part of the annual premium during the early years of the contract. Much of the premium is credited toward the savings accumulation of the policyholder. This savings accumulation is referred to as the cash value of the policy. The accumulation of this investment portion of the insurance contract makes it possible for an individual to pay a level or fixed premium throughout his life or for a specified number of years despite the higher costs of insurance that accompany advancing age.

Term life insurance provides for much less capital accumulation for the insurance companies than does whole-life insurance, since the annual premiums for term insurance correspond more directly with the basic cost of insurance protection. It is through whole-life insurance and the types of contracts discussed in the following paragraphs, with their large accumulations of savings, that the tremendous amounts of capital of the life insurance companies are generated. Life insurance companies in turn make this capital available to the economy in general by investing in the securities of government and business.

There are two types of whole-life insurance: *straight life,* on which a fixed premium is paid throughout the life of the insured; and *limited payment life,* on which premiums are payable for a specified number of years, or until death if death occurs before the end of the specified period. Under a limited payment plan the payments may extend from an immediate single sum payment of the total premium to a thirty-year payment period or longer, although most limited payment plans are written on a twenty- or thirty-year basis. The face value of the policy is not payable at the completion of the payment period but only upon the death of the insured.

Endowment Insurance. Like the term plan of life insurance, *endowment insurance* is written for a specified number of years. In contrast, however, if the insured person survives to the end of the stipulated period, the face amount of the policy is payable to the insured. Such policies may be written as twenty- or thirty-year endowment contracts, or for such other time spans as may be desired. Endowment policies may also be written to mature at a specified age, in which case the term of the endowment is the difference between the age of the insured at the time the policy is contracted for and the age so specified in the policy. Like the limited payment plan of life insurance, the endowment policy may involve a single premium to be paid immediately upon the writing of the contract with the endowment to be made at some specified future period. Some endowment policies provide for payment of benefits over a period of years rather than in a single lump sum. Such policies involve a combination of the endowment and annuity contract. Endowment policies are especially important as outlets for family savings.

Annuity Contracts. Annuity insurance has often been described as "insurance in reverse." The basic purpose of life insurance is to create an estate, while the annuity contract provides for the disposition of an estate through its systematic liquidation. Under an annuity contract, the annuitant agrees to pay a stipulated sum of money to the insurance company, either in the form of a single lump-sum payment or in a series of regular payments, in return for a regular income from the company for a specified time, such as a number of years or for life. Typically, annuities are purchased to meet the possibility that the buyer may outlive his earning period and will need a regular income to sustain him in the years beyond retirement.

For example, if a man 60 years of age has $20,000 on which to live for the rest of his life plus the earnings that he may receive during the remainder of his productive career, he may buy a life annuity with the $20,000 that will provide him with a monthly payment of approximately $107. If after the payment of only one such installment by the insurance company the annuitant should die, the company has no further obligation. On the other hand, if the annuitant should live to a very old age, the insurance company would be bound to make annuity payments throughout the life of the individual. Through the annuity contract, therefore, the person may assure himself that he will not live so long that his accumulated savings will be exhausted. Obviously the younger the age at which the insurance company is to begin payments to the annuitant, the more expensive will be the annuity contract.

Because many prospective purchasers of annuity contracts object to the prospect of the life insurance company being relieved of further responsibility for income payments in the event of an early death of the annuitant, perhaps after a single payment, several modifications of this basic type of annuity contract exist. These modified plans of annuity contracts generally provide for some sort of refund or guaranteed payment period to beneficiaries in the event of an early death of the annuitant.

Annuities may be purchased also by turning over the face amount of an endowment insurance policy. Also, a beneficiary of a life insurance policy may, upon the death of the insured, reinvest the proceeds of the policy payable to him in exchange for an annuity contract.

Extent of Life Insurance Protection

There are more than 100 million insurance policyholders in the United States. In 1956 this insurance was represented by 261 million life insurance policies, providing an aggregate of $412 billion of insurance protection. The average amount of life insurance owned per family in 1956 was $7,600, more than twice as much as ten years before. Life insurance savings of $1,400 per family in the form of policy reserves provided savings for more families than any other form of long-term savings. In addition, there were 5.3 million annuity contracts in force.[1]

Life insurance protection and annuities were provided by 1,144 United States companies. Of this total, Texas had 348 chartered companies; Louisiana was second with 102 companies; Alabama was third with 48 companies; and South Carolina was fourth with 39 companies. Although the above states claim the largest numbers of life insurance companies, such companies are for the most part relatively small. Since the turn of the century six states have accounted for between 80 and 90 per cent of all of the assets of life insurance companies. These states are New York, New Jersey, Massachusetts, Connecticut, Wisconsin, and Pennsylvania.

The Investment of Life Insurance Company Funds

Although life insurance companies usually are able to meet the payments for which they are obligated each year out of funds received from insurance premiums and from earnings on their investments, the companies maintain vast reserves. Through the investment of these reserves the life insurance companies make their principal contribution to the flow of long-term capital in the economy. The investments customarily made by life insurance companies may be described as a *fixed income type* in which the purpose of investment is primarily one of safety of principal and stability of income. Such investments usually take the form of United States Government securities, state and municipal bonds, the securities of business and industry, real estate mortgages, direct investment in real estate, and policy loans.

State laws, in general, place severe restrictions on the types of investment that life insurance companies may make. These

[1] *Life Insurance Fact Book,* Institute of Life Insurance, 1957.

laws stem for the most part from the Armstrong investigation of life insurance companies in New York in 1905. In the process of this examination it was found that life insurance companies had participated in many underwriting syndicates and had secured control of other corporations, including banks and mortgage companies, through stock ownership. This investigation encouraged enactment of legislation of the strictest nature; and in many states investments of life insurance companies were limited to securities of the federal government and other political subdivisions, highly secure corporate bonds, and mortgage loans secured by improved real estate worth at least 50 per cent more than the amount so loaned.

Since those early days of the twentieth century there has been a slow but gradual liberalization of the laws as they apply to investments of life insurance companies. Among other things, these companies have been permitted to invest directly in such income-producing assets as housing projects, real estate for lease-back purposes, and, to a limited extent, common stocks. Although there has been considerable controversy relative to the merits of life insurance company investment in common stocks, most states now permit such investments to a limited extent.

The tremendous growth of life insurance company assets has posed a major problem for the investment departments of these organizations. Government securities, with their low yields, provide only part of the answer to the problem of the insurance company, and the diligent search for new investment outlets will continue. To the extent that the insurance companies are able to expand their areas of investment, the long-term capital needs of the economy are more adequately served.

It has been suggested that the life insurance companies could profitably enter the small-loan field, both through business and personal loans, if state regulation made this possible. It has also been suggested that life insurance companies make small loans in conjunction with commercial banks. This has been tried by at least one New York life insurance company. Finally, a vast area of investment is opening up to the life insurance companies through direct investment in income-producing properties. The redevelopment housing programs in the major cities offer an excellent opportunity for financing by the large insurance companies. An example of this type of arrangement is the Garden City Apartments in New York City, which are financed by the Metropolitan Life Insurance Company and others. Some states permit life insurance companies to invest in commercial and industrial real estate properties. In such cases, the properties acquired are leased to commercial or industrial enterprises, generally on the basis of a fixed annual rental.[2]

ACCIDENT AND SICKNESS INSURANCE

When disability strikes a person, he may suffer financial loss in two ways: through his loss of income while disabled, and through the medical costs relating to the disability. *Accident and sickness insurance* provides indemnity to the insured for loss of income because of accident or sickness and provides for the expenses of hospital and surgical requirements. This form of insurance has enjoyed a rate of growth in recent decades far greater than that of any other form of insurance.

Types of Accident and Sickness Insurance

Accident or sickness insurance may be written as one or a combination of the following: disability income insurance, hospital, medical, and surgical expense insurance, and major medical expense insurance.

Disability Income Insurance. The increasing recognition that the earning power of the head of a household is usually the most important asset of the family has resulted in a greater consciousness of the need not only for life insurance but also for protection against loss of income because of accident or sickness. Disability income insurance provides this form of financial protection. Under such insurance a person may receive weekly payments of a stated amount for total disability, or a fraction of such a stated amount for partial disability.

Because disability may be defined in various ways, the definition clauses in such policies are of great importance. Most companies make a distinction between the inability of the insured to perform the duties of his own occupation because of accident or sickness as opposed to the inability to perform the duties of an alternative occupation. For example, the loss of the use of a hand

---

[2] The lease is described in greater detail in Chapter 12.

by a commercial airline pilot would make it difficult if not impossible to continue with his occupation, but it would not prevent a productive career in another occupation. It is common practice for insurance companies to provide for protection against loss of income due to a person's inability to perform the duties of his own occupation for one year, and beyond one year—up to the time limit of the policy—to provide protection against the inability to perform the duties of any occupation. Although some companies provide benefits for the entire duration of the disability, most policies limit the period of benefits to one, five, or ten years.

Hospital, Medical, and Surgical Expense Insurance. Hospitalization insurance, together with medical and surgical insurance, is relatively new to the insurance field. This type of insurance, as the name implies, agrees to reimburse within stipulated limits either the insured or the hospital for certain hospital, medical, and surgical expenses that result from accident or sickness. Insurance of this type may be issued as a group policy, covering all of the employees of a business firm, for example, or it may be issued to cover an individual or a family. Hospital, medical, and surgical expense insurance, in addition to being written by private companies, is written in large volume by certain organizations formed on a nonprofit basis for this specific purpose. Prominent among the latter group are the "Blue Cross" and "Blue Shield" organizations.

Major Medical Expense Insurance. An increasingly popular form of personal insurance is that which provides for large medical expenses. Although such expenses arise infrequently, when they occur, accumulated family savings may be wiped out. In other instances, needed medical treatment of a costly nature may not be available to a family because of a lack of financial resources. *Major medical insurance,* sometimes called "catastrophe insurance," provides protection against the expenses of the most serious of accidents or sicknesses. Although such insurance is usually written under group policies, a few companies have offered such protection to individuals and to families.

Several features are typically embodied in these contracts. First, in order to provide protection against major medical expenses only, a deductible clause is usually included. For example, expenses of less than $300 may be excluded by such policies. When the major medical expense insurance is written as a supplement to a basic medical expense plan, such as Blue Cross, the deductible amount may be specified as a minimum amount or "corridor" between the maximum benefits of the basic plan and the benefits of the major medical insurance plan. Under this arrangement the first $300 of a $900 medical expense may be covered by the basic medical expense plan, the next $100 must be provided by the insured, with the protection under the major medical insurance plan applying to the remaining $500 of expense.

A second common provision of the major medical insurance plan is that of coinsurance; that is, the insured and the insurance company participate jointly in the medical expense according to a predetermined ratio. If the coinsurance is stated to be 25 per cent on the part of the insured, in our example above the insured would pay the $100 deductible or corridor amount plus $125 (one quarter of the remaining medical expense liability). A third provision of this insurance establishes a maximum limit to the liability of the company for any one cause of illness. This maximum limit, however, is usually quite liberal.

PROPERTY INSURANCE

Basically, the purpose of *property insurance* is either to protect the insured against loss arising out of physical damages to his own property or loss arising from damages to others for which the insured may be held liable.

Types of Property Insurance

For purposes of describing the types of property insurance, it will be convenient to follow the broad classification of fire, marine, and casualty and surety insurance.

Fire Insurance. The basic form of *fire insurance* offers protection to the insured against the destruction of physical property as a result of fire. Such insurance does not provide for protection against loss to the insured of the use of such facilities. For example, the owner of a store would receive payment for the physical damage resulting from fire to the store premises, but he would not receive compensation for the loss of trade caused by the fire loss.

Such protection may be provided by the fire insurance companies in the form of a modification of the basic fire policy, but at an increased premium. In addition, fire insurance companies may write policies that protect against such related perils to property as explosion, windstorm, and riot. The fire insurance companies find these risks convenient to undertake, since it is often difficult to determine the extent to which damage results from these perils or from the fires that often follow such disasters.

Marine Insurance. Marine insurance is one of the oldest forms of commercial insurance. These policies were written originally to protect against the perils of the sea. Such protection was offered not only against the natural dangers of sea transportation but piracy and other man-created dangers as well. Marine insurance later was extended to include protection over transportation of merchandise from the seller to the purchaser, including land transportation as well as marine transportation. A distinction is customarily made between insurance written on shipments over land by such carriers as railroads and trucks, which is referred to as *inland marine insurance,* and those that involve sea perils, referred to as *ocean marine insurance.*

Casualty and Surety Insurance. Casualty and surety insurance is of more recent origin than the other forms of insurance discussed. In brief, casualty and surety insurance may be assumed to include all forms of coverage not included as marine, fire, or life insurance. An example of casualty insurance is the well-known automobile liability insurance that owners of vehicles carry as protection against claims resulting from injuries to other persons. Another example of insurance of the casualty type is that offering protection against burglary or robbery. Other forms of casualty insurance include insurance of a business against excessive bad-debt loss as a result of sales to customers on open account and protection against the breakage of plate glass.

Business firms protect themselves against claims resulting from occupational accidents through the purchase of a form of casualty insurance known as *workmen's compensation and employers' liability insurance.* Under workmen's compensation laws of the various states, employers are liable for most of the accidents that take place in connection with their business operations. Even for accidents not covered by workmen's compensation laws the employer may be sued for damages under common law. Workmen's compensation and employers' liability insurance assumes the expenses of compensation, medical, surgical, and hospitalization requirements as determined by the compensation laws of the state.

The *surety contract* generally provides that one party, the surety company, becomes answerable to a third party, the insured, as a result of failure on the part of a second party to perform as required by contract. For example, the businessman who contracts for the construction of a new building may secure a surety bond protecting him against failure of the contractor to complete the structure by a certain time, or protecting him against unsatisfied claims of laborers or suppliers of materials as a result of failure of the contractor to meet his obligations.

The *fidelity bond*, as a special form of surety contract, provides that the surety company reimburse employers for the losses incurred as a result of the dishonest acts of employees. Banks, savings and loan associations, and other businesses in which employees have access to large sums of money invariably carry fidelity bonds.

Property Insurance Companies

Historically, fire and marine insurance on the one hand and casualty and surety insurance on the other have been handled by separate companies. It was believed that the strict separation of these two broad types of insurance operations was to be desired in the light of the risk that a single company could undertake. The tremendous growth of the major property insurance companies, however, has long since provided sufficient diversification of risk to permit *multiple-line insurance underwriting*. Since 1950 there has been a steadily increasing number of multiple-line companies in which fire and marine insurance companies are writing a steadily increasing volume of casualty and surety insurance, and casualty and surety insurance companies are building up fire and marine insurance lines. The practice of affording complete property insurance in one package has encouraged mergers and affiliations of fire and marine insurance companies with casualty and surety insurance companies. A recent development in the insurance field involves life insurance underwriting along with multiple-line property insurance underwriting.

Multiple-line insurance has permitted the writing of insurance risks at lower total cost to the insured than would be possible under a system of insurance with several different companies, each for a specified risk. This decreased cost to the insured results from decreased administrative costs. The complete property insurance requirements of an individual or business may be handled in a single contract without the individual processing of policies required when insurance lines are written by separate companies.

In expanding insurance activities to include multiple lines of protection, it has been necessary for companies to organize new administrative departments. This has involved the usual problems of recruiting and training new personnel, the development of new forms and contracts, and the establishment of new procedures to integrate the multiple lines. For these reasons it has been easier for companies to expand their insurance lines by acquiring existing firms through merger than by internal expansion.

The Investment of Property Insurance Company Funds

Property insurance, like life insurance, is big business. As of December 31, 1957, the assets of all property insurance companies totaled approximately $23 billion. In order to provide an extra guaranty of ability to pay losses, property insurance companies maintain large capital funds. In addition, they have the reserves

Chart 11–1

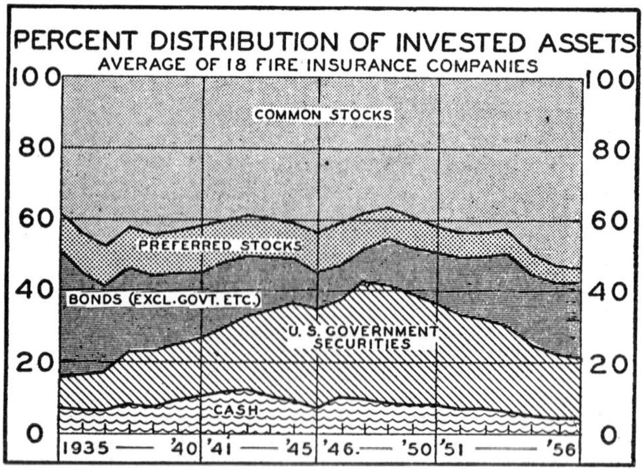

PERCENT DISTRIBUTION OF INVESTED ASSETS
AVERAGE OF 18 FIRE INSURANCE COMPANIES
COMMON STOCKS
PREFERRED STOCKS
BONDS (EXCL. GOVT. ETC.)
U. S. GOVERNMENT SECURITIES
CASH
1935 — '40 '41 — '45 '46 — '50 '51 — '56

SOURCE: Standard and Poor's Corporation

accumulated out of premiums that are collected on insurance policics in advance. All of these items provide the funds that must be invested and which in turn produce investment income.

Life insurance companies are permitted to invest only in high-grade securities, plus limited amounts of the highest quality common stocks. Fire and casualty insurance companies are not so restricted. The property insurance company may have a substantial investment in the common stocks of industrial, railroad, public utility enterprises, and banks. As of December 31, 1956, the common stock investments of a selected group of large fire and marine insurance companies constituted approximately 61 per cent of total investments; for a selected group of casualty and surety companies, common stocks represented approximately 33 per cent of total investments. The pattern of investments of these companies since 1935 may be observed from Chart 11-1 for fire and marine insurance companies and from Chart 11-2 for casualty and surety insurance companies.

Chart 11–2

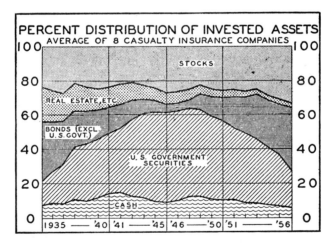

SOURCE: Standard and Poor's Corporation

QUESTIONS

1. Describe the financial contributions made by insurance companies to the economy of the United States.
2. Outline the specific types of insurance that are classified as personal insurance and those classified as property insurance. What is the major distinction between personal insurance and property insurance?
3. Distinguish between the basic features of term insurance as opposed to whole-life insurance.
4. From the viewpoint of financial contribution to the economy, is there any substantial distinction between term insurance and whole-life insurance?
5. Under what circumstances would the straight term life insurance contract be most appropriate as a form of insurance protection?
6. Under what circumstances would you recommend strongly against the use of straight term life insurance? Would modification of the basic plan of term insurance to include a renewal and convertible privilege eliminate your objection completely to term insurance?
7. Describe the nature of the whole-life insurance contract. In what way are fixed premiums made possible? Distinguish between straight life and limited payment life types of whole-life insurance.
8. Compare endowment insurance with both term life insurance and whole-life insurance.
9. Discuss the fundamental difference in objectives of life insurance, on the one hand, and annuity insurance on the other.
10. Describe the types of investments made by life insurance companies. Why have life insurance companies invested their funds to only a limited extent in common stocks? Comment on any change in pattern of investments of life insurance companies over the last 15 years.
11. Describe the principal forms of accident and sickness insurance.
12. Describe the various major types of property insurance contacts.
13. What is meant by multiple-line insurance underwriting? What advantages or disadvantages does it offer?
14. Compare the pattern of investments of property insurance companies with that of life insurance companies.

SUGGESTED READINGS

KULP, C. A. *Casualty Insurance*; Third Edition. New York: The Ronald Press Company, 1956.

MACLEAN, JOSEPH B. *Life Insurance*; Eighth Edition. New York: McGraw-Hill Book Company, Inc., 1957.

MAGEE, JOHN H. *General Insurance*; Fifth Edition. Homewood, Illinois: Richard D. Irwin, Inc., 1957.

MEHR, ROBERT I., and OSLER, ROBERT W. *Modern Life Insurance*; Revised Edition. New York: The Macmillan Company, 1956.

RODDA, WILLIAM H. *Fire and Property Insurance*. Englewood Cliffs, New Jersey: Prentice-Hall, Inc., 1956.

Chapter 12

Other Sources of

Long-Term

Business Financing

In addition to the institutions providing long-term funds for business discussed in the preceding chapters, many other types of institutions play an important part in providing such financing. Some of these institutions are discussed in greater detail elsewhere in this book because they engage in short-term lending as their principal activity. Their long-term lending operations, however, are discussed in this chapter. Other institutions and sources of long-term financing discussed in this chapter are concerned almost entirely with long-term financial arrangements. In still other cases, institutions have been established for the specific purpose of providing long-term financial assistance to businesses that cannot obtain such financing on reasonable terms from other sources. Such institutions are generally sponsored by federal, state, or local governments.

The sources of long-term business financing to be discussed in this chapter are as follows:

Commercial banks
Mutual savings banks
Business corporations
Eleemosynary institutions
Regional development companies
The Small Business Administration
Investment development companies
Individual investors
The lease arrangement and equipment trust financing

219

COMMERCIAL BANKS

In Part I the commercial banking system was described as providing the foundation for business credit throughout the nation. It was observed that commercial banks invest primarily in short-term business loans. These banks, however, must be discussed with respect to two additional forms of lending activity. These are bank investments in long-term corporate securities and term loans to business.

Long-Term Corporate Investments by Banks

During the 1920's commercial banks invested heavily in long-term corporate bonds. Because of heavy losses suffered by the commercial banks of the nation as a result of the forced sale of such securities to meet depositors' demands during the depression of the thirties, there was a widespread shift to municipal, state, and federal securities.

As the law now stands, commercial banks are generally permitted to invest in corporate bonds as long as they are of investment quality and are marketable under ordinary circumstances with reasonable promptness at fair value. Bonds that have a wide public interest and investment holding are preferred in this connection because the breadth of the market enhances the market ability of the securities. The law generally restricts banks to an investment of not more than 10 per cent of their capital and surplus in the securities of any one corporation.

Despite these restrictions and the general preference of banks today for government securities, long-term corporate securities continue to be held to a limited extent. As of midyear 1957, commercial banks held more than $6 billion of corporate securities as investments.[1]

Term Loans by Commercial Banks

The *bank term loan* represents an interesting and significant development in the lending practices of commercial banks. This type of loan differs from the usual bank business loan in that it

---

[1] Federal Deposit Insurance Corporation, Report No. 47, "Assets, Liabilities, and Capital Accounts Commercial and Mutual Savings Banks" (Washington, D. C.: June 6, 1957), p. 3.

has a maturity exceeding one year. Also, the term loan requires repayment in installments throughout the life of the loan. Such installment repayments may be on a monthly, a quarterly, or a yearly basis.

Development of Term Loans by Banks. Term lending on the part of the commercial banks of the nation appears to have begun during the depression years of the thirties. Although the term loan was contrary to the generally accepted concept of bank lending activity, there were several reasons for its rapid growth and acceptance by the banks of the nation. First, banks utilized the term-loan arrangement as a convenient means of investing their surplus funds. These surplus funds accumulated in large part from a decline in the demand on the part of business establishments for short-term credit. Second, a higher return could be realized on the term loans than on the usual business loan. Third, the Securities Act of 1933 made it more difficult for the corporations of the nation to secure money through public distribution of securities, and the incentive was strong on the part of business corporations to negotiate directly with banks to finance their intermediate-term capital needs. Fourth, the commercial banks were encouraged by the federal government to engage in this type of lending activity. This encouragement took the form of direct recommendations, which were reflected in the reports of bank examiners. Finally, the term loan provided banks with an alternative to investment in the securities of the federal government and of the states and municipalities. The yields on government securities had been reduced to unprecedented lows.

In the post-World War II period the American Bankers Association lent its support to the term lending arrangement and encouraged its members to explore more fully the potential offered by such loans. By 1940 the tremendous growth and popularity of term loans had established them as one of the most important and significant lending innovations by the banks of the nation. During World War II term lending declined because of the inability of businesses to establish long-range plans for expansion and because special governmental lending programs were established to care for the financing of war production. In the postwar period, however, the volume of such loans increased at a very rapid rate. In 1946 a survey by the Federal Reserve System revealed 144,000 term loans outstanding to commercial and industrial concerns by member banks. These loans represented a total of $4.6 billion or 34 per cent of the banks' total business loan volume. Nearly three fourths of all member banks had such loans outstanding.[2] As of December 31, 1955, the proportion of term loans to total business loans remained at approximately one third.

The Term Loan Agreement. The *term loan agreement* takes the form of a detailed written contract between the bank and the borrower. Term loans may be secured by specific property as collateral or they may be unsecured, depending upon the situation that prevails in each case. Among other things, the bank frequently requires a business to maintain a certain minimum amount of net working capital. In the event the net working capital of the business should fall below the stipulated amount, dividends or the salaries of executives may be reduced or curtailed until such time as the appropriate level of net working capital is re-established.

It is also frequently stipulated in the agreement that the business is not to dispose of its fixed assets without the permission of the bank or to incur other indebtedness without specific permission. Another common provision is that insurance must be carried on the lives of key men of the business establishment with the bank as beneficiary. Some banks carry blanket insurance policies on the lives of executives of companies receiving term loans. Another requirement may be that changes in management personnel, changes in production methods or items of production, and increases in executive salaries or bonuses be approved by the bank before being undertaken by the business.

Despite the restrictive nature of the many protective covenants that usually accompany the term loan, businessmen have generally found the arrangement to their advantage. In any event, the protective covenants establish only fair and reasonable protection against undesirable business activities of management. Also, the simplicity of the term loan arrangement, as well as its cost, renders it far more desirable under many circumstances than funds secured through the public sale of securities or through other media.

---

[2] Duncan McC. Holthausen, "Term Lending to Businesses by Commercial Banks," *Federal Reserve Bulletin*, May, 1947, p. 498. See also, Albert R. Koch, "Business Loans of Member Banks," *Federal Reserve Bulletin*, March, 1947, pp. 253-261.

MUTUAL SAVINGS BANKS

Mutual savings banks are legally regarded as banks and are eligible for insurance under the provisions of the Federal Deposit Insurance Corporation. Similarity to commercial banking operations, however, ends with the deposit of the customer's savings. Mutual savings banks provide no checking account facilities and concentrate entirely upon serving as savings institutions. These institutions are located primarily in New York, New Jersey, and in the New England states.

Mutual savings banks invest in bonds and notes of railroads, utilities, and industrial companies, and in commercial and residential real estate mortgages. In addition, a few of the mutual savings banks own the common stock of business organizations. In 1951 New York State amended its laws to permit savings banks to invest in common stocks. As of midyear 1957 mutual savings banks had total assets of more than $33 billion. Approximately 12 per cent of mutual savings banks' total assets are invested in the long-term securities of business enterprises.[3]

BUSINESS CORPORATIONS

The business corporations of the nation not only are large users of funds but also play a significant part in providing long-term capital for other businesses. Such capital is provided in several ways. First of all, a corporation may invest capital in a subsidiary company for purposes of control. In other cases, a corporation may invest in the securities of another company when that company is an important supplier of materials to the investing company. Such investment is often undertaken to insure a smooth flow of materials required for manufacture. For example, in 1950 one of the large automobile manufacturing companies loaned a substantial sum of money to one of the major steel corporations in return for which the automobile company received an appropriate interest return plus a guarantee of a priority over other purchasers of supplies of steel.

In still other cases, corporations in setting up sinking funds for retirement of their own outstanding bonds may direct the sinking

---

[3] *Federal Reserve Bulletin* (Washington, D. C.: Board of Governors of the Federal Reserve System), January, 1958, p. 43.

fund trustee to invest accumulated contributions to the fund in the securities of other corporations. When the maturity of their own bonds is reached, these investments are liquidated and their own bonds are retired with the funds so received. The practice of investing sinking funds in the securities of other companies is now the exception to the rule. Such funds are generally used to retire regularly the bonds for which the sinking funds are set up. Finally, and most important, the large sums that are accumulated by the employee pension funds of corporations are invested in the long-term securities of business and government.

Employee Pension Funds

The establishment of pension funds for the benefit of workers has been a part of the American economy for many years. A major form of pension planning today is that provided by the Social Security Act. Somewhat earlier than this Act, the Railroad Retirement Act provided for a retirement benefit for railroad employees, and still other legislation provided for benefits for retired government employees. In recent years employers have shown a willingness to establish private pension plans, generally as a supplement to the Federal Old-Age and Survivors Insurance System.

Although the first private pension was adopted by the American Express Company in 1875, a large proportion of the private pension plans now in existence have been established since 1945. Their rapid development since that time has been due in part to union pressure and to the desire of employers to reduce labor turnover by providing greater economic security for their employees. The governmental wage restrictions of the World War II period also played a direct role in encouraging the establishment of employee pensions funds by business corporations. The Steel Industry Board in 1949, while disapproving a direct increase in wages for workers in the steel industry, recommended strongly the establishment of private pension plans for the workers. This made it possible for the unions to satisfy the workers' demands without contributing directly to the inflationary pressures that a direct increase in wages would have produced. Corporations were encouraged further to contribute toward pension funds because of high corporate profits taxes. Corporate pension contributions are tax credits for corporate income tax purposes.

Extent and Administration of Pension Funds

It has been estimated that there are more than 15,000 pension funds of all types with assets of nearly $29 billion. More than 10 million persons are covered by such plans. In 1956 the addition to pension fund reserves amounted to $3.6 billion.[4]

The majority of pension funds are administered by trust companies or trust departments of banks. In contrast with the regular trust-management functions of the trust companies, there are no general legal restrictions imposed upon the handling of the private pension plans placed under their management. Rather, each trust agreement is complete in itself and provides all of the details relative to administration of funds. Life insurance companies handle approximately one third of all funds paid into pension accounts. A few large pension funds, such as those of Sears, Roebuck and Company and United States Steel Corporation, are administered by the companies directly.

The Investment of Pension Funds

The funds accumulating under pension agreements with trust companies, trust departments of banks, and life insurance companies are invested primarily in high-grade corporate bonds. The distribution of investments of all pension funds other than those managed by life insurance companies is shown in Table 12-1. Note that common stock is the second most important form of investment. Because of the general increase in common stock values, the proportion of common stock relative to other investments at market value is considerably greater than at book value.

Trust institutions have generally avoided investing funds in the securities of corporations from which such funds have been derived, partly as a matter of sound financial policy and partly as a result of certain requirements on such investments imposed by the United States Treasury Department.[5] Pension funds managed by life insurance companies are combined with the general investable funds arising out of regular life insurance activities. These funds are then invested largely in corporate debt securities and residential and commercial real estate mortgages.

---

[4] *Corporate Pension Funds, 1956.* Statistical Series Release Number 1474 (Washington, D. C.: Securities and Exchange Commission), August 16, 1957.

[5] Roger F. Murray, "Investment Aspects of the Accumulation of Pension Funds," *The Journal of Finance* (May, 1952), p. 255.

Table 12–1

PENSION FUND ASSETS *

December 31, 1956

	Book Value		Market Value	
	Millions of Dollars	Per Cent of Total	Millions of Dollars	Per Cent of Total
Cash and deposits	332	2.0	332	1.9
U. S. Government securities	2,293	13.8	2,192	12.5
Corporate bonds	8,704	52.3	7,904	45.0
Own company	776	4.7	682	3.9
Other companies	7,928	47.6	7,222	41.1
Preferred stock	570	3.4	524	3.0
Common stock	3,774	22.7	5,648	32.2
Own company	505	3.0	864	4.9
Other companies	3,269	19.6	4,784	27.2
Mortgages	230	1.4	229	1.3
Other assets	736	4.4	735	4.2
Total assets	16,639	100.0	17,565	100.0

* Does not include corporate pension funds administered by insurance companies. Reserves in such funds were $12.3 billion as of December 31, 1956.

SOURCE: *Corporate Pension Funds, 1956.* Statistical Series Release Number 1474, Securities and Exchange Commission, Washington, D. C., August 16, 1957.

ELEEMOSYNARY INSTITUTIONS

The assets of such organizations as educational institutions, charitable organizations, philantropic institutions, hospitals, and religious bodies have been increasing at a rapid rate throughout most of the history of the United States. The assets of these institutions now total many billions of dollars, much of which is currently invested in stocks and bonds of business corporations. The *World Almanac* for 1958 lists 129 colleges and universities with endowments in excess of $5 million. The total amount shown for these endowments is $3.2 billion. This publication also lists 62 foundations, public trusts, and funds with assets of $1 million or more, having a total of more than $3 billion. In addition there were 6,966 registered hospitals.[6] Many of these hospitals have endowments of considerable volume, and it is reported that the endow-

[6] *The World Almanac and Book of Facts for 1958* (New York: *New York World-Telegram* and *The Sun*), pp. 309, 480, and 486.

ments of a few of the larger metropolitan hospitals amount to many millions of dollars.[7]

As an indication of the investment pattern of some of these institutions, Scudder, Stevens & Clark, a Boston investment counseling firm, reported in 1954 that the funds of 23 leading educational institutions were invested largely in long-term corporate securities. Common stocks constituted 52 per cent of total investments; preferred stocks, 7 per cent; bonds, 34 per cent; and real-estate mortgages and miscellaneous, 7 per cent. In comparing this pattern of investment with the results of a similar survey in 1931, the most striking change is that of the proportion of common stocks. In 1931, common stocks accounted for only 11 per cent of the total assets of these institutions. During this period the ownership of real estate and real estate mortgages was greatly reduced. Recent studies reveal a continuing trend toward common stocks. The increase in the popularity of common stocks for educational institutions apparently is to be explained by the fact that these institutions have been attempting to offset the low yields on high-grade corporate bonds and the increases in maintenance costs and general expenses.

Although figures are not available to reveal the investment pattern of all eleemosynary institutions, the total of their resources is significant with respect to the capital markets. The resources of these institutions will probably continue to increase as a result of the encouragement given by the government through tax credits to corporations and individual donors for philanthropic purposes.

REGIONAL DEVELOPMENT COMPANIES

Another source of long-term capital is that provided by organizations which attempt to encourage the establishment of new businesses in their particular geographical areas. Several of these organizations have been in operation for many years and have a fine record of success. Funds for the operations of regional development companies are usually provided by local business firms or associations. For example, La Crosse, Wisconsin, has an Industrial Association which was organized in 1910 by the Board of Trade of

[7] James W. Wooster, Jr. "Current Trends and Developments in the Investment Practices of Endowments and Pension Funds," *Law and Contemporary Problems* (Durham, North Carolina: Duke University), Winter 1952, p. 162.

that city. This organization is authorized to assist in the establishment of new businesses in that city by purchasing stock or by making loans to assist individuals or corporations in beginning their operations. The Association reports that it has aided about fifty manufacturing concerns during its period of operation.[8]

Louisville, Kentucky, has supported such an organization since 1916. This organization, the Louisville Industrial Foundation, will lend up to $100,000 to each concern that it feels inclined to support and, during the earlier years of the operation of this fund, financial support was occasionally given through the purchase of preferred stock. The Louisville Industrial Foundation reports a long list of very successful corporations in that area which owe their establishment and early growth to the support lent them by this organization.

Easton, Pennsylvania, has a Guarantee Fund which is authorized to make loans to prospective business enterprises to be located in that city. Scranton, Pennsylvania, Baltimore, Maryland, and many others have similar funds for encouraging the establishment of business enterprises in their communities.

An interesting development in the financial support of new enterprises has occurred in New England since World War II. This idea was sponsored by a group of men in private industry in Maine in 1950. This organization, called the Development Credit Corporation, made loans to 50 small companies totaling $1.6 million in the first seven years of its existence. The funds of this organization were obtained from 77 Maine individuals, business concerns, and utilities, which subscribed to $50,000 of capital stock each. In addition, to supplement its capital stock funds, this corporation borrows from commercial banks, savings banks, trust companies, building and loan associations, and insurance companies in that state.

A similar corporation was established in New Hampshire in the year following the creation of the Maine Development Credit Corporation. Rhode Island established a like corporation in 1953, and the legislatures of Vermont and Connecticut have passed enabling legislation for the creation of development credit corporations. In 1954 Massachusetts established such a corporation

---

[8] Carl A. Dauten, *Business Finance*, (Englewood Cliffs, New Jersey: Prentice-Hall, Inc., 1956), p. 169.

and in the first three years of operation extended 94 loans for a total amount of $10.6 million. The New York Business Development Corporation was established in 1956 and in its first six months of operation made 16 loans totaling nearly $51.5 million.

The development credit corporations are designed to make it possible for businesses with good prospects of success, but without adequate financial resources, to become established, as well as to permit established companies to expand and employ a greater number of people. This plan is in contrast with that utilized by the cities of several of the southern states, which attempt to encourage the establishment of new businesses by the construction of factory buildings financed through the sale of tax-exempt municipal bonds and the leasing of such buildings to businessmen who are willing to operate their businesses in those communities.

Although the total amount of long-term funds provided to business through these regional development companies is not large compared with the total of business credit, it does represent a strategic outlay of funds for the establishment of new businesses and permits the growth of established businesses that are otherwise handicapped by a lack of adequate financial resources.

THE SMALL BUSINESS ADMINISTRATION

The Small Business Administration was described in Chapter 6 as an agency of the federal government that was established, in part, to provide financial assistance to small firms which are unable to obtain loans through private channels on reasonable terms. It is sufficient here to note that the Small Business Administration provides long-term loans as well as short-term loans. Such long-term loans may not exceed a maturity of ten years.

INVESTMENT DEVELOPMENT COMPANIES

Since World War II a new type of financial organization that has as its primary purpose the provision of venture capital for new and growing business organizations has developed. These companies, in most cases, represent the association of a few wealthy persons interested in taking advantage of growth opportunities of selected speculative enterprises. These venture capital companies, commonly referred to as *investment development companies* are privately established profit-seeking organizations whose primary function is to provide venture capital not otherwise available to new and growing business ventures. They usually supply equity capital, but some loan capital has been provided when its use seemed appropriate.

In addition to providing the financial backing for new companies, the investment development companies take an active and continuing interest in the companies they finance although they do not necessarily require voting control. They offer expert management counsel and guidance and continuing financial assistance as the companies pass through the various stages of their development. Only one of the investment development companies has offered its securities for public sale. A list of the principal investment development companies and their locations is shown in Table 12-2.

Table 12–2

PRINCIPAL INVESTMENT DEVELOPMENT COMPANIES OF THE UNITED STATES, 1951

Name of Company	Location	Form of Organization	Date Org.*
American Research and Development Corporation	Boston	Corporation—public sale of securities	June 1946
New Enterprises, Inc.	Boston	Corporation—restricted distribution of securities	Feb. 1946
Rockefeller Brothers, Inc.	New York	Corporation—restricted distribution of securities	1946
Industrial Capital Corporation	San Francisco	Corporation—restricted distribution of securities	May 1946
J. H. Whitney & Company	New York	Partnership	Feb. 1946
Wm. A. M. Burden & Co.	New York	Partnership	June 1949
Payson & Trask	New York	Partnership	June 1917
Henry Sears & Co.	New York	Partnership	Sept. 1949
Fox, Wells & Company	New York	Partnership	Feb. 1951
T. Mellon & Sons	Pittsburgh	Partnership Association	Jan. 1946
Nathan W. Levin	New York	Proprietorship	Sept. 1937

* None of the above-named companies had discontinued operations as of April, 1951.

SOURCE: Carl A. Dauten and Merle T. Welshans, "Investment Development Companies," *The Journal of Finance*, September, 1951, p. 277.

These organizations generally prefer to invest in enterprises that have new processes or products or make use of new ideas with competitive advantages. They will also provide funds to develop new products or processes that offer prospects for the establishment of profitable business ventures. Investments are usually disposed of by the investment development companies when the success of the venture that has been financed is assured and the securities can be sold at a substantial profit.

Although this type of company is quite new and the total money invested by all such companies to date is perhaps no more than a few million dollars, it represents an interesting development in the financial field and, if successful, can be expected to become more widespread throughout the United States. It is of particular importance because it represents an attempt on the part of private financial facilities to adapt their operations to the needs of a dynamic economy rather than to depend on government assistance to carry the burden of speculative financial assistance for new ventures.

INDIVIDUAL INVESTORS

The role of the individual in supplying long-term funds for business purposes cannot be ignored despite the fact that institutional suppliers of funds are of primary interest to us. Institutional investors, such as the insurance companies, trust companies, and commercial banks, derive most of their investable funds from the savings of individuals. In addition, however, individuals annually invest large sums directly in the securities of business organizations. Until recently there was little reliable evidence to indicate the amount of participation on the part of individuals of the nation in such business securities as corporate bonds, real-estate mortgages, and corporate stocks. In 1952, however, a study was made of share ownership in the United States.[9] This study, which was conducted by the Brookings Institution at the request of the New York Stock Exchange, offers reliable evidence of the important role of the individual investor in public securities.

The individual investor is more inclined to invest in corporate stocks than he is in corporate bonds and real-estate mortgages. Corporate bonds are of primary interest to the large institutional investors, many of which are restricted entirely to that form of investment. As of December, 1951, 6,490,000 individuals in the

[9] Lewis H. Kimmel, *Share Ownership in the United States* (Washington, D. C.: The Brookings Institution, 1952).

United States owned shares in publicly owned stocks, that is, stocks that were traded on the securities exchanges and other security markets. This represented ownership of publicly owned stocks by approximately one of every sixteen adult persons in the United States and represented 4.2 per cent of the entire population.[10] In contrast with ownership of stock on the part of individuals, 2,670,000 individuals owned real-estate mortgages and corporate bonds. This number represented 1.7 per cent of the total population of the United States.[11]

Individuals of the nation who hold ownership in life insurance policies, savings accounts, United States Savings Bonds, and other forms of investment greatly outnumber those who own corporate stocks and bonds. Ownership of nine forms of investments by individuals is shown in Table 12-3. This study revealed that 55 per cent of all family units with incomes of $10,000 a year and over were owners of one or more issues of securities, while for family units having annual incomes of from $4,000 to $5,000 the incidence of share ownership is a little over 7 per cent.[12] Individuals fifty years of age or older accounted for approximately 54 per cent of all individual share owners.

Geographically, the proportion of individuals owning shares is highest in the Far Western states, averaging approximately 6 per cent of all individuals in those states. Eastern states rank second with 4.3 per cent of the population owning shares, while the North Central states are third with 4 per cent of all individuals owning shares.

With respect to size of cities, share ownership appears to be more frequent in medium-sized cities than in the larger cities and small-town and rural communities. In cities of 25,000 to 100,000 population, 6 per cent of all individuals held share ownership, representing the highest incidence of ownership of all size groups. Cities of from 100,000 to 500,000 ranked second with 5.5 per cent of individuals owning shares, with cities of 10,000 to 25,000 and cities of over 500,000 population having equal average share holdings of 4.6 per cent. As of December, 1951, the market value of shareholdings of individuals was approximately $78.3 billion.[13]

10 *Ibid.*, p. 89.
11 *Ibid.*, p. 119.
12 *Ibid.*, p. 95.
13 *Ibid.*, p. 69.

Table 12–3

OWNERSHIP OF NINE FORMS OF INVESTMENTS BY INDIVIDUALS

December, 1951

Type of Investment	Per Cent of Total Population Who Are Owners	Estimated Number of Owners
Life insurance [a]	67.1	104,340,000
Saving accounts	34.0	52,850,000
U. S. Series "E" bonds	27.8	43,190,000
Annuities and pensions [b]	9.3	14,520,000
Publicly owned stocks	4.2	6,490,000
Other Government bonds [c]	2.4	3,720,000
Privately held stocks	1.9	3,020,000
Real estate mortgages and bonds	1.2	1,880,000
Corporate bonds	0.5	790,000
One or more of nine forms of investments	78.9	122,760,000

[a]) Includes government life insurance held by veterans and servicemen.

[b]) Does not include coverage under the federal old age and survivors insurance system.

[c]) Includes all federal government bonds (except Series E), state, county, and municipal bonds; also includes foreign government bonds.

SOURCE: Lewis H. Kimmel, *Share Ownership in the United States,* Washington. D. C., The Brookings Institution, 1952, p. 118.

THE LEASE ARRANGEMENT AND EQUIPMENT TRUST FINANCING

The lease arrangement and equipment trust financing do not represent special types of credit flowing from any single form of financial institution; rather, they represent a type of financing arrangement that may be utilized in connection with existing financial institutions.

The Lease Arrangement

It has been estimated that more than 80 per cent of all retail establishments rent their places of business under lease arrangements. Many manufacturing corporations also find it to their advantage to rent their plant facilities. One refinement of the typical lease arrangement is that of the construction of certain facilities for the specific use of a particular company. For example, Safeway Stores tries to interest local real-estate groups and other persons with the necessary capital to construct buildings to their specifications. After construction, such buildings are leased to Safeway for a period of years in accordance with a predetermined agreement. Through this means the company is benefited by the acquisition of new retail facilities without having to make an outlay of cash or to increase its corporate indebtedness.

The lease arrangement is not confined to real-estate transactions, and its use has now extended far down the line through the equipment and other facilities of some firms. In 1951 the Mutual Life Insurance Company received permission from the New York State Insurance Department to engage in leasing operations for passenger automobiles. These automobiles are leased to big companies, such as Sunshine Biscuits, Incorporated, Johnson and Johnson, and Minneapolis-Honeywell Regulator Company. Mutual Life Insurance Company in 1951 owned for rental purposes 2,000 cars, representing an investment of more than $2½ million. The administrative arrangements are generally handled by an intermediary firm. The companies that make use of leased automobiles benefit from the arrangement much as they would from the lease of real property in that it releases capital that would otherwise be tied up in equipment.

In 1953 Reo Motors, Incorporated, established a subsidiary— Reo Truck Leasing, Incorporated—for the purpose of leasing trucks to business establishments. Although this appears to be the first attempt of a truck manufacturer to go directly into leasing operations, independent truck leasing companies have been in operation for some time. The National Truck Leasing system, which is made up of a network of nationwide leasing companies, estimated that approximately 75,000 trucks were under lease in 1952. Cases have also been reported where firms have leased their office equipment, including typewriters, file cabinets, and other items, in an effort to free as much capital as possible for use in the business.

The Sale and Lease-Back Arrangement. Another lease arrangement involves the sale of property owned by a company and its lease back to the selling company. One important reason for this sale and lease-back arrangement is to acquire additional working capital for business operations. Such funds obtained from the sale of fixed assets may be used to take advantage of increased business possibilities at a time when it is either impossible or undesirable to increase the debt or equity of the business. The earnings resulting from the application of these funds put into business operations may far outweigh the rental cost of the facilities that the company has sold. Also, the rental that is paid thereafter to the new owner of the property is considered to be an expense and, as such, is chargeable against earnings for income tax purposes. It is true, of course, that the business which retains its fixed physical facilities is permitted to charge off against its earnings an amount each year for depreciation purposes; however, the amount that is chargeable for depreciation is limited to a proportion of the improvements on the land. Improvements made on leased property may be amortized for tax purposes over the term of the lease rather than for the number of years specified by the Internal Revenue Service.

As a rule, under the sale and lease-back arrangement the lessee (the user of the property) is required to carry an appropriate amount of property insurance, to pay property taxes that may be levied upon the property, and otherwise to maintain the property as if he were the owner.

In addition to the benefits that may accrue to a company which engages in the sale and lease-back arrangement with respect to its working capital position, the sale of fixed assets often makes possible the retirement of existing debt that may be carried against such assets on the balance sheet. Under these circumstances the capital structure of the firm is simplified, which, in turn, may result in a stronger credit position.

Examples of the Sale and Lease-Back Arrangement. An example of the sale and lease-back arrangement between industrial or commercial enterprises and institutional investors is that of Sears, Roebuck and Company, which in December, 1946, sold store properties in several large cities to a life insurance company, in turn leasing them back on a long-term basis. In 1951 the Owens-Illinois Glass Company of Toledo sold its Sayreville, New Jersey, plant to the United States Steel & Carnegie Pension Fund, but it continued to occupy the plant under a 28-year lease. In 1954 Federated Department Stores, Inc., sold its five Fedway Division stores to the Mallard Realty Corporation of New York with an agreement to lease the property for thirty years. The Bridgeport Brass Company sold a new tubing plant to the Knights of Columbus with a lease agreement for twenty years. In 1954 a pension fund represented by Bankers Trust Company of New York bought the land under F. W. Woolworth Company's Fifth Avenue Store in New York City. At the expiration of Woolworth's lease on the land in 1979, the property will belong to the fund.

An interesting sidelight on the sale and lease-back arrangement is that in which the sale of properties is made to a university and leased back for normal business operations. For example, Vanderbilt University in 1951 acquired four going concerns as investments for lease-back purposes. These were a $1¼ million terminal on the Mississippi River at St. Paul, Minnesota, which was purchased from the Wood River Oil and Refining Company and leased to the Texas Company. Previously, Vanderbilt University had purchased a Textron mill at Charlotte, North Carolina, a sporting goods equipment plant at Tullahoma, Tennessee, and a New Orleans warehouse.

Equipment Trust Financing

An important method of financing the purchase of heavy rolling stock, such as locomotives and tank cars, by railroads and expensive equipment in general by other types of businesses is that of the *equipment trust arrangement.* As an alternative to the outright purchase of rolling stock, this device provides for the transfer of title to the equipment by the seller to a trustee. The trustee, generally a trust company or a trust department of a commercial bank, holds title to the equipment but leases it to the railroad that is to make use of it.

The railroad usually pays from 20 to 25 per cent of the cost of the equipment as an initial rental payment. This is comparable to the down payment that is customarily made in connection with a direct purchase. The balance of the cost of the equipment is financed through the sale of *equipment trust obligations* issued by the trustee against the collateral value of the rolling stock to which the trustee holds title.

It is generally the responsibility of the railroad to maintain the equipment properly, to pay all taxes and insurance charges, as well as to keep the trustee informed of the location and the condition of the equipment. After the railroad has met the stipulated number of rental payments over a period of years, title to the rolling stock is turned over to the railroad. The periodic lease or rental payment is used by the trustee to pay interest on and gradually retire outstanding obligations. When a railroad acquires rolling stock under this arrangement, a metal plate is usually attached to each piece of equipment showing the name of the trust institution that holds title to the property.

Examples of Equipment Trust Financing. As an example of the use of equipment obligations, the Gulf, Mobile, and Ohio Railroad Company obtained new equipment at an estimated cost of $3,823,700 on July 1, 1957. The title to the equipment was placed with the First National Bank of Mobile, Alabama, as trustee. The Railroad paid 20 per cent of the cost price in cash, and the trustee sold equipment obligations to finance the remaining 80 per cent. These equipment obligations provide a 4¼ per cent return to the investor and are retired at the rate of $101,000 semi-annually to July 1, 1972. The equipment involved included 250 fifty-ton box cars, 100 seventy-ton covered hopper cars, 10 seventy-ton steel tank cars, and 50 seventy-ton gondola cars. In addition to the 20 per cent cash payment paid to the trustee for this equipment, the Railroad also unconditionally guarantees the equipment trust obligations. The holders of the equipment obligations, therefore, have a lien on the rolling stock and a general claim against the Railroad for the amount of the obligations.

Although in some instances it has been considered desirable for the seller of the equipment to underwrite or guarantee the equipment trust obligations, this is not ordinarily required. In fact, equipment trust obligations have an extremely favorable investment rating, and very few losses on them have been recorded in recent decades. This excellent record of equipment trust obligations has resulted in part from the fact that the rolling stock of railroads has been in extremely short supply in recent decades and a trustee can easily reclaim the equipment for the benefit of the holders of the equipment obligations in the event of a default on

the part of the railroads. In earlier years a great proportion of
the railroads of the country found it necessary to default on their
other fixed financial charges, but they have been loath to miss the
regular rental payments on equipment acquired through the equipment trust obligations device, since loss of the equipment would
generally impair seriously the efficiency of operations.

Although this financial arrangement came into existence originally as a result of the need on the part of the weaker railroads to
obtain additional new rolling stock, it is now the typical process
by which railroads acquire rolling stock. A partial list of the
equipment obligations of the New York Central Railroad is shown
in Table 12-4.

Table 12–4

PARTIAL LIST OF EQUIPMENT OBLIGATIONS OF THE NEW YORK CENTRAL RAILROAD

Name Of Issue	Interest Payable	Maturity	Original Issue	Cost of Equipment	Paid in Cash	Security
N.Y.C.R.R. Eq. 3⅜, 1952 1st	F & A (Feb. & Aug.)	1954–67	$ 8,850,000	12,003,119	25%	95 locomotives
N.Y.C.R.R. Eq. 3⅛, 1952 2nd	M & N	1954–67	5,220,000	7,103,987	25%	42 locomotives 7 cars
N.Y.C.R.R. Eq. 3¼, 1952 3rd	F & A	1954–67	8,475,000	11,004,250	25%	64 locomotives 16 cars
N.Y.C.R.R. Eq. 3⅛, 1953 1st	J & J	1954–68	11,625,000	15,219,900	25%	60 locomotives 1,500 cars
N.Y.C.R.R. Eq. 3⅝, 1953 2nd	M & S	1954–68	9,375,000	12,500,000	25%	2,501 cars

Advantages of Equipment Trust Financing. For the strong
companies, the equipment trust device offers the advantage of a
low interest cost because of the security offered the investors. For
the weaker companies, it makes possible acquisition of equipment
that otherwise could not be obtained. The manufacturer of the
equipment is benefited inasmuch as it makes possible the payment
to him of cash upon delivery of the equipment. The investor is
benefited by being provided with extremely high-grade investment
instruments. The trust institution, of course, is benefited to the
extent that it earns a fee for serving as trustee in the handling of
equipment trust obligations.

Although it may appear that these various parties to the transaction benefit at the expense of the existing creditors of the railroad, this is not necessarily the case. The acquisition of modern equipment may be required to achieve the efficiency necessary to make possible the payment of all debts of a company. Yet a complicated debt structure in a business may result in a deadlock among the creditor groups with respect to subordination of their claims to those of new creditors who would be asked to finance additional equipment. The equipment trust device affords an automatic subordination of claims on the part of existing creditors, inasmuch as the railroad does not come into possession of title of the equipment until it has actually been paid for through rental payments.

Equipment trust financing has been used by oil companies that have purchased tank cars under this arrangement and by some air transport companies for the acquisition of airplanes. Except in the railroad industry, however, where the arrangement has been proven to be successful, and perhaps indispensable, its application to other industries is as yet undetermined with respect to successful operations.

QUESTIONS

1. Describe the role of term loans in commerical banking. As a borrower would you regard a bank term loan to be an acceptable and attractive source of capital?

2. On what logical basis could you as a business borrower object to the protective covenants that are generally incorporated into a term loan agreement?

3. Distinguish between commercial banking and mutual savings banking. Describe the role of mutual savings banks in providing long-term financing for business.

4. Describe the various aspects of corporate business enterprises that place them in the role of a provider of long-term funds as well as a user of long-term funds.

5. Discuss the growth of employee pension funds. How are the pension funds of corporations administered?

6. Discuss the investment of pension funds. In particular, compare the investment of funds administered by life insurance companies with funds managed by administrators other than life insurance companies.

7. Discuss the relationship between eleemosynary institutions and long-term business financing.

8. Describe the pattern of operations of regional development companies. Do you consider such efforts to be worth while and generally desirable? Can you describe possible undesirable consequences of such operations?

9. Describe the operations of development credit corporations.

10. Describe the nature and operations of investment development companies. Discuss the special features of these organizations with emphasis on their basic objectives and methods of long-term financing.

11. Discuss the role of individuals in providing long-term funds for business.

12. In what way may the lease arrangement be considered a form of long-term financing? As a businessman, would you favor or object to the use of the lease arrangment in general? Describe the reasons for the growing popularity of the sale and lease-back arrangement.

13. Describe the mechanics of financing long-term equipment requirements through the use of the equipment trust arrangement.

SUGGESTED READINGS

Dauten, Carl A. *Business Finance*; Second Edition. Englewood Cliffs, New Jersey: Prentice-Hall, Inc., 1956. Chapter 8.

Dauten, Carl A., and Welshans, Merle T. "Investment Development Companies," *Journal of Finance* (September, 1951), pp. 276-290.

Jacoby, Neil H., and Saulnier, Raymond J. *Term Lending to Business.* New York: National Bureau of Economic Research, Inc., 1942.

Kimmel, Lewis H. *Share Ownership in the United States.* Washington, D. C.: The Brookings Institution, 1952.

Murray, Roger F. "Investment Aspects of the Accumulation of Pension Funds," *Journal of Finance* (May, 1952), pp. 252-259.

Ninth Semiannual Report. Small Business Administration. Washington, D. C.: For six months ending December 31, 1957.

Prochnow, Hebert V. *Term Loans and Theories of Bank Liquidity.* New York: Prentice-Hall, Inc., 1949.

Robinson, Roland I. *The Management of Bank Funds.* New York: McGraw-Hill Book Company, Inc., 1951. Chapter 10.

Steiner, William H. "Mutual Savings Banks," *Law and Contemporary Problems* (Winter, 1952), pp. 86-107.

Survey of Corporate Pension Funds, 1951-1954. Washington, D. C.: Securities and Exchange Commission. October 1, 1956.

Wooster, James W., Jr. "Current Trends and Developments in the Investment Practices of Endowments and Pension Funds," *Law and Contemporary Problems* (Winter, 1952), pp. 162-171.

Chapter 13

Merchandising and

Facilitating Agencies for

Long-Term Financing

The preceding five chapters were devoted to the organizational forms taken by businesses, the instruments and methods of long-term finance, and the sources of capital for long-term business investment. In this chapter we shall explore the processes by which the borrowers and the lenders of long-term capital are brought together. Specifically, we shall describe the activities of the investment bankers as they relate to the origination, distribution, and sale of long-term corporate securities, and the activities of the over-the-counter market and securities exchanges in serving as facilitating media for the transfer of outstanding securities.

INVESTMENT BANKING

The process of marketing to the general public securities issued by private corporations is complicated and time consuming. Corporations usually find it convenient to use independent distributors in selling their products; they find it even more to their advantage to utilize the services of professional groups whose primary activity is that of marketing securities. The average corporation has infrequent occasion to issue long-term securities, and the technicalities of such issues are so great that it is difficult for corporate executives to keep abreast of legal requirements or investor attitudes.

The groups whose function it is to market long-term securities are generally referred to as *investment bankers*. These investment bankers, therefore, are the middlemen between corporations and the general public in the accumulation of investment funds. The legal form of organization used for investment banking purposes includes both the partnership and the corporation.

Functions of Investment Bankers

Although the specific activities of investment bankers may differ, depending upon the size and the financial resources of the company, the primary functions of investment banking in general are:

1. Originating
2. Purchasing and underwriting
3. Wholesaling and retailing

(1) Originating. The investment banker assists the issuing corporation by offering recommendations as to the types and the terms of securities that should be sold and by aiding the corporation in the registration processes required by the Securities and Exchange Commission. Before an investment banking firm undertakes to originate an issue of securities, it makes a detailed study of the corporation in order to determine the feasibility of security distribution. Most of the larger investment banking firms engage in the originating function.

(2) Purchasing and Underwriting. Investment bankers not only offer the facilities through which securities are channeled to the investing public, but they also assume the risk arising from the possibility that such securities may not be purchased by investors. To accomplish this, the investment banking firm enters into a purchase agreement with the issuing corporation. The securities are then purchased in their entirety by the investment banking firm after which they are offered for sale to investors at a price sufficiently higher than their cost to assure a profit from operations. Under these circumstances the corporation issuing the securities is free to contract for the construction of additional plant facilities or to make other commitments without having to wait until the securities have been sold.

Under the laws of several states, when a corporation issues additional shares of voting stock or any security that may be converted into voting stock, such securities must be offered for sale first to the existing holders of voting stock in the corporation. The purpose of this regulation is to permit existing stockholders to maintain their proportion of voting power, claim to assets, and earnings in the company. This priority with respect to the purchase of new securities is referred to as the *pre-emptive right*. Corporate charters of individual companies may provide for such priority on the part of existing stockholders in states that do not require it. To make the new issues of securities attractive to existing stockholders, the company will generally offer the securities at a discount from the market price.

It may appear, then, that the investment banking firm serves its purpose only with respect to the initial issue of securities for public sale by a company and that subsequent issues are simply offered to the holders of the company's earlier issues of voting stock. Despite the discount price at which new issues of securities may be offered to a company's existing stockholders, however, a severe break in the market price of the stock during the period when the additional stock is being issued may eliminate the company-established discount from market price. Under this circumstance investors will not be inclined to invest further in the company on the basis of the price of the securities set by the company. As a result, the company has an unsuccessful flotation and does not receive the money from the sale of securities on which it may have been depending to carry out its commitments.

In view of the uncertainty of an unsuccessful issue of securities, even when offered to existing stockholders at a discount price, the investment banking firm may again enter the picture. The investment bankers enter into a *stand-by underwriting agreement* whereby they agree to purchase from the corporation all securities not taken by the stockholders or the public. This stand-by function of the investment bankers permits the corporation to proceed with its plans with the assurance of receiving its funds from the sale of securities, notwithstanding the uncertainties of the securities markets. The issuing corporation pays the investment banking firm a fee for their assumption of the risk of an unsuccessful flotation of securities. Although there is a clear distinction between the purchasing and the stand-by underwriting activities of the investment bankers, the term "underwriting" is generally used to include both activities.

A third category of investment banking activity for corporations issuing securities is that of *best-effort selling*. Under this arrangement the investment banking firm makes a best-effort to sell the securities of the issuing corporation, but it assumes no risk for a possible failure of the flotation. The investment bankers are paid a fee for those securities that they sell. Securities are handled on a best-effort basis for either of two reasons. First, the investment bankers may anticipate so much difficulty in selling the securities that they are unwilling to assume the underwriting risk; and second, the issue of securities may appear to be so certain of successful sale, because of the strength and reputation of the company, that the issuing company itself is willing to assume the risk of an unsuccessful flotation.

(3) Wholesaling and Retailing. A few of the large investment banking houses confine their activities entirely to the originating, underwriting or purchasing, and wholesaling functions, depending upon the sale of securities to retail security brokers for their disposition. These organizations, represented by such firms as Morgan, Stanley, and Company and Kuhn, Loeb, and Company, maintain only a central office. The vast majority of large investment banking houses, however, not only wholesale their securities to independent security brokerage houses, but they also maintain their own retail outlets in the major cities of the country.

In addition to the retail outlets maintained by the large investment banking houses, there are many independently owned and operated retail brokerage outlets. Many of these independent brokerage houses, while of insufficient size and strength to participate in originating and underwriting functions, purchase small blocks of securities for resale from the underwriters. Like the underwriters, they depend upon the resale of the securities for a price above their cost to cover their expenses and provide profit from operations.

Competitive Bidding

In contrast with private corporate issues, governmental bodies generally require competitive bidding by investment banking houses before awarding issues for underwriting purposes. This is true also of railroad securities and of some public utilities.

Under these circumstances there may be little initial negotiation between the investment houses and the issuer. Rather, the issuer decides upon the size of issue and the type of security which it wishes to sell and invites the investment banking houses of that region or of the nation to offer a bid for handling the securities. The investment banking house offering the highest price for the securities and providing information to indicate its ability to carry through a successful flotation of the securities will generally be awarded the contract. From that point on, the process of security distribution may be much like that of the handling of securities of an industrial corporation.

A great deal of controversy has existed with respect to the relative advantages and disadvantages of competitive bidding by investment banking houses. Investment bankers contend vigorously that the continuing counsel which they make available to the corporations served is essential to an economical and efficient distribution of the securities of such companies. Others contend that competitive bidding results in a higher price being paid to the issuer for the securities than would otherwise be the case. Much evidence has been presented by both sides, and it is safe to say that required competitive bidding is not likely to be extended to all issuers of securities in the near future for lack of evidence of abuse of the system as it now exists.

Market Stabilization

Investment bankers generally consider the stabilization of market prices for the securities that they are attempting to sell to be an essential feature of their operations. Because the steady flow of the new securities to the market may depress the price temporarily and because purchasers of the new securities may resell their securities after holding them but a few days, it is sometimes necessary to "buy in" some of the securities in order to relieve the market of its congestion. After the market has been re-established, the investment bankers again move their issues into circulation. Although the action of investment bankers to stabilize the markets for the issues that they are distributing is often regarded as a form of manipulation, its objective is the elimination rather than the creation of wide price fluctuations. It is also argued that market stabilization interferes with the normal operations of supply and demand, and that it may lead to the overpricing of securities.

Although the Securities Exchange Act of 1934 prohibits manipulation of this sort on the part of all others, underwriters are permitted to engage in the activity for purposes of reasonably maintaining the price of the securities that they are marketing. When market stabilization is intended, however, it is necessary to state that fact in the information or *prospectus* that is provided for purchasers of registered securities.

Direct Placements

In addition to the securities distributed by investment bankers, corporations also sell a substantial volume of securities directly to investors. Because of the unusually large supply of investable funds on the part of such institutions as life insurance companies and trust companies in the post-World War II period, the securities of well-known corporations could be sold easily by the corporations. Such direct placements eliminate the complexities of security registration with the Securities and Exchange Commission. Although the relative proportion of direct placements to those handled through the investment bankers has declined, it remains a substantial amount.

Even in connection with direct placements, the issuing corporation may find it convenient to seek the assistance of the investment banker in negotiating the arrangement. As for best-effort selling, the investment banker serves only as an agent and assumes no risk, receiving for its efforts a fee based on services rendered. A study published by the Securities and Exchange Commission in 1952 revealed that investment bankers served as agents or finders in approximately 50 per cent of all private sales, and for this service they were paid average fees ranging from 20 cents per $100 of proceeds for the largest issues to $1.70 per $100 of proceeds for the smallest issues.[1]

Regulation of Investment Banking

Federal regulation of investment banking is administered primarily under the provisions of the Securities Act of 1933. The

[1] *Privately Placed Securities—Cost of Flotation,* Securities and Exchange Commission, 1952, p. 9.

chief purposes of the Act are to provide full, fair, and accurate disclosure of the character of securities offered for sale in interstate commerce or through the mails and to prevent fraud in the sale of such securities. Disclosure is achieved by requiring the filing of a registration statement with the Securities and Exchange Commission and the delivery of a prospectus to prospective investors. The Securities and Exchange Commission does not pass upon the investment merits of securities, and it is illegal for a seller of securities to represent the Commission's approval of a registration statement as constituting a recommendation of investment quality. The philosophy underlying the Act is that the most effective regulatory device is the requirement of complete and accurate information on which investment decisions may be made. The Securities and Exchange Commission, however, does not guarantee the accuracy of any statement made by an issuer of securities in a registration statement or prospectus. Legal recourse may be taken against officers and other representatives of the issuing company for incorrect statements and misrepresentations.

In addition to federal regulation of investment banking, most of the states have blue sky laws to protect investors from fraudulent security offerings. *Blue sky laws* apparently receive their name from the efforts of some unscrupulous operators to sell portions of the blue sky—operators for whom the sky is the limit in their security dealings. Although the laws of the various states differ with respect to the specific nature of regulation of security selling, the efforts of the states are limited in their effectiveness by the difficulties of administering interstate security operations. Because of this handicap, the regulatory actions of the federal government provide the principal basis for regulation of investment banking.

OVER-THE-COUNTER MARKET

The security houses that make up the over-the-counter market serve not only to distribute new securities to the investing public but also to provide a second-hand market for securities for the public in general; that is, they stand ready to buy or to sell outstanding issues of securities. It is important at this point to distinguish between over-the-counter operations and the operations of security exchanges.

In the over-the-counter markets, securities are purchased and sold by dealers who act as principals. They buy from and sell to the public, other dealers, and commission brokers for their own account. In a sense, they operate in somewhat the manner of any merchant; they have an inventory, comprised of the securities in which they specialize, which they hope to sell at a figure high enough above the purchase price to provide a profit.

The security exchanges, which will be discussed later in this chapter, represent convenient market places for the trading of such securities only. The nonmember investor does not have access to the floor of the exchange; hence he must secure the services of a person who does have membership and floor-trading privileges. The brokers that represent the public in floor-trading activities on the exchange serve only as agents and hence must represent their customers to the best of their ability.

Securities Traded in the Over-the-Counter Market

Among the securities handled exclusively through the over-the-counter market may be included real estate bonds, Federal Land Bank and Federal Home Loan Bank bonds, state bonds, municipal bonds, and equipment trust obligations. Bank and insurance company stocks are also handled exclusively through the over-the-counter market. In addition, the over-the-counter market handles the securities of smaller industrial and utility corporations in which there is very little interest. Some securities of industrial, utility, and railroad companies are handled both on the exchanges and through the over-the-counter market.

Making a Market

When an over-the-counter dealer stands ready to buy or sell a particular security or group of securities at specified prices, he is said to be *making a market* for the security. Under these circumstances he will offer for the security a price at which he feels he can profit from a resale of the security to other investors. The quotation which is made by a dealer making a market for a given security is referred to as the *bid-and-asked price,* the bid being that price he is willing to pay for the securities and the asked price being the figure at which the dealer is willing to sell the security. Hence, the margin or spread between bid and asked price for a security is readily apparent from its quotations. Quotations shown in Table 13-1 indicate the spread for a few of the over-the-counter issues as of March 14, 1958.

Table 13–1

SELECTED OVER-THE-COUNTER QUOTATIONS
NEW YORK MARKET

March 14, 1958

	BID	ASKED	PREV. BID
AMP Inc	18¼	19⅝	18
Aerovox Corp	4⅛	4¾	4⅛
Air Products	28	29⅞	27½
Am Box Board	29¼	31½	28¾
Amer Cement	23⅛	24⅝	23⅛
Am Com'l Barge	16	17½	16
Am Express	39¾	42¼	39⅜
Am Hospital Sup	42	44⅞	42
Am Marietta	33½	35½	33⅜
Am Pipe Constr	27	29⅛	27
Am Res & Dev	25¾	27¾	25¾
Am Window Gl	10	11	10⅛
Anheuser Busch	19	20¼	19
Arden Farms	14⅜	15½	14⅜
Arden Farms pf	49¾	53¼	49¾
Arizona Pub Ser	28⅜	30	28⅜
Arkansas Mo P	18⅝	19⅞	18⅜
Arkansas W Gas	18¾	20⅜	18¾
Art Metal Const	28	30⅛	28
Assoc Spring	19½	21¼	19½
Avon Products	44	47¾	44
Aztec Oil & Gas	12¾	13¾	12¾
Bareco Inv	6½	7⅜	6¼
Bates Mfg	5⅝	6⅛	5⅝
Bausch & Lomb	20	21½	20⅛

SOURCE: National Association of Security Dealers.

A security that is traded frequently and has a ready market can be expected to have a narrower spread than a security that is traded infrequently. Since an over-the-counter dealer cannot make a market for the many thousands of securities in existence, he confines his activities to a limited number of securities. However, the over-the-counter dealer will buy securities and will provide a sale for securities in which he does not necessarily specialize. This is accomplished through an arrangement whereby the dealer contacts other investment dealers making a market for the securities in question. The over-the-counter dealer who receives a request for the purchase or sale of securities in which he does not specialize will immediately contact by telephone, wire, or other means dealers who are known to make a market for the security. After a reply is received indicating the quotation, the dealer will contact his customer and negotiate the transaction. In such a case the profit is divided between the dealer making the market for the security and the dealer who has contact with the customer.

For the more popular issues, the process of contacting a dealer specializing or making a market in the security may require only a phone call to a nearby dealer in the same community. In some cases, however, a security presented for sale or requested for purchase may be so little known to the dealer that he may have to determine from among the thousands of over-the-counter dealers of the country which dealers make a market for the security in question. This process is not so difficult as might seem at first, since the National Quotation Bureau, Inc., provides a service which reveals the dealers throughout the nation that are making a market or specializing in specific securities.

National Quotation Bureau, Inc.

This organization has three divisions—an eastern division with its main office in New York, a western division with its office in Chicago, and a Pacific Coast division located in San Francisco. Each day subscribers to this service, that is, participating dealers, who wish to present their quotations on securities on which they are making a market will forward such information by telephone or wire to the office of their district. These quotations, generally sent in the morning, are sorted in the early afternoon and reproduced for distribution. These daily quotations may run more than a hundred pages and contain several thousand bond and stock issues. By early evening the reproduced quotations are ready for delivery to subscribing dealers throughout the country. By the time the dealers open their offices for business the following morning, they have on their desks the quotations offered by specializing dealers that are less than 24 hours old.

Through the use of this service, a dealer in any part of the country is able to quote a recent quotation on practically any security for which there is a public market.

Regulation of the Over-the-Counter Market

Under the Securities Exchange Act of 1934, all brokers and dealers doing business in interstate commerce must be registered with the Securities and Exchange Commission. Under the Maloney Act of 1938, brokers and dealers were authorized to form national associations to govern and to establish practices of fair trade for their industry. This was one instance where regulation was requested of the government by business itself, and it appears to stem from the fact that reputable dealers in the investment field had little protection against bad publicity resulting from the unscrupulous practices of a few over-the-counter dealers. Under this provision only one such national association, the National Association of Security Dealers, has been formed.

The National Association of Security Dealers has established a lengthy set of rules and regulations intended to insure fair play and responsibility on the part of the member associations. Any broker or dealer engaged in that type of business is eligible to become a member of the NASD as long as he can prove a record of responsible operation and if he is willing to accept the code of ethics provided by the NASD. At present nearly 3,000 of the nation's approximately 4,000 registered security firms are members of this Association.

SECURITY EXCHANGES

At present there are seventeen security exchanges in the United States and one located in the Territory of Hawaii. These exchanges are outgrowths of informal arrangements for trading in securities at convenient locations in the nation's cities. The New York Stock Exchange, for example, had its beginning under the shade of a certain buttonwood tree on Wall Street. At a later date, because of the popularity of this meeting place, traders began to transact business in behalf of others as their agents. Eventually these traders moved indoors and now enjoy spacious and well-equipped quarters and facilities.

The New York Stock Exchange and the other exchanges of the nation have applied the latest developments in electronic communications. The present methods of transmitting information within cities and between cities is in sharp contrast with the devices used before the introduction of telegraph in 1844. It has been reported that quotations were conveyed between New York and Philadelphia through semaphore signals in the daytime and light signals at night from high point to high point across the state of New Jersey. Although cumbersome compared with modern methods of communication, quotations were often transmitted in as short a space of time as ten minutes.

The stock exchanges appear to have come into existence primarily to facilitate trading in local issues; and although there are now only seventeen such exchanges in operation, records indicate the existence of more than one hundred exchanges during the nation's history. As recently as 1929 thirty exchanges were in operation. Not only has the number of stock exchanges been reduced, due in part to the development of better means of communication between investors in the smaller communities and the large city exchanges, but the nature of their operations has also changed. No longer do these stock exchanges of the nation restrict their trading to local issues, but rather they deal in some securities that are also traded on other exchanges and in the over-the-counter market.

Of the seventeen exchanges, only two may be considered to be truly national in scope. These are the New York Stock Exchange and the American Stock Exchange, both of which are located in New York City. Together these exchanges account for more than 90 per cent of the dollar volume of security trading on all exchanges. The relative importance of the security exchanges may be observed from Table 13-2, which shows the number of shares and market value of stock traded on the exchanges for a month's operations.

Because of the tremendous relative importance of the New York Stock Exchange and because in most respects its operations are typical of those of the other exchanges, the following description of exchange organization and activities will relate primarily to the New York Stock Exchange.

Exchange Organization

The New York Stock Exchange is a voluntary association of 1,375 members. Like all the stock exchanges of the nation, its objective is to provide a convenient meeting place where buyers and sellers of securities or their representatives may transact busi-

Table 13–2

MARKET VALUE AND VOLUME OF SALES EFFECTED ON REGISTERED AND EXEMPTED SECURITIES EXCHANGES

December 1957

	TOTAL MARKET VALUE (DOLLARS)	STOCKS		BONDS	
		MARKET VALUE (DOLLARS)	NUMBER OF SHARES	MARKET VALUE (DOLLARS)	PRINCIPAL AMOUNT (DOLLARS)
ALL REGISTERED EXCHANGES					
Breakdown of December 1957 Data by Exchanges					
All Registered Exchanges	2,649,532,948	2,529,193,132	96,083,912	109,561,914	129,460,152
American Stock Exchange	145,760,454	141,250,266	16,797,247	1,396,996	1,662,000
Boston Stock Exchange	20,192,783	20,182,117	497,751	0	0
Chicago Board of Trade	0	0	0	0	0
Cincinnati Stock Exchange	2,248,784	2,244,381	58,814	1,932	4,000
Detroit Stock Exchange	11,901,169	11,898,524	471,004	0	0
Midwest Stock Exchange	70,555,643	70,450,824	2,512,753	0	0
New Orleans Stock Exchange	82,327	82,327	4,444	0	0
New York Stock Exchange	2,315,825,241	2,200,335,496	68,264,570	108,148,983	127,775,252
Pacific Coast Stock Exchange	51,775,721	51,702,440	2,747,554	0	0
Phila.-Balto. Stock Exchange	27,713,750	27,569,681	824,396	14,003	18,900
Pittsburgh Stock Exchange	3,035,259	3,035,259	110,962	0	0
Salt Lake Stock Exchange	163,008	163,008	1,713,212	0	0
San Francisco Mining Exchange	242,703	242,703	1,996,870	0	0
Spokane Stock Exchange	36,106	36,106	84,335	0	0
ALL EXEMPTED EXCHANGES [1]					
Breakdown of December 1957 Data by Exchanges					
All Exempted Exchanges	457,159	457,159	31,735	0	0
Colo. Springs Stock Exchange	421	421	1,621	0	0
Honolulu Stock Exchange	398,882	398,882	27,764	0	0
Richmond Stock Exchange	45,997	45,997	1,335	0	0
Wheeling Stock Exchange	11,859	11,859	1,015	0	0

[1] The exchanges that are exempt from registration with the Securities and Exchange Commission are small and specialize in certain types of securities such as mining shares and other securities of local interest.

SOURCE: *Statistical Bulletin*, United States Securities and Exchange Commission, February, 1958, p. 9.

ness. In addition, the New York Stock Exchange provides facilities for the settlement of exchange transactions, establishes rules relative to the trading processes and the activities of its members, provides publicity for the transactions on the Exchange, and establishes standards for the corporations whose securities are traded on the Exchange. The New York Stock Exchange, then, serves primarily to facilitate the transfer of outstanding securities from investor to investor, and in so doing it contributes significantly to the financial processes of the nation. The existence of a highly efficient second-hand market in securities, as in most fields of activity, provides assurance to the purchaser of new securities that his investment can be readily sold should alternative investments appear more attractive or if funds are needed for other purposes.

Although the number of shares, or seats as they are commonly referred to, on the New York Stock Exchange was increased from 1,100 to its present level of 1,375 in 1929, it is improbable that the number will again be increased because the physical accommodations for trading activity are limited. As might be expected, membership shares carry a considerable value; and in order to purchase a share it is necessary to negotiate with other shareholders who may be willing to dispose of their membership. During the height of stock market activity in 1929, membership shares on the New York Stock Exchange sold for as much as $625,000, while in 1942 shares sold for as low as $17,000. The cost of shares in the post-World War II period has been within the range of $60,000 to $100,000. Membership on the exchanges may be grouped into four classes: commission brokers, floor traders, specialists, and odd-lot dealers.

Commission Brokers. The largest group of members on the New York Stock Exchange, the *commission brokers,* maintain offices for the purpose of soliciting business from investors. Many members maintain offices throughout the country.

Floor Traders. *Floor traders* hold membership on the Exchange primarily for their own use. Not only do the floor traders avoid commission charges on their transactions by virtue of their access to the floor of the exchange, but also they are able to determine by direct contact with traders the temper and strength of the market for a security at a particular time. The speculative advantage of such a position is apparent. Because the floor traders are constantly in search of opportunities for even modest profits, their activities give breadth to the entire market. They provide bids and offers when they may not be available from other sources.

Specialists. *Specialists* buy and sell securities for their own account and generally limit their interest to a very few stocks. They also serve as floor brokers for other brokers who place transactions with them.

Odd-Lot Dealers. The *odd-lot dealers* facilitate the purchase and sale of securities in less than round lots. Since the customary trading unit on the Exchange is a round lot of 100 shares of stock, the commission broker who receives an order to buy or sell stock in quantities of less than 100 shares must complete the order in a different way than that used for round-lot orders.[2] The odd-lot dealer "makes" a market for these fractional orders by buying full units of a security through the regular trading facilities and selling these securities in odd lots. Similarly, odd lots that are purchased by these dealers are accumulated until they can be resold as full units. For this service the odd-lot dealers charge a commission which is in addition to the commission that the customer would otherwise pay if he were dealing in lots of 100 shares.

Listing of Securities

The New York Stock Exchange requires that all securities must be listed before they may be traded on the Exchange. To qualify for listing on the New York Stock Exchange, application for such listing, showing evidence of the firm's strength and of the interest in the firm's securities on the part of investors throughout the nation, must be submitted. If the corporation's security is accepted for listing by the New York Stock Exchange, the corporation must then pay a fee for the privilege. The acceptance of the security for listing on the "big board" (the New York Stock Exchange) does not guarantee investment quality of the security, but rather it indicates that the corporation has shown the existence of a national interest in the security and has otherwise proved its suitability for public trading. It also means that the corporation has agreed to certain requirements stipulated by the exchange with regard to the publication of reports periodically and the preparation of such other information for public distribution as will make possible an intelligent analysis of the firm's securities. The securi-

[2] For a very few stocks listed on the New York Stock Exchange, the round lot is ten shares.

ties of approximately 1,200 corporations are listed on the New York Stock Exchange.

The American Stock Exchange and all of the regional exchanges permit unlisted trading privileges as well as listed trading privileges. The distinction between these two lies primarily in the method by which the security is placed on the exchange for trading. For unlisted securities, the initiative is taken by the exchange itself instead of the issuing corporation in recommending such securities for trading privileges. Unlisted trading privileges must be approved by the Securities and Exchange Commission. The securities of approximately 1,000 corporations carry unlisted trading privileges on the nation's stock exchanges.

Security Exchange Operations

Orders for the purchase or the sale of securities listed on the New York Stock Exchange may be placed with any one of the approximately 1,500 offices maintained for that purpose by members of the Exchange throughout the nation as well as in some foreign countries. In addition, orders may be placed with approximately 2,500 other firms that have correspondent relations with members of the Exchange. The larger firms maintain a large board on which security prices are recorded for the customer's observation and study. Within the city of New York it is possible to dial by telephone for the quotation on some of the leading securities.

Market Orders. The firm that receives an order to purchase 100 shares of stock listed on the New York Stock Exchange at the best price immediately available wires the order to the New York office of the firm, where the order is transmitted by telephone to the floor of the Exchange. An order for immediate execution at the best possible price is referred to as a *market order*. The floor of the Exchange is ringed with telephone booths. These facilities are rented by the commission brokers for the purpose of communicating with their central offices. When the message has been relayed to the floor of the exchange, an employee of the commission broker takes the call and signals to the broker. The broker is called to the telephone to pick up the message by two annunciator boards on which a number is flashed. Each broker has a specified number; and upon seeing his number lighted, he immediately goes to his booth to pick up the order.

Having received the order, the broker proceeds to the location on the floor of the Exchange where trading in the security to be purchased is being carried on. Since securities are always traded at the same location or post, the broker knows exactly where to go to make the purchase. These posts carry the names of stocks traded at that location, the last price at which the security was traded, and a plus or a minus sign indicating whether the last transaction was at a price above or below that for the previous transaction.

As the broker in our example approaches the post, he may hear bids and offers being called out by other brokers. Our broker then participates in the bidding until he obtains as low a price as possible for the security that he is commissioned to purchase. Should the activity in that particular security be negligible at that moment, the broker may have to ask for the last quotation. If the quotation is $43\frac{1}{4}$ bid ($43.25), $43\frac{7}{8}$ offered ($43.875), the broker could immediately make the purchase by accepting the existing offer. In attempting to make the purchase at as low a price as possible for the customer, however, he will probably begin by bidding $43\frac{3}{8}$, then $43\frac{1}{2}$, and on up by increments of $\frac{1}{8}$ of 1 point until the bid is accepted.

Upon making the stock purchase, a memorandum is sent via pneumatic message tubes to the ticker room of the Exchange where it is recorded and sent throughout the United States. The ticker tape service is operated through the facilities of the Western Union Company. A section of New York Stock Exchange ticker tape and an explanation of the symbols are shown below.

Figure 13–1

SECTION OF TICKER TAPE OF NEW YORK STOCK EXCHANGE

DMY	KN	GM	LLT	PE
19	$63\frac{3}{8}$	$59\frac{7}{8}$	$2s17\frac{1}{8}$	$1000s32\frac{1}{4}$

Explanation: Dresser Industries Incorporated, 100 shares sold at 19; Kennecott Copper, 100 shares sold at $63\frac{3}{8}$; General Motors, 100 shares sold at $59\frac{7}{8}$; Long Island Lighting, 200 shares sold at $17\frac{1}{8}$; Philadelphia Electric Company, 1,000 shares sold at $32\frac{1}{4}$.

Ticker abbreviations appear on the upper line of the tape. Immediately below the last letter of the abbreviation are the number of shares and the price. When the sale is for a round lot of 100 shares, only the price is shown. For multiples of 100 shares from 200 through 900, the first digit of the sales figure is shown by an "s." All volume figures are shown for sales of 1,000 shares and over. The letters "ss" are used to separate the volume from the price for stocks traded in units of 10's rather than 100's. Errors and corrections are written out.

The purchase transaction is also sent by memorandum to the broker's telephone booth where the information is transmitted to the central office and then by wire to the brokerage office where the order was originally placed. Several days later the customer will receive a stock certificate indicating his ownership of 100 shares of the stock.

Limit Orders. As an alternative to the market order, the customer may establish a maximum price that he is willing to pay for the security, or in the case of the sale of securities he may establish a minimum price at which he is willing to dispose of his securities. When such limitations are placed upon the broker, the transaction is referred to as a *limit order.*

In our example, if a limited purchase order of 43 had been placed by the customer for the security in question, the order could not have been filled at that moment since other brokers were bidding as high as 43¼. The broker then would have waited until such time as a price of 43 or less became available. Usually, such limit orders away from the current market price are turned over to a specialist who enters it in his book and acts upon it for the commission broker when the price comes within the limit range. Of course, if the price of the stock progressed upward rather than back down as far as 43, the order would not be completed. Limit orders may be placed to expire at the end of one day if not consummated, one week, one month, or on a G.T.C. (good-till-canceled) basis.

Stop-Loss Orders. The holder of stock may limit his possible loss or protect part of a past increase in the price of his stock by placing a *stop-loss order* at a price a few points below the prevailing market price. In this way the stock is automatically offered for sale when the price of the security falls to the stop-loss price. For example, the purchaser of stock in our example may place a stop-loss order on his stock at a price of 40. The commission broker makes no effort to sell the stock until the price falls to that figure, whereupon it is sold for as high a price as possible. This type of order does not guarantee a price of 40 to the seller, since by the time the stock is actually sold the price may have declined rapidly to well below 40.

Short Sales. The *short sale* may be defined as the sale of securities that the seller does not own but which are borrowed for that purpose in anticipation of a price decline in the security. In the event that a price decline does occur, the short seller covers his short position by buying enough of the securities borrowed to repay the lender of securities. The difference between the price at which the securities were sold and at which they were repurchased to repay the loan less commissions is the profit of the short seller.

As an example of the operation of a short sale, assume that a person believes that the price of a certain security is going to fall. If the individual owns that particular stock, he may dispose of it as quickly as possible in order to avoid the loss resulting from a price decrease. In addition, he may turn the situation to his advantage by selling short, that is, by selling stock in excess of that held in his portfolio. As an alternative to selling his presently held stocks, he may engage in a short sale to protect his position. Any loss in value of stock owned would be offset by the profit resulting from the short sale. The short sale may be made by any person who has established favorable customer relations with one of the brokerage firms. It is not necessary that the person have this particular security in his portfolio at this time or at any other time.

In our example we shall assume that 100 shares of a particular stock are to be sold short. The order is placed through the seller's broker who in turn arranges to borrow the necessary stock to be sold short. The brokerage house handling the order for the customer may secure the stock for the short sale from the securities held by the brokerage house for its other customers. Permission must be granted by the customers whose securities are to be used for this purpose. When the brokerage house is unable to draw upon its own customers' holdings for this purpose, it bargains with another brokerage house.

Having sold the securities which have been borrowed for that purpose, the brokerage house delivers to the lender of the securities the proceeds of the sale of the securities to be held by him as collateral. If the price at which the securities were sold was 50, then the proceeds from the sale of 100 shares, $5,000, would be turned over to the lender of the stocks. Regulation T of the Board of Governors of the Federal Reserve System, as well as regulations of the New York Stock Exchange, require the short seller to maintain a margin or deposit with the broker equivalent to a specified percentage of the value of the stock sold short. Loans of stock are callable on 24 hours' notice. If the short seller covers his short position at the end of thirty days by which time the stock has dropped to a price of 40, he pays $4,000 for 100 shares to be returned to the lender of the stock. The short seller receives the $5,000 that was posted as collateral and has a $1,000 profit from the transaction, minus brokerage fees. Should the price of the security move upward rather than downward, the short seller must, of course, cover his short position by paying more for the stock than the price at which it was sold, with the result that a loss rather than a gain is experienced.

Because short sales have an important effect on the market for securities, the Securities and Exchange Commission now regulates the circumstances under which such sales may be made.

Margin Purchases. Securities may be purchased by delivering to the broker only part of the purchase price and using the securities so purchased as collateral for a loan to make up the balance of the purchase price. This is known as *buying on the margin.* The purchaser of the securities need not arrange the financing personally since the brokerage houses have constant contact with banks for this purpose. If the price of the securities that have been offered as collateral begins to decline, the customer may be required to reduce the loan by paying additional cash or by placing additional securities as collateral. In the event of a continuing decline in the market for securities pledged as collateral and the failure of the customer to re-establish the required margin, the bank or brokerage house may sell the securities in order to protect itself.

Because of the inflationary aspects of a large volume of margin trading, the federal government has limited the extent to which securities may be purchased under this arrangement. In earlier times it was unusual but possible for a person to buy securities by paying in only 10 per cent of the purchase price and borrowing the remainder. The leverage that is obtained from such an action is obvious. If the individual should purchase securities having a market price of $10,000 by contributing only $1,000 in cash and by borrowing $9,000, a 10 per cent increase in the price of the securities would increase their market value to $11,000, which, if sold, would result in a 100 per cent gain to the person making the margin purchase. Of course, if the market price should drop by 10 per cent, the purchaser's entire investment is wiped out.

For a period during World War II the Board of Governors of the Federal Reserve System, through which margin requirements are regulated for the federal government, prohibited margin trading because of its inflationary implications. Since World War II margin requirements have been changed frequently.

Regulation of Security Trading

At the present time corporations issuing securities for public distribution are subject to both state and federal regulation. Although state laws and controls, sometimes referred to as *blue-sky laws*, are generally administered well, the very size of many corporations has rendered it necessary to have some form of national control over their activities. The basis of most federal regulation over security trading is the Securities Exchange Act of 1934. It was the purpose of this Act to facilitate the analysis of securities for investment purposes (1) by requiring that information pertinent to that end be made readily available to investors and other interested parties; (2) by maintaining fair and orderly markets and eliminating fraudulent acts, and by establishing rules for the activities of exchange members and others representing investors in the securities markets; (3) by limiting and regulating the use of credit in security trading; (4) by regulating the activities of officers of corporations and other insiders having access to information not available to the general public. These objectives are accomplished in part by requiring the registration of securities, exchanges, and broker dealers.

QUESTIONS

1. Describe the basic economic function of investment banking institutions.
2. Describe in detail each step of the investment banking process.
3. Discuss the assumption of risk by investment bankers in the process of marketing securities of corporations. How do investment bankers minimize the risks accompanying the investment banking process?
4. Distinguish between the purchase function and the stand-by function in investment banking.
5. When additional stock of a company is to be offered to existing stockholders at a discount from the market price, why would the services of investment bankers be utilized?
6. The over-the-counter market has been described as a second-hand market. As a second-hand market, what is the contribution of the over-the-counter market to the economic growth of the nation?
7. Describe some of the types of securities traded in the over-the-counter market.
8. Describe the steps involved in the completion of an over-the-counter transaction.
9. Explain how over-the-counter market operations are regulated.
10. Describe the types and nature of operations of the nation's securities exchanges.
11. List the various reasons for ownership of membership shares on one or more of the nation's stock exchanges.
12. Describe the steps involved in the completion of a round-lot market order on the New York Stock Exchange. How does the completion of an odd-lot order differ from that of a round-lot order?
13. Margin purchases are usually made in expectation of a rising price level for securities purchased. Short sales are made in expectation of a declining price level for securities sold. Explain.

SUGGESTED READINGS

BELLEMORE, DOUGLAS H. *Investments.* New York: B. C. Forbes and Sons Publishing Company, Inc., 1953. Chapters 8 through 12.

BOGEN, JULES I. (Editor). *Financial Handbook;* Third Edition. New York: The Ronald Press Company, 1950. Sections 1 and 2.

CLENDENIN, JOHN C. *Introduction to Investments;* Second Edition. New York: McGraw-Hill Book Company, Inc., 1955. Chapters 8 through 12.

GUTHMANN, H. G., and DOUGALL, H. E. *Corporate Financial Policy;* Third Edition. New York: Prentice-Hall, Inc., 1955. Chapters 15 through 17.

Investment Bankers Association of America. *Fundamentals of Investment Banking.* New York: Prentice-Hall, Inc., 1949. Chapters 1, 2, 16, 17, and 18.

JORDAN, DAVID F., and DOUGALL, HERBERT E. *Investments;* Sixth Edition. New York: Prentice-Hall, Inc., 1952. Chapters 14 through 16.

ROBBINS, SIDNEY M. *Managing Securities.* New York: Houghton Mifflin Company, 1954. Chapters 2 through 5.

Financing

Special

Areas

Financing Agriculture

The rapid shift of the population of the United States to urban living since the turn of the century has been one of the results of an expanding industrial economy. Agriculture, in turn, with a decreasing proportion of the population devoted to farming has had to provide ever-increasing quantities of food and fibers to sustain a rapidly increasing total population. Such production has been made possible by the more skillful utilization of land by the application of modern machinery to farm tasks, and by improved methods of storage and preservation, and of transporting farm products to the population centers. Just as industrial activity has reflected an increasing productivity based on scientific research and technological experimentation, agriculture has responded in similar fashion. Agriculture has, in fact, become increasingly commercialized.[1]

PROBLEMS IN FINANCING AGRICULTURE

The demands for increased productivity in agriculture has made it necessary for farmers to invest ever-increasing sums of capital in land, buildings, machinery, livestock, fertilizers, and general supplies. Because the typical farm in the United States remains a combination of home and business, funds for operation of the farm must include operation of the home as well.

As an indication of the size of the investment in agriculture in the United States, as of January 1, 1957, total farm assets approximated $177 billion.[2] Table 14-1 reveals the pattern of agricul-

[1] For those persons having a special interest in the field of agricultural credit, the following reference is strongly recommended: I. W. Duggan and Ralph U. Battles, *Financing the Farm Business* (New York: John Wiley & Sons, Inc., 1950). This reference has been used frequently in the preparation of this chapter.

[2] "The Balance Sheet of Agriculture, 1957," *Federal Reserve Bulletin*, August, 1957, p. 903.

Table 14–1

COMPARATIVE BALANCE SHEET OF AGRICULTURE
UNITED STATES, JANUARY 1, SELECTED YEARS, 1940-57
[In billions of dollars]

ITEM	1940	1950	1956	1957
ASSETS				
Physical assets:				
Real estate	33.6	75.3	102.7	109.5
Non-real-estate:				
Livestock	5.1	12.9	10.7	11.2
Machinery and motor vehicles	3.1	11.2	16.5	17.0
Crops stored on and off farms	2.7	7.6	8.3	8.4
Household furnishings and equipment	4.3	7.7	11.6	12.0
Financial assets:				
Deposits and currency	3.2	9.1	9.5	9.5
United States savings bonds	.2	4.8	5.6	5.7
Investments in cooperatives	.8	2.1	3.3	3.5
Total	53.0	130.7	168.2	176.8

SOURCE: "The Balance Sheet of Agriculture, 1957," *Federal Reserve Bulletin*, August, 1957, p. 903.

tural assets for selected years. Note that the item of machinery and motor vehicles has increased in importance from 6 per cent of total assets in 1940 to 10 per cent in 1957. Such an increase reflects clearly the increasing capital requirements for mechanization of farms.

Methods of Agricultural Financing

The person who is intent on farming but with no farm of his own nor sufficient capital to acquire a farm may work for others until he is able to acquire a tract of land of his own. As a possible alternative, the farmer may establish partnership relationships with one or more other persons in order to finance the purchase of farm land and equipment. He may also lease land for farming purposes, either on the basis of a fixed rental or for a fixed proportion of the crops grown on the land. Finally, the farmer may borrow. We are principally concerned with the facilities that are available for borrowing for agricultural production and for the acquisition of farm assets.

Although many farmers own their farms and have adequate financial resources for current farming operations without recourse to borrowing, other farmers spend many years of their lives repaying indebtedness—indebtedness arising from the purchase of land and from the credit purchases of machinery, livestock, and requirements for the home. Nor is such indebtedness by the farmer to be avoided if the farm is to be operated with efficiency. The farmer who has the capacity and the equipment to cultivate 120 acres but who has only 80 acres of land of his own will do well to acquire additional land on the basis of borrowed capital, if such land and borrowing are available at a reasonable cost. So too, the farmer with much land but little equipment may be well advised to use his credit to acquire such equipment in order that his land may be utilized fully.

The farmer who has only sufficient financial resources to carry the family through the year would be foolish to reduce his cultivation because he is unable on a cash basis to meet the costs of harvesting his crops before such crops are marketed. Such a farmer would be expected to borrow prior to the harvest period in anticipation of his expected income. Without ample credit, farms could no more function efficiently than could the business institutions of the nation. Farming, in fact, is only another form of business activity, operating generally as a single proprietorship.

Special Considerations in Agricultural Financing

Most farm production is highly seasonal in nature. As such, the bulk of the annual income from farming activities may be received by the farmer within a very few weeks during each year. It may be both necessary and profitable to borrow to meet the operational costs of farming, repaying the loan when the crops have been harvested. The traditional source of such financing for the farmer has been the commercial bank. Banks in the farming regions have at times found it difficult to meet adequately the heavy seasonal demands for operating capital on the part of the farmers. In addition, the term of such loans must be adjusted to the growing period of crops and livestock, a term that is generally longer than that of the typical working capital loan to industry.

The small size of the average farm loan as compared with industrial loans and the difficulty of appraising farm resources have resulted in an interest charge somewhat higher than that to industry. Also the purchase of farm land requires a long amortization period, due to the uncertain year-to-year volume and value of agricultural production. Although the twenty-five and thirty-year urban home mortgage is still relatively new, forty-year mortgages have been common for many years in agriculture.

As a result of the complexities and difficulties of agricultural finance, there have been ever-recurring complaints that agricultural financial facilities were not adequate. This special problem of agricultural financing was recognized as early as World War I by the United States government. Since that time the government has sponsored several special agencies for the relief of these problems.

SOURCES OF FARM CREDIT

The sources of farm credit may be grouped broadly as private sources and public sources. Although most discussion of farm financing seems to center about the many public agencies established by the government for that purpose, private sources of agricultural credit continue to provide a preponderance of all financing required by the farmer. The public sources serve as supplementary financial facilities. Among the principal sources of private agricultural credit are the commercial banks, life insurance companies, individuals, merchants, and dealers. The governmental facilities for farm financing are almost all within the jurisdiction of the Farm Credit Administration. Both private and governmental facilities for farm financing are discussed in this chapter.

Private sources include the following:

1. Commercial banks
2. Life insurance companies
3. Individuals, merchants, dealers, and others

Commercial Banks

The commercial banks of rural areas have been the primary institutional source of short-term agricultural credit throughout the history of this country. In addition, commercial banks provide a substantial amount of long-term farm mortgage credit. Unlike the larger urban communities with many types of financial institutions, the small town in the agricultural area may have the commercial bank as its only financial institution. It is not surprising then that the commercial banks have played such a dominant role in agricultural financing.

Because of the high degree of liquidity required of commercial bank assets, short-term loans for production and operating purposes have been the principal contribution of commercial banks to farm finance. Short-term loans are generally based on the current earnings prospects of the farm rather than on land or equipment as mortgage collateral for the loans. The restrictive provisions of federal regulation in connection with real estate lending on the part of national banks has made long-term loans secured by real estate less suitable than short-term loans. The banking laws of many states also limit the scope of long-term lending based on real estate collateral by state chartered commercial banks. As indicated by Table 14-2 commercial banks provided only 14 per cent of all real estate loans, while they provided more than 41 per cent of all non-real estate farm loans.

Life Insurance Companies

Life insurance companies have for many years been a significant source of long-term mortgage loans for the farmer. As revealed in Table 14-2 they are the most important institutional source of farm mortgage loans. Excluding noninstitutional farm mortgage lenders, the life insurance companies of the nation held approximately 25 per cent of the farm mortgage debt as of January 1, 1957. Yet, because of the tremendous resources of life insurance companies, farm mortgages represent but a small percentage of their total assets.[3]

Since the objective of life insurance companies for most of their investments in farm mortgages is safety of the loan and a

[3] In 1956, only 2.8 per cent of total life insurance company assets were in farm mortgages. *Life Insurance Fact Book*, Institute of Life Insurance, 1957, pp. 62, 75.

Table 14–2
AMOUNT OF LOANS TO FARMERS AND PER CENT OF TOTAL
HELD, BY TYPES OF LENDERS, UNITED STATES [1]
January 1, 1957

TYPE OF LENDER	AMOUNT (MILLIONS)	PER CENT OF TOTAL
	REAL ESTATE LOANS	
Federal land bank [2]	$1,722	17.4
Insurance companies	2,477	25.0
Commercial banks [3]	1,386	14.0
Farmers Home Administration [4]	290	2.9
Individuals and others	4,033	40.7
Total	$9,908	100.0
	NON-REAL ESTATE LOANS	
Production credit associations [5]	$ 699	8.8
Federal intermediate credit banks [6]	60	.7
Commercial banks [3][5]	3,280	41.2
Farmers Home Administration [7]	431	5.4
Individuals and others	3,500	43.9
Total	$7,970	100.0

[1] Excludes territories and possessions.
[2] Includes regular mortgages, purchase money mortgages, and sales contracts.
[3] Includes national and State commercial, mutual, and stock savings, and private banks.
[4] Includes tenant-purchase, farm-enlargement, farm-development, and project-liquidation loans, and loans for these purposes from State corporation trust funds.
[5] Excludes loans held or guaranteed by Commodity Credit Corporation.
[6] Loans to and discounts for private financing institutions only.
[7] Includes production and subsistence loans, disaster loans, and emergency crop and feed loans in liquidation.

SOURCE: Agricultural Research Service, U. S. Department of Agriculture.

modest yield, it is not surprising that the volume of long-term farm mortgage lending by the life insurance companies has diminished during periods of agricultural difficulties. Some authorities believe, however, that the insurance companies were far more lenient toward distressed mortgagors during the depression of the 1930's than most other private mortgagees. The emphasis of the life insurance companies on the factor of safety has resulted in their restriction of farm mortgage loans to the better farming areas and to the better farms.

At the present time, long-term life insurance company loans to the farmer carry maturities of up to forty years, with repayment arrangements based upon the farmer's financial position. In some cases the amortization schedule is such that the payments decrease in size from year to year, while in other cases where it is expected that ability to repay will increase in the future, the principal payments increase. The fact that insurance companies restrict their mortgage loans to the better risks makes it possible for them to charge lower interest rates than is true of most other private farm mortgage lenders. The low interest rates of life insurance companies on mortgage loans, together with the fact that prepayments of principal are generally permitted without penalty, make these loans very desirable from the viewpoint of the farmer.

The large insurance companies, often located far from the agricultural loan areas of their choice, make such loans through branch offices, local banks, or local loan agents. Branch offices are generally established in choice agricultural areas for the purpose of selecting high-grade long-term farm loans. These branch offices must be staffed with personnel trained in both the mortgage loan field and in agriculture. Farmers needing loans are contacted through the company's local underwriters, through casualty and property insurance underwriters who generally receive a fee for such information, or through individuals who may suggest loan prospects. Branch managers are generally responsible directly to the home office of the insurance company they represent.

In recent years the insurance companies have made funds available to qualifying farmers in less popular lending areas through the establishment of purchase agreements with local banks. Such purchase agreements involve a commitment to purchase qualifying loans from the bank within a two-year period after the loans are made. To qualify for purchase by the insurance companies, such loans must meet prescribed requirements with regard to appraisal standards, loan-to-value ratios, loan terms, and other pertinent factors. The purchase-agreement arrangement has the advantage to the bank of permitting temporary ownership of long-term investment instruments and the advantage to the insurance company of long-term investments in isolated areas without the trouble of local title and financial settlement details. To the local bank, details of loan settlement and administration are not difficult because they may handle the matters directly rather than by correspondence. The bank generally sells such long-term mortgages to the insurance company at a price somewhat above par as compensation for originating the loan.

Local loan agents also serve the insurance companies in areas where branch offices are not practicable. The loan agents may be real estate agents, contractors, insurance agents, or farm association representatives who have close contact with farmers. Such agents generally receive a fee based on a percentage of the amount of the loan.

Individuals, Merchants, Dealers, and Others

This group of lenders accounts for well over one third of all short- and long-term agricultural loans. Loans from individuals generally arise out of a property sale in which the seller takes a mortgage as part payment for the sale price, or from a sale in which the purchaser borrows from close friends or relatives. As might be expected, there is little standardization of individual lending practices and there is generally no appraisal of the property by a trained appraiser.

Typical of the loans from merchants and dealers are the equipment loans. Such loans are offered to facilitate the purchase of heavy farm equipment, such as tractors and combines. Although these loans are arranged to permit systematic and periodic repayment, lending agencies rely to a large extent on the collateral value of the equipment for the safety of the loan. While interest rates are usually quite high, the inability of many farmers to secure adequate financing through customary channels often leaves no alternative to the use of such credit. Credit by merchants is sometimes extended for such purchases as fertilizers, feed, farm supplies, and family living.

Among the miscellaneous category of "other lenders" are the mortgage loan companies. Mortgage loan companies make long-term farm mortgage loans with the express purpose of reselling such mortgages to institutional investors. Sale of such mortgages is generally at a premium, and the mortgage companies sometimes continue to service the loans by handling the collection of payments for which they receive a fee. Endowment funds of educational and other institutions are in some cases invested in farm mortgages.

THE FARM CREDIT ADMINISTRATION

The Federal Farm Loan Act of 1916 gave rise to the first of many governmental credit institutions that were to be established to aid the farmer. In 1933 most of these federal credit institutions were consolidated in the Farm Credit Administration, and others have been added since that time. The Farm Credit Administration functioned as an independent agency of the government until 1939 at which time it was placed under the control of the United States Department of Agriculture. Under the provisions of the Farm Credit Act of 1953 the Farm Credit Administration has again become an independent agency in the executive branch of the government.

The new act established a 13-member, part-time, policy-making Federal Farm Credit Board to direct, supervise, and control the Farm Credit Administration. Twelve members of the Board, one from each farm credit district, are appointed by the President of the United States, with the advice and consent of the Senate, after giving consideration to nominations made by national farm loan associations, production credit associations, and cooperatives borrowing from the district banks for cooperatives. Thus, farmers through their cooperatives have a voice in the selection of the national board. The thirteenth member is appointed by the Secretary of Agriculture as his representative.

The Farm Credit Act of 1953 provides that the Federal Farm Credit Board shall function as a unit without delegating authority to individual members and prohibits the Board from operating in an administrative capacity. All administrative powers, functions, and duties of the Farm Credit Administration are exercised and performed by the Governor of the Farm Credit Administration, who is its chief executive officer. The Federal Farm Credit Board appoints the Governor of the Farm Credit Administration.

The Farm Credit Administration has three principal credit divisions: the Land Bank Service, the Short-Term Credit Service, and the Cooperative Bank Service. The organizational structure of the Farm Credit Administration is shown in Chart 14-1. Frequent reference to this chart by the student will facilitate an

ORGANIZATION OF THE FARM CREDIT ADMINISTRATION

Chart 14–1

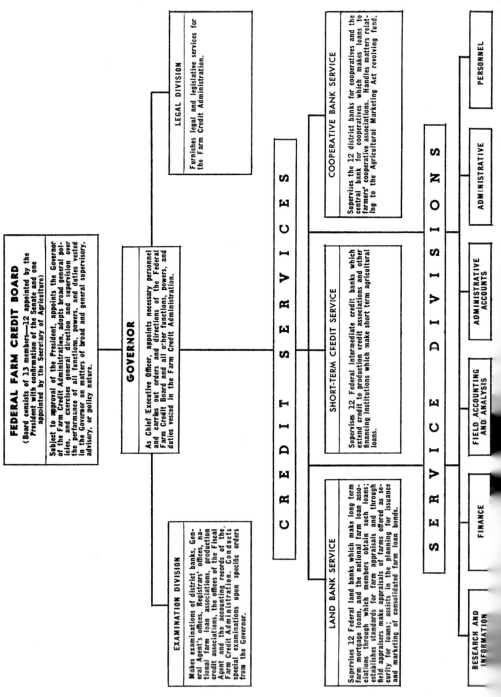

FEDERAL FARM CREDIT BOARD

(Board consists of 13 members—12 appointed by the President with confirmation of the Senate and one appointed by the Secretary of Agriculture)

Subject to approval of the President, appoints the Governor of the Farm Credit Administration, adopts broad general policies, and exercises general direction and supervision over the performance of all functions, powers, and duties vested in the Governor on matters of broad and general supervisory, advisory, or policy nature.

GOVERNOR

As Chief Executive Officer, appoints necessary personnel and carries out orders and directions of the Federal Farm Credit Board and all other functions, powers, and duties vested in the Farm Credit Administration.

LEGAL DIVISION

Furnishes legal and legislative services for the Farm Credit Administration.

EXAMINATION DIVISION

Makes examinations of district banks, General Agent's offices, Registrars' offices, national farm loan associations, production credit associations, the offices of the Fiscal Agent and the accounting records of the Farm Credit Administration. Conducts special examinations upon specific orders from the Governor.

C R E D I T   S E R V I C E S

LAND BANK SERVICE

Supervises 12 Federal land banks which make long term farm mortgage loans, and the national farm loan associations through which members obtain such loans; establishes standards for farm appraisals and through field appraisers make appraisals of farms offered as security for loans; assists in the planning for issuance and marketing of consolidated farm loan bonds.

SHORT-TERM CREDIT SERVICE

Supervises 12 Federal intermediate credit banks which extend credit to production credit associations and other financing institutions which make short term agricultural loans.

COOPERATIVE BANK SERVICE

Supervises the 12 district banks for cooperatives and the central bank for cooperatives which makes loans to farmers' cooperative associations. Handles matters relating to the Agricultural Marketing Act revolving fund.

S E R V I C E   D I V I S I O N S

| BRESEARCH AND INFORMATION | FINANCE | FIELD ACCOUNTING AND ANALYSIS | ADMINISTRATIVE ACCOUNTS | ADMINISTRATIVE | PERSONNEL |

SOURCE: Farm Credit Administration

understanding of the administrative relationship among the agricultural lending agencies.

THE FEDERAL LAND BANK SERVICE

Under the authority of the Federal Farm Loan Act of 1916, twelve farm credit districts were created. Each farm credit district is served by a federal land bank located, as a rule, in one of the principal cities of the district. The location of these banks and the district boundaries are shown in Figure 14-1.

Sources of Funds

The original capital of the federal land banks was provided almost entirely by the United States Treasury through the purchase of stock. Each bank was to be capitalized at $750,000 with additional funds to be obtained through the issue of debenture bonds, and these bonds were to be secured by the first mortgages of borrowers or United States Government bonds. With increased subscriptions from other sources the government-held stock was largely retired by 1932; however, emergency legislation in that year provided for an increased investment of $125 million in the stock of the banks to increase their supply of loanable funds. No dividends were paid on stock held by the government, and all such stock held by the government has now been retired.

Consolidated federal farm loan bonds, sold to investors, are now the principal source of funds for making land bank loans. These bonds are the joint and several obligations of the twelve federal land banks. They are not guaranteed either as to principal or interest by the United States government. On June 30, 1957, outstanding consolidated federal farm loan bonds amounted to more than $1.6 billion. In addition to the consolidated federal farm loan bonds, the federal land banks owed commercial banks $18 million and national farm loan associations $19 million.[4]

Purposes of Federal Land Bank Loans

Federal land bank loans may be made for the following purposes: (1) to buy land for agricultural uses; (2) to provide build-

[4] *Annual Report of the Farm Credit Administration,* 1956-57 (Washington, D. C.), pp. 26, 27.

Figure 14-1

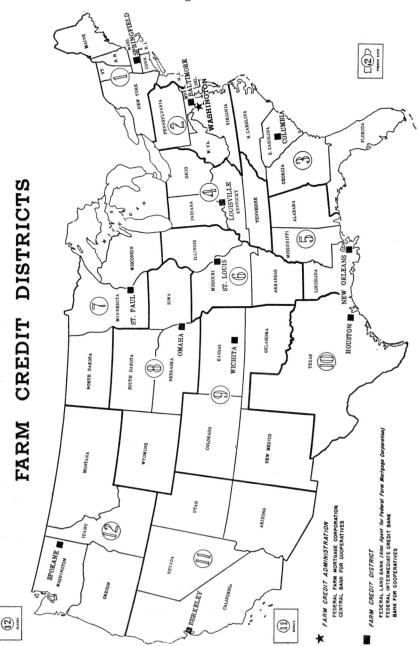

FARM CREDIT DISTRICTS

FARM CREDIT ADMINISTRATION
FEDERAL FARM MORTGAGE CORPORATION
CENTRAL BANK FOR COOPERATIVES

FARM CREDIT DISTRICT
FEDERAL LAND BANK (Also Agent for Federal Farm Mortgage Corporation)
FEDERAL INTERMEDIATE CREDIT BANK
BANK FOR COOPERATIVES

SOURCE: Farm Credit Administration

ings and to improve the farm lands; (3) to buy equipment, fertilizers, and livestock necessary for the proper operation of the farm; (4) to refinance indebtedness of the borrower incurred for agricultural purposes, or incurred at least two years prior to the date of the application; and (5) to provide the borrower with funds for general agricultural purposes. The maximum loan to any one borrower is $200,000; the minimum loan is $100. A loan may not exceed 65 per cent of the appraised normal value of the farm to be mortgaged.

National Farm Loan Associations

Federal land bank loans are negotiated through the national farm loan associations. These associations exist to provide the connection between the farmer and the land bank and to facilitate the orderly and prompt consideration of loan applications through a system of decentralization of functions and responsibilities.

National farm loan associations may be described as cooperative credit organizations. They are chartered by, and operated under, the supervision of the Farm Credit Administration in accordance with the provisions of the Federal Farm Loan Act. The associations are composed of groups of farmers who assume certain mutual responsibilities to provide a source of long-term farm mortgage credit for their community. They are usually organized on a community or county basis and, to be eligible for a charter, a group of at least ten farmers with a total loan demand of at least $20,000 is required. Where the total demand for funds is less than this amount or the number of persons wanting loans is less than ten, applications may be made directly to the land bank of that district. The stockholders of each association elect a board of directors, which in turn appoints a president, a secretary-treasurer, and a loan committee. The secretary-treasurer, upon whom most of the administrative work falls, is not required to be a stockholder. The primary duties of the national farm loan associations consist of assisting the farmer in the determination of his loan needs, initiating the loan application, and servicing the loan through the collection of payments, placing of insurance, and in some cases the disposition of property forfeited for nonpayment of debt.

Membership. Each borrower is required to purchase stock in his association to the extent of 5 per cent of the amount of his loan. As a stockholder-borrower, he is entitled to one vote irrespective of the amount he borrows.

Each loan that is made by a federal land bank through a national farm loan association is guaranteed by the association, resulting in a limited guarantee of each member of the association for all of the loans made through his association. This guarantee is made effective through the requirement that the association hold stock of its federal land bank in an amount equal to 5 per cent of total loans made through the association. Should mortgage losses of an association exceed normal dividends due from the federal land bank, recourse may be had to the stock held by the borrower-stockholder.

An example of a loan application and approval may best illustrate the functioning of the federal land bank system. Assume that a farmer has applied for a loan of $6,500 to provide for the purchase of land for agricultural use, or for other reasons acceptable to the land bank. The loan committee of the association examines the application to establish a preliminary appraisal of the property to be mortgaged and the acceptability of the applicant as a mortgagor. If the loan application is acceptable to the loan committee, it is presented to the board of directors of the association where, if acceptable to the board, it is forwarded to the federal land bank of that district. The federal land bank then has the property appraised by one of its own appraisers, a requirement established by the Federal Farm Loan Act. If the appraiser submits a favorable report and the application is satisfactory in other respects, the loan may be granted. The maximum loan-to-value ratio is 65 per cent; hence, the property in this example must have an appraised value of at least $10,000.[5]

On the assumption that this loan is approved, upon clearance and transfer of title to the property, the $6,500 is delivered to the

---

[5] As a result of substantial losses sustained by the federal land banks and associations due to appraisals based on inflated property values in the early 1920's, appraisals have been based on assumed "normal" agricultural values since 1933. This permitted loans to be made in excess of 65 per cent of sale prices during the depression because property values were below normal, and at the present time it limits loan participation to much less than 65 per cent because of higher property values. The annual Report of the Farm Credit Administration for 1949-50 indicated that appraisals made in 1949 resulted in reported "normal" agricultural value of only 56 per cent of the average price of those particular farms.

national farm loan association through which the loan was initiated. The association in turn brings together the parties to the transaction and delivers the money to the seller of the property after the loan settlement arrangements are completed.

The borrower is required to purchase stock in his association in the amount of $325 (5 per cent of $6,500). This amount in turn is paid by the association to the land bank for stock. The borrower is liable, therefore, not only for his indebtedness, but also to the extent of his stock ownership for the loans of his fellow association members. If losses of the association prove to be negligible, the borrower may surrender his stock upon payment of his loan and receive his $325. Should losses of the association be large because of numerous defaults, the borrower may recover only a part or none of his stock investment, depending on the amount of the stock fund required to offset the loan losses. This system of requiring a joint responsibility for all loans of an association by all borrowers results in a greater selectivity of risks and a local control otherwise difficult to achieve.

Loans, Interest Rates, and Dividends. The federal land banks, through the 1,052 national farm loan associations, made 52,715 loans for a total of $475 million during the year ending June 30, 1957. Under the Federal Farm Loan Act the contract interest rate on loans made through national farm loan associations cannot be more than 1 per cent above the interest rate on the last series of bonds issued by the bank making the loans, except with the approval of the Governor of the Farm Credit Administration. In no case may the interest rate exceed 6 per cent per year. As of June 30, 1957, the interest rate of all new loans of federal land banks with the exception of those located in Baltimore, Maryland; Columbia, South Carolina; Spokane, Washington; and Springfield, Massachusetts, was 5 per cent. The interest rate of the federal land banks located in those cities was 5½ per cent.[6]

Dividends of over $115 million were paid by the federal land banks for the period June 30, 1944, to June 30, 1957. Practically all of these dividends were paid to national farm loan associations, which in turn declared dividends in relatively substantial sums to their member-borrowers. During the fiscal year ending June 30,

[6] *Ibid.*, p. 26.

1957, dividends were declared by the federal land banks in the amount of $7.5 million.[7]

THE FEDERAL SHORT-TERM CREDIT SERVICE

The Federal Short-Term Credit Service supervises and coordinates the operations of the 12 federal intermediate credit banks, which in turn work closely with the 497 production credit associations on all phases of their operations. It provides leadership and guidance in all major phases of the operations of the institutions concerned, including their capitalization, development of credit standards, investment of funds, disposition of earnings, and other factors related to sound lending and management practices. It approves the borrowing of money and the issuance of debentures by the federal intermediate credit banks.[8]

The Federal Intermediate Credit Banks

Federal assistance in the field of long-term credit for the farmer was followed by attempts to provide supplementary sources of intermediate and short-term credit. This was accomplished through the establishment of 12 federal intermediate credit banks under the Agricultural Credits Act of 1923. Congressional inquiry had revealed that agricultural and livestock industries needed a more adequate and stable supply of intermediate and short-term credit than was available to them through existing sources.

The federal intermediate credit banks themselves do not make loans directly to farmers; they discount agricultural and livestock paper and make loans to local financial institutions that do finance the credit needs of the farmer. Representative of the kind of institutions receiving such financing are the production credit associations, agricultural credit corporations, livestock loan companies, and commercial banks. These loans are generally made for production and general farm operation purposes and may carry maturities of up to five years. The usual loan term, however, is

---

[7] *Ibid.*, p. 29.

[8] On January 1, 1957, after 23 years of operation, the 12 production credit corporations were terminated by merger in the 12 federal intermediate credit banks in their respective farm credit districts. The corporations were established under the Farm Credit Act of 1933 to aid farmers in organizing local production credit associations, to supply the associations with initial capital, and to provide the supervision and assistance necessary to enable them to make sound credit available to farmers and stockmen.

for one year or less, maturities being based on the time for marketing crops or livestock.

Sources of Funds

The federal intermediate credit banks obtain the bulk of their funds from the sale of consolidated collateral trust debentures in the financial markets to the investing public. Although maturities of up to five years are permitted, the average maturity has been from three to twelve months. For the year ending June 30, 1957, the average maturity was eight months. Debentures issued in 1957 carried a total cost to the banks of 3.81 per cent. Each bank's participation in the outstanding debentures must not exceed ten times the amount of its capital and paid-in surplus. The twelve banks are jointly and severally liable for these obligations. The debentures are not guaranteed by the federal government, either as to principal or interest. Sales and distribution are usually made through security dealers and dealer banks for delivery on the first of each month. Such sales are made on the basis of estimates of cash needs, but unexpected demands make it necessary from time to time to obtain funds for short periods between sales.

The federal reserve banks are also authorized to loan to the intermediate credit banks under Section 13 of the Federal Reserve Act for periods of fifteen days, such loans to be secured by debentures maturing within six months. Debentures of similar maturities may also be purchased outright by the federal reserve banks.

The original capital of each federal intermediate credit bank, $5 million, was supplied by the United States Treasury. The total capital and surplus of the twelve banks as of January 1, 1957, was $150 million.

Management and Supervision

Each intermediate credit bank operates under its own corporate management and under the direction of a board of directors, which serves as the board for the other three permanent credit units of each district. The operations of the banks are supervised by the Intermediate Credit Division Commissioner, who is responsible to the Governor of the Farm Credit Administration.

Interest and Discount Rates

The board of directors of a federal intermediate credit bank together with the Commisisoner fix the discount and interest rates. Except with the approval of the Governor of the Farm Credit Administration, however, the rate fixed may not exceed by more than 1 per cent per annum the rate of the last preceding issue of debentures in which the bank participated. The rate charged by a bank, therefore, is governed primarily by the cost of money which, in turn, is related closely to the prevailing rates on other prime securities in the market. As of June 30, 1957, the interest and discount rate of the federal intermediate credit banks ranged from 4 to 4½ per cent.[9]

Institutions that rediscount with an intermediate credit bank are permitted to charge their borrowers on such loans not more than 4 per cent per annum in excess of the discount rate of the intermediate credit bank. The intermediate credit banks pay an annual franchise tax to the United States of 25 per cent of their net earnings remaining after paying all operating costs, charge-offs of determined losses, and necessary adjustments for reserves. From the beginning of operations to the close of June 30, 1957, the banks had paid $10 million in franchise taxes.

The twelve federal intermediate credit banks during the fiscal year ending June 30, 1957, extended credit amounting to $2.3 billion.[10]

Production Credit Associations

The Governor of the Farm Credit Administration is authorized to charter cooperative lending organizations, known as production credit associations, making short-term loans to farmers for agricultural uses. Typically, such loans are used for purposes of breeding, raising, and fattening of livestock and poultry; dairying; the growing, harvesting, and marketing of crops; the purchase and repair of farm machinery; and the refinancing of short-term debts. Associations now serve every rural county in the United States and Puerto Rico, each association's territory of operation being prescribed by the Governor of the Farm Credit Administration.

9 *Ibid.,* p. 60.
10 *Ibid.,* p. 56.

Capital Stock. Each production credit association has two classes of capital stock: Class A, which is nonvoting; and Class B, which is voting. Class B stock may be owned only by borrowing farmers. The Class A stock, owned by the Governor of the Farm Credit Administration, is preferred as to assets in case of liquidation of an association, but all stocks share proportionately in dividends. Borrowers are required to purchase Class B stock of an association to the extent of $5 for each $100 of loan. Such stock may be retained and used regularly for borrowing purposes. Should the borrower prefer to discontinue his membership after his indebtedness to the association has been retired, he may list it for sale to another eligible borrower. As in the case of members of the national farm loan associations, each borrower has one vote. Such voting must be accomplished in person, voting by proxy not being permitted. Holders of Class B stock are required to sell their stock in the event that two years elapse after the repayment of a loan and no new loan has been negotiated. The purpose of this limitation is to restrict control of the production credit association to active borrower members.

Management. Voting stockholders elect their association's board of directors at their annual meetings. The board is generally composed of five members, each selected for three years on a staggered basis. It is the responsibility of these directors to elect the association officers and appoint its employees.

Source of funds. The production credit associations secure loan funds by borrowing from the federal intermediate credit bank of their district, or by turning over to the intermediate credit banks loans that they have made to their customers. Loans are made to farmers and ranchers for general agricultural purposes to finance sound short-term credit needs. These loans are generally secured by a first lien on crops, livestock, and equipment, and interest is charged ony on the amount of the loan actually outstanding. Interest rates in 1957 averaged from 6 to 7 per cent.

The production loan associations also charge a loan service fee to cover the cost of appraising, reviewing, and administering the loans. Short-term credit secured from the production credit associations is often sufficient to cover a member's entire credit needs for a season or a year. Farmers usually get their installments as they need the money and repay their loans when they sell the products financed. Budgeted loans of this nature reduce the number of days each dollar is outstanding and reduce correspondingly the amount of interest paid by the borrower. Farmers had 275,603 loans outstanding for a total of $1.6 billion from the 497 production credit associations as of June 30, 1957.[11]

THE COOPERATIVE BANK SERVICE

For many years the federal government has encouraged the establishment of farmers' marketing and purchasing cooperatives. Such encouragement has taken the form of immunity from the antitrust laws, tax advantages, and financial assistance. The provision of financial assistance is accomplished through a system of banks for cooperatives.

Under the provisions of the Farm Credit Act of 1933 the Governor of the Farm Credit Administration chartered twelve district banks and one Central Bank to provide a permanent system of credit for farmers' cooperatives. One of the banks for cooperatives is located in each of the farm credit districts and the Central Bank is located in Washington, D. C.

Functions of the Banks for Cooperatives

The thirteen banks make loans to cooperatives engaged in marketing agricultural products, purchasing farm supplies, and furnishing farm business services. The Central Bank makes loans that are too large for the district banks to handle or to cooperatives operating in more than one farm credit district. The Central Bank for Cooperatives also participates in many loans made by the district banks. District banks, in turn, participate in loans made by the Central Bank.

Capital and Other Sources of Loanable Funds

The initial capital for the banks for cooperatives was subscribed by the Governor of the Farm Credit Administration from funds made available by the federal government. Changes in this initial capital have been made from time to time as the demand for credit has varied. Stock held by the government is nonvoting,

[11] *Ibid.*, p. 39.

but it is eligible to participate in dividends. In addition, borrowing cooperatives are required to purchase stock to the extent of $100 for each $2,000 of loans extended to them.

The banks for cooperatives are authorized to borrow from, or turn their own loans over to, other banks for cooperatives, the federal intermediate credit banks, and commercial banks. The Central Bank for Cooperatives is authorized to issue debentures in an amount not to exceed five times its paid-in capital and surplus.

Management

General supervision of the banks for cooperatives is exercised by the Cooperative Bank Commissioner acting under the direction of the Governor of the Farm Credit Administration. The district banks have as their board of directors the farm credit board of each district. In addition to the officers elected by the board, each of the banks has a staff composed of business analysts, appraisers, accountants, and clerical employees. The Central Bank for Cooperatives has a board of seven directors, six of whom are appointed by the Governor of the Farm Credit Administration. The seventh member is the Cooperative Bank Commissioner, who also acts as chairman of the board.

Eligible Borrowers

To be eligible to borrow from a bank for cooperatives, an association must be a cooperative operated for the mutual benefit of its members, in which farmers act together in doing one or more of the following: (1) processing, preparing for market, handling, or marketing farm products; (2) purchasing, testing, grading, processing, distributing, or furnishing farm supplies; or (3) furnishing farm business services.

Types of Loans

Three types of loans are made to cooperatives: (1) short-term loans secured by appropriate commodities in storage; (2) operating capital loans to supplement the borrowing cooperatives' working capital; (3) loans for the purpose of assisting in financing the cost of construction, purchase, or lease of land and the acquisition of buildings, equipment, or other physical facilities. Although maturities of twenty years are permitted, in most cases they are for much shorter periods.

OTHER FEDERAL AGRICULTURAL CREDIT FACILITIES

The trend in recent years has been toward administrative centralization of the many sources of government sponsored agricultural credit under the Farm Credit Administration. There remain, however, several financial operating organizations directly under the control of the Secretary of Agriculture. Two of these are the Commodity Credit Corporation and the Farmers Home Administration.

The Commodity Credit Corporation

The Commodity Credit Corporation was organized in 1933 to provide a more orderly and stable market for farm products. Loans and loan guarantees are used by the Corporation in order to support the price of basic commodities such as wheat, tobacco, corn, and cotton. These basic commodities serve as collateral for Commodity Credit Corporation loans. The maximum loan value on farm products is based on a percentage of "parity" prices established at the beginning of the year. A condition of the availability of such loans, however, is that the borrowing farmer shall have complied with governmental restrictions concerning the number of acres allotted to that farmer for the planting of that crop. He can borrow from the Commodity Credit Corporation a stipulated percentage of the parity value of the crop even though such parity value is above the prevailing market value of that product. Purchase by the government of the farm products used as collateral for the commodity credit loan becomes effective by default if the loan is not repaid. This amounts to a conditional purchase plan by the government to effect a price floor on farm products.

The Commodity Credit Corporation also gives support to farm prices through the outright purchase and storage of crops and it has participated in general supply programs in cooperation with other federal agencies, foreign governments, and international relief organizations.

The capital of the Commodity Credit Corporation is provided entirely by the United States government. The Corporation has a capital of $100 million plus a reserve of $500 million. It is authorized to borrow an additional $4,750 million on the credit of the United States government. From the time of organization of the CCC in 1933 to July 1, 1956, over $22 billion in loans and loan guarantees had been issued. As of July 1, 1956, there was $2.3 billion of such loan and loan guarantees outstanding.[12]

The Farmers Home Administration

The Farmers Home Administration was created in 1946 by the merger of the Farm Security Administration and the Emergency Crop and Feed Loan Division of the Farm Credit Administration. It has been authorized to make loans and to insure loans for farmers who are otherwise unable to obtain credit at appropriate rates of interest and suitable maturities. Preference has been given to veterans to enable them to purchase farms. Loans for terms up to forty years are made for purposes of purchase, improvement, or repair of farms and farm buildings.

Responsibility for the administration of the following has been given the Farmers Home Administration: (a) administration of rural resettlement projects; (b) financing the purchase of farm property for tenant farmers; (c) emergency loans to low-income farmers; and (d) loans to facilitate farmers' community and cooperative enterprises that would be classified as rehabilitation or resettlement projects. Loans of up to $20,000 are made for such purposes as the purchase of livestock, seed, fertilizer, farm equipment, supplies, and other farm needs, as well as for financing indebtedness and family subsistence. Such loans have maturities of from 1 to 7 years. Funds for the loans of the Farmers Home Administration are provided by Congress. As of July 1, 1956, the Farmers Home Administration had $788 million in loans outstanding, of which the largest part was for production and subsistence purposes and the next largest use was for farm ownership.[13]

QUESTIONS

1. Compare the credit needs for farming with the credit needs of industrial manufacturing.

[12] *Agricultural Finance Review*, Volume 19 (February, 1957) (Washington, D. C.), p. 119.

[13] *Ibid.*, p. 108.

2. Farm financing is often described as being an especially difficult problem. Explain.
3. Discuss the importance of commercial bank lending for agricultural purposes. Do commercial banks provide credit for all agricultural purposes?
4. To what extent and for what purposes do life insurance companies provide funds for agriculture?
5. How do the life insurance companies of the nation maintain contact with farmers for purposes of extending mortgage loans?
6. Describe some of the private sources of agricultural credit other than commercial banks and life insurance companies.
7. Describe the evolution and present structure of the principal governmental facilities for farm credit.
8. Trace the principal steps involved in the making of a federal land bank loan from the original application by the farmer to the receipt of the loan.
9. Discuss the method by which the federal land banks shift part of the risk of mortgage lending to other groups.
10. Describe the role of the federal intermediate credit banks in agricultural financing.
11. Discuss the sources of loan funds for the federal land banks and for the federal intermediate credit banks. To what extent are the obligations of these organizations liabilities of the federal government?
12. Describe the role of the production credit associations in agricultural financing.
13. For what purposes were the banks for cooperatives established?
14. Outline the types of loans available to farmers through the Farmers Home Administration.

SUGGESTED READINGS

Agricultural Credit. New York: American Institute of Banking, 1954.
Agricultural Finance Review, published annually by the Agricultural Research Service, United States Department of Agriculture.
Agricultural Production Financing. New York: Agricultural Commission, American Bankers Association.
Annual Reports, published by the Farm Credit Administration.
ARNOLD, L. L. *Problems of Capital Accumulation in Getting Started Farming.* Station Bulletin 638. Lafayette, Ind.: Purdue University, February, 1957.
DUGGAN, I. W., and BATTLES, RALPH U. *Financing the Farm Business.* New York: John Wiley and Sons, Inc., 1950.
Farm Equipment Financing by Banks. New York: Agricultural Commission, American Bankers Association.
Farm Real Estate Financing. New York: Agricultural Commission, American Bankers Association.
Intermediate-Term Bank Credit For Farmers. New York: Agricultural Commission, American Bankers Association.

International Finance

The productive capacity of the United States economy is the result of many factors, including vast natural resources, suitable climatic conditions, and a population that has had the courage and the ability to profit by these natural advantages. Of equal importance to the productive growth of the nation has been the existence of a form of government that has encouraged this development through stimulation of individual effort. Not the least of the contributions of the government in this respect has been that of facilitating trade between the areas of the nation, in turn making it possible for each geographical area to specialize in those activities for which its individual natural resources best equip it.

It is difficult to imagine the situation that would exist if each of the forty-eight states tried to be self-sufficient. Under these circumstances, we could expect the northern industrial states to enjoy little of the citrus fruits that they now import from Florida and the West Coast. Nor could we expect the tobacco-growing states to have the full benefit of farm machinery for their operations, since the market for machinery in a single state is hardly sufficient to warrant production on a scale necessary for economical manufacture.

While these principles of specialization with regard to geographical areas of the United States are obvious enough, it may be somewhat more difficult to appreciate the extension of these principles of specialization beyond the borders of the country; yet the basic principles underlying specialization of effort within a nation hold true with equal force among nations. The very size of the United States is such as to lead a person not otherwise familiar with the vast amount of goods and services transported between the United States and foreign countries to believe that the nation is nearly self-sufficient. It is true that many items which were formerly imported are now produced in the country, making us less dependent upon foreign sources; however, there is an effective limit to the self-sufficiency that any nation may attain. For example, the development of sufficient coffee production within the nation to satisfy the current domestic demand for the product would probably be impossible.

In addition to the many items for which other nations possess a natural productive advantage, other items are not available within our own national borders under any circumstances. Examples of such items include tin, magnesium, and certain other minerals, as well as extracts from certain tropical plants used in the preparation of medicines. Although there are some legitimate reasons for curtailing temporarily, and in some cases permanently, certain types of trade flows, it is undoubtedly true that a specialized concentration of effort on the part of the nations of the world is to the general benefit of everybody concerned.

The benefits which arise as a result of specialization of effort are made possible only to the extent that the persons participating in such specialization are assured that there will be a market for the fruits of their effort. A market for goods and services is made effective only if adequate financial facilities exist to make possible the settlement of claims between the parties. Just as there has developed within the United States an intricate and smoothly operating system of finance to provide for the exchange of goods and services among persons and institutions, so too there has developed a system of international finance whereby settlement of international claims may be effected. It is with this process of settlement of international claims that this chapter is concerned.

INTERNATIONAL PAYMENTS

As a citizen of the United States tours our country during his vacation, he desires to pay his lodging bills, his gasoline costs, and other vacation expenses with dollars. Similarly, the motel and hotel operators and the service station attendants wish to be paid for their goods and services in the form of dollars. The large mail-order houses located in Chicago also demand dollars for the goods that they are willing to ship to all parts of the country, and the persons ordering such goods are prepared to pay in terms of dollars.

On the other hand, a person who orders leather goods from Mexico, glassware from Italy, or a year's subscription to *The London Times*, must arrange for payment for these items not in dollars but rather in the money of the particular country from which the items have been ordered. Payment for the subscription to *The London Times*, for example, must be made in pounds sterling.

In some cases, a foreign exporter may be willing to take dollars in payment for his goods or services, but only because he expects to be able to convert the dollars into the currency of his own country. For the most part, however, an importer must make arrangements to pay the seller of goods or services from another country in the legal tender of the seller's country. But the purchaser need not secure actual possession of the foreign money; in fact, it is entirely probable that many persons have made international purchases for many years without ever having seen currency other than that of the United States.

In the case of a year's subscription to *The London Times*, the subscriber need only go to the bank and buy a claim against British pounds equivalent to the subscription cost of the paper. This claim, which is purchased in the United States with American dollars, may be in the form of a bill of exchange, a telegraphic order, or similar instruments. An oversimplified example will illustrate how these claims may be purchased and the actual acquisition of the foreign currency avoided.

If the person who is purchasing a subscription to *The London Times* must secure a claim for two pounds, six shillings, he could conceivably seek out a British tourist who at that moment might be touring the United States. If that tourist had brought his checkbook with him, he might be induced to write a check against his own local bank in England for two pounds, six shillings in return for the appropriate number of dollars, which he would expect to spend while a tourist in this country. In addition, of course, the English tourist might expect a slight additional payment to compensate him for the trouble of rendering this service. The individual to whom the check is written could then endorse it and send it together with his order for *The London Times* to England where the check would be deposited for collection with the bank with which that paper does business. In this instance, the subscriber of the paper from the United States purchased nothing more than a claim to pounds.

This is rather an awkward process, however, and it is hardly to be expected that an importer would be required to seek out some foreign visitor to this country. Instead, the banking system along with other institutions provides this service for a nominal fee. Although all banks do not have departments that sell foreign exchange to their customers, practically all banks do have correspondent relations with banks located in the major seaport towns or cities which do offer that facility. Hence, it is only necessary to go to a local bank in order to secure a claim against foreign money. If the local bank does not itself have a claim to foreign currency, it can purchase such a claim for its customers from a bank with which it deals for that purpose. The banks that deal directly in foreign exchange may do so by maintaining monetary deposits in banks in foreign countries, against which they may draw drafts for sale to their home customers. In other cases, banks may operate branches in the foreign countries. The Federal Reserve Act authorizes banks to establish branches abroad and, as of the end of 1956, there were 115 such branches in 26 foreign countries or dependencies of the United States.

Foreign banking corporations likewise have their own network of foreign contacts. In addition to maintaining correspondent relations with United States banks, foreign banks are permitted to operate agencies and to set up subsidiaries in this country. Most of these organizations are located in New York City and must, of course, comply with the state banking laws. They are limited as to the type of business in which they may engage, primarily that of dealing in foreign exchange. Subsidiary banking corporations established by foreign banks are not subject to any special restrictions because of foreign ownership.

EXCHANGE RATES

The conversion ratio, or *exchange rate* as it is generally referred to, is the rate at which a given unit of foreign currency is quoted in terms of domestic currency. For example, if the British pound is quoted at $2.80 in the foreign exchange rate section of the daily newspaper, it means that purchases of claims on pounds sterling were made on the basis of a ratio of 2.8 dollars for one British pound. For the individual who cares to buy claims on pounds sterling, this exact ratio would not necessarily prevail since it is a record of the exchange ratio of large unit transfers within the foreign exchange market itself. The prices quoted to the individual are always in favor of the seller of the exchange, which, of course, makes possible a margin of profit for the seller. The seller or dealer in our example is a bank.

The balance in the foreign account of a bank is subject to constant drain as a result of the bank's activities in selling claims to individuals in the United States who wish to import goods or services from other countries. These banks may re-establish a given deposit level with their correspondent banks through either the sale of dollar claims in the foreign country concerned or by buying claims from another dealer in the foreign exchange. The question may arise, however, as to what happens if during a period of time the volume of trading is decidedly unbalanced and the demand for claims against British pounds is substantially greater than the corresponding demand by British businesses and individuals for American dollars. Since the exchange ratio reflects the forces of supply and demand for these two currencies, such a situation would be expected to cause the ratio to rise to a point above $2.80 for each pound sterling. At some point, the number of dollars available in exchange for pounds would become high enough to induce the owners of British pounds to invest in American dollars.

Like the price of all commodities, exchange rates vary from one period to another, although the degree of variance is as a rule not large over a short period of time. Changes of a few cents may be noticed in weekly comparisons between the exchange ratios of currencies of other countries and that of the United States. As a result of varying exchange rates, the importer or exporter may be financially benefited or hurt in much the same manner that he may be affected by changes in the price level of the commodity which he purchases or sells. Foreign exchange rates between the United States and the principal countries of the world as of April 9, 1958, are shown in Table 15-1.

Arbitrage

Arbitrage may be defined as the simultaneous, or nearly simultaneous, purchasing, as of commodities, securities, or bills of ex-

Table 15–1
FOREIGN EXCHANGE

	—IN DOLLARS—	
	WEDNESDAY	PREV. DAY
Canada (Free Dollar)	1.03¼	1.03 1-64
England (Pound)	2.81 23-32	2.81 25-32
30-day Futures	2.80⅞	2.80 25-32
90-day Futures	2.79 3-16	2.79 1-16
Transferable	2.79⅜	2.79 17-32
Switch (or Security)	2.78⅜	2.78¼
Australia (Pound)	2.25⅜	2.25½
New Zealand (Pound)	2.80 25-32	2.80 25-32
South Africa (Pound)	2.82 3-32	2.82 5-32
Belgium (Franc)	.0200⅝	.0200 9-16
Holland (Guilder)	.2642	.2641
Switzerland (Franc)	.2334	.2334
West Germany DM (Freely Convert.)	.2381	.2381
DM (Liber. Cap.)	.2381	.2381
DM (Lim. Convert.)	.2380	.23805

LATIN AMERICA:

Argentina ("Free" Peso)	.0249	.0254
Brazil ("Free" Cruzeiro)	.0090	.0092
Chile ("Free" Peso)	.0014	.0014
Colombia ("Free" Peso)	.1300	.1330
Mexico (Peso)	.0802	.0802
Peru (Sol)	.0460	.0460
Uruguay ("Free" Peso)	.1675	.1695
Venezuela (Bolivar)	.3000	.3000

NEAR EAST:

Iraq (Dinar)	2.82¾	2.82⅞
Lebanon (Pound)	.3200	.3200

FAR EAST:

India (Rupee)	.2113	.2113½
Pakistan (Rupee)	.2116½	.2117
Hong Kong (H. K. Dollar)	.1755	.1755

change, in one market where the price is lower than in another market, and selling in the latter. In international exchange variations in quotations between countries at any time are quickly brought into alignment through the arbitrage activities of international financiers.

For example, if the exchange rate in New York was reported at £1 = $2.81 and in London the rate was quoted at £1 = $2.80, alert international financiers would simultaneously sell claims to British pounds in New York at the rate of $2.81 and have London

Table 15–1 (Concluded)

FOREIGN EXCHANGE

These buying prices were quoted at 4 p.m. by the First National City Bank of New York for foreign banknotes (official rates in parenthesis where officially-sanctioned fluctuations are too small to warrant daily comparison):

	—IN DOLLARS—	
	WEDNESDAY	PREV. DAY
England (Pound)	2.78	2.78
France (Franc) (.0024)	.00221	.00222
Holland (Guilder)	.2620	.2620
Italy (Lira) (.00161)	.00160	.00160
Spain (Peseta) (.0236)	.0187	.0187
Germany (DM)	.2370	.2370
Argentina (Peso)	.0242	.0246
Brazil (Cruzeiro)	.0086	.0087
Chile (Peso)	.0010	.0010
Colombia (Peso)	.1250	.1300
Uruguay (Peso)	.1625	.1700
Egypt (Pound) (2.881)	1.67	1.67
Turkey (Lira) (.3575)	.0675	.0675
India (Rupee)	.1950	.1950
Pakistan (Rupee)	.1300	.1300
Hong Kong (H. K. Dollar)	.1600	.1600
Japan (Yen) (.0028)	.00255	.00255
Philippines (Peso) (.4992)	.3100	.3100

Inactive currencies: Cuba (1.001); Denmark (.1452); Iran (.0135); Norway (.1403); Portugal (.0350); Sweden (.1937).

SOURCE: *The Wall Street Journal*, April 9, 1958.

correspondents sell claims on American dollars in London at the rate of $2.80 for each pound sterling. Such arbitrage would be profitable only when dealing in large sums. If an arbitrager, under these circumstances, sold a claim on £100,000 in New York, he would receive $281,000. The corresponding sale of claims on American dollars in London would be at the rate of £100,000 for $280,000. Hence, a profit of $1,000 would be realized.

The effect on exchange rates of such arbitrage activities would be the elimination of the variation between the New York and the London quotations, for example, since the sale of large amounts of claims to American dollars in London would drive the price for pounds sterling up and in New York the sale of claims to pounds sterling would force the exchange rate down. A quotation differential of as little as one-sixteenth of one cent may be sufficient to encourage arbitrage activities.

Exchange Quotations

In inquiring at the local bank as to the exchange rate for a foreign currency at a specific time, a banker's sight draft rate will generally be given. A *banker's sight draft*, or *banker's check* as it is more commonly termed, differs from the common bank check only in that it is drawn by one bank on another bank. When presented for payment at the foreign bank, the balance of the drawing bank is reduced. Several days or weeks may elapse between the time the check is issued by the bank and the time it is presented for payment at the foreign bank or foreign correspondent bank. During this interval, the foreign balance of the issuing bank is not affected by the transaction.

If specifically requested, the quotation may be based on a cable rate. The bank may cable to its foreign correspondent or foreign branch to credit to the account of a specified individual or business establishment a certain amount of money. The cost of a cable order of this sort is more expensive to the purchaser than that of the banker's check since it reduces the balance of the bank's foreign deposit almost immediately. A rate which is lower than either the banker's check rate or the cable rate is that of the *banker's time draft*, sometimes called long exchange or a long bill. Such instruments are payable at specified future dates, usually thirty days or some multiple thereof. The quotations on these time drafts are, of course, lower because they involve a reduction in the balance of the foreign branch or correspondent only after a specified period of time.

Exchange Rates Between Gold Standard Countries

When the currency of two nations is convertible freely into gold at a fixed price and both nations permit unlimited flow of gold in and out of the country, the exchange rate of the two gold-standard currencies fluctuates but very little from the mint parity. The *mint parity* may be defined as the ratio between the volume of gold into which the standard monetary unit of one gold-standard country is convertible and the volume of gold into which the standard monetary unit of another country is convertible. For example, before World War I and during the late 1920's, both the United States and Great Britain were on an unqualified gold standard. At that time, the gold dollar contained 23.2200 grains of pure gold, while the British gold sovereign contained 113.0016 grains of pure gold. The exchange rate between United States dollars and British pounds, therefore, based upon the ratio of these two quantities of gold contained in the monetary units of the respective countries, was $4.8665 for one British pound (113.0016 ÷ 23.2200 = 4.8665).

The purchaser of imported goods could pay for his shipment in two ways under this situation. He had the alternative of either shipping an appropriate amount of gold to pay the exporter, or he could buy foreign exchange to the extent of the amount due the foreign exporter. Other things being equal or nearly so, the average person would prefer to deal in foreign exchange rather than go to the trouble of shipping the gold, since such shipment involves the cost of transportation, packing, insurance, and other charges. However, if in the process of purchasing foreign exchange to satisfy a claim, the importer feels that a price is being charged him which is greater than that warranted by the additional expense of shipping the gold itself, he may prefer to deal directly in gold. It is to be expected, therefore, that exchange rates under a gold-standard arrangement would fluctuate around the mint-parity price but within the limit established by the cost of shipping the metal itself, since any attempt to charge an amount in excess of the actual expenses of transporting the metal would result in individuals dealing directly in gold.

The exchange rate during the pre-World War I period fluctuated over a range of 2 cents plus and minus the mint-parity, and so long as the exchange rate remained within this range, there was no actual flow of gold. The exchange rate at which importers found it more economical to ship gold itself was referred to as the *gold-export point.* The *gold-import point,* of course, was that point at which foreign importers found it convenient to satisfy claims of exporters in this country through the shipment of gold rather than the purchase of foreign exchange. The profits that dealers in foreign exchange could make through the sale of claims of foreign money under the gold standard were limited to the spread between the mint-parity price and the gold-export or the gold-import point minus the cost of such activities.[1]

[1] Stephen Enke and Virgil Salera, *International Economics* (New York: Prentice-Hall, Inc., 1947), p. 124.

FINANCING INTERNATIONAL TRADE

One of the substantial financial burdens of any industrial firm is that of carrying the cost of the goods being produced through the process of manufacture itself. In the case of a United States manufacturer who ships his goods to such far distant places as India or Australia, his funds are tied up not only for the period of manufacture, but also for a lengthy period of transportation. In order to solve this problem and so reduce the burden of carrying these financial costs, the manufacturers may stipulate that the foreign importer is to provide payment for the goods as soon as the goods are placed in transportation to their destination. In any case, a substantial financial burden exists either on the part of the exporter or on the part of the importer.

Financing by the Exporter

Should the exporter have confidence in his foreign customers and be in a financial position to carry sales to his customers on open-book account, there is no reason why the arrangement should not operate very much as it operates in domestic trade, subject, of course, to the complications involved in any international transaction.

Sight and Time Drafts. As an alternative to the shipment of merchandise on the basis of open-account financing, the exporter may use a collection draft. A *draft* or bill of exchange is an unconditional order in writing, signed by the person drawing it, requiring the person to whom it is addressed to pay on demand or at a fixed or determinable future time a sum certain in money to order or to bearer. A draft may require immediate payment by the importer upon its presentation, or it may only require acceptance on the part of the importer, providing for payment at a specified future time. Those instruments requiring immediate payment are classified as *sight drafts*; those requiring payment later are classified as *time drafts*. These drafts may require remittance in the currency of the country of the exporter or of the importer, depending upon the terms of the transaction. An example of a sight draft form is shown in Figure 15-1.

Drafts may be either documentary or clean. A *documentary draft* is accompanied by an order bill of lading and such other

Figure 15–1

$2,500.00	New Orleans, Louisiana,	August 15, 19 59

At sight - PAY TO THE

ORDER OF__John Smith_____

Two thousand five hundred no/100 - - - - - - - - - - - - - - - - - DOLLARS

VALUE RECEIVED AND CHARGE TO ACCOUNT OF

TO Brazilian Import Company_____   NEW ORLEANS EXPORT COMPANY

No.11678   Rio de Janeiro, Brazil   _Thomas Jones_

Sight Draft or Bill of Exchange

papers as insurance receipts, certificates of sanitation, and consular invoices. The *order bill of lading* represents the written acceptance of goods for shipment by a transportation company and the terms under which the goods are to be conveyed to their destination. In addition, the order bill of lading carries title to the merchandise being shipped, and only its holder may claim the merchandise from the transportation company. (See Figure 15-2.) The documentary sight draft is generally referred to as a D/P draft (documentary payments draft) while the documentary time draft is referred to as a D/A draft (documentary acceptance draft).

A *clean draft* is one that is not accompanied by any special documents and is generally used when the exporter has confidence in the importer's ability to meet the draft when presented. In such a case, once the merchandise is shipped to the importer, it is delivered to him by the transportation company irrespective of any action he may take with regard to acknowledgment of the draft.

Bank Assistance in the Collection of Drafts. An importer will generally try to avoid making payment for a purchase before the goods are actually shipped because he must wait several days and perhaps weeks before receiving the goods. It is equally true that the exporter is seldom willing to send the draft and documents directly to the importer for payment or acceptance unless a substantial amount of confidence exists between the exporter and the importer. Under these circumstances the exporter will work through his commercial bank.

Figure 15–2

UNITED STATES LINES CO.

(SPACES IMMEDIATELY BELOW FOR SHIPPERS MEMORANDA—NOT PART OF BILL OF LADING)

FORWARDING AGENT—REFERENCES	EXPORT DEC. No.
John Doe Shipping Co., #E6776 F.M.B. #9786	X67-90687

DELIVERING CARRIER TO STEAMER:	CAR NUMBER — REFERENCE
New York Central R.R. Co.	876528

BILL OF LADING

(SHORT FORM)

(NOT NEGOTIABLE UNLESS
  CONSIGNED "TO ORDER")

SHIP American Banker	FLAG	PIER 61 N.R.	PORT OF LOADING
PORT OF DISCHARGE FROM SHIP Liverpool	AM.	THROUGH BILL OF LADING	NEW YORK
(Where goods are to be delivered to consignee or On-carrier)			
If goods to be transshipped beyond Port of Discharge, show destination Here ➡ To			

SHIPPER....Midwest Printing Company

CONSIGNED TO: ORDER OF....M. T. Wilson & Co.

ADDRESS ARRIVAL NOTICE TO....Same at 15 Dock St., Liverpool, E.C. 3

PARTICULARS FURNISHED BY SHIPPER OF GOODS				
MARKS AND NUMBERS	NO. OF PKGS.	DESCRIPTION OF PACKAGES AND GOODS	MEASUREMENT	GROSS WEIGHT IN POUNDS
M. T. W. & CO. Liverpool 1/59	56	Books		10,145
		SPECIMEN		

FREIGHT PAYABLE IN   NEW YORK

(10,145) @ PER 2240 LBS.. $		
@ PER 100 LBS.. $		
FT. @ PER 40 CU. FT. $		
545 FT. @ $1.05 PER CU. FT... $	572	25
$		
$		
$		
$		
TOTAL . . $		

(TERMS OF THIS BILL OF LADING CONTINUED FROM REVERSE SIDE HEREOF)

IN WITNESS WHEREOF,
THE MASTER OR AGENT OF SAID VESSEL HAS SIGNED....**3**

BILLS OF LADING, ALL OF THE SAME TENOR AND DATE, ONE OF WHICH BEING ACCOMPLISHED, THE OTHERS TO STAND VOID.

UNITED STATES LINES COMPANY

BY............J.J.

FOR THE MASTER

B/L No.   ISSUED AT NEW YORK, N. Y.
M-105

January	12	1959
MO.	DAY	YEAR

Order Bill of Lading

A New York exporter, who is dealing with a foreign importer with whom he has had little relationship in the past, may ship goods on the basis of a documentary draft that he deposits for collection with his local bank. That bank, following the specific instructions set out regarding the manner of collection, then forwards the draft together with the accompanying documents to its correspondent bank in the foreign country involved. The correspondent bank is instructed to hold the documents until payment is made if a sight draft is used, or until acceptance is obtained if a time draft is used. Remittance is made to the exporter when collection is made on the sight draft.

Financing Through the Exporter's Bank. It is important to recognize that throughout this transaction the banking system has provided only a service to the exporter and has in no way financed the transaction itself. The exporter's bank, however, may offer considerable assistance in this respect by allowing the exporter to borrow against the security of a documentary draft. The amount of the bank loan under these circumstances is less than the face amount of the draft. Such loans have not only the financial strength of the exporter to support them but also that of the importer, since the documents permitting acquisition of the merchandise are released only after the importer has accepted the draft. The amount that the exporter can borrow against the draft depends in large measure upon the credit standing of both the exporter and the importer. In some cases, a substantial percentage of the draft may be advanced when the exporter is financially strong, even though the importer may be little known to the exporter's bank, since the credit position of the exporter will offer suitable protection to the bank. In other cases, a substantial advance may be made where the exporter has only modest financial strength but where the importer is financially strong.

In addition to the financial strength of the exporter and the importer, the character of the goods shipped will also have an important bearing upon the amount loaned against a draft since the goods shipped offers collateral security for the advance. Goods not subject to breakage or perishability offer a better form of collateral than goods of a highly perishable nature. Also, goods for which there is a ready market are preferred as collateral over those for which the market may be very limited.

Financing by the Importer

As in the case of the exporter, the importer may arrange for the payment of goods that he orders without access to the credit of his bank. Payment may be made in full with the order, or a partial payment may be offered. The partial payment offers some protection to both the exporter and the importer. It protects the exporter against arbitrary rejection of the goods so shipped on the part of the importer. It also assures the importer of having some control over the transaction in the event the merchandise purchased is damaged in shipment because of poor packing or because it otherwise does not measure up to specifications. In other cases where the importer is required to make payment with his order but wishes some protection against failure of the exporter to make shipment in accordance with the provisions of the order, the order may be sent directly to the exporter but payment therefor is sent to a representative bank in the community of the exporter. The bank is instructed not to release payment until certain documents are presented to the bank to evidence shipment of the goods according to the terms of the transaction. The bank, of course, charges a fee for providing this service.

Financing Through the Importer's Bank. In the field of foreign trade, because of the language barriers that exist and because of the difficulty in obtaining credit information between companies of the various countries, the use of the banker's acceptance is common. The *banker's acceptance* differs from the trade draft in only one respect. The former instrument is drawn on a bank and is accepted by a bank rather than by the importing firm. An example of a banker's acceptance is shown in Figure 15-3. The importer must, of course, make arrangements with his bank in advance of such an action. The exporter, too, must know before shipment is made whether or not the bank in question has agreed to accept such a draft. This arrangement is facilitated through the use of the commercial letter of credit. The *commercial letter of credit* may be described as a written statement on the part of the bank to an individual or firm guaranteeing acceptance and payment of a draft up to a specified sum if presented to the bank in accordance with the terms of the commercial letter of credit. (See Figure 15-4.)

Figure 15-3

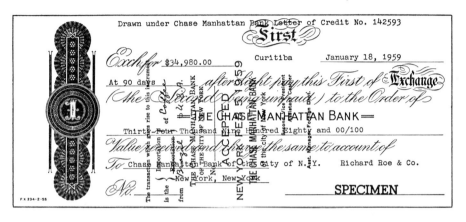

Banker's Acceptance

Importer Bank Financing—An Example. The issuance of the
the letter of credit and its application to international finance may
be observed from the following example. The owner of a small
but exclusive shop located in Chicago may wish to import expensive perfumes from Paris. Although the firm is well known locally,
its financial reputation is not known widely enough to permit it
to make direct purchases from foreign exporters on the basis of
an open-book account arrangement or on the basis of drafts drawn
on the firm. Under these circumstances the firm would substitute
for its own credit that of its bank through the use of a commercial
letter of credit. This would be accomplished by making application to its bank for a letter of credit. Before the bank will issue
such a commitment, it must be entirely satisfied that its customer
is in a satisfactory financial condition.

The letter of credit is addressed to a specific French exporter
from whom the perfumes are to be purchased. The exporter, upon
receipt of the commercial letter of credit, has little reason to hesi-
tate in making the shipment. Although he has perhaps never
heard of the firm that has placed the order, the bank which has
issued the commercial letter of credit may be well known to the
exporter or to the exporter's bank. The French exporter, then,
makes shipment of the perfumes and at the same time draws a draft
in the appropriate amount on the bank that has issued the letter
of credit. This draft is presented to the exporter's bank along

Figure 15–4

IRREVOCABLE
COMMERCIAL
LETTER OF CREDIT

The Chase Manhattan Bank

INTERNATIONAL DEPARTMENT
EIGHTEEN PINE STREET
NEW YORK 15, N. Y.

...$35,000.00 U.S.Cy...

No. 142593   New   York   January 29, 1959

┌   ┐
  Richard Roe & Co.
  Curitiba
  Brazil
└   ┘

GENTLEMEN:
    WE HEREBY AUTHORIZE YOU TO DRAW ON The Chase Manhattan Bank, New York City

BY ORDER OF John Doe & Co.
             New York, N. Y.
AND FOR ACCOUNT OF John Doe & Co.
UP TO AN AGGREGATE AMOUNT OF THIRTY-FIVE THOUSAND DOLLARS U.S. CURRENCY.....

AVAILABLE BY YOUR DRAFTS AT 90 days sight, for full invoice value, in duplicate..
ACCOMPANIED BY Commercial Invoice in triplicate....
                Consular Invoice in duplicate...
                Full set of onboard Bills of Lading to order of The
Chase Manhattan Bank, New York, marked Notify John Doe & Co., New York,
N. Y., and bearing a separate onboard endorsement signed by the Master
and dated not later than January 31, 1959, also marked freight collect
at port of destination...

evidencing shipment of 500 Bags of Coffee, FOB vessel at Paranagua from
Paranagua, Brazil to any U.S. Atlantic and/or U.S. Gulf Port.

...Any charges for negotiation of the draft(s) are for your account.
...Marine and war risk insurance covered by buyers.

    DRAFTS MUST BE DRAWN AND NEGOTIATED NOT LATER THAN February 5, 1959.

EACH DRAFT MUST STATE THAT IT IS "DRAWN UNDER LETTER OF CREDIT OF THE CHASE MANHATTAN BANK,
NEW YORK, NO. 142593 DATED January 29, 1959 ", AND THE AMOUNT ENDORSED ON THIS
LETTER OF CREDIT.
    WE HEREBY AGREE WITH THE DRAWERS, ENDORSERS, AND BONA FIDE HOLDERS OF ALL DRAFTS DRAWN
UNDER AND IN COMPLIANCE WITH THE TERMS OF THIS CREDIT, THAT SUCH DRAFTS WILL BE DULY-HONORED
UPON PRESENTATION TO THE DRAWEE.
    EXCEPT SO FAR AS OTHERWISE EXPRESSLY STATED, THIS CREDIT IS SUBJECT TO THE UNIFORM
CUSTOMS AND PRACTICE FOR COMMERCIAL DOCUMENTARY CREDITS FIXED BY THE THIRTEENTH CONGRESS
OF THE INTERNATIONAL CHAMBER OF COMMERCE.

                         YOURS VERY TRULY

SPECIMEN

                    ASSISTANT VICE PRESIDENT   ASSISTANT TREASURER
                    ASSISTANT TREASURER   FOR PROCURATION

Irrevocable Commercial Letter of Credit

with the other papers as required by the commercial letter of credit. The exporter's bank transmits the draft and the accompanying documents to its New York correspondent where it is forwarded to the importer's bank. The importer's bank, upon receipt of the documents, makes a thorough inspection of the various papers that accompany the draft to determine if all the provisions of the letter of credit have been met. If upon examination of the document the bank is satisfied that the terms of the commercial letter of credit have been met, the draft is accepted and the appropriate officials of the bank enter their signatures on the draft. The accepted draft, now known as a banker's acceptance, may be held until maturity by the exporter, at which time it is rerouted to the accepting bank for settlement, or the exporter may sell it to other investors.

After having accepted the draft, the bank notifies its customer that the shipping documents are in its possession and that he is to come to the bank and make arrangements to take over the documents. As the merchandise is sold, the firm is able to build up its account with the bank by daily deposits until sufficient deposits are available to retire the acceptance. The bank then is in a position to meet its obligation on the acceptance without advancing its own funds at any time.

In releasing shipping documents to a customer, the bank may prefer to establish an agency arrangement between the firm and the bank whereby the bank retains title to the merchandise. The instrument that provides for the retention of title to the merchandise by the bank is called a *trust receipt*. (See Figure 15-5.) Should the business fail, the bank would not take the position of an ordinary creditor in order to establish its claim on the business assets, but rather, it would be able to repossess the goods and place them with another agent for sale since title had never been transferred to the customer. As the merchandise is sold under the trust receipt arrangement, it is generally required that the business deliver to the bank the proceeds from the sale until such time as the total amount of the acceptance has been deposited with the bank.

In summary, the banker's acceptance and the commercial letter of credit involve four principal parties: the importer, the importer's bank, the exporter, and the exporter's bank. Each benefits

Figure 15–5

RETURN TO	THE CHASE MANHATTAN BANK	INTERNATIONAL DEPARTMENT

TRUST RECEIPT AND
RECEIPT FOR DOCUMENTS

EIGHTEEN PINE STREET

COMMERCIAL L/C DIVISION

NEW YORK, Feb. 5, 1959

FROM
John Doe & Co.
New York
N.Y.

WE HAVE ACCEPTED DRAFT OF	DRAWN UNDER L/C NO.	COMMISSION %
Richard Roe & Co. Curitiba, Brazil	142593	

FOR ACCOUNT OF
John Doe & Co.

WE DEBIT YOUR ACCOUNT

TENOR	PAYABLE DATE	MATURITY DATE	AMOUNT	
90 D/S	May 6, 1959	May 6, 1959	$34,980.00	Please officially sign the trust receipt appearing on the reverse side hereof, and return this form to us.

COVERING SHIPMENT OF		PER S/S	
500 Bags Coffee			

FROM Parangua, Brazil TO New York, N.Y.   MORMACSURF

ACCEPTED AGAINST	INVOICE	INSURANCE CTF.	CONSULAR INVOICE	B/L	PAR. POST RECEIPTS	DELIVERY ORDER	FORWARDERS RECEIPT	CERTIF. OF ORIGIN	SPECIF.	INSPECTION CTF.	WEIGHT CTF.
ORIGINAL DOCUMENTS ENCLOSED	–1		1	2/4							
DUPLICATE DOCUMENTS TO FOLLOW											

Trust Receipt
No. 1675

MARKS AND NUMBERS	REMARKS
	We are advised remaining documents are coming by second mail and will be delivered as soon as received.

SPECIMEN

HRC/MIO

Trust Receipt and Receipt for Documents

to a substantial degree through this arrangement. The importer benefits in that he is able to secure adequate credit even though his own financial credit is not established on an international basis. The importer's bank benefits because it has charged a fee for the issuance of the commercial letter of credit and for the other services provided in connection therewith. The exporter has been benefited in that he has been given the assurance of definite payment for the shipment of merchandise. A sale is made possible that may have otherwise been rejected because of lack of certainty of payment. Finally, the exporter's bank benefits if it discounts the acceptance for the exporter since it receives a high-grade credit instrument with a definite, short-term maturity. Acceptances held by commercial banks provide a low but certain yield, and a bank can liquidate them quickly if it should need funds for other purposes.

TRAVELER'S LETTER OF CREDIT

A purchaser for a firm traveling abroad may not know in advance from whom purchases are to be made. For example, an art buyer who tours several countries may not know in advance from which individuals or firms purchases may be made. In this case, the buyer might carry American currency that could be exchanged in the foreign countries for their currency. This involves the possible physical loss of the money, and occasionally conversion into the currency of the foreign country is accomplished only at a substantial discount. A traveler's letter of credit provides the necessary convenience and protection for this purpose.

The *traveler's letter of credit* is issued by a bank in one country and is addressed to a list of banks abroad. These foreign banks to which the letter of credit is addressed are usually correspondents of the issuing bank and have agreed to purchase upon sight drafts presented to them by persons displaying such letters of credit. At the time a letter of credit is issued by a bank, a copy of the signature of the person to whom the letter of credit is issued is sent to each of its foreign correspondent banks. When the individual presents a draft for payment in foreign currency to one of these foreign correspondent banks, he is asked to present his signature, which is then compared with the signature forwarded directly to these banks by the issuing bank. In addition, the individual presenting the draft may be asked for supplementary identification documents.

As in the case of the regular letter of credit, a maximum amount is stipulated for draft purposes on the part of the holder of the letter of credit. In order that an individual holding such a letter of credit may not exceed his authorized withdrawals, each bank to which the letter of credit is presented will enter on the letter of credit the amount of the draft that it has honored. In this way the individual presenting the letter of credit is unable to draw an amount in excess of that authorized.

TRAVELER'S CHECKS

Traveler's checks, which are offered by banks, express companies, and other agencies, are generally issued in denominations of $10, $20, $50, and $100. These checks, generally purchased by an individual before leaving for a trip, involve a promise to pay on demand even amounts as indicated by the face of the traveler's check. Each check must be signed twice, once at the time it is purchased and again at the time it is presented for payment. In this manner, the firm or institution to which the traveler's checks are presented for payment may be able to determine the authenticity of the signature by requiring the signing in its presence. Such traveler's checks are usually sold for their face amount plus a charge of one per cent. The use of the traveler's check is widespread and offers many advantages to the traveler, including protection in the event of loss of the traveler's checks and certainty of acceptance on the part of the firms to which they are presented for payment.

QUESTIONS

1. Describe the process by which an importer in the United States is able to purchase goods from suppliers located in many countries, paying for each purchase with money of the country of the exporter.
2. How do commercial banks provide for the financial settlement of international transactions. Describe the institutional arrangements of commercial banks for maintaining deposits in foreign countries.
3. Explain the role of supply and demand as it relates to the establishment of exchange rates between countries.
4. Describe the activities and economic role of the arbitrager in international finance.
5. Foreign exchange quotations may be given in terms of sight drafts, cable drafts, and time drafts. What is the relative cost of these different types of drafts? Why should such cost differentials exist?
6. Explain how the exchange ratio is determined between countries whose currency is freely convertible into gold.
7. Explain the significance of gold-export points and gold-import points as they relate to importers in gold-standard countries.
8. Describe the various ways by which an exporter may finance an international shipment of goods. How may commercial banks assist the exporter in the collection of drafts?
9. How may an importer protect himself against improper delivery of goods when he is required to make payment with his order?
10. Describe fully the process by which an importer may substitute the credit of his bank for his own in financing international transactions.
11. How may a bank protect itself after having issued a commercial letter of credit on behalf of a customer?
12. Distinguish between a commercial letter of credit and a traveler's letter of credit.

SUGGESTED READINGS

(See Suggested Readings for Chapter 16.)

International Finance
(Concluded)

Part III

Chapter **16**

In the preceding chapter the mechanical details relating to the settlement of international claims were discussed without regard to the ultimate sources of foreign exchange claims. But, just as it is true that a single financial institution, such as a bank, cannot continue to sell foreign drafts to residents of the United States without replenishing its own claims on foreign exchange for such sales, it is also true that all financial institutions in a given country can provide foreign exchange to their customers only to the extent that such foreign exchange becomes available to the nation.

International finance is a two-way street: when we export goods and services to a foreign country, we create claims against that country; and when we import goods and services from foreign countries, claims are established against those countries. To expect to sell goods and services abroad on a permanent basis without in turn making it possible for foreign businesses and individuals to pay for them by selling goods and services to this country would be as unreasonable as to expect the average family to subsist by continually spending without a corresponding inflow of income.

FACTORS AFFECTING EXCHANGE RATES

It was shown in the preceding chapter that in a free market substantial changes in the balances of international trade are reflected in variations in exchange rates. Exchange rates are not only affected by changes in international trade, but by all of the factors that affect the flow of funds between countries. In this first section of this chapter attention will be directed to several such factors. Consideration will first be given to the normal flow of funds between nations arising out of regular business and investment activities. Then the influence of unusual capital transfers will be considered. This will be followed by an analysis of governmental policies that affect trade and direct governmental influences on exchange rates.

Regular Receipts and Payments

A country receives foreign exchange from various sources. The most important are generally the sale of goods and services to individuals and businesses in foreign countries. A country may export raw materials and finished goods. It may also sell services such as transportation and financing of trade and it may sell goods and services to foreigners traveling within its borders. A country may also receive income from investments by its citizens in foreign countries.

Claims for foreign exchange may also arise because foreigners are investing money in a country on a long-term or on a short-term basis. This may be done by buying bonds of the government or of private corporations, or by buying common stock or investing directly in a business.

A country also receives foreign exchange from gifts and grants. These may be received from foreign governments, businesses, institutions, or private citizens. Lastly, foreign exchange may also be received by exchanging gold for it.

The reverse of these transactions require payments of foreign exchange. Whenever a country or its citizens import goods or services, buy investments in foreign countries, make gifts or grants to foreign countries or their residents, or buy gold, payments of foreign exchange must be made.

The balance between the total volume of receipts of a country and the total volume of payments is referred to as its *balance of payments*. The balance between exports of goods and imports of goods is called the *balance of trade*. The receipts and payments of foreign exchange arising out of the balance of trade between two countries need not balance, but the total balance of payments must of course be in balance since goods, services, and investments will not be sold in international trade unless they are paid for or loans are arranged to pay for them.

Influence of Unusual Capital Transfers on Exchange Rates

We have seen that the flow of capital investments between nations provides a balancing factor for the difference in value between the total volume of exports of goods and services and the volume of imports of goods and services of a country. When the volume of international capital flows is larger than necessary to balance payments between countries, however, exchange rates are affected significantly. For example, if a nation is threatened with military invasion, there is an understandable reluctance to invest in such a country. Also, liquidation of existing investments as quickly as possible is effected by many persons and such capital reinvested in other nations in less danger of military threat. Such widespread shifts of capital investments from one country to another result in a prolonged and perhaps exaggerated condition of undervaluation of the currency of the nation subject to military threat, while there is a corresponding overvaluation in the currency of the nations to which such investments are shifted. Moreover, the continuing shift of such capital investments between nations prevents the exchange rate from being re-established at the old level as a result of normal trade influences. Large-scale shifts of capital may result from such additional causes as the possibility of political revolution or any event which would cause people to expect a fall in the exchange rate of the currency of a country.

Governmental Policies Affecting International Trade

Exchange rates are influenced to a significant degree by government policies that affect the flow of international trade. These may take the form of the establishment of tariffs against imports, the payment of subsidies to exporters, the creation of quotas with respect to volumes of import, the licensing of exports, the negotiation of trade agreements, and others. When, for example, higher tariffs are established by this country, the effect upon trade is to limit the number of dollars offered in foreign exchange with a resulting increase in the value of the dollar in international trade. The increase in the value of a nation's currency resulting from protectionist measures is accounted for by the fact that it becomes increasingly difficult for the nationals of a foreign country to obtain dollar claims when the market for the goods which they hope to sell to Americans is reduced. Since the volume of dollar claims is reduced, it becomes increasingly expensive for foreigners to make purchases in this country.

On the other hand, the adoption by the government of one nation of policies to stimulate or to restrict trade generally results in a change in governmental policies on the part of other nations. Restrictive policies on the part of one government may encourage similar actions on the part of the governments of other nations with which it deals, eliminating the benefits that may have temporarily accrued to the initiating nation, and the same is true of policies designed to increase the trade of one nation at the expense of other nations.

Direct Governmental Influences on Exchange Rates

The financial crisis that began in central Europe in 1931 and eventually spread throughout the world marked the end of most free foreign exchange markets in the world. World War II with its accompanying financial dislocations increased the degree to which foreign exchange was dominated by governments, and it even brought about new restrictions upon exchange rates. The United States, like most other nations, found it necessary to engage in control over exchange rates during World War II and in the postwar period.

The most common form of direct governmental influence on exchange rates has been that of the establishment of official exchange rates. These rates, which must be paid by all persons requiring foreign exchange, determine the conversion price of foreign exchange claims received by persons in this country. In addition, governments have at times restricted private dealing in foreign currency, and in other cases governments have engaged in large purchase and sale operations of foreign currencies in order to maintain desired exchange rates.

Among the reasons why governments impose direct controls on international exchange is the desire to eliminate widespread flights of capital from one nation to another as a result of serious disturbances to a nation's economic system. Unless widespread capital flights are checked, a nation's entire reserves may be depleted and its position in international trade damaged seriously. At other times nations have imposed these controls in order to conserve an existing supply of foreign monetary claims when it was anticipated that additional foreign claims would not become available for certain vital imports.

In still other cases, governments have had to resort to exchange controls as a result of the slackening of international investment upon which many governments depended to refinance their existing indebtedness. Such governments, through the use of exchange controls, have attempted to meet their foreign obligations by relying upon the foreign claims resulting from the exports of the country.

During periods of armed conflict, also, governments have used their power to freeze the claims of foreign belligerents. During World War II vast sums of investments representing claims by German nationals were frozen in the United States. Another reason for the establishment of exchange controls has been to permit the development of military strength and self-sufficiency. The Axis powers by engaging in such controls prior to and during World War II made it possible for their own strategic war industries to develop without having to compete with foreign producers, which at the same time resulted in the control of small adjoining countries in such a way as to utilize their productivity to the benefit of the growing strength of the Axis.

STABILIZATION OF EXCHANGE RATES

Central banks of most countries have for many years participated in foreign markets in an effort to stabilize exchange rates. They have done so because without some degree of stability of exchange rates, commerce between nations is hampered. Sellers of merchandise may be reluctant to make shipments when there is a possibility that the money of the country in which payment is to be made may fall in value between the time of shipment and the final date of payment of the cost of the goods or services. For the same reason there is a general reluctance to make long-term investments when the repayment of the debt may be made with cheap money as a result of depreciation of the currency of the country in which the investment is made. It is apparent, therefore, that economic development is dependent upon stable exchange rates and, in turn, economic development may contribute to stable exchange rates by eliminating the need for currency depreciation.

Central Bank Stabilization Activities

In order to maintain a reasonable stability of foreign exchange rates, many central banks during the 1920's purchased monetary claims of other countries, and at other times they sold their holdings of foreign monetary claims.

If, for example, the rate of exchange between the American dollar and the British pound had increased from $4.86 for each pound sterling in London to $4.90, the Bank of England would purchase additional claims to American dollars, paying for them with British pounds. The withdrawal of American dollars from the market and the freeing of additional British pounds tended to re-establish the original rate of exchange. When the exchange rate moved in the other direction to the point where, for example, it required only $4.80 to purchase one pound sterling, the Bank of England would sell its holdings of claims to American dollars and get pounds for them. The increased supply of claims to American dollars, along with a declining volume of pounds, tended to reduce the rate of exchange to the former level.

Stabilization Funds

The scope of exchange operations by the central banks of the various nations reached such proportions that special organizations were established to engage solely in this activity. The British Exchange Equalization Account was established for this purpose in 1932, and two years later the United States Exchange Stabilization Fund was created. Shortly thereafter, other nations established similar organizations.

Many people assumed that the exchange stabilization funds established by the various countries of the world would confine their operations to the elimination of short-term fluctuations in the exchange rates while the long-term trend of exchange rates would be established by the free interplay of supply and demand. In the light of the severe burden of economic depression which resulted during the early years of the operation of these funds, however, it is not surprising that attention was given not only to the elimination of short-term fluctuations in exchange rates but also to the manipulation of the long-term trend.[1] To the extent

---

[1] Lester V. Chandler, *The Economics of Money and Banking* (Revised Edition; New York: Harper & Brothers, 1953), p. 674.

that a nation was able to depress the value of its own currency in foreign exchange, the export market of that nation was benefited because of the increased purchasing power of the foreign importer. It is obvious, of course, that once such a policy was undertaken by one country, other nations were encouraged to do the same for defensive reasons.

International Cooperation

Although officials of the various exchange stabilization funds of the nations of the world conferred from time to time and made superficial efforts at cooperation, it was recognized that without a stronger system of international cooperation there could be no permanent solution to the problems of international exchange. Recognition of the necessity for international cooperation found expression in 1943 when the United States Treasury proposed the establishment of an international stabilization fund. Only a day later the British government offered a proposal for the establishment of a fund somewhat similar to the plan proposed by the United States. Later the Canadian government offered a counterproposal and, following publication and public discussion of these various plans, a meeting was called to consider the establishment of such a fund. The United Nations Monetary and Financial Conference, meeting at Bretton Woods, New Hampshire, in the summer of 1944, proposed the establishment of two new agencies, the International Monetary Fund and the International Bank for Reconstruction and Development. After most of the nations that participated in the Conference ratified the proposals, these agencies were established early in 1946.

THE INTERNATIONAL MONETARY FUND

The International Monetary Fund was established primarily to provide for the expansion and balanced growth of international trade and to promote exchange stability. The primary objectives of the fund were to be accomplished through the establishment of an international organization that would provide for cooperative effort among the member nations for the settlement of their international monetary problems. In addition, it was believed that the existence of such an institution would help to promote confidence among member countries by making available to those countries financial assistance and the opportunity to eliminate maladjustments in their balance of payments. It was hoped that these facilities of the International Monetary Fund would help the nations of the world to attain and maintain full employment of their manpower and to achieve a steadily rising real income on the part of the population. In accomplishing its objectives, the International Monetary Fund has gained respect and prestige.

Structure and Organization

The International Monetary Fund has its executive offices in the United States. The organization is directed by a Board of Governors that is appointed by the member countries. Although each member nation is entitled to a single appointee to the Board of Governors, the more important nations exercise a larger influence than do the smaller nations through greater voting strength on questions that come before the organization. Each member has 250 votes plus an additional vote for each paid-in share. These shares have a par value of an equivalent of $100,000. Since the United States holds nearly a third of the shares in the International Monetary Fund, it exercises a preponderant voice in the affairs of the organization. As of April 30, 1957, there were 60 members of the Board of Governors representing the 60 member nations. To the extent that a nation borrows from the Fund, its voting privilege is reduced accordingly. A nation that lends funds to the International Monetary Fund receives additional voting privileges.

Although the Board of Governors of the International Monetary Fund directs the major activities of that organization, much of the detailed work is the responsibility of the Executive Directors of the Fund. As of April 30, 1957, there were seventeen Executive Directors, five of whom are appointed regularly by the five largest contributing members of the Fund. These five nations in the order of the size of their contribution to the Fund are: the United States, United Kingdom, China, France, and India. The remaining eleven Executive Directors are elected by groups of other member countries of the International Monetary Fund. The Executive Directors of the International Monetary Fund and their voting power as of April 30, 1957, are shown in Table 16-1.

Financial Resources

The International Monetary Fund has financial resources consisting of a pool of gold and foreign exchange of approximately $9 billion. These resources were obtained through contributions of member nations, quotas for which were established on the basis of each member nation's national income and volume of international trade. As might be expected, the quota of the United States is by far the largest of any of the countries. This quota is $2.75 billion, representing approximately one third of the total for all nations. The United Kingdom is next in size with a quota equivalent to $1.3 billion, representing approximately one sixth of the total. China has a quota equivalent to $550 million, France $525 million, and India $400 million.

Operations of the Fund

Under the terms of membership in the International Monetary Fund, a nation agrees to effect no direct changes in the value of its currency without consulting and receiving the permission of the appropriate authorities of the Fund. A nation, however, may depreciate its currency up to 10 per cent without the permission of the International Monetary Fund if it considers its currency to be overvalued in international exchange. If a 10 per cent depreciation in a nation's currency still does not establish an exchange rate that the nation considers to be appropriate, it must obtain permission from the International Monetary Fund for additional adjustments. If, after study of the problems of the nation in question, the authorities of the Fund feel that further depreciation is warranted, such adjustments are authorized. The International Monetary Fund permits such major changes in exchange rates only when it feels that there is a long-run disequilibrium and not because of what may be considered to be a short-term shortage of foreign exchange on the part of a nation.

In addition to the regulatory features, the Fund assists member nations that experience temporary shortages of foreign exchange. For example, when the principal export crop of a small nation fails, leaving that nation in an unsatisfactory position to make its purchases abroad in that year, the nation is permitted to borrow from the Fund claims on the foreign currency of the country from which it wishes to make its import purchases. The amount that

Table 16-1

INTERNATIONAL MONETARY FUND

EXECUTIVE DIRECTORS AND VOTING POWER

as of April 30, 1957

DIRECTOR _Alternate_	CASTING VOTES OF	VOTES BY COUNTRY	TOTAL VOTES [1]	PER CENT OF TOTAL
APPOINTED				
Frank A. Southard, Jr. _John S. Hooker_	United States	27,750	27,750	26.60
G. F. Thorold _R. E. Heasman_	United Kingdom	13,250	13,250	12.70
Beue Tann _Ching-Yao Hsieh_	China	5,750	5,750	5.51
Jean de Largentaye _Jean-Maxime Leveque_	France	5,500	5,500	5.27
P. S. Narayan Prasad _P. J. J. Pinto_	India	4,250	4,250	4.07
ELECTED				
Ahmed Zaki Saad (Egypt) _Albert Mansour (Egypt)_	Afghanistan Egypt Ethiopia Iran Iraq Jordan Lebanon Pakistan Philippines Syria	350 850 310 600 330 280 295 1,250 400 315	4,980	4.77
Andre van Campenhout (Belgium) _Maurice Toussaint (Belgium)_	Austria Belgium Korea Luxembourg Turkey	750 2,500 375 350 680	4,655	4.46
Pieter Lieftinck (Netherlands) _H. M. H. A. van der Valk (Netherlands)_	Israel Netherlands Yugoslavia	325 3,000 850	4,175	4.00
Carlo Gragnani (Italy) _Costa P. Caranicas (Greece)_	Greece Indonesia Italy	650 1,350 2,050	4,050	3.88
Takeshi Watanabe (Japan) _Prayad Buranasiri (Thailand)_	Burma Ceylon Japan Thailand	400 400 2,750 375	3,925	3.76

[1] Voting power varies on certain matters with use by members of the Fund's resources.

INTERNATIONAL MONETARY FUND (Continued)

EXECUTIVE DIRECTORS AND VOTING POWER

as of April 30, 1957

DIRECTOR *Alternate*	CASTING VOTES OF	VOTES BY COUNTRY	TOTAL VOTES [1]	PER CENT OF TOTAL
Rodolfo Corominas-Segura (Argentina) *Julio Gonzalez del Solar* *(Guatemala)*	Argentina Bolivia Chile Ecuador Paraguay Uruguay	1,750 350 750 350 285 400	3,885	3.72
B. B. Callaghan (Australia) *Vacant*	Australia Union of South Africa Viet-Nam	2,250 1,250 375	3,875	3.71
Octavio Paranagua (Brazil) *Helvecio Xavier Lopes (Brazil)*	Brazil Colombia Dominican Republic Haiti Panama Peru	1,750 750 350 270 255 500	3,875	3.71
Torben Friis (Denmark) *Jouko J. Voutilainen (Finland)*	Denmark Finland Iceland Norway Sweden	930 630 260 750 1,250	3,820	3.66
Jorge Sol (El Salvador) *Jorge Hazera (Costa Rica)*	Costa Rica Cuba El Salvador Guatemala Honduras Mexico Nicaragua Venezuela	300 750 275 300 275 1,150 325 400	3,775	3.62
Otmar Emminger (Federal Republic of Germany) *Wilhelm Hanemann (Federal* *Republic of Germany)*	Federal Republic of Germany	3,550	3,550	3.40
Louis Rasminsky (Canada) *Alan B. Hocklin (Canada)*	Canada	3,250	3,250	3.12
			104,315	100.00[2]

[2] This total is not equal to the sum of the items because of rounding.

SOURCE: International Monetary Fund, *Annual Report, 1957*, Washington, D. C., pp. 154-155.

a nation may draw or borrow from the common pool of gold and currencies of the International Monetary Fund is limited in any one year to 25 per cent of a nation's subscription quota and an over-all limit of twice a nation's quota. When a nation borrows from the fund, it must offer as collateral an amount equivalent to the sum borrowed in its own currency; hence, the Fund has as its security against the loan to a nation, that nation's original contribution to the Fund plus the nation's currency placed as collateral for the loan. A nation borrowing from the resources of the Fund must pay a service charge, the amount of the charge varying with the length of time that the nation retains the borrowed funds. Loans from the Fund are not available automatically, but rather they may be extended only when their use is compatible with the objectives and purposes of the International Monetary Fund itself.

The International Monetary Fund, therefore, seeks to obtain its objectives of a balanced growth of international trade and an increasing level of real income for the participating countries in two basic ways: first, through international cooperation, eliminating the arbitrary action of individual nations with respect to currency depreciation; and second, by providing for a system of loans to nations temporarily in need of foreign exchange. From the beginning of operations to April 30, 1957, the International Monetary Fund had extended loans of more than $2,350 million. A large proportion of this amount was extended to member nations during the first two years of operation of the Fund. These loans were taken for the most part by countries that were later given assistance under the European Recovery Program. Over $1 billion was made available to members in the fiscal year ending April 30, 1957, largely to help nations adjust to the shifts in foreign trade resulting from the Suez Canal crisis. Of the total loans extended by the International Monetary Fund, an overwhelming proportion of the total has been in the form of American dollars as opposed to the currencies of other countries.

THE INTERNATIONAL BANK FOR RECONSTRUCTION AND DEVELOPMENT

In contrast with the objectives of the International Monetary Fund, the International Bank for Reconstruction and Development, or the "World Bank" as it is popularly referred to, was established to promote long-term capital loans between nations for productive purposes. Although the citizens of highly industrialized nations such as the United States can well afford to invest capital in the underdeveloped regions of the world, political instability of the governments of many of the underdeveloped countries makes such action virtually impossible without the protection of such an organization as the World Bank. Until 1929, private investors in the United States invested freely abroad; however, the large losses later sustained made investors wary of foreign commitments. The World Bank plays an important part in encouraging private foreign investments by underwriting or guaranteeing the loans.

Like its sister institution, the International Monetary Fund, the World Bank was an outgrowth of the Bretton Woods agreement. In order to be a member of the World Bank, it is necessary to be a member of the International Monetary Fund also. As of June 30, 1957, all members of the International Monetary Fund were also members of the World Bank.

Structure and Organization

The management of the World Bank is very similar to that of the International Monetary Fund. Each member nation is represented by a Governor, and in turn there is a group of seventeen Executive Directors of the bank that handle the day-to-day operations of the institution. As for the International Monetary Fund, five of the Executive Directors of the World Bank are appointed by the five largest subscribing nations, and the remaining Executive Directors are elected by groups of nations. The World Bank has its principal office in Washington, D. C., and occupies the same building as the International Monetary Fund. The operations of these two organizations, however, are separate and distinct.

Financial Resources of the World Bank

The capital of the World Bank is provided by subscriptions of member nations. As of June 30, 1957, it had total subscriptions of $9,268 million, of which amount the United States had subscribed more than one third. The United Kingdom had subscribed approximately one seventh of the total, with China,

France, and India subscribing the next largest amounts. Despite the large sums subscribed, however, each member nation's subscription is far larger than the amount actually paid into the fund. Only 20 per cent of each nation's full quota has been called up to the present time, and the Bank does not plan to call the other 80 per cent if it can be avoided. In any event, the remaining 80 per cent can be called only to meet the bank's obligations that it may incur. Although only a small portion of the total subscription of each nation has been called, the remainder provides a vast reservoir of strength for the World Bank should it become necessary to draw upon it.

In addition to this primary source of loanable funds, and of even greater importance, the World Bank may issue its own debenture bonds for sale to the public, the proceeds from which may be used for general loan purposes by the bank. As of June 30, 1957, the World Bank had outstanding the equivalent of over $1 billion of debenture bonds. These bonds have a multiple protection: first, there is the promise of the borrowers from the bank to pay their loans; second, the cash and other reserves of the bank built up out of its earnings; and third, the right of the World Bank to call upon its member nations to pay the remainder of their 80 per cent subscription. The principal purchasers of such bonds in the United States have been the mutual savings banks, life insurance companies, commercial banks, and pension and trust funds. Among the purchasers of bonds outside the United States are the central banks of some of the member nations.

In addition to the direct issue of debentures, the World Bank can insure or guarantee international loans. A premium is charged for such a guarantee.

Operations of the Bank

Three conditions must exist before a nation may secure a loan from the World Bank. In the first place, it must be a member of the Bank; in the second place, the loan must be recommended by a committee of the Bank; and finally, the borrower must present evidence that a comparable loan is not available from another source on reasonable terms. The World Bank makes extensive surveys in order to determine whether the proposed use for loans is economically justifiable and within the scope of the objectives

Table 16–2
LOANS OF THE INTERNATIONAL BANK FOR RECONSTRUCTION AND DEVELOPMENT CLASSIFIED BY PURPOSE AND AREA

June 30, 1957

Expressed in Millions of United States Dollars

				AREAS		
PURPOSE	TOTAL	AFRICA	ASIA	AUSTRAL-ASIA	EUROPE	WESTERN HEMI-SPHERE
Grand Total	3,025	367	575	317	1,088	678
Development Loans: Total	2,528	367	575	317	591	678
ELECTRIC POWER						
Generation and Distribution ...	869	178	145	29	186	331
TRANSPORTATION	715	145	137	127	59	247
Railroads	353	117	80	26	3	127
Shipping	12	..	..	..	12	..
Ports and Inland Waterways ..	83	3	37	..	37	6
Roads	196	25	..	57	..	114
Airlines and Airports	57	..	6	44	7	..
Pipelines (natural gas)	14	..	14	..	..	..
COMMUNICATIONS						
Telephone, Telegraph and Radio	24	2	..	..	..	22
AGRICULTURE AND FORESTRY	276	..	46	104	71	55
Farm Mechanization	115	..	..	88	2	25
Irrigation and Flood Control ..	115	..	31	6	57	21
Land Clearance and Improvement	26	..	14	6	2	4
Crop Processing and Storage ...	7	..	..	..	4	3
Livestock	3	..	1	..	..	2
Forestry	10	..	..	4	6	..
INDUSTRY	439	2	172	57	185	23
Iron and Steel	190	..	153	14	23	..
Pulp, Paper and Board	70	..	4	1	45	20
Fertilizer and Other Chemicals .	29	..	..	..	29	..
Other Industries	76	..	5	26	43	2
Mining	28	..	..	16	12	..
Development Banks	46	2	10	..	33	1
GENERAL DEVELOPMENT	205	40	75	..	90	..
Reconstruction Loans: Total	497	..	..	..	497	..

SOURCE: International Bank for Reconstruction and Development, *Twelfth Annual Report,* 1956-57, Washington, D. C., p. 51—of appendices.

of the World Bank. In contrast with privately negotiated loans, the terms of repayment are quite flexible. The borrowing nation may petition for the extension of the maturity of a loan if temporary conditions warrant such an extension.

As an example of the lending activities of the World Bank, during the period from July 1, 1957, through January 31, 1958, 22 loans aggregating the equivalent of $404.6 million were made to 13 countries. This brought the number of loans since the start of operations to 192 in 46 countries, and raised the gross total of loans to over $3.5 billion.[2]

One of the loans made during this same period was a $40 million loan for 18 years at 6 per cent interest to the Belgian Congo for a 4-year highway construction program. Another was a $25 million 10-year loan at $5\frac{3}{4}$ per cent to the Union of South Africa to expand its railway system. A third loan was a $32.5 million $13\frac{1}{2}$-year loan at 6 per cent made to India to enable the privately owned Tata Iron and Steel Company Limited to expand its capacity. Other loans were for irrigation projects, electric power projects, water supply systems, and the expansion and modernization of coal-mining operations.[3]

The total of the Bank's loans classified by purpose and area is shown in Table 16-2.

In addition to its lending activities, the World Bank, in connection with its normal course of work on loan proposals and projects, gives a wide range of technical, financial, and administrative assistance.

It is to be hoped that the World Bank will set an entirely new standard for international lending and will serve to institute a highly efficient system of loan analysis as well as to increase emphasis on the use of such loans for productive purposes.

[2] International Bank for Reconstruction and Development, *Supplement to the Twelfth Annual Report, July 1, 1957 to January 31, 1958*, Washington, D. C., pp. 1-4.
[3] *Ibid.*

QUESTIONS

1. Discuss the nature of international trade.
2. What is meant by the balance of payments? How is the balance of trade related to it?
3. How are exchange rates determined?
4. Describe the influence of unusual capital transfers on exchange rates.
5. How do governmental policies affecting international trade affect exchange rates?
6. Describe the nature of direct governmental influences on exchange rates. Why have they been used?
7. Discuss the basis for stabilization of exchange rates.
8. Describe and evaluate the operations of stabilization funds.
9. Why was the International Monetary Fund established?
10. Describe the structure and organization of the International Monetary Fund.
11. What are the financial resources of the International Monetary Fund?
12. Discuss the methods of operation of the International Monetary Fund?
13. What is the basic function of the International Bank for Reconstruction and Development or World Bank?
14. Describe the structure and organization of the World Bank.
15. What are the financial resources of the World Bank?
16. Discuss the methods of operation of the World Bank.

SUGGESTED READINGS

BOGEN, JULES I. (Editor). *Financial Handbook*; Fifth Edition. New York: The Ronald Press Company, 1950. Chapter 15.

CHANDLER, LESTER V. *The Economics of Money and Banking*; Revised Edition. New York: Harper & Brothers, 1953. Chapters 29-32.

ENKE, STEPHEN S., and SALERA, VIRGIL. *International Economics*; Second Edition. Englewood Cliffs, New Jersey: Prentice-Hall, Inc., 1951.

EVITT, HERBERT E. *A Manual of Foreign Exchange*; Fourth Edition. London: Pitman Publishing Company, 1955.

GORDON, WENDELL C. *International Trade*. New York: Alfred A. Knopf, Publisher, 1958. Part V.

International Bank for Reconstruction and Development. Annual Reports. Washington, D. C.

International Monetary Fund. Annual Reports. Washington, D. C.

PRITCHARD, LELAND J. *Money and Banking*. Boston: Houghton Mifflin Company, 1958. Part V.

YOUNG, JOHN P. *The International Economy*; Third Edition. New York: The Ronald Press Company, 1951.

Financing

the

Consumer

Chapter 17

Consumer Credit

in the Financial

Structure

In this chapter consumer credit will be defined so as to distinguish it from business, agricultural, and government credit. The functions of consumer credit will then be considered, showing how development and adaptation took place to meet changing needs. Changes in the volume of consumer credit will be analyzed in the light of the factors that affect the demand for such credit. Then attention will be directed to the users of various types of installment credit.

NATURE OF CONSUMER CREDIT

Consumer credit may be defined as credit used by consumers to help finance the purchase of commodities and services for personal consumption or to refinance debts originally incurred for such purchases. Its use to finance personal consumption distinguishes it from business credit used for production purposes. For example, when an individual uses credit to buy an automobile for personal or family use, the credit extended to him is consumer credit; when a cab driver uses credit to buy a similar automobile for use as a taxi, the credit extended to him is business credit. The distinguishing feature is the use to which the goods or services bought on credit are to be put.

Problems of Classification

In applying such a definition of consumer credit, several practical problems are encountered. Credit extended to farmers who

329

are operating a family farm may be used for consumption, for production, or for both purposes. It is often difficult for a farmer himself to know just how the money will be divided between different uses. Banks therefore make no attempt to divide farm loans into loans for production and loans for consumption. Furthermore many institutions loan money exclusively to farmers. Therefore, agricultural credit is usually treated as a separate category of credit even though it is part consumer credit and part producer credit.

A similar problem of classification of credit arises at times in the nonagricultural sector of the economy. A consumer may use credit to buy an automobile that is intended primarily for personal use. It may be used in part, however, for business purposes, such as making business trips. Since there is no practicable way of allocating such credit between consumption and production, all of it is classed as consumer credit.

Long-Term Consumer Credit

Our definition of consumer credit includes credit used to purchase residential real estate and to make repairs or to modernize such property, since in each of these cases the purpose is to finance or refinance the purchase of goods or services for personal consumption. The major difference between financing the purchase of an automobile and a home is usually in the time period involved in repayment of the loan. Both are durable goods; but a house usually lasts many times as long as a car, it costs much more, and payments for it therefore are made over a longer period of time.

Credit used to purchase homes is treated as long-term consumer credit; that used for other purposes, as intermediate and short-term credit. Such a distinction is frequently made in practice and in studies of consumer credit.[1] Following such a division, credit for home repairs and modernization is treated as part of short-term and intermediate-term consumer credit. Credit for financing the purchase of a home is, then, the only case of long-term consumer financing.

[1] See Gottfried Haberler, *Consumer Installment Credit and Economic Fluctuations* (New York: National Bureau of Economic Research, Inc., 1942), p. 18; and *Proceedings of the Michigan Consumer Credit Conference* (Albion, 1952), p. 3.

This distinction is followed in this part of the text. Chapters 18 and 19 deal with short-term and intermediate-term consumer credit, and Chapter 20 deals with long-term credit for financing urban residential real estate.

FUNCTIONS OF CONSUMER CREDIT

The basic function of consumer credit is to enable the con-sumer to maximize the satisfaction he obtains by using his income for consumer goods. This assistance to the consumer takes several forms: (1) the provision of a convenient form of payment, (2) help in periods of financial stress, and (3) a plan for the payment of durable goods while they are being used.

(1) Convenient Form of Payment

One reason for using consumer credit is the convenience of paying for goods and services. The typical charge account involves purchases from a retail store that are paid once a month, usually by check. This plan makes small purchases more convenient than when cash is paid at the time of each purchase. Normally, about the same amount is spent each month whether goods are charged or paid for in cash. Since many people are paid monthly or semi-monthly, it is a convenience for them to be able to pay for goods as their wages and salaries are paid to them. At times charge accounts may be used to carry the consumer for a longer period of time. Some customers may occasionally be one or two months in arrears in paying their bills. This is especially true after heavy purchases for the Christmas season.

Services are also frequently paid for on a charge basis. This is true of electric, gas, and some telephone services that are billed once a month. Utilities may require deposits by members of lower-income groups, those renting their homes, those whose credit they do not feel is sound, and similar groups. The usual arrangement, however, is to grant credit for a period of about six weeks since bills are sent out once a month and ten days to two weeks are allowed for payment. As a rule, doctors, dentists, lawyers, and other professional people also send out statements once a month, thus providing a convenient method of monthly payment.

(2) Aid in Financial Emergencies

A second function of consumer credit is to help consumers meet periods of financial stress. This function has been referred to as the safety-valve function of consumer credit. Most families with incomes of $5,000 or below, and many with larger incomes, do not have sufficient liquid assets to meet emergencies. They have such assets as homes, life insurance policies, automobiles, and household equipment of considerable value, but they do not have much cash to meet unforeseen contingencies. In fact, over half of these families do not have cash on hand equal to one-month's income.[2]

When an emergency strikes, such as a serious illness, an accident, temporary loss of a job, or loss from a fire, a tornado, or a theft not covered by insurance, the cash reserve of these families is soon depleted. Consumer credit can perform a valuable function in tiding a family over such a period. In other cases the financial difficulty may result from poor planning of family expenditures or poor budgeting of family resources. In such cases unpaid bills have probably accumulated, and a consumer loan to consolidate these bills and to pay them in installments may provide a way out of the difficulty.

(3) Buying Durables on Installments

The third function performed by consumer credit is to aid consumers in financing the purchase of durable goods by paying for them in installments. There is a demand by consumers for housing, refrigeration, transportation, and so on. These demands are satisfied in our economy by means of consumer goods that provide such services for a period of time. A house may provide a place to live for 40 to 50 years, an electric refrigerator may provide refrigeration service for 10 or more years, and an automobile may provide transportation for 5 or more years.

The day-by-day satisfactions from durable goods are made available to consumers in several ways. In the case of some goods, most commonly houses, it is possible to enjoy their use by renting them. Renting is becoming more widespread in the case of automobiles and some appliances, especially television sets.

2 Wallace P. Mors, *Consumer Credit Facts For You* (Cleveland: Bureau of Business Research, Western Reserve University, 1952), p. 1.

Another way of enjoying the services of durable goods is to purchase them, either new or used. These goods may be bought for cash or on the installment plan. To pay cash, the average consumer would have to save for a period of time until he accumulated the purchase price. For most consumers, this is not feasible as a method of acquiring a home since by the time a sufficient amount could be saved, the family would be grown and away from home. Therefore, most houses are paid for while the owners are deriving housing services by living in them.

The situation in regard to durables other than housing is similar. Most consumers would take several years to save enough to buy an automobile, furniture, and other major durable goods even if they followed through with a savings program. In the meantime they would have to do without these services, and the price of waiting may be very high or even prohibitive. It does little good to save enough money to buy a refrigerator two years after the old one has failed to function, or to buy a car to drive to a new job at a place inaccessible by public transportation a year after the job has begun. Therefore, a system of paying for such durables as they are being used is a real service to consumers.

Under most payment plans these durable goods are paid for in a period that is materially shorter than their useful life. For example, a house that usually is serviceable for 40 years or more, is paid off in installments in 20 to 25 years. A refrigerator, which lasts 10 years or more, is usually paid for in 2 years; and so on. Financing such purchases on installments, therefore, is also an aid to the consumer in building up his stock of durable goods since, when the article is paid for, a substantial proportion of unused services exists.

Another effect of selling durable goods on installments is to accelerate the movement of manufactured goods, since consumers buy such goods sooner than they could if they had to save the full purchase price first. This effect is especially important in the case of a new durable good because manufacturers are able to achieve volume sales more rapidly than they could in a cash-sale economy.

DEVELOPMENT OF CONSUMER CREDIT

Consumer credit is probably as old as the human race itself. Before money was used, primitive peoples developed credit to make barter more flexible. This was consumer credit because almost all goods were consumer goods in those days. Such a form of consumer credit based on a barter system is still used by primitive societies in remote parts of the world today.[3]

In a primitive economy no charge was made for the loan of goods because it was a problem for a nomadic people to carry around excess goods, such as food and clothing. If such articles were repaid in kind later on, the borrower and the lender both benefited because the borrower had the goods when needed and the lender did not have the problem of moving them around with him.

Development of Cash Lending

Records indicate that the lending of money for use in buying consumer goods developed almost simultaneously with the development of money as a medium of exchange. The business of lending cash to wage earners in the United States probably began after the Civil War in the cities of the Middle West. Such loans were made for short periods of time. The smallest loans were payable in a week, two weeks, or a month; and the largest, in less than a year.

Some degree of specialization developed in this early business of lending cash to consumers. One group of lenders attached wages as security, that is, they had the borrower sign an agreement to have a part of future wages paid to the lender in the event the loan was not paid on time. These salary lenders made loans of from $5 to $50 and charged interest rates of from 10 per cent to 40 per cent a month, depending upon the size of the loan. Another group loaned on unsecured notes, relying on their ability to get a court order to attach wages to collect on defaulted loans. A third group used chattel mortgages on household furniture as security. Their loans generally ranged from $10 to $300, and their charges were between 5 per cent and 20 per cent a month.

This loan business was illegal under the usury laws that existed in most states then, just as it is now. But it was difficult to prove the usurious nature of the transactions since interest charges were disguised as fees for services, notes often had to be signed before the loans were completed, the amount of the loan

[3] *Proceedings of the Consumer Credit Conference for 1950*, p. 6.

was turned over without witnesses, receipts were not given, and so on. Many borrowers were also so glad to be accommodated that they did not press charges.

As these abuses were brought to light, especially by the Russell Sage Foundation, small-loan legislation was passed in state after state, and legal lending of cash to consumers was developed by consumer finance companies, and later also by commercial banks.

Factors Responsible for the Development of Cash Lending

Several factors account for the development of cash lending to consumers on an organized basis. The structure of our society was undergoing some pronounced changes in the period following the Civil War. One of the most important was the shifting of workers from rural to urban areas. In 1790 only 5.1 per cent of the population of the United States lived in urban areas, that is, in communities of 2,500 or more. By 1840 this percentage had increased to 10.8 per cent, and after that it went up more rapidly. By 1860 the percentage had about doubled, reaching 19.8 per cent; and it about doubled again by 1900 when it was 39.7 per cent. Although it has gone up more slowly since then, it is at about 60 per cent today.[4]

A farmer can get along for a period of time during an emergency with practically no cash. As soon as he moves to an urban area, however, he is dependent upon current income, past savings, credit, or charity. Thus, the growing urbanization led to a demand for cash loans to meet emergencies.

This need was further accentuated by the changing character of industry and of the position of the laboring class. In 1860 this country was primarily agricultural, but by 1900 it was predominantly an industrial nation. It had an established factory system and a permanent body of industrial workers. The average size of the factory increased markedly, and relationships between employer and employee became more and more impersonal. This was especially true in such fields as iron and steel where the capital per establishment went up from $160,000 in 1869 to almost $2,300,000 in 1909. Small independent producers began to disappear, and laborers were organized into plants of a thousand men

4 Richard U. Ratcliff, *Urban Land Economics* (New York: McGraw-Hill Book Co., Inc. 1949), p. 52.

or more.[5] In many cases employers continued to maintain a close relationship with employees and financed them during periods of difficulty. In other cases the employer no longer had such a relationship with his workers, and emergencies found the workers on their own.

Development of the Financing of Durable Goods Purchases

The use of credit for the payment for durable goods while they were being used also developed early in our economy. At first it was extended in the form of sales credit with long periods for repayment. A very large part of the trade in colonial Philadelphia was carried on by means of credit sales. For example, the records of a cabinetmaker for the period from 1775 to 1811 showed that 92 per cent of all sales were on credit. A linen merchant of the same period expected few of his customers to pay him in less than a year. Benjamin Franklin took over nine months, on the average, to pay for the books he bought.[6]

Under such conditions the volume of bad debts was bound to be high. One bookseller who allowed some customers over two years to pay their bills had bad debts averaging 10 per cent of sales. As was to be expected, some people misused credit and got into financial difficulties. The debts of some southern planters to mercantile houses in London were passed from father to son for several generations.[7]

Debts that could not be repaid during a lifetime gave rise to a peculiar marriage custom in colonial days. A man who married a widow whose former husband left unpaid debts was required to have the marriage ceremony take place in the middle of the King's highway with the bride dressed only in her slip to avoid taking on her former husband's debts.[8]

The first known examples of installment selling occurred in eastern cities. Stores that sold factory-made furniture on installments were established, but no records remain to show the extent of such trade or the terms of such sales. Early in the 19th century clock manufacturers in New England also began to sell their

[5] Bogart and Kemmerer, *Economic History of the American People* (New York: Longmans, Green, and Co., 1943), p. 539.

[6] *Proceedings of the Consumer Credit Conference, op. cit.,* pp. 6, 7.

[7] *Ibid.*, p. 7.

[8] *Ibid.*, pp. 7, 8.

products on installments. By 1850 a considerable business was done in the sale of pianos and organs on installments. By that year Singer Sewing Machine Company also had begun to sell its machines through agents on the installment plan, and its competitors soon copied this practice. By the end of the century, the installment system had spread to most of the country east of the Mississippi, and even beyond in some cases. This plan was used for a wide variety of goods and was made available to consumers with relatively low incomes.[9]

The real giant of installment buying, the automobile, appeared shortly after 1890, but it did not develop into a widely used consumer good until World War I days and later. In 1900 less than 4,200 cars were built, and the total production of cars and trucks first passed 100,000 in 1909.[10] Sales of cars paid for on installments probably began in 1910, and advertisements offering cars on time payments appeared in New York City in 1914. Thereafter the development of such financing grew at a phenomenal rate, especially after the end of World War I in 1918. As new consumer goods, such as refrigerators, vacuum cleaners, washing machines, and stokers, were developed, they also were sold on installments, which helped increase the volume of such financing.

Factors Responsible for the Growth of Installment Buying

One of the basic reasons for the growth of installment credit was the increase in the investment in durable goods by consumers. It is impossible to construct estimates of stocks of durable goods in the hands of consumers before 1900. It is possible, however, to obtain a fairly accurate picture of the durable goods owned by typical families in 1860.[11] In the homes of the better-housed workers in northern cities a kitchen range was generally the only stove in the house. Candles frequently were the only source of light. Furniture was often homemade or, if factory-made, it was of very poor quality and there was little of it in the house. Dishes, silverware, and cooking utensils were of the cheapest grades. The poor, of course, got by with even less equipment. Farmers, espe-

[9] Reavis Cox, *The Economics of Installment Buying* (New York: The Ronald Press Company, 1948), pp. 62-63.

[10] Clyde William Phelps, *The Role of Sales Finance Companies in the American Economy* (Baltimore: Commercial Credit Company, 1952), p. 23.

[11] E. W. Martin, *The Standard of Living in 1860* (Chicago: The University of Chicago Press, 1942).

cially those in the West, lived in log houses. What little furniture they had was homemade, and a fireplace served both for cooking and for heat.

The stock of durable equipment in American homes increased between 1860 and 1900, but at the turn of the century it was still not large by today's standards. One authority has estimated that the moderately well-to-do home in 1900 had an original investment of not over $200 in such devices as a sewing machine, an ice refrigerator, a cooking stove, and a few odds and ends of laundry, cleaning, and transportation equipment. Today such a home will probably have an automobile, a mechanical refrigerator, a vacuum cleaner, a washing machine, one or more radios, a television set, several small appliances such as irons and toasters, and perhaps other items, having a total purchase price of $2,500 to $5,000.

This increase in the ownership of durable goods has led to a large total investment in such goods. Estimates of the value of the stocks of consumer durables have been prepared for January 1, 1940, and January 1, 1943, showing the depreciated value of the goods in use in 1939 and 1942. Even though such estimates cannot be precise, they are accurate enough to show the magnitude of consumer investment in plant and equipment. On January 1, 1940, consumers had over $35 billion of durable and semidurable goods. Household furniture, fixtures, and equipment accounted for the largest investment, slightly over $15 billion. Over $9 billion was invested in clothing, jewelry, and accessories; and $3.3 billion in recreational equipment, books, and maps. Automobiles and accessories, including luggage for travel, were valued at $7.2 billion. By January 1, 1943, after more than a year of World War II, consumer investment had increased by $5 billion over 1939 in terms of 1939 prices.[12]

Detailed estimates such as these have not been developed for later years, but in the post-World War II period consumers have spent large sums on durable and semidurable goods. Expenditures were unusually large because of the increase in family formation and also because durable goods were not available during the war. According to one study, the equity of consumers in durable goods, after depreciation, on June 30, 1957, was $179 billion.[13]

[12] Reavis Cox and Ralph Breyer, *The Economic Implications of Consumer Plant and Equipment* (Washington: Retail Credit Institute of America, Inc., 1944), pp. 17-18.
[13] *Consumer Finance News*, December, 1957, p. 4.

Basic Causes for Increased Investment in Durables

This increase in consumer expenditures on durables was the major factor leading to an increase in installment credit. Several factors were responsible for these increased expenditures. Methods of producing durable goods in large quantities at a low price were important. It is, of course, also true that a market had to exist for large quantities of goods to make the economies of large-scale, assembly-line production possible.

This mass market was provided because incomes were increasing and money was available for items other than necessary food, clothing, and minimum shelter. Changing modes of living also provided the incentive to purchase such goods. More and more people moved to the cities and wanted conveniences equal to those of their neighbors. Increased activities put a greater premium on leisure time, thus leading to a demand for laborsaving devices.

Development of Urban Residential Real Estate Financing

Lending money to individuals to buy homes appears to have begun almost as soon as people lived in established communities. The earliest form of real estate financing was through loans by one individual to another, and such direct loans are still an important source of financing in this field. The first formal organization to set up a plan for home financing was organized in Frankford,[14] Pennsylvania, in 1831.[15] It was a cooperative agency for the purpose of lending funds pooled by the shareholders to the members for building or purchasing houses. It was not an American invention but was patterned after similar European institutions with which some of the immigrants were familiar. As time went on, more of these institutions were established and developed into present-day savings and loan associations. Over the years other agencies engaged in home financing.

Factors Responsible for the Development of Lending on Urban Real Estate

The growth of manufacturing and of urbanization after the Civil War led to an increased demand for housing in the cities.

[14] Now a part of the city of Philadelphia.
[15] Henry M. Bodfish and A. D. Theobald, *Savings and Loan Principles* (New York: Prentice-Hall, Inc., 1938), p. 27.

In rural areas it was freqeuntly possible to build a log house with the help of the neighbors, but this was impossible in urban areas.

The demand for housing was also increased by the large number of immigrants entering this country, most of whom were between 15 and 45 years of age. Some of them went onto farms, but most of them remained in cities, especially in the East. Few of these immigrant families or other families had the necessary cash to buy or build a house. Many rented their homes, but over the years an increasing number became homeowners. In 1890, 37 per cent of nonfarm families owned their own homes. This increased to 41 per cent in 1940, to 53 per cent in 1950, and to 60 per cent in 1956. This increase in home ownership was possible not only because of increased incomes but also because financial institutions developed procedures by means of which homes could be paid for while the owners lived in them.

VOLUME OF CONSUMER CREDIT

Consumer credit has become one of the most important segments of financing. Statistics compiled by the Federal Reserve System show that total consumer credit outstanding at the end of 1956 was $41.9 billion. The magnitude of this figure can better be appreciated when it is compared with short-term and intermediate lending to business. As of December 31, 1956, all insured commercial banks had commercial loans to business of $38.6 billion outstanding.[16]

The largest segment of consumer credit is represented by *installment credit*, that is, credit which is to be repaid in regular installments usually on a monthly basis. At the end of 1956 this was $31.6 billion or 75 per cent of the total, and noninstallment credit was $10.3 billion or 25 per cent of the total. Over 70 per cent of all installment credit was sale credit used to finance the sale of durable goods, and the rest was installment cash loans. Sale credit was higher than these figures show because some personal installment loans are used to finance the purchase of other durables, particularly automobiles. Credit used to buy automobiles on time was the largest part of installment sale credit, accounting for almost 65 per cent of such credit outstanding at the end of 1956.

[16] *Federal Reserve Bulletin*, November, 1957, pp. 1248 and 1268.

The biggest part of noninstallment credit is convenience credit in the form of charge accounts and services that are paid for monthly. At the end of 1956 charge account credit was 46 per cent and service credit 21 per cent of noninstallment credit. The remaining 33 per cent consisted of singe-payment loans made by commercial banks and pawnbrokers. Complete figures on consumer credit outstanding by types since 1939 are presented in Table 17–1.

Relationship of Consumer Credit to Disposable Income

Another way to gauge the importance of consumer credit is to compare it with disposable personal income, that is, income available for personal consumption expenditures after paying personal income taxes. Since 1929 the monthly average of consumer credit outstanding has been between 5 per cent and 15 per cent of disposable personal income, except during the period 1943-1946 when consumer durables were in short supply because of World War II restrictions. In prosperous years, when goods are freely available, consumer credit outstanding has averaged between 8 and 15 per cent of disposable personal income. These relationships for the period from 1929 through the first half of 1955 may be seen graphically in Chart 17-1. During this period the volume of consumer credit outstanding did not exceed 12 per cent of disposable income. It exceeded this level in the second half of 1955 and then continued to increase more rapidly than income in 1956 and 1957.

Since consumer credit fluctuates with disposable personal income, the volume of credit outstanding changes in response to changes in economic activity. A study of Chart 17-2 shows that total consumer credit reached a high point at the end of 1929 and again in 1937, and turned down in each case with business activity. The next high point was at the end of 1941 when World War II restrictions cut the supply of durable goods. In 1946 credit started upward again and has continued upward except for a minor dip in 1954 when business experienced a minor adjustment.

The volatile segment of consumer credit is installment credit as Chart 17–2 clearly shows. The other forms of credit have remained fairly stable, but they do show some adjustments to income changes and to changing price levels.

Table 17-1
SHORT- AND INTERMEDIATE-TERM CONSUMER CREDIT
CONSUMER CREDIT, BY MAJOR PARTS

[Estimated amounts of short- and intermediate-term credit outstanding, in millions of dollars]

End of year or month	Total	Instalment credit					Noninstalment credit			
		Total	Automobile paper[1]	Other consumer goods paper[1]	Repair and modernization loans[2]	Personal loans	Total	Single-payment loans	Charge accounts	Service credit
1939	7,222	4,503	1,497	1,620	298	1,088	2,719	787	1,414	518
1941	9,172	6,085	2,458	1,929	376	1,322	3,087	845	1,645	597
1945	5,665	2,462	455	816	182	1,009	3,203	746	1,612	845
1949	17,305	11,590	4,555	3,706	898	2,431	5,715	1,532	2,795	1,388
1950	21,395	14,703	6,074	4,799	1,016	2,814	6,692	1,821	3,291	1,580
1951	22,617	15,294	5,972	4,880	1,085	3,357	7,323	1,934	3,605	1,784
1952	27,401	19,403	7,733	6,174	1,385	4,111	7,998	2,120	4,011	1,867
1953	31,243	23,005	9,835	6,779	1,610	4,781	8,238	2,187	4,124	1,927
1954	32,292	23,568	9,809	6,751	1,616	5,392	8,724	2,408	4,308	2,008
1955	38,670	28,958	13,472	7,634	1,689	6,163	9,712	3,002	4,579	2,131
1956	42,097	31,827	14,459	8,510	1,895	6,963	10,270	3,253	4,735	2,282
1957—Jan.	41,138	31,568	14,410	8,305	1,872	6,981	9,570	3,199	4,111	2,260
Apr.	41,247	31,786	14,691	8,017	1,862	7,216	9,461	3,374	3,735	2,352
July	42,592	32,968	15,329	8,189	1,921	7,529	9,624	3,406	3,810	2,408
Oct.	43,274	33,504	15,579	8,236	1,988	7,701	9,770	3,405	3,991	2,374

[1] Represents all consumer instalment credit extended for the purpose of purchasing automobiles and other consumer goods, whether held by retail outlets or financial institutions. Includes credit on purchases by individuals of automobiles or other consumer goods that may be used in part for business.

[2] Represents repair and modernization loans held by financial institutions; holdings of retail outlets are included in other consumer goods paper.

SOURCE: *Federal Reserve Bulletin*, December, 1957, p. 1400.

Chart 17-1

CONSUMER CREDIT OUTSTANDING VS. DISPOSABLE
PERSONAL INCOME

1929-1955

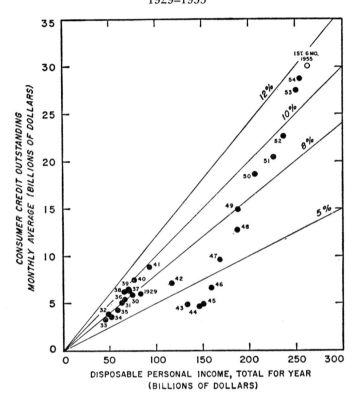

SOURCE: *Survey of Current Business*, August, 1955, p. 8.

The most pronounced fluctuation in installment credit is in that type used to finance the purchase of durable goods. It fluctuates widely because the sales of such goods have wide fluctuations as economic conditions change.

Relationship of Consumer Credit to Consumer Expenditures

Another measure of the importance of consumer credit is the amount of new credit granted in relationship to personal consumption expenditures. Total installment credit extended was 5.8 per cent of personal consumption expenditures in 1946. It increased year by year until it reached 11.1 per cent in 1950. It

Chart 17–2

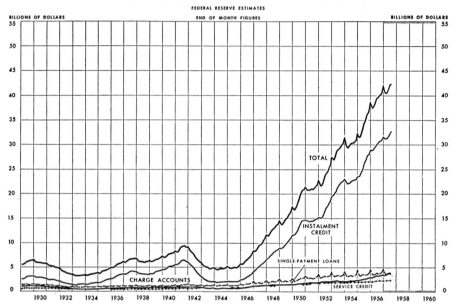

SHORT- AND INTERMEDIATE - TERM CONSUMER CREDIT OUTSTANDING

FEDERAL RESERVE ESTIMATES
END OF MONTH FIGURES

SOURCE: *Federal Reserve Chart Book,* Historical Supplement, September, 1957, p. 72.

stayed at about this level in relationship to consumption expenditures in 1951 and then increased to over 13 per cent in 1952, 1953, and 1954. In 1955 it increased to over 15 per cent and remained at about this level in 1956 and 1957. Such figures for the period from 1946 through 1956 are shown in Table 17–2.

Real Estate Credit

At the end of 1956, $99 billion of mortgage debt was outstanding on one- to four-family houses in urban areas. Of this total, over $83 billion was loaned by financial institutions, and over $15 billion by individuals and other lenders. The volume of nonfarm mortgage debt since 1940 can be seen graphically in Chart 17–3.

Chart 17–3 also shows the volume of new loans made on urban residential property. A comparison of this line with the value of residential construction shows that new loans fluctuate closely with such construction.

Table 17–2
THE RELATIONSHIP OF INSTALLMENT CREDIT EXTENDED
TO PERSONAL CONSUMPTION EXPENDITURES
1946–1956

YEAR	PERSONAL CONSUMPTION EXPENDITURES	INSTALLMENT CREDIT EXTENDED	INSTALLMENT CREDIT AS A PERCENTAGE OF CONSUMPTION EXPENDITURES
	(Billions of Dollars)		
1946	146.6	8.5	5.8
1947	165.0	12.7	7.7
1948	177.6	15.5	8.7
1949	180.6	18.1	10.0
1950	194.0	21.6	11.1
1951	208.3	23.6	11.3
1952	218.3	29.5	13.5
1953	230.5	31.6	13.7
1954	236.6	31.1	13.1
1955	254.4	39.0	15.4
1956	267.2	40.1	15.0

SOURCE: *Economic Indicators*, May, 1955, pp. 2, 29, and *Survey of Current Business*, July, 1957, p. 9.

Total Consumer Credit

The full significance of the debts of consumers in urban areas can be gained by combining all types of consumer credit. At the end of 1956 the total of short-term, intermediate, and long-term consumer credit outstanding was $141 billion. For the complete picture, it is necessary to add the consumer-credit portion of farm real estate credit and of short-term and intermediate-term farm credit. At the end of 1956, $9.9 billion of farm real estate credit was outstanding. Much of this credit, but not all of it, was used to finance farm homes.

Some consumer credit was also involved in the loans of over $4 billion made to farmers at the end of 1956 by insured commercial banks and in the $6.7 billion of government credit to agriculture outstanding at the end of 1956.[17] Probably half or more of this total of credit extended to farmers should be included as part of long-term or short-term consumer credit. Thus, total consumer credit outstanding, short-term, intermediate, and long-term, for housing was probably $150 billion or more at the end of 1956.

[17] *Federal Reserve Bulletin*, November, 1957, pp. 1248, 1256, 1265.

Chart 17–3

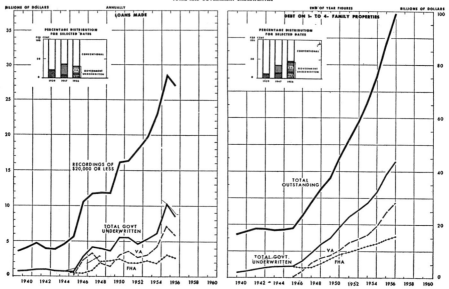

SOURCE: Board of Governors of the Federal Reserve System.

WHO USES CONSUMER CREDIT

The large amounts of consumer credit of all types outstanding indicate that its use is widespread. This is borne out by the Federal Reserve Board annual surveys of consumer finances. The figures for early 1957 are typical of the post-World War II period, especially the period after the Korean War. That survey includes all short-term and intermediate-term consumer debts except charge accounts that were being paid regularly as due. The survey revealed that 58 per cent of all spending units in the country had some debt.[18] Of these, almost half had debts of less than $500 and only 16 per cent of all spending units had debts of over $1,000.

This debt is by no means concentrated in any one income classification, either low or high, although the lowest income group shows a higher percentage having no debt than any other group. Of those spending units having a money income in 1956 of under $1,000 before taxes, 71 per cent had no installment debt.

[18] These data and those which follow on the distribution of consumer debt are taken from *Federal Reserve Bulletin*, August, 1957, p. 899.

This percentage drops to 30 for units with incomes between $7,500 and $10,000. It is 53 per cent for those in the $10,000 and above income bracket.

There is also some variation in the frequency of debt by the age of the head of the family or spending unit. The highest percentage of units having some debt is for the group in which the head is between 25 and 34 years of age. In this group 76 per cent had some debt. This percentage decreases as the head of the unit advances in age, as shown in Table 17-3.

CALCULATING THE INTEREST RATE PAID ON INSTALLMENT LOANS

In comparing costs of alternative sources of credit, the total dollar cost for the loans should be compared. It is also helpful to calculate the annual rate of interest that is being paid. Suppose that a borrower receives a loan of $100 repayable in 12 monthly installments and that the charge for the loan is $10. The $100 loan and $10 charge will most likely be repaid in equal monthly installments of $9.17 ($110 ÷ 12). Since the loan is being repaid monthly, the borrower has the use of $100 for the first month, $91.67 for the second, and so on as follows:

1st month	$100
2nd "	91 2/3
3rd "	83 1/3
4th "	75
5th "	66 2/3
6th "	58 1/3
7th "	50
8th "	41 2/3
9th "	33 1/3
10th "	25
11th "	16 2/3
12th "	8 1/3
Total	$650

The borrower has owed an average amount of $54.17 for the year ($650 ÷ 12). Then, dividing the loan charge of $10 by the average amount owed of $54.17 gives an interest rate of 18.5 per cent.

This rate may also be calculated by means of a simple formula:

$$R = \frac{2mI}{P(n+1)}$$

Table 17-3

PERSONAL DEBT OF SPENDING UNITS WITHIN INCOME AND AGE GROUPS, EARLY 1957

[Percentage distribution of spending units]

Income and age	Number of cases	All cases	No debt	Some debt	Amount of personal debt [1]					
					$1–$99	$100–$199	$200–$499	$500–$999	$1,000 and over	Not ascertained
All spending units [2]	3,041	100	42	58	9	6	12	11	16	4
1956 money income before taxes:										
Under $1,000	224	100	71	29	10	5	7	4	2	1
$1,000–$1,999	310	100	56	44	14	6	11	6	4	3
$2,000–$2,999	325	100	45	55	10	9	15	10	6	5
$3,000–$3,999	352	100	35	65	10	6	14	16	14	5
$4,000–$4,999	395	100	31	69	10	5	17	15	17	5
$5,000–$7,499	761	100	32	68	5	6	15	13	26	3
$7,500–$9,999	327	100	30	70	8	4	12	12	31	3
$10,000 and over	347	100	53	47	4	2	5	8	22	6
Age of head of spending unit:										
18–24	271	100	39	61	9	7	13	13	16	3
25–34	600	100	24	76	8	6	17	16	25	4
35–44	686	100	29	71	9	7	13	13	23	6
45–54	586	100	40	60	8	5	14	13	16	4
55–64	433	100	59	41	10	5	11	6	7	2
65 and over	420	100	75	25	10	3	4	2	2	4

[1] Includes all short- and intermediate-term consumer debt other than charge accounts; excludes mortgage and business debt.
[2] Includes cases in which age of head of spending unit was not ascertained.

SOURCE: *Federal Reserve Bulletin*, August, 1957, p. 899.

In this formula,

R equals the annual interest rate expressed in decimal form.

m equals the number of installment payment periods in a year (12 for monthly payments; 52 for weekly payments).

I equals the total amount of the charge for the loan in dollars and cents.

P equals the net amount of the credit made available to the borrower (in the case of an installment sale contract, this is the amount of the unpaid balance that remains to be paid after the buyer has received credit for any down payment including trade-in allowance; in the case of a cash loan this is the amount of cash actually received by the borrower).

n equals the number of installment payments specified in the contract.

In the example used, m is 12 since the loan is repaid monthly, and I is $10. P is $100 since that is the amount he has actually received, and n is 12 since the loan is for 12 months.

Substituting these items in the formula gives the following results:

$$R = \frac{2 \times 12 \times \$10}{\$100 \ (12 + 1)} = \frac{\$240}{\$1300} = .185$$

or 18.5 per cent per year.

INSTITUTIONS GRANTING CONSUMER CREDIT

A large number of institutions are engaged in granting consumer credit. Cash is loaned to consumers by many institutions. The major ones are consumer finance companies, credit unions, industrial banks and loan companies, and commercial banks.

A number of agencies are also engaged in lending money to consumers to aid them in purchasing goods and services. Retail stores, utilities, other service agencies, and professional persons grant credit as a convenience to their customers. Installment sales credit is extended primarily by sales finance companies and commercial banks, but also to some extent by other financial institutions. The lending activities of these institutions will be discussed in the chapters that follow.

QUESTIONS

1. Define consumer credit in such a way as to distinguish it from other types of credit.
2. Briefly discuss several problems that arise in applying your definition of consumer credit.
3. What difference, if any, is there between credit used to finance the purchase of a house and to finance the purchase of an automobile?
4. Describe the economic functions performed by consumer credit.
5. Discuss several alternative ways in which consumers may provide themselves with the services of durable goods. Give several examples of each method.
6. Describe the early development of consumer lending.
7. Describe the development of cash lending to consumers in the United States.
8. Briefly trace the development of the financing of durable goods.
9. Discuss the factors responsible for the growth of installment buying.
10. Briefly describe the factors responsible for the growth of lending on urban real estate.
11. From data in the latest Federal Reserve Bulletin, bring Table 17-1 on page 342 up to date.
12. Discuss the relationship of consumer credit to disposable income.
13. Why is installment credit the volatile element in consumer credit?
14. From a knowledge of the factors that cause changes in the volume of various types of consumer credit, account for the changes in the volume of consumer credit from 1950 to the present. (Use data developed in your answer to Question 11)
15. Discuss the relationship of nonfarm mortgage debt to residential construction.
16. Describe the users of consumer credit by income groups and family status. Use data in the *Federal Reserve Bulletin* showing the users of consumer credit in the past year. Account for differences between your data and that presented in the text on page 348.
17. Calculate the annual rate of interest on the following loan: $300 loaned for a period of one year to be repaid with a loan charge of $45 in equal monthly installments.

SUGGESTED READINGS

Consumer Credit Facts for You, Educational Pamphlet Number 1. Cleveland: Bureau of Business Research, Western Reserve University, 1952.

Cox, Reavis. *The Economics of Instalment Buying*. New York: The Ronald Press Company, 1948.

Dauten, Carl A. "A Fresh Approach to the Place of Consumer Credit in Economic and Financial Thinking," *Journal of Finance* (May, 1954), pp. 111-123.

Haberler, Gottfried. *Consumer Instalment Credit and Economic Fluctuations*. New York: National Bureau of Economic Research, Inc., 1942.

The Role of Consumer Demand and Consumer Credit. New York: Proceedings of the National Consumer Credit Conference for 1953, New York University, 1953.

Chapter 18

Institutions Financing

the Consumer

In the preceding chapter the three functions of consumer credit were described. The first function, providing a convenient form of payment, is largely performed by retailers, service institutions, and professional men as an added service to their customers. Recently banks and specialized agencies have developed plans to help them render this service.

To perform the second function, that is, to provide aid in time of stress, cash loans must be made available to consumers. This has been done by consumer finance companies, industrial banks and loan companies, credit unions, and personal loan departments of commercial banks.

Cash loans from any of these agencies may also be used to perform the third function of consumer credit, that is, to pay for durable goods while they are being used. The major portion of durable-goods financing, however, is done as part of the sales transaction under an arrangement between the seller and a financial institution. Such financing was first developed by a specialized agency set up for this purpose, the sales finance company. In more recent years industrial banks and personal loan departments of commercial banks have also engaged in direct sales financing, and some of the large consumer finance companies also have sales finance subsidiaries.

The development of each of these institutions that finance the consumer will be analyzed in this and the following chapter. Consideration will also be given to their methods of operation, the results of their operation, and their current problems and trends.

Several institutions serve to facilitate consumer financing. These include various credit checking agencies that report on the credit standing of individuals and some specialized insurance companies which insure loans of various types. Their functions and problems will be considered briefly, especially their relationship to the consumer financing process.

Consumer finance companies, industrial banks and loan companies, and credit unions will be covered in this chapter; sales finance companies, commercial banks, and the facilitating agencies will be considered in the next chapter.

CONSUMER FINANCE COMPANIES

Consumer finance companies were developed to perform the second function of consumer credit, that is, to provide aid in time of financial emergency. They made loans in the early years of their existence primarily to low-income borrowers who found it impossible to obtain credit elsewhere. As time went on they expanded their scope of operations until today most of them make loans to a cross section of middle-income as well as low-income families.

Development of Consumer Finance Companies

As was pointed out in the last chapter, organized cash lending to consumers in this country probably began in cities of the Middle West after the end of the Civil War. Since the laws of the states not only made no provisions for institutions to lend money to consumers, but also made profitable legal operation impossible because of usury laws, such lending was carried on in violation of the law. Interest rates were seldom less than 5 per cent a month and were often as high as 40 per cent a month. Such lenders were referred to as loan sharks because they took advantage of borrowers in need.

Loan sharks flourished because there was a need for credit for emergencies that was not being met in any other way. They still flourish today when no adequate law exists to provide for loaning small sums to consumers. Kansas, for example, which had no small-loan law until recently, relied upon a usury statute setting 10 per cent per year as the maximum legal interest rate. A survey by the Junior Bar Conference of the American Bar Association showed that loan sharks flourished there despite all attempts to stop them. One illegal lender in Topeka made over

2,000 loans on which he charged rates of from 192 per cent to 418 per cent a year. Additional charges were made when loans were renewed. This is typical of what happened in all parts of Kansas. Similar situations still exist in states that have no small-loan law and in those states in which the law is largely or wholly inoperative.[1]

Remedial Action. Several steps were taken to combat the loan-shark problem in the period before World War I. Late in the nineteenth century legislation was passed that was designed to encourage the establishment of semiphilanthropic organizations to make small loans to consumers. As a result, in several cities, especially in the East, remedial loan societies were sponsored by social-minded citizens who devoted their time to these organizations without compensation. Although these societies helped many people, they hardly made a dent in the loan-shark problem. They did, however, provide factual data on small-loan operations and especially on the costs of doing such business.

At this stage the Russell Sage Foundation became interested in this field. They supplied funds for fellowships for special studies of social problems, and several of the recipients decided to study the small-loan field. The Foundation began to crystallize public opinion around its findings, and bills were introduced in various state legislatures to help solve the problem.

The first comprehensive small-loan legislation was passed in Massachusetts in 1911, and New Jersey followed suit in 1914. In the next year such legislation was passed in New York, Ohio, and Pennsylvania. With the experience in these states as a guide, the Russell Sage Foundation published a model Uniform Small Loan Law in 1916.

Several features are basic in a small loan law if illegal lending is to be eliminated. Maximum rates of charge must be set and these must be high enough to permit profitable operations. The charge is an over-all charge for expenses, services, and interest and it is the only charge permitted. It is computed on the unpaid balance of the loan each month or oftener if payments are made more frequently. Provision must be made for licensing lenders based on character, fitness to conduct the business, and financial

---

[1] Wallace P. Mors, *Small Loan Laws of the United States* (Cleveland: Bureau of Business Research, Western Reserve University, 1955), pp. 8-11.

responsibility. There must also be state supervision of the business and penalties against nonlicensees who charge more than the maximum rates permitted by the usury law, or against licensees who violate any of the provisions of the law. The early laws set the maximum size of loan permitted under the law at $300. Today it is $600 in many states and $1,000 or higher in some states.

Present Status. The number of consumer finance companies has grown over the years under the Uniform Small Loan Law. In the fall of 1957 there were about 10,000 consumer finance offices in the states that had effective small-loan legislation. Many of these are part of several national chains, others are part of a local or regional chain, many are independent offices.

The consumer finance companies had $2.4 billion of loans outstanding at the end of 1956 and made loans of $3.8 billion during the year.[2] This was much less than the total volume of loans of all types made by personal loan departments of commercial banks, but more than the volume of personal installment loans made by banks and substantially more than the volume of loans of industrial banks and loan companies, and credit unions.

Organization of Consumer Finance Companies

The Uniform Small Loan Law does not require any special form of organization for consumer finance companies. At first most of the lenders were individual proprietorships and partnerships, but the corporate form has become increasingly important. In the early years of licensed lending most of it was done by individual offices, but since 1920 chain operations have become increasingly important. This growth may be seen from the increase in the number of offices of some of the major chains. Household Finance Corporation, which is the largest of the chains in volume of loans outstanding, had 35 offices in 1918 and 832 at the end of 1956. Beneficial Finance Company, which had 54 offices in 1922, had 1,023 at the end of 1956. The American Investment Company of Illinois had 16 offices in 1929 and had increased this number to 409 at the end of 1956.

At the end of 1956 the Household Finance Corporation, the Beneficial Finance Company, and the American Investment Com-

2 *Consumers Finance News,* March, 1957, p. 21; and earlier issues.

pany of Illinois [3] held about half of the outstanding dollar balances of loans in the country. Despite the increasing dominance of the chains, however, many independent offices are operating profitably, not only in those communities in which they have no competition, but also in cities and towns that have one or more chain offices.

Chains have grown because they enjoy some advantages over independent offices. They have easier access to capital because they are able to raise funds in the security markets. They also find it easier and cheaper to obtain short-term bank loans. In addition they benefit from the mobility of capital since they can shift funds from office to office as they are needed. They gain a further advantage from geographic diversification of risks, not only economic, but also the risk of reduction in legal rates of charge. There may well be some economics from large-scale operation due to centralization of financing, supervision, accounting, and statistical work. There is, however, little saving that comes from having larger offices as such because the industry is basically one of more or less constant costs.[4] Since this is true, some independent operators have been able to offset the advantages of chain operation by particularly skillful administration, building community goodwill, or enjoying a good location for their office, and have therefore operated profitably in competition with the chains.

Sources of Funds

In the earliest stages consumer finance companies were financed almost entirely through the investments of the owners and the retention of earnings. As time went on, the larger companies gained access to sizable amounts of credit from commercial banks and were also able to sell their own promissory notes to investors through the commercial paper market. They also found it possible to sell securities to the investing public and to sell some issues of notes and bonds directly to institutional investors, such as insurance companies and banks. Individuals and partner-

---

[3] The small-loan offices of the Amercan Investment Company are operated under the names of such subsidiaries as Public Loan Corporation, Domestic Finance Corporation, and Ohio Finance Company.

[4] For a thorough anaylsis of this point, see R. Miller Upton, *The Importance of Direct Costs in the Granting of Consumer Installment Credit* (Unpublished Dissertation, Northwestern University, Chicago, 1948).

ships have had some access to bank credit, and independent corporations have also been able to raise a small amount of money by means of bond issues. For example, at the end of 1956 Household Finance Corporation had raised funds equal to 17 per cent of the assets employed in the business by short-term borrowing and 48 per cent by long-term borrowing. Preferred stock was 20 per cent of the capital and surplus of the corporation at this time. At the end of 1956 Beneficial Finance Company and subsidiaries had raised funds equal to 11 per cent of the assets used in the business by short-term borrowing and 55 per cent by long-term borrowing. Preferred stock was equal to only 3 per cent of capital and surplus.[5]

Characteristics of Loans and Borrowers

The major purpose of cash loans made by consumer finance companies is to tide consumers over a period of financial emergency. This is evident from the statistics of the stated use of funds from loans from the American Investment Company offices in 1957. Figures for this company are used because it is reasonably representative of the industry in this respect. Over a third of all loans were for the consolidation of existing debts, and an additional 8 per cent were for medical, hospital, and funeral expenses. The remaining loans were for the purchase of clothing, furniture, travel, education, repairs, and the like. The complete breakdown is presented in Table 18-1.

Table 18–1

PURPOSE OF LOANS MADE BY AMERICAN INVESTMENT COM-
PANY SUBSIDIARIES DURING 1957

Purpose of Loan	Per Cent of Total Loans
Consolidation of existing debts	37.91
Repairs and automobiles	14.90
Clothing, fuel, rent, food	8.96
Furniture and appliances	15.37
Medical, hospital, dental, funeral	8.37
Travel, vacation, education, assist relatives	8.72
Taxes, mortgages, interest, and insurance	5.77

SOURCE: Data furnished by the American Investment Company.

[5] From annual reports of the companies.

The average size of the loan made by personal finance companies has been increasing as loan limits have been raised in some states and as the price level has increased. The American Investment Company, for example, made an average loan of $148 in 1929. In 1956 the American Investment Company made an average loan of $385, the Household Finance Corporation of $399, and the Beneficial Finance Company of $398.

The majority of loans are made to individuals in the middle-income groups. Most borrowers have incomes between $50 and $100 a week although a sizable proportion have incomes as high as $150 a week and some even higher. In 1956, for example, the average income of borrowers from Household Finance Corporation was $83 a week, and it was the same for borrowers from Beneficial Finance Company.[6]

Loans are made to a cross section of the American population but primarily to skilled and unskilled laborers. A survey made in 1955 of a cross section of consumer finance offices throughout the United States showed that 59 per cent of all loans were made to skilled and semiskilled workers and 11 per cent to unskilled and domestic workers. A detailed breakdown for loans to all groups is presented in Table 18-2.

Table 18–2

OCCUPATIONS OF CONSUMER FINANCE COMPANY CUSTOMERS

(Based on a survey of 1,800 offices throughout the United States in 1955)

Skilled and semiskilled workers	58.77%
Office and other nonmanual skills	7.06
Managers, superintendents, foremen, farm managers and in business for selves	5.24
Salesmen and saleswomen	5.59
School teachers	.80
Unskilled and domestic workers	11.16
Professional and semiprofessional	1.82
Persons with independent incomes	1.26
Protective services, members of the Armed Services, and other service workers	7.61
Occupations not reported and miscellaneous	.69
Total	100.00%

SOURCE: *Consumer Finance Facts and Figures*, 1956-1957. Washington: National Consumer Finance Association, 1956, p. 14.

6 *Ibid.*

Operations of Consumer Finance Companies

Consumer finance companies have from the beginning carried on active promotion campaigns to attract customers. They have done so by newspaper and direct mail advertising and also by establishing offices in busy shopping centers. An established office obtains many of its customers from former borrowers. Several of the chains have found that they get over half of their business from this source.

Factors in Granting Loans. Several factors must be checked in granting loans to keep loss ratios at a minimum. These factors are basically the ability of the borrower to repay the loan and his willingness to pay it. This means that the size of the income of the prospective borrower and expectations as to its stability must be checked. Since ability to pay may also be impaired because of heavy expenditures, such as medical expenditures, the possibility of such contingencies must be checked. Willingness to pay can best be gauged by the past payment record of an individual and his reputation for honest dealings.

The size of the payments to be made on the loan must also be checked in relationship to the expected income of the borrower and his other necessary expenses. This requires checking on other debts and, in the case of property owners, on the size of the payments on any mortgage. Owning property is usually a favorable factor in a credit evaluation, but in some cases payments may be so large in relation to current income as to make default almost inevitable.

Before a loan is made, the complete financial position of the applicant is usually reviewed. It may at times be possible to plan his finances in such a way that with a larger loan he can pay off some of his pressing debts and reduce his monthly payments to a level that he can meet.

In the early days of lending, all loans were made with chattel mortgages on automobiles, furniture, or store fixtures as collateral or with a comaker or guarantor of the loan. Today an increasing number of loans are being made without security or comaker.

When the loan is made, most states require the lender to give the borrower a Statement of Loan, which sets forth the lender's name and address, the interest rate, the date of the loan, the amount of the loan, the number of the loan in the lender's records, the number and amount of each payment, the date of the month when payments are due, and the date when the final payment is due. Some states require a detailed explanation of these items, and some require certain excerpts from the law or the regulation to appear on this statement. The lender usually provides a payment section on this same form on which the lender enters the payments as they are made by the borrower. Some lenders provide a separate payment book, and a few still use a receipt for each payment received.

The original plan of consumer finance companies was to have the borrower repay an equal amount of principal each month and a smaller sum as interest each month as the outstanding loan balance was reduced. In the last few years most lenders have changed their loan schedules to provide for equal payments each month. Some have so adjusted the amount of the loan as to provide for equal dollar payments each month.

Loan Record. The loss experience of most small loan companies when compared with the total dollar volume of loans made has been favorable. The experience of the American Investment Company is again fairly typical. The net amount charged off in the post-World War II period, after allowing for recoveries, varied between 1.11 per cent and 2.34 per cent of the monthly average of notes outstanding. The amount was larger during the depression of the thirties when it reached almost 4 per cent of average monthly notes outstanding in 1934. It is, however, much higher as a percentage of gross revenue from interest on loans. In 1947 when losses after allowing for recoveries reached 2.34 per cent of average monthly notes outstanding because uncollectible accounts of service personnel, which had been deferred during the war, were charged off, they were 8.5 per cent of gross revenue. In the worst year of the depression, 1934, losses after recoveries were 12 per cent of gross revenue.

Charges. The last draft of the Uniform Small Loan Law provided for a maximum rate of interest of 3 per cent per month on the unpaid balance of a loan up to $100 and 2 per cent per month on the amount above $100.

Some small loan laws still permit a top rate of 3½ per cent on all or part of the first $300, but most have set the top rate at 3 per cent and some at 2½ per cent. In Missouri it is now 2.218

per cent on loans up to $400, or $15 per year on each $100 of the original amount of the loan. Many of the smaller companies have regularly charged the top legal rates. The large chains have often set lower rates to attract business. This is not done as much as it was before World War II because of higher costs under inflationary conditions.

Profits. Profits of consumer finance companies have never been unusually high and have been dropping materially in the last few years as costs have gone up and rates have remained fixed or have been reduced somewhat. For example, Beneficial Finance Company had net income equal to 4.29 per cent of average assets employed in the business in 1956, a decline from 4.44 per cent in 1955. Because of substantial trading on equity by means of short-term and long-term borrowing, net income available for common stock was 15.3 per cent of common stock and surplus.[7]

Problems of Consumer Finance Companies

The consumer finance business, like any dynamic business, always has problems that it must meet in adapting to changing demands by the consumer and changing economic conditions. Several such problems that are peculiar to this business will be discussed in this section.

Public Understanding of the Nature of the Business. One of the biggest problems facing the consumer finance industry is the lack of understanding of the nature of its operations. The idea is still current in some quarters that these companies are charging rates far above the cost of the services they render.

In considering the rates of consumer finance companies, several things should be kept in mind. First of all, the charge is only on the unpaid balance, while competing institutions usually quote rates as a per cent of the original amount of the loan. This latter method makes rates appear to be much lower than they really are because in a loan repaid in equal installments the average amount outstanding is only about half of the original amount of the loan.

Secondly, consumer finance companies make no other charges of any kind in most states, that is, they have no investigation fee,

[7] Beneficial Finance Company, *Annual Report,* 1956.

notary fee, recording fee, and the like. Some states do permit insurance to be sold to cover the borrower in case of death or accident. Some companies have sold such insurance, others have not.

In the third place, many costs are almost as great for a small loan as for a large loan. It costs about as much to investigate a credit applicant if he wishes to borrow $50 as if he wants $1,000. Bookkeeping and collection costs are just as high for monthly payments of $5 as for $100 or more. The expenses of trying to collect past-due accounts are not affected much by the size of the account.

Small loan companies also have special costs that other consumer lending agencies do not have. These costs arise out of the regulations of the small-loan law. The small-loan law requires the lender to give the borrower a loan statement with detailed information on it. There are also provisions concerning the types of records that must be kept and the reports which must be made to the regulatory agency. The provision of the small-loan law that payments must be accepted in advance and that the borrower can be charged only for the time he has had the money also increases clerical work and raises costs.

Inflated Costs. One of the major problems is that of maintaining profits in the face of cost increases due to inflation during and after World War II. Maximum loan charges are set by law, and most have not been increased since before World War II although the price level has doubled. Consumer finance companies have been able to operate profitably under such conditions because the size of the average loan on which the interest income is calculated has about kept pace with the price level. Furthermore, these companies have resorted to the use of more and more borrowed funds, which they have been able to obtain at a rate of interest that is lower than the earnings on these funds. Since many costs do not vary with the size of the loan, revenue has increased sufficiently to keep up in large part with increased costs. However, the maximum loan limit must be raised if the companies are to gain the full cost advantage of larger loans and this has not been done in some states.

The cost problem became more serious in 1953 when the Federal Reserve System acted to restrain inflation and interest was increased as a result of these policies. This increased the major variable cost and so offset in part the advantage of larger loans. The full effect will be felt only after some lapse of time, however, since a large part of borrowed funds are on a long-term basis. If interest rates stay up for several years, consumer finance companies will be hard put to keep up profit rates unless they are permitted to charge higher interest rates or can make larger loans.

Credit Life, Health, and Accident Insurance. In recent years many lending institutions and insurance companies have developed plans to sell insurance in connection with consumer loans. The amount of insurance is usually equal to the unpaid balance on the loan each month. It may be group insurance, or a separate policy may be written for each loan. When borrowers have been given a choice, they have usually been willing to pay reasonable fees for life insurance on a loan, but health and accident insurance has been much less popular.

The sale of credit insurance creates a problem in the consumer finance field. The uniform laws have been based on the all-inclusive rate of charge. Insurance has usually been paid for as a special item when used in connection with loans from other lending agencies. Many in the consumer finance field feel that insurance should be sold on the same basis in their field. But others believe that, if any fees are allowed over and above the all-inclusive rate, the way is open for unscrupulous lenders to get back into the field and to load up borrowers with unwanted and unneeded insurance at high rates.

INDUSTRIAL BANKS

Substantial amounts of consumer credit are extended by institutions called industrial banks, industrial loan companies, or Morris Plan banks after one of the earliest groups of such banks to be developed.[8] Their distinguishing characteristic is that they have a thrift function as well as a loan function. They have always stressed their operation as a thrift institution. When the law permits, they accept deposits; in other cases they sell investment

---

[8] These banks are also at times referred to as industrial savings and loan companies, finance and thrift companies, or discount companies.

certificates that pay interest. These certificates may be bought on installments, and thus they provide a means of saving in small sums. Since they are cashable on demand, they become essentially the equivalent of a time deposit in a regular bank.

The second basic functon of industrial banks is to make loans to individuals for consumption purposes. These loans are of relatively small size even though they are somewhat larger than those of consumer finance companies. These loans are generally repaid in regular installments. This type of lending distinguishes industrial banks from commercial banks, which do diversified lending to businesses as well as to consumers.

Development of Industrial Banks

The first unit of this type of financial institution was established in the United States in 1901 when an immigrant from Latvia, David Stein, founded the Merchants and Mechanics Savings and Loan Association at Newport News, Virginia. It was patterned after the consumer banks and loan associations that had been developed in Europe to make loans to workers. Its name is similar to that of present-day organizations granting real estate credit, but it was established to make general consumer loans for small amounts and to provide a means of saving small amounts.

Other banks of this type were not started until 1910, when Arthur J. Morris set up the Fidelity Savings and Trust Company at Norfolk, Virginia. This institution proposed to lend money to people employed in industry; hence the name industrial bank or loan company. Morris also planned to obtain at least part of his funds by selling investment certificates that would carry a definite rate of interest. Since these certificates could be paid for in installments, they also provided a means of saving in small amounts.

In 1911 Mr. Morris copyrighted the name the "Morris Plan" and began to promote such units actively in large cities throughout the country. By 1917 he had established over 70 companies in the major cities of the country and also in some smaller ones. Growth of Morris Plan banks has been much slower since then; their total number still is under 100.

While the Morris Plan banks were being developed, other organizations and individuals were setting up similar units. Several other systems of banks were established, but these have all been dissolved. In the early thirties two new systems of banks that have offices in the South and Southeastern parts of the United States were established. The total number of industrial banks and loan companies is still under 500 according to the American Industrial Bankers Association.

The total volume of outstanding loan balances of industrial bank and loan companies at the end of 1952 was $795 million.[9] In addition to personal cash loans, loans were made for home repair and modernization, and retail installment paper was purchased from dealers to aid in sales financing.

Most states have special statutes governing industrial banks. These provide for consumer loans repayable in installments and for the acceptance of deposits or the issuance of investment certificates. Various regulations pertain to charges and penalties for delinquency. There is no uniformity in these laws, such as exists in the small-loan field, because the approach to the problem was piecemeal.

At present seven states have industrial-bank laws that give these institutions bank status and allow them to call their savings accounts "deposits." These states are Arizona, Colorado, Connecticut, Florida, Maine, New York, and North Carolina. Michigan and Ohio formerly had such laws, but now industrial banks are chartered as regular state banks in these states. The industrial banks in these nine states may become members of the Federal Deposit Insurance Corporation and thus have their deposits insured.

In twenty-two states industrial-loan laws authorize corporations chartered under them to accept savings under some form of investment certificate.[10] These corporations cannot call themselves banks or call the money received under savings plans "deposits." The remaining states have no special laws, but in some a few industrial banks have been established under the general corporation law or general banking statutes.[11]

---

[9] *Federal Reserve Bulletin*, March, 1953, p. 277. These are the latest figures that are available. Data for industrial banks and loan companies as a separate group are no longer published.

[10] These states are: Arkansas, California, Georgia, Indiana, Iowa, Kansas, Kentucky, Maryland, Massachusetts, Minnesota, Missouri, Montana, Nebraska, New Hampshire, Oregon, Rhode Island, Tennessee, Texas, Utah, Virginia, Washington, and West Virginia.

[11] *The Industrial Banker*, September, 1952, p. 11.

Organization of Industrial Banks

Most of the industrial-bank and loan laws have some provisions governing the organization of such banks. Almost all prescribe a minimum capital, which is usually between $25,000 and $50,000 but is higher in some states in the larger cities. Several states also provide that a charter can be granted only if an additional bank would serve the convenience and the advantage of the community.

Provisions in regard to loans also vary. Some forbid loans on real estate as security; some allow them under definite restrictions. Loan maturities are almost always set for short-term loans, usually between 12 and 24 months. The maximum loan size is usually higher than that for consumer finance companies—many laws set $1,000 as a limit, some $2,000, and some as high as $5,000.

Industrial-banking laws also as a rule regulate the maximum charges that can be made on loans by setting maximum discount rates per annum, delinquency fees, and investigation fees or service charges. Some laws provide for a maximum discount and no other fees, but most laws allow some fees. Discounts are usually from 6 to 8 per cent when other fees can be charged. This, of course, means that the true interest rate is well over twice this amount per annum. Discount rates are usually 10 to 12 per cent when no other fees are allowed, which means that the true interest rate is in the 20 to 25 per cent range.

When industrial banks were first set up, they frequently were able technically to operate within an 8 per cent usury statute by combining an investment certificate with a loan. During the life of the loan an investment certificate equal to the face of the loan was bought on installments. At the maturity of the loan this certificate was offset against the loan account. Thus, technically, the whole sum was in use for the life of the loan. Some companies still use this technique even though most laws specifically allow a certain maximum per cent of discount on loans paid in installments.

There is practically never a requirement for reserves against losses on loans. When industrial banks accept deposits, however, they are subject to the same reserve requirement as regular commercial banks in the state. This is usually between 5 and 10 per cent of deposits.

Source of Funds

In the banks insured with the FDIC, depositors provide about 90 per cent of all funds. The amount is less for banks which cannot accept deposits by that name but is still about two thirds of all funds. Owners provide most of the remainder of the funds through stock ownership and retained earnings. Some industrial banks borrow from commercial banks. A few also have raised some funds by means of long-term notes and bonds.

Characteristics of Loans and Borrowers

The first industrial banks made comaker loans almost exclusively. Some diversification was obtained by insisting that the comaker be in an industry different from that of the borrower. For example, if the borrower was employed in a shoe factory, he might get a friend who worked for a local public utility to sign the note for the loan with him. Comaker loans still account for an important part of industrial bank loans, but they have tended to decline in importance and loans made on the signature of the borrower have become more common. Such loans are made especially to superior credit risks. Group life insurance on the unpaid balance is regularly required.

An increasing percentage of loans is also being made with collateral to minimize the risk when no comaker is used. A wide range of items is used as collateral—stocks, bonds, insurance policies, fully paid investment certificates, savings passbooks, and household furniture. Industrial banks have also entered the field of sales financing, especially of automobiles.

Borrowers from industrial banks are from somewhat higher income groups than those from consumer finance companies. This difference in type of borrower is due to several factors. Industrial banks and loan companies were not established to provide credit primarily to low-income groups who had been the victims of loan-shark activities. They offered their services to a somewhat higher income group in which some members had funds available to put on deposit in the bank or loan company. Their rate structure has also not been high enough to make lending of small sums profitable. This has been especially true in the post-World War II period, since inflation has increased costs of operation and rates have not been increased.

Operations of Industrial Banks

Industrial banks have always carried on a vigorous promotion campaign for loan business and for deposits. They have used newspaper and radio advertising, and other media. Major emphasis is usually placed, however, on direct-mail advertising because they want to attract only acceptable applicants. Advertising has followed a seasonal pattern, stressing the needs for funds for Christmas, Christmas savings clubs, money for new clothing, and the like.

Losses on loans compared with the total volume of loans have been quite small. They have usually been less than 1.0 per cent of dollar loan volume and have averaged only 0.34 per cent for a representative group of banks since 1936.[12] Losses are, of course, a higher percentage of total operating income. In 1934 charge-offs for insured industrial banks wcrc 13.74 per cent of operating earnings. This dropped to 3.51 per cent in 1939 and went up somewhat again in 1940. Since 1943 charge-offs have been exceeded by recoveries in several years, and net charge-offs have been very small.[13]

Industrial banks have consistently operated at a profit which has usually been higher than that of commercial banks, but not so high as that in some industrial fields. Their percentage of income on loans has been going down; but since the average loan size has gone up, they have managed to maintain profitable operations.[14]

In 1952 the average net profit of industrial banks was 1.25 per cent of the volume of loans made. In the five-year period before World War II the average net profit was 2.53 per cent of the volume of loans made. Figures are not available on net profit as a percentage of average receivables outstanding, but the level is somewhat higher. Net profit was 1.79 per cent of all assets in 1952.[15] Since the major part of the funds of industrial banks is supplied by depositors, net profit on net worth has been much higher than on assets, but not so high as that in many industrial fields.

---

12 *The Industrial Banker*, April, 1953, p. 17.
13 Earnest A. Dauer, "Radical Changes in Industrial Banks," *Harvard Business Review*, Autumn, 1947, p. 620.
14 *Ibid.*, p. 618.
15 *The Industrial Banker*, April, 1953, p. 17.

Problems of Industrial Banks

Industrial banks grew rapidly when they were first established, but their growth has not been fast since the late twenties. Commercial banks opposed the creation of additional industrial banks as being unnecessary to serve the needs of the community. Attempts to get legislatures in the remaining states to provide for industrial banking met with little success. This was due to the change in the philosophy of commercial banks. They entered the field of consumer credit and thus began to meet the needs of of the consumer for credit. These commercial bank programs were pushed vigorously in the thirties and have been promoted ever since.

The industrial banks that were in the states which permitted them to accept deposits gradually expanded their scope of activities. The larger banks especially increased the percentage of demand deposits they held. Industrial banks also made loans on real estate as security and some commercial loans.

Many industrial banks have taken out charters as state banks. Michigan and Ohio have gone so far as to abandon industrial bank laws and to give these banks the status of state banks. This changing pattern has progressed rapidly in the postwar period in those states in which industrial banks can accept deposits and call themselves banks. In fact it has gone so far that one authority, after studying the record of industrial banks whose accounts are insured by the FDIC, concluded: "There is no doubt; in a very real sense the industrial bank is fast disappearing as a clearly distinguishable type of financial institution." [16]

These banks in the other states are still a somewhat more distinct type of institution. They are designated by the Federal Reserve System as industrial loan companies to distinguish them from the deposit-taking industrial banks. Even these institutions, however, are not as clear-cut a type as they were formerly. Various states have raised the limits on the size of loans of consumer finance companies so that industrial loan companies compete in the same loan class. Many industrial loan companies have also set up sales finance divisions, as have some of the small loan companies. At the same time some of the sales finance companies have taken out licenses as consumer finance companies. The

[16] Dauer, *op. cit.*, p. 624.

trend is toward the disappearance of the industrial loan company as such and the development of a more diversified form of consumer finance institution.

CREDIT UNIONS

A third agency that extends credit to consumers is the credit union. The *credit union* is a cooperative society that supplies its members with consumer credit. It is organized in an industrial plant, in a parish, in a social group, or in a small community to provide a means for accumulating savings of its members and for loaning such funds at moderate rates of interest to those in the organization who need funds for a provident or productive purpose.

Development of Credit Unions

The American credit union is an adaptation of the cooperative financial institutions that developed in Germany and other parts of Europe in the latter half of the nineteenth century. One type was begun by Schulze, then mayor of Delitzsch, Germany, to meet the needs for commercial credit of small entrepreneurs. The rural counterpart was set up by Raiffeisen, a wine merchant and burgomaster of a group of small villages. It was made up of farmers who pooled their credit so that members might borrow funds through their society.

The first credit union on the American continent was set up in 1900 near Quebec by a member of the Canadian Dominion legislature, Alphonse Desjardins. Some nine years later he also helped organize one of the first American credit unions among French Canadians residing at Manchester, New Hampshire, which was given a special charter in 1909. Prior to that time several cooperative credit associations had been operating in Massachusetts, and in 1909 that state passed the first credit-union law. Some progress was made in passing enabling legislation after that time, but the process was slow. Real progress began in 1921 when the late Edward A. Filene, a Boston merchant, became interested in credit-union development and set up the Credit Union National Extension Bureau. Filene put a large sum of money into his organization and, under the guidance of an excellent promoter, Roy F. Bergengren, adequate credit-union laws were passed in state after state. At the beginning of 1955 there were credit-union laws in 44 states.

In 1934 Congress was persuaded to pass a national credit union law. A Credit Union Division was created in the Farm Credit Administration to supervise credit unions with United States charters and to render various services to such organizations. This division has been shifted several times and is now organized as the Bureau of Federal Credit Unions in the Department of Health, Education, and Welfare.

As the number of credit unions in a state grew, a state credit-union league was formed. In 1935 these leagues formed the Credit Union National Association, which took over the promotional work of the Credit Union National Extension Bureau.

The number of credit unions grew rapidly until World War II and again after the war. As of early 1956 there were over 17,000 credit unions in the United States with over 9 million members and assets of over $3.3 billion. Over half of these are still state-chartered credit unions, but the federally chartered credit unions have been growing faster than the state.[17] At the end of 1956 credit unions had $2,048 million of loans outstanding, and the volume had increased to $2,405 million by the end of September, 1957. The loan volume of credit unions has been increasing over the years. At the end of 1939 their loans outstanding amounted to $132 million or 4.3 per cent of the total of consumer installment loans outstanding at financial institutions. At the end of 1956 this item had increased to 7.6 per cent of the total volume of loans outstanding. Thus credit unions are obtaining a larger proportion of total consumer installment loans than they did fifteen years ago.[18]

Organization of Credit Unions

Since the credit union is a cooperative, the power to run it resides in the general meetings of the group. All who have paid the entrance fee, which is usually 25 cents, and have subscribed to at least one share are eligible to vote. The general administration of the organization is placed in the hands of a board of directors elected at the annual meeting.

[17] *The Credit Union Yearbook*, 1957, p. 6.
[18] *Federal Reserve Bulletin*, December, 1957, p. 1400.

A credit committee, which usually consists of three members, is the heart of the organization since it must pass on all loan applications. Also elected is a supervisory committee, which usually has three members. It is an auditing committee that has the duty of going over the books at frequent intervals to be sure that operations are being carried on in line with the by-laws of the association and the law under which it was chartered. Many credit unions also have an education committee that tries to educate the members in thrift and the proper use of credit.

The funds of the credit union and its financial records are handled by the treasurer, who is elected at the annual meeting. He may employ clerical assistance to aid him in his duties. The treasurer may also be paid for his duties, but he is the only elected official who may receive any compensation. The salary is usually low because almost all who work for the credit union do it on a part-time basis. Most of the time spent on credit union affairs is donated by the elected officers and committees. Office space is generally also donated by the firm or organization sponsoring the credit union. Total costs can be kept at a low level.

The typical credit union is a fairly small organization. The average assets of credit unions are about $80,000, but some are, of course, much smaller and a few much larger. The credit union serving the employees of the City of New York has over 30,000 members and assets of more than $10 million, and several others have assets in excess of $1 million.

Sources of Funds

Almost the only source of funds of credit unions is the money invested in them by the members. Shares are usually sold for $5 each and may be paid for in installments. Some of the state laws, but not the federal law, permit credit unions to accept deposits from members as well as to sell shares. Even where this is possible, the bulk of the funds has come from shares. When deposits are accepted, they are treated as creditor obligations and as such have priority over shares in liquidation. They also usually receive a somewhat lower rate of return than is paid on the shares. Some credit unions have at times obtained additional funds to meet their loan demands by borrowing from other credit unions that had an excess of funds.

Characteristics of Loans and Borrowers

Loans are made for any provident or productive purpose. Some are made for very small amounts, but the average loan is somewhat larger than that of many consumer-finance company offices. The average size of the loans made by federal credit unions in 1954 was $394.[19]

Under most laws, loans cannot be made for more than $400 unless they are secured. The maximum amount loaned to one individual cannot exceed 10 per cent of the assets of the credit union. Loans under $400 are usually made on the signature of the applicant, or in some cases with a comaker, but a few credit unions require collateral for all loans. When collateral is required, it may be household goods and appliances or an automobile. If the loan is used to purchase a major appliance or an automobile, a chattel mortgage is usually placed on that property as security.

Little information is available on the borrowers from credit unions. A study of the lending activities of a small group of credit unions in Illinois and Ohio in 1950 and 1951 indicated that their borrowers were somewhat similar to those from consumer finance companies in the same period. Most of them were in the same income brackets. They were also divided between white-collar workers and manual workers in about the same proportions, that is, about one quarter were in the former group and three quarters in the latter. Within these broad classifications there were several significant differences. Credit unions made about three quarters of all loans in the white-collar group to clerks, whereas consumer finance company loans were spread more evenly over all groups in this category. Credit unions also made a significantly larger proportion of loans to operatives and a smaller proportion to skilled and semiskilled craftsmen and foremen than did consumer finance companies.[20]

Operations of Credit Unions

Most laws set 1 per cent per month on the unpaid balance of a loan as the maximum charge allowed. Some states set no figure

---

[19] *1954 Report of Operations—Federal Credit Unions*, p. 6.
[20] W. David Robbins, *Consumer Installment Loans* (Columbus: The Bureau of Business Research, The Ohio State University, 1955), p. 60.

but simply state that the charge must be reasonable. In actual practice 1 per cent per month on the unpaid balance has become the top rate charged and some credit unions charge less.

Life insurance on the unpaid balance of the loan is provided through a mutual insurance company, Cuna Mutual Insurance Society, at no additional cost to the borrower. Under most of the laws, penalties may be charged for being late in payment on loans, but in actual practice this is seldom done.

Most credit-union funds are tied up in short-term loans to members. Laws in many of the states also permit loans secured by real estate. Such loans have been growing in popularity, especially in California, Massachusetts, Minnesota, Rhode Island, and Wisconsin. In the states in which real estate loans are made, they now account for about 30 per cent of the total volume of loans.

At times some credit unions, especially the larger ones, have funds that are not borrowed by members of their group. These may be loaned to other credit unions that have a demand for loan funds which is greater than the available savings of the group.

Most state laws also allow credit unions to invest in bonds of various governmental units. Most investments have been made in United States government bonds. A few states give credit unions wider discretion in making investments, allowing them to invest in any security eligible for savings banks. Few, however, have availed themselves of these wider investment opportunities.

The credit-union laws provide for setting up a reserve as insurance against losses on accounts. All entrance fees and also a percentage of net earnings are put into this reserve fund. The federal law requires that a minimum of 20 per cent of net earnings must be put into this fund each year before any dividends can be paid. This fund, however, need only be built up until it equals 20 per cent of the total value of shares outstanding. Some credit unions have by a vote of the members put a larger amount into the reserve fund. Most credit unions do not pay out all of their earnings above reserve requirements each year. This constitutes an additional cushion against losses.

Results of Operations

Credit unions are usually successful enough to pay dividends of at least 2½ to 3 per cent on shares outstanding. Most federal credit unions are paying between 3 and 5 per cent and some as much as 6 per cent. This is possible on their rates of charge because, as cooperatives, they pay no income taxes. Profits are larger than dividend payments, as a rule, and some funds are retained in the business.

Not all credit unions, however, fulfill their objectives. About 1 out of 5 credit unions is liquidated, according to William W. Pratt, Executive Director of the Pennsylvania Credit Union League.[21] Most of them have been liquidated at better than 100 cents on the dollar, but a few have not. Between 1935 and 1951, 1,840 federal credit unions were liquidated—1,468 at 100 per cent or more of shareholders investments and 372 at less than 100 per cent.[22] In most cases of liquidation at less than 100 per cent the losses have been small. Credit unions have usually been liquidated, however, not because of poor finances but because of a lack of interest on the part of members and officers, lack of expected growth, loss of a capable treasurer who could not be replaced, or the dissolution of the group in which the credit union was organized.

Problems of Credit Unions

The credit-union movement has prospered much more than has any other form of cooperative in the United States. It is still growing, but it is not taking over so large a part of the consumer-credit business as some of its enthusiastic supporters hoped that it would. Several problems have been encountered in the expansion of the credit-union program. One is to get trained workers to handle the work of the treasurer's office, the loan committee, and the supervisory committee. This is usually not a serious problem in groups of office workers, but it is a real problem in groups of laborers, mechanics, and the like. The Credit Union National Association has sought to overcome this problem by training workers in new credit unions and by developing simplified forms for record keeping.

Another problem is to maintain the interest of the members in the group. Most members use a credit union as an institution

---

[21] Wm. W. Pratt, "Credit Unions—Objectives and Operating Principles," in *Consumer Credit Course* by Frank Parker (Philadelphia: University of Pennsylvania, 1951).
[22] Bureau of Federal Credit Unions, *Federal Credit Union* (Washington: Government Printing Office, 1952), p. 10.

for saving money and for borrowing money, but they have little interest in its affairs beyond that. It is a real problem in many credit unions to keep members interested in their activities and willing to devote time to serve as officers and committee members. The spirit of belonging to a cooperative effort has not taken hold as it has in some European cooperatives.

The dominant group in the credit-union field has the true cooperative spirit and stresses service to the members. Other credit unions have become more conservative and are interested primarily in running a successful financial institution. In fact, they have almost made the credit union another type of bank peculiarly suited to the needs of factory and office workers. The Credit Union National Association has taken the lead in urging credit unions to strengthen their educational activities and to learn the value of working together in a democratic organization. If the credit union is to prosper, it must move in this direction. If it is just another form of bank, it has no right to expect that service will be donated to it.

QUESTIONS

1. Describe the methods used by loan sharks to carry on their business.
2. What part did the Russell Sage Foundation play in the consumer credit problem?
3. (a) Outline the provisions of an effective consumer finance act.
   (b) Discuss the need for each provision as part of an effective law.
4. Indicate the present status of consumer finance company lending.
5. (a) What is the status of chains in the consumer finance company field?
   (b) Discuss the advantages and disadvantages of chains compared with individually owned offices.
6. Discuss the sources of funds of consumer finance companies.
7. Discuss the purpose of loans made by consumer finance companies.
8. Describe the characteristics of borrowers from consumer finance companies.
9. Analyze the factors that are considered in granting loans.
10. (a) Comment on the loss record of consumer finance companies.
    (b) How does it compare with the loss record of commercial banks?
11. Discuss the charges and profits of consumer finance companies.
12. What would be likely to happen if the top rate of interest in a state in which it is 2½% on the first $150 is cut to 1½%?

13. Discuss the following problems of consumer finance companies:
    (a) Public understanding of the nature of the business, especially its costs, charges, and profit margins.
    (b) The effect of inflation on consumer finance companies.
14. What are the distinguishing features of industrial banks?
15. Briefly trace the development and current status of industrial banks.
16. What is the legal basis on which industrial banks operate?
17. Discuss the operation of industrial banks, including their source of funds, characteristics of loans made, promotional activities, loss record, and profits.
18. Discuss current problems in the field of industrial banking.
19. What are the distinguishing features of a credit union?
20. Briefly trace the development of credit unions.
21. Discuss the operation of credit unions including such items as sources of funds, organizational structure, types of loans made, charges, and the results of operations.
22. Discuss current problems in the credit union field.
23. From your knowledge of the nature and operations of consumer finance companies, industrial banks, and credit unions, discuss the effect on each of the following:
    (a) Increase in salaries paid office workers greater than increases in other fields.
    (b) Inflation of the price level to twice its previous level.
    (c) Substantial increase in interest rates.

SUGGESTED READINGS

BOARD OF GOVERNORS OF THE FEDERAL RESERVE SYSTEM. *Consumer Instalment Credit* (Part I, Volume 1). Washington: Government Printing Office, 1957, Chapters 3-6.

DURAND, DAVID. *Risk Elements in Consumer Instalment Financing.* New York: National Bureau of Economic Research, Inc., 1941.

GILES, RICHARD Y. *Credit for the Millions.* New York: Harper & Brothers, 1951.

NEIFELD, M. R. *Trends in Consumer Finance.* Easton, Pennsylvania: Mack Publishing Co., 1954.

ROBBINS, W. DAVID. *Consumer Instalment Loans,* Columbus: The Ohio State University, 1955.

Chapter 19

Institutions Financing

the Consumer *(Concluded)*

Consumer finance companies, industrial banks and loan companies, and credit unions developed at about the same time to meet the needs of consumers for cash loans. A few years later another type of institution, the sales finance company, was developed to finance the sale of durable goods on installments. In the early 1920's a few small commercial banks also entered the field of consumer lending, and in the 1930's the majority of banks entered this field. The lending activities in the consumer-credit field of these two types of institutions will be considered in this chapter. Consideration will also be given to the services rendered by several facilitating agencies in the consumer financing field.

SALES FINANCE COMPANIES

The basic function of sales finance companies, which is to finance the purchase of durable goods by consumers, is accomplished by purchasing from retail merchants or dealers the promissory notes signed by consumers who have bought goods on time payments. These notes are bought at a discount, which gives the sales finance company its return for the services it renders. The sales finance company usually also collects the installment payments as they come due.

A second function involves the financing of wholesale purchases by the merchant or dealer from the manufacturer. Since cash payment is required by the manufacturer for automobiles and most appliances, the majority of dealers need continuous financing of their stocks. Such financing is business credit, but for convenience it is provided by the same company that finances retail sales.

Some sales finance companies also make loans to individuals for repair and modernization of their homes, and for other purposes. Such loans are usually handled by subsidiaries or divisions set up for the purpose.

Development of Sales Finance Companies

The sale of durable goods on installments goes back to the early years of the nineteenth century when furniture was sold by some cabinetmakers on that basis. It received its real impetus in the last part of that century when sewing machines, pianos, and sets of books were frequently sold on installments.

The big growth of sales financing came with the rapid development of the automobile industry in the period shortly before World War I and again after the war. The first corporation to finance auto sales, which was organized in 1915, was immediately swamped with business.[1] Shortly thereafter the Commercial Credit Company developed a plan to finance automobile sales. This company had been founded earlier to finance accounts receivable for manufacturers and wholesalers. It developed its automobile sales financing activities rapidly and is today one of the "Big Three" of the sales finance field.

The second of the "Big Three," C.I.T. Financial Corporation, went into business shortly after the Commercial Credit Company did. The third of the "Big Three," General Motors Acceptance Corporation, was incorporated in 1919 to do sales financing but also to make wholesale loans to General Motors dealers who were having trouble getting enough funds to finance the purchase of new cars from the manufacturer.[2] Sales finance companies were formed rapidly after the first ones began to operate.

Before 1938 the major sales finance companies had arrangements with automobile dealers to handle the financing of the sales of their cars. General Motors Acceptance Corporation was established to provide wholesale and retail credit to General Motors dealers. The Ford Motor Company established the Universal Credit Corporation for the same purpose. In 1933 Ford Motor Company sold a controlling interest in this company to

---

[1] Clyde William Phelps, *The Role of Sales Finance Companies in the American Economy* (Baltimore: Commercial Credit Company, 1952), p. 55.
[2] *Ibid.*, p. 56.

the C.I.T. Financial Corporation. Commercial Credit Company was affiliated with Chrysler Motor Corporation, which owned stock in it from 1934 to 1938. Both C.I.T. and Commercial Credit handled financing for dealers of other automobile manufacturers and also for retail stores selling appliances and other durables.

The Department of Justice, questioning these preferred relationships, brought antitrust proceedings against the "Big Three" and their related automobile companies. Late in 1938 Chrysler and Ford entered into consent decrees under which the companies agreed to discontinue preferential arrangements with any of the sales finance companies. General Motors and General Motors Acceptance Corporation refused to agree. After years of legal bickering, however, they finally agreed to a consent decree in 1952, freeing their dealers to finance their sales as they saw fit without discrimination.

Present Status. By the end of 1956 sales finance companies had $9,100 million of credit outstanding to consumers, divided as follows: [3]

> Automobile paper ....$7,283 million
> Other consumer goods paper ...... 1,227 million
> Repair and modernization paper.. 23 million
> Personal loans .... 567 million

Large as this volume is, it is only about 40 per cent of all outstanding installment accounts at the end of the year arising out of the sale of goods. Outstanding automobile accounts, however, are 50 per cent of the total.[4]

Reasons for Development of a New Type of Institution. Commercial banks did not engage in this type of financing on a large scale until twenty years or more after the sales finance companies pioneered in its development. Several factors account for the failure of the banks to meet the need for sales financing. One basic factor is that this new type of financing was contrary to the basic philosophy under which commercial banks were operating. This philosophy held that commercial banks should restrict themselves to short-term business loans that were self-liquidating. Ac-

[3] *Federal Reserve Bulletin,* November, 1957, p. 1269.
[4] *Ibid.,* pp. 1268, 1269.

cording to this point of view, long-term business credit should be raised in the capital markets. There was no place for credit for consumption, which conservative opinion frowned upon as being nonproductive. Not only was the banking philosophy contrary to the development of this new field, but banks could utilize all of their funds profitably in making business loans.

Several other factors were also involved. Automobile financing was a new type of business that required new methods and a different outlook from regular banking. Risks were likely to be great until a substantial volume was built up. The average businessman is reluctant to risk losses in a new field while he can continue to employ his funds profitably in others.

Bankers also had an obligation to depositors that did not exist in sales finance companies. It was not until the depression of 1929 had run its course that it became clear that sales credit could be extended safely. Therefore, many bankers refused to take a risk with depositors' funds when what appeared to be safe short-term business loans were available.

The ability of sales finance companies to set up branches where they chose also gave them an advantage over banks, which in many states can have no branches and are greatly restricted in others. Sales finance companies could set up branches in centers in which cars were being sold.

A last factor was the usury laws that limited banks to rates lower than those necessary to cover costs of this type of lending. These laws were changed and regulations revised when banks began to enter the field. The factors that finally led banks to make all types of consumer loans are considered in the next section, which deals with the role of banks in consumer financing.

Organization of Sales Finance Companies

The basic legal doctrine under which sales financing has been developed in the United States is the "time-price theory." Under this doctrine the sale price of an article sold on credit is a matter of contract between the seller and the buyer, and the difference between a cash price and a time price is a matter of negotiation between the parties to the contract. Such a differential is not construed as interest upon money loaned and therefore does not come under the usury laws.

Since most retailers do not have sufficient capital to carry credit obligations to maturity, they refinance them through sales finance companies or other financial institutions. The contracts between the seller and the buyer calling for time payments are sold to a financial institution at a discount. This discount is determined by competition between the various institutions buying such paper. The courts have held that this sale of the paper is also a sale of a thing rather than a loan of money. Thus this whole process has been exempted from the usury statutes. Beginning with Indiana in 1935, however, about half of the states have passed special statutes dealing with installment sales and financing. Some of the laws control charges that can be made, while others only require a detailed disclosure of the items added to the cash price to establish the installment sale price. Practically all of the statutes have provisions regarding the refund of charges if the contract is paid in full before final maturity. Some govern repossession practices, and some, charges for delinquency.

Most of the laws require sales finance companies to be licensed. Generally the licenses are issued on application and the payment of a license fee, but without specific requirements that must be met or investigation of the applicants. The licenses may generally be revoked if a material misstatement is made in the application, for a willful violation of the law, or for fraud.

Sources of Funds

When sales finance companies first began operations, they had to rely almost exclusively on the funds of the owners. As time went on, they found it possible to obtain credit from commercial banks and also from the security markets. More recently insurance companies have bought some of their senior securities.

Complete data on the sources of funds used by sales finance companies are not available. A study has been made, however, of the financial position at the end of 1956 of 78 sales finance companies of various sizes. On the average they raised 40 per cent of their funds by short-term borrowing, including bank loans and commercial paper. Another 40 per cent was raised by long-term borrowing. About a fourth of the long-term borrowing was done by the sale of subordinated debentures, the rest primarily by senior debenture bonds. The subordinated debentures, which are subordinated to bank loans, are usually sold to insurance companies. These debentures usually run from 5 to 15 years and are usually retired out of profits. The senior debentures are usually sold to insurance companies for a 5- to 15-year period.

Common stock and surplus accounted for about 10 per cent of all sources of funds. Preferred stock was only 1.4 per cent and miscellaneous liabilities, such as accounts payable and taxes payable, accounted for the balance of the funds used.

The larger companies relied more heavily on long-term borrowing and much less on short-term borrowing than did the smaller companies. The smaller companies also obtained a higher percentage of funds from common stock and surplus than did the larger ones and also made more use of preferred stock.[5]

Characteristics of Loans and Borrowers

The standard down payment in most of the auto industry is one third for new and used cars. Many dealers, however, work on a 25 per cent or even a 20 per cent down payment, and a few on even less. The maximum repayment period is 36 months, occasionally 42 months. On late model used cars (the current model and two previous models) the maximum period is usually 18 months, and on older used cars usually 12 months.

New cars are usually financed for a charge of 6 per cent a year figured on the total amount financed. This total includes not only the unpaid balance of the price of the car, but also fire, theft, and collision insurance, and perhaps also group life and health and accident insurance. The following example shows how this finance charge is calculated:

Cash selling price	$1,800.00
Down payment (1/3 of C.S.P.)	600.00
Cash unpaid balance	$1,200.00
Basic insurance (coverage itemized)	120.00
Special features (coverage itemized)	18.00
Amount financed	$1,338.00
Finance charge (6% per year for 18 months)	120.42
Amount of contract	$1,458.42
Repayable 17 @ $81.02 \} equals	$1,458.42
1 @ 81.08	

[5] Robert W. Johnson, "Financial Position of Sales Finance Companies—1956," *Time Sales Financing* (November, 1957), p. 3.

Late model used car charges may be as high as 9 per cent a year, and charges on older cars as much as 12 per cent a year, which means that effective interest rates are as high as 18 and 24 per cent a year.

Down payments are generally a lower percentage of the purchase price for appliances and furniture than for automobiles. They are frequently 10 per cent or less. Most loans do not run longer than a year or a year and a half for most purchases, and two years on larger purchases.

Since the size of the account is smaller, finance charges are higher for other durables than they are for cars. There is frequently a flat charge to cover acquisition costs, a collection charge based on the number of payments, a charge of 2 per cent of the amount financed to cover losses, and a financing charge calculated on a 6 per cent discount basis.

No detailed studies are available on the characteristics of individuals who finance their purchases of automobiles and other durable goods on installments through sales finance companies. Since the dealer usually selects the sales finance company or a bank that handles the financing of his accounts except in those cases in which the customer handles his own financing, there is probably little difference between those who obtain sales finance credit from sales finance companies and those who get such credit from banks. Such information as is available on those who finance on installments indicates that they are a cross section of the population, excluding very low and very high income groups. There is some concentration of borrowers in the 18-44 year age group who are married and have children under 18 years old.

Operations of Sales Finance Companies

The basic procedures for financing the sale of automobiles and other consumer goods are the same. Some differences exist in details of the methods employed, however, due to the different character of the goods being financed.

Financing Automobiles. The original contract is drawn up between the automobile dealer and the purchaser of a car. The usual procedure is to have the purchaser sign a *conditional sales contract,* which provides that the seller retain title to the car until the agreed purchase price has been paid. In some cases a separate note is signed for the unpaid balance, in others the sales contract is all that is required.

The finance company takes over the contract from the dealer. This may be done under what is known as the *full recourse plan,* in which case the dealer endorses the paper and is fully liable in case the buyer defaults. A second method is to sign a *repurchase agreement* under which the dealer is obligated to buy back the equipment in the event of default. This is usually for the balance of the account remaining unpaid, but it may be for less if the car shows signs of abuse or unusual wear. A third method is the *nonrecourse plan* under which the dealer has no further liability. This method is used less frequently than the other two because under recourse plans the seller is likely to exercise more care in arranging the loan. Most sales finance companies employ all three methods, or a combination of them, but some still adhere solely to the full recourse plan.

Payments are usually made by the purchaser of the car direct to the sales finance company. The usual method is to give the customer at the time he buys the car a book that has a coupon for each payment, showing when it is due and the amount due. The proper coupon is detached and mailed with each payment.

Wholesale Financing of Automobiles. As part of the service rendered in financing the sale of automobiles, the sales finance companies also finance the stock of cars in the hands of the dealer. Since automobile manufacturers insist on cash payment before cars are delivered to the dealer, most dealers find it necessary to finance their inventory of cars.

As the cars are rolled off the assembly line and assigned for delivery to dealers, they are paid for by the finance company under a prearranged plan. The contract used to effect the arrangement usually is in the form of a trust receipt, under which the finance company releases the cars to the dealer who agrees to hold them in trust for the finance company. The dealer is given the right to sell the car as an agent for the finance company and agrees to account to the lender for the proceeds.

As a part of this wholesale plan, insurance is provided for each car against loss from theft, fire, lightning, tornado, and the like. If the car is driven to the dealer's place of business, collision insurance may also be obtained from the finance company.

The usual practice is to extend wholesale financing for a period of three months with a provision that the car is to be paid for as soon as it is sold. If the car is not sold in 90 days, it is either paid for or the financing is extended for 30, 60, or 90 days. When this is done, a partial payment is frequently made to the finance company.

The rate for wholesale financing is usually just about equal to costs. It consists of a flat charge, which is normally ⅛ of 1 per cent of the amount financed plus interest for the actual time that the money is used. Low charges for wholesale financing are used as a promotional device to obtain retail financing business.

Financing Other Durables. In most respects the financing of other durable goods, such as refrigerators, washers, and television sets, is similar to that of automobiles. The relationships between the dealer and the purchaser are much the same, but some differences exist in the relationship between the dealer and the finance company.

Most finance companies have several plans of financing available. One plan is the full recourse plan under which the dealer has full responsibility for all paper. He has no alternative but to pay the full amount of the unpaid balance on any contract if the customer defaults. The finance company, however, generally sets aside a part of the finance charge as a reserve to compensate the dealer for losses. The standard amount set aside is usually 10 per cent of the finance charge, but it may be somewhat higher at times.

A number of limited recourse plans are in use. Under one, a dealer has full responsibility for default during the first sixth of the contract period, that is, for example, for 3 months on an 18-month payment plan. After that, he may have no further responsibility under an arrangement whereby the manufacturer assumes responsibility for the remainder of the period. In other cases in which the manufacturer is not a party to the arrangement, the dealer may assume the responsibility of taking over repossessed merchandise in the event of default, but for less than its resale value to compensate him for selling it again.

In wholesale financing, the major difference from automobile financing is that manufacturers or distributors at times agree to repurchase merchandise that the dealer does not sell. Advances are usually for only 90 per cent of the wholesale price, whereas they are almost always 100 per cent for cars. Charges are higher, the flat charge generally being ½ per cent to 1 per cent of the amount financed and the interest charge may also be somewhat higher.

Results of Operations. No complete data on reserves, expenses, and profits of sales finance companies are available. The First National Bank of Chicago has compiled data based on the financial statements of all sales finance companies carrying a line of credit with their bank. In 1954 total expenses, including taxes, were 86.9 per cent of gross income. Gross income was 6.71 per cent of total retail and wholesale paper purchased, and net income was only .83 per cent. This figure has not been above 1.11 per cent during the past ten years. The net income on average accounts receivable outstanding, however, is substantially larger because money used in wholesale financing is turned over several times during the year. For this reason and since a substantial proportion of the capital comes from preferred stockholders and creditors, net profit on net worth was 12.3 per cent in 1954. Since 1941 the highest profit figure on net worth was 17.4 per cent in 1950 and the lowest 11.0 per cent in 1941.[6]

Problems of Sales Finance Companies

Since the late thirties, and especially in the post-World War II period, commercial banks have taken over a substantial proportion of the sales finance business, both by engaging in sales financing and by making loans to consumers directly to buy durables. There is every indication that banks will remain in this field. The sales finance field therefore promises to become even more competitive than it has been.

As the automobile business became intensely competitive in late 1954 and 1955, a problem arose because some dealers felt that in order to sell cars they had to lengthen the time period for installment payments and to reduce the down payments. It may appear as if terms of 30 or 36 months are sound because automo-

[6] Article by Earl O'Keefe on "Sales Credit Company Operations" in *Proceedings of the National Consumer Credit Conference for 1952* held at Indiana University, 1952, p. 161; and Elmer E. Schmus, *Ratios of the Installment Sales Finance and Small Loan Companies* (Chicago: The First National Bank of Chicago, 1955), pp. 18-19.

biles last for eight or ten years. An analysis of the situation in the summer of 1955 by the American Finance Conference, however, shows that such was not the case when down payments were no larger than those being made at that time. They checked the status of various loan arrangements on a Ford Customline V-8 four-door sedan with a cash selling price of $2,200 and a Buick Super Riviera with a cash selling price of $3,500. Insurance and interest were added on the basis of actual charges at the time, and the value of used cars was based on the NADA *Used Car Guide* for the Midwest.

They found that in the case of the Ford, if it were sold on a bona fide down payment of one third and 24 months for repayment, the owner's equity exceeded the used-car value after five months. On a 36-months contract, however, this was not true until the seventeenth month. For most of the first year, debt exceeds the wholesale value of the car by over $200. If the down payment is only 25 per cent and the contract for 30 months, the owner has no equity for more than 14 months, and it takes 21 months if repayment is spread over 36 months.

Such a situation reduces the incentives to keep up payments and is likely to lead to increased repossessions, which will be made at a loss since owners have built up little or no equity. It also makes refinancing all but impossible if the owner has a decline in income or if an emergency arises, because he has built up no equity of any proportion. It could also affect future sales of cars since, when little or no equity is built up in a car, it makes trading more difficult for those who formerly used their equity as down payment on a new car. Such a situation can also lead to poor public relations for the sales finance industry. To hold such problems to a minimum, the American Finance Conference has made every effort to point out to its members the hazards inherent in payment terms longer than 24 months combined with low down payments.

Another problem is one of increasing regulation, which creates new problems for the industry. Every year bills are introduced into state legislatures to regulate one or more phases of sales financing. Pressure for regulation comes in part because of the undesirable practices of a few companies. In some cases no clear statement of charges is given to a customer so that he does not know what he is paying for interest, fees, insurance, and the like, and legislators feel that the law should step in to protect him. Competition can work effectively only if the customer knows what the facts are so that he can make a deal intelligently.

Another area of criticism regards the fees or kickbacks paid to dealers by finance companies. Under the plan in which there is full recourse to the dealer in the event of default, the finance company frequently returns part of the finance charges to cover losses. Larger sums may be returned to compensate the dealer for obtaining business for the finance compay. This practice can lead to abuses and overcharging of the customer. Compensation for losses and for services rendered to the finance company is justifiable, but larger payments to attract business that are passed on to the consumer are not. This could not happen, of course, if all consumers knew all the facts and shopped around, but it does happen when such is not the case. To make further regulation unnecessary, sales finance companies must continue to work to eliminate such practices by the few and to educate the consumer so that competition can work effectively.

COMMERCIAL BANKS

The largest volume of consumer credit is granted by the commercial banks of the country. At the end of 1956 they had outstanding total installment credit of $11.7 billion. This included credit for financing the sale of durable goods, repair and modernization loans, and personal cash loans repayable in installments. In addition single-payment loans made to individuals, which were used for consumption purposes, added $2.1 billion to the total volume of consumer credit outstanding at commercial banks. Since the total of short-term and intermediate consumer credit outstanding at the end of 1956 was $41.9 billion, commercial banks had granted a third of it.[7]

Development of Consumer Lending by Commercial Banks

Banks have achieved their position in consumer lending even though they entered this field after most of the other financial institutions had been active for 15 or more years. Some banks had made loans to consumers on a 30- 60,- or 90-day basis in the same way that they made commercial loans to business. Some

[7] *Federal Reserve Bulletin*, December, 1957, p. 1400.

credit extended to farmers was also used for consumption purposes. In the middle 1920's a few smaller banks set up personal loan departments, but the growth was slow. According to one authority only 9 banks were known to have had such departments at the end of 1925, 13 more set them up in 1926, and 14 in 1927.[8] In 1928 impetus was given to the movement when the National City Bank of New York, one of the largest banks in the country, set up a personal loan department. In 1929 the Bank of America in San Francisco, California, which has branches all over the state, entered the field. Growth was somewhat faster after that, but by the end of 1933 there were still probably fewer than 250 banks engaged actively in the consumer lending field.

In the summer of 1934 the United States government initiated a program that gave real impetus to the expansion of bank lending to consumers. In an effort to stimulate employment and economic activity in general, the Federal Housing Administration was authorized to guarantee loans to authorized lenders who would extend credit for home repair and modernization. Under the program as originally set up, loans were to run for not over 60 months, could not exceed $2,000, and had to be repaid in equal monthly installments. These loans were known as FHA Title I loans.

The first period for which the program was announced was for 20 months. A guaranty fund equal to 20 per cent of the total amount of loans made, against which losses could be charged, was provided by the FHA. This first guarantee was made without cost to the lending institution. The guarantee was later reduced to 10 per cent. It soon became apparent, however, that even under very bad economic conditions and with inexperienced lenders losses were much below 10 per cent.

During the first 20 months under Title I, almost 6,000 banks reported loans made. Losses paid to the banks by the FHA were only 2.4 per cent of the loan volume, and a substantial part of such losses were later recovered by the FHA.

By no means all of the banks that made FHA loans, however, entered the consumer-loan field immediately. In fact, in 1936 and early 1937, when the guarantee was cut to 10 per cent, less

---

[8] Rolf Nugent, "A Census of Personal Loan Departments," *Banking* (November, 1937), p. 29.

than 4,000 banks made Title I loans. The record of FHA loans and their experiences with them, however, convinced many bankers that consumer loans could be made without undue losses so as to yield a reasonable profit. At that time many banks also had unused funds which they were anxious to put to work. The fact that the banks were indirectly financing the consumer anyway by heavily financing the finance companies also argued for getting into direct financing.

The Bankers Association for Consumer Credit, which was formed in 1938, gave added impetus to the movement. In 1940 it merged its activities with those of the American Bankers Association, which had recognized the importance of consumer financing by banks. Consumer lending by banks became more widespread, especially during the World War II years. At the present time about 90 per cent of all commercial banks of the country make consumer loans.

Organization of Commercial Banks

One problem that had to be met in the development of consumer loan business by banks was the passage of enabling legislation. Most states have set 6 per cent interest as the maximum that banks may charge on regular loans, but consumer financing in small sums cannot be done at this rate. It was necessary for most states to pass enabling legislation to permit Title I FHA loans at a 5 per cent discount rate.

Most states have passed legislation permitting rates above 6 per cent interest for consumer financing. Usually the maximum has been set at 6 per cent discount, which amounts to 11.78 per cent simple interest per annum. Many of the states also allow fees to be charged for credit investigation, for late payments, and for insurance premiums, or they permit a general service charge. Some of the states have passed special legislation covering other phases of consumer lending, such as licensing and examination.

Banks have generally set up a separate department to handle consumer loans. Many banks have bought out a small sales finance company or other consumer lending agency to obtain trained personnel and an established system for handling consumer loans. Consumer loan departments usually are open for more hours than the rest of the bank. This is done to accommodate borrowers and also to remain competitive with other agencies that are open many hours more during a week than most banks. A separate consumer loan department has also been formed by many bankers since many people feel a bank is interested only in business loans and are reluctant to ask regular loan officers for a consumer loan.

Sources of Funds

One basic difference in operation between other finance companies and commercial banks is their source of funds. Commercial banks secure a part of their funds from the investment of the owners in original capital contributions, reserves, and retained earnings, but the bulk of it comes from depositors. These deposits are, in the main, demand deposits on which the banks are not allowed to pay interest. Since deposits in many banks are between 10 and 15 times the capital accounts, and even more in some banks, most of the funds come from this source.

This use of depositors' money on which no interest is paid does not mean that funds are available to the bank without cost. In exchange for the use of such funds banks furnish services to their customers, especially by providing checking privileges. In prosperity periods when all bank funds are in use, the opportunity cost of using the funds for other types of loans must also be considered.

Characteristics of Loans and Borrowers

Even though banks were slow in entering the field of consumer lending, many now engage in all phases of it. In providing consumer credit directly, some banks make personal loans of various types and also engage in sales financing. The loans made by commercial banks are often divided into five groups, as follows:

1. Home repair and modernization loans
2. Personal loans
3. Automobile loans
4. Home equipment loans
5. Charge account loans

As pointed out previously, the first consumer loans that many banks made were home repair and modernization loans under

Title I of the FHA. Many banks still make such loans today, but frequently they are no longer insured by FHA. Banks have found that they can operate safely by setting up reserves for losses and thus carry these loans without the government guarantee.

Personal loans are made to take care of the needs of individuals for cash to pay accumulated bills or to meet emergencies. Some are single-payment loans, but most are repayable in installments. They may be made on the signature of the borrower, with a comaker, or by using collateral as security.

The most important field for many of the larger banks is automobile financing. This may be done by a direct loan to the purchaser of the car or by an arrangement with an automobile dealer to buy his notes. Under such an arrangement with a dealer, it is usually necessary to finance the stock of cars he has on hand in order to get the note business.

Of increasing importance to many banks is the financing of household durable goods, such as appliances, furniture, radios, and television sets. This may also be done by a direct loan to the consumer or by an arrangement with a dealer to buy his notes.

The most recent field that banks have entered in consumer financing is the provision of charge-account credit. Under this system charge purchases made by approved customers at stores that are in the system are credited directly to the account of the store upon receipt of the sales check by the bank.

(1) Home Repair and Modernization Loans. The original home repair and modernization loans under Title I of the FHA were guaranteed by the government without cost to the banks. Since 1939, an insurance premium of ¾ of 1 per cent of the net proceeds to the borrower must be paid to the FHA as compensation for insuring loans up to 10 per cent of the dollar amount of loans made. The making of insured loans under Title I is not limited to banks, but they have always made the major portion of such loans.

Several types of loans may be guaranteed under Title I. Loans for repairs or improvements to a dwelling for one family may have a maximum maturity of 3 years plus 32 days if they are for $600 or less and 5 years and 32 days if they are for over $600. The maximum amount for such Title I loans is $3,500. For dwellings for 2 or more families, the loan may run for 7 years plus 32 days and may be as large as $15,000. The maximum discount rate is $5 per $100 per year up to $2,500, and $4 per $100 per year on any portion of the loan above $2,500. Loans may also be made up to $3,500 to build new structures other than residences in urban and rural areas. The major activity has been in repair and improvement loans on single-family residences; most of the remainder consists of such loans on multifamily dwellings.

Even though substantial numbers of repair and improvement loans are made with FHA guarantees, some banks have chosen to carry their own programs without such security. The low loss record experienced by FHA shows that this is safe for any bank that checks loan applications with reasonable care.

(2) Personal Loans. The procedure for handling personal loans is much the same as that used by other institutions making such loans. Banks differ somewhat from other financial institutions in the type of security required. A large proportion of all bank personal loans are still made on a comaker basis. This was the basic requirement of most banks when they first started personal loan departments, and it has been continued. Some banks achieve the same end by having a note endorsed or guaranteed by one or two individuals.

As personal loan departments have had more experience and have tried to increase their volume, they have shifted from comaker loans to loans on an individual signature. In some cases these loans are made to teachers, employees of public utilities, and other groups under an arrangement whereby payments are deducted from pay checks and sent directly to the bank. Some personal loans are made with collateral, but much less reliance is placed on household goods than is true of other institutions. Collateral may consist of savings accounts, marketable securities, the cash value of life insurance policies that have been assigned to the bank, savings and loan shares, and the like.

(3) Automobile Loans. Most financing through the purchase of notes from dealers is done by the larger banks. The methods used follow closely those developed by the sales finance companies.

The practice of making direct loans to individuals to finance car purchases has been developed by many commercial banks into a major outlet for funds. Frequently it is based upon an arrangement between insurance agents or brokers and the bank. Since sales finance companies often require that insurance be carried in specified companies, insurance agents and brokers have lost regular accounts when a new car was purchased. To keep this business, they have teamed up with commercial banks to have these banks finance the purchase directly while they handle the insurance.

Some auto dealers have arrangements with banks whereby they send purchasers to the bank to work out a direct loan. Banks also make such loans to their regular customers, and some advertise actively for such business.

The form of instrument used to attach the car as security for the unpaid balance of the purchase price is usually a conditional sales contract when it is permitted by law. Where this instrument is not available, a chattel mortgage is used. Whenever a loan is made for other purposes but a car is used as collateral, a chattel mortgage must be used because conditional sales contracts are valid only in connection with a genuine sale. To simplify making payments and to aid in record keeping, coupon books are used just as they are used in sales financing.

(4) Home Equipment Loans. Banks also do a substantial volume of business in financing the purchase of other durable goods. A part of this is direct financing, most of which arises from the purchases of notes from dealers. This financing is done in much the same way as sales financing by sales finance companies. Banks also do wholesale floor planning for the dealers as a method of securing their consumer notes.

(5) Charge-Account Loans. A recent innovation is the financing of charge accounts. Franklin National Bank of Franklin Square, Hempstead, New York, was one of the first to use the plan, and its operation is typical of the basic methods followed. Stores arrange with the bank for the plan and receive application blanks for their customers to fill in. The bank screens these applications and, if a customer is approved, he receives a credit card that is good at any member store. When he makes a charge purchase of over $5, the store first checks with the bank by phone. The store sends the sales slip to the bank, and the bank credits the amount shown on the sales slip, less a 5 per cent service

charge, to the merchant's account. The bank then bills the customer monthly for all of his purchases. This bill is paid by check or cash just like any other bill even when the customer has an account at the bank.

Some banks have charged as much as 8 per cent for the service charge on charge-account loans. There has been some criticism that charges of 5 to 8 per cent are too high. In some retail fields credit department costs probably approach 5 per cent of credit sales, although complete cost records are often not kept. The bank charge also includes a payment for the use of money since the account of the merchant is credited immediately, even though the account is not collected until after the first of the next month or later. In addition to the cost, some merchants do not believe that it is good neighborhood merchandising to turn credit decisions over to an outside agency. They believe that, in order to maintain a hold on their customers, they should retain control over who gets credit at their store and how much he gets.

Size of Loan. Little definite information is available on the average size of consumer loans made by commercial banks. Loans to finance automobiles are usually made for two thirds of the purchase price, which means a loan of $1,200 or more. Loans on appliances and on other durables are, of course, much smaller. Personal loans are probably somewhat larger on the average than those of the consumer finance companies. Some banks refuse some of the smaller loans, and such legal restrictions on the size of bank loans that do exist are much more liberal than are those in consumer finance company laws. Some information on the average size of loans by banks is included in a study of loans made by 22 commercial banks in 10 states and 18 consumer finance companies operating 2,262 offices in 38 states.[9] The average size of loan made by the banks included in this study was $534 in 1950-51.[10]

Borrowers. The individuals who borrow from banks to make repair and modernization loans, auto loans, and personal loans are probably a cross section of the middle-income groups. One study, which compared the occupations of customers of the per-

[9] The operations of 7 credit unions in 2 states were also studied.
[10] W. David Robbins, *Consumer Installment Loans* (Columbus: The Bureau of Business Research, Ohio State University, 1956), p. 41.

sonal loan department of the National City Bank in New York with those of several major consumer finance companies, showed that the two types of institutions attracted somewhat different groups as customers. Only 15 per cent of the bank borrowers were wage earners, whereas 57 per cent of the borrowers from the consumer finance companies were in this class. Over 70 per cent of the borrowers from the bank were in white-collar jobs, but only about 40 per cent of consumer finance company borrowers were in this class. In the study of loan activities by banks and consumer finance companies referred to earlier, about half of the bank borrowers were white-collar workers and half were manual workers, whereas only about one quarter of the consumer finance company borrowers were white-collar workers and three quarters were manual workers. Bank borrowers in the main came from a somewhat higher income group than consumer finance company borrowers. Fewer bank borrowers were under 30 years of age and more over 40 years than were consumer finance company borrowers.[11]

The degree of overlapping between potential bank and consumer finance company borrowers is probably not very great even though some loans are made to persons in the same occupational groups. Several students of the field have placed the overlap at not over 5 to 10 per cent, but some men in the consumer finance business feel it may be as high as 15 per cent.[12]

Operations of Commercial Banks

The operating procedures used by banks resemble those of other institutions in the consumer-financing field. In fact, some banks have taken over consumer finance companies or sales finance companies to obtain experienced personnel and an efficient system of operation.

Rates charged by banks are lower than those of consumer finance companies and some sales finance companies. Charges of 5 to 8 per cent on a discount basis are normal, which means effective interest rates between 10 and 16 per cent. In addition, a flat service charge may be made for smaller loans. Insurance of

[11] *Ibid.,* pp. 60, 66, 74.
[12] See Clyde William Phelps, "How Banks Are Faring in Consumer Credit," *Commercial and Financial Chronicle* (Dec. 29, 1949), and Wallace P. Mors, *Consumer Credit Facts for You* (Cleveland: Western Reserve University, 1952), p. 9.

various types is frequently required, and many banks charge penalties for late payments.

The loss experience on most types of consumer loans has not been high, and part of the amounts originally written off have been recovered. Banks have set aside reserves to take care of these losses. Some banks figure them as a percentage of net earnings, setting aside 10 to 15 per cent of earnings to meet losses. Others calculate losses as a percentage of loans made. Reserves are usually allowed to accumulate until they reach a specified percentage of loan volume outstanding. This is usually 3 to 5 per cent, but some banks have set it at 10 per cent. After the specified reserve is accumulated, only enough is added to the reserve to keep it at the required percentage of the volume of loans outstanding.

General profit figures on bank consumer lending are not available. Many banks do not calculate such figures. Indications are, however, that the business is profitable or it would not be pushed so vigorously or have spread to so many banks.

The rate of profit on loans is probably somewhat lower than that for other financial institutions. When compared with owners' equity, it is, however, substantial since many banks have funds to work with that are equal to 10 or more times their capital accounts.

Problems of Commercial Banks

Banks increased their share of the consumer-financing business materially in the late thirties and in the post-World War II period. This was done during a period when the total volume of business was increasing rapidly. The volume of business will continue to grow as real income and population increase, but at a slower rate than during recent years. It will also move up and down with the level of business activity. Under these conditions it will become more difficult to obtain an increasing share of the total business.

Banks are at a competitive disadvantage since they are forbidden to set up branches in many states and are restricted as to their location in others. National sales finance companies have the advantage of being able to work out uniform policies for financing in various parts of the country. As a result, concerns that distribute their products over a wide area find it simpler to deal with branches of a large sales finance company than with individual banks with varying requirements. Sales finance companies can also achieve the advantages of diversification. This has been possible only for banks in the western part of the United States where the Bank of America has a large number of branches and the Transamerica Corporation holds stock in subsidiary banks in five states. Offsetting this disadvantage, however, banks are able to meet the needs of their community by adjusting their policies to changing local conditions.

Banks also have a problem in regard to rates, especially in used-car financing. The typical discount rates of 6 per cent, or even 8 per cent, are not high enough to cover the cost of financing older used cars. If costs continue upward, this problem will become more serious.

Some banks are still faced with the problem of customer acceptance as a source of consumer lending. Banks were traditionally austere institutions that frightened many would-be borrowers, and some of them have not succeeded in completely dispelling this attitude.

There has also been a hesitancy on the part of some banks to cooperate with other consumer-lending agencies. If consumer lending is to be carried on safely, it is necessary to exchange information on the amount of credit that has been extended to individuals because some people will get hopelessly into debt if given a chance. Another area of cooperation, consumer education, is equally important. Banks must cooperate in educating the consumer on the wise use of credit, on charges, and the like, if the industry is to be governed to a large extent by competition rather than by detailed regulation.

FACILITATING AGENCIES

The merchandising function plays only a minor role in the intermediate- and short-term consumer credit fields. All agencies in these areas do some merchandising by using sales promotion programs to increase their business. But in the sense of selling consumer paper to other institutions or individuals, little is done. Some sellers of durables do carry their own paper for a period and later look for a purchaser for such paper, but there is little organized activity of this kind.

Credit Exchanges

Several facilitating agencies, however, play a role in the consumer credit field. In most cities of any size the consumer finance companies operating under the small-loan law have set up a credit exchange to provide information on loans. Some of the earliest of these exchanges operated on a one-loan plan under which an individual or a married couple could have only one loan from a small-loan company outstanding at any time. This was in keeping with the philosophy that one of the functions of a small-loan company is to help a man plan his finances so as to get out of debt and that this can be done best if he has to deal with only one company.

The one-loan exchanges met with opposition from new companies entering a territory. These companies felt that a one-loan rule made it almost impossible for them to develop a profitable volume of business, and they therefore refused to join the exchange. An exchange to which some companies do not belong cannot be effective, and as a result many exchanges changed their rules to permit two or three loans, and in a few cases even more.

As some of the small-loan companies increased their resources, they entered the field of durable goods financing either by setting up sales-finance subsidiaries or by buying notes from businesses that had taken them when they sold durables on installments. This created a new problem for restricted-loan exchanges since these loans were of a somewhat different nature from the regular loans to help an individual in financial difficulty. As a result, some exchanges amended their rules so as to allow several loans to an individual so long as the same collateral was not used as security for more than one loan. Under this revised rule, for example, a loan could be secured by a chattel mortgage on household goods, but the purchase of a new washing machine by that same family could be financed by using that machine as security.

More recently the consumer finance companies in some cities, as for example St. Louis, have developed clearinghouse exchanges in which no restrictions are placed on loans, but each company furnishes the exchange with complete information on all loans and on all notes they purchase. Each lender can then obtain full information on the other loans of a prospective borrower, but he is free to use his own discretion regarding the granting of an additional loan. This type of exchange has overcome the objections of new companies to joining an exchange, but some of the older companies have held that it defeats one of the purposes of the small-loan law, which is to help an individual in financial straits to plan his way out of debt.

Credit Bureaus

Another important facilitating agency is the credit-checking agency or credit bureau. Most cities of any size have a credit bureau that keeps files on the paying records of individuals. It is organized by local merchants and finance companies to serve as a central exchange for data on the credit extended to individuals. The latest data in the file is usually furnished by telephone, teletype, telautograph,[13] or messenger. When more detailed information is required, a special report may be prepared. It gives general data on the applicant, such as his age, marital status, family, permanence of residence, mode of living, and reputation. Data are also given on his estimated income, his investments, and bank accounts, and any suits against him or liens are noted. Information is also provided on his buying and paying habits at the stores where he has accounts.

For information on an individual who lives out of town, data may be obtained from a credit bureau in his town. Several national concerns also prepare reports on the financial status of individuals, primarily for insurance purposes, but also for credit evaluation.

Credit bureaus work well when all important credit-granting agencies cooperate. To get them to do this is, however, a real problem. Some will not join, while others refuse to report all loans or they give incorrect data. It is especially difficult to get some used-car dealers to furnish information, and their data are very important since a used-car loan may represent by far the largest debt of a borrower, especially if he does not own his home. Some progress toward cooperation by all is being made, but the problem is one that will probably never be solved completely or permanently.

---

[13] The telautograph is a device whereby what is written with a stylus in the credit department of the firm seeking information is reproduced on a pad by a receiving pen in the credit bureau office.

Insurance Agencies

Insurance of various types, such as fire, theft, and comprehensive, is usually carried on durables when they are financed. This may be handled by regular insurance companies or by special companies writing insurance only in connection with financing. In automobile financing, collision insurance is also required.

To an increasing extent group life insurance is being used to insure the unpaid balance of consumer loans. Special companies are active in this field, but of late some of the leading life insurance companies have entered it. There is also increasing emphasis on accident and disability insurance on a group basis to protect borrowers against these contingencies.

Even though all types of insurance coverage are growing, there is disagreement as to the advisability of requiring some types. Some of the finance companies, especially in the consumer finance field, oppose any kind of insurance even when it is allowed by state law. Others feel that, although group life insurance is desirable, accident, disability, and the like are of limited usefulness. Limited surveys made by some of the companies indicate that consumers by and large want group life coverage, but they are not agreed on the desirability of other types.

There is a real danger that insurance may be abused by some. A borrower may be sold policies he does not need or want at high rates so as to yield unreasonable profits to the lender. This need not happen, but it offers an opportunity for the unscrupulous that some have taken advantage of.

QUESTIONS

1. Briefly describe the functions of sales finance companies.
2. Trace the development of sales finance companies before World War II.
3. Describe the present status of the sales finance field.
4. Account for the development of a specialized type of institution to do sales financing.
5. Outline the legal regulations under which sales finance companies operate.
6. Where do sales finance companies obtain their funds?
7. Describe the methods of operation of sales finance companies in financing consumer purchases of durable goods.
8. Describe the procedures used in wholesale financing of automobiles.
9. Comment on the results of operations of sales finance companies.
10. Discuss current problems and trends in sales financing.

11. Discuss the development of consumer financing by commercial banks.
12. Why were banks slow in entering this field?
13. How does the source of funds of commercial banks differ from that of other financial institutions?
14. Which types of personal loans do commercial banks make at the present time?
15. Describe the procedures used in making home repair and modernization loans.
16. Discuss the results of operations in this field.
17. Describe bank lending in the personal-loan field.
18. Discuss the activities of banks in automobile and other durable goods financing.
19. How does the development of bank charge-account financing fit into the long-range development of monetary and credit instruments?
20. Describe the characteristics of borrowers from consumer credit departments of banks. How do they differ from borrowers at consumer finance companies? How does the size of loan differ?
21. Discuss the rates charged by bank consumer credit departments, their loss experience, and their profits.
22. Discuss current problems and trends in the field of bank lending to consumers.
23. Describe the services of facilitating agencies in the consumer finance field.
24. From data in a recent *Federal Reserve Bulletin* make a table showing the following data for each year since 1950 for banks and for sales finance companies:

Total installment credit
Automobile paper
Other consumer goods paper
Repair and modernization loans
Personal loans

Have there been any changing patterns of financing by banks and sales finance companies during this period? Discuss possible reasons for changing patterns.

SUGGESTED READINGS

CHAPMAN, JOHN M., AND ASSOCIATES. *Commercial Banks and Consumer Instalment Credit.* New York: National Bureau of Economic Research, Inc., 1940.

PHELPS, CLYDE WILLIAM. *Instalment Sales Financing—Its Services to the Dealer.* Baltimore: Commercial Credit Company, 1953.

————. *The Role of the Sales Finance Companies in the American Economy.* Baltimore: Commercial Credit Company, 1952.

————. *Using Instalment Credit.* Baltimore: Commercial Credit Company, 1955.

PLUMMER, WILBUR C., AND YOUNG, RALPH A. *Sales Finance Companies and Their Credit Practices.* New York: National Bureau of Economic Research, Inc., 1940.

Chapter 20

Financing Urban

Residential

Real Estate

Financing the purchase of residential real estate is classified as long-term consumer financing. In 1956 the total volume of nonfarm mortgages of $20,000 or less recorded on 1- to 4-family dwellings was in excess of $27 billion. Savings and loan associations made somewhat more than a third of these loans, commercial banks one fifth of the total, and mortgage companies somewhat less than one fifth. Individuals made 13 per cent of the total volume of loans, and life insurance companies and ~~commercial~~ *mutual* banks each made 7 per cent of the total volume.[1]

The percentage of total mortgage debt outstanding on 1- to 4-family homes at the end of 1956 is somewhat different for these groups than the proportion of loans made by each in that year. The percentage of outstanding loans held by life insurance companies and mutual savings banks is materially higher than the percentage of loans made by them in 1956; and the percentage of loans held by mortgage companies, individuals, and others is materially lower. This difference is due in part to some changes in the percentage of loans made by various lenders over the years. It exists primarily, however, because life insurance companies and mutual savings banks buy substantial quantities of mortgages from mortgage companies. Such companies perform the merchandising function by handling the original loan transactions and then selling mortgages in large blocks to permanent investors. See Table 20-1 for additional information.

[1] *Federal Reserve Bulletin*, November, 1957, pp. 1265-67.

Table 20-1

DISTRIBUTION OF MORTGAGE DEBT ON NONFARM HOMES
BY TYPES OF LENDERS

(For the Year 1956 and on December 31, 1956)

	PERCENTAGE OF TOTAL LOANS MADE IN 1956	PERCENTAGE OF TOTAL OUTSTANDING DEBT HELD AS OF DECEMBER 31, 1956
Savings and loan associations	35	34
Life insurance companies	7	20
Commercial banks	20	18
Mutual savings banks	7	13
Mortgage companies	18	} 12
Individuals and others	13	
Federal National Mortgage Association ..		3

SOURCE: Based on data in the *Federal Reserve Bulletin*, November, 1957, pp. 1265-67, and *Savings and Loan Fact Book 1957*, p. 33.

The basic procedures followed by all of the agencies financing urban residential real estate will be considered first. Then consideration will be given to special features of each of the major financing agencies and to the results of their operations in this field. The role of real estate brokers and mortgage companies in merchandising mortgages will also be analyzed. Some consideration will also be directed to those agencies that facilitate this process of financing. This is done by such organizations as appraisal companies and title insurance companies, but primarily by various governmental agencies. The activities in this area of several federal agencies are so important that consideration will not only be given to the governmental financing programs, but also to the influences they have had on real estate financing.

PROCEDURES IN RESIDENTIAL REAL ESTATE FINANCING

As in all lending operations, the procedures used in urban residential real estate financing are determined in large part by the characteristics of such financing. The financing is almost entirely long-term except for loans for construction, and even these are usually replaced by long-term loans. Long-term loans are possible because houses last for long periods of time, often 40 or 50 or more years. Special risks are also involved in real estate financing. The value of the collateral is affected by such factors as the changing economic status of the area, the city, and the neighborhood, as well as by business fluctuations, changing price levels, and the like. There are legal technicalities to consider to be sure that the prospective borrower has a clear title. The property must also be maintained adequately if it is to maintain its value. The present and prospective income and other obligations of the borrower are also significant in determining the safety of a loan.

These special factors, along with the fixed location of the collateral, have resulted in mortgage markets being more localized than are the markets for many other types of investments. In recent years the scope of the mortgage markets has been broadened, but local forces still have a great influence.

The Mortgage

A loan made to finance the purchase of residential real estate is typically secured by means of a mortgage against such property. The real estate mortgage, in one form or another, has probably been used as long as the right of private property has been recognized. The form used in this country is patterned after that of the English common law and equity law. In early England, a borrower of money would actually turn over possession of his land to the lender, and the lender would have use of the land until the debt was paid. The word "mortgage," which stems from the terms "mort-gage" or "dead-pledge," was therefore rather appropriate in that the land was to all intents and purposes dead so far as the borrower was concerned until such time as the loan was repaid. The borrower in such a loan transaction was called the *mortgagor*; the lender, the *mortgagee*.

Modifications of this form of mortgage arrangement were developed which provided in some cases that the income from the land should apply to the payment of the debt, and in other cases that possession of the land by the lendor was not to be obtained unless the borrower failed to abide by the terms of the contractual agreement. Later the English Court of Equity began to take the view that it was unreasonable that a mortgagee should retain the full value of the property if the borrower defaulted since it was merely conveyed to him to secure a debt and therefore a mortgagor had a right in equity to redeem his property upon full payment of the obligation, even though the maturity date of the loan had passed. In technical parlance this right has come to be known as the *equity of redemption.*

Along with the development of the equity of redemption came the procedure of foreclosure. The foreclosure was necessary to prevent an undue burden upon the lender because of the uncertainty of the period of equity of redemption. It provided that on the petition of the mortgagee the courts would fix a time within which the mortgagor was required to pay the debt. If the mortgagor failed to pay within this time, the decree provided that his equity of redemption was thereby "barred and foreclosed."

In the United States the theory of the mortgage varies from one state to another, although in practice the legal distinctions are not too significant. Specifically, some states continue to regard the mortgage as a transfer of legal title to the mortgagee with the agreement that if the debt is paid as agreed, the transfer is void; while other states regard the mortgage as simply a lien on the property to secure the debt.

Typical Mortgage Provisions. The typical mortgage form begins with a statement of the amount of the debt, the interest rate, and the terms under which it is to be repaid. The next provision mortgages the property that is described in the mortgage. Then follows a group of covenants or agreements of the mortgagor beginning with his agreement to pay the debt according to the terms specified in the mortgage. He also agrees to keep the property insured in an amount large enough to protect the interest of the mortgagee and to pay all taxes and assessments on the property. Also typical is an agreement not to remove or alter any buildings without the consent of the mortgagee. Another typical clause is an acceleration clause, which provides that in the event of a failure to make a payment on principal or interest or to pay taxes which are due, the mortgagee may declare the full amount of the debt as due immediately.

Junior Mortgages. At times a mortgagor may want to borrow more money on a piece of property than the lender on a mortgage is willing to lend him. He may find a lender who will lend him an additional sum, usually at a higher rate of interest, provided he gives him a claim on his equity in the property that is not covered by the existing mortgage. When this is done, the existing mortgage is called the first mortgage; the new mortgage, the second mortgage. At times three or more mortgages may be placed on one piece of property.

State laws provide for the recording of mortgages in order to protect the interests of all parties. An unrecorded mortgage is binding between the parties to the agreement. The law provides, however, that the first mortgage to be recorded is the senior mortgage, so all mortgages should be recorded promptly.

Foreclosure Procedure. In the event of default by the mortgagor the mortgagee will usually try to work out whenever possible an arrangement whereby the payments in default may be met. If he feels that his interests are in jeopardy, he will bring a suit asking the court to foreclose on the mortgage and to hold a foreclosure sale. The mortgagee may bid at the foreclosure sale, and he occupies a strategic position since he can use his claim to pay for his bid while other bidders must pay cash. Foreclosure costs are paid first out of the proceeds of the sale of the property. If the proceeds are large enough so that a surplus exists after foreclosure costs and the mortgage debt are paid, the mortgagor is entitled to the surplus. If part of the debt is unpaid, the court grants the mortgagee a deficiency judgment for this amount. This may be collected from other assets of the mortgagor. If he has insufficient assets, the claim will remain on record for a period of time. Such an unpaid claim makes it almost impossible to get a mortgage loan in the future.

Land Contracts. In some cases a *land contract*, instead of a mortgage, is used to finance the sale of real estate. It is a contract for the sale of property in which the deed to the property does not pass to the purchaser until the terms of the contract have been fulfilled. It generally provides for regular payments, usually monthly, of interest and part of the principal. In cases in which the purchaser does not have sufficient money to finance the purchase of property by means of a mortgage, he may be able to do so by means of a land contract; and in this way he can build up enough equity to get mortgage financing or in some cases to pay the full cost of the property. The seller may be willing to make such an arrangement since he holds the deed to the property until the terms of the contract have been fulfilled.

Mortgage Loan Procedures. The purchaser of a home who desires to finance part of the purchase price has several alternatives. He may have the real estate broker make the arrangements for a loan, or he may do it directly. The real estate broker may have contacts with a bank, an insurance company, or a savings and loan association that handles financing on his sales when suitable arrangements for a loan can be made. Some of the large real estate firms operate in close contact with mortgage companies that will make the loan in the first instance and then sell the mortgage to an institution such as a life insurance company.

The purchaser may also arrange the financing directly through a bank or a savings and loan association. In the New England states and in New York, New Jersey, and Pennsylvania he has another possible source of financing, the mutual savings banks that invest a substantial part of their loanable funds in real estate mortgages.

The loan applicant must provide data about himself and his financial affairs and also information on the house to be financed. The lender investigates the borrower's credit, and he makes an appraisal of the property or has it made by an appraisal company. The officers or a loan committee in the lending institution review the loan, and if it appears to be desirable, approve it subject to an examination of the title. If the title is satisfactory, the loan is closed by having the borrower sign the mortgage and a note or series of notes to evidence the debt.

Government Guarantees. During the depression of the thirties the federal government set up the Federal Housing Administration to stimulate home building by guaranteeing mortgages on urban residential real estate. A prospective borrower who wants to obtain an FHA loan applies for such a loan at a savings and loan association, a commercial bank, or other lending institution approved for such loans. The required application papers are sent to the local FHA office for approval. They appraise the property and check the ability of the applicant to make the required loan payments.

The Serviceman's Readjustment Act, or GI Bill as it is popularly known, authorized the Veterans' Administration to guarantee loans on homes purchased by veterans. Such loans were first made available to World War II veterans and later also to veterans of the Korean War. Details of FHA and VA loan guarantee programs are covered in the discussion of government agencies and programs in the real estate field.

Amortized Loans. All loans guaranteed by the Federal Housing Administration and by the Veterans' Administration must be *amortized loans,* that is, loans on which the borrower agrees to make regular payments on principal as well as of interest. Many loans made without such guarantees are also made on this basis. The payments are calculated so that the loan is retired within an agreed period of time. Often the lender also requires that the borrower add an amount equal to one twelfth of the annual property insurance and annual property taxes to his payments.

Monthly payments required to repay the principal and to pay interest are reduced materially as the time period of the loan is extended. For example, a $1,000 amortized loan at 5 per cent interest requires monthly payments of $10.61 if amortized in 10 years and $6.60 if amortized in 20 years. Table 20-2 shows monthly payments for various time periods and interest rates.

Table 20–2
MONTHLY PAYMENT NECESSARY TO RETIRE AN AMORTIZED MORTGAGE LOAN OF $1,000

Loan Period	4½%	5%	6%
10 years	$10.36	$10.61	$11.11
15 years	7.65	7.91	8.44
20 years	6.33	6.60	7.17
25 ycars	5.56	5.85	6.45
30 years	5.07	5.37	6.00

Financing New Home Construction

If a loan secured by a mortgage is to be used to finance the construction of a new house, the lender requires copies of the plans and specifications of the house and an estimate of the cost prepared by the builder. The credit and reliability of the builder must then be investigated also. The down payment is often paid to the lending institution, which then disburses money to the builder as work progresses.

Builders of subdivisions follow a somewhat different procedure to make sure that financing is available on the houses when they are ready for sale. The builder obtains a short-term loan from a commercial bank to meet his construction costs. Before obtaining such a construction loan, he gets a commitment for permanent financing from an investor such as an insurance company or a savings bank. The terms of the loans are specified in the commitment. This commitment may be obtained directly by the builder, but especially for FHA and VA loans, it is usually obtained by a mortgage company that will handle the details of financing for the builder.

In periods in which credit is difficult to obtain, the mortgage company may find it impossible to get a commitment from a permanent investor to take its mortgages. In such a case the company may arrange for a standby commitment by a commercial bank. The bank gives the mortgage company a firm commitment to buy the mortgages at a future date at an agreed price below the face value of the mortgages and to hold them for a limited period of time during which the mortgage company attempts to find a purchaser for the mortgages. If this cannot be done in the stipulated time period, the bank agrees to buy the mortgages at the price agreed upon.

SAVINGS AND LOAN ASSOCIATIONS

After the development of the first savings and loan association in 1831, the movement spread to surrounding towns and cities and gradually over most of the eastern part of the country. Many of these early associations were called building and loan associations, and this name is still used by some associations today. After 1855, the establishment of new associations spread into the Mississippi and Ohio valleys and also into Texas, California, and a few other states. Between 1880 and 1890 associations were chartered at a rapid rate in all sections of the country. Up to this time all associations were local institutions serving their immediate communities. Late in the decade many national associations were chartered. Many were organized as promotional ventures for the benefit of the organizers. Most of these organizations failed during the several periods of depressed business activity between 1890 and 1901. As a result, several states passed laws preventing national organizations from doing business in their state. This experience has kept the business local in character since that time.

The big development came after 1920 and again after World War II. Today savings and loan associations do a greater volume of residential real estate financing than any other type of institution.

There are over 6,000 savings and loan associations with total loans outstanding of over $36 billion at the end of 1956.[2] Some have passed the $100 million mark in assets, but most of them in metropolitan areas have assets of $5 million to $50 million. Some in suburban areas and many in small communities are much smaller.

Organization and Operation

A savings and loan association may be chartered under a state charter or, since 1933, under a federal charter. At the end of 1956 over 70 per cent had state charters. The average size of the federal associations was larger than that of the state associations so that the federal group had over 50 per cent of the total assets of all the associations.[3]

Usually five or more responsible citizens may apply for a charter. To obtain a state charter, they must demonstrate their fitness to receive a charter and the need for the services of the proposed savings and loan association. To obtain a federal charter, they must demonstrate: (1) the good character and responsibility of the applicants, (2) the necessity for such an institution in the community, (3) the reasonable probability of its usefulness and success, and (4) that it can be established without undue injury to properly conducted existing local thrift and home-financing institutions.[4]

Both savers and borrowers are members of savings and loan associations. Since most of these associations are cooperatives, the savings put into them are shares of ownership in the association. This distinguishes them from deposits in a commercial bank, which are liabilities of the bank. Payments on savings and loan shares are *dividends,* not interest. In recent years, as part of their competitive strategy to attract savings, savings and loan associations have to a large extent dropped the use of the word "shares" in their literature and referred instead to "savings accounts."

---

[2] United States Savings and Loan League, *Savings and Loan Fact Book 1957*, p. 45.
[3] *Ibid.*, p. 42.
[4] Federal Savings and Loan Associations (Washington, D. C.: Home Loan Bank Board, 1951), p. 5.

Many account holders treat their accounts much like a deposit account rather than like a share of ownership. In 1956, for example, over $15.5 billion was put into savings accounts and $10.5 billion was withdrawn, leaving a net increase in savings accounts of about $5 billion. This brought the amount in savings accounts at the end of the year to $37.3 billion.[5]

The usual provision is that a borrower must buy at least one share in the association so he usually has just one share and one vote. A saver has one vote for each $100 or fraction thereof he has invested in the association with a limit of 50 votes per member. The members consider the affairs of the association and elect the board of directors at an annual meeting.

The directors have full responsibility for conducting the business of the association. They usually engage a full-time executive to run the association and restrict their function to the determination of general policies.

Loans and Investments

Savings and loan associations devote themselves almost exclusively to making loans on residential real estate. Federal associations may lend a maximum of 85 per cent of their total resources only upon the security of first liens on new homes or combination home and business properties located within 50 miles of the home office of the association. These associations may lend up to 80 per cent of the appraised value of the property, but not over $20,000, on a monthly amortized basis for not over 20 years. Unamortized loans may also be made for not over 5 years. FHA and GI loans may be made in accordance with the terms specified by these agencies.

Up to 15 per cent of the resources of federal savings and loan associations may be invested in first liens on apartment and business properties. The maximum percentage of the loan to the appraised value varies between 50 and 66⅔ per cent, depending on the type of property and the terms for repayment. There is no top dollar limit or geographical limitation on such loans.

State laws usually allow broader discretion in the type of property that can be used to secure a loan, but about 90 per cent of all loans are on single-family dwellings. The most frequent provision

---

[5] United States Savings and Loan League. *Savings and Loan Fact Book 1957*, p. 49.

allows loans up to 80 per cent of the value of the property on one to four-family dwellings, and smaller percentages on other types of property. The maximum loan is usually set between $15,000 and $25,000, with $20,000 the most common figure. Most state laws specify no maximum term for the loan, and those that do have a maximum set either 15, 20, or 25 years for amortized loans and 3 to 5 years for unamortized loans. Many loans are written for less than the maximum period; 10, 12, 15, and 20 years are the most common terms.

Many savings and loan associations also make loans to finance the construction of new homes. In 1956 such loans represented over one third of all loans made. They may also make property improvement loans insured by the Federal Housing Administration.

Both federal and state associations may invest in direct and guaranteed obligations of the United States government. About three fourths of the states allow investment in bonds of their state and its municipalities. Some grant wider investment powers.

Membership in the Federal Home Loan Bank System

Federal savings and loan associations must join the Federal Home Loan Bank System. State associations may join, and over half of them have done so. This gives them access to their regional Home Loan Bank for credit. The associations may obtain a loan from this bank by using their mortgages as collateral. These loans may run for as long as 10 years and must be repaid in quarterly installments. Short-term loans may also be made to meet seasonal needs, often without security.

Supervision

Federal savings and loan associations are supervised by the Home Loan Bank Board and state associations by agencies in their respective states. The associations must submit reports at least annually, and they are subject to examinations that are usually made once a year. The purpose of such examinations is to be sure that the associations are complying with the law, that they are not insolvent, and that they show no signs of future difficulties. The integrity of the management and personnel in handling the affairs of the association is also checked.

Results of Operations

Most savings and loan associations have operated successfully. The maximum interest rate they can charge is influenced by FHA rates. Usually charges on other than FHA or GI loans are not above 5½ or 6 per cent. Expenses range between 1 and 1½ per cent of the volume of loans outstanding. The typical savings and loan association has transferred between 25 and 35 per cent of its earnings to reserves and undivided profits.

Although some losses occur on mortgages, they have seldom been serious enough to cause difficulty for the association except during the depression of the thirties. Between 1929 and 1940 no fewer than 68 associations failed in any one year, and in 1938 the number reached 277.[6] Since 1940 the number of failures has been small, and in most post-World War II years none failed at all. Dividend rates are typically 3 or 3½ per cent at the present time. A few associations pay 2½ per cent and a sizable number 4 per cent or even more.

COMMERCIAL BANKS

State banks have made loans on real estate mortgages almost from their beginning, helping to finance the westward movement of the population. National banks were not permitted to loan money on real property as security under the National Bank Act of 1864, but there was some evasion of this provision. The Federal Reserve Act allowed loans on farm land, and an amendment in 1916 provided for one-year loans on urban real estate. In later years much more liberal provisions for real estate loans were enacted. At present national banks may make amortized loans on improved residential properties for not over 66⅔ per cent of their appraised value and for not over 20 years. Nonamortized loans may be made for not over 50 per cent of the appraised value of the property and for not over 5 years. National banks may make FHA and VA loans according to the provisions of these programs. The total volume of real estate loans of a national bank excluding VA loans may not exceed the unimpaired capital and surplus of the bank or 60 per cent of the time or savings deposits, whichever is the greater.

[6] *Statistical Abstract of the United States* (Washington, D. C.: United States Government Printing Office, 1951), p. 406.

State banking laws are much more liberal than the national banking laws. Over half of the states have no restriction on the length of the loan or on the loan-to-value ratio. Those which do have restrictions have more liberal provisions than the national banking acts as a rule.

Loans

The length of time of the loan and the ratio of the loan to the appraised value of the property for FHA and VA loans are generally at or near the upper limits allowed under these programs. Conventional loans on one- to four-family properties are usually also amortized loans made in most cases for periods of 15 years or less, and the loan-to-value ratios are generally between 40 and 70 per cent. Interest rates generally range from 5 per cent to 6 per cent on conventional loans. Interest rates on VA and FHA loans are generally at the upper limits permitted under these programs.

Results of Operations

Since accounting practices vary among banks, it is difficult to determine exact net income figures. Lending costs other than losses, however, probably average 1 per cent to 1½ per cent. Since gross income has averaged somewhat below 5 per cent, net income after allowing for losses and for other lending costs has been about 3 per cent to 3½ per cent of the average dollar amount of loans outstanding.

MUTUAL SAVINGS BANKS

Mutual savings banks are an important source of real estate credit in a few geographical areas. Of over 600 such banks in operation, practically all are in the New England states and in New York, New Jersey, and Pennsylvania.

Loans

Mutual savings banks invested in real estate mortgages from the beginning of their existence. In fact, until the depression in 1929 such mortgages were their preferred form of investment. Due to losses in the thirties, however, many banks no longer considered mortgages attractive forms of investment. In the post-World War

II period, mutual savings banks have again invested heavily in mortgages on residential property, especially owner-occupied dwellings.

Prior to 1937 mutual savings banks could write mortgages up to 60 per cent of the appraised value of property. In 1937 this was raised to 70 per cent for amortized loans for not over 20 years, and in 1943, to 75 per cent. After 1935, FHA loans could be made in line with the regular procedures for such loans; and in the post-World War II period, VA-guaranteed loans were also permitted.

Results of Operations

The record of mutual savings banks in lending on real estate as security has been good. Foreclosures were negligible before 1928. Beginning with 1929 foreclosures went up rapidly, reaching a high point in 1933. During and after World War II, foreclosures decreased just as rapidly and again became negligible.

No up-to-date records exist on the rates of return earned by mutual savings banks. They have, however, in recent years been able to pay interest on savings accounts at about the same rate as dividends of savings and loan associations. Such records as are available indicate that their net return on the average dollar amount of real estate loans outstanding has been somewhat higher on the average than that of commercial banks on such loans.

LIFE INSURANCE COMPANIES

Life insurance companies have been lending substantial sums on real estate for over a century. Mortgages have varied somewhat in importance as a source of investment for their assets. In 1890 over 40 per cent of their assets were in mortgages. This figure declined, especially after 1929, until in 1945 it was but 15 per cent. Mortgages have been purchased in large amounts in the post-World War II period, and at the end of 1956 accounted for more than 30 per cent of the assets of life insurance companies.[7]

Loans

The state laws under which insurance companies operate place some restrictions on their investment in mortgages. Loans are

7 *Life Insurance Fact Book* (New York: Institute of Life Insurance, 1957), p 75

generally restricted to first liens on improved real estate. The maximum amount of a loan is often restricted. A typical provision sets the top limit at $25,000 or 2 per cent of the total admitted assets of the insurance company, whichever is greater. Some laws, such as those of New York, limit mortgages to 40 per cent of the company's assets.

FHA and VA loans are permitted under the regular provisions for such loans. For other loans maximum loan-to-value ratios are usually set at 66⅔ per cent, but at times at 50 per cent. Loans for larger ratios may be made in some states if they are fully amortized in prescribed periods of time, such as 15 years.

Geographic restrictions on the location of property are quite liberal. Many states allow loans in all 48 states; some allow loans in several states in the region in which the insurance company is located.

Insurance companies frequently concentrate in particular types of loans. Companies with portfolios under $20 million usually limit themselves to FHA and VA loans and/or to conventional loans on one- to four-family dwellings. Companies with portfolios of over $100 million often concentrate heavily in non-residential lending.

Insurance companies make some loans directly either through the home office or branch offices. Most loans, however, are purchased from brokers, mortgage companies, or other institutions. This may be done through branch offices, by appointing a broker or mortgage company as a correspondent to bring loans to the attention of the loan department of the insurance company, or by buying mortgages in blocks from mortgage companies that have made the loans with the intention of selling the mortgages to permanent investors.

Results of Operations

The over-all record of life insurance company investments in mortgages has been good. Just as with other institutions, however, foreclosures were numerous during the depression of the thirties. When final losses are spread over the period from 1920 through 1946, they are not high. Losses in the post-World War II period have been negligible for most companies. Detailed cost records are not available on the net income earned on mortgage loans.

Such evidence as is available indicates that insurance companies have earned on the average about the same rate on mortgage loans as have commercial banks.

MERCHANDISING AND FACILITATING AGENCIES

In real estate financing the merchandising function is performed by some real estate brokers, but primarily by mortgage companies. The procedures involved have already been covered in the discussion of mortgage financing. The nature of mortgage companies will be considered somewhat more fully in this section. The activities of several facilitating agencies will also be considered.

Mortgage Companies

One of the developments that has made possible a national market for real estate mortgages has been the growth of mortgage companies. These companies not only negotiate the loans but continue to service them by collecting interest and principal payments and forwarding them to the owner of the mortgage. This requires facilities for receiving such payments and for sending out notices of accounts due and past due. Servicing also includes checking to be sure that proper insurance is carried and that all taxes are paid.

Mortgage companies as they operate today for all practical purposes began with the introduction of FHA mortgage insurance in 1934. These companies first concentrated their activities on FHA loans and later also on VA loans, but they have handled some conventional loans. Their growth was especially rapid in the decade from 1945 to 1955. The number of such companies doubled and their assets increased tenfold during this period.[8]

Mortgage companies are usually closely-held private corporations. They have a relatively small capital investment compared with the volume of business they do. They get most of their money from short-term bank borrowing. In most postwar years almost 90 per cent of the money these companies have tied up in mortgages has come from bank borrowing.[9]

[8] Saul B. Klaman, "Mortgage Companies in the Postwar Mortgage Market," *Journal of Finance* (May, 1957), p. 151.
[9] *Ibid.*, p. 153.

Facilitating Agencies

Several agencies also facilitate the process of mortgage financing. One is the professional appraisal concern that makes careful appraisal of all types of property based on such factors as location, the trend of the neighborhood, the type of construction, and the condition of the property. This is done by government appraisers for FHA and VA loans.

Another facilitating agency, the title company, assures the purchaser of real estate or the mortgagee who is loaning money on real estate that the title to the property is clear. The title to most land in the United States was originally held by a state or by the federal government. It has gone through a series of title transfers until it has reached the present owners. The record of such transfers is recorded in public record books in chronological order. If all titles in the series of sales were defined completely and accurately at the time a transfer was made, if all the proper instruments that might affect the title were properly recorded, and if all complicating factors, such as suits over title arising out of litigation over the bequests in a will, were properly handled, the present title would be clear. There are so many chances for defects in a title that checking the records to be sure a title is clear has become a specialized activity carried on by title companies. They will search the records for a fee and issue an opinion on the character of the title being examined.

Important as a clear title to property is, there are very few titles about which there is absolutely no question. Most defects are minor and do not affect the transfer of title. Since it is impossible in most cases to be absolutely sure about a title, some companies have developed title insurance. They, of course, insure only titles that they believe from their examination are sound. The amount of insurance is stated in the policy and is usually the full value of the property at the time the insurance is written. The premium is paid only once, at the time the policy is purchased.

GOVERNMENTAL ASSISTANCE IN REAL ESTATE FINANCING

Several agencies of the federal government are instrumental in facilitating the financing of urban residential real estate. One group is the Federal Home Loan Bank Board and the Federal Home Loan Banks and the Federal Savings and Loan Insurance Corporation that are under its jurisdiction. Another group includes the Federal Housing Administration and the Federal National Mortgage Association that are under the jurisdiction of the Housing and Home Finance Agency. The Veterans' Administration is also engaged in facilitating real estate financing through its program of loan guarantees under the GI Bill.

Federal Home Loan Bank Board

The Federal Home Loan Bank Board directs operations of the Federal Home Loan Bank System and the Federal Savings and Loan Insurance Corporation. These two agencies were established by Congress during the depression period as permanent organizations that were to encourage home ownership and sound home financing and protect the savings of small investors. The Board is responsible also for the supervision of federal savings and loan associations.

Federal Home Loan Bank System. The act establishing the Federal Home Loan Bank System in 1932 provided for twelve regional banks, but their number was later reduced to eleven. Each bank is administered by a board of twelve directors, four of whom are appointed by the Federal Home Loan Bank Board for terms of four years and eight of whom are elected by the members for terms of two years. Membership is open to all state and federally chartered financial institutions, other than commercial banks, that are engaged in long-term home financing, provided the character of their management and their policies are consistent with standards established under the Act. The great majority of the present member institutions are savings and loan companies. A few mutual savings banks and insurance companies, however, have also become members of these federal home loan banks.

The funds of the federal home loan banks are obtained from the proceeds of sales of their capital stock to members, sales of consolidated Federal Home Loan Bank obligations to the public, and deposits of surplus cash by member institutions. Each member bank of the system is required to buy stock in its federal home loan bank equal to at least 2 per cent of the total of the unpaid principal of its home mortgage loans and other home purchase contracts. The original capital was provided by the purchase of stock by the United States government as well as by member institutions, but the members took over all of the government-owned stock in the post-World War II period. The investment in the banks is also increased by the provision that 20 per cent of net earnings must be transferred to a reserve account semiannually until such reserve equals the paid-in capital. After that, 5 per cent of net earnings must still be added to the reserve.

The system of banks also raises funds by issuing consolidated Federal Home Loan Bank obligations. These have usually been notes that have run for a year or less. At the end of 1956, $963 million was outstanding in such notes.[10] These obligations are jointly and severally guaranteed by the eleven banks but are not guaranteed by the United States government.

The excess cash of a district federal home loan bank may be deposited with another of the eleven district banks of the System. This is one means by which credit may be transferred from a region of surplus funds to an area of need for funds.

The district banks make long-term or short-term loans to their member institutions on the security of the home mortgages that the members have in turn obtained from their borrowers, or on the security of government bonds. Short-term unsecured loans are also available under certain conditions. Secured loans outstanding on December 31, 1956, reached a total of over $800 million and unsecured loans over $400 million.[11]

The federal home loan banks are entirely self-supporting and have paid dividends regularly since their establishment. The eleven banks do not pay uniform dividends since their operations are not uniformly profitable. In 1956 dividends ranged from 2 per cent to $2\frac{3}{4}$ per cent.[12]

Federal Savings and Loan Insurance Corporation. The Federal Home Loan Bank Board also has supervision over the Federal Savings and Loan Insurance Corporation. Although this agency is entirely separate from the Federal Deposit Insurance Corporation, it functions in much the same manner and has increased public confidence in and encouraged the flow of savings to savings

[10] United States Savings and Loan League, *Savings and Loan Fact Book 1957*, p. 68.
[11] *Ibid.*, p. 71.
[12] *Ibid.*, p. 70.

and loan associations. The law requires federal associations to be insured, while state-chartered associations may become insured upon application and approval. Insured associations are subject to annual examination and to the rules and regulations of the Federal Savings and Loan Insurance Corporation.

As of December 31, 1956, there were 3,666 insured institutions with total assets of almost $40 billion. Over 90 per cent of the assets of the entire savings and loan business are held by the insured group.[18]

The Federal Savings and Loan Insurance Corporation insures the safety of savings against loss up to a maximum of $10,000 for each account holder. If an insured association must be liquidated because it is in financial difficulties, the Corporation may pay the insured accounts in cash or may make accounts in other insured associations available to the account holders of the association in liquidation.

Besides its function of paying off investors in case an insured association is ordered liquidated, the Federal Savings and Loan Insurance Corporation possesses broad preventive powers by coming to the assistance of an association in the early stages of any difficulty. For instance, in order to prevent a default or to restore an insured association in default to normal operations, the Insurance Corporation may make a cash contribution or loan to such an institution.

Insured associations other than the federal associations which are required by law to be insured have the right of terminating their insurance, provided they meet certain legal requirements. Also under the provisions of the insurance law, the Corporation has the right to cancel the insurance of any insured association for a violation of the law or the rules and regulations of the Corporation, but it has never found it necessary to do so.

The Federal Housing Administration

The Federal Housing Administration was established under the provisions of the National Housing Act in 1934 for the purpose of stabilizing the mortgage market and to make money available to finance the construction of new homes and also to finance needed repairs to homes and other property. This organization

[18] *Ibid.*, p. 74.

was to accomplish its objectives through the insurance against loss of certain types of loans made by private lending institutions.

Insurance of property improvement loans is authorized under Title I of the National Housing Act. These loans made to finance alterations, repairs, and improvements to existing structures were considered in Chapter 19.

The principal activity of the Federal Housing Administration is the insurance of mortgages on both new and existing one- to four-family homes, authorized under Title II of the Act. All FHA loans are amortized loans. The payments include part of the principal, interest at not over 5 per cent per year, mortgage insurance premiums,[14] fire and other hazard insurance premiums, real property taxes, and special assessments, if any. The maximum maturity on FHA loans is 30 years. The Commissioner of the FHA may reduce this maximum period by administrative action when he feels this is desirable. The maximum loan cannot exceed 95 per cent of the first $9,000 of appraised value plus 75 per cent of the appraised value over $9,000. For example, on a house appraised at $15,000 the maximum loan eligible for FHA insurance is $13,050 calculated as follows:

95% of the first $9,000	=	$ 8,550
75% of the remaining $6,000	=	4,500
		$13,050

The maximum loan guaranteed by FHA may not exceed $20,000.

The FHA is also authorized to insure mortgages on cooperative housing projects. The mortgagor must be a nonprofit housing corporation in which the permanent occupancy of the dwellings is restricted to members or a nonprofit corporation organized for the purpose of building homes for its members. Special more liberal provisions are made if such cooperative housing is for occupancy by elderly persons. FHA insurance is also available to assist in financing the rehabilitation of existing housing, the replacement of slums with new housing, and the construction of housing for essential civilian employees of some defense installations. The Federal Housing Administration also provides insur-

14 Payments of mortgage insurance premiums to the Mutual Mortgage Insurance Fund are of a mutual nature, and if the loss experience of a given class of mortgages is favorable, a portion of the paid-in insurance may be returned to the mortgagor upon termination of the loan.

ance on mortgages on certain types of rental property both during and after construction.

Veterans' Administration

The "GI Bill" provided for the guarantee or insurance of loans made by private lending institutions to veterans of World War II. The insurance provided by the Veterans' Administration was patterned after that of the Federal Housing Administration. The terms, however, are somewhat more liberal than those of the convential insured loan.

The Veterans' Administration offers a guarantee for real estate loans to qualified veterans of $7,500 or 60 per cent of the total loan, whichever is smaller. This guarantee differs from that of the Federal Housing Administration in that the entire loan is not covered by the guarantee. Before a lender may lose because of a default on payments, however, the resale value of the property must have decreased by more than the amount of the insured portion of the mortgage. For example, if a house that was bought for $13,000 had a VA loan of $12,000, the lender would not lose so long as the property could be sold for $4,500 since he had a guaranty of $7,500 of the loan from the VA.

The large surpluses of loanable funds at the war's end resulted in widespread participation in the Veterans' loan insurance program. As these funds were substantially reduced, however, the 4 per cent limitation resulted in a lack of interest on the part of many lenders to continue lending on this basis. In 1953 maximum interest rates were raised to 4½ per cent to attract more funds for GI loans.

Proportion of FHA and VA Loans

FHA and VA loans have been made by all types of lenders. Commercial banks and insurance companies have made about two thirds of the dollar value of all of their real estate loans on this basis in recent years and mutual savings banks somewhat over one half. Savings and loan associations have made a much smaller proportion of these loans than banks and insurance companies. Since many mortgage companies specialize in these loans, such loans are three quarters or more of the dollar value of all loans made by them. Table 20-3 shows the proportion of loans of each type made in 1956 by each group of lenders.

Table 20–3

PERCENTAGE DISTRIBUTION OF TYPES OF MORTGAGE LOANS ON RESIDENTIAL REAL ESTATE BY TYPES OF LENDERS IN 1956

(Based Upon Dollar Volume of Total Recordings)

	CONVENTIONAL	FHA	VA	TOTAL
Savings and Loan Associations ..	84.3%	3.5%	12.2%	100.0%
Commercial Banks	66.3	17.0	16.7	100.0
Insurance Companies	68.6	16.4	15.0	100.0
Mutual Savings Banks	53.3	11.7	35.0	100.0
Mortgage Companies	25.4	17.2	57.4	100.0
Others	97.7	0.7	1.6	100.0
ALL LENDERS	68.6%	9.7%	21.7%	100.0%

SOURCE: *Savings and Loan Fact Book 1957*, p. 33.

The Federal National Mortgage Association

The Federal National Mortgage Association was organized in 1938 as a subsidiary of the Reconstruction Finance Corporation, and was later transferred to the Housing and Home Finance Agency. It originally was brought into existence to provide an additional market for the FHA insured mortgages of lenders. In the postwar period its authority was broadened to include mortgages insured by the Veterans' Administration. It was recognized that a retarded flow of savings to the mortgage market would curtail the activities of lenders and in turn have a cumulative effect on the activities of builders, materials suppliers, and other groups dependent upon construction. The plan was to provide a pool or reservoir of funds that would supplement the flow of mortgage money during periods when such flow was low and would drain off an excess flow of funds at other times through the sale of mortgages previously purchased, so as to help to maintain a more stable construction industry.

The Federal National Mortgage Association accumulated a rather substantial portfolio of mortgages prior to the war, indicating the general need for a supplementary source of funds. During World War II this process was reversed because construction of new homes was largely curtailed during this period, resulting in a dearth of investments in mortgages on new properties. The mortgages previously sold to the Federal National Mortgage Association were purchased by private organizations.

Following the war, the volume of mortgages purchased by the Association again began to increase as it purchased large sums of mortgages insured by the Veterans' Administration and also by the FHA. As credit became more difficult to obtain from private institutions in the period after 1955, especially at the maximum rates established on FHA and VA loans, the Federal National Mortgage Association increased its activities greatly. In 1957 alone over $1 billion was invested in residential mortgages, three fourths of which were VA mortgages and one fourth FHA mortgages.

The FNMA is also authorized to enter into standby commitments made before construction is begun to purchase mortgages on new housing projects at the time the houses are completed and sold. During 1957 the FNMA entered into such commitments for mortgages totaling $132 million.[15]

FNMA has several sources of funds for its mortgage-buying activity. The principal source is debenture bonds that are sold to private investors. A second source is preferred stock that is held entirely by the Treasury Department, and a third source is common stock. Sellers of mortgages to FNMA must buy common stock in the Association based on the amount of mortgages sold. The percentage of stock to the value of mortgages sold may be set by FNMA, but it may not be below the legal minimum of 1 per cent. This percentage has usually been set at 2 per cent, but has at times been 3 per cent and at other times at the minimum.

GOVERNMENTAL INFLUENCES ON REAL ESTATE FINANCING

The difficulties of real estate financing institutions in the early phases of the depression of the thirties were of such a magnitude that even the best-run organizations were strained to remain solvent. It is possible that another experience of this nature would again plunge many institutions into bankruptcy and home owners into foreclosure. Yet, there is reason to believe that much of this may be averted because the difficulties of real estate finance in the early thirties were due in part to the techniques of mortgage lending, which have been substantially altered since that time. These changes relate to loan maturities, interest rates, loan-to-value ratios, and other terms of the loan.

---

[15] Data released by Office of Public Affairs.

Loan Maturity and Repayment

One of the most obvious changes in mortgage lending practice is the loan maturity and repayment. Before 1933 in many parts of the United States, loans were commonly written on a one-, three-, or five-year basis, and on occasions were even written "on demand." It was commonly understood that these notes and mortgages would be renewed periodically, if the interest, taxes, and other obligations were paid currently. Not only did the short maturities carried by these loans make it difficult to retire them without several renewals, but also, since amortization of the principal was seldom required, there was no plan for a systematic reduction of the loan. Although mortgage lenders of this period generally cooperated in renewing the notes of borrowers, it was often necessary during depression periods to insist upon payment. Such action frequently resulted in loss of property on the part of the borrower. The FHA and other governmental loan programs were based upon maturities of twenty or more years and the insistence upon amortization of loan principal during the entire period of the loan term. The success of the FHA program and later the VA program led many lenders to make conventional loans on the same basis so that today the typical loan is an amortized loan for a long period of years.

Loan-to-Value Ratio

Another influence of the federal agencies on real estate finance concerns the loan-to-value ratio. The high loan percentage relative to the appraised value of the property replaced the multiple-mortgage system that was prevalent prior to the depression. The effect of the multiple-mortgage system was to place a very high, if not unbearable, debt obligation on the mortgagor at interest rates that added to the difficulty of retiring the indebtedness. The modern mortgage, therefore, not only extends the term of the loan, making possible smaller installment payments, but also reduces the cost of home purchase financing because it eliminates the high cost of second and third mortgages.

Control Over Planning and Construction

A final factor that should be mentioned relative to the influence of federal institutions on real estate finance is that of control over the planning and construction of new houses. Prior to the establishment of the Federal Housing Administration, loans were negotiated between borrower and lender on a take-it-or-leave-it basis. If the lender did not approve of the location or construction of an improvement, he simply refused the loan, in which case the applicant had to seek another lender. The Federal Housing Administration established definite standards of location, construction, and materials on the loans it was willing to insure. The borrower generally found it convenient to conform to these standards in order to qualify for the favorable terms that accompanied the insured loan.

CURRENT PROBLEMS

Governmental assistance to urban real estate financing has led to some beneficial changes, but it has also raised serious problems. Governmental agencies have a major role in real estate financing today. They are in a position to encourage or restrict credit by the policies they follow. They can add to inflationary pressures by an easy credit policy in periods of high levels of building activity or give added impetus to deflation when the housing market is saturated. In addition to the general problem of the proper role of government, several special problems exist in this field.

Despite all of the machinery for home financing set up by the federal government, it is doubtful whether the system is organized so as to function effectively in an emergency. Even with the existence of the eleven federal home loan banks and the Federal National Mortgage Association, no fully effective mortgage market exists. A secondary mortgage market should exist in which lenders could convert their mortgages into cash when they need funds, either by selling mortgages or by getting a loan on the basis of such mortgages as collateral. They should also be able to purchase mortgages when they have excess funds. FNMA does not provide such a market since it can only deal with the originating institution for FHA and VA guaranteed mortgages. The federal home loan banks lack authority to buy or sell mortgages. Thus there are two sets of machinery, neither of which may be adequately set up to do the job required in an emergency.

A true secondary mortgage market must have an assured source of funds in an emergency that is available even if debentures cannot be sold. This means access to the federal reserve banks for loans or to the Treasury, preferably the former. Such a secondary market could also encourage a wider geographic distribution of mortgage funds and could cushion sudden wide fluctuations of funds to the mortgage market.

In inflationary periods such an institution could help achieve stability by operating only on a restricted basis or not at all. In such periods interest rates should be free to equate the supply of and demand for mortgage funds. The full supply of funds should come from current savings, not from governmental credit of any type if price rises are to be avoided.

QUESTIONS

1. Indicate the importance of various financial institutions in financing the purchase of urban residential real estate.
2. Discuss the characteristics of residential real estate financing that distinguish it from other forms of financing.
3. Describe a typical mortgage and explain how it is used in real estate financing.
4. Describe the mortgage loan procedures followed in financing real estate.
5. Discuss the role of government guarantees in real estate financing.
6. Describe the development of savings and loan associations.
7. Describe the organization of a savings and loan association and the procedures followed in making loans.
8. Discuss the results of the loan operations of savings and loan associations.
9. Describe the place of commercial banks in real estate financing.
10. Discuss the operations of commercial banks in the real estate field and the results of such operations.
11. Describe the role of mutual savings banks in real estate financing.
12. Discuss the results of the operation of mutual savings banks in real estate financing.
13. Describe the activities of life insurance companies in real estate financing.
14. Discuss the operations of life insurance companies in this field and the results of such operations.
15. Describe merchandising and facilitating agencies in the real estate financing field.
16. It is often said that the nature of the liabilities of a financial institution determine the use it makes of its funds. What relationship, if any, exists between the nature of the liabilities of savings and loan associations, mutual savings banks, commercial banks, and life insurance companies and their position in the field of urban real estate finance?

17. Compare and contrast short-term and intermediate consumer financing with long-term financing of urban real estate. Account for any differences.
18. Describe the organization and operation of the Federal Home Loan Bank System.
19. Discuss the operations and record of the Federal Savings and Loan Insurance Corporation.
20. Describe the mortgage loan policies of the Federal Housing Administration.
21. Describe the role of the Veterans' Administration in urban real estate financing.
22. What are the functions of the Federal National Mortgage Association?
23. Discuss the major influences that government agencies and regulations have had on real estate financing.
24. From data in a recent *Federal Reserve Bulletin* make a table showing the following for commercial banks, insurance companies, and savings and loan associations for each of the last five years:

> Total loans outstanding
> FHA insured
> VA insured
> Conventional or other

Discuss the pattern of loans made during this period by each of the agencies. Give possible explanations for changing patterns.

SUGGESTED READINGS

BEHRENS, CARL F. *Commercial Bank Activities in Urban Mortgage Financing.* New York: National Bureau of Economic Research, Inc., 1952.

BODFISH, HENRY MORTON, and THEOBALD, A. D. *Savings and Loan Principles.* New York: Prentice-Hall, Inc., 1938.

COLEAN, MILES L. *The Impact of Government on Real Estate Finance in the United States.* New York: National Bureau of Economic Research, Inc., 1950.

HOAGLAND, HENRY E. *Real Estate Principles*; Third Edition. New York: McGraw-Hill Book Company, Inc., 1955, Part Two.

LINTNER, JOHN. *Mutual Savings Banks in the Savings and Mortgage Markets.* Boston: Harvard University, 1948.

MORTON, J. E. *Urban Mortgage Lending: Comparative Markets and Experience.* New York: National Bureau of Economic Research, Inc., 1956.

SAULNIER, R. J. *Urban Mortgage Lending by Life Insurance Companies.* New York: National Bureau of Economic Research, Inc., 1950.

The

Monetary

System

Chapter 21

Monetary System

of the United States

The functions performed by money were discussed in Chapter 1. The essential role of a monetary system in the operation and development of financial institutions to supply credit to business, agriculture, consumers, and the government was also explained. In this part the nature of the monetary system and its development and administration in the United States will be explored more fully. This chapter considers the monetary system of the United States. Alternative types of monetary systems are also considered briefly.

THE EARLY DEVELOPMENT OF MONETARY STANDARDS

In any monetary system it is necessary to have a *monetary standard,* which states the unit of value and the value of the various types of money in use. In early economies there was no need for a monetary standard since there was usually only one or, at the most, two or three types of money. Such money had intrinsic value because it was demanded to meet some need or for use in adornment or decoration, and it therefore had value as a commodity, which gave it value as money. Later when governments began to develop coins on which kings placed their seals to guarantee the weight and the quality of the metal, the unit of account came to be the basic coin that was minted by the government. In more modern times governments developed the monetary system further to help facilitate commerce. The basic monetary unit of the country was established by law, and the weight and fineness of the precious metal in such a coin was stipulated. Any other money in use had its value expressed in terms of the standard money.

Thus, monetary standards were developed, some based on gold, some on silver, and some on both metals. In recent years the standard in some countries has been paper money issued by the government.

Not only have different monetary standards been used at different times and in different places, but also there has been little agreement as to the best type of money standard. At the outbreak of World War I in 1914, gold was generally used, but the gold standard was largely abandoned during the war and has never been fully restored.

MONETARY STANDARDS

In this section the characteristics of the major types of standards will be considered: first, the various forms of gold standards; and then in turn silver standards, bimetallic standards, and paper money standards.

Gold-Coin Standard

The earliest gold standards were based on gold coins and for that reason were known as *gold-coin standards.* The monetary unit was defined in terms of a coin containing a certain amount of gold of prescribed purity or fineness,[1] and all other types of money were kept at a parity with gold. Gold that was presented to the mint was minted into coins at little or no cost to the suppliers of the metal. It was also legal to melt down at will gold coins in any quantity. These provisions were necessary to keep the monetary value of gold and its value as metal the same.

All other types of money that were in use, either coins or paper, were freely convertible into gold at its face value at the option of the holder. In this way the value of all types of money in use was stabilized in terms of the standard gold money since they could be exchanged for gold money at will. Under the gold-coin standard free export and import of gold was also allowed. This kept the value of domestic gold in line with world gold prices. It also had a tendency to keep domestic prices in line with prices in other countries on a gold standard since prices in all gold coun-

---

[1] Gold coins do not contain pure gold since it is too soft. They are an alloy of gold and baser metals. Frequently, the gold content is 90 per cent, and baser metals, 10 per cent. Such a coin is referred to as nine-tenths fine.

tries were based on the price of gold that was determined by international supply and demand.

Most nations dropped the gold standard during World War I, but they planned to return to it in the postwar period. Many found, however, that they did not have sufficient gold or they feared the loss of gold if it became freely available, and therefore some of these nations adopted a gold-bullion standard.

Gold-Bullion Standard

Under a *gold-bullion standard* gold is not coined and gold coins are not allowed to circulate. The government or central bank still buys gold at a set price in unlimited quantities. The gold, however, is kept by the government or central bank, and other forms of money not convertible into gold are issued to pay for it. In addition to stopping the coinage of gold when a gold-bullion standard is set up, other forms of money are no longer converted into gold or gold coin in any amount requested by the holder. It is possible, however, to get gold bars of a specified weight that are usually worth several thousand dollars. For example, England in the period following World War I was on a gold-bullion standard and used bars worth somewhat over $7,500 each.

This use of gold bars having a large value cuts down the demand for gold. Less gold is demanded because gold coins no longer circulate and are not available for hoarding. Gold is available only to those having sufficient money to buy one or more gold bars. Since gold bars are available, however, for use in industry, to pay for goods bought from foreign countries, or for hoarding if the purchaser prefers to hold gold bars rather than other forms of money or other assets, the value of gold for money and as a commodity in the arts remains about the same.

In some countries, especially the United States in 1933, a modification of the gold-bullion standard, known as the *limited gold-bullion standard*, was adopted. Under a full gold-bullion standard, persons with large sums of money at times requested gold and hoarded it, especially when they feared inflation. This is not possible under the limited gold-bullion standard since gold is under the control of the government and may be dealt in only under government regulations. All gold must be turned into the treasury or central bank, and gold bars are available only when a permit is issued for their use in foreign exchange.

Under a limited-gold bullion standard the price of gold as a money metal and its price for nonmonetary uses need not be the same. Persons who desire gold but cannot get it under the regulations may pay a price above the official price. If the official price is below the world price, gold may be smuggled out of the country instead of being turned over to the government or central bank as required by law. These modifications of the gold standard have given central banks and governments more freedom in monetary management. The gold holdings of the government or central bank are generally larger than under a full gold-standard, thus making ordinary changes in the gold supply of less significance since there is less danger of reducing the gold supply to a level so low that a loss of confidence in money would result. Under a limited gold-bullion standard the possibilities of a serious reduction in the gold supply are even less than under a gold-bullion standard since holding gold for hoarding is made illegal.

The concentration of gold in the hands of the government or central bank and the decreased demand for gold also make it possible to issue a larger amount of money on the same gold base. This gives the monetary authorities more flexibility in regulating the money supply and thus makes monetary management easier.

Gold-Exchange Standard

Some countries which have felt that their gold supply was too limited for a gold-bullion or limited gold-bullion standard have tied their currency to gold by basing it on the currency of another nation that has one of those standards. Such an arrangement is referred to as a *gold-exchange standard*. Under this standard the money of a country is not redeemable in gold but in the currency of a foreign country that is based on a fixed amount of gold. Part or all of the monetary reserves of the country may be kept in the form of claims against the money of the foreign country to which its currency is tied.

Some of the nations in the British Empire have used this system to tie their money to the British pound. For a time the Philippines were on a gold-exchange standard based on the American dollar. Their monetary unit, the peso, was not directly redeemable in gold, but in United States dollars to which the Filipino government had a claim because they had deposits in American banks. Indirectly it was possible to get gold for the peso by first getting dollars and then converting the dollars into gold. Thus the value of the peso was kept on a parity with the dollar and with gold.

Operation of the Gold Standard

When a nation is operating on a gold standard, the flow of gold into or out of a country changes the money supply. As gold flows into a country, the money supply and the basis for credit expansion are increased; when it flows out, they are reduced. This tends to correct imbalances in trade. As gold flows in, for example, the money supply is expanded, prices tend to rise, and therefore a smaller quantity of goods is sold and the gold inflow is stopped.

The gold standard, when in full operation, also tends to promote stability in exchange rates between currencies of different countries that are on the gold standard. This is true because exchange rates are all fixed in terms of gold. The gold standard also tends toward equality of prices for goods in all countries on this standard. If prices are low in a country, purchases in that country are increased and gold flows in to pay for them. This flow leads to higher prices and a new equilibrium.

If these advantages of a gold standard are to be achieved, certain rules must be followed. Each country must have a supply of gold which is large enough so that changes in the gold supply will lead to significant changes in the supply of money. Trade between nations must be in reasonable balance so that minor fluctuations can be smoothed out by changes in the general price level caused by changes in the gold supply. The economies must be stable so that political factors do not lead to shifts of gold out of a country. Competition must exist to such a degree that changes in the money supply willl affect prices and through prices affect economic activity. Also, trade between nations must be reasonably free or adjustments cannot take place.

The automatic features of the gold standard have much to commend them. The conditions outlined above, which are necessary if the gold standard is to work, do not exist in most parts of the world today, however, and, as a result, the gold standard has been abandoned in most countries.

Silver Standard

The monetary standard can be based upon silver as the standard metal. Most of the early monetary systems were based upon silver, but such a standard has been used very little since the middle of the nineteenth century. The steps needed to set up a silver standard and to keep it in operation are the same as those described for a gold standard. Modifications of the silver standard, such as a silver-bullion standard, would be possible, but these have been used little because silver standards existed primarily in a period in history when governments did little to manage their monetary systems.

Bimetallic Standard

A *bimetallic standard* is one based upon two metals—in practice, silver and gold. Such standards were widely used in the nineteenth century. The American monetary system before 1900 was based on bimetallism, and controversies over the monetary role of silver have been some of the most bitter in our history. Under a bimetallic standard the unit of value is kept constant in terms of both gold and silver. This means unlimited coinage at a nominal charge of both metals, the right to demand either gold or silver coins for other types of money and to melt them down if desired, and the free import and export of gold and silver. The basic money unit, such as the dollar in America, must be stated in terms of prescribed weights of both metals.

If such a system is set up and the government or central bank freely coins both metals and makes both available in any quantities desired, the relative prices of the two metals tend to remain fixed at their monetary value. They will not be worth less because the metals can be taken to the mint and coined at the prescribed weights and fineness of metal. They cannot be worth more in the market as long as they are available from the government or central bank in exchange for other types of money. It may not be possible to maintain this ideal relationship as will be seen in the discussion below of the disadvantages of a bimetallic standard.

Several advantages have been claimed for a bimetallic standard. While some nations were on a gold standard, some on silver, and some on both, the proponents of bimetallism claimed that it would tend to stabilize prices of goods bought and sold in foreign trade since the value of gold and silver would be stabilized. Some proponents also claimed that it would tend to stabilize all prices since the value of gold and silver together would be likely to be more stable than the value of either gold or silver.

These contentions have some merit, but the advantages were not gained in actual practice because one of the metals usually disappeared from circulation in a country. This could not happen if all countries on bimetallism used the same ratio between gold and silver in their money units and if this ratio was also in line with the over-all supply and demand relationships for the two metals for nonmonetary as well as monetary uses. In actual practice, however, such has not been the case, and one metal or the other has gone out of circulation. Suppose that 15 to 1 was the correct relationship of the metals to keep both in circulation, that is, the silver dollar, for example, had 15 times as much metal in it as did the gold dollar. If a country adopted a ratio of 14 to 1, it would find itself actually on a silver standard because gold would be worth 15 times as much as silver for nonmonetary uses and only 14 times as much for monetary uses, and would therefore not be minted. If, on the other hand, the ratio were set at 16 to 1, silver would not be minted since its value for nonmonetary uses would be one fifteenth that of gold and for monetary purposes only one sixteenth.

When one of the metals is undervalued as money, it will not remain in circulation, while the metal that is relatively overvalued will circulate. This is an example of the operation of *Gresham's Law*, which states that when several types of money exist in an economy, the one which is most overvalued as money in relationship to the others will circulate while the other types will disappear from circulation. It is often expressed less formally by saying that *bad* money drives *good* money out of circulation.

Inconvertible Paper Standard

Governments have from time to time, and especially in more recent years, set up monetary systems based upon paper money as the standard. This type of standard is usually referred to as an *inconvertible paper standard*. Under systems of this type all kinds of money in circulation are kept equal in value by having them interchangeable on request to the central bank or government. No attempt is made to keep the value of the paper at any set relationship to any metal. At times the government has stores of metal on hand as a backing for the paper money, or it continues to purchase metal for monetary reserves, but it does not redeem paper money in metal.

At present paper standards are used in some cases because a country is short of metals and in other cases because it is felt that a metallic base for the monetary system is unnecessary. In the past, however, paper standards have been associated with extreme cases of inflation. This has been due in large part to the issuance of large quantities of paper money to meet emergency needs during wars or severe, protracted depressions.

Since paper money standards have been used in emergency periods, some have drawn the conclusion that they are undesirable and should be avoided if at all possible. This does not necessarily follow since the past record of paper standards shows that they were introduced when other monetary standards had already deteriorated or broken down completely. Today no monetary standard is allowed to work without management by governmental or central bank authorities. The success of any standard in use today thus depends on the efficiency with which it is managed. There is still some difference of opinion among economists as to which type of standard can be managed most effectively, one based on metals or an inconvertible paper standard. Others advocate a return to a gold-coin or gold-bullion standard whenever the international financial situation is stable enough to warrant it because they feel that such a system can be more effective in promoting economic progress than any managed monetary standard.

Commodity Standard

Some authorities have advocated a *commodity standard* in which the monetary unit is based on a fixed quantity of a group of commodities in the same manner that the gold standard is based on a fixed quantity of gold. The commodities could be such basic ones as wheat, corn, cotton, coffee, sugar, petroleum, coal, pig iron, and tin. The monetary authority would exchange a unit of money for the package of commodities or some multiple of it, and likewise it would exchange those commodities for a unit of money. This plan is advocated in part because it is believed that it would tend to stabilize the economy. As business declined, the monetary authority would buy commodities and so cushion the decline. It would sell them in prosperous times, thus reducing the degree of inflation. If most nations adopted such a standard, its advocates believe it would stabilize exchange rates and prices in various countries just as the gold standard would tend to do if it were working automatically.

But the plan has serious shortcomings. It would be hard to agree on the package of commodities initially. To change the package as one or more of the commodities become less significant would be almost impossible politically. For example, if the demand for zinc in industry had declined because other materials were replacing it, zinc would tend to decline in price since the demand was lower. In such a case the proportion of zinc in the package of commodities should also be reduced to reflect its changed importance in the economy. Since this would decrease demand for zinc even further, zinc producers would be likely to exert political pressure to prevent the change. Another shortcoming is that the monetary authority would be swamped with commodities if price trends were downward or it would have its stocks depleted if price trends were upward. The stock of commodities held in storage could also become quite large if it was increased as the money supply was increased to take care of the needs of an expanding economy. It would have to be increased or a way found to issue money without backing, and this action would defeat the whole plan.

TYPES OF MONEY

Early monetary systems used the standard money to meet the needs of the economy for a medium of exchange. Under a gold standard, silver standard, or bimetallic standard, coins that were circulated had their full monetary value of metal in them. Such coins are known as *full-bodied money* because their value as a commodity is as great as their value as money.

In order to facilitate the process of exchange as time went on, governments issued paper money for hand-to-hand circulation while keeping the full monetary value of such money in gold or silver on deposit in their vaults. It was much easier to carry or hold a large sum of money in bills than in gold coins or silver coins. This plan was also more economical since gold or silver coins are worn down in use. When gold or silver was brought to the government, the holders accepted gold or silver certificates of equal value in exchange, and the metal was stored either as bullion or as minted coins. Such paper money with full metallic backing is known as *representative full-bodied money.*

At the present time in the United States neither full-bodied money nor representative full-bodied money is in circulation. The money we use is *credit money,* that is, money which has a greater value than the value of the material out of which it is made. This includes coins, paper money, and checking deposits.

The use of coins with less metal in them than their value as money developed from the experience with full-bodied money. In earlier times governments issued coins including those to be used for small transactions with the full value of metal in them. When the market prices of metals for nonmonetary uses increased, the coins were often melted down for metal. To prevent this, *token coins* were made with less than their full weight of metal. In the United States monetary system the silver dollar is a token coin, for it does not contain a dollar's worth of silver at present silver prices. The monetary developments that led to this status for the silver dollar will be considered in the next section of this chapter, which briefly traces American experience with monetary standards.

Silver certificates backed by silver coins or bullion in the hands of the Treasury have also been issued. These silver certificates are *representative token money* under our present system since the silver used as backing is not equal to the value of the money at current prices of silver.

Governments have also from time to time issued paper money without any backing in metal. This money is backed by the credit of the government and is in effect a government promissory note. It is often referred to as fiat money.

As commercial banks developed, they also issued paper money or bank notes, at first largely without regulation, but as time went on, under more and more stringent regulation. These were promissory notes of the bank or bank credit money. As central banks developed, they also issued such credit money and have in most countries become the only banks with this privilege. These forms of money are at times referred to as fiduciary money.

The most widely used form of money in modern times is not currency of any kind, but deposits in commercial banks that are transferred by means of checks. Checks have replaced currency to such an extent that most authorities have classified demand deposits subject to checks as a form of money.

These various types of money may be summarized as follows:

A. Full-bodied money
B. Representative full-bodied money
C. Credit money
    a. Token coins
    b. Representative token money
    c. Government promissory notes
    d. Commercial bank promissory notes
    e. Central bank promissory notes
D. Demand deposits subject to checks

AMERICAN EXPERIENCE WITH MONETARY STANDARDS

The first monetary act, which was passed under the new constitution in 1792, provided for a bimetallic standard. The dollar, which was set up as the unit of value, was defined as 371.25 grains of pure silver or 24.75 grains of pure gold. Thus the metal in the silver dollar was 15 times the weight of the metal in the gold dollar, or there was a ratio of 15 to 1 between the metals at the mint. Provision was made for gold coins in denominations of $2.50, $5, and $10, and for silver coins in denominations of $1, 50¢, 25¢, 10¢, and 5¢. All of these coins contained silver equal to their full face value, the 10¢ piece one tenth as much as the silver dollar, and so on. Provision was also made for one-cent copper coins and for half-cent copper coins.

From 1792 to 1834

Prior to 1792 many foreign coins circulated in the United States, but it was hoped that the provision for minting gold and silver would provide enough American coins to meet the demands of the economy. Until American coins were produced in sufficient quantities, however, provision was made for the use of foreign coins. Spanish dollars weighing 415 grains of silver nine-tenths fine, which gave them a silver content of 373.5 grains,[2] were to be accepted as full *legal tender*, that is, they had the legal power to be used to discharge debts and creditors could not insist on payment in any other type of money if the debt was stated in dollars. All lighter Spanish dollars and all other foreign coins were to be accepted only for their actual value in metal. These provisions were unrealistic since to carry them out meant weighing coins at every transaction. Most foreign coins were light due to long periods of use, while the American coins were of full weight. The result was that American coins were kept on hand and foreign coins were circulated. Therefore the early bimetallic standard resulted in a monetary system making almost exclusive use of foreign coins. This is again an example of the operation of Gresham's law.

Another problem was that the market ratio between silver and gold, which was about 15 to 1 in 1792, changed somewhat in later years to about 15.5 to 1 and France adopted this ratio. As a result, little gold was brought to the mint because it was worth more in the general market than at the mint, and the few gold coins that were minted soon disappeared from circulation.

Even though the government issued no paper money, the First and Second Banks of the United States were given permission to do so, and the various states also chartered state banks with the power to issue bank notes. Even though these notes were supposed to be redeemable in specie, in actual practice they often were not kept at a parity in value with metal coins. Our first monetary system therefore consisted of a gold and silver standard with a varied collection of foreign coins of light weights, many types of paper money of varying values issued by state banks, and the notes of the First and Second Banks of the United States during their periods of existence.

From 1834 to the Civil War

In 1834 Congress acted in an effort to remedy the situation. The Congressional committee recommendation was for a ratio between gold and silver of 15.6 to 1, which was about in line with the current market ratio. Congress, however, chose to make the

---

[2] The American silver dollar had 371.25 grains of silver.

ratio 16 to 1. As a result, silver was undervalued at the mint. Consequently, practically no silver was presented for coinage, but gold did start to come into the mint. Silver coins also were melted down since they had more silver in them than their monetary value. Thus not only silver dollars but also small silver coins disappeared from circulation. To fill the gap, banks issued paper money for use as change. Not only was this inconvenient to use, but bank paper money was not of uniform or stable value, and the supply was not large enough to meet the needs of the economy. Therefore, in 1853 Congress provided for fractional silver coins, which did not have their full weight in silver, thus making silver coins token coins.

From the Civil War to World War I

During the Civil War the United States went on an inconvertible paper standard. To finance the Civil War Congress authorized the issuance of $450 million of paper money known as *greenbacks,* and some $430 million was issued. These notes were made full legal tender, but they were not redeemable in gold or silver. The money supply was about doubled between 1860 and 1865, and wholesale prices more than doubled. Banks refused to redeem their notes in metal, and coins of all types disappeared from circulation.

At the end of the Civil War there was no immediate return to a metallic standard. Congress provided for the redemption of paper money in metals by 1879. In effect, the country was placed on a gold standard at that time since no provision was made for coining silver dollars but only for gold dollars at the prewar gold content, that is, 23.22 grains of gold. The supply of paper money was also restricted since no additional greenbacks were issued, state bank notes were taxed out of existence, and national bank notes could only be issued with specified government bonds as backing. As a result, by 1879 prices dropped to less than 50 per cent of 1865 levels.

In 1879 the dollar was made convertible into gold, and the country was for all practical purposes on a gold standard. Even before 1879, however, there was strong agitation again to do something for silver, and some of the silver debates in the period to 1900 were among the most bitter in our history. The demand for the use of silver for monetary purposes came from two sources, the silver producers and the groups that were affected unfavorably by declining price levels and therefore wanted to increase the money supply as a means of raising prices.

As a result of the silver movement, Congress passed the Bland-Allison Act in 1878. It directed the Secretary of the Treasury to buy from $2 million to $4 million of silver a month to be coined into silver dollars. In 1890 the Sherman Act went further and called for the purchase of 4 million ounces of silver a month. These purchases were not large enough to raise the market price of silver to the mint value, that is $1.29 an ounce. The Sherman Silver Purchase Act was repealed in 1893 because the Treasury found it almost impossible to keep gold reserves since the paper money issued to pay for the silver was turned in for gold. In 1896 William Jennings Bryan ran for president on a platform of returning to bimetallism at a 16 to 1 ratio. His defeat in 1896 and again in 1900 settled the silver issue for the time being, but it came back again in later years.

In 1900 the Gold Standard Act was passed, clearly putting the United States on a gold standard. Most major nations of the world had money systems based on gold, and it appeared as if gold had become established as the monetary base.

From World War I to the Present

During World War I, which began in 1914, most nations left the gold standard as they resorted to inflationary methods of war finance. They planned to return to gold after the war, and many of them did so. The United States did not redeem currency in gold during the war period but restored full convertibility in 1919 at the prewar gold content of 23.22 grains. Gradually other nations returned to gold, and by 1928 the important commercial nations were again on gold, but most were on gold-bullion or gold-exchange standards.

The great depression that began in 1929 again caused most countries to abandon gold, a few in 1929 and 1930 and most of the remaining countries, except for the United States, in 1931 and 1932. In 1933 the United States also abandoned gold under the new Democratic Administration due to a deliberate policy to reverse the downward trend of prices during the depression.

Legislation that was enacted in May, 1933, gave the President a broad grant of powers over the monetary system. This included the power to fix the gold value of the dollar but not to reduce it by over 50 per cent, to fix the silver value of the dollar and re-establish bimetallism if he saw fit, and to accept up to $200 million in silver at a price not to exceed 50 cents an ounce in payment of debts by foreign governments. The Treasury bought gold on order of the President at increasing prices until in January, 1934, it was paying almost $35 an ounce.

At the end of January, 1934, Congress passed the Gold Reserve Act of 1934, which provided for a modified gold standard. The President was given the power to fix the gold value of the dollar at not less than 50 nor more than 60 per cent of its former value. This meant that he could fix the dollar between 11.61 and 13.93 grains of gold, which amounted to a price range for gold of between $34.45 and $41.34 an ounce. Acting under this authority, the President set the dollar at 13.71 grains of gold or $35 for an ounce of gold. All gold was ordered turned into the Treasury, and no more gold was to be coined. Gold reserves were held in the form of gold bars and the Treasury laid down regulations under which gold could be held, transported, imported, or exported.

The changing of the gold content of the dollar created a problem since many mortgage and bond contracts had been written in terms of gold coins of the weight and fineness current at the time such contracts were executed. Congress passed a resolution which made all future gold clauses void and provided that such obligations in existing contracts could be settled by any coin or currency which was legal tender, and all coins and currency were designated as such. The Supreme Court held in a split decision that the gold clause resolution was constitutional.

The Gold Reserve Act placed the United States on a limited gold-bullion standard. Gold was available from the Treasury under regulation for use in settling foreign balances, but not for private holding. The United States has been on this standard since 1934 except for the period during World War II when restrictions on the use of gold were so stringent that for all practical purposes our country was off the gold standard.

Even though the United States adopted a limited gold-bullion standard in 1934, programs to aid silver continued. Some silver

Table 21-1

KINDS OF UNITED STATES CURRENCY OUTSTANDING AND IN CIRCULATION

[On Basis of Compilation by United States Treasury. In Millions of Dollars]

Kind of Currency	Total Outstanding Dec. 31, 1957	Held in the Treasury — As Security Against Gold and Silver Certificates	Held in the Treasury — Treasury Cash	Held in the Treasury — For F.R. Banks and Agents	Held by F.R. Banks and Agents	Currency in Circulation [1] — Dec. 31, 1957	Currency in Circulation [1] — Nov. 30, 1957	Currency in Circulation [1] — Dec. 31, 1956
Gold	22,781	22,117	[2]664		2,816	32	32	33
Gold certificates	22,117		60	19,269	1,552			
Federal Reserve notes	28,643	[3]2,408	36		339	27,031	26,887	27,038
Treasury currency—total	5,146					4,771	4,742	4,720
Standard silver dollars	488	196	23		6	263	260	247
Silver bullion	2,213	2,213						
Silver certificates and Treasury notes of 1890	[3]2,408				251	2,157	2,135	2,174
Subsidiary silver coin	1,411		8		44	1,358	1,353	1,309
Minor coin	498		2		7	489	486	471
United States notes	347		2		28	316	320	316
Federal Reserve Bank notes	128		1		1	126	127	140
National Bank notes	61		([4])		([4])	61	61	63
Total—Dec. 31, 1957	([5])	24,525	761	19,269	4,706	31,834		
Nov. 30, 1957	([5])	24,510	761	19,267	4,892		31,661	
Dec. 31, 1956	([5])	23,714	775	18,454	4,529			31,790

[1] Outside Treasury and Federal Reserve Banks. Includes any paper currency held outside the continental limits of the United States. Totals for other end-of-month dates are shown in table above.

[2] Includes $155,039,431 held as reserve against United States notes and Treasury notes of 1890.

[3] To avoid duplication, amount of silver dollars and bullion held as security against silver certificates and Treasury notes of 1890 outstanding is not included in total Treasury currency outstanding.

[4] Less than $500,000.

[5] Because some of the types of currency shown are held as collateral or reserves against other types, a grand total of all types has no special significance and is not shown.

SOURCE: *Federal Reserve Bulletin*, February, 1958, p. 155.

was accepted in payment of war debts, and silver was bought and added to our monetary reserves under the provisions of the 1933 monetary legislation. Pressure existed to do more for silver, however, and Congress passed the Silver Purchase Act in June, 1934. This Act directed the Secretary of the Treasury to buy silver until the silver stocks were equal to one fourth of the combined silver and gold stocks or until silver increased in price to $1.29 an ounce, its former monetary value under bimetallism. Large amounts of silver were bought under this program. In 1939 Congress directed that the buying price should be 71.11 cents for all newly mined domestic silver, and in 1946 it fixed a minimum buying and selling price of 90.5 cents an ounce. Thus, even though the United States is on a limited gold-bullion standard, monetary reserves are kept in both gold and silver and the government continues to add to its silver stocks year by year.

THE PRESENT MONETARY SYSTEM OF THE UNITED STATES

The present monetary system of the United States is based on a limited gold-bullion standard. The dollar contains 13.71 grains, or one thirty-fifth of an ounce, of pure gold. Stated somewhat differently, gold is worth $35 an ounce for monetary purposes. The gold stocks of the country are held by the Treasury, and at the end of December of 1957 amounted to over $22 billion.[3] Gold certificates are issued against this gold and are held by the federal reserve banks and their agents.

Federal reserve notes issued by the federal reserve banks are obligations of the United States and also a first lien on all the assets of the federal reserve bank that issues them. They are secured by deposit with the federal reserve agent of at least 25 per cent backing in gold certificates and the remainder in any combination of eligible commercial paper, gold certificates, or direct obligations of the United States government. On December 31, 1957, almost $29 billion of federal reserve notes were in circulation.[4]

As a backing for silver certificates, the Treasury also has stocks of silver primarily in bullion form. It held over $2 billion of silver bullion on December 31, 1957, and almost $200 million of stand-

[3] *Federal Reserve Bulletin*, February, 1958, p. 155.
[4] *Ibid.*

ard silver dollars. There were also at this time $263 million of silver dollars in circulation. The silver stocks of the Treasury also serve as a backing for Treasury notes of 1890 issued under the Sherman Silver Purchase Act, which are being retired whenever they are received by banks or the Treasury.[5]

On December 31, 1957, there was also over $1.4 billion of subsidiary coins outstanding and $500 million of nickels and pennies.[6]

Data on each of these types of money and on the amounts of each held by the treasury, federal reserve banks and agents, and in circulation are shown in Table 21-1.

As of December 25, 1957, demand deposits in commercial banks were just under $109 billion dollars.[7]

QUESTIONS

1. Briefly trace the development of monetary standards.
2. Describe the operation of the gold-coin standard.
3. Describe the operation of the gold-bullion standard and the limited gold-bullion standard.
4. How does shifting from the gold-coin standard to a gold-bullion standard affect monetary management?
5. What is the gold-exchange standard? Why has it been used?
6. Describe the bimetallic standard. What are its advantages over a single-metal standard? its disadvantages?
7. What is an inconvertible paper standard? Why has it often been associated with inflation?
8. Describe the operation of a commodity standard. What problems would arise if such a standard were adopted?
9. Outline the various types of money in use in the United States. Discuss the nature and relative importance of each in our money supply.
10. Briefly trace American experience with monetary standards before World War I.
11. Discuss our experience with monetary standards from World War I to the present.
12. Describe our present monetary standard.

SUGGESTED READINGS

DEWEY, D. R. *Financial History of the United States.* New York: Longmans, Green & Company, Inc., 1924.

LAUGHLIN, J. L. *The History of Bimetallism in the United States.* New York: D. Appleton & Co., 1892.

"Monetary System of the United States," reprint from *Federal Reserve Bulletin,* February, 1953.

ROGERS, J. H. *America Weighs Her Gold.* New Haven: Yale University Press, 1931.

[5] *Ibid.*
[6] *Ibid.*
[7] *Federal Reserve Bulletin,* February, 1958, p. 156.

Chapter 22

Expansion and

Contraction of the

Money Supply

This chapter will consider the operation of the monetary system, especially the ways in which the supply of money can be expanded and contracted to meet the changing needs for funds. The supply of money can be changed by changing the supply of currency, or by changing the supply of deposit credit extended by the commercial banking system. The federal reserve banks can also increase or decrease the amount of money and credit in use, in part through the effect their policies have on the activities of commercial banks and in part through direct action. The federal government can also increase or decrease the money supply by means of its fiscal policies. Each of the factors affecting the supply of money will be considered in turn.

CHANGES IN THE MONETARY STOCK OF GOLD AND SILVER AND REPRESENTATIVE MONEY

Since the monetary system of this country is based on gold, changes in the gold supply can lead to changes in the total money supply. This is true not only directly because increases or decreases in the gold supply change the amount of money available, but also indirectly because federal reserve notes are backed in part by gold and more can be issued as the gold backing for doing so increases.

Changes in the Monetary Supply of Gold and Silver

The monetary supply of gold is increased whenever newly mined gold is sold to the Treasury Department. The gold is held in bullion form, and gold certificates can be issued against it. Since these certificates may legally be held only by the twelve federal reserve banks, the seller of gold receives for it some other form of currency, demand deposits, or federal reserve notes. Since little gold is mined domestically, most of the increase in the gold supply comes from foreign countries, especially South Africa.

Gold is also brought to this country or shipped out of it to settle balances in international transactions. Foreigners may pay us by transferring gold to this country, thus increasing our gold supply; or Americans may use gold obtained by application to the Treasury Department to make payments abroad. The actual transfer is usually handled through the New York Federal Reserve Bank, but the net effect is an increase or a decrease in the supply of monetary gold held by the Treasury.

The monetary gold stock of the United States increased rapidly during the thirties as a result of the gold buying policy of the Treasury. Since any gold presented to it was bought at $35 an ounce, in international financial operations an ounce of gold and $35 were kept equal in value. During World War II gold flowed out of this country to meet American purchases of goods abroad. After the war, this flow was reversed as the rest of the world looked to this country as a source of sorely needed food, machinery, and other goods. Gold started to flow out again as the United States government purchased goods abroad to carry on the Korean War. Table 22-1 shows the changes in the monetary gold stock in recent years. Especially noteworthy is the rapid increase in the thirties that laid the basis for the credit expansion during World War II.

Table 22–1

GOLD MONETARY STOCKS 1934-1957

(Dollar amounts in millions as of June 30)

1934	$ 7,856.2	1942	$22,736.7	1950	$24,230.7
1935	9,115.6	1943	22,387.5	1951	21,755.9
1936	10,608.4	1944	21,173.1	1952	23,346.5
1937	12,318.3	1945	20,213.0	1953	22,462.8
1938	12,963.0	1946	20,269.9	1954	21,927.0
1939	16,110.1	1947	21,266.5	1955	21,677.6
1940	19,963.1	1948	23,532.5	1956	21,799.1
1941	22,624.2	1949	24,466.3	1957	22,622.9

SOURCE: *Treasury Bulletin.*

As a rule when gold is turned into the Treasury Department either by domestic producers or by foreign central banks through the federal reserve banks, the balances held in bank accounts increase. Such additional new or primary reserves provide the basis for further expansion of the money supply as will be explained later.

Sterilization of Gold Imports. This addition to the deposits and the reserves of the banking system can be counterbalanced by an action of the Treasury Department known as *sterilization of gold imports.* Under the normal procedure the gold is paid for by issuing gold certificates to one of the federal reserve banks. When the Treasury desires to sterilize gold imports, however, payment for the gold is made from other government funds. Thus the increased funds arising in the banking system from gold purchases by the Treasury are offset by an equal amount of funds withdrawn by tax collections or borrowing. This process of sterilization of gold imports was carried on for several years during the thirties to offset some of the inflationary potential resulting from large-scale gold purchases.

Changes in Silver Stocks. The money supply can also be increased by increases in the monetary silver stocks. The present silver purchase program of the Treasury dates back to the Silver Purchase Act of 1934. Under this Act the Secretary of the Treasury was directed, at his discretion, to purchase silver at a price not in excess of $1.29 an ounce.[1] The plan was to purchase silver until at a value of $1.29 an ounce it was equal to one fourth of the combined gold and silver monetary stocks of the country. Later legislation removed the discretion of the Secretary as to purchases and directed him to buy all silver offered by domestic producers at a set price. The price for all domestic silver mined after July 1, 1946, was set at 90.5 cents per fine ounce. This legislation also authorized the Treasury to sell any "free" silver not needed to back silver certificates at a price not less than the buying price, and the Treasury set a selling price of 91 cents per fine ounce.

Just as gold purchases are made by issuing gold certificates, the Secretary of the Treasury pays for silver by the issuance of silver

---

[1] He was to pay not more than 50 cents per ounce for silver stocks existing in the United States on May 1, 1934.

Table 22–2

SILVER MONETARY STOCKS 1934-1955

(Dollar amounts in millions as of June 30)

1934	$ 898.2	1942	$4,306.3	1950	$3,671.5
1935	1,463.1	1943	3,298.5	1951	3,718.5
1936	2,249.5	1944	3,947.9	1952	3,768.5
1937	2,542.1	1945	3,685.8	1953	3,814.3
1938	3,066.4	1946	3,508.4	1954	3,863.1
1939	3,605.2	1947	3,525.7	1955	3,922.4
1940	3,939.6	1948	3,571.0	1956	3,994.5
1941	4,148.7	1949	3,618.3	1957	4,116.6

SOURCE: *Treasury Bulletin.*

certificates. He may issue silver certificates in an amount up to $1.29 for each ounce of silver purchased, but he has done so only for the actual purchase price. The purchase of silver, just as of gold, places new funds into the economic system and adds to bank reserves. Thus it not only increases the money supply but also provides the basis for credit expansion.

Silver purchases could be sterilized by using other government funds to pay for them, but this has not been considered necessary since the amount involved annually is small in relationship to total money supply. When the Treasury sells silver as it did to relieve the shortage for nonmonetary uses during World War II, the money supply is reduced and so are bank deposits and credit expansion potentials.

Changes in the Volume of Federal Reserve Notes

Although silver and silver certificates are used in day-to-day transactions, the total volume is small compared with the amount of federal reserve notes in circulation. These notes may be issued by the Federal Reserve System with a backing of at least 25 per cent in gold certificates and 75 per cent in commercial paper, United States government bonds, or additional gold certificates. As the level of business activity increases, the volume of commercial paper also increases, thus increasing the backing available for the issuance of federal reserve notes. The use of notes and drafts is not common in American business transactions, however, and as a result the commercial paper held by the banking system has fallen far short of monetary needs. Federal reserve notes, therefore, have been backed to a large extent by government bonds and gold certificates. On January 29, 1958, for example, the backing for $29.5 billion in federal reserve notes was $12.3 billion of gold certificates, $49.1 million of eligible paper, and $17.2 billion of United States government securities.[2]

The volume of federal reserve notes has increased to meet the needs of the country for currency. The largest increases took place during World War II, although there was a fairly rapid rate of increase beginning in 1933. The increases before 1933, except for a brief period during World War I, were largely to meet the needs of an increasing population and a rising standard of living. Part of the increase after 1933 was due to government efforts to raise the level of economic activity. During World War II a major part of the increase was due to the rapid increases in the volume of payments resulting from war activities.

Before the onset of the 1929 depression, the backing for federal reserve notes was gold and commercial paper. The volume of commercial paper was large enough and grew rapidly enough to permit increases in this part of the money supply to keep pace with the increasing level of business activity. During the depression the supply of commercial paper in the portfolios of the federal reserve banks dropped to a level so low that extra gold had to be used as backing for federal reserve notes. When gold flowed out of the country due to the uncertainties of the world economic situation, it became almost impossible to provide sufficient monetary backing. As a result Congress passed the Glass-Steagall Act in 1932 that permitted government bonds to be used along with gold and commercial paper as backing for federal reserve notes. Since that time government bonds have been used to an increasing extent as backing for the federal reserve bank currency. This made possible the large increases in currency needed during World War II when the volume of commercial paper did not increase materially.

Federal reserve notes still maintain their elastic character even though they are not tied to changes in business volume as directly as when they were backed to a large extent by commercial paper. The supply does expand and contract, however, to meet changes in the demand for funds. For example, when the Christmas shop-

2 *Federal Reserve Bulletin*, February, 1958, p. 153.

ping season ends, the public has less need for funds, and money accumulated in the hands of businessmen is deposited in their banks. The commercial banks turn these excess funds over to their federal reserve bank, which exchanges the excess federal reserve notes for its collateral with the federal reserve agent, thus reducing the supply of federal reserve notes.

Federal reserve notes have also become elastic with respect to government deficit expenditures. As the government debt grows, more bonds are available to be used as collateral for federal reserve notes. Therefore, when large-scale government operations, such as those of World War II, result in a greatly increased demand for currency, the basis exists for meeting this demand by the issuance of additional federal reserve notes as long as the gold supply is adequate to meet the 25 per cent reserve requirement. The amount of federal reserve notes in circulation at present is far short of the volume that could be issued on the basis of present gold reserve requirements and monetary gold stocks.

THE EXPANSION AND CONTRACTION OF DEPOSIT CREDIT

The supply of money is much larger than the supply of currency since the largest part of the dollar volume of transactions is carried on by means of checks drawn against demand deposits. Demand deposits are a part of the total money supply that can be spent at will. At the end of December of 1957, the volume of demand deposits was almost $110 billion while the total currency outside banks was about $32 billion.

The banking system of the United States can expand and contract the volume of deposit credit as the needs for funds by individuals, businesses, and governments change. The process by which this is done is not easily understood from a study of the operations of an individual bank but requires a study of the operations of the banks as units in a banking system. Furthermore, an understanding of this process requires a study of the relationship of bank loans to deposits and to bank reserves.

In analyzing the process of bank credit expansion, it is helpful to make a distinction between primary deposits and derivative deposits. The former arise whenever cash and all forms of checks drawn against other banks are placed on deposit in a bank.

or whenever a bank receives money from a bond coupon or other item left for collection. The derivative deposit arises out of a credit to a depositor's account when he receives a bank loan. Since most businessmen pay all their bills by check except for petty cash items, they do not withdraw the loan funds but leave them on deposit and write checks against them. The commercial banks must keep reserves against their deposits irrespective of whether they are primary or derivative.

Credit Expansion

When reserves were first required by law, the purpose was to assure depositors that the bank had the ability to meet their needs for the withdrawal of cash. The minimum reserves required by law today, however, must be kept with the federal reserve banks. They cannot be used to meet demands for cash, except to a limited extent as required reserves are freed when deposits are reduced. The basic function they serve is to regulate the credit expansion process since such reserves must be set aside for all deposits.

The process of credit creation takes place as a result of the operations of the whole system of banks, but it arises out of the independent transactions of individual banks. To explain the process, therefore, the loan activities of a single bank will first be considered without regard to their effects on other banks, and then in relationship to a system of banks. This approach is somewhat artificial since a bank practically never acts independently of the actions of other banks, but it has been adopted to clarify the process. Furthermore, it helps to explain the belief of many bankers that they cannot create credit since they only loan funds placed on deposit in their bank by their depositors. This analysis shows how a system of banks in which each bank is carrying on its local activities can do what an individual banker cannot do.

For illustration, let us assume that a bank which must keep reserves of 20 per cent against deposits receives a primary deposit of $10,000. The bank statement, ignoring all other items, would then show the following:

ASSETS		LIABILITIES	
Reserves	$10,000	Deposits	$10,000

Against this new deposit of $10,000, the bank must keep required reserves of 20 per cent or $2,000, so that it has $8,000 of excess reserves available.

It may appear at first glance as if the banker could proceed to make loans for $40,000 since all he needs is a 20 per cent reserve against the resulting demand deposits. If he attempted to do this, however, he would soon find himself in difficulty. Since bank loans are usually obtained just prior to the demand for funds, checks would undoubtedly be written against the deposit accounts almost at once. Many of these checks would be deposited in other banks, and the bank would be faced with a demand for cash as checks were presented for collection. This demand could reach the full $40,000. Since the bank has only $8,000 to meet it, it could not follow such a course and remain in business.

The amount that the banker can safely lend is the $8,000 of excess reserves. If he lends more, he runs the risk of having to make payments on checks that he cannot meet. After such a loan, his books would show the following situation:

Assets		Liabilities	
Reserves	$10,000	Deposits	$18,000
Loans and discounts.	8,000		

If a check were written for the full amount of the derivative deposit ($8,000) and sent to a bank in another city for deposit, the lending bank would lose all of its excess reserves. This may be seen from its books, which would appear as follows:

Assets		Liabilities	
Reserves	$ 2,000	Deposits	$10,000
Loans and discounts.	8,000		

In practice a bank may be able to loan somewhat more than the $8,000 since banks frequently require their customers to keep an average deposit balance of something in the neighborhood of 20 per cent of the loan. The whole of the additional $2,000 cannot safely be loaned since an average balance of $2,000 does not prevent the full amount of the loan being used for a period of time. With an average balance in each derivative deposit account, however, all accounts will not be drawn to zero at the same time and some additional funds are available for loans.

It may be argued that a banker will feel sure that some checks written against his bank will be redeposited in his bank and that he can therefore lend larger sums. The banker, however, since his is one of approximately 14,000 banks, can usually not anticipate such redeposits of funds, and he cannot run the risk of being caught short of reserves. Thus, when an individual bank receives a new primary deposit, it cannot lend the full amount of that deposit but only the amount available as excess reserves. From the point of view of an individual bank, therefore, credit creation appears impossible. Since a part of every new deposit cannot be loaned out due to reserve requirements, the volume of additional loans is less than new primary deposits.

Credit Expansion in an Economy with Two Banks

What cannot be done by an individual bank is being done by the banking system when many banks are expanding loans and derivative deposits at the same time. To illustrate this point, assume that we have an economy with just two banks, A and B. This example can be realistic if we assume further that Bank A represents one bank in the system and Bank B, all other banks combined. Bank A, as in our previous example, receives a new primary deposit of $10,000 and is required to keep reserves of 20 per cent against deposits. Its books would then appear as follows:

BANK A

ASSETS		LIABILITIES	
Reserves $10,000		Deposits $10,000	

A loan for $8,000 is made and credited to the account of the borrower as follows:

BANK A

ASSETS		LIABILITIES	
Reserves $10,000		Deposits $18,000	
Loans and discounts. 8,000			

Assume that a check is drawn against it almost immediately and deposited in Bank B. The books of the two banks would then show the following:

Bank *A*

Assets		Liabilities	
Reserves	$ 2,000	Deposits	$10,000
Loans and discounts.	8,000		

Bank *B*

Reserves	$ 8,000	Deposits	$ 8,000

The derivative deposit arising out of a loan from Bank *A* has now been transferred by check to Bank *B* where it is received as a primary deposit. Bank *B* must now set aside 20 per cent as required reserves and may lend or reinvest the remainder. Its books after such a loan would appear as follows:

Bank *B*

(After a loan equal to its excess reserves)

Assets		Liabilities	
Reserves	$ 8,000	Deposits	$14,400
Loans and discounts.	6,400		

Assume that a check is drawn against the derivative deposit of $6,400 arising out of the loan by Bank *B*. This reduces its reserves and deposits as follows:

Bank *B*

Assets		Liabilities	
Reserves	$ 1,600	Deposits	$ 8,000
Loans and discounts.	6,400		

The check for $6,400 will most likely be deposited in a bank, in our example in Bank *A* or Bank *B* itself, since we have assumed that only two banks existed. In the American banking system it may be deposited in one of the approximately 14,000 banks in the system.

This process of credit expansion can take place in the same way when a bank buys securities as when it makes a loan. Assume, as we did in the case of a bank loan, the following situation in Bank *A*:

Bank *A*

Assets		Liabilities	
Reserves	$10,000	Deposits	$10,000

Securities costing $8,000 are purchased and the proceeds credited to the account of the seller, giving the following situation:

BANK *A*

ASSETS		LIABILITIES	
Reserves	$10,000	Deposits	$18,000
Investments	8,000		

Assume that a check is drawn against the deposit and is deposited in Bank *B*. The books of the two banks would then show the following:

BANK *A*

ASSETS		LIABILITIES	
Reserves	$ 2,000	Deposits	$10,000
Investments	8,000		

BANK *B*

ASSETS		LIABILITIES	
Reserves	$ 8,000	Deposits	$ 8,000

Just as in the case of a loan the derivative deposit has been transferred to Bank *B* where it is received as a primary deposit.

At each stage in the process, 20 per cent of the new primary deposit becomes required reserves and 80 per cent excess reserves that can be loaned out. In time, the whole of the original $10,000 primary deposit will have become required reserves and $50,000 of deposits will have been credited to deposit accounts of which $40,000 will have been loaned out.

Required reserves may be above or below 20 per cent for central reserve cities and may be not over 20 per cent for reserve city banks and not above 14 per cent for country banks. Average required reserves in the United States probably approximate 15 per cent. The possibilities of credit creation with a 15 per cent required reserve is shown in Table 22-3.

Offsetting Factors

The process of credit creation can go on only to the extent that the activities described actually take place. If for any reason the proceeds of a loan are withdrawn from the banking system, no new deposit arises to continue the process. A new deposit of $10,000 permits loans of $8,000 under a 20 per cent required re-

Table 22–3

THE MULTIPLYING CAPACITY OF MONEY IN BANK OR COMMODITY TRANSACTIONS

		Amount Received or Deposited	Amount Lent	Amount for Legal Reserves
Transaction	1	$100.00	$ 85.00	$ 15.00
	2	85.00	72.25	12.75
	3	72.25	61.41	10.84
	4	61.41	52.20	9.21
	5	52.20	44.37	7.83
	6	44.37	37.71	6.66
	7	37.71	32.05	5.66
	8	32.05	27.24	4.81
	9	27.24	23.15	4.09
	10	23.15	19.68	3.47
	11	19.68	16.73	2.95
	12	16.73	14.22	2.51
	13	14.22	12.09	2.13
	14	12.09	10.28	1.81
	15	10.28	8.74	1.54
	16	8.74	7.43	1.31
	17	7.43	6.32	1.11
	18	6.32	5.37	.95
	19	5.37	4.56	.81
	20	4.56	3.88	.68
Total for	20	$640.80	$544.68	$ 96.12
Additional transactions		25.86	21.98	3.88
Grand total		$666.66	$566.66	$100.00

SOURCE: Board of Governors of the Federal Reserve System, *The Federal Reserve System—Its Purposes and Functions,* Washington, D. C., 1947, p. 18.

serve; but if this $8,000 were used in currency transactions without being deposited in a bank, no credit could be created. It is the custom of carrying on business by means of checks which are deposited on the same or next business day after they are received that makes credit creation possible.

In the examples above, no allowance was made for currency withdrawal. In actual practice, as the volume of business in the economy increases, some additional cash is withdrawn for hand-to-hand circulation and to meet the needs of business for petty cash. Larger balances are also kept in the deposit accounts of businesses and individuals. Banks likewise must keep larger sums to meet day-to-day needs for funds and thus must keep larger till reserves over and above the required reserves.

Money may also be withdrawn from the banking system to meet the demand for payments to foreign countries, or foreign banks may withdraw some of the money they are holding on deposit in American banks. The United States Treasury may withdraw funds it has on deposit in commercial banks. The volume of demand deposits may be reduced because individuals shift some of their funds into time deposits or savings accounts. All of these factors reduce the multiplying capacity of primary deposits.

Furthermore, this process can go on only if excess reserves are actually being loaned by the banks. This means that banks must be willing to lend the full amount of their excess reserves, and that acceptable borrowers must be available who have a demand for credit.

Contraction of Credit

When the need for funds by business decreases, this process can work in reverse. Expansion takes place as long as the demand for new bank loans exceeds the repayment of old loans. When old loans are being repaid faster than new loans are being granted and banks are not immediately investing the funds so freed, contraction of the supply of deposit credit will take place.

Let us assume that Bank A has no excess reserves and see the effect of the repayment of a loan. Before the borrower began to build up deposits to repay the loan, its books were as follows:

BANK A

ASSETS		LIABILITIES	
Reserves	$ 2,000	Deposits	$10,000
Loans and discounts.	8,000		

The borrower of the $8,000 must build up his deposit account by $8,000 in order to be able to repay the loan. This is reflected on the books as follows:

BANK A

ASSETS		LIABILITIES	
Reserves	$10,000	Deposits	$18,000
Loans and discounts.	8,000		

After the $8,000 loan is repaid, the books show the following:

ASSETS		LIABILITIES	
Reserves	$10,000	Deposits	$10,000

If no new loan is made from the $10,000 of reserves, credit contraction will result. This is true because $8,000 of funds have been taken out of the banking system to build up deposits to repay the loan and are now being held idle by Bank *A* as excess reserves. The result of taking out $8,000 of reserves may be cumulative on the contraction side just as it was during expansion.

Assume that the $8,000 of deposits built up to repay the loan came from Bank *B*, which before these funds were withdrawn had no excess reserves and showed the following situation on its books:

BANK *B*

ASSETS		LIABILITIES	
Reserves	$ 2,000	Deposits	$10,000
Loans and discounts.	8,000		

The withdrawal of $8,000 of deposits would require a sale of securities that might be held by the bank or a loan from its federal reserve bank or from another bank that might have excess funds to lend. If we assume that a loan was made, its book would appear as follows:

BANK *B*

ASSETS		LIABILITIES	
Reserves	$ 400	Deposits	$ 2,000
Loans and discounts.	8,000	Loan from federal reserve bank	6,400

Reserves must remain at $400 since this amount is the required reserve on the $2,000 of deposits. In order to pay off its debt to the federal reserve bank, this bank will probably refuse to renew the $8,000 loan when it comes due. In order to pay the loan, the borrower builds up his deposit by $8,000. The books now appear as follows:

BANK *B*

ASSETS		LIABILITIES	
Reserves	$ 8,400	Deposits	$10,000
Loans and discounts.	8,000	Loan from federal reserve bank	6,400

This enables the bank to pay its loan to the federal reserve bank as follows:

BANK *B*

ASSETS		LIABILITIES	
Reserves	$ 2,000	Deposits	$10,000
Loans and discounts.	8,000		

After the $8,000 loan from the bank is repaid the situation is as follows:

BANK *B*

ASSETS		LIABILITIES	
Reserves	$ 2,000	Deposits	$ 2,000

In building up the $8,000 deposit to repay the loan, the lender took $8,000 out of another bank in the system. This in turn led this bank to refuse to renew loans for this amount, and in building up deposit balances to repay the loans, funds were withdrawn from other banks. This process of contraction is thus cumulative just as the process of expansion is, nor can it be stopped if a bank sells securities to meet a demand for funds it does not have available as excess reserves. When securities are sold, the purchaser will withdraw funds from some bank in the system to pay for them, thus leading to contraction just as when the adjustment to a deficiency in reserves is a loan from the federal reserve bank that is repaid by reducing the amount of loans outstanding.

EXPANSION AND CONTRACTION THROUGH THE FEDERAL RESERVE SYSTEM

The expansion of credit can be carried even further through the operations of the Federal Reserve System. Under present laws the federal reserve banks are required to keep reserves of 25 per cent in gold certificates against federal reserve notes and against the deposits of member banks. These deposits consist of the required reserves and such excess reserves as member banks choose to leave at their federal reserve bank. The federal reserve banks can make new reserves available to the banking system by means of loans and advances to member banks, the purchase of securities or commercial paper in the open market, or by accepting currency that has been deposited in the banks and is no longer needed to meet the demands of the customers of the bank.

If a member bank has used up all of its excess reserves except for vault cash needed to meet the day-to-day demands of depositors, it can obtain additional funds to loan to businessmen by borrowing from its federal reserve bank. It may do this by discounting notes in its possession or by getting a loan, using bonds or commercial paper as collateral. In fact, the federal reserve banks may make a loan to a member bank based on any sound assets as collateral. These funds will then be available to the banking system as additional primary deposits and can result in additional credit expansion by the system of banks.

The Federal Reserve System through its Open Market Committee may take the initiative by buying securities in the open market. This is usually done by purchasing government bonds, especially short-term obligations. Such funds will also add to the primary reserves of the banking system.

Credit can similarly be contracted when the Federal Reserve System sells securities and thus takes funds out of the commercial banking system.

CREDIT CREATION BY MEANS OF GOVERNMENT DEFICIT FINANCING

Since 1933, and especially during World War II, one of the most important sources of credit expansion has been the deficit financing of the United States Treasury. This process can best be explained by a description of the techniques used to finance World War II deficits. During the first year of the war the commercial banks bought about half of all war bonds issued by the Treasury. After 1942 the banks were no longer allowed to buy the savings series of war bonds directly, but they were encouraged to invest in short-term government obligations, that is, Treasury bills issued for three months and Treasury certificates issued for a year. The commercial banks kept most of their excess reserves in such short-term government obligations. In addition to not being able to buy bonds directly from the Treasury, the banks also could not hold bonds that had maturities more than ten years in the future.

There is normally an inverse relationship between bond prices and interest rates. As interest rates rise, the price of bonds that are outstanding falls; and as interest rates fall, the price of such bonds rises. The change in price is just great enough so that the yield on the currently outstanding bonds would be the same if they were held to maturity as the yield on newly issued bonds of the same quality. An investor, for example, who held a 10-year, $1,000 bond paying 4 per cent interest would not sell it for $1,000 if interest rates had dropped and the same quality of bonds were being issued currently at $3\frac{1}{2}$ per cent interest. Nor could he expect to get $1,000 for his bond if interest rates had risen so that newly issued bonds of the same quality were now paying $4\frac{1}{2}$ per cent.

When interest rates change, the price of bonds currently outstanding changes until an investor buying such bonds receives exactly the same yield if he holds them to maturity as he does on newly issued bonds of the same quality. This means that the change in price becomes greater as the number of years to maturity of the bond increases. An example will help show why this happens. Suppose a bond pays 4 per cent or $40 per year on a $1,000 bond. If interest rates rise to 4.5 per cent, a new bond of like quality will pay $45 a year. If the bond has two years to run, a prospective purchaser will pay about $990 for it since he will be about equally well off whether he buys this bond at $990 and gets an extra $10 when he is paid $1,000 at maturity or buys a new bond at $1,000. (*Old bond:* $40 a year interest for 2 years = $80 + $10 received at maturity = $90. *New bond:* $45 interest for 2 years = $90.) The price a prospective borrower can afford to pay for the bond decreases the longer the period to maturity since the $5 a year smaller interest payment is received for more years.

During World War II the normal expectation was for interest rates to rise due to the increased demand for funds and for bond prices to decline. The banks were assured that such price declines would not occur since the federal reserve authorities adopted a policy of purchasing all government bonds on demand at par or above. This policy of supporting government bonds at par or above was adopted to aid the sale of war bonds by eliminating the fear of drastic price declines should interest rates rise. Many bond buyers remembered the record of the Liberty Bonds used in financing World War I, which fell to $820 for a $1,000 bond in 1920, as interest rates rose in the postwar period. To assure the sale of World War II bonds, therefore, especially at the low interest rate pattern which existed at the beginning of the war, the Treasury felt that a commitment to redeem all bonds at par or above on demand was essential. This policy facilitated the credit creation that resulted from the deficits of the federal government. Since war bonds paid materially higher interest rates than Treasury bills or certificates and carried no risk of a price decline below par, the banks naturally preferred to have them in their portfolios.

Between the war bond drives, therefore, the banks bought bonds from private investors, usually paying them a premium due to their large demand for such bonds. To get the funds to buy these bonds, the banks sold their holdings of bills and certificates to the Federal Reserve. This process added new funds made available by the Federal Reserve to the supply of money. Since the funds received by the bondholders who sold their securities to the banks were also usually redeposited, there was little loss of funds by the banks from the process. The funds received from the Federal Reserve for the bills and certificates thus were additional funds. These new funds were new reserves that formed the basis for multiple credit expansion as they were spread throughout the banking system and thus also the basis for additional purchases of government securities by the commercial banks.

Such credit creation by means of monetizing the debt was used extensively to finance World War II. During the war, reserve bank holdings of United States obligations increased by over $20 billion and bank holdings by over $80 billion.[3]

CONSOLIDATED CONDITION STATEMENT FOR BANKS AND THE MONETARY SYSTEM

The various factors that have been dicussed, which tend to expand the money supply and to contract it, may be summarized as follows:

FACTORS TENDING TO INCREASE THE MONEY SUPPLY

1. Increase in the monetary gold stock.
2. Increase in treasury currency outstanding.
3. Increase in federal reserve holdings of loans and securities.
4. Increase in commercial bank holdings of loans and securities.
5. Decrease in foreign deposits.
6. Decrease in Treasury holdings of cash and deposits.
7. Decrease in time and savings deposits.
8. Decrease of capital accounts of the banks.

[3] *Federal Reserve Bulletin*, January, 1952, p. 50.

FACTORS TENDING TO DECREASE THE MONEY SUPPLY

1. Decrease in the monetary gold stock.
2. Decrease in treasury currency outstanding.
3. Decrease in federal reserve holdings of loans and securities.
4. Decrease in commercial bank holdings of loans and securities.
5. Increase in foreign deposits.
6. Increase in Treasury holdings of cash and deposits.
7. Increase in time and savings deposits.
8. Increase of capital accounts of the banks.

Since so many factors affect the supply of money, it is helpful to have data on all of them in summary form so as to be able to analyze the changes that have taken place. Such information is published monthly in the *Federal Reserve Bulletin* in the form of a Consolidated Condition Statement for Banks and the Monetary System. This statement shows a balance between the assets of the banking and monetary system and the liabilities in the form of deposits and currency and the capital accounts of the banks. The items on each side of this equation are as follows:

ASSETS

Gold
Treasury currency outstanding
Bank credit
    Loans
    Investment in U. S. Government securities
    Investments in other securities

LIABILITIES AND CAPITAL

Capital and miscellaneous accounts
Foreign bank deposits
U. S. government balances
Demand deposits
Time deposits
Currency outside banks

Table 22-4 shows this Consolidated Condition Statement for various midyear and year-end dates between 1929 and the middle of 1957.

By studying the increases and the decreases in each of these items, it is possible to see the method by which the money supply has been expanded or contracted, and by studying figures for a period of time, to see trends being developed. For example, the

Table 22-4

CONSOLIDATED CONDITION STATEMENT FOR BANKS AND THE MONETARY SYSTEM [1]

[Figures Partly Estimated Except on Call Dates. In Millions of Dollars]

| DATE | ASSETS | | BANK CREDIT | | U. S. GOVERNMENT OBLIGATIONS | | | | | TOTAL ASSETS, NET—TOTAL LIABILITIES AND CAPITAL, NET | LIABILITIES AND CAPITAL | |
	GOLD	TREASURY CURRENCY OUTSTANDING	TOTAL	LOANS, NET	TOTAL	COMMERCIAL AND SAVINGS BANKS	FEDERAL RESERVE BANKS	OTHER	OTHER SECURITIES		TOTAL DEPOSITS AND CURRENCY	CAPITAL AND MISC. ACCOUNTS, NET
1929—June 29	4,037	2,019	58,642	41,082	5,741	5,499	216	26	11,819	64,698	55,776	8,922
1933—June 30	4,031	2,286	42,148	21,957	10,328	8,199	1,998	131	9,863	48,465	42,029	6,436
1939—Dec. 30	17,644	2,963	54,564	22,157	23,105	19,417	2,484	1,204	9,302	75,171	68,359	6,812
1911—Dec. 31	22,737	3,247	64,653	26,605	29,049	25,511	2,254	1,284	8,999	90,637	82,811	7,826
1945—Dec. 31	20,065	4,339	167,381	30,387	128,417	101,288	24,262	2,867	8,577	191,785	180,806	10,979
1947—Dec. 31	22,754	4,562	160,832	43,023	107,086	81,199	22,559	3,328	10,723	188,148	175,348	12,800
1950—Dec. 30	22,706	4,636	171,667	60,366	96,560	72,894	20,778	2,888	14,741	199,009	184,384	14,624
1952—Dec. 31	23,187	4,812	192,866	75,484	100,008	72,740	24,697	2,571	17,374	220,865	204,220	16,647
1954—Dec. 31	21,713	4,985	210,988	85,730	104,819	77,728	24,932	2,159	20,439	237,686	218,882	18,806
1955—Dec. 31	21,690	5,008	217,437	100,031	96,736	70,052	24,785	1,899	20,670	244,135	224,943	19,193
1956—June 30	21,799	5,032	216,563	105,420	90,511	64,917	23,758	1,836	20,632	243,394	223,585	19,807
1956—Dec. 31	21,949	5,066	223,742	110,120	93,161	66,523	24,915	1,723	20,461	250,757	230,510	20,246
1957—June 26*	22,600	5,100	222,200	113,000	87,800	63,400	22,900	1,600	21,400	249,900	229,100	20,900

DETAILS OF DEPOSITS AND CURRENCY

| DATE | U. S. GOVERNMENT BALANCES | | | | DEPOSITS ADJUSTED AND CURRENCY | | | | | | | SEASONALLY ADJUSTED SERIES [5] | | |
| | FOREIGN BANK DEPOSITS, NET | TREASURY CASH HOLDINGS | AT COMMERCIAL AND SAVINGS BANKS | AT F. R. BANKS | TOTAL | TIME DEPOSITS [2] | | | | DEMAND DEPOSITS [4] | CURRENCY OUTSIDE BANKS | TOTAL DEMAND DEPOSITS ADJUSTED AND CURRENCY | DEMAND DEPOSITS ADJUSTED | CURRENCY OUTSIDE BANKS |
						TOTAL	COMMERCIAL BANKS	MUTUAL SAVINGS BANKS [3]	POSTAL SAVINGS SYSTEM					
1929—June 29	365	204	381	36	54,790	28,611	19,557	8,905	149	22,540	3,639	......	......	......
1933—June 30	50	264	852	35	40,828	21,656	10,849	9,621	1,186	14,411	4,761	......	......	......
1939—Dec. 30	1,217	2,409	846	634	63,254	27,059	15,258	10,523	1,278	29,793	6,401	......	......	......
1941—Dec. 31	1,498	2,215	1,895	867	76,336	27,729	15,884	10,532	1,313	38,992	9,615	......	......	......
1945—Dec. 31	2,141	2,287	24,608	977	150,793	48,452	30,135	15,385	2,932	75,851	26,490	......	......	......
1947—Dec. 31	1,682	1,336	1,452	870	170,008	56,411	35,249	17,746	3,416	87,121	26,476	111,100	85,200	25,900
1950—Dec. 30	2,518	1,293	2,989	668	176,916	59,247	36,314	20,009	2,923	92,272	25,398	114,300	89,800	24,500
1952—Dec. 31	2,501	1,270	5,259	389	194,801	65,799	40,666	22,586	2,547	101,508	27,494	124,700	97,800	26,900
1954—Dec. 31	3,329	796	4,510	563	209,684	75,282	46,844	26,302	2,136	106,550	27,852	129,700	102,800	26,900
1955—Dec. 31	3,167	767	4,038	394	216,577	78,378	48,359	28,129	1,890	109,914	28,285	133,200	105,800	27,400
1956—June 30	3,115	768	5,537	522	213,643	80,615	49,698	29,152	1,765	104,744	28,284	134,300	106,700	27,600
1956—Dec. 31	3,306	775	4,038	441	221,950	82,224	50,577	30,000	1,647	111,391	28,335	134,400	106,700	27,700
1957—June 26* ...	3,400	800	4,800	500	219,700	86,400	54,000	30,900	1,500	105,600	27,800	135,200	107,300	27,900

* Preliminary.

[1] Represents all commercial and savings banks, Federal Reserve Banks, Postal Savings System, and Treasury currency funds (the gold account, Treasury currency account, and Exchange Stabilization Fund).

[2] Excludes interbank time deposits; U. S. Treasurer's time deposits, open account; and deposits of Postal Savings System in banks.

[3] Prior to June 30, 1947, includes a small amount of demand deposits.

[4] Demand deposits other than interbank and U. S. Govt., less cash items reported as in process of collection.

[5] Seasonally adjusted series begin in 1947 and are available only for last Wednesday of the month. For back figures, see BULLETIN for July 1957, pp. 828-829.

SOURCE: *Federal Reserve Bulletin*, January, 1958, p. 40.

period from December 31, 1941, to December 31, 1945, the period
of World War II, shows the following increases and decreases in
the various accounts in the statement:

ASSETS

		MILLIONS OF DOLLARS
Gold		— 2,672
Treasury currency		+ 1,092
Loans		+ 3,782
U. S. government obligations		
Commercial and savings banks	+75,777	
Federal reserve banks	+22,008	
Other banks	+ 1,583	+ 99,368
Other securities		— 422
		+101,148

LIABILITIES AND CAPITAL

Capital accounts	+ 3,153
Foreign bank deposits	+ 643
U. S. government balances	+ 22,895
Demand deposits	+ 36,859
Time deposits	+ 20,725
Currency outside banks	+ 16,875
	+101,150 *

* Figures do not total exactly the same due to rounding.

From these figures it is apparent that the major factor leading
to an increase in the money supply was bank investment in United
States government obligations, although some increase also took
place in bank loans to business and in the supply of treasury
currency. This increase in bank holding of treasury obligations
made possible the large increases in United States government
balances, demand deposits, time deposits, and currency outside
banks.

It is interesting and informative to see the contrast in the
picture during the inflationary period of the Korean War. The
increases and decreases that occurred between June 30, 1950, and
December 26, 1951, are shown at the top of page 473.

During this period the major source of the expansion of purchasing power was loans, although the purchase of securities other
than those of the government also provided a sizable sum. Bank
reserves were cut down by the loss of gold. In order for the banks
to get excess reserves to start the process of credit expansion, they
sold over $5 billion of government obligations to the federal re-

Assets

		Millions of Dollars
Gold		— 1,631
Treasury currency		+ 93
Loans		+15,701
U. S. Government obligations		
Commercial and savings banks	—5,620	
Federal reserve banks	+5,169	
Other banks	— 358	— 809
Other securities		+ 2,160
		+15,514

Liabilities and Capital

Capital accounts	+ 1,082
Foreign bank deposits	— 255
U. S. Government balances	— 1,049
Demand deposits	+13,060
Time deposits	+ 1,461
Currency outside banks	+ 1,115
	+15,414

serve banks. The major part of the credit expansion during this period was in the form of demand deposits, although currency outside banks and time deposits also increased.

There is thus a decided difference between the credit creation of the two periods. During World War II it took place primarily through the sale of government obligations to the banking system, whereas during the Korean War it occurred largely because of the extension of bank loans to business. Studies of figures in the consolidated condition statement can be used during any period to show what is happening in the monetary and credit system, and especially the extent and type of inflationary pressures being developed.

QUESTIONS

1. Explain how changes in the gold supply can change the money supply.
2. What is meant by sterilization of gold imports? How does it affect the money supply?
3. Explain how changes in the supply of silver can change the money supply.
4. How is the supply of federal reserve notes expanded and contracted to meet the needs of the economy?
5. Trace the effect on its accounts of a loan made by a bank that has excess reserves available from new deposits.

6. Describe the process of credit expansion in an economy with two banks.
7. Explain how credit expansion can take place when a bank buys securities.
8. Explain the potential for credit expansion when required reserves average 15 per cent.
9. Discuss the various factors that affect the potential for credit expansion.
10. Explain the process of credit contraction.
11. Explain the role of the Federal Reserve System in credit expansion and contraction.
12. How may government financing lead to credit expansion? How was this done during World War II?
13. Summarize the factors that can lead to an increase in the money supply. A decrease.
14. Compare and contrast the factors that led to an increase in the money supply during World War II and during the Korean War.

SUGGESTED READINGS

Board of Governors of the Federal Reserve System. *The Federal Reserve System—Its Purposes and Functions.* Washington, D. C.: Board of Governors, 1954. Chapters 2, 6, 7, 8.

Currie, L. *The Supply and Control of Money in the United States.* Cambridge: Harvard University Press, 1934.

Phillips, C. A. *Bank Credit.* New York: The Macmillan Co., 1926.

Shaw, E. S. *Money, Income, and Monetary Policy.* Homewood, Illinois: Richard D. Irwin, Inc., 1950.

Chapter 23

Federal Reserve

Instruments of Monetary

and Credit Control

Control over the monetary and credit policies of the country is shared today by the Board of Governors of the Federal Reserve System and various agencies of the United States government, especially the Treasury Department. When the Federal Reserve System was set up, it had almost exclusive authority in this field. The government did have the right to set the monetary standard and to regulate the value of the dollar, and it had some influence on money and credit through its fiscal policy. Monetary standards, however, were changed infrequently and the impact of fiscal policy was small except in wartime. In the early days of the Federal Reserve System, government influence on the economic affairs of the country was still negligible.

OBJECTIVES OF THE FEDERAL
RESERVE SYSTEM

In line with the philosophy of government at the time, the original objectives of the Federal Reserve System were conceived in narrow terms. The founders of the System felt that it should provide an elastic currency for the country, that it should provide facilities for the discounting of commercial paper held by member banks, and that it should improve the supervision of banks. Over the years, however, as the attitude toward the role of government in economic affairs has changed, the objectives of the Federal Reserve System have been broadened. Amendments to the original law contained phrases such as "the maintenance of sound credit conditions and the accommodation of commerce, industry, and agriculture" and "preventing the excessive use of credit" for speculative purposes. The law as amended also refers to the effect of certain actions "upon the general credit situation of the country." The objectives were expanded during World War I to include aid in financing the government. The Board of Governors stated in a publication in 1947 that the objectives of the System are to help prevent inflation and deflation, and to share in creating conditions favorable to sustained high employment, stable values, and a rising level of consumption,[1] as well as carrying out the original objectives for which the Federal Reserve System was established.

MONETARY AND CREDIT CONTROL POLICIES

In attaining these objectives, policies directed toward these ends must be followed. Even though there is general agreement on basic objectives, opinions on the policies needed to attain these objectives vary. Furthermore, there is disagreement as to the possibility of carrying out some of the policies. The important policies that have been advocated to achieve the objectives of the System will be considered as a background to the study of the instruments of Federal Reserve policy and their use by the System. These are:

1. Protection of the monetary standard.
2. Regulating the use of money.
3. Aiding foreign governments and central banks.
4. Stabilization of price levels and the volume of employment.
5. Promotion of sound banking.

These policies will be discussed in this order.

(1) Protection of the Monetary Standard

The earliest central bank policy, as developed in Europe and especially by the Bank of England, was to protect the monetary standard, that is, to make certain that a sufficient supply of gold remained in the vaults of the government and of the banks and in general circulation for the gold standard to operate effectively.

[1] The Board of Governors of the Federal Reserve System, *The Federal Reserve System, Its Purposes and Functions* (Washington, D. C.: 1947), p. 1.

For example, when gold was sent out of the country in a volume so large as to threaten the effective operation of the gold standard, the Bank of England acted to raise interest rates so as to make investment of funds at home more profitable, thus reducing the export of gold. This policy was of some importance in this country while we were on the unregulated gold standard; but under the present modified gold-bullion standard it is of minor significance, since federal reserve action has been replaced by direct Treasury controls over gold. A somewhat broader policy in this same area, that is, the safeguarding of the soundness of the monetary and banking system, is being followed, however.

(2) Regulating the Use of Money

Another central banking policy is to regulate the use of money so that it is channeled into productive activities rather than speculative activities. Allied to this is the use of monetary policy to prevent inflation. The Federal Reserve System as originally set up provided for an elastic supply of currency, which expanded as business needs for currency expanded, thus providing money for productive activities. Since the Federal Reserve has acted from time to time to curb speculation and to help prevent inflation, it has followed this policy in a general way.

Central banking policy has also traditionally been concerned with interest rates. In countries that are to a large measure dependent on foreign trade, of which England is a good example, interest-rate policy is an important factor in determining whether available funds are to be used in foreign or domestic investment since, when interest rates are higher at home, fewer funds are invested abroad. This effect of shifts in the interest rate is of limited importance in the American economy. Interest rates do have some effect on the rate of use of capital in the domestic economy, but economists are not in agreement as to the extent of this effect or its exact nature. As a result, there has been disagreement as to the general interest-rate policy, if any, to pursue. This will be considered in the discussion of recent monetary and credit policies in the last chapter of this book.

There has been little disagreement with the policy to reduce, in so far as possible, seasonal variations in interest rates due to different demands for funds at different times during the year, as for example at Christmas. Likewise there is general agreement on the policy to eliminate regional differences in interest rates due to the uneven distribution of available funds in various sections of the country and the lack of complete mobility of such funds.

Another policy is to regulate the supply of money so as to aid the Treasury in its financing. There is no question about the Federal Reserve helping the Treasury in financing emergency needs, such as those of World War I, the 1929 depression, and World War II. In recent years, however, a controversy has developed concerning Federal Reserve policies of monetary ease to aid Treasury financing in a period of inflationary pressures and a large government debt. This controversy is related to the interest-rate controversy that will also be considered in the last chapter of this book.

(3) Aiding Foreign Governments and Central Banks

A policy followed by the Federal Reserve from time to time is one of aid to foreign governments and their central banks. For example, historians of federal reserve policy are of the opinion that the easy money policies followed by the System in the twenties, especially in 1924 and 1927, were designed to prevent the flow of gold to the United States, which would have made it difficult for foreign central banks to establish and maintain the gold standard. From time to time, assistance has been extended directly to foreign central banks, as for example, in 1925 when the Bank of England was authorized to draw on the Federal Reserve for gold if it was needed to re-establish the gold standard in Great Britain. This policy has been of limited significance since the end of World War II because such assistance has been made available in part through the International Monetary Fund and also by direct aid from our government to foreign governments.

(4) Stabilization of Price Levels and Employment

The fourth group of policies advocated to obtain the objectives of the Federal Reserve System are concerned with the stabilization of price levels and high levels of employment. Bills have been introduced into Congress specifically to direct the Federal Reserve System to maintain a stable price level even though there is a serious question about the feasibility of such a program. This doubt was expressed in 1939 by the federal reserve authorities before additional problems were created by the large federal government deficits of World War II as follows:

> Experience has shown . . . that (1) prices cannot be controlled by changes in the amount and cost of money; (2) the Board's control of the amount of money is not complete and cannot be made complete; (3) a steady average of prices does not necessarily result in lasting prosperity; and (4) a steady level of average prices is not nearly as important to the people as a fair relationship between the prices of the commodities which they produce and those which they must buy.
> Steady prices and lasting prosperity cannot be brought about by action of the Federal Reserve System alone, because they are affected by many factors beyond the control of the Federal Reserve System.[2]

Not only is there doubt about the ability of the Federal Reserve to maintain a stable price level, but also there is some question about its desirability. Some economists have advocated a gradually decreasing price level under which the benefits of increased technology would be spread to all by means of lower prices. On the other hand, some have favored a gradually rising price level, since they feel that full employment is easier to maintain when prices are rising.

There is more or less general agreement that monetary policies should be designed so as to help maintain a high level of employment. There is, however, no agreement as to the type of policies that should be followed to achieve this goal. Fluctuations in business activity are due to a complex interrelationship of factors of which monetary and credit conditions are only one. Their relationship to economic stability will be discussed in Chapter 27.

(5) Promotion of Sound Banking

Another objective of the Federal Reserve is the promotion of sound banking. This not only includes the promotion of sound individual banks, but also an effective and efficient system of banks that can meet the needs of the economy as a whole. This objective is accomplished in part by bank examinations, which have already been considered in the section on commercial banks. It is also accomplished by regulations governing bank activities, such as those designed to prevent speculative loans. The services of the Federal Reserve in expeditiously clearing checks, holding reserves

[2] *Federal Reserve Bulletin*, April, 1939, p. 255.

of member banks, transferring funds, and providing banks with currency to meet regular as well as unusual demands for funds all help to achieve this objective.

Consideration will be given next to the instruments in the hands of the Federal Reserve System to carry out its policies. Later chapters will discuss the relationship of federal reserve and treasury policies to price levels, interest rates, and economic stability.

THE DISCOUNT RATE

One of the most important instruments of federal reserve policy, in the minds of the framers of the act, was the use of the discount rate for making the amount of currency and credit correspond to the needs of business. The plan was for a businessman who needed help to finance his current operations to obtain a short-term loan, using as collateral the notes and other commercial paper that he received upon the shipment of goods to his customers. If his bank was short of funds, it could in turn discount such commercial paper with its federal reserve bank. The reserve bank could, if necessary, use this paper as the basis for issuing federal reserve notes. The reserve bank, it was felt, could encourage or discourage this process by raising or lowering the rate that it charged the member banks for discounting commercial paper in their portfolios.

The discount power was given to the reserve authorities as a basic part of the monetary and credit system because it was felt that it would be effective in regulating the volume of money and credit in use in the economy. This expectation was based upon the experience of the Bank of England, which for decades had been successful in controlling the general credit situation in Great Britain by the manipulation of discount rates.

Rationale of Discount Policy

The early rationale of discount policy was developed by the Bank of England before the Federal Reserve System was established. Stated in somewhat oversimplified terms, discount policy was intended to work in the following fashion. An increase in the discount rate would lead to a general increase in interest rates and a restriction of the extension of credit. This in turn would lead to a postponement of the establishment of new production facilities and therefore to a decreased demand for capital goods. As a consequence, income would decrease and with it the demand for consumer goods. Holders of inventories carried by means of borrowed funds would liquidate their stocks in an already weak market. The result would be a drop in prices that would tend to stimulate the demand for and to reduce the supply of goods, thus restoring economic balance. A reduction in the discount rate was expected to have the opposite effect.

Few economists would ascribe such influence to interest rates today. Business fluctuations depend upon a whole series of real and psychological factors that affect the demand for and the supply of capital, not upon interest rates alone. Increases in the discount rate, however, along with other actions of the reserve authorities, cause banks to curtail their borrowing from the federal reserve banks. This slows down the rate of expansion of bank reserves and may, if carried far enough, lead to a reduction in bank reserves and to a contraction of credit. Therefore, banks not only raise interest rates on their loans to meet the higher cost for money, but also they reduce the amount of credit extended to their customers since the available supply is lower.

Decreases in the discount rate affect the banking system and the economy somewhat differently. As the cost of money to banks is lowered, they should find it advantageous to borrow more from the federal reserve banks. Since such borrowing adds new reserves to the banking system, it can serve as the basis for credit expansion. Usually, however, when discount rates are lowered, the demand for funds has been declining so that borrowing from the federal reserve banks has not increased immediately. Open-market operations or a reduction in reserve requirements have in most cases also added to bank reserves in the first stages of a downturn, and as a result banks have had no need to borrow to increase reserves. As expansion in economic activity increases the demand for loans to such a degree that reserves are fully used, low discount rates make borrowing from the federal reserve banks attractive and such borrowing leads to further bank lending, further credit expansion, and expansion of economic activity.

Experience with the Discount Rate

Discount-rate policy helped finance World War I largely because the discount rate was kept below the interest rate on government bonds used as collateral for loans that were encouraged by the reserve authorities. It contributed to easy money conditions in the twenties and may have helped to start the stock market boom. Increases in discount rates in 1928 and 1929 were too late to stop the boom, and there is serious question whether that boom could have been stopped even if discount rates had been raised sooner. Profits in a rising stock market, in which stocks could be bought with 10 per cent cash and a 90 per cent loan, were too large to be influenced by a difference between 4 and 5, or 6, or even 8 per cent a year in interest charges. Low rates during the depression were powerless by themselves to increase business materially. During World War II low rates helped war financing. Banks were encouraged to expand credit since they knew that additional funds were available at very low rates if needed, and they were urged to make use of such borrowing to help meet the credit needs of the war effort.

Discount policy alone has not been effective as a method of monetary and credit control. It has been augmented over the years by open-market operations, authority to change reserve requirements, and direct controls over various types of lending. It has had some effectiveness, however, as part of a coordinated monetary and credit policy.

RESERVE REQUIREMENTS

The Board of Governors of the Federal Reserve System has the power to raise or lower the requirements for reserves against deposits to be held at the federal reserve banks within limits prescribed by law. For time deposits these limits are 3 and 6 per cent, and for demand deposits the limits are set by the geographic location of the bank. For central reserve city banks, that is, those in New York and Chicago, the limits are 13 and 26 per cent; for the reserve city banks they are 10 and 20 per cent; and for country banks, 7 and 14 per cent.

When the Federal Reserve Act was passed, reserves were set by law at a fixed amount without provision for change except by an act of Congress. A change was made in 1917 as part of the process of adjusting from the National Banking System to the Federal Reserve System, but after that reserves remained fixed until 1933. At that time, an amendment to the Agricultural Adjustment Act provided for the present authority of the Board of Governors to set reserves within prescribed limits. In 1948 the Board was given temporary powers to increase maximum reserve requirements as part of the program to combat inflation,[3] but this provision was allowed to lapse the following year.

Early Developments in Bank Reserves

The original provision for fixed legal reserve requirements was based on banking experience in pre-federal reserve days. The practice in Europe was to leave the determination of bank reserves largely to the discretion of the bankers, but this did not work well in the United States due to the speculative atmosphere in developing a new continent. The practice of keeping reserves against deposits dates back to the earliest beginnings of banking when money was placed on deposit with goldsmiths for safekeeping in their vaults. They not only kept gold, silver, and precious stones on deposit, but they also bought and sold them and made loans on them.

The goldsmiths soon discovered that most of the deposits were not called for at one time, and that, in fact, the bulk of them continually remained on deposit. They found, therefore, that they could lend some of the money placed on deposit and thus carry on lending operations with reserves equal to only a portion of deposits. Conservative bankers kept a large percentage of the deposits on hand to meet any and all demands of depositors. Reserves thus served to provide liquidity for these early bankers.

As this early banking process developed, customers found it convenient to make payments by endorsing and transferring receipts for deposits rather than withdrawing the coins and transferring them. Some also found it convenient to have receipts issued in round numbers to use in transferring funds. Thus the practice of issuing bank note currency began. At first notes were issued only against the funds of the banker and of depositors, but experience soon showed that some could be issued against the credit of the

---

[3] Maximum reserve requirements were set as follows: time deposits, 7½%; demand deposits: central reserve cities, 30%; reserve cities, 24%; country, 18%.

bank since coins would not be called for at once by any large number of depositors. Some reserves had to be kept to meet the demands of depositors. This need for reserves thus limited the ability of the banker to extend credit. As the banking system developed in Europe, bankers themselves determined the amount of reserves needed for liquidity and safety of note issue and a tradition of conservative banking developed.

American Experience with Bank Reserves

In colonial days American banks likewise were not required to keep reserves against notes or deposits. Many American banks printed and issued their own money in the form of bank notes with very little backing and failed to keep adequate reserves against deposits. In the early part of the nineteenth century voluntary plans for keeping reserves in key centers developed, and gradually state laws setting minimum reserves were enacted. However, these laws, except in Massachusetts and Louisiana, required reserves only against notes, not against deposits. When the National Bank Act was passed, reserves were required against deposits as well as notes. A geographic division of banks for reserve purposes with country, reserve city, and central reserve city banks was adopted, and different reserve requirements were set for each division of banks. The original fixed reserve requirements of the Federal Reserve Act were based on the procedures developed in the National Banking System.

Factors Affecting Bank Reserves

Before considering the effect that changes in reserve requirements have had as an instrument of monetary and credit control, it is desirable for an understanding of the principles involved to review the factors that affect bank reserves and to consider their functions under modern conditions of required reserves. In the previous chapter the factors that govern the ability of the banking system to expand or contract credit were considered. The net result of these factors is to increase or decrease bank reserves. The reserves held by banks in excess of those required by law or the regulatory authorities are available for additional credit expansion.

The most important factors that influence member bank reserves, which are the basis of the money supply, are gold movements, currency in circulation, and federal reserve credit, which depends largely on discounts and advances to member banks and open-market purchases of government securities.

Functions of Required Reserves

The difference between total reserves and those required to be held at the federal reserve banks constitute the excess reserves available for credit expansion. Thus, the major function of required reserves is to control the process of bank credit creation. If required reserves are increased, a smaller amount of reserves is available for credit expansion. For example, assume that required reserves are at a level of 20 per cent of deposits and that excess reserves of $1 billion exist in the banking system. These reserves could lead to a total extension of credit of $5 billion if no offsetting factors, such as an increase in currency in circulation, were at work. Suppose the Federal Reserve increases required reserves to 21 per cent and as a result of this increase $800 million more is needed to meet reserve requirements. Excess reserves are now reduced to $200 million and the potential for credit extension to somewhat less than $1 billion. The potential for credit expansion has been reduced primarily because a large part of the excess reserves are now required reserves no longer available for expansion and also because the potential for expansion is somewhat smaller when required reserves are 21 per cent than when they are 20 per cent.

Another function often associated with required reserves is liquidity. This is provided directly to only a very limited degree since required reserves are not available for use. As depositors call for their funds, reserves on such funds are freed, and this does provide a limited degree of liquidity. Of more importance for liquidity are the indirect effects. Since bankers are reluctant to be in debt to their federal reserve banks for any length of time, they have to provide for reserves over and above the required reserves. They do this by keeping vault cash to meet any demand for funds that might normally be expected and also by keeping secondary reserves in short-term government securities.

Many banks, especially the smaller ones, also keep more than the required amount of reserves with their federal reserve bank to make certain that an error in their books or in calculating reserves or an unexpected reduction of their reserve account because of an unusual volume of checks charged against it in the process of clearing checks will not find them short of required reserves. Not only are banks reluctant to be short of required reserves because it is considered a sign of poor bank management, but there is also a monetary penalty assessed by the Federal Reserve whenever a member bank is short of required reserves. Thus indirectly required reserves lead to liquidity since bankers keep reserves over and above required reserves.

American Experience with Changing the Level of Required Reserves

Required reserves have been changed on several occasions since the Board of Governors was given authority to do so in 1933. In 1936 and 1937, as excess reserves increased materially due to large gold imports, the Board raised required reserves until they were at the upper limits. In 1938 they were lowered somewhat again to try to stimulate activity after the business recession of 1937. Large excess reserves were built up after 1938, as can be seen from Table 23-1, but the reserve authorities did not raise reserve requirements until 1941. During the war required reserves were cut in central reserve city banks, but they were raised again in the postwar period.

They have been changed several times since then as the Federal Reserve has used them to make credit more easily available as the pace of business has slackened and to restrict credit expansion when the economy was operating at or near full-employment levels.

There has been some question about the effectiveness of changing reserve requirements as an instrument of monetary policy, and also some people are of the opinion that it is not a desirable form of control even if effective. Before World War II large gold imports made the policy ineffective since even at maximum levels large excess reserves remained. In the early postwar period large government bond holdings by banks reduced the effectiveness of raising required reserves. As reserves were raised, banks sold government bonds to the federal reserve banks and so obtained the funds to meet the higher reserves. Thus credit was not restricted to any great degree. This was especially true as

Table 23–1

REQUIRED AND EXCESS RESERVES OF MEMBER BANKS
SELECTED DATES FROM 1929–1957

(Millions of Dollars)

MIDYEAR OR YEAR-END	MEMBER BANK RESERVES		
	TOTAL	REQUIRED	EXCESS
1929—June	2,356	2,333	23
1933—June	2,292	1,817	475
1939—December	11,653	6,444	5,209
1941—December	12,450	9,365	3,085
1945—December	15,915	14,457	1,458
1947—December	17,899	16,400	1,499
1950—December	17,681	16,509	1,172
1952—December	19,950	20,520	− 570
1953—December	20,160	19,397	763
1954—December	18,876	18,618	258
1955—December	19,005	18,903	102
1956—December	19,059	19,089	− 30
1957—December	19,034	19,091	− 57

SOURCE: *Federal Reserve Bulletin*, February, 1958, p. 148.

long as the bonds could be sold at par or better under the federal reserve program of supporting government bonds. Several indirect effects no doubt did help restrain credit expansion. Having to meet higher reserve requirements made it clear to all bankers that it was the policy of the Federal Reserve System to restrict credit expansion. Also cutting down bond holdings reduced bank liquidity and so helped curb potential future credit expansion.

Even when effective, there is some question about the advisability of changing reserve requirements very often as a means of monetary control. Excess reserves are not spread evenly throughout the banking system. When required reserves are raised, some banks are forced to restrict credit to meet the requirements, whereas others can do so without a change in lending policy because they have excess reserves. Reserves are not necessarily short in those areas in which credit should be restricted most, and so the change may not work equitably or effectively. Thus most monetary authorities feel that reserve requirements should be changed only when some basic monetary or economic change has taken place. However, in the last several years the Board of Governors has not followed this policy but has changed reserve requirements in coordination with changes in the discount rate and open-market operations to control the availability of credit.

The 100 Per Cent Reserve Proposal

From time to time proposals have been made for changing the law on required reserves. The most drastic proposal is the 100 per cent reserve plan. Under it banks would have to keep 100 per cent reserves against all checking accounts and could make loans only out of time deposits. This would stop credit expansion by the banks, and it is proposed to put such powers in the hands of the Treasury. To start the plan, banks would have to be given reserves by the Federal Reserve or the government or allowed to use government bonds for the purpose.

The 100 per cent reserve plan would affect the American economy materially. Its sponsors hope that it would stabilize business by preventing credit expansion and thus also speculative booms, but this is not generally agreed to. The adoption of such a plan would present some new problems. Political pressure would no doubt be brought to bear on the officials in the Treasury from time to time for credit expansion they did not feel was wise. Banks would also have to raise service charges to operate profitably, since bank funds available for lending would be greatly reduced.

Other Proposals

A more moderate proposal is to require reserves in government bonds above the present maximum reserves. This action would force banks to hold these bonds and so not make them available for sale or as collateral for a federal reserve loan. This would prevent further expansion of credit for business purposes. Such a bond reserve could be used, however, to help insure credit expansion by means of government deficits since, if bond reserves were raised, banks would be forced to buy bonds to comply with the rules.

Another proposal is to keep present requirements but to grant authority to the Board to impose higher requirements on all new deposits received after a certain date. This would not force contraction of loans by any bank but would provide the means to stop further credit inflation. Such a plan would allow 100 per cent reserves against new deposits and could at any time prevent further credit expansion. In a war period the plan would make it possible for reserve banks to buy government bonds but would subject the funds paid out by the government to 100 per cent reserves and so prevent their use for further credit expansion, as was done in World War II.

A proposal of a technical nature is to abolish geographic divisions of cities for required reserves and to have uniform reserves for the country based on types of deposits. Usually suggested as classifications for different regulations are time deposits, deposits of other banks, and all other demand deposits. Advocates of this scheme feel that geographic differences are much less significant than they were when reserves were first required, some 85 years ago, and therefore the present differentials are inequitable.

OPEN-MARKET OPERATIONS

One of the most important instruments of monetary and credit policy is open-market operations, that is, the purchase of securities by the federal reserve banks to put additional reserves at the disposal of member banks or the sale of securities to reduce member bank reserves. The original Federal Reserve Act did not provide for open-market operations. This policy instrument developed out of the experience of the early post-World War I period.

From the beginning of their operations the reserve banks bought government securities with their funds to earn money for meeting expenses, and to show a profit in order that dividends on the stock held by member banks could be paid. All twelve banks usually bought and sold such securities in the New York market, and at times their combined sales were so large that they disorganized that market. Furthermore, the funds used to buy the bonds got into the hands of New York member banks, and this situation enabled them to reduce their borrowing at the New York Federal Reserve Bank. This made it difficult for the New York bank to maintain effective credit control in its area. As a result, an open-market committee was set up to coordinate buying and selling of government bonds. In 1933 the Open Market Committee was established by law, and in 1935 it was given its present composition of the Federal Reserve Board of Governors plus five members elected by the twelve federal reserve banks.

The Open-Market Process

Open-market operations differ from discount operations in that they increase or decrease reserves at the initiative of the federal reserve, not of individual bankers. The process in simplified form works as follows: If the Open Market Committee wants to buy government securities, it notifies dealers in such securities and they supply the desired securities. The dealers receive checks for the securities from the federal reserve banks, and these checks are deposited with member banks. They in turn deposit the checks at their federal reserve banks, thus adding new excess reserves that form the basis for additional credit expansion.

If the Federal Reserve wants to reduce reserves, it sells government securities to the dealers. The dealers pay for them by a check in favor of a federal reserve bank drawn on a member bank, and the reserve bank then deducts the amount from the reserves of the member bank.

Open-market operations may not lead to an immediate change in the volume of bank credit. This is especially true when bonds are sold to restrict credit. As bonds are sold by the reserve banks, some banks lose reserves and are forced to borrow from their reserve bank. Since they do not like to be in debt to the Federal Reserve, they use funds from loans that mature to repay the reserve bank. Thus credit is gradually restricted as a result of the adjustments banks make to the effects of open-market operations.

Reserve banks also buy banker's acceptances in the open market, but the amount has not been large in recent years. Such purchases are similar to discounts in that the initiative to sell them comes from the individual bank. They are, however, similar to open-market bond operations in that the reserve banks will buy the banker's acceptances from others than member banks, and they do not place member banks in debt to the reserve banks. The effect of these operations in increasing or decreasing bank reserves is the same as purchases and sales of government bonds.

Experience with Open-Market Operations

From the beginning of the use of open-market operations in 1922 until 1941, such operations were gradually coordinated with changes in the discount rate. For example, between 1929 and and 1933 large-scale purchases of government securities were made and discount rates were reduced. These were important factors in the decline of interest rates during this period. During World War II open-market operations were directed toward war financing. Bank reserves were kept adequate to insure a low interest-rate pattern. Between the bond drives large sums of government bonds were purchased to support the market and to place banks in a liquid position for additional war financing.

In the postwar period Federal Reserve open-market operations in the money market were hampered, however, by the large holdings of bonds by member banks and the policy of supporting governments at par or above. The sale of bonds by the reserve banks to reduce reserves was met by the sale of bonds by member banks, which had their reserves reduced. Since the Federal Reserve stood ready to buy such bonds at par or above to maintain their price, the net result was a purchase of bonds that offset the prior sale. Thus open-market operations were rendered ineffective as long as bonds were purchased at par or above. This policy was abandoned early in the Korean War for a more flexible bond buying policy, and open-market operations again became an effective instrument of credit policy.

The Significance of Open-Market Operations

Although not provided for in the original organization of the Federal Reserve System, open-market operations have become the most important and effective means of monetary and credit control. They can effectively take funds out of the market and thus raise short-term interest rates and help restrain a boom. They can also provide for easy money conditions and lowered short-term interest rates. Of course, such monetary ease will not of itself start business on the recovery road after a recession. When used with discount policy, open-market operations are an effective way of restricting credit or making it more easily available.

In order for open-market operations to be effective, the Federal Reserve must be free to buy and sell as it sees fit. This of course could not be done during the post-World War II period, when it was committed to buy government bonds whenever such action was necessary to maintain the price above par. Open-market operations work only when there is no obligation on the part of the Federal Reserve to buy bonds to maintain bond prices. Nevertheless, open-market operations must be carried on with the financing needs of the Treasury in mind. It would be impossible to maintain the present government debt with all of the refunding operations required without the active help of the reserve authorities. This problem will be considered more fully in the next chapter when government actions affecting monetary and credit conditions will be considered.

SELECTIVE CREDIT CONTROLS

The instruments of monetary and credit policy so far considered all work uniformly to control credit in all areas of the economy. The Federal Reserve also has power to control credit in special fields. It has permanent power to regulate stock-market credit and has had emergency grants of power to regulate consumer credit and real estate credit. These selective controls of credit in strategic areas are intended to supplement the general credit controls in those areas in which the terms of the credit, other than the interest cost, are most important, that is, such factors as the percentage of down payment required and the length of time allowed for repayment.

Margin Requirements

The Federal Reserve Act enjoins the Federal Reserve authorities to restrain the undue rise of bank credit for speculation in securities, real estate, or commodities. The Federal Reserve issued several warnings against the growth of stock-market credit during and immediately after World War I. Early in 1926 it began publishing current figures on loans to brokers in an effort to use publicity as a method of control. In 1929 the Board issued emphatic warnings against the further expansion of stock-market credit. It also instituted a campaign to have the reserve banks insist that member banks in debt to them either repay their indebtedness or reduce their loans for carrying stocks.

Despite these attempts to curb stock-market credit, it expanded greatly and was in part responsible for the extreme character of the 1929 stock-market boom and subsequent crash. To avoid a repetition of this experience, Congress, first in the Banking Act of 1933 and then more fully in the Securities Exchange Act of 1934, gave the Board of Governors the power to regulate stock-market credit.

This regulation is accomplished by setting the amount that holders of stocks may borrow upon them, either from banks or from securities brokers and dealers. The difference between the amount of the loan and the current market value of the stock at the time the loan is made is called the *margin*. For example, if a loan of $7,500 is made against stock having a market value of $10,000, the margin is $2,500 or 25 per cent. The Board's regulations apply to the minimum margin required and thus prescribe maximum loan values. They apply only at the time securities are purchased and only to credit obtained for the purpose of buying or carrying securities registered on a national securities exchange. They do not apply to loans based on stocks as collateral if the proceeds are to be used for commercial purposes.

Margin requirements for the purpose of restraining stock-market credit can greatly reduce the speculative demand for stocks in a boom period, as can be seen from the following example. Suppose that without margin requirements $10,000 of stock could be bought for a $1,000 margin and a $9,000 loan, as was often the case before the 1929 crash. If the stock rose in price by 10 per cent, the purchaser had a $1,000 profit on a $1,000 investment.[4] Under margin requirements of 50 per cent, $1,000 can be used to buy $2,000 worth of stock. A similar 10 per cent rise would yield a profit of $200 on the investment of $1,000. High margins greatly reduce the profit to be made out of market movements and in the same manner also reduce the loss. If $1,000 is used to purchase $10,000 of stock, a 10 per cent decline in the price of the stock wipes out the $1,000 put up by the purchaser. If margin requirements are 50 per cent, a 10 per cent decline reduces the total value of stock purchased by only $200, thus leaving $800 of the $1,000 put up by the purchaser intact. In like manner, high margins remove the pressure of forced selling that is necessary to protect a loan in a declining market when margins are small. In the example above of a $10,000 purchase with a $1,000 investment by the purchaser, a 10 per cent drop will wipe out all of the equity of the owner. If the purchaser cannot put up additional money or if the bank cannot get in touch with him as the market is falling, the bank will sell the stock in order to protect its loan.

High margin requirements also restrict the amount of pyramiding which can take place in a rising market, that is, traders adding to their holdings of stock in a rising market without putting up

[4] Not counting the cost of the loan or brokerage commissions.

additional money or securities. Suppose that $10,000 of stock bought on a $1,000 or 10 per cent margin rises in market value to $15,000. The $5,000 increase in price under 10 per cent margins would permit the purchase of $45,000 more of the stock, since the holder now has a margin of $6,000, that is, his original $1,000 and the increase in market value of $5,000. This gives him a 10 per cent margin on $60,000 of stock in total, the $15,000 of old stock at present prices and $45,000 of additional stock. Under a 50 per cent margin, only $5,000 more of stock could be bought, since $2,500 of the gain would be needed for additional margin on the original stock if it is used for collateral for an additional stock purchase, which leaves but $2,500 margin to purchase additional stock.

The regulation of margin requirements has been effective as one of the means of preventing the "boom and bust" character of stock trading. It can be given a large amount of credit for this, but not exclusive credit, since stock-market procedures have also been changed and many more investments are being made on the basis of analysis of the prospects of the company, rather than for short-run speculation in the hope of a quick price rise.

Consumer Credit Regulation

During World War II the Federal Reserve was given temporary powers to regulate consumer credit and did so under Regulation W of the Federal Reserve Board. That regulation prescribed minimum down payments and maximum repayment periods for installment loans. The scope of the regulation was broadened later to include a larger number of items and also charge accounts and single payment loans. These regulations under more limited scope were continued on and off for several years after the war and were reintroduced during the Korean War.

The purpose of Regulation W during the war was to discourage the buying of articles that were scarce in relationship to the demand for them. Those who argue for such regulation under more normal conditions do so because they feel that consumer credit is an important source of inflationary credit. Others feel that the restriction of the use of credit during prosperity will defer some demand for durables to a later period and so help even out the sales of durables. Many economists do not believe that there is evidence to support either of these contentions. Thus there is some difference of opinion as to the effectiveness or desirability of consumer credit regulation. Beyond question it could be effective if made stringent enough. Some oppose it because they are opposed to any direct government intervention in the economy. Others oppose it because they believe that credit controls should be general in nature, regulating only the over-all volume of credit to prevent inflation and not the volume in specific sectors of the economy. Those affected have in some cases opposed it because of the extra work involved in record keeping.

Regulation W did reduce the use of consumer credit during World War II. The reduction was greatest for commodities, such as automobiles, which were in shortest supply. The reduction, however, was due to the lack of goods to purchase as well as to Regulation W, and for that reason it is impossible to assess its effectiveness during this period. In 1946 and 1947 consumers had such large amounts of liquid funds that it is imposssible to tell if Regulation W had much effect. In early 1949, some authorities felt that Regulation W was having a very dampening effect on consumer durable goods purchases, and the lifting of regulations led to increased sales in the latter part of that year. The reimposition of Regulation W in September, 1950, slowed down the rise in installment credit [5] but such credit expanded in 1952 after controls were removed. The price level during this period, however, was about stable.

The regulation of consumer credit may be a valuable tool of credit policy in periods of war or national emergency. There is, however, no agreement that it would be desirable to make it a part of the permanent powers of the Federal Reserve.

Real Estate Credit Regulation

During the Korean War, the Board was given temporary power to regulate real estate credit to restrain the building boom in a period of high defense and foreign aid expenditures involving the use of many of the same materials as needed for home building. The Board laid down the rules in Regulation X that regulated credit first for residential construction and then also for some

[5] R. J. Saulnier, "An Appraisal of Selective Credit Controls" in *Papers and Proceedings of the American Economic Association*, May, 1952, p. 260.

nonresidential construction. The required amount of down payment was prescribed and so were maximum repayment periods.

This regulation differed from Regulation W in that, as the
price of the house went up, the percentage of down payment increased. This was intended to discourage the building of higher
priced homes to a greater degree than low-priced homes. The goal
of reducing the number of homes built in 1951 to 850,000 from a
rate close to 1,400,000 was not achieved, but building was reduced
materially. There was too little experience with this type of credit
regulation, however, to be sure how much of the drop was due
to credit restrictions and how much to other factors, such as uncertainty in a war period. In 1952 construction levels exceeded
those of 1951, but the reason for this is not entirely clear since as
inflation appeared to have been arrested, the terms of the regulation were eased somewhat, especially for lower priced homes.
Certainly regulation of real estate credit can be effective if made
stringent enough. It can cut demand in those fields in which
down payments have been very small. It also appears to be effective in reducing building of multifamily apartments built for
rental. Just what it will do in other areas is not clear. At present
it appears unlikely that the Federal Reserve will be given the
power to regulate real estate credit except in war or emergency
periods.

OTHER FEDERAL RESERVE ACTIONS IN
CONTROLLING MONEY AND CREDIT

Direct action by federal reserve authorities also has some influence on monetary and credit policy. Banks have from time to
time been advised to follow loan policies in line with the objectives of the Federal Reserve. After World War I banks were urged
to sell their government securities; in 1929 pressure was put on
them to decrease stock market loans; and during the early days of
World War II they were directed to discourage loans for carrying
large inventories of consumer goods. During the Korean War a
voluntary credit restraint program was put into operation to discourage all credit for nonessential uses and to restrict other credit
not related to the defense effort.

To enforce such policies, if necessary, the Board of Governors
could take action against bank officers or directors. The Board

has the power, after due warning and a chance to be heard, to remove a bank officer or a director for violating banking laws or for following unsound banking practices. Every opportunity must be given the officer or the director to cease and desist from his action. Every director of the bank must be kept informed of proceedings which, except for such notice, are kept secret.

Direct action has not been used frequently as an instrument of credit policy. It is available, however, to supplement other regulations if need be. It can be used to help direct bank credit away from undue speculative activity into productive uses. It is especially worth while in emergency periods, such as in World War II and the Korean War.

Such direct policies are much more effective in countries such as England that have a small number of banks with many branches. They are much more difficult to carry out effectively in our system, which has thousands of banks under different ownership and direction.

QUESTIONS

1. What were the objectives for which the Federal Reserve System was established?
2. How have these objectives been broadened over the years?
3. Briefly describe the various policies that have been followed by the Federal Reserve.
4. Describe the effect of federal reserve policies on interest rates. What are they designed to accomplish?
5. How has the Federal Reserve aided foreign central banks? Why is such a policy of limited significance at present?
6. Discuss the possible effectiveness and desirability of a policy to stabilize the price level.
7. How may the discount rate be used to carry out federal reserve policy?
8. Discuss the rationale of discount policy.
9. What was the original function of bank reserves? What is their function in the American banking system today?
10. How may changes in reserve requirements be used to carry out federal reserve policy?
11. Describe American experience with reserve requirements during the thirties and in the period following World War II.
12. Evaluate the changing of reserve requirements as a means of monetary control.
13. Discuss several proposals for changing the law on required reserves.

14. Discuss the process by which open-market operations affect the monetary situation.
15. Describe American experience with open-market operations in the thirties, during World War II, and in the period after World War II.
16. Evaluate open-market operations as a means of monetary control.
17. Explain the process by which margin requirements can control speculative financing of the purchase of stocks and pyramiding.
18. Explain how consumer credit was regulated under Regulation W. Discuss the effectiveness and desirability of consumer credit regulation.
19. Explain the regulation of real estate credit under Regulation X. Discuss its effectiveness.
20. Discuss direct action by federal reserve authorities as a method of credit control.

SUGGESTED READINGS

ADAMS, E. SHERMAN. *Monetary Management.* New York: The Ronald Press Company, 1950.

BACH, G. L. *Federal Reserve Policy-Making.* New York: Alfred A. Knopf, Inc., 1950.

Board of Governors of the Federal Reserve System. *The Federal Reserve System—Its Purposes and Functions.* Washington, D. C.: Board of Governors, 1954. Chapters 2, 3, 4, 9.

GOLDENWISER, E. A. *American Monetary Policy.* New York: McGraw-Hill Book Co., Inc., 1951.

HERSEY, A. "Historical Review of Objectives of Federal Reserve Policy," *Federal Reserve Bulletin*, April, 1940, pp. 279-289.

Chapter 24

Treasury Powers

Affecting the Supply

of Money and Credit

The final authority over monetary and credit policy was granted to the federal government when the framers of the Constitution gave the government the right to coin money and to regulate its value. The government has always exercised the exclusive power to set the monetary standard and to provide coins, but it has allowed private banks to issue paper money and to extend credit. In fact, state banks issued bank notes until such notes were taxed out of existence after the National Bank Act was passed.

Gradually more and more of the monetary and credit powers have been taken out of private hands and concentrated in the hands of public authorities. As part of the banking legislation enacted during the depression of the thirties, national banks are no longer allowed to issue bank notes. The power to issue paper money has been concentrated in the hands of the Treasury Department and the Federal Reserve System. Although the federal reserve banks are owned by the member banks, supervision of monetary and credit functions is in the hands of the Board of Governors appointed by the President of the United States.

When the Federal Reserve System was first established in 1913, most of the power to regulate money and credit was placed in its hands. The power to change the monetary standard or its value or the basis of issuing paper money Congress reserved to itself. However, as the public debt grew during World War I, during the 1929 depression, and especially during World War II, the Treasury became vitally interested in credit conditions. Policies that affect interest rates and monetary ease or stringency affect the Treasury directly, since it is the largest borrower in the nation on both a short-term and a long-term basis. Furthermore, in managing the large public debt and various trust funds placed under its jurisdiction, the Treasury has acquired the power to influence the money market materially.

This chapter will consider Treasury powers and policies affecting monetary and credit conditions. Consideration will be given first to Treasury powers relating to the monetary standard and the gold and silver stocks. The problems of the Treasury in managing its cash balances so as not to disrupt monetary and credit conditions will be analyzed next. Budget operations will then be considered, including especially the monetary and the credit effects of government surpluses and deficits and the way they are handled. Lastly, debt management will be considered as it affects monetary and credit conditions. Such debt management concerns the policy regarding types of securities to issue, interest rate patterns, maturities, refunding policies, and the like.

POWERS RELATING TO THE MONETARY STANDARD AND GOLD AND SILVER STOCKS

The monetary standard of this country is based on gold, with an ounce of fine gold the equivalent of $35. All gold must be held by the Treasury, and gold can be obtained only to settle foreign balances and then only upon application to the Treasury. The Treasury acquired the ability to spend sums it had not collected in taxes or received from the sale of bonds when the dollar was devalued during the depression in the thirties. The value of an ounce of gold before devaluation was $20.67, and after devaluation it was $35. This change increased the value of the gold supply held by the Treasury by 69 per cent. Some of the profit made by the devaluation has been spent at the direction of Congress, but some of it still remains in the hands of the Treasury. This accounts for the value of gold held by the Treasury being in excess of the volume of gold certificates.

Gold Purchases by the Treasury

Whenever new gold is added to the monetary stock, the reserves of the banking system are increased and thus also the potential for credit expansion is increased. This is true whether the gold is newly mined domestic gold, it is reclaimed from artistic or other uses, or it is imported into the United States. In each case the gold must be turned over to the Treasury. It is usually deposited in a commercial bank and then turned over to a federal reserve bank or the Treasury. If received by a federal reserve bank, it can be turned over to the Treasury for gold certificates. The funds received for the gold are usually deposited in a commercial bank; and since they are new funds, they add to the primary reserves of the banking system.

The Treasury has usually followed a passive policy in regard to the effect of gold buying on bank reserves. For a period from December, 1936, until April, 1938, however, the Treasury prevented increases of bank reserves by sterilizing gold purchases, that is, paying for them with other funds rather than gold certificates backed by the gold being purchased. From December, 1936, until the middle of February, 1938, this policy was followed for all gold purchased at a cost to the Treasury in excess of a billion dollars. It was modified at that time to apply only to increases in the monetary gold stock in excess of $100 million in any quarter, but the policy was dropped in April of that year.

There was widespread criticism of the policy since it increased the public debt and interest charges on it. There was also a serious question about its effectiveness since gold stocks were already large enough to support a much greater credit structure. Furthermore, the program could succeed only as long as the newly issued government bonds were not used as a basis for credit expansion. If the Federal Reserve purchased the bonds in its open-market operations, additional reserves would be added to the banking system thus nullifying the effects of the Treasury policy of sterilizing gold imports. Treasury policy in this area, as well as Treasury policy in the money-and-credit area generally, cannot be successful if it is counteracted by Federal Reserve policy, and Federal Reserve policy cannot succeed if the Treasury follows policies having an opposite effect.

Silver Purchases by the Treasury

Silver purchases under the silver buying program increase primary reserves just as gold purchases do, but the amounts in-

volved are smaller. Most silver is purchased from domestic producers whereas most gold comes from abroad, but the effect on
bank reserves as the silver is turned over to the Treasury is similar.
When the Treasury pays for the silver by means of a check drawn
on its account at the federal reserve banks, new reserves are
created. If the silver is received by a federal reserve bank, it can be
turned over to the Treasury for silver certificates.

Present laws prescribe the purchase by the Treasury of all
newly mined domestic silver offered to it at 90.5 cents per fine
ounce. The Secretary of the Treasury has discretion with regard
to the purchase of foreign silver and the price to be paid for it.
He may also set the terms under which silver will be sold from
the silver stocks. Thus, to this limited extent, the Secretary of the
Treasury can affect bank reserves by buying foreign silver and
setting the price to be paid for it and by selling monetary silver
and thus reducing bank reserves.

The Treasury has an additional power that it has never used
and which, even if used, would not have a substantial effect on
bank reserves. Congress has prescribed that, although silver certificates must be issued for at least the purchase price of the silver,
they can be issued for the monetary value of the silver, that is,
$1.29 an ounce. Issuing these additional certificates would in-
crease bank reserves by an additional amount as the silver is purchased or when the Treasury spends the proceeds received from
turning silver certificates over to the federal reserve banks.

Issuing Irredeemable Paper Money

On several occasions, bank reserves have been increased by
the issuance of paper money by the Treasury that had no gold or
silver backing. Such action, which can only be authorized by
Congress, was taken to aid in financing the Revolutionary War,
the War of 1812, and the Civil War. An amendment to the Agricultural Adjustment Act of 1933 gave the President the power to
order the issuance of such unsecured paper money or greenbacks
up to $3 billion. If such greenbacks had been issued, they would
have increased bank reserves and the credit expansion potential.
This power was never used, and it was revoked in June, 1945.
Most Americans are strongly opposed to fiat money even in
periods in which large-scale credit expansion is taking place.

MANAGING THE TREASURY'S CASH BALANCES [1]

The operations of the Treasury are carried out on a large scale. It is necessary to maintain a large cash balance, especially since funds are not paid into the Treasury at an even rate throughout the year and are not paid out on a regular basis either. This makes it imperative for the Treasury to handle its cash balances in such a way as to avoid credit ease during parts of the year and credit stringency during others. The Treasury has developed detailed procedures for handling its cash balances so as to affect bank reserves as little as possible.

A part of the Treasury funds are kept on deposit in the federal reserve banks and their branches. Some deposits are also kept in insular, territorial, and foreign depositaries to provide a convenient place for depositing funds and in a few cases to permit disbursing officers to make payments in local funds. Some funds are kept in insured domestic banks designated as "General Depositaries" in areas in which no branch of the federal reserve bank is conveniently located. The Treasury also has some cash in a cash room in Washington where currency may be obtained or Treasury checks cashed.

Treasury Tax and Loan Accounts

The bulk of Treasury balances are kept in special deposit accounts, called *Treasury Tax and Loan Accounts,* that are maintained at about 11,000 designated banking institutions in the United States. These depositaries are divided into three groups: those having Tax and Loan Account balances on March 19, 1958, of $150,000 or less are in Group A; those with balances over $150,000, in Group B, if their *total* deposits are under $500 million, and in Group C if their *total* deposits are $500 million or more.

Several types of government receipts are deposited in these Treasury Tax and Loan Accounts. Employers have the option of paying withheld income, old-age insurance, and railroad retirement taxes either to federal reserve banks or to one of the special depositaries, and most employers have paid them to the latter.

The Treasury may also make large payments of income and profits taxes eligible for deposit in Tax and Loan Accounts.

[1] The material in this section is based to a large extent on articles in *The Treasury and the Money Market,* New York, Federal Reserve Bank of New York, 1954.

Shortly before each quarterly income tax payment is due, the Treasury announces whether or not large payments are eligible for such deposit. The dividing line that has been used to select large payments has been $10,000. These checks are separated by the Directors of Internal Revenue and deposited in the federal reserve banks, which inform the depositary banks daily of the amount of checks written against their bank eligible for credit in Tax and Loan Accounts. The banks execute a certificate indicating that they have credited the funds to the Treasury's account and return it to the federal reserve bank.

These funds accumulated in the Treasury Tax and Loan Accounts from large quarterly tax checks are called X balances. They are not included in the account balances in determining whether a depositary is in Group A or Group B. At first the Treasury withdrew these X balances before withdrawing other funds in the Tax and Loan Accounts. Since large checks were concentrated in a minority of banks, however, this reduced funds in these banks and so restricted credit unnecessarily. Therefore at present, withdrawals are based on the need for funds and on the state of the money market.

Since July, 1953, many excise taxes may also be paid either to a federal reserve bank or to a qualified depositary with a Tax and Loan Account. The proceeds from a large proportion of the sales of new government securities also flow into the Tax and Loan Accounts. The proceeds from the sale of nonmarketable securities are always eligible for deposit in such accounts. Most marketable issues are also sold with the privilege of credit to these accounts. Treasury bills, however, have rarely been made eligible for credit to Tax and Loan Accounts. A two-weeks notice is usually given when funds are withdrawn from Treasury accounts in the Class A depositaries and shifted to Treasury accounts in the federal reserve banks, and 4- to 7-days notice for funds in Class B depositaries. Funds may be withdrawn from Class C depositaries on the day the notice of the call for such funds is given to the bank.

Outlays

Almost all governmental operating expenditures are paid by checks that are collectible at any reserve bank or reserve bank branch or at the Treasury Department. Only a small part of the payments made when the Treasury retires government securities, however, are made by means of checks. When banks present securities from their portfolios, or those of correspondent banks or their customers, to their district reserve bank, they receive a direct credit to their account at this bank. Series A and Series E Savings Bonds may be redeemed by banks and a few other financial institutions, which are reimbursed in turn by the federal reserve banks from Treasury accounts without the use of a check. Most interest payments are also made without the use of checks since banks present the coupons directly to their federal reserve bank for payment.

Direct Purchase of Certificates of Indebtedness

Since 1942 the Federal Reserve System has been granted authority on a temporary basis, which has been renewed periodically as it expired, to buy up to $5 billion of direct or fully guaranteed government obligations. This authority was used with some frequency during World War II, and it has been used from time to time since then. It is used to finance expenditures when funds will be available shortly to the Treasury. In the months in which quarterly tax payments are to be made, the Treasury often finds that it has a large volume of disbursements to make just a few days before the funds from tax payments become available after the fifteenth of the month. By selling Special Treasury Certificates directly to the federal reserve banks, rapid short-run changes in funds available to the banking system are prevented.

The Effect of Handling Cash Balances on the Money Market

The Treasury has sought to handle its cash receipts, outlays, and balances in such a way as to avoid large changes in bank reserves. To do this, the Treasury tries to keep its balances in its accounts at the federal reserve banks relatively stable. Almost all Treasury disbursements are made by checks drawn against its deposits at the federal reserve banks. Most Treasury receipts are deposited in the Tax and Loan Accounts at the commercial bank depositaries, but some are deposited directly in the Treasury accounts at the federal reserve banks. The Treasury adjusts the withdrawal of funds from its accounts at the commercial bank depositaries, or calls on these accounts as they are referred to, in such a way as to keep its balances at the federal reserve banks as stable as possible. This means that the funds shifted from depositary banks and the funds deposited in the federal reserve banks directly must day by day be equal to the volume of Treasury checks that are likely to be presented to the federal reserve banks for collection.

When the Treasury account at the reserve banks is kept at the same level, bank reserves are not changed. This is possible only if accurate forecasts are made of the daily receipts and expenditures from the Treasury account so that funds from the Tax and Loan Accounts may be shifted in the right amounts at the right time. If such forecasts and procedures for shifting balances in depositary accounts had not been worked out with a reasonable degree of success, the operations of the Treasury would cause bank reserves to fluctuate a great deal over short periods of time.

POWERS RELATING TO THE GOVERNMENT BUDGET AND TO SURPLUSES OR DEFICITS

The government may also influence monetary and credit conditions indirectly through the effects of taxation and expenditure programs, and especially by having a significant cash deficit or surplus. Decisions in the budget-making area rest with Congress and are usually based on the needs of the government and on political considerations without giving much weight to the monetary and credit effects. Because of the magnitude of the government budget, government income and expenditures may be one of the most important factors in determining credit conditions.

Effects of Tax Policy

The tax policy and tax program may effect monetary and credit conditions in several ways. The level of taxes in relationship to national income may affect the volume of saving and thus of the funds available for investment without credit expansion. The tax structure may also help determine whether saving is done largely by the upper-income groups, middle-income groups, or by all groups. This fact could affect the amount of funds available for different types of investment. Persons in middle-income groups may be more conservative than those with more wealth and may tend to favor bonds or mortgages over equity investments.

Changes in corporation tax rates may also affect the amount of funds available for short-term investment in government bonds and the balances kept in bank accounts. This is true in part because larger tax payments reduce the amount of money a corporation has available for current expenditures. Also, if tax rates are raised with little advance warning, as has been done at times in the past, a corporation may be forced to use funds it was holding for future use to meet the higher tax payments. Some concerns that are short of funds may be forced to borrow to meet the tax payments. In either case a smaller amount of credit is available for other uses than before.

Effects of Deficit Financing

The government spending program also has an effect on monetary and credit conditions, especially when cash disbursements exceed receipts. When spending is at a faster rate than taxes and other funds are collected, the resulting cash deficit will affect the monetary and banking system. The effect will depend on how the deficit is financed.

Sale of Bonds to Individuals. If treasury securities are sold to individuals, business corporations, insurance companies, or any institution other than commercial banks or federal reserve banks, there is no permanent effect on bank reserves. As the securities are sold, the government may keep the funds on deposit in the Tax and Loan Accounts at the commercial banks. This does not affect bank reserves; but as the government gets ready to spend the funds, it will transfer them to its account at the federal reserve bank and so cut reserves. They are increased again, however, as soon as the funds are spent.

Temporary changes in reserves occur as the funds are shifted to the federal reserve banks. The Treasury can influence credit conditions by keeping newly borrowed funds in commercial banks or by transferring them immediately to the Federal Reserve, and by the length of time that elapses between borrowing operations and the expenditure of the borrowed funds.

Sales of Bonds to Commercial Banks. When government bonds are sold to commercial banks, deposits are increased but primary reserves are not. If the bonds are sold to banks having a Treasury Tax and Loan Account, the funds are at first transferred to that account. In time, however, they are shifted to the Treasury Account at the federal reserve bank, thus reducing bank reserves. These are restored again, however, as the funds are spent. The net result is that some funds which were not previously in use are now being used because of borrowing by the government. The process of credit expansion is carried on just as it is if the bank funds are used for a loan to a business. It can, of course, take place only if there are excess reserves available in the banking system, and it reduces such reserves as part of them become required reserves for a larger total of deposits. If the bank holding the government bonds sells them to the federal reserve banks, primary reserves are increased. Thus the purchase of government bonds by the banks not only leads to credit expansion, but it also provides a liquid asset that can be used to increase primary reserves, especially if bond prices remain stable.

Sale of Bonds to Federal Reserve Banks. Primary reserves and deposits are also increased directly when bonds are sold by the government to the federal reserve banks. Deposits are increased at the commercial banks as the funds are spent. These are primary reserves since they have been added to the commercial banking system from the Federal Reserve and were not previously withdrawn as in the other cases. Such direct sale was authorized during World War II, but it was not used to any large extent. When bank-held bonds are bought by the Federal Reserve, however, as they were between bond drives in World War II, the final effect is the same.

Effects on the Volume of Credit and on Reserves. The Treasury can thus influence the credit conditions of the country by the methods used to borrow funds to meet a deficit. If bonds are sold to nonbank investors, credit is not expanded; but when bonds are sold to bank investors, the basis for credit expansion is laid. During periods of high level of business activity and of a large demand for funds, the credit expansion process will probably take place. During depression periods checks may not be drawn against the new deposits, since private spending is at low levels, and then the credit expansion process will not take place even though added reserves have been made available.

Just the reverse process takes place when government surpluses are used to retire bonds. As the money is raised by taxes, bank deposits are reduced by the checks made payable to the Treasury. Primary reserves are also reduced as these funds are deposited at the federal reserve banks or kept in the Treasury. If bonds held by individuals are retired, both deposits and reserves are restored to former levels as the checks received from the government are deposited in commercial banks.

If bonds held by commercial banks are retired, reserves are again restored as the banks receive the funds from the Treasury. The assets of the bank have changed since it now has cash instead of bonds, but deposits are not restored. The bank, however, can extend credit since it now has additional cash available.

If securities held by the federal reserve banks are retired, both reserves and deposits are permanently reduced. They were reduced when the funds were raised by taxes, and they are not increased since the federal reserve banks now have fewer bonds and more cash. Their potential ability to expand credit in the future is increased, but this is not significant since they have at no time expanded credit to anything like the volume possible under the law.

DEBT MANAGEMENT

Since World War II, debt management has also become an important Treasury function affecting credit conditions. Since the government debt is so large, what the government does in handling its debt is one of the most important factors in the money markets.

Debt management includes the types of securities to sell, the interest-rate patterns to use, the types of refunding to do, and decisions on callable issues. Debt management is at times used in a wider sense to include budget policy, the financing of deficits, the methods used to pay off debt, and borrowing more than immediate requirements. These were discussed in the previous section, leaving the technical problems of debt management for this section. Before considering the techniques of debt management, in order to evaluate them it is desirable to consider the objectives to be achieved.

Objectives of Debt Management

One of the basic objectives of debt management has been to handle the debt in such a way as best to promote the interests of the economy. This has been done by encouraging a wide distribution of the debt, especially in such periods as World War II, in an effort to encourage saving by large numbers of individuals. It has also been done during periods in which inflationary pressures were strong by issuing bonds that contained a provision prohibiting their sale or transfer to a commercial bank, thus making it impossible to use them for bank credit expansion.

Debt management can also be conducted in such a way as to maintain conditions that will help assure economic stability. During prosperity the Treasury can borrow money when that becomes necessary for new financing or refinancing by selling bonds to nonbank investors so as not to add to the money supply. During depressions the Treasury can borrow in ways that are least likely to compete with private demands for funds. This can be done by selling short-term securities so as to attract idle short-term funds and especially idle bank reserves. Thus there will be no restriction of credit for business and individuals. Credit will be available in larger amounts to the extent that bank purchases of bonds lead to credit expansion.

Some advocate that the Treasury go further in this area and affect the supply of long-term funds so as to promote stability. If long-term bonds are issued at attractive rates, funds can be taken out of the long-term market. This action can reduce the supply of available funds for home construction, capital development, and the like. There is no agreement that the Treasury should use debt management in this way, and no serious attempt has been made to apply such a policy.

Another objective of debt-management policy is to hold down Treasury interest costs. The influence of Treasury policies may also tend to reduce all interest rates, and lower interest rates tend to stimulate home building, the construction of business plant and equipment, commercial building, and the like. This objective and the first one may, however, conflict at times when higher interest rates may be helpful to restrain inflationary pressures.

A somewhat more restricted objective is to maintain satisfactory conditions in the government securities market. This means that investor confidence should be maintained in government securities. It also means that wide price swings should be discouraged and that buying and selling should be orderly.

More technical objectives are to issue securities of different types so as to fit the needs of various investor groups and to obtain an evenly spaced scheduling of debt maturities so as to facilitate debt retirement if funds are available, or refunding when that is necessary.

Types of Securities Issued

One of the important areas of debt management is the determination of the types of securities to issue. This involves such factors as maturity, interest rates, marketability, and eligibility for various investor groups. Of the total gross debt of $275 billion of the federal government at the end of 1957, $164 billion was in marketable securities.[2] These were of various types from 90-day issues to 40-year bonds.

Short-Term Securities. The shortest term obligations are Treasury bills, which usually mature in 90 or 91 days. They are offered for subscription about four times a month and are sold at a discount below face value. The Treasury asks subscribers to indicate the maximum amount they are willing to pay for the bills. It allots the bills to the bidders in order of bid prices down to the lowest bid needed to raise the necessary funds. Treasury bills are issued in denominations of $1,000 and larger amounts.

Certificates of indebtedness are usually issued for a year, but they have been issued for 11 months and 13 months. Certificates are issued at par and have coupons for interest payments. They are offered for public subscription several times a year. At the end of 1957 there was $26.9 billion of Treasury bills outstanding and $34.6 billion of certificates of indebtedness. The volume of bills has fluctuated between $19 billion and $29 billion for the past five years. The volume of certificates has fluctuated between about $15 billion and $35 billion [3] during the same period.

Treasury Notes. Treasury notes are intermediate-term securities running for more than 1 year but not over 5 years. They are

[2] *Federal Reserve Bulletin,* February, 1958, p. 484.
[3] *Ibid.*

generally issued in coupon form. At the end of 1957, $20.7 billion of notes was outstanding. During the last 5 years the amount of notes outstanding has varied from about $17 billion to almost $50 billion.[4]

Treasury Bonds. Treasury bonds have a maturity in excess of 5 years and have been issued for periods as long as 40 years but usually for less than 20 years. Most are available in either coupon or registered form. Most bonds are available in denominations of from $500 to $100,000. As of January 31, 1958, there were 26 separate issues outstanding with coupon rates ranging between $2\frac{1}{8}$ and $3\frac{1}{4}$ per cent. The volume of bonds was $82.1 billion at the end of 1957. It has fluctuated between $77 billion and the present level for the last 5 years.[5] The Treasury also had $9.5 billion of a convertible bond issue outstanding at the end of 1957. These $2\frac{3}{4}$ per cent bonds were not marketable but were convertible into marketable Treasury notes.

Nonmarketable Issues. Nonmarketable issues totaled $53.4 billion, of which almost $52.5 billion was in savings bonds and the rest in such special issues as armed forces leave bonds.[6] Various series of savings bonds have been issued. The most popular are Series E bonds, which are offered continuously by banks, post offices, and some other financial institutions. They are sold at 75 per cent of face value in denominations at maturity of from $25 to $10,000. They run for 9 years and 8 months, and earn 3 per cent if held to maturity. They may be held for another 10 years at 3 per cent compound interest if the investor so desires. They are not salable, but they may be surrendered for cash any time after 60 days from the date of issue. The redemption price is fixed so that no interest is earned if they are held for 60 days or less, and after that the rate of interest increases progressively to maturity. If held for one year, the bonds pay only about 1.5 per cent interest. An individual may not buy more than $20,000 of Series E bonds in any one year.

Series H bonds provide for semiannual interest payments. They are sold at par and also run for 9 years and 8 months as do Series E bonds, but they cannot be extended. Interest payments

[4] *Ibid.*
[5] *Ibid.*
[6] *Ibid.*

begin at 1.65 per cent the first year and increase year by year so as to average 3 per cent for the whole period. A $20,000 limit on purchases in one year is in effect just as for Series E bonds.

Series J bonds are of the same type as Series E. They run for 12 years and sell for $72 for a $100 maturity value. Denominations are as low as $25 and as high as $100,000. These bonds earn 2.76 per cent if held to maturity. The limit on purchases in any one year is much higher than for Series E or H bonds since an individual may buy up to $200,000 a year of Series J and Series K bonds combined. Series K bonds are bonds that are sold at par and pay 2¾ per cent interest. They are issued for 12 years in denominations of from $500 to $100,000. They may be cashed after 6 months, but the cash value is below the face value until maturity to encourage holding them to maturity. Like all savings bonds, these bonds cannot be transferred except to heirs or business successors and have no collateral value.

Special Issues. The last type of government bonds includes the special issues for United States government investment accounts, such as the Federal Old-Age and Survivors Insurance Trust Fund, the Government Life Insurance Fund, the National Service Life Insurance Fund, and the Federal Deposit Insurance Corporation. At the end of 1957 special issues amounted to $45.8 billion.[7]

Effect on the Money Market. Varying the proportions of long-term, intermediate-term, and short-term securities and of marketable and nonmarketable issues has a pronounced effect on different sectors of the money market by increasing the supply of one type of security and reducing the supply of others. For example, as of June 30, 1949, the Treasury had only about $3.6 billion of notes outstanding.[8] This small amount of intermediate-term government borrowing increased the demand for medium-term municipal securities and thus helped local financing of public works.

The money market has been affected in the past by restrictions on bank ownership placed in some bond issues. The policy of issuing bank ineligible bonds and of shifting the debt to such bonds can restrain credit creation. When bonds are sold to non-bank investors, credit expansion does not take place. Preventing

[7] *Ibid.*
[8] *Federal Reserve Bulletin*, February, 1952, p. 177.

banks from buying bonds outstanding forces them to use idle investment funds for short-term government and for other securities. Insofar as bonds other than government issues are bought, the liquidity of a bank portfolio is also reduced somewhat.

Interest-Rate Patterns

Interest-rate patterns on government bonds likewise have an effect on the money markets. The rates paid by the government on short-term borrowing affect short-term rates on other securities and on bank loans. Banks will not invest in other securities unless the rates are as good as, or better than, those on government securities, and they also demand a reasonable margin over short-term government rates to compensate for the added work and risk of commercial loans. The same is true of medium- and long-term rates.

The government, even as the largest borrower in the country, cannot set the pattern of interest rates without regard to the supply of and demand for investment funds in general. But it can exert an influence over different sectors of the money market by varying interest rates on short-term, intermediate-term, and long-term security issues. Interest rates, maturities, and types of securities issued must be geared to the needs and the desires of investors if the public debt is to be financed most expeditiously.

For example, in 1954, when business was in a minor recession, average rates of interest on various types of government securities were as follows: [9]

Bills (rates on new issues)	.953%
Certificates	.92 %
Notes	1.82 %
Bonds	2.53 %

By the end of October, 1957, when business was at boom levels, rates had increased as follows: [10]

Bills (rates on new issues)	3.591%
Certificates	3.94 %
Notes	3.99 %
Bonds	3.73 %

The short-term rates were increased far more during this period than were long-term rates, and also more than rates on

[9] *Federal Reserve Bulletin*, May, 1956, p. 477.
[10] *Federal Reserve Bulletin*, February, 1958, p. 165.

notes. The rate on notes was well below that on bonds in 1953 but above it in 1957.

Some have advocated the funding of a large part of the short-term debt by issuing long-maturity bonds at interest rates above those presently used. This would ease the burden on the Treasury, which now has over $1.5 billion of securities coming due each week. It would not, however, serve the economy best. Short-term government bonds have become a regular source of investment for short-term funds of banks, institutions, businesses, and wealthy individuals. The government thus is filling a need in financing as it has, as well as saving interest costs. Any decided change would have pronounced repercussions on the short-term and long-term money markets.

Debt management thus exerts important influences on the total money market and especially on various sectors of it as patterns of securities and interest rates are changed.

TRUST ACCOUNT OPERATIONS

The Treasury can also influence the money markets by the use it makes of funds in the trust accounts under its supervision, such as the Federal Old-Age and Survivors Insurance Trust Fund. As of November 30, 1957, government investment accounts were in excess of $55 billion. About $46 billion was invested in special issues designed only for government trust funds, and over $9 billion was in issues that could be held by the general public.[11] The funds in these accounts increase rapidly in prosperous years.

When the Treasury buys regular bonds in the market with these funds instead of special issues, it affects the demand for such bonds. It has also engaged in selling such bonds and shifting to special issues. As long as a substantial part of these funds is in general issues, the Treasury is in a position to influence the money markets both by buying and selling government bonds. Open-market operations are thus no longer the exclusive province of the Federal Reserve.

Both the Treasury and the Federal Reserve thus can substantially influence monetary and credit conditions. If working at cross purposes, each could offset the actions of the other. Cooperation is needed if credit is to be governed so as to serve the needs

[11] *Ibid.*, p. 172.

of industry, commerce, and the government in the best possible manner. This problem will be considered more fully in the last chapter in which recent monetary and credit policies and problems will be analyzed.

QUESTIONS

1. Describe the process by which gold that is sold to the Treasury is paid for. How are bank reserves affected?
2. Describe the procedures followed in sterilizing gold purchases. Why was this policy criticized?
3. Describe the silver buying program of the Treasury. How are bank reserves affected when silver is purchased?
4. List the various depositaries in which the Treasury keeps funds. Why is each one used?
5. Describe the three types of Treasury Tax and Loan Accounts.
6. Define X balances. What effect do they have on Treasury Tax and Loan Account balances?
7. Explain the handling of government receipts.
8. Explain how government outlays are handled.
9. How does the direct purchase of certificates of indebtedness by the Federal Reserve System aid the Treasury in handling its accounts?
10. Discuss the effects of tax policy on monetary and credit conditions.
11. How does deficit financing affect the supply of credit when bonds are sold to individuals? to commercial banks? to federal reserve banks?
12. Discuss various objectives of debt management.
13. Prepare a table listing the various types of securities issued by the United States government and the major characteristics of each type.
14. Discuss the effects on the money markets of varying the proportions of various types of securities issued by the government.
15. Discuss the pattern of interest rates on various types of government securities and its effect on the money market.
16. How may Treasury handling of the trust accounts under its supervision influence the money markets?
17. What is the relationship between Federal Reserve and Treasury powers in the money and credit field?

SUGGESTED READINGS

ADAMS, E. SHERMAN. *Monetary Management.* New York: The Ronald Press Company, 1950. Chapters 7, 8, 9.

Federal Reserve Bank of New York. *The Treasury and the Money Market.* New York: The Federal Reserve Bank of New York, 1954.

Institute for International Finance, Bulletin No. 189. *Credit and Debt Management Policies for a Changing Economy.* New York: New York University, 1954.

POOLE, KENYON E. (ed.). *Fiscal Policies and the American Economy.* New York: Prentice-Hall, Inc., 1951. Chapters 2, 4, 5.

Monetary

Policies and

Problems

Chapter 25

Monetary Policies

and the Price Level

Monetary policies have an effect on many phases of economic activity, but especially on the level of prices and on interest rates and the money markets. This chapter will be concerned with the relationship of monetary policies to price changes and the effects of such changes on the economy in general.

BASIC FACTORS AFFECTING PRICES

In a free enterprise economy, competition acts as the basic regulator of production and distribution. This influence of competition is exerted through changes in the prices of individual commodities. Under perfectly competitive conditions, prices are set by supply and demand through impersonal market forces. Such factors as a change in the availability of raw materials or of skilled labor and a change in the cost of capital affect the supply of a product and thus its price. Changes in the number of consumers, changes in consumer income, changes in taste, and similar factors that affect demand also affect the price of a product.

Although a producer has some control over his prices in most markets in actual practice, supply and demand are still the dominant price factors. Changes in the factors that affect supply will have an influence on a producer's costs and thus on his decisions regarding his selling prices. Factors affecting demand will determine how many units of a product consumers will demand at different prices. A producer must consider his demand schedule along with cost data in determining the prices for his products. He may do it experimentally by observing the results on sales and profits of his price policies, but supply and demand factors are the basic determinants of his policy.

Factors Affecting Supply and Demand in General

Some of the factors affecting the supply of and demand for individual products, and through them the prices of those products, have a general influence on the prices of almost all commodities. Producers are competing with other producers for the supply of labor in general and for some specialized types of skilled labor, and for the supply of some types of raw materials and of capital. Since the consumer must allocate his income among various types of purchases, without a change in his income an increase in his expenditures on one product must lead to a decrease in his demand for others or a decrease in savings.

Not only are supply and demand factors thus interrelated, but various general economic influences affect all of them in varying degrees. The long-term trend in productivity of labor and capital affects supply, and the development of new goods affects demand. Customs such as those associated with Christmas and Easter have an effect upon both the demand and the supply of goods during various seasons of the year.

More pronounced influences arise out of the forces associated with the recurrent fluctuations in general business activity known as business cycles. Such cycles affect most phases of business activity at about the same time, but they are not regular in occurrence nor of the same severity from one cycle to the next. When demand in general drops considerably, prices and production are affected. As incomes are cut and unemployment spreads, demand is cut in a cumulative process and prices follow suit. Some consideration of this phenomena of cycles and the relationship of monetary policies to the cycle will be given in Chapter 27.

Monetary Influences on Prices

Another general influence on prices comes from the operation of the monetary and credit system itself. A change in the supply of money while other factors remain the same will affect demand and so have an influence on price. This change in price will in turn influence supply, and thus the effect will spread over the whole economy. Any factor that changes the value of the money unit will affect the whole economy by affecting both the demand for and the supply of goods. The changes that arise from changes in the monetary system are the topic for this chapter. As a background for understanding such changes, a brief examination will be made of past price changes of an unusual nature, especially in the United States.

SOME OUTSTANDING PRICE MOVEMENTS IN THE PAST

Changes in the money supply or in the amount of metal in the money unit have influenced prices materially from time to time since the days of the earliest records of civilization.

Early Experiences

The money standard in Babylon shortly before 2000 B. C.[1] was in terms of silver and barley. According to records of the period, one shekel of silver was supposed to be equal to 300 measures of grain. The earliest price records show that it was equal to only 240 measures of grain. At the time of Hammurabi, which was just before 2000 B. C., a shekel of silver declined to between 150 and 180 measures of grain, while in the Twentieth Century B. C. it declined to 90 measures. Much later, that is after the conquest of Babylonia by Persia in 539 B. C., the value of the silver shekel was between 15 and 40 measures of grain.

The largest inflationary period in ancient history was probably initiated by Alexander the Great when he captured the large gold hoards of Persia and brought them to Greece. The effect on prices was pronounced for some years, but twenty years after the death of Alexander a deflationary period began that lasted over fifty years.

The first recorded instances of deliberate currency debasement occurred in the Greek city states. Currency was debased by calling in all coins and issuing new ones containing less of the precious metals. This must have proved a popular form of inflation since there are many such cases in the records of Greek city states.

Roman Experience

Similar inflationary situations occurred in Roman history. Caesar Augustus brought such large quantities of precious metals

[1] The material in this section draws heavily on the book by Paul Einzig, *Inflation* (London: Chatto and Winders, 1952).

from Egypt that prices rose and interest rates fell. During the Punic wars devaluation led to inflation as the heavy bronze coin was reduced in stages from one pound to one ounce. From the time of Nero, debasements were frequent. The weight of gold coins was gradually reduced and silver coins had baser metals added to them so that they finally contained only 2 per cent of silver. Few attempts were made to arrest or reverse this process of debasement of the coinage. One such attempt by Aurelian to improve the coinage by adding to its metallic content was resisted so vigorously that it led to armed rebellion.

Experience in the Middle Ages and Early Modern Times

During the Middle Ages debasement of coinage was frequently practiced. This device was used as a source of revenue for princes and kings. The rulers of France used it in this way more than others, and records show that profit from debasement at times exceeded the total of all other revenues.

One of the outstanding examples of inflation followed the discovery of America. Gold and silver poured into Spain from Mexico and Peru; and since they were used to buy goods from other countries, they were distributed over the continent and to England. Prices rose in Spain and in most of Europe, but not in proportion to the increase in gold and silver stocks. This was due to the demands of increased trade resulting from the discovery of America and to large-scale hoarding of the precious metals.

Paper money was not used generally for domestic exchange until the end of the Seventeenth Century. The first outstanding example of inflation due to the issuing of an excessive amount of paper money was in France where John Law was given a charter in 1719 for a bank that could issue paper money. The note circulation of his bank amounted to almost 2,700 million livres [2] against which he had coin of 21 million livres and bullion of 27 million livres. Prices went up rapidly, but they fell just as fast when Law's bank failed and the money supply was again restricted.

The next outstanding example of inflation is the American experience during the Revolutionary War. This will be considered in the next topic, which deals with American monetary

[2] The livre was the monetary unit in use at that time in France.

experiences. Shortly after this American inflation, the government of the French Revolution issued paper currency in huge quantities. This currency, called assignats, declined to ½ per cent of its nominal value. This experience was so disastrous that the French financed the Napoleonic wars without inflation, but such inflation did take place in the countries that opposed Napoleon.

Inflation During World Wars I and II

The only outstanding case of inflation in the period between the Napoleonic Wars and World War I took place in the United States during the Civil War. Inflation during World War I was widespread, but it was held in check to some degree by government action. The most spectacular inflation took place in Germany when in 1923 prices soared to astronomical heights.

More attempts were made to control inflation during World War II, and they met with some measure of success. Runaway inflation, however, occurred in some countries, especially China and Hungary.

MAJOR AMERICAN PRICE MOVEMENTS

Prices in the United States have been affected in a pronounced way by monetary factors on several occasions. This has been especially true during major wars beginning with the War of Independence.

War of Independence

The war that brought this nation into being was financed to a large degree by inflationary means. The Second Continental Congress had no real authority to levy taxes and thus found it difficult to raise money. As a result this Congress decided to issue notes, at first for only $2 million. More and more were issued until the total rose to over $240 million, and the individual states issued $200 million more. Since the notes were crudely engraved, counterfeiting was easy and this fact helped to swell the total of circulating media. This continental currency depreciated in value so rapidly that the expression "not worth a Continental" has become a part of the American language.

War of 1812

During the War of 1812 attempts were made to avoid the inflationary finance of the Revolutionary War. But since the war was not popular in New England, it was impossible to finance it by taxation and borrowing. Paper currency was issued in a somewhat disguised form by putting out bonds in small denominations, bearing no interest and having no maturity date. Wholesale prices based on 1913 as 100 rose from 152 in 1812 to 221 in 1814. They declined to about the prewar level by 1816 and continued downward as depression engulfed the economy.[3]

War Between the States

The Mexican War did not involve the total economy to any extent and led to no inflationary movements in prices. The Civil War, however, was financed in part through the issuance of paper money. In the early stages Congress could not raise enough money by taxes and borrowing to finance all expenditures, and therefore it resorted to inflation by issuing United States Notes with no backing, called "greenbacks." In all, $450 million of such paper money was authorized. Even though this was but a fraction of the cost of the war, prices went up substantially. Wholesale prices on a 1913 base increased from 87 in 1860 to 189 in 1865.[4] Attempts to retire the greenbacks at the end of the war led to deflation and depression in 1866, and as a result the contraction law was repealed and the greenbacks are still a part of our money supply today.

World War I

During World War I no resort was made directly to printing-press money, but inflationary policies were nevertheless followed. About one third of the cost of the war was raised by taxes and two thirds by borrowing. A substantial part of this credit was obtained from the banking system and thus added to the supply of purchasing media. In fact, individuals were even persuaded to use Liberty Bonds as collateral for bank loans to buy such bonds. Prices rose from 100 in 1913 to 221 in 1920, and then as credit

[3] Albert Gailord Hart, *Money, Debt, and Economic Activity* (New York: Prentice-Hall, Inc., 1948), p. 270.

[4] *Ibid.*

expansion was finally restricted in 1921 they dropped to a level of 140 in 1922.[5]

World War II

During World War II a much larger proportion of the cost of the war was met by noninflationary means. Nevertheless, large sums of bonds were still taken up by the banking system. By the end of the war, the debt of the federal government had increased by $207 billion. Bank holdings of government bonds had increased by almost $60 billion.[6] Prices went up by only about a third during the war as they were held in check after the first year by price and wage controls, but they rose rapidly after the controls were lifted in the postwar period. In 1947 wholesale prices had risen to 205 from a level of 110 in 1939, using 1913 as a base (100).[7]

ANALYSIS OF MONETARY FACTORS DETERMINING PRICES

The record of outstanding monetary changes throughout history shows that inflation usually occurred because the supply of money was increased faster than was the supply of goods. In the earliest cases this was true because large stocks of gold and silver were acquired as part of the booty of war. Later on, governments increased the money supply by cutting the metal content of existing coins and using the extra metal to issue more coins. Beginning in the Eighteenth Century paper money was issued without backing, which led to higher prices. In the last half of the Nineteenth Century, and especially in the Twentieth Century, bank credit expansion was the basis for inflation, and credit contraction was the basis for deflation.

Such changes in the volume of money were probably the most important factor affecting prices. They were by no means the only influence, however. Prices did not always go up in proportion to the increases in money supply. This was especially true in connection with the increase in the money supply as gold and silver

---

[5] *Ibid.*
[6] Committee for Economic Development, *Flexible Monetary Policy* (New York: Committee for Economic Development, 1953), p. 25.
[7] Hart, *Op. Cit.*

were brought to the Old World from Mexico and Peru. Trade went up at the same time, and so more money was needed to meet the demand of such commerce. Hoarding of precious metals also took place, or in other words, the rate at which the money was used in the market to buy goods was slowed down.

Equation of Exchange

Changes in the volume of money, in the rate at which money is used, and in the volume of goods being exchanged must be considered together to understand their relationship to price changes. These factors have been put into an equation, known as the *equation of exchange* or the quantity equation, which serves as a ready frame of reference for analysis. In the simplest form, the equation may be stated as follows:

$$MV = \Sigma\, pQ$$

In this equation M is the total supply of money in circulation, and V is the velocity of circulation or turnover expressed as the average number of times the money supply is used to purchase goods during the year. On the goods (right) side of the equation there is a summation of the amounts spent on all goods, which is equal to the average price of each article sold, as for example, bushels of wheat, multiplied by the quantity sold. For convenience, the right side of the equation may be written as PT with P a weighted average of all average prices, or p's, and T the sum of all the Q's. The equation then becomes $MV = PT$.

Often the equation is rewritten by adding bank credit and its velocity as separate factors, M' and V'. The equation then becomes $MV + M'V' = PT$.

This equation can aid in understanding the factors involved in general price changes. It views two identical quantities from different points of view. The total money value of goods and services sold is viewed from the point of view of the price of the goods by summing the quantities of goods multiplied by a weighted average of prices, and from the point of view of the sum of the money transactions to buy such goods. These two magnitudes must of course be equal, but valuable information on the economy can be gained from a study of the factors that are at work to make them equal.

Effect of Changes in the Factors in the Equation of Exchange on Prices

An oversimplified picture of the way in which the various factors affect prices may be obtained by varying one factor while others are assumed to remain constant. Let us begin by seeing how changes in M will affect prices. Suppose that the government debases coinage under a monetary system based on metals alone and issues two coins for each old one. The denomination of each coin remains the same, but the amount of metal is cut in half. There are now two lighter coins for each one that was formerly outstanding, for example, two $5 coins of half the former weight for each $5 coin outstanding before, and so on. If all other factors remain the same and time lags are ignored, prices must double to keep the equation in balance. The result will be the same if the government does not debase the coinage but simply duplicates each coin in existence. If twice as many coins are in existence as before and are used at the previous rate to make purchases, prices must also double to keep the equation in balance.

The same principles hold for the total of M and M'. If the quantity of purchasing media is doubled and all other factors remain the same, prices must double; if it is cut in half, prices must drop to half of their former level.

The same is true of other factors in the equation. If V and V' change and other factors remain constant, prices must change in the same proportion. If T increases by 50 per cent but the other factors do not change, prices must drop by a third to keep the equation in balance, that is, to keep the product of $P \times T$ the same.

Changes in M and M' and Other Factors

This analysis is too simplified to be a satisfactory explanation of monetary phenomena in the real world. When one factor such as M changes, other factors will probably also change so that the effect on prices may not be proportionate, or a change may not occur at all. For example, the supply of money, that is, the total of M and M', may double; but the rate of use, or V and V', may be cut in half. Then the other side of the equation need not be affected at all. Or, V and V' could decrease somewhat and prices go up somewhat to again balance the situation.

So far the effect of a change in M, M', V, or V' has been assumed to be on P. It is possible, however, for T to be affected. If in a period of unused resources M and M' are increased and V and V' do not decrease, or at least not proportionately, T can go up to balance the PT side of the equation. Thus it can be seen that the actual situation is likely to be far more complex than the situation in which a change in M, V, M', or V' leads to a proportionate change in P.

The Cash Balances Approach

An alternative way of analyzing the effect of money changes on prices is through an analysis of the cash balances held by the public. Several equations are used to explain the relationship of money to prices and trade. One of the most useful is the following: $M = KTP$. In this equation M is the money supply, T is the physical volume of trade to be transacted with money during a year, and P is the price level of the things included in T. The new factor, K, is the amount of money held in the form of cash balances, that is, cash plus bank deposits. It is expressed as the fraction representing the ratio of cash balances to the amount of transactions in a given period of time, such as a year, a quarter, or a month.

K is thus related to the velocity of the circulation of money. If the amount of cash balances held is equal to one fifth of a year's transactions, V is 5 and K is 1/5. In other words, K and V are reciprocals of one another, that is, $K = \dfrac{1}{V}$. The cash balances equation therefore can be written $M = \dfrac{1}{V}(TP)$ or $MV = TP$.

Thus this cash balances equation and the quantity equation are but somewhat different ways of looking at the same thing. There is an advantage, however, to using both equations as alternative approaches to the factors affecting prices. The equation of exchange focuses attention on the rate at which money is spent and the reasons for spending it at that rate. The cash balances equation puts special emphasis on the reasons for holding money as cash balances, as well as on the reasons for spending it, by stating the relationship between the money supply on one side and the demand for money to be held as cash balances and to be used in trade on the other side. It is therefore possible to use traditional economic supply and demand analysis to help understand what is happening to prices.

Effect of Changes in Cash Balances

One or two brief examples will show how the cash balances approach can be useful in analysis. For example, an increase in the supply of money through government deficits is likely to affect cash balances. If there is less than full employment at that time, the volume of trade will go up and there may also be an abnormal increase in cash balances. This will occur if business-men do not feel that future propects for a continuing volume of business at profitable levels are good and therefore do not spend normal amounts on replacement of inventory, repairs and maintenance, and capital expenditures. As a result, the increased government expenditures at such a time will not have the same effect on the volume of business as they would have had if the outlook for the future were more optimistic. This was the situa-tion during the thirties when government deficits led to ab-normal increases in cash balances.

If government deficits, however, increase the money supply when the expectation is for a continued increase in business at profitable levels and for inflation, as is true during a war, cash balances, or K, will not increase. They may even be reduced as businessmen rush to buy raw materials and machinery and equipment before prices advance. On the other hand, if prices are held in check by price controls as they were during World War II, cash balances, or K, will increase greatly. When price controls are lifted, these additional cash balances will be used to buy goods and services and prices will rise at that time. Thus inflation has not been avoided but only repressed for a time and shifted to a period when more goods are available.

FACTORS INFLUENCING THE MONEY SUPPLY, VELOCITY, AND THE VOLUME OF TRADE

To provide a background for understanding the types of adjustments that are likely to occur in actual practice, some of the factors which may affect each variable in the equation will be considered.

The Money Supply

Since a detailed analysis was made in Chapter 22 of the factors affecting the supply of money, M and M', in the American monetary system, they will only be reviewed briefly here. The monetary gold and silver stocks depend upon past accumulations of these metals and current additions to them. Such additions depend on the proportion of newly mined or imported metals devoted to monetary rather than nonmonetary uses. To get at the basic factors determing the total quantity of metals available, as well as the percentage that becomes part of the money supply, involves an analysis of the price of the metals as money that is set by the government, the cost of production that is influenced by costs of labor and capital in general, the intensity of demand for nonmonetary uses, and the like. The total currency supply is also influenced by government and banking policies that determine the amount of subsidiary coinage and paper money outstanding, as well as by the demands of the public for cash.

The largest part of the supply of money today is bank credit. The amount of such credit is determined by the demand for holding such credit as deposits in checking accounts and for borrowing such credit by private individuals and the government, and by the policies of the commercial banks and central bank authorities that govern its availability. The basic reasons for holding a certain level of money in checking accounts are complex. They will be considered under the factors determining V and V', since the amount of money a community decides to hold at any time determines the rate at which it will be turned over in use.

The amount of borrowing from banks by private individuals depends on a whole host of factors, such as the volume of business, expectations concerning the outlook for business, the amount of working capital the firm obtains from nonbank sources, and the relative cost and availability of bank and nonbank credit. Government demand for bank credit depends on the need for funds, which in turn depends on such factors as government receipts and expenditures, and the financing of deficits by the use of bank or nonbank funds. Political considerations are often the dominant factors in such decisions.

The Velocity of Money

The velocity of money is the relationship between two factors; the volume of monetary transactions; and the amount of cash balances (cash and bank deposits) that individuals, business units, institutions, and the government feel they must keep on hand to meet demands for funds and to tide them over emergencies. These factors in turn depend upon the organization of the financial system of the community and the state of expectations concerning the future.

The organization of the financial system is an important factor in determining the needs for money and bank credit. If money can be borrowed easily, quickly, and at a reasonable cost, smaller money balances will be kept by individuals, businesses, and government. A highly developed system of savings institutions that provides safety, liquidity, and some income on savings also increases velocity since individuals will place funds in such institutions rather than hoard the money. The degree to which such funds can be kept fully invested by such institutions also affects velocity. If, for example, a savings and loan association can get a loan from a home loan bank when it has an unusual or unexpected demand for funds, it can keep its resources more fully utilized than it could if it were entirely on its own.

The mechanics of the system of money receipts and payments in a community also has an important effect on velocity. The more rapidly checks can be sent from place to place and cleared, the faster the velocity of money. The frequency of money receipts and payments affects velocity too. If income is received every thirty days and spent regularly day by day, velocity is lower than if it is received every seven days, since in the former case cash balances are higher and expenditures are the same day by day.

Velocity is also affected by the timing of receipts and disbursements. The closer they correspond, the smaller the need for cash balances and the greater is the velocity of money. This may be seen by comparing three different ways of receiving the same income for a month and paying for the same volume of purchases. In the first case, income is received daily and expenditures are made daily. This means that cash balances are at a relatively low level in relationship to purchases for a month and the average velocity for the month is relatively high.

Assume in the second case that income is received once a month and expenditures are made daily. In this case cash balances at the beginning of the month and on the average during the month are much higher in relationship to expenditures during the month than in the first case, and velocity is much lower.

Assume that in the third case income is received once a month and that goods are bought more or less regularly during the month, but they are bought on credit, using charge accounts that are to be paid once a month. In this case, cash balances at the end of the month are the same in relationship to monthly expenditures as in the second case. Monthly expenditures in relationship to average cash balances, or velocity, however, are much higher since cash was on hand only long enough to pay the charge account. If in this last case an individual received his monthly income on the 20th of the month and did not pay for his purchases until the end of the month, his average cash balances would be higher and velocity lower than if he received his income on the last of the month and paid his charge account on the same or the following day.

Business cash balances and the velocity of payments are also affected in various ways by the timing of receipts and disbursements. A business may sell for cash only and receive its income from sales more or less regularly throughout the month. If payments are made more or less regularly during the month as might be the case, for example, for a huckster who sells fruit and vegetables that he buys and pays for daily, cash balances can be lower and average velocity will be higher than in the case of a dry goods store that pays for its merchandise and most other expenditures once a month.

A business such as a wholesale establishment may sell almost all of its goods on credit. If it gives discounts to its customers for payment by the tenth of the month, it may receive most of its cash shortly after the tenth. If this business must in turn make its payments by the tenth in order to take advantage of discounts, cash balances that must be kept to make such payments will be relatively high in relationship to sales for the month and velocity will be relatively low.

Another major factor affecting velocity is the state of expectations about the future level of economic activity. Consumers will spend more freely when they feel that money income will remain stable or will increase than they will when they expect incomes to decrease. They will also spend their money more rapidly when they feel prices are likely to increase in the near future. Businessmen keep smaller sums of money on deposit to meet emergencies when they feel the future outlook is favorable than when it is doubtful or unfavorable. This is especially true when they expect the prices of the goods they have to buy to increase. They also defer expenditures on capital equipment and cut purchases for inventory when expectations are for a decline in business, and this reduces the velocity of money. Expectations regarding interest rates and the future level of security prices may make new financing more or less desirable and so increase or decrease velocity.

The Physical Volume of Trade

Not only the volume and velocity of purchasing media, but also the physical volume of trade is subject to many influences, some of which lead to changes in prices. The basic volume of trade is determined by such factors as the size of the population and the labor force and its technical competence, the quantity and the quality of the natural resources and man-made capital, and the techniques of production, distribution, and administration. The extent to which resources are fully used is equally important. The volume of trade effected by means of money transactions depends upon the extent of barter and upon the number of times goods and services are exchanged for money before sale to the final consumer. This is affected by the degree of specialization in production, the degree of integration from raw materials to finished products in one concern, and the number of middlemen in the distribution process. Since T includes financial transactions, it also depends upon the volume of new securities issued and the frequency with which already existing securities are sold. The same is true of the volume of sale of durable goods, such as houses, that were produced and sold in the first instance in an earlier period.

The general price level is thus the result of the interaction of all of these factors that affect M, M', V, V', and T. Changes in the money supply can lead to changes in prices, but many other factors are involved.

AN ANALYSIS OF CHANGES IN THE GENERAL PRICE LEVEL

On the basis of all of these factors that affect the price level, it is possible to analyze various types of changes in the general price level somewhat further.

Price Changes Initiated by a General Change in Costs

It is possible for the general price level to increase without the original impulse coming from either the money supply or its velocity. If costs are increased materially, as in the case of wages being increased faster than productivity, selling prices will increase in a period in which the demand for goods is strong in relationship to the supply. The added need for funds to meet production and distribution at higher prices usually leads to increases in the money supply or velocity, or both. Thus these factors have increased, but the basic influence was from costs and prices to the money supply and velocity. These may not go up, however, if the monetary authorities restrict credit expansion, but in that case only the most efficient concerns will have enough demand to operate profitably and as a result some resources will be unemployed.

Price Changes Initiated by Changes in the Money Supply

The interrelationship of the factors that affect prices in actual practice is quite complex. In this topic additional consideration will be given to the adjustments that take place when the primary change is in the money supply or its velocity. In the following chapters the more complex interrelationships arising out of changes in both the money supply and goods side of the equation during business cycles will be considered.

Several types of inflation may be due to an increase in the supply or turn-over of money. Inflation may be generated by an increase in the supply of purchasing power, such as was the case when the supply of metals was increased or their value was cut. In modern times such inflation is usually initiated by government deficits financed by credit creation. If this is done in periods of less than full employment of men and resources, the volume of trade will go up and prices may at first be affected but slightly, if at all. As unused resources are brought into use, however, prices will be affected. Some items, such as metals, may become scarce while other resources are still in plentiful supply, and the prices of the scarce items will rise. As full use of any resource is approached, expectations of future price rises will force prices up. Attempts to buy before such price rises will also increase demand above current needs and thus force prices up. Since some costs such as interest costs and wages set by contract will lag, profits will rise and this will tend to increase the demand for capital goods. Such changes will be considered more fully in the discussion of monetary factors in business cycles in Chapter 27.

After resources are fully employed, the full effect of the increased money supply will be on prices. It may be more than proportional for a time as expectations of higher prices lead to a faster rate of spending and so raise V and V^1. The expansion will continue until trade and prices are in balance at the new levels of the money supply. Velocity will probably drop somewhat from those levels during the period of rising prices since the desire to trade money for goods before they go up in price has disappeared.

Even if the supply of purchasing media is increased in a period of relatively full employment of men and resources, prices may not go up proportionately. Higher prices will increase profits for a time and so lead to a demand for more capital and labor. This may lead to an increase of the labor force by inducing married women, retired workers, and similar groups to enter the labor force. Capital will also probably be utilized more fully by such devices as having two or three shifts use machines.

Speculative Type of Inflation

Inflation due to an increased money supply can lead to additional price pressure of the speculative type. Since prices have risen for some time, the idea becomes current that they will keep on rising. This may become self-generating for a time since instead of higher prices resulting in decreased demand, people may buy more to get goods before they go still higher. This may not happen in all sectors of the economy but may be confined to certain areas, as it was to land prices in the Florida land boom in the 1920's or to security prices in the 1928-1929 stock market boom. Such a price rise leads to an increase in V and V' since speculators try to turn over their funds as rapidly as possible and many others try to buy ahead of needs in anticipation of further price rises. Such an inflation can only lead to collapse since speculators will hold goods or securities only if they feel they are going higher. When they are no longer sure of price increases and try to liquidate, prices collapse as they did in the commodity markets in 1920 and the the stock market in 1929.

QUESTIONS

1. Discuss the several factors that have an effect on the demand for and supply of all goods and services.
2. Describe the process by which inflation took place before modern times.
3. Discuss the early periods of inflation based on the issue of paper money.
4. Discuss the basis for inflation during World Wars I and II.
5. Discuss the causes of the major periods of inflation in American history.
6. State the equation of exchange. Identify each factor in it. Why are the two sides of the equation equal?
7. Analyze the effect of changes in M, M', V, V', and T on the price level.
8. State the cash balances equation and identify each factor in it.
9. How may focusing attention on cash balances be useful in analyzing the factors affecting the price level?
10. Outline and discuss the major factors affecting the money supply, the velocity of money, and the physical volume of trade.
11. Explain the process by which price changes may be initiated by a general change in costs.
12. Explain the process by which a change in the money supply leads to a change in the general price level.
13. Discuss the speculative type of inflation.

SUGGESTED READINGS

American Economic Association, Lutz, Friedrich A., and Mints, Lloyd M. (eds.). *Readings in Monetary Theory.* Homewood, Ill.: Richard D. Irwin Company, 1951.

Einzig, Paul. *Inflation.* London: Chatto and Winders, 1952.

Fisher, Irving. *The Purchasing Power of Money.* New York: The Macmillan Co., 1926.

Kemmerer, E. W. *Money.* New York: The Macmillan Co., 1935. Chapters 10-13.

Robertson, D. H. *Money.* New York: Harcourt, Brace & Company, Inc., 1929.

Chapter 26

Monetary Policies,

Interest Rates, and

the Money Market

In this chapter the effect of monetary policies on interest rates and on the money markets will be analyzed. Consideration will be given first to the demand for loanable funds and to the supply of such funds since these are the basic factors in determining interest rates. The major factors that affect the supply of loanable funds and the demand for them will be analyzed next. Then consideration will be given to the effects of the policies of the Federal Reserve System and the Treasury on the demand for and the supply of funds. The final section of the chapter considers the New York money market, which is the sector of the capital market in which final adjustments between the demand for and the supply of loanable funds are made.

INTEREST RATES

The basic price that equates the demand for and the supply of loanable funds in the capital markets is the interest rate. The quoted interest rate for any type of loan is a combination of several factors. Part of it is a fee for the administrative costs of making a loan, and another part of it is a payment for the risk involved. The remainder is a payment for the use of money itself. This payment is made because the borrower has the use of the money during the period of the loan and can employ it to his advantage. It is also in part a compensation to the lender for parting with liquidity. Instead of having money that he can use at will for investment or consumption expenditures, he now has a claim for repayment at a future date.

Quoted interest rates for different types of loans are not the same but vary depending upon the use to which the funds are to be put. The costs incurred in making short-term or long-term loans to business, short-term or long-term loans to governmental units, loans to religious and charitable institutions, and loans to consumers to buy real estate, to finance the purchase of durable goods, or to tide them over emergencies vary significantly, and these variations account for differences in quoted interest rates. The same is true of the way in which lenders assess the degree of risk involved in various types of loans. The part of the quoted interest rate that is paid for the use of the money itself and for parting with liquidity, however, is determined by general supply and demand factors in the market for loanable funds.

Supply of Loanable Funds

There are two basic sources of loanable funds, savings and bank credit. The supply of savings comes from all sectors of the economy. Individuals may save part of their income, either as direct savings or through an indirect savings program such as that involved in purchasing whole-life or endowment life insurance policies or annuity contracts. Governmental units at times have funds available in excess of current expenditures, and so do non-profit institutions. Corporations may have savings available because they are not paying out all of their earnings as dividends. Depreciation allowances which are not being used currently for the purchase of new capital equipment to replace that which is wearing out may also be available for lending.

Another source of savings consists of the many pension funds, both governmental and private, in existence in this country. These funds, which are building up large reserves to meet future commitments, are available for investment.

Some savings are invested as ownership equity in business either directly in single proprietorships or partnerships, or by buying stock in a corporation. The bulk of such savings is available as loanable funds.

Some lending is done directly as, for example, when an individual lends money to a friend who is in business to enable him to expand his operations. As we have seen, however, one of the basic functions of financial institutions is the accumulation of savings, and most savings are made available to borrowers through such institutions.

The other basic source of loanable funds is bank credit. Banks are not only the major suppliers of credit, but they can create deposits which are the most widely used forms of money in our economy.

The supply of loanable funds can be grouped in various ways. They may be divided into short-term funds and long-term funds. The supply of funds can also be grouped by types of credit, such as business credit, consumer credit, agricultural credit, and government credit, and by the institutions supplying each type, as has been done in this book.

Factors Affecting the Supply of Loanable Funds

Many factors affect the supply of loanable funds from savings and from the extension of bank credit. Some factors primarily affect one of these types of sources, others both of them. The factors affecting each of them will be considered in turn, and then attention will be directed to a major factor affecting both of them.

Volume of Savings. The major determinant of the volume of savings, corporate as well as individual, is the level of national income. When income is high, savings are high; when it is low, savings are low. Important in the level of savings, too, is the pattern of income taxes, that is, both the level of the tax and the tax rates in various income brackets.

Also important from the standpoint of the individual is the stage in his life cycle. Little saving is done by young people, especially young married people with children of school age. When the children have finished school, a family usually saves money for a period of time until the wage earner retires or has his income reduced or cut off completely because of physical disability. An economy in which a substantial proportion of the families are young couples with children will have a smaller amount of savings in the aggregate than one in which older people predominate.

The volume of savings is also dependent upon the factors that affect indirect savings. The more effectively the life insurance industry promotes the sale of whole-life and endowment insurance policies, the larger will be the volume of savings. The larger the demand for private pension funds in which funds are built up during working years to be used to make payments upon retirement, the larger the volume of savings. The effect of interest rates on such savings is often just the reverse of the normal effect of price on supply. As interest rates decrease, more money must be paid for insurance to provide the same type of coverage since a smaller amount of money is available from the reinvestment of earnings. Inversely, as interest rates rise, less money need be put into reserves to obtain the same objectives. The same thing is true of savings put into annuities and pension funds.

In the case of savings associated with the use of consumer credit, the effect of interest rates is felt only with quite a lag. When, for example, a car is bought on payments over a two-year period, savings must go on for two years to repay the loan. This saving to meet monthly payments is unrelated to current changes in interest rates. There may even be an inverse effect in the case of a loan for the purchase of a house, since if interest rates drop substantially, the loan can be refinanced so that the same dollar payments provide a larger amount for repayment of principal, that is, for saving.

The availability of long-term credit of different types also depends upon the policies of the many different suppliers of such credit. As we have seen, these include commercial banks, commercial credit companies, savings and loan associations, mutual savings banks, insurance companies, investment companies, and individuals. Since commercial banks are by no means dominant in this field, credit is not expanded directly to any appreciable extent to meet long-term credit demands. Indirectly, however, their policies and those of the Federal Reserve are very important because, if funds are being supplied by the banking system for short-term needs, a larger proportion of the supply of loanable funds may be made available for long-term credit.

During the post-World War II period, the policies of the Federal Reserve and the Treasury influenced the supply of long-term funds materially. As part of the program of supporting bond prices, the Federal Reserve bought all bonds offered for sale at par or better. This meant that federal reserve credit was available for long-term investment since government bonds could be sold without fear of loss of principal to get additional funds for current lending.

Volume of Bank Credit. The availability of short-term credit depends to a large extent upon the lending policies of the commercial banks of the country and upon the policies of the Federal Reserve System that affect the banks. The attitude of bankers is important, and this is influenced by such factors as present business conditions and future prospects. The volume of bank reserves is also important, and this is determined not only by the Federal Reserve to a large extent but also by governmental borrowing policies. Thus the policies of commercial banks, the Federal Reserve, and the government are the important factors.

Liquidity Preference. A significant factor at times in determining the available supply of loanable funds, both long-term and short-term, is the attitude of lenders regarding the future. Lenders may feel that the economic outlook is so uncertain that they are reluctant to lend their money but prefer to keep it in liquid form. This liquidity preference may be so strong that large amounts of idle funds accumulate as they did in the depression of the thirties. Lenders may also have a preference for liquidity because they feel that interest rates will be higher in the near future or opportunities for direct investment more favorable, and they will therefore hold funds idle rather than lend them at present rates. Thus liquidity preference may hold some funds idle that would normally be available for lending.

Demand for Loanable Funds

The demand for loanable funds also comes from all sectors of the economy. Business borrows to finance current operations and to buy plant and equipment. Farmers likewise borrow to meet short-term and long-term needs. Institutions such as hospitals and schools borrow primarily to finance new buildings. Individuals borrow on a long-term basis to finance the purchase of a home, and on an intermediate- and short-term basis to finance the purchase of durable goods or to tide them over emergencies. Governmental units borrow to finance public buildings, to bridge the gap between expenditures and tax receipts, and to meet budget deficits.

Factors Affecting the Demand for Loanable Funds

The factors affecting the demand for loanble funds are different for different types of borrowers. They have been considered in detail in the analysis of the various types of credit. Therefore, the only factor to be considered here will be the effect of interest rates on the major types of credit.

One of the biggest borrowers is the federal government, and Congress is generally little influenced in its spending program by interest-rate considerations. Short-term business borrowing for some purposes may be affected but little by minor changes in interest rates. For example, a change in interest rates is of minor significance in deciding on a loan to hold goods in inventory for 90 days longer than normal because prices are expected to advance 10 per cent or more. A change in interest rates from 4 to 6 per cent a year changes carrying costs from 1 per cent of the value of the goods to $1\frac{1}{2}$ per cent, a negligible factor when compared with possible changes in prices, costs, and profits.

Fluctuations in long-term interest of $\frac{1}{4}$ or $\frac{1}{2}$ per cent do, however, have an effect on long-term business borrowing. Most corporations will defer long-term borrowing when such a rise in rates has taken place but only if prospects are favorable for lower rates in the near future.

Moderate changes in interest rates have little effect upon consumer borrowing. The administrative costs of consumer lending are so high in relationship to the pure money cost that the total effect of a small change in interest rates on the repayment schedule is minor. For example, if a $1,200 loan on a car for two years could be obtained for a 5 per cent discount, the monthly payment, excluding insurance, is $55. If the rate is raised to a 6 per cent discount, payments are only increased to $56 a month, hardly enough to deter purchase of the car on credit. The effect may be somewhat greater when loans are used to buy homes, but even on a $10,000 mortgage repaid over a period of 20 years a change of $\frac{1}{2}$ per cent in interest rates from 5 to $5\frac{1}{2}$ per cent would change monthly payments by only about $2.80.

No doubt in all fields some marginal borrowers are affected by moderate changes in interest rates. But for many types of loans the demand for credit is not very responsive to minor changes in the cost of borrowing.

Role of the Banking System and the Government

Interest rates do not directly or quickly change the supply of some types of loanable funds. The demand for loanable funds of many types is likewise not directly or immediately affected by interest rates. On the other hand, both the supply of and the demand for loanable funds are affected materially by the actions of the banking system and the government. When credit is expanded through short-term loans made by commercial banks, the supply of loanable funds is increased; and when credit is contracted, the supply of loanable funds is decreased. All actions of the Federal Reserve in setting rediscount rates, in buying securities in the open market, and in changing reserve requirements also affect the supply of loanable funds. In fact, all factors that were described in Chapter 22 as affecting the supply of purchasing media affect the supply of loanable funds in the market.

Furthermore, on the demand side government borrowing has now become a major influence and will remain so in the foreseeable future. Government surpluses or deficits make funds available in the market or take them out of the market in substantial amounts. Treasury policies regarding debt management materially affect the supply-and-demand relationships for short-term, intermediate, and long-term funds, as was seen in Chapter 24.

The capital markets are thus under the influence of the Treasury and the Federal Reserve and are likely to remain so. Their policies are thus important factors in these markets. They affect the demand for funds to a limited degree, but they have important influences on the supply. In fact, their real influence is through the effects their policies have on the availability of credit of various types.

Final adjustments between supply and demand in such a complex market can only be made quickly and effectively because a highly organized national money market exists in New York City. The organization and operation of this money market will be considered next.

THE NEW YORK MONEY MARKET

The national money market in New York City is not a definite organization, such as the New York Stock Exchange, but an intangible relationship between various participants that demand and supply funds in this market. It has been described by the New York Federal Reserve Bank as: [1]

---

[1] *Money Market Essays.* Federal Reserve Bank of New York, 1952, p. 1.

. . . the Central national market in New York City where temporary surplus funds of various types of organizations (including secondary reserves of the banks) go to find income-producing employment
without sacrifice of liquidity, and where short-term needs for funds are
satisfied, usually at interest rates that are advantageous to the borrower. It is a place where final adjustments between the supply of funds
and the demand for funds are made for the country as a whole, after
much regional clearing has been effected. In general, it is an impersonal market involving the usual lender-customer relationships only
to a limited extent. The open-market borrower frequently has certain
sources from which he expects to obtain part of the funds he needs
fairly regularly, but he usually feels no obligation to go to any particular lender or group of lenders for his financing any longer than he
considers that to be in his interest, and he gets his money from whatever source he can on the most favorable terms. Similarly, the lender
in the money market ordinarily assumes no responsibility for financing
the borrower any longer than suits his convenience.

As is to be expected in a market of final money adjustments,
most credit is extended for short periods of time, some of it on a
day-to-day basis. The procedure is largely on an impersonal basis
since borrowers and lenders do not have a regular demand for or
supply of funds but are in and out of the market so as to adjust
their finances.

Sources of Funds in the New York Money Market

Many institutions and governmental units supply funds to
the New York money markets from time to time. Included are
commercial banks, businesses, investing institutions (especially
insurance companies), state and local governments, foreign central
banks and commercial banks, and the federal reserve banks. Each
of these will be considered in turn.

Commercial Banks. Commercial banks are usually the most
important source of funds in the money market. Banks throughout the country have correspondent relations with New York City
banks. Many banks keep some funds on deposit with these banks.
This is especially true of state banks that are not members of the
Federal Reserve System, since they frequently keep part of their
primary reserves with their New York City correspondent banks.
Some banks also send temporarily idle funds to their New York
correspondent for investment in the money market.

This concentration of funds in New York City was greater
before the establishment of the Federal Reserve System. Many

banks then kept reserves in New York that they now must keep with their federal reserve bank as required reserves. It was expected that the establishment of twelve regional reserve banks would end this concentration of funds in New York City, and it has decreased it considerably.

New York City banks not only lend the funds of correspondent banks but also their own funds. Day by day some of the large New York City banks and also a few large banks in other cities have some funds available over and above the demands of their customers and required reserves at the Federal Reserve Bank of New York. These temporarily excess reserves or *federal funds* as they are called are loaned on a day-to-day basis to banks that are temporarily short of reserves. This process involves the transfer of reserve balances on the books of the federal reserve bank from the reserve account of the lending bank to the reserve account of the borrowing bank. The lending for a one-day period is generally done by an exchange of checks. One is drawn by the lending bank on the federal reserve bank and is payable immediately, thus giving the borrowing bank funds at the reserve bank for that day. A second check is made out by the borrowing bank and is payable through the clearinghouse on the next day, thus effecting repayment of the loan. Most of these transactions are between New York City banks, but at times large banks in other cities enter the New York money market, usually as lenders, but also as borrowers. In such cases, the borrowing and repayment are effected by telegraphic transfer of funds held at the federal reserve banks.

Businesses. Another major source of supply of funds is the temporarily idle funds of business concerns. Many large concerns keep all of their funds in New York City banks except those needed to meet day-to-day operating needs. Funds often accumulate that will be idle for a foreseeable period of time, such as funds to be used to pay property taxes, to pay dividends, and to buy machinery. When new issues of securities are sold, funds are also usually available for a period of time before they are needed for construction projects or other capital improvements. Many concerns invest these funds temporarily in the New York money market.

Investing Institutions and Governmental Units. Another source of funds, but smaller in amount, includes the idle funds of investing institutions, especially insurance companies. Their funds are put into longer-term investments, but they may not be invested immediately upon receipt. Such institutions may hold their funds for more favorable market conditions or to buy securities of a new issue to come out shortly. In the meantime, these funds are often put to use in the money markets. From time to time state and local governments and their agencies, as well as some agencies of the federal government, supply funds to the market. Funds may be available because a bond issue was sold to finance a construction program over an extended period, or because funds are being accumulated to retire bonds. This source of funds, however, is minor and irregular.

Foreign Banks. Of more importance are the funds of foreign central banks and commercial banks. Since World War I, New York City has become one of the most important international financial centers. Foreign central banks frequently keep some of their funds in New York City in the form of gold especially earmarked for their account or in dollar assets of various kinds. These dollar assets, by and large, are kept on deposit in the reserve banks. More than twenty-five years ago the Federal Reserve Bank of New York offered to use the temporarily idle funds of foreign central banks to buy banker's acceptances, which it guaranteed for a fee. The supply of banker's acceptances has been too small recently to meet such demands, and some central banks have asked that their funds be invested in Treasury bills and in other short-term government securities.

Foreign commercial banks also have correspondent relationships with New York banks or have offices in New York City. Through them they supply sizable sums to the money market, especially for loans to security dealers and for investment in short-term government securities.

Federal Reserve Banks. The last source of funds is the federal reserve banks themselves. The Federal Reserve Bank of New York supplies funds when it buys government securities in the market either for its own account or for the System as a result of operations of the open-market committee. This source of funds is of special significance since changes in open-market operations by the Federal Reserve have their first effect on the supply of funds in this market.

Demand for Funds in the New York Money Market

There are also many types of demand for funds in this final money market in New York City. These are in the form of security dealer and broker loans, commercial paper, banker's acceptances, tax anticipation notes, treasury bills and certificates, and federal funds.

Security Dealer and Broker Loans. Before 1929 the most important demand for funds was from security dealers and brokers. They borrowed either on demand or on a time basis to finance the buying of securities on margin by their customers and to carry their own portfolio of securities. Most of the borrowing was on a demand or "call loan" basis, that is, the loan was repayable through the clearinghouse on one day's notice. Such loans were referred to as "Street loans" from their use in Wall Street. As the character of the security markets has changed and as regulation has reduced the percentage of the purchase price of stock that can be borrowed, such loans have decreased in importance.

Commercial Paper. Another source of demand for funds is open-market commercial paper. The market for short-term notes of well-known concerns with strong credit ratings is relatively less important than it was in the twenties. In recent years, however, a new type of commercial paper has become more important than the notes of well-known business concerns. It is the short-term notes of several of the major finance companies, which are known as *finance company commercial paper* or simply as *finance company paper*. The volume of such paper grew rapidly in the fifties and far exceeds that of regular commercial paper.

Banker's Acceptances. A third source of demand also involves the sale of business paper, that is, the banker's acceptance. This form of paper became important as a source of demand because it was encouraged and supported by the Federal Reserve System. Since this paper, which is used to finance exports, imports, and the storage of staple commodities, is also the unconditional obligation of the accepting bank, it has a rating as top-quality business paper. The use of such paper has also declined since 1929 due to the use of direct loans from banks, but it has shown some tendency to increase in recent years.

Tax Anticipation Notes. Occasionally state and local governmental units enter the money market for funds for a short period of time. This is usually done by selling tax anticipation notes to provide funds until tax payments are received. Much of this borrowing is done locally, but some of it is done in the New York money market.

Treasury Bills and Certificates. The most important source of demand since 1929 is the sale of Treasury bills, which usually run for 90 or 91 days. They are sold at a discount through competitive bidding. These bills are offered in all parts of the country, but most of them are bought in New York City. Almost all of the trading after they are issued is done there. As early as the World War I period, the Treasury raised short-term funds by selling certificates of indebtedness for a fixed price, commonly for a one-year period. During part of the thirties no certificates were issued, but their use was resumed on a large scale during World War II. In addition, government instrumentalities, such as the Federal Intermediate Credit Banks, are a minor source of demand for funds from time to time.

Federal Funds. The final source of demand is the commercial banks, primarily the large city banks. Banks that are temporarily short of required reserves borrow federal funds on a one-day basis from banks that have excess funds.

Organization of the New York Money Market

As already pointed out, the New York money market has no formal market organization but depends upon the interactions of the institutions that supply and demand funds with help from brokers who facilitate borrowing and lending. The large New York City banks are an important part of the market organization. They are often referred to as "Wall Street" banks although most of them are not on Wall Street. Most of the transactions in the money market are cleared through their books, and most funds that flow to or from New York go through their accounts on the books of the Federal Reserve Bank of New York. They are major lenders and borrowers of funds of all types. Some of the large New York City banks and a few Chicago banks also act as dealers in government securities.

The federal reserve banks, and especially the New York Federal Reserve Bank, are an important part of the money market. They buy and sell large quantities of government obligations and also some banker's acceptances. They also loan money to banks when they need it to maintain required reserves.

There are several groups of dealers in the money market—dealers in securities, especially government securities, dealers in commercial paper, and dealers in banker's acceptances. One organization may act as a dealer in several of these areas. For example, a government security dealer will probably also be a dealer in other securities. He may also carry on a brokerage business. In fact, the dealer function may be subsidiary to the brokerage business.

There are also some money brokers in the New York money market. Their function is to know who has quickly available funds and who has a need for funds. Their role is becoming less and less important, however, as the various dealers and banks are in almost constant contact with each other by direct telephone lines.

Changing Character of the New York Money Market

The character of the New York money market is a changing one as business and economic conditions change. The whole complexion of the market has changed since the twenties, and especially since 1933. Both the supply of funds and the demand for funds have increased greatly. The supply went up due to the monetary and fiscal policies under the New Deal, and the demand increased because of the great increase in the volume of short-term government securities offered for sale. Business borrowing through commercial paper and banker's acceptances has decreased as banks have made more direct loans on just as favorable a basis as funds could be gotten in the money market. Call loans have all but disappeared as an important factor in the money markets. These changes in the use of funds in the money market are shown clearly in Table 26-1, which shows the volume of different classes of loans outstanding in 1925 and 1956.

The use of federal funds has increased greatly and has in fact become the final source of funds before resort to borrowing from the federal reserve banks. As a result, the rate on federal funds has become the most sensitive interest rate in the market. Its lower

Table 26–1

VOLUME OF LOANS AND SHORT-TERM SECURITIES
AVAILABLE IN THE MONEY MARKET,
1925 AND 1956

(Approximate amounts outstanding in millions of dollars)

	1925	1956
Brokers' Loans	2,000-3,000	500-800
Commercial Paper	600-800	475-550
Acceptances	600-800	625-700
U. S. Short-term Securities	2,500-3,000	58,000-60,000
Federal Funds (daily volume) ...	100-175	800-1,200

SOURCE: *The Federal Funds Market,* Federal Reserve Bank of Boston, 1957, p. 9.

limit is almost zero, and its upper limit is the federal reserve discount rate. Fluctuations in the federal funds rate may be seen clearly in Chart 26-1, which shows selected short-term money market rates for the 1953-57 period.

Relationship of Monetary Policy to the Money Market

As the final money market, the New York money market is affected directly or indirectly by all factors that affect the supply of and the demand for loanable funds. A demand for additional funds in St. Louis, for example, would first be met locally. If it continued, however, funds would be obtained from balances held by New York correspondent banks and by the sale of short-term governments, probably in the New York market. Similarly, excess funds of banks and businesses tend to flow to the New York market. The most important determinant of day-to-day conditions in that market is the reserve position of New York City banks. When excess reserves exist, they are made available; when reserves are low or practically nonexistent, credit is tight in this market. Conditions in the New York market and in other markets are also equalized quite rapidly. If reserves are short in New York but plentiful elsewhere, funds will flow to the money market. Likewise, if funds are available in New York, they will be loaned out and find their way into the channels of trade throughout the country. Therefore, any policy that affects the money market will affect the supply of loanable funds throughout the country.

Changes in federal reserve policy have a pronounced effect upon this market. In fact, the direct impact upon the economy

Chart 26-1

SELECTED SHORT-TERM MONEY MARKET RATES
1953-1957
MONTHLY AVERAGES

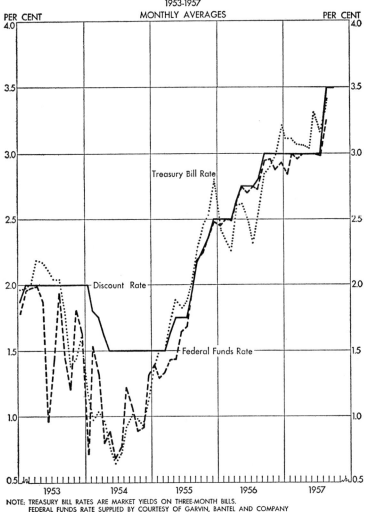

NOTE: TREASURY BILL RATES ARE MARKET YIELDS ON THREE-MONTH BILLS.
FEDERAL FUNDS RATE SUPPLIED BY COURTESY OF GARVIN, BANTEL AND COMPANY

SOURCE: *The Federal Funds Market,* Federal Reserve Bank of Boston, 1957, p. 26.

of changes in federal reserve policies is often through this New York money market. Changes in reserve requirements directly affect the market for federal funds. Changing the rediscount rate changes the top rate on federal funds; and by influencing this most sensitive of all rates, it has an effect on the whole market. Open-market operations have their first impact almost entirely in the New York money market as government securities are bought or sold in this market. Treasury financing by means of short-term securities is also largely done in this market. Thus Treasury policies regarding money management have an important influence. In fact, all types of changes in monetary policy influence the money market materially. Since it is a sensitive market, it does not take major changes to affect it substantially. Monetary policy has a more direct and immediate effect on the availability of funds than it would have if this final market for balancing supply and demand did not exist or was not organized as well as it is.

QUESTIONS

1. Discuss the various types of costs involved in a rate of interest such as the quoted rate of interest on a high-grade bond.
2. Why do interest rates for different types of loans vary widely?
3. What are the basic determinants of the rate of interest?
4. What are the basic sources of loanable funds?
5. Which factors affect the volume of savings? the volume of bank credit?
6. What is the relationship of liquidity preference to the supply of loanable funds?
7. What are the sources of demand for loanable funds?
8. Which factors affect the demand for loanable funds?
9. What is the nature of the influence of the Federal Reserve System and the Treasury in the market for loanable funds?
10. Define the money market.
11. What are federal funds? What is their relationship to the money market?
12. List and briefly discuss each of the sources of supply of funds in the money market.
13. What is the nature of the demand for funds in the money market?
14. Describe the organization and operation of the money market.
15. Discuss the major changes in the money market as it has been adapted to changes in the financial structure of the economy.
16. Explain how federal reserve policies affect the money market.

SUGGESTED READINGS

BOULDING, KENNETH E. *Economic Analysis*. New York: Harper & Brothers, 1955, Chapter 18.

Federal Reserve Bank of Boston. *The Federal Funds Market*. Boston: The Federal Reserve Bank of Boston, 1957.

Federal Reserve Bank of New York. *The Treasury and the Money Market*. New York: The Federal Reserve Bank of New York, 1954.

ROOSA, ROBERT V. *Federal Reserve Operations in the Money and Government Securities Markets*. New York: The Federal Reserve Bank of New York, 1956, Chapters 2-5.

Chapter 27

Monetary Policies

and Business

Fluctuations

In the two previous chapters an analysis was made of the effect of changes in monetary policies upon the price level and upon interest rates and money markets. Since price changes and fluctuations in interest rates are strategic variables in the continually recurring cycles in business activity, their role in the cyclical process will be analyzed more thoroughly in this chapter.

Since business records have become available, and especially since business activity has been carried on almost exclusively by means of monetary or credit transactions in an economy with highly developed financial institutions, business has fluctuated between prosperity (inflation) and recession or depression. These recurring fluctuations in business activity have come to be known as *business cycles* even though they are not of equal intensity. They have ranged from such mild downturns as those in 1927 and 1954, which most people were hardly aware of, to the deep depression of the early thirties in which about a third of the labor force was out of work. They are also of unequal length varying from a little over a year to almost nine years in duration.

In order to understand the role of monetary policies in such cycles, consideration will first be given to the conditions under which the economy would remain in equilibrium and the role of monetary policy in maintaining such equilibrium, especially the policy relating to the long-run trend of prices. Then some of the factors that are at work in the business cycle will be considered, especially those related to price level and interest rate changes.

The role of monetary factors in the upswing and downturn in the cycle will be emphasized.

ECONOMIC EQUILIBRIUM

To understand the nature of business cycles, it is necessary to understand the conditions under which the economy would remain in *equilibrium,* that is, all of the productive resources of the community were being effectively utilized and no factors were at work that would cause some of them to be in short supply or to be unused in the future. In analyzing the nature of economic equilibrium, attention will first be directed to the circular nature of economic activity and the resulting circular flow of money in the economy. This will be done because in a pecuniary economy such as ours equilibrium can exist only when money flows through the economy smoothly and without interruption. The nature of equilibrium will then be explored more fully. To focus attention on the nature of such equilibrium in a growing economy, consideration will first be given to the nature of equilibrium in a static economy and then to the requirements for equilibrium in a growing economy.

The Circular Nature of Economic Activity

Economic activity is a circular process. Spending by consumers, businesses, governmental units, and others leads to production of goods and services; as goods are produced income is paid for wages, interest, rent, and profits; such income is used to buy more goods, which leads to more production; and so on. In this circular process expenditures of one individual or group are receipts to another individual or group. For example, wages are an expense of doing business, but they are income to the wage earner. When a wage earner spends part of his pay check for shoes, his expenditure is a receipt for the merchant. When the latter orders shoes to replace those he has sold, his expenditures to replenish his stocks are receipts to the wholesaler or manufacturer, and so on.

To understand the nature of equilibrium, it is necessary to look at this circular process in the total economy. This aggregative picture is the combined result of the circular flows of money from individual consumers to business units and back again to consumers, from individuals and businesses to the government as taxes and back again to individuals and businesses as government expenditures, and other money flows in the economy.

In the act of producing producer goods, consumer goods, and services, money is paid out to the factors of production in the form of wages, interest, rent, and the distribution of profits. Money is also paid to the government in the form of taxes on income and indirect taxes, licenses, etc. Some money is transferred to other agencies and individuals in the form of gifts and grants. The remaining money is kept in the business—some as depreciation allowances to provide for the replacement of plant and equipment, and the remainder as retained profits to increase the equity of the owners.

The money paid out in the production process is received by individual consumers, nonprofit institutions, businesses, and governmental units. They in turn decide how they will spend this money on goods and services of various types, and the proportion of it they will save. They may also make use of credit and in this way spend more for a period of time than the money they receive. From time to time, such debts may be paid off at a faster rate than new credit is extended. The goods and services consumers, businesses, governments, and institutions purchase determine what is produced in the next round.

Money kept in the business as depreciation allowances and as retained earnings, and savings of individuals and institutions must also enter the expenditure stream to complete the circular flow of money. Depreciation allowances and retained earnings may be spent by the business on plant and equipment, or additional goods for inventory, and so enter the expenditure stream. If the business does not have an immediate need for these funds, it may make them available for investment in the money market and the borrower will then spend them. Savings may enter the spending stream by being invested directly in real estate, equipment, or other assets, or they may be put into financial institutions and enter the spending stream when they are spent by the borrower.

The monetary and banking system is used by individuals, institutions, government, and businesses to facilitate the transfer of money in the circular flow of activity. The operation of the banking system can create a problem in maintaining equilibrium since money may at times accumulate in the banking system rather than be spent or invested. At other times individuals, businesses, or governments may have money available for expenditure that did not arise out of the circular flow of economic activity but which came from credit creation by the banking system.

The Nature of Equilibrium

In order to understand business fluctuations, it is necessary to see under what conditions the circular flow of money would remain in equilibrium. This requires a balance between production, money flows, and expenditures on goods and services. Our economy produces a vast array of different types of goods and services. This includes producer goods, such as machinery and equipment; consumer goods of all types, including homes, durable goods, nondurable goods, and services; military and other equipment for the government and governmental services, such as postal service; and equipment for public and private institutions, such as schools and hospitals. The quantities and the types of all of the different kinds of goods and services being produced during any period of time constitute the pattern of production.

The production of goods and services provides income for the factors of production, and such income is paid to individuals, corporations, private institutions, pension and trust funds, and governmental units. Part of the income is not available to those who received it because they are required to pay part of it in taxes. When taxes are spent on goods and services, they give rise to income payments. Some taxes are used by the government to make payments for which no goods or services are currently received, such as payments to farmers for cooperating with programs to decrease the amount of agricultural land in cultivation. These payments are known as *transfer payments*. Some private transfer payments also shift money as, for example, donations to the Red Cross that are used to help victims of a flood. Additional funds may be available for spending because credit has been created through bank loans. The amount and the different kinds of all such income payments, transfer payments, and money from credit creation constitute the pattern of money flow receipts in the economy during any period of time.

Money is used to buy goods and services of all types by all individuals and groups in the economy. The amount and the type of such expenditures on consumer goods, producer goods, and government purchases of goods and services constitute the pattern of expenditures in any period of time or the pattern of money flow disbursements.

Equilibrium would exist if the pattern of production of goods and services and credit creation and transfer payments gave rise to a pattern of money flow receipts which was used for a pattern of expenditures that took the goods which were being produced off the market at prices that yielded a return on capital which businessmen considered adequate. These patterns would not only have to be in balance currently, but anticipated patterns of production, money flow receipts, and consumption would have to be in balance or adjustments would be taking place or would be contemplated to bring them into balance in the future.

In order to understand the role of monetary factors in achieving such a balance, this equilibrium situation must be analyzed further. Let us first analyze the nature of this equilibrium in a static economy in which total production is remaining stable and no appreciable changes are taking place in technology. Not only must aggregative money flows and plans for their expenditures balance with present and projected patterns of production, but all of the sectors of these patterns must also be in balance. This means that the government budget must be met without resort to credit creation. Borrowing could go on out of current income of individuals, institutions, or businesses, but no money creation could be taking place, for if it were, adjustments would be in process to adjust the economy to the higher level of money flows.

Savings and investment must also be in balance. The balance between savings and investment is one of the strategic variables in maintaining equilibrium. Income spent on consumption gets back into the expenditure stream directly, and money paid to the government as taxes is sure to be spent, even if some lag exists; but savings are not automatically spent on investment goods. The interest rate does not equate the supply of and demand for investable funds quickly or completely. Some savings may increase cash balances at times instead of being used for investment purposes. Past accumulations of savings can also be spent, thus adding new funds to the supply of investable funds, or credit creation can have the same effect. Thus all of the factors that affect the money markets affect this most strategic economic variable.

Equilibrium in a Dynamic Economy

Equilibrium in the patterns of the flow of goods, the flow of money receipts, and the flow of expenditures as described above is a static concept. But the economy is dynamic. Even in the absence of fluctuations in economic activity, there would still be the long-term trend in the economy. The trend of business activity in the United States has been generally upward even though it has been interrupted at times by severe depressions such as that of the thirties. This upward trend is due to such factors as increased population, a larger percentage of married women working, and increased technology resulting in more and better capital equipment. In a dynamic economy in which production is increasing, equilibrium between the patterns of production, money flows, and consumption could be achieved if credit creation was taking place at a rate just fast enough to finance the added production due to the rising trend of the economy. Equilibrium could also exist without credit creation if all economic plans were made on the basis of a decreasing price level due to the transaction of a larger volume of business with a fixed supply of purchasing media. Next the various types of monetary policies that may be followed to achieve equilibrium in the long run are analyzed further.

Monetary Policies and Dynamic Equilibrium

If the economy remained in equilibrium and if the supply of purchasing power was not increased as the supply of goods increased, the long-run price trend would be downward. Before the establishment of the Federal Reserve System, this was the underlying situation. Prices rose during war periods due to inflationary war financing, but they dropped gradually thereafter. The monetary agitation in the period from the end of the Civil War to 1896 was due in a large measure to the deflation caused by increased supplies of goods and a relatively fixed money supply. The two major exceptions were in the late 1840's and after 1896. The money supply was increased greatly in the first of these periods by the discovery of gold in California, and in the second period by increased world gold production due to new discoveries of the precious metal and improved techniques for separating it from gold-bearing ores.

The Federal Reserve Act provided for the issuance of federal reserve notes with a backing in gold and commercial paper. This was designed to allow the money supply to increase along with the needs of business. The present limited use of commercial paper has rendered this automatic adjustment largely inoperative. Therefore, the size of the money supply depends to a large extent on government and Federal Reserve policy. If they keep the money supply fixed, prices will drop as the production of goods and services increases. If they allow the money supply to increase as the production of goods and services increases, long-run prices will remain about stable. If they allow the money supply to increase faster than does the supply of goods and services, prices will rise.

Fixed Money Supply. A case can be made for each of these types of long-run price policies. Some persons argue that the money supply should remain fixed or at most be increased only in proportion to the increase in the labor force. In this way increases in technology would result in lower prices and so would be spread to all sectors of the economy including those on fixed incomes. This would, of course, imply more or less fixed money wages with increased real wages. Opponents of such a price policy maintain that it is unrealistic in an economy with highly organized labor groups to expect them not to press for increases in money wages. They also feel that the prices of many manufactured goods will not be adjusted downward rapidly, and as a result prices of raw materials would bear the brunt of the decline, since many of them are still set in more or less free markets.

Money Supply Related to Production. Many feel that the disadvantages of a fixed money supply so far outweigh its advantages that the money supply should be adjusted to the level of production. One group favors a monetary policy that would increase the supply of purchasing media as the volume of production goes up. This would maintain more or less stable long-run prices. It would permit money wage increases equal to increases in productivity and would lead to no serious price disparities.

Some persons contend, however, that a gradually rising price level is to be preferred to either of the other alternatives. This means that the money supply would be increased faster than the volume of production. The proponents of this policy argue that business is more likely to be prosperous when prices are rising, since profits are easier to make because inventories are gradually increasing in value and expectations for the future are likely to be brighter if no severe deflation is foreseen.

Another argument for this long-run monetary policy is that it could provide a way to retire the interest-bearing debt with less use of tax revenues. Part of the debt could be monetized each year to increase the money supply. This could be done by having the federal reserve banks buy government bonds for permanent holding and then trade them for non-interest-bearing bonds, which could be used as backing for federal reserve notes.

The gains under a rising price level, however, are not made without cost to the economy. Any profits from increased prices of inventories or from costs lagging behind selling prices are at the expense of fixed income groups; so are the increased real incomes of some groups, which can keep income increases ahead of price rises. Such gains by some groups at the expense of others are not equitable whether due to rapid inflation as in wartime or to gradual inflation.

THE ROLE OF MONETARY POLICY IN CYCLICAL FLUCTUATIONS

As has already been shown, monetary changes are important in the cyclical process because of their effect on interest rates. Their influence is more pervasive than this, however. In fact, modern business cycles could exist only in an economy with a banking system that has the ability to expand and contract credit. In the analysis of the factors at work in the cyclical process, expansion will be considered first. An analysis will be made of the factors that can initiate an upturn in economic activity and of the cumulative process which occurs after the upturn has begun. This same type of analysis will be made for the downturn. Monetary factors will be seen to play an important role in all stages of this cyclical process.

Initiating Factors Leading to an Upswing

Many factors can initiate an upswing in economic activity. First, factors arising out of changes in the patterns of production, money flows, and consumption will be considered; then actions of the government; and last, monetary and banking changes.

General Initiating Factors. Any change in the pattern of production, of money flows, or of consumption can be the factor that initiates an upswing in business activity. The pattern of production may be changed because of unusually good crops, and this will affect other sectors of the economy. Unusually large crops will lead to lower prices for the commodities in bountiful supply. Many consumers already buy all of the food they need and want so they will have money left for other goods or for saving. If they increase expenditures on other goods, production of such goods will be increased and such increased production will require additional expenditures for the factors of production.

When a new consumer good, such as a television set, is introduced, consumers also adjust their expenditure patterns. The demand for the new item will lead to increased production and increased expenditures on plant and equipment to make the added production possible. Expenditures on other items or savings or both are reduced to free money for the purchase of the new good. The pattern of production will be changed to turn out the new pattern of consumer goods.

Since supply of a new product falls short of demand for a time, prices will be high enough to yield a larger profit than in industries in which supply and demand are in approximate balance. These above-normal profits will temporarily alter the pattern of money flow receipts and are likely to lead to additional expenditures by those receiving the added money income.

New inventions in the producer-goods field may also make it possible to turn out goods at lower prices. Such inventions may make present equipment obsolete and so lead to a demand for capital goods, which would not otherwise have existed.

Increases in the rate of foreign spending may also initiate fluctuations in the domestic economy by increasing the total demand for goods. Fluctuations can also occur if the types of products demanded by foreigners are changed materially even though total expenditures remain much the same. This may happen, for example, when crop failures abroad lead to an increased demand for American farm products and a reduced demand for manufactured goods. Since the increased demand will raise the price of farm products, farmers' income will increase and they are also likely to increase expenditures, especially on farm machinery.

Actions of the Government. Under present conditions the most important initiating factors in business cycles arise from the actions of government. The effects of increased expenditures during periods of defense and war production need no further explanation. Increases in government expenditures during any period of time, even though of a smaller magnitude, initiate increases in economic activity. The same is true of changes in the methods of financing such expenditures. A shift from the payment of government expenditures through taxation to payment by borrowing or credit creation materially affect the economy by increasing the incomes of those individuals whose taxes have been cut and also by affecting the supply of loanable funds.

Governmental bodies can also influence business conditions and thus initiate upward movements in economic activity by changing the legal rules under which business is carried on as, for example, in such fields as tariff and banking legislation. The introduction of a high protective tariff after the existence of low rates causes a demand for producer goods to produce the items that were formerly imported. The higher prices for the domestically produced goods, likewise, will lead to a change in consumer expenditure patterns.

Monetary and Banking Changes. Initiating forces may also be set in motion in the monetary and banking fields. Since gold is the basis of the monetary system of the United States, a new discovery of gold increases purchasing power without a corresponding increase in the supply of goods other than gold and thus changes the pattern of consumption. Changes in the banking system can also initiate fluctuations in the economy. If credit is made easily available at low rates, businessmen are more likely to spend money on the improvement and expansion of plant and equipment. Similar increases in activity can also take place in the housing markets and durable consumer-goods markets if credit is made more readily available or is made available at lower interest rates.

The Cumulative Process During Expansion

After one of the initiating factors has begun an upswing, various intensifying factors may reinforce the upward movement. As the demand for goods rises, prices will also tend to rise, especially if the supply cannot be augmented immediately. Such increases or prospective increases in price that businessmen expect from past experience will cause them to increase their orders for goods above current demands so as to lay in a supply of goods before the price rise. This leads to an accumulation of inventories above current consumption needs on the upswing of the cycle and so reinforces the upward movement.

The increased prices and the increased volume of business, along with a lag in costs, lead to an increase in profits. This increase in profits induces businessmen to expand production facilities and, by doing so, they add to the increasing income stream.

As prosperity spreads, it is also carried along by the psychological reactions of businessmen according to the process that has been described as "waves of optimism." When business is good, a businessman is led to believe that it will be still better, especially when other businessmen have the same reaction to the situation. This emotional response leads to a demand for goods greater than that which is justified by the underlying situation, especially during the period when capital goods are being produced. Increased expectations of profit also raise the potential earnings from additional capital equipment and thus intensify the demand for capital goods.

During the upswing of the cycle, it becomes comparatively easy to raise money by means of the sale of securities and in this way to obtain the necessary funds for capital expansion. Some of these securities are purchased with funds that were previously idle, and the introduction of this money into the income stream also has an inflationary effect. During the expansion period speculation also plays a part and helps reinforce the cumulative upward movement of business. Speculators buy goods and securities in anticipation of price rises and so increase the demand for them. Such capital gains as are made are usually spent more readily than regular income and in a different pattern from that of ordinary consumer expenditures. Furthermore, when they are spent on consumer goods, money that was intended for saving is shifted to the consumption sector of the economy. If, for example, a man sells for $1,500 common stock for which he paid $1,000, he considers the $500 capital gain as current income. The men who paid him the $1,500, however, usually take it from savings so that $500 intended for saving has now been shifted to consumption expenditures.

Another factor that intensifies the upswing as the demand for consumer goods increases is the derived demand for additional producer goods. The demand for producer goods increases by a larger percentage than that for consumer goods due to the operation of the accelerator principle. Since capital goods last for a relatively long period of time, only a small proportion needs to be replaced each year. For example, if capital goods last for ten years, 10 per cent will be replaced each year on the average. At a time when all of the capital equipment is being utilized fully, a 10 per cent increase in consumer demand may lead to a doubling of the demand for capital goods, 10 per cent of the current stock for normal replacement, and another 10 per cent to meet the added demand for consumer goods. The effect of such a 10 per cent increase in demand and of further increases will be clearer from the following example:

DEMAND FOR CONSUMER GOODS	PRODUCER GOODS NEEDED TO PRODUCE THE CONSUMER GOODS	NORMAL REPLACEMENT OF PRODUCER GOODS
1,000 units	100 units	10 units
1,100 units	110 units	10 units
1,200 units	120 units	10 units

ADDED DEMAND FOR PRODUCER GOODS TO MEET ADDED CONSUMER DEMAND	TOTAL DEMAND FOR PRODUCER GOODS	PERCENTAGE INCREASE IN DEMAND FOR PRODUCER GOODS
. . . .	10 units	. . .
10 units	20 units	100
20 units	30 units	50

In actual practice, as the upswing begins, unused plant and equipment are first brought into use. As capacity is approached, the magnified demand for producer goods is felt. At the same time equipment that is old and partially obsolete is replaced so that the firm may operate more efficiently to meet the increased demand for goods. After full employment of men and resources is approached, there is pressure on prices of capital goods as the derived demand for them continues to exert itself because of continued increases in the demand for consumer goods.

The accelerator principle also is at work during the upswing in the durable consumer-goods field. It magnifies the increase in demand for new houses over the increase in demand for all houses, both old and new. The same is true of the increase in demand for new automobiles, new refrigerators, and all other new durable goods.

This whole process is aided and given added impetus by the expansion of credit through the banking system. Since the additional funds needed to finance the expansion need not come from current income or saving but can be created by the banking system, there is additional purchasing power over and above that created in the production of goods. Since there are no added goods coming into the market when this purchasing power is put into the system, it leads to an inflation of the price level. Credit is not only used during the expansion by businessmen, but it is also used to an increasing degree by consumers as they become more optimistic about the future and businessmen and bankers become more liberal in granting credit.

Relationship of Monetary Factors to Intensifying Factors in the Expansion

In the final analysis, all of the intensifying factors are related to credit creation or the use of previously idle cash balances. When businessmen build up inventories in anticipation of price rises or expand production as profits increase, they either use previously idle funds or increase short-term borrowing. This borrowing has been an important source of added purchasing media in past cycles.

Speculation in commodity and security markets is also aided by credit expansion. The same has usually been true of government deficit financing during an upturn. Long-term business financing is primarily done from current savings, but in the early stages of an upturn idle cash balances are drawn into the investment markets. Some funds made available to a business from bank loans may also find their way into permanent investment in plant and equipment.

The accelerator principle would apply even if credit could not be expanded, but its effect on the economy would be far different. As the demand for producer goods increased, prices could rise only if some other prices declined or if velocity of money increased. This would lead to adjustments of a different nature from those that now take place. Also, interest rates would rise faster than they do under a sytsem that allows credit to expand, and this would make capital expansion less profitable.

The credit that is created as a result of the various factors at work in the upswing leads to inflation since the supply of money is being expanded faster than the supply of goods. Inflation helps to intensify the upward movement in business, and also it pushes the economy further away from equilibrium. A rise in the price level reduces the *real income* of consumers, that is, the quantity of goods which can be bought with a given number of dollars of income. Some groups, such as organized labor, will suceed in getting wage increases to offset the increase in prices and so restore their real income. Other groups, such as those living on pensions or on income from bond investments, cannot increase their money income and so suffer a loss in real income. Others, such as government workers and teachers, may experience a considerable lag in getting their incomes increased and so suffer a loss in real income for a considerable period of time during the upswing.

This reduction in real income by some groups in society is called *forced saving* since these individuals have been forced to do without their former volume of goods and services. These goods and services have been made available to those groups who received additional money from credit creation. The concept of forced saving must be considered from the viewpoint of the total economy since the individuals who have suffered a loss in real income have nothing to show for it. The level of consumption in the economy, however, has been reduced; and investment in plant, equipment, inventory, and houses has been increased through the expenditure of the new money that has been created, and so in real terms the saving of the economy has been increased.

Forced saving unbalances the pattern of money flows since some groups have more money to spend and others have less real income to spend. Unbalance is continued because the groups that have suffered a loss of real income will make every effort to get their money incomes increased so as to restore their former level of real income.

Thus the whole nature of the expansion in business is determined by the character of the monetary system, especially its expansibility. Monetary policy is thus one of the important factors in the cycle.

Initiating Factors Leading to a Downturn

The downturn in business may be brought about by an initiating factor from outside the circular flow of economic activity, such as a decrease in government spending or a reduced availability or higher price for bank credit. Changes, however, are going on during the expansion period that tend to slow business down or even to cause a downturn. Costs tend to rise faster than do selling prices after a period of time, and the cut in profits reduces the motive for expansion. Inefficiency also increases, and this in turn also reduces profits.

During the expansion period maladjustments occur in the structure of production. As business expands and the capital-goods industries expand at a much faster rate than the rest of the economy, various bottlenecks develop that cause expansion to take place at an uneven rate. Basic raw materials especially become short and increase rapidly in price. This makes it unprofitable to produce some of the goods that are needed for a balanced structure of production. It also means that cost and price relationships in other fields are unstable and will shift radically when the pressure of the demand for the basic commodities eases somewhat.

Inflation and forced saving also lead to distortions that cannot help but result in unbalance in the system. Prices of some commodities rise faster than others, and so they lead to a shift in both the patterns of consumption and production. As money incomes are increased, consumers again strive to re-establish the old relationships so that the economy is continually kept off balance. After prices have risen for some time and incomes of some groups have been increased several times to offset the price rises, serious maladjustments may occur. Those having fixed incomes and those not sharing fully in the increases in income are forced to alter their pattern of consumption materially. This may reduce demand for luxury items and durable goods to such an extent that overproduction exists in these fields and unemployment results.

Furthermore, errors of forecast made during the upswing do not show up while activity is expanding rapidly. After a while, however, it becomes apparent that all of the goods that some businessmen thought would be demanded in their field cannot be sold at prices to yield a reasonable profit, and this factor also slows down the expansion. These errors of forecast result in more production in some fields than is demanded by consumers under present income patterns. Since the economy is not perfectly competitive, production is likely to be cut, rather than prices, in order to correct the unbalance. As production is cut in these over-expanded fields so as to bring effective supply and demand into balance, there is a downward pressure on income working counter to the other upward pressures.

During the period of business expansion there is also an increase in interest rates because the demand for funds rises faster than the supply. This makes it less profitable to finance expansion by means of bonds and also makes capital investment less desirable. At the same time that interest rates are rising, the marginal efficiency of capital, that is, the expected rate of return which can be earned by adding additional units of capital equipment falls, first in a few fields and then in others. This is true because expectations of future profits are reduced as supply becomes larger in relation to demand and costs press against selling prices. The result is a decrease in the expenditures on new plant and equipment.

Also, as the cycle develops and full employment is approached, the main effect of the accelerator is an increase in the price of capital goods. According to studies by the National Bureau of Economic Research, the maximum rate of advance in quantity in the capital-goods field takes place during the early part of the upswing, while the maximum rate of increase in price takes place during the last part.[1] This rapid increase in the price of capital goods during the last segment of the upswing along with reduced profit expectations makes it less desirable to expand the use of capital equipment.

Monetary Factors in the Downturn

Monetary factors are strategic in the forces making for a downturn. Inflation and forced saving have caused some of the basic unbalances that need to be corrected to bring again money flows and goods flows into balance. Monetary factors are also strategic in determining the rate of interest, which together with the prospect for return from capital determines the level of investment. Rising interest rates, along with declining prospects for return

[1] Frederick C. Mills, *Price-Quantity Interactions in Business Cycles* (New York: National Bureau of Economic Research, Inc., 1946), pp. 41 and 79.

from investments in producer goods, lead to a reduction in investment, which is one of the most important factors leading to a downturn. Thus monetary factors are also important factors that initiate the downturn.

The Cumulative Process During Contraction

The process of income generation, decreasing profits and future expectations of smaller profits, credit contraction, and increasing pessimism, intensify the downturn just as their converse did the upturn. The fall in prices now causes businessmen to buy less than is needed to meet current demands since they want to cut inventory losses. Inventories from the past prosperity period are reduced below the point where they are adequate to take care of the current volume of business so as to cut losses from future price declines. Hoarding on the part of individuals and businessmen takes funds out of the current economic stream, whereas credit creation had added additional funds during the upswing. In the Keynesian terminology liquidity preference is increased during the downturn and this intensifies the depression. Furthermore, funds that would normally be used to buy consumer goods are used to retire debts because of the fear of the future, and such payments are usually saved by the recipients so that funds which would normally go into consumption now become a part of saving. As profits are reduced and gross errors of forecast become apparent in some fields, there is a liquidation of many businesses. This leads to a forced sale of assets to pay off debts and to distress prices, which further complicate the business picture and intensify the depression.

Factors Leading to Another Upswing

In many past cycles initiating factors arising outside the circular flow of economic activity have started business on a new upward movement. These have included such things as new inventions leading to increased business spending, new consumer goods leading to increased consumer and business spending, increased foreign purchases in the United States, and increased governmental expenditures. Even in the absence of such outside initiating forces, the economy will gradually generate the momentum for an upturn.

QUESTIONS

1. Describe the circular nature of economic transactions.
2. Describe the circular flow of money in the total economy.
3. What is the relationship of funds from depreciation allowances, retained corporation earnings, and savings to the circular flow of money?
4. What is the role of the banking system in the circular flow?
5. Describe the patterns of production, of money flow receipts, and of expenditures.
6. Describe the conditions under which the economy would be in equilibrium. What is the relationship of government financing to equilibrium? What is the relationship of savings and investment to equilibrium?
7. What are the requirements for equilibrium in a dynamic economy?
8. Discuss the role of different types of monetary policies in achieving dynamic equilibrium.
9. Analyze the general factors that may initiate an upwing in economic activity. Show in each case why the rate of economic activity would be increased. Do the same for initiating factors arising out of the actions of government and out of monetary and banking changes.
10. Describe the various intensifying factors that may reinforce the upward movement in business. Show in each case how the rate of economic activity is speeded up.
11. Describe and discuss the relationship of monetary factors to the intensifying factors on the upswing.
12. Discuss the operation of the factors that may lead to a downturn.
13. Describe and discuss the role of monetary factors in initiating a downturn.
14. Describe the cumulative process during contraction.
15. Analyze the factors that may lead to a renewed upturn in economic activity.

SUGGESTED READINGS

CLARK, J. M. *Strategic Factors in Business Cycles.* New York: National Bureau of Economic Research, Inc., 1934.

DAUTEN, CARL A. *Business Fluctuations and Forecasting.* Cincinnati: South-Western Publishing Co., 1954. Chapters 13, 16.

Federal Reserve Bank of Philadelphia. *The Quest for Stability.* Philadelphia: The Federal Reserve Bank of Philadelphia, 1956.

HABERLER, GOTTFRIED VON. *Prosperity and Depression.* Geneva: League of Nations, 1939. Chapters 9-12.

MITCHELL, W. C. *Business Cycles and Their Causes.* Berkeley: University of California Press, 1941.

SCHUMPETER, JOSEPH. *Business Cycles.* New York: McGraw-Hill Book Co., 1939. Vol. 1, Chapters 2, 3, 4.

Chapter 28

Recent Monetary

and Credit Problems

and Policies

Monetary and fiscal policies have been important factors in the post-World War II economy. There has frequently been a cleavage of opinion since the end of the war as to the type of policies to follow. This led to open disagreements for a time between the Treasury and the Board of Governors of the Federal Reserve System. Even after they reached an accord, opinion was still divided at times as to the proper course to follow. In order to understand the issues involved, it is necessary to look at the financing of World War II, which gave rise to the problems that created this divergence of viewpoint concerning the proper course of action.

THE MONETARY SITUATION IN THE PERIOD PRIOR TO WORLD WAR II

During the depression of the thirties, and especially after the passage of the Glass-Steagall Act in 1932, which permitted government bonds to serve as collateral for federal reserve notes, the Federal Reserve System took steps to maintain easy money conditions. Government bonds were purchased by the federal reserve banks in sufficient quantities not only to allow member banks to pay off all debts at the reserve banks but also to give them substantial excess reserves. Between February, 1932, and October, 1933, the federal reserve banks increased their holdings of government securities from $740 million to $2,400 million.[1]

[1] Karl R. Bopp and others, *Federal Reserve Policy* (Washington, D. C.: Federal Reserve System, 1947), p. 13.

After 1933 gold came into this country in large quantities due to the gold buying program of the Treasury. This increased reserves much faster than the banking system was able to put funds to work. As a result, in 1940 excess reserves reached almost $7 billion.[2]

MONETARY POLICY DURING WORLD WAR II

When the international situation worsened in the spring of 1939, the Federal Reserve System took steps to meet any serious disturbances in the securities markets. The Open Market Committee authorized its executive committee to make large purchases of government securities to prevent disorderly conditions in the market and to exercise an influence toward maintaining orderly conditions. When war broke out later in the year, the System purchased almost a half billion dollars of government bonds and announced that all the federal reserve banks stood ready to make advances on government securities at par to both member and nonmember banks. These actions helped to maintain an orderly market in government securities.

As our country increased the production of war material and as European countries bought larger quantities of such goods here, the purchasing power of civilians expanded faster than did the supply of consumer goods, thus creating inflationary pressures. The Board of Governors helped to restrain these pressures by raising reserve requirements to the legal limits in the early fall of 1941.

When the United States entered the war in December, 1941, the financing of war expenditures became the major concern of the Treasury and the Board of Governors of the Federal Reserve System. In order to accomplish this end, the Federal Reserve System had two primary objectives: [3] (1) to maintain relative stability in the market for government securities so as to make sufficient funds available to the Treasury at low interest rates, and (2) to restrict the creation of purchasing power to the lowest amount consistent with the first objective.

To emphasize its willingness and ability to supply all the funds needed to meet the needs of the government and of private

2 *Ibid.*
3 *Ibid.*, p. 18.

business, the following statement was issued by the Federal Reserve Board shortly after the United States entered the war in December, 1941: [4]

> The financial and banking mechanism of the country is today in a stronger position to meet any emergency than ever before.
> The existing supply of funds and of bank reserves is fully adequate to meet all present and prospective needs of the Government and of private activity. The Federal Reserve System has powers to add to these resources to whatever extent may be required in the future.
> The System is prepared to use its powers to assure that an ample supply of funds is available at all times for financing the war effort and to exert its influence toward maintaining conditions in the United States Government security market that are satisfactory from the standpoint of the Government's requirements.
> Continuing the policy which was announced following the outbreak of war in Europe, Federal Reserve Banks stand ready to advance funds on United States Government securities at par to all banks.

Interest-Rate Pattern

Another step to meet the needs of the government for funds was an agreement with the Treasury on a pattern of interest rates that would be maintained by federal reserve open-market operations. It was decided to stablize rates to keep down the cost of borrowing and also to remove any incentive to wait for higher rates later instead of buying bonds when funds were available.

The pattern agreed on was much the same as that prevailing during the depressed period of the thirties. The rate was fixed at ⅜ per cent on 90-day bills, ⅞ per cent on certificates of indebtedness, 2 per cent on 8-year to 10-year bonds, and 2½ per cent on the 15-year maturities.

Having agreed on this pattern for financing the war, the Federal Reserve System took steps to maintain such a pattern. To maintain the ⅜ per cent rate on bills, the federal reserve banks announced that they would purchase any quantity of such bills offered in the market at a price necessary to maintain that rate. They also agreed to give the seller an option to repurchase his bills at the same rate. This in effect made bills as liquid as cash and enabled the banks to invest their excess reserves at ⅜ per cent. This was done to keep excess reserves in the hands of the banks at a minimum.

[4] *Ibid.*, pp. 18, 19.

Rates on other securities were prevented from rising by open-market purchases of securities of all issues in amounts large enough to keep the price at par or above. To help encourage bank participation in war financing, discount rates were set at 1 per cent. On advances secured by government securities that were due or callable in one year or less, a preferential rate of ½ per cent was set. This was to encourage banks to invest in short-term government securities.

Shift to Longer Maturity Bonds

As the war went on, there were strong incentives for banks to purchase bonds of longer maturities. The deposits of most banks were rising due to the increased business and money supplies resulting from war production, and they invested them in what they considered to be a balanced proportion between bonds of various maturities. As they needed reserves, they tended to sell the shorter issues, and thus they increased their proportion of long-term bonds.

Nonbank investors and some banks consciously adopted a policy of carrying mostly longer-term bonds. They felt that if a pattern of rates was to be maintained through open-market operations, all maturities would be equally liquid since the investor was assured of being able to sell them at any time at par or better. This gave them the advantage of higher interest rates on the long-term bonds for funds intended for short-term investment.

There was another advantage to holding longer issues for a period of time. As they approached maturity, the price went up, due to increased demand since such bonds were now attractive to investors who had money to invest for only a short period of time. The price increased until the rate of return on them was brought into line with that on securities of shorter duration. Therefore some institutions and individuals bought longer maturities, sold them later at a premium, and bought newly issued long-term issues. This process became known as *playing the pattern of rates*.

Reserve System Bond Purchases

The process of maintaining rates forced the reserve system to buy large quantities of short-term securities. The large volume of short-term securities issued by the Treasury also led to almost continuous refunding operations. To sell all of the securities needed required either interest rates high enough to meet the demands of the market or a continuous increase in the money supply. The latter course was followed as reserves were supplied by open-market purchases, especially of short-maturity securities.

The details of this process are interesting since they show how the banking system was used to inflate the money supply. Many banks were designated as special depositaries in which the Treasury kept war-loan accounts. Such a bank could pay for new issues of government securities purchased for its own account or for the account of its customers by crediting the war-loan account rather than transferring the funds to the federal reserve bank. These accounts were made exempt from reserve requirements and were not assessed for deposit insurance in order to encourage their use to the fullest extent. After this was done, a bank no longer needed additional reserves against deposits resulting from its own purchases of government securities. When its customers bought bonds, reserves were freed as the funds were shifted out of regular deposit accounts to reserve-free war-loan accounts. These excess reserves were used by the banks to buy government securities. As the government spent its funds, deposits were shifted from war-loan accounts to regular deposit accounts requiring reserves. To get the necessary reserves, banks sold securities, especially the short-term ones. These were bought by the Federal Reserve System to maintain the pattern of rates, and thus new reserves were created and the money supply increased.

Bank Purchases of Securities

Even though it was part of the Treasury policy to sell as many bonds as possible to nonbank investors and banks were practically excluded from the last six bond drives, banks still bought large quantities of securities. During bond drives savings institutions and other corporations sold bonds they held, and these were bought by banks. These bonds were usually sold at a premium, and the sellers then bought bonds of the new issues at par. The real result of the war-bond drives was an expansion of bank credit even though banks were excluded from the direct purchase of securities from the Treasury. As the government spent the money it raised during a bond drive, that money was deposited in the accounts of businesses and individuals. The increase in deposits increased the amount of reserves required to be held against these deposits. The banks obtained the money for the additional reserves by selling some of their government securities to the Federal Reserve. Thus in the final analysis the Federal Reserve supplied a large quantity of the primary reserves that made the whole operation possible.

This was a case of wartime money inflation just as definitely as the continental currency or greenback inflation, but the process was more complex and hence less generally understood. It is true that after the third bond drive the Federal Reserve discouraged banks from participating unnecessarily in the absorption of government securities. As long as the pattern of interest rates made expansion of bank credit profitable, however, it was not unusual that many bonds were bought by the commercial banks and the Federal Reserve System when individuals and institutions found it desirable to dispose of them at a premium.

Effects of War Financing

The magnitude of war financing changed the whole character of the financial structure of the American economy. The federal debt increased from somewhat over $40 billion in 1939 to nearly $280 billion in February, 1946, a sevenfold increase. The total was so large that it exceeded the total of all other regular debts. Some idea of the magnitude may be gained from the fact that interest payments on this debt were larger than total government receipts in any peacetime year before 1941.[5]

Not only did the government become the biggest factor in the demand for funds, but also government bonds assumed a new and often dominant importance in the investments of many institutions. Government securities were 26 per cent of the assets of member banks of the Federal Reserve System in December, 1939, but they had gone up to 57 per cent at the end of 1945. They were 18 per cent of the assets of legal reserve life insurance companies in the earlier year and 46 per cent in the latter year. The proportion of funds of the federal reserve banks in government securities increased from 14 per cent to 54 per cent during the same period.

---

[5] Charles Cortez Abbott, *The Federal Debt* (New York: The Twentieth Century Fund, 1953), p. 3.

Government securities also increased in importance as an investment medium for liquid assets. Financial business corporations, such as real estate companies, finance companies, and investment companies, had 29 per cent of liquid assets in government securities at the end of 1939 and 56 per cent at the end of 1945. The proportion of liquid assets of regular business corporations invested in government securities increased from 14 per cent to 46 per cent during the same period, and that of unincorporated businesses from 17 per cent to 36 per cent.[6]

POSTWAR MONETARY PROBLEMS AND POLICIES

It may seem in retrospect that at the end of World War II steps should have been taken to reduce the money supply or at least not to allow it to increase further. Many governmental officials were afraid to tighten credit, however, because of the fear of a major depression. It had taken the demands of all-out war to eliminate the persistent large-scale unemployment of the thirties. Now government spending was to be cut from $100 billion a year to $40 billion or even less. Predictions were common that as many as eight million would be unemployed in 1946.

The rapid reconversion from war production to consumer goods production, however, was almost as miraculous an achievement as the rapid build-up of production to meet the needs of war. Consumers had buying power and pent-up desires for goods from the wartime period and spent it on goods as fast as they were available. The government also failed to cut expenditures as fast or as far as some had predicted. As a result, there was no depression in the early postwar period.

Situation in 1946 and 1947

Practically all economic controls were abandoned in 1946, however, and prices went up sharply through 1947 and until the fall of 1948. Price controls had held prices in check sufficiently so that wholesale prices rose from 79 to only 107 (1926 = 100) during the war. At the beginning of 1948 they had increased to 170.[7]

[6] *Ibid.,* p. 18.
[7] E. A. Goldenwiser, *Monetary Management* (New York: McGraw-Hill Book Company, Inc., 1949), p. 75.

Even though economic controls were abandoned quickly, monetary policies changed slowly. This was due in part to economic uncertainty and to fears of a postwar depression. The new situation in which government bonds dominated the market also led to cautious action as both the Federal Reserve System and the Treasury Department were working out policies under these changed conditions. There was also a reluctance to do anything that might unsettle the security markets since the large volume of government securities with short maturities called for frequent large refunding operations.

The action of Congress was also on the inflationary side. Controls were abandoned, and in 1948 taxes were cut sufficiently to increase the amount of money available for consumer spending by over $5 billion.

Action was gradually taken, however, to get away from the wartime pattern of interest rates. In the summer of 1946, the preferential discount rate on advances secured by short-term government securities was discontinued. This had no immediate effect on the market since banks were not borrowing, but the action was opposed for a time by the Treasury for fear it might unsettle the market for government securities. It was the middle of 1947 before the buying of Treasury bills at a price to yield ⅜ per cent was discontinued, and it was some time after that before yields on certificates of indebtedness were allowed to rise. Treasury bills were then allowed to rise in yield from ⅜ to over 1 per cent, and certificates from ⅞ per cent to 1¼ per cent. Long-term government bonds, however, continued to be supported, but the support price was dropped to near par from levels that had been as high as 108.[8]

Retirement of Bank-Held Debt

One of the factors that restrained credit expansion in 1946 and 1947 was the retirement of bank-held debt by the Treasury. The Victory Loan in the fall of 1945 had been oversubscribed, and this gave the government an unusually large cash balance. Furthermore, the Treasury did not need as much cash after the war as it did during the war. Treasury balances were used to retire bank-held debt, and the record shows that there was a

[8] *Ibid.*, p. 78.

contraction of bank credit. The effect was largely on the books, since the funds from the bond sale had not been used and were now again offset against the bonds. It did, however, reduce an inflationary potential, which would have become real if the funds had been spent. A Treasury surplus in 1947 was also used to retire bank-held debt, and this restrained inflationary pressures.

As the money supply was being cut by government action, however, it was being expanded by business borrowing. From a level of under $20 billion in 1943, bank loans rose to almost $40 billion early in 1948. The net result was that except for the reduction of the large government deposit accounts built up to meet war needs, the volume of money after allowing for seasonal fluctuations expanded continuously until early 1948.

The Situation in 1948

By the middle of 1948 inflationary pressures were again strong. Tax reduction had increased consumer expenditures, world tension led to higher military expenditures by the government, and large sums were also appropriated for foreign aid. Since the Treasury no longer had excess cash balances and since no substantial surpluses were in sight, there was no hope for restraint from this area. The Federal Reserve System, which held over $20 billion in government securities, was technically in a position to tighten the money supply by bond sales. The policy, however, was one of attempting to hold the money supply about constant so as to avoid deflation as well as inflation.

A new situation developed, however, in the summer and fall of 1948. Insurance companies and other financial institutions sold large amounts of government bonds in order to invest in mortgages and corporate bonds at more attractive interest rates. Commercial banks bought many of these bonds, and the Federal Reserve had to buy most of the remainder of these bonds to prevent them from dropping below par. The commercial banks sold short-term securities in order to get the funds to buy the longer-term bonds, and the Federal Reserve was also forced to buy many of these to carry out its policy of maintaining an orderly market for government securities. The Federal Reserve made every effort to sell short-term securities whenever possible to keep total bank reserves from increasing materially. This situation, however, made it impossible to make bank credit tighter to reduce inflationary pressures.

To meet this situation, Congress was asked to give the Federal Reserve additional powers. An increase in required reserves of 4 points on demand deposits and 1½ points on time deposits was authorized by a special session of Congress in the summer of 1948. This increased the maximum level to which reserve requirements could be raised on demand deposits of member banks to 30 per cent for central reserve city banks, 24 per cent for reserve city banks, and 18 per cent for country banks. The new maximum on time deposits was 7½ per cent for all member banks. This action enabled the Federal Reserve System to absorb more government bonds so as to keep the market above par and to offset the additions to bank reserves by raising reserve requirements. The Federal Reserve also asked for power to set additional reserve requirements in government bonds, but Congress refused to act upon this request.

The Federal Reserve System handled a large volume of government securities in 1947 and 1948 as it bought bonds of longer maturities and sold shorter-term obligations. Total transactions of government securities in those two years amounted to almost $80 billion, but the net change in the total portfolio was small.

Inflationary pressures abated late in 1948 as the increase in government expenditures slowed down and as private borrowing for capital expansion and especially for increasing inventories decreased. There was a minor recession in business activity in 1949, but consumer expenditures did not decrease appreciably. To ease money conditions, reserves were reduced in May and June of 1949 and again in August. This reduction in reserves freed bank funds and the demand for government bonds on the part of banks increased. Bond prices rose, and yields on short-term securities fell. The Federal Reserve System moderated this increase by selling a part of its portfolio of securities.

Federal Reserve Action in Early 1950

As business again picked up in the early part of 1950, the Federal Reserve System acted to tighten money supplies. Insurance companies, pension funds, and personal trusts had funds available for long-term investment from extensive current savings and also as a backlog from past accumulations. To take some of these funds off the market so as to prevent overextension of private long-term financing, the Federal Reserve sold a substantial amount of long-term government bonds not eligible for bank holding, thus reducing the supply of funds in the market.

MONETARY PROBLEMS AND POLICIES SINCE THE KOREAN WAR

When the Korean War started in June of 1950, the increased demand for goods led to renewed inflationary pressures. Government deficits were not the cause of price rises in the last half of 1950, since the Treasury had an excess of cash income over cash outgo in the last half of the year of almost a billion dollars. The explanation lies in private spending. Consumers, fearing the shortages of World War II, spent large sums on various types of durable and semidurable goods. Business also spent heavily for inventories and for capital investment. The annual rate of gross private domestic investment went up over $12 billion from the second to the fourth quarter of 1950. Loans of insured commercial banks rose nearly $7.5 billion from June to December.[9] Life insurance companies also supplied long-term funds by selling government bonds and putting the funds in mortgages and corporate obligations.

Treasury-Federal Reserve Controversy

Under these conditions reserve bank credit increased materially. The Board of Governors of the Federal Reserve System wanted to act to restrict expansion, but it could not so long as it felt obligated to support the bond market by buying all government securities at par or better. The Treasury wanted to follow a pattern of low rates as it did in World War II and this, of course, required price-support operations, since interest rates would have gone up in a free market as the demand for funds increased.

The controversy between the Treasury and Federal Reserve System developed into an open conflict in the summer of 1950, especially after the Reserve System had to engage in large-scale open-market operations to assure the success of some financing at

[9] Abbott, *op. cit.*, pp. 92, 93.

a rate the market did not find attractive. When the Secretary of the Treasury stated in a speech in January, 1951, that the Treasury had not changed its position and was not willing to allow even fractional increases in interest rates, the controversy became acute. Not only Federal Reserve officials but the press and the members of Congress entered it. Such a situation could not last long, and the President appointed a committee to study ways and means to provide the necessary restraint on private credit expansion and at the same time to maintain stability in the market for government securities. Before this committee could report, however, an agreement between the Treasury and the Federal Reserve System was announced in March, 1951.

Basis of the Opposing Viewpoints

Before looking at this agreement, it is desirable to see the basis of the opposing viewpoints. Treasury officials were interested in keeping interest rates on the debt at a low level. They favored low rates not only to keep the cost of servicing the debt at a minimum, but also from a belief that low interest rates were necessary to keep investment in plant, equipment, housing, local public works, and the like at high levels. The Treasury also emphasized orderly conditions in the bond markets since stable interest rates were as important for debt management as low interest rates. The Treasury officials believed that the emergency arising out of the Korean War should be met by direct controls, such as materials allocation, rationing, and price controls.

Federal reserve officials felt that in the absence of all-out war such controls were unnecessary if proper monetary and fiscal policies were followed. They believed that if the government kept cash outgo and income reasonably in balance, monetary controls would be sufficient to prevent inflation. Such a course would also prevent the building up of idle funds by consumers as was done during World War II and which resulted in inflationary pressures when controls were taken off.

The Accord

The accord that was announced in March, 1951, was designed to check credit expansion without the use of direct controls. One direct result of the accord was the offer to exchange long-term 2½ per cent bonds that were being sold to the Federal Reserve in quantities for an nonmarketable 29-year issue at 2⅔ per cent. These bonds were also nonmarketable, but they could be exchanged at the option of the holder into marketable 5-year 1½ per cent notes. At the same time government bonds were no longer bought in the market by the Federal Reserve to the same degree as before, and the price pegs were no longer rigidly adhered to. Toward the end of the year the longest-term government bonds had dropped to below 97 in a free market.

The Federal Reserve did not stay out of the market completely but continued to buy and sell some securities so as to maintain an orderly market. As the private demand for funds increased due to a boom in residential building and in the capital markets, interest rates rose and long-term securities dropped somewhat further.

Policies Under the Republican Administration

The Republican Administration elected in November, 1952, followed the same general line of policies reached in the accord in the spring of 1951. They decided to issue long-term government securities whenever funds were available in the market. Early in 1953 the Treasury issued 30-year bonds at 3¼ per cent. As available funds were already at a low level, this helped to tighten the money markets and to raise interest rates.

The Federal Reserve also acted to restrict credit in the early part of 1953. There was much debate about the correctness of monetary policies during this period. Many felt that credit was restricted too severely and that this restriction was in part responsible for the downturn in business later in the year.

Since it was not the policy of the federal reserve authorities to force deflation, reserve requirements were lowered in the early summer to provide the funds needed to meet a sizable government deficit. As funds were needed for seasonal use, the Federal Reserve System bought government securities to provide such funds. When signs appeared during the summer that a business readjustment was in prospect, credit was eased still further. As business turned down somewhat in a minor recession, the Federal Reserve used all the instruments at its command to reverse the recession. The reserve banks reduced discount rates, the Board of Governors reduced member bank reserve requirements, and the Open Market Committee acted to maintain more than adequate reserves. Under this policy of "active ease" the free reserves of member banks rose materially.

This policy of active ease was followed during most of 1954. As a result, interest rates dropped to the lowest level in several years. This reduction did not prevent a slight decline in short-term business loans or consumer loans during the year; but it did help increase loans on real estate materially and thus activity in the home building field.

Business started to expand late in 1954 and continued upward in 1955. When it became apparent that a business boom was developing, steps were again taken to restrict credit. The Open Market Committee reduced the holdings of government securities. Discount rates were increased in April and May and again several times later on in the year. Margin requirements on stock purchases were also raised, first to 60 per cent and then to 70 per cent. By the last quarter of the year borrowing from the federal reserve banks exceeded excess reserves by $350 million.[10] As credit became more and more restricted, interest rates rose, especially short term and intermediate-term rates.

There was little question raised about this reversal of policy from credit ease to credit restraint during most of 1955. When more price pressures developed in 1956, the Federal Reserve acted to tighten credit still further. The rediscount rate was raised again, and general tightness of credit was maintained through open-market operations.

The advance in general economic activity was slowed materially in 1956, especially due to lower automobile sales and some decrease in residential building. For a time it appeared as if a new controversy might develop when the Secretary of the Treasury stated publicly that he felt that the last increase in the rediscount rate was not only unwise but might lead to a downturn in business. Businessmen in various lines also questioned the policy of credit restriction. The Federal Reserve made credit somewhat easier in early summer of that year through open-market operations, but it did not believe that economic conditions at the time called for a major reversal in policy. Economic activity, however, continued upward in 1956 as business capital expenditures increased to record levels. Economic activity continued to expand

[10] *Federal Reserve Bulletin*, February, 1956, p. 101.

during the first three quarters of 1957 as business capital expenditures continued to increase and state and local government expenditures kept on increasing.

Beginning in 1956 and through 1957 prices of consumer goods began to advance after having been more or less stable for several years. To hold inflationary forces in check, the Federal Reserve followed a policy of active restraint through open-market operations and also by raising the rediscount rate on several occasions. Their policies were designed to curb the price rises and speculative excesses at the top of a cycle. They were also designed to counter what the Chairman of the Board of Governors referred to as "the alarming spread of the belief, not only in this country but also abroad, that creeping inflation under modern economic conditions was to be a chronic and unavoidable condition." [11] Federal reserve policy during the whole period of expansion was marked by an independence from the policies and actions of the Treasury. It was also carried on without regard to criticism that was at times vociferous in the business community and in Congress.

In the late fall of 1957 business began to decline and federal reserve policy shifted from credit restraint to one of making credit easier to obtain and cheaper. The policy was applied cautiously, however, since price rises continued in the early stages of the downturn.

QUESTIONS

1. Describe the monetary situation in the period prior to World War II.
2. What were the primary objectives of the Federal Reserve System in its policies designed to aid in financing the war?
3. Describe the interest-rate pattern the Federal Reserve System and the Treasury agreed on for financing the war. How was this pattern maintained?
4. Why did many individuals and institutions carry mostly long-term bonds during the war?
5. Describe the process of playing the pattern of rates.
6. Describe the process by which bond sales led to credit creation during World War II.
7. Describe the effects of war financing on the financial structure of the American economy.

[11] In a statement by William McChesney Martin, Jr., Chairman. Board of Governors of the Federal Reserve System, before the Joint Economic Committee of Congress, February 6, 1958.

8. Describe the economic and financial situation in the immediate post-war period. What was the role of monetary policy in this period?
9. Why were inflationary pressures strong in 1948? What steps were taken to combat them?
10. What was the major cause of inflation during the Korean War?
11. Describe the Treasury–Federal Reserve controversy during this period. Discuss the opposing viewpoints.
12. What was the nature of the accord they reached?
13. Describe the monetary policies followed during the first part of the Republican Administration and the policies of the Federal Reserve System.
14. Why was a policy of active ease adopted in the second half of 1953 and followed during most of 1954?
15. Describe and evaluate federal reserve policy during the prosperity period from late 1954 to late 1957.

SUGGESTED READINGS

"Bank Credit and Money in 1957." *Federal Reserve Bulletin* (Washington, D. C.: Board of Governors of the Federal Reserve System), (February, 1958), pp. 113-121.

GOLDENWEISER, E. A. *American Monetary Policy.* New York: McGraw-Hill Book Co., Inc., 1951.

MARTIN, WILLIAM McCHESNEY. "Flexible Monetary Policy." Statement before the Joint Economic Committee of Congress, February 6, 1958. *Federal Reserve Bulletin* (Washington, D. C.: Board of Governors of the Federal Reserve System), (February, 1958), pp. 134-140.

SPROUL, A. "Monetary Management and Credit Control." *American Economic Review* (June, 1947), pp. 339-350.

United States Congress, Joint Committee on the Economic Report-Subcommittee on General Credit Control and Debt Management. *Monetary Policy and Management of the Public Debt.* Washington: Government Printing Office, 1952.

INDEX